JESUS AND THE PEOPLE OF GOD

New Testament Monographs, 21

Series Editor
Stanley E. Porter

Jesus and the People of God

Reconfiguring Ethnic Identity

Joseph H. Hellerman

Sheffield Phoenix Press

2013

Copyright © 2007, 2013 Sheffield Phoenix Press

First published in hardback, 2007
First published in paperback, 2013

Published by Sheffield Phoenix Press
Department of Biblical Studies, University of Sheffield
Sheffield S3 7QB

www.sheffieldphoenix.com

All rights reserved.
No part of this publication may be reproduced or transmitted in any form or by any means, electronic or mechanical, including photocopying, recording or any information storage or retrieval system, without the publishers' permission in writing.

A CIP catalogue record for this book
is available from the British Library

Typeset by CA Typesetting Ltd
Printed on acid-free paper by Lightning Source

ISBN 978-1-909697-20-1 (paperback)
ISBN 978-1-906055-21-9 (hardback)
ISSN 1747-9606

Dedication

No one writes in isolation, and I owe much to the thoughts and ideas of many who have contributed to my intellectual and spiritual development over the years, in print and in person. My debt to the various pioneers of recent scholarly work on the interface between early Christianity and Second Temple Judaism (E.P. Sanders, N.T. Wright, and James D.G. Dunn) will be immediately apparent to all who are familiar with the literature. Readers will encounter a host of additional dialogue partners, as well, as they work their way through the book.

A number of colleagues, friends, and acquaintances provided timely input during the writing of the book, making *Jesus and the People of God* somewhat of a community endeavor. Those who interacted with portions of the manuscript include several of my colleagues at Talbot School of Theology, Biola University: Drs Alan Hultberg, Jon Lunde, Walt Russell, Mike Wilkins and Matt Williams. Dr Kevin Pittle, a cultural anthropologist from Biola's School of Intercultural Studies, exposed me to current literature on the subject of ethnic identity formation (Chapter Ten). I also received helpful input from Scott Bartchy (UCLA), who critiqued the material dealing with Jesus and sacred food (Chapter 7), and from Larry Helyer (Taylor University), who specializes in Second-Temple Jewish Literature, and who was kind enough to read and respond to Chapters 2 and 3 of the book. Finally, I assigned a relatively polished version of the manuscript to students in a graduate seminar on the social history of the early Christians. A number of my students' insights have found their way into the discussion, and their collective proof-reading (along with that of my secretary, Michelle Cutrona) was of no little help in cleaning up the manuscript prior to publication.

The bulk of the project was completed during a Fall 2005 Sabbatical provided by Biola University. A further monetary grant during the Spring of 2007 facilitated the editing process. Thanks to my Dean, Dr Dennis Dirks, and to Dr Chris Grace, Vice-Provost of Faculty Development, for making the funds available. I count it a delight to work in an environment like Biola, where faculty such as myself enjoy a remarkable degree of collegial encouragement, as well as ample institutional support. I dedicate *Jesus and the People of God* to my dear colleagues in the School of Theology.

CONTENTS

Abbreviations	xi
INTRODUCTION	1
1. Some Methodological Considerations	4
2. Charting our Course Together	6

Chapter 1
BOUNDARIES AND CRISIS: THE STORY OF A PARTICULAR PEOPLE OF GOD ... 10
  1. Boundaries in the Eyes of Non-Judeans ... 11
  2. Boundaries in the Hebrew Scriptures ... 20
  3. The Crisis of Hellenization ... 27

Chapter 2
INTERPRETING RECENT HISTORY
THE MACCABEAN THEOLOGICAL ENTERPRISE ... 37
  1. 1 Maccabees ... 39
  2. 2 Maccabees ... 45
  3. *4 Maccabees* ... 53
  4. Conclusion ... 59

Chapter 3
RECRAFTING ISRAEL'S STORY: THE GENRE OF THE REWRITTEN BIBLE ... 61
  1. *Jubilees* ... 61
  2. Pseudo-Philo ... 73
  3. Judith ... 78
  4. Additions to Esther ... 84
  5. Conclusion ... 88

Chapter 4
JESUS AND JEWISH NATIONALISM: ISSUES OF APPROACH AND METHODOLOGY ... 90
  1. The Canonical Gospels and the Jesus of History: An Overview ... 91
  2. Tradition History and a *Gesamtbild* of the Historical Jesus ... 94
  3. Behind the Scenes: Cultural Scripts and Gospel Interpretation ... 102
  4. Nationalism, Legalism, and the Not-So-New Perspective ... 107
  5. Conclusion ... 120

Chapter 5
JESUS AND SACRED TIMES — 123
1. Jesus and Sabbath — 124
2. Jesus and the Jewish Festivals — 145
3. Conclusion — 166

Chapter 6
JESUS AND SACRED SPACE — 167
1. Territoriality and the Cultic Topography of the Jerusalem Temple — 168
2. Predictions of the Temple's Destruction — 172
3. Jesus' Action in the Temple — 177
4. Neither on This Mountain Nor in Jerusalem — 188
5. Summary: Jesus and Sacred Space — 202

Chapter 7
JESUS AND SACRED FOOD — 204
1. Food, Social Relations, and Jewish Sectarianism — 206
2. Dismantling Intra-Jewish Boundaries — 213
3. Table Fellowship with Gentiles — 221
4. 'He Declared All Foods Clean' — 227
5. Summary: Jesus and Sacred Food — 234

Chapter 8
JESUS AND HIS EARLIEST FOLLOWERS: ANTICIPATING OBJECTIONS — 236
1. A Purity-Friendly Jesus? — 239
2. Jesus, Jewish Identity, and the Post-Easter Church — 242
3. Factor #1: Roman Abuses and the Persistence of Maccabean Ideology — 242
4. Factor #2: The Jewish Make-up of the Post-Easter Church — 254
5. Factor #3: The Nature of Jesus' Teachings — 255
6. Factor #4: Jewish Eschatological Expectations — 257
7. Some Related Evidence: The Case of Paul — 260
8. Conclusion — 263

Chapter 9
JESUS' VISION FOR A FAMILY OF GOD — 265
1. Mediterranean Family Values — 266
2. Jesus and Family: Readjusting the Pendulum — 270
3. Jesus and Family: Adjusting the Pendulum Back Again — 272
4. Surrogate Family Language in the Gospel of Matthew — 277
5. Some Concluding Thoughts — 285

Chapter 10
JESUS AS AN ETHNIC ENTREPRENEUR — 288
1. 'Ethnic Group' and 'Ethnicity': Some Definitions — 289
2. Aspects of a Shared Past: A Threefold Typology — 291

3. Considering the Aims of Jesus	296
4. Kinship and Ethnicity	297
5. Jesus and Patriarchy	301
6. Conclusion	305

Conclusion
JESUS AND THE PEOPLE OF GOD   309
   1. Summary   309
   2. Opening the Canopy of Historical Methodology   316
   3. A Brief Epilogue: Jesus Then and Now   324

Bibliography   328
Index of Ancient Sources   362
Index of Authors   375
Index of Subjects   381

ABBREVIATIONS

AB	Anchor Bible
ABD	David Noel Freedman (ed.), *The Anchor Bible Dictionary* (New York: Doubleday, 1992)
ABRL	Anchor Bible Reference Library
ANRW	Hildegard Temporini and Wolfgang Haase (eds.), *Aufstieg und Niedergang der römischen Welt: Geschichte und Kultur Roms im Spiegel der neueren Forschung* (Berlin: W. de Gruyter, 1972–)
BASOR	*Bulletin of the American Schools of Oriental Research*
BGBE	Beiträge zur Geschichte der biblischen Exegese
Bib	*Biblica*
BibInt	*Biblical Interpretation: A Journal of Contemporary Approaches*
BJRL	*Bulletin of the John Rylands University Library of Manchester*
BTB	*Biblical Theological Bulletin*
BBR	*Bulletin for Biblical Research*
BR	*Biblical Research*
BZ	*Biblische Zeitschrift*
CAH	Cambridge Ancient History
CBQ	*Catholic Biblical Quarterly*
CBQMS	*Catholic Biblical Quarterly*, Monograph Series
ConBNT	Coniectanea biblica, New Testament
DJG	*Dictionary of Jesus and the Gospels*
EKKNT	Evangelisch-Katholischer Kommentar zum Neuen Testament
EphTheolLov	*Ephemerides Theologicae Lovanienses*
EQ	*Evangelical Quarterly*
ET	*Expository Times*
FRLANT	Forschungen zur Religion und Literatur des Alten und Neuen Testaments
HTKNT	Herders theologischer Kommentar zum Neuen Testament
HNT	Handbuch zum Neuen Testament
HTR	*Harvard Theological Review*
HUCA	*Hebrew Union College Annual*
ICC	International Critical Commentary
IEJ	*Israel Exploration Journal*
Int	*Interpretation*
JAAR	*Journal of the American Academy of Religion*
JETS	*Journal of the Evangelical Theological Society*
JBL	*Journal of Biblical Literature*
JJS	*Journal of Jewish Studies*
JQR	*Jewish Quarterly Review*
JR	*Journal of Religion*
JSJ	*Journal for the Study of Judaism in the Persian, Hellenistic and Roman Period*
JSNT	*Journal for the Study of the New Testament*

JSNTSup	*Journal for the Study of the New Testament*, Supplement Series
JSOT	*Journal for the Study of the Old Testament*
JSOTSup	*Journal for the Study of the Old Testament*, Supplement Series
JSPSup	*Journal for the Study of the Pseudepigrapha*, Supplement Series
JSS	*Journal of Semitic Studies*
JTS	*Journal of Theological Studies*
NCB	New Century Bible
NIBC	New International Biblical Commentary
NovT	*Novum Testamentum*
NovTSup	*Novum Testamentum*, Supplements
NTS	*New Testament Studies*
OTP	James Charlesworth (ed.), *Old Testament Pseudepigrapha*
PEQ	*Palestine Exploration Quarterly*
RevQ	*Revue de Qumran*
RB	*Revue biblique*
SBL	Society of Biblical Literature
SBLDS	SBL Dissertation Series
SBLSBS	SBL Sources for Biblical Study
SBLSP	SBL Seminar Papers
SJT	*Scottish Journal of Theology*
SNTSMS	Society for New Testament Studies Monograph Series
SUNT	Studien zur Umwelt des Neuen Testaments
THKNT	Theologischer Handkommentar zum Neuen Testament
TSAJ	Texts and Studies in Ancient Judaism
VT	*Vetus Testamentum*
WMANT	Wissenschaftliche Monographien zum Alten und Neuen Testament
WTJ	*Westminster Theological Journal*
WUNT	Wissenschaftliche Untersuchungen zum Neuen Testament
ZAW	*Zeitschrift für die alttestamentliche Wissenschaft*
ZNW	*Zeitschrift für die neutestamentliche Wissenschaft*

Introduction

In 167 BCE, at the instigation of an influential faction of Jewish elites, the Syrian king, Antiochus IV, began a program of forced Hellenization which prohibited behaviors and altered institutions that were particularly defining for Jewish identity:

> 44 And the king sent letters by messengers to Jerusalem and the cities of Judah; he directed them to follow customs strange to the land, 45 to forbid burnt offerings and sacrifices and drink offerings in the sanctuary, to profane sabbaths and feasts, 46 to defile the sanctuary and the priests, 47 to build altars and sacred precincts and shrines for idols, to sacrifice swine and unclean animals, 48 and to leave their sons uncircumcised (1 Macc. 1.44-48a).

The king also proscribed Jewish dietary laws, and the eating of unclean food became something of a litmus test for faithfulness to Antiochus's directives. Finally, imperial authorities destroyed copies of the Torah—the sacred source for Jewish religious practices—and determined possession of the law to be a capital offense.

Antiochus's goal was transparently socio-political: 'that [his whole kingdom] should be one people, and that each should give up his customs' (1 Macc. 1.41-42).[1] The king perceptively discerned that, in order to achieve his desired ends, he would have to abolish traditional Jewish distinctions between sacred and profane foods, times, and places. For the 'customs' associated with these distinctions (along with male circumcision) had served to set apart Jewish inhabitants of the empire as the chosen people of Yahweh and thereby obstruct any attempt to render the Jews 'one people' with their Greek overlords.[2]

---

1. Scholars have generally abandoned attempts to explain Antiochus's actions on religious grounds. As Grabbe observes, 'Antiochus was concerned with politics, and religious matters were only incidental to his principal goals, which were those of most politicians: money and power' (Grabbe [1992a: 256]). See also Mørkholm (1966: 186). Nongbri sees in the decree 'a slightly overdue reorganization and attempted pacifying of a rebellious province' (2005: 98).

2. Note Cummins's summary: 'In brief, what was at stake was the Jewish way of life; the repressive measures of the enemy, climaxing in the persecution and suffering under Antiochus IV Epiphanes, were designed to replace Israel's central symbols—Temple, Torah, circumcision, and so forth—with various Hellenistic distinctives' (Cummins [2001: 30]).

The ensuing history is a familiar one and I will return to it at various points in the pages that follow. Suffice it to say that a series of successes on the part of the Maccabees and their supporters ultimately garnered for Judeans both religious and political independence from their Syrian Greek oppressors. My intention is to consider the effects of the crisis of 167–164 BCE upon later Jewish convictions regarding those symbols of socio-religious identity proscribed by Antiochus, and then to interpret the aims of Jesus of Nazareth against this background.

The motivation for this study comes from my work in the social history of early Christianity. I have elsewhere identified the patrilineal kinship group as the primary model adopted by Paul and others who sought to construct a vision for the social organization of early Christian communities.[3] As is widely acknowledged, this vision can be traced back to Jesus of Nazareth, who explicitly spoke of his followers in terms of surrogate family relations (Mk 3.31-35; 10.28-31).

A parallel trend in Jesus studies, which at first appears unrelated to the fictive family construct, interprets Jesus' critiques of Jewish symbols such as sabbath, dietary laws, and the Jerusalem temple as challenges to a defensive, nationalistic posture characteristic of Judeans in Palestine during the Roman period.[4] No longer is it sufficient (or even acceptable, for many) to view Jesus' conflicts with Jewish leaders over purity against a background of current beliefs about meritorious works of righteousness. Instead, Jesus is challenging symbols of national identity.

Although not as optimistic as some about the extent of its explanatory power, I am, nevertheless, quite attracted to this 'new perspective' on Jesus. Additionally, I am now inclined to view Jesus' critiques of these familiar symbols of Jewish identity, on the one hand, and the establishment of his followers as a surrogate kinship group, on the other, as two parts of the same social project. That is, in his challenges to contemporary practices and values relating to Sabbath, temple, and dietary laws, Jesus begins (nega-

---

3. Hellerman (2001).
4. Most prominently, Wright (1996) 369-442. My use of the terms 'nationalistic' and 'nationalism' should not be interpreted anachronistically to refer to the concept of a modern nation-state. Rather, such expressions will function in a way loosely related to the semantic fields of ethnicity and ethnic identity. A definition may prove helpful. Brass understands ethnic identity (loosely, 'nationalism', in the chapters that follow) to consist of the subjective, symbolic or emblematic use by a group of people of any aspect of culture, in order to create internal cohesion and differentiate themselves from other groups (Brass [1991: 19]).

This, of course, would be an unworkable description of a modern nation-state, but it quite accurately articulates, at a high level of abstraction, the strategies of first-century Judeans, as they sought to negotiate a place for themselves in the context of Roman imperial occupation.

tively) to deconstruct the idea of God's people as a localized *ethnos* that had prevailed since Sinai, in order simultaneously (positively) to reconstruct the social identity of the people of God in terms of surrogate family. This, in turn, sets the stage for Pentecost and the Gentile mission to follow, when persons from every *ethnos* will become 'children of God through faith in Christ Jesus' (Gal. 3.26). The thesis can be summarized with a series of assertions:

1. The Maccabean crisis (167-64 BCE) generated a heightened concern on the part of the Jewish people to preserve those marks of national identity that had been proscribed by Antiochus IV. Post-Maccabean Jewish literature thus evidences:

    (a) a pronounced preoccupation with the defining mark of circumcision and with distinctions between sacred and profane food, space, times, and people—distinctions which are specifically associated in these texts with the identity of the Jews as the chosen people of God.

    (b) a profoundly ideological historiography that directly attributes the varying fortunes of the Jews during the Seleucid period to their faithfulness (or lack thereof) to Torah legislation relating to circumcision, sacred food, sacred times, and sacred space. Maccabean historians trace the initial successes of the pogrom of Antiochus IV to the actions of Hellenized Jewish elites who deserted the temple and compromised Jewish purity laws. According to a pattern common in the Hebrew Scriptures, God allowed a pagan monarch to judge a faithless Israel. The same writers proceed to interpret the ensuing change in fortunes— consisting of the Hasmonean victories and the purification of the temple—as God's response to the faithfulness of Jewish martyrs who sacrificed their lives in order to preserve Jewish distinctives.

2. The ideology outlined above continued to occupy a central place in the symbolic universe of future generations of Jews and served as a vibrant cultural script informing Jewish convictions under Roman rule during the genesis of the Jesus movement.

3. Jesus intentionally challenged traditional distinctions between sacred and profane times, space, and food, thereby offering a pointed critique of Maccabean ideology and bringing into question the deeply entrenched idea of the people of God as *ethnos* in the context of Roman imperial hegemony.

4. Jesus' alternative to God's people as *ethnos* was to reconstitute the people of God as a surrogate family. No longer would the Abrahamic

patriline be determinative for membership among God's eschatological remnant. According to the social vision of Jesus, the person who belongs to the people of God is the one who 'does the will of God'.
5. Jesus' relativization of national symbols such as Sabbath-keeping, food-laws, sacred space (the temple), and the Jewish calendar—and the corresponding establishment of his followers as a surrogate family—provided the ideological foundation and symbolic framework for the expansion of the Jesus movement beyond the boundaries of ethnic Judaism during the decades immediately following Jesus' ministry in Galilee and Judea.

Some assertions will, of course, prove easier to support than others. I suspect that I will satisfactorily demonstrate to most readers the accuracy of the first and second statements above. Evidence for post-Maccabean preoccupation with Jewish identity markers abounds in the literature, and these values appear to have taken root and thrived well out into the Roman period. Framing the social organization of the Jesus movement in terms of surrogate family (#4) should also provoke little controversy. Even scholars who are least optimistic about the historical reliability of the canonical Gospels generally find vestiges of the historical Jesus in passages like Mk 3.31-35. The appropriation of the surrogate family construct by later leaders of the Jesus movement is, moreover, simply historical reality (#5).

Assertion #3 will likely prove more problematic, particularly for scholars who have difficulty imagining a Jesus who would challenge common Jewish praxis in the area of purity. I have in mind here primarily my minimalist readers, but even those with more confidence in the historical reliability of the Gospels may reject the contention that Jesus subverted traditional markers of national identity. I refer the latter group to the discussion that follows. For minimalist readers a word about historical methodology is in order. My own social location as an evangelical scholar encourages me to adopt a robust view of the reliability of the Gospels, and I gladly acknowledge the effects of my philosophical and theological views upon my work as a social historian. I hope to demonstrate that optimism about the canonical Jesus traditions makes good historical sense, as well.

1. *Some Methodological Considerations*

The essence of historical reconstruction consists of the postulation of cause-and-effect, and it is often the case that the latter elucidates the former. As Gerald Downing has cleverly observed, 'It is only in the light of what happens next that you can hope to understand and explain what has been happening'.⁵ In the present case 'what has been happening' continues to generate vigorous scholarly debate, and little agreement obtains in the guild about the teachings and activities of the historical Jesus. The general framework of 'what happens next', however, rests upon somewhat more secure historical bedrock. I have in mind here the genesis of the Jesus movement among Palestinian Jews in the first decades after Jesus' death.

We can be assured that reconstruction of various details surrounding the earliest years of the Jesus movement will continue to resist scholarly consensus. Few, however, will question (a) the origins of the movement among a rag-tag group of Jesus' followers and (b) early Christianity's subsequent growth and expansion throughout the eastern Roman empire. As Larry Hurtado has recently demonstrated, moreover, the high Christology which characterizes Pauline literature and, to a lesser degree, the Synoptic Gospels can be traced to Jewish-Christian circles in the earliest years of the movement. Devotion to Jesus as divine, and the practice of establishing communities of followers organized around what Hurtado calls a binitarian form of worship, 'erupted suddenly and quickly, not gradually and late, among first-century circles of followers'.⁶ Post-Easter activities among Jesus' followers in Jerusalem cry out for historical explanation.

A minimalist view of Jesus, which correspondingly maintains that the early church generated most of the material in the canonical Gospels, struggles satisfactorily to account for the historical phenomenon of the early Jesus movement, as outlined above. The problem cannot be easily dismissed, whether one's Jesus is a social reformer, a charismatic holy man, or a Jewish peripatetic philosopher. To be sure, some of these portrayals make reasonable sense of Jesus as a Second-Temple Jew in his own social and historical context. This is the strength of any reconstruction that emphasizes what Jesus shared with his contemporaries, while dismissing those portions of the tradition that present Jesus as in some way unique. A minimalist Jesus of whatever stripe, however, makes less sense of ensuing developments among Jesus' earliest followers in Judea. This is no small matter. If the Jesus of history lived the life, and died the death, that some minimalist scholars claim he did, then the Jesus movement surfaces as an anomaly in Second-Temple Judaism.⁷

Schooled readers will be quick to reply that to take the Jesus of the Gospels at face value is to argue for an equally anomalous Second-Temple

---

5. Downing (1992: 167).
6. Hurtado (2003: 650). See also Bauckham (1999) and Wright (1998). Contra Casey (1991).
7. Some time ago, in a programmatic essay, Catchpole wrestled with this fundamental historical issue. What decisive impulse within Second Judaism, he asked, could have generated a movement like early Christianity? The answer he offered to his own query makes as much sense today as it did when Catchpole wrote it: 'the most probable answer to that question is Jesus' (1977: 177).

Jew. I concur with this judgment and happily take on the burden of such an argument. I should add, however, that it is often the case that Jesus' apparently anomalous activities and teachings—particularly his challenges to markers of Jewish identity—find their conceptual roots in the writings of the Hebrew prophets which, of course, contain both inclusive and exclusive streams of proclamation, where Israel and the nations are concerned. In the end, however, the Jesus who surfaces in the pages that follow will inevitably stand out among his contemporaries in first-century Palestine. It will become immediately apparent that I prefer an anomalous Jesus to an anomalous Jesus movement. And I hope to demonstrate that such a perspective is a historically reasonable one.

2. *Charting Our Course Together*

The discussion that follows unfolds in a straightforward manner. Chapter 1 first examines Jewish social distinctives from the perspective of Greco-Roman writers, and then proceeds to consider the origins and ideological underpinnings of these practices, as outlined in the Hebrew Scriptures. The chapter concludes with a survey of postexilic Jewish history, giving special consideration to the defining years of the early Maccabean period, when Antiochus IV proscribed Judean socio-religious distinctives and ignited a rebellion among pious Jews which resulted in the purification of the temple in 164 BCE.

Chapters 2 and 3 offer a rather detailed survey of Jewish nationalism during the post-Maccabean era, based on evidence from seven representative works of literature: 1–2 Maccabees and *4 Maccabees, Jubilees,* Pseudo-Philo's *Biblical Antiquities,* Judith, and the Additions to Esther.[8] I am particularly interested here to highlight authorial preoccupation with defining socio-religious practices such as circumcision and the preservation of distinctions between sacred and profane times, space, and foods. It will become quite evident that the experiences of 167–164 BCE generated a distinct theological outlook where these markers of Judean identity were concerned. As later Jews looked back upon the watershed era of early Hasmonean history, many concluded that the quality of their relationship with Yahweh depended directly upon their faithfulness to the social distinctives outlined above. Compromises with Hellenism had, in their eyes, rendered Jerusalem and her temple vulnerable to the abuses of Antiochus IV in 167 BCE, when Yahweh removed his hand of divine protection in response to the disobedience of his people. And it was, in contrast, the faithfulness of the Maccabean martyrs to Torah injunctions related to circumcision and the food laws which ultimately restored God's blessing, as evidenced by a series of

---

8. I have listed the works in the order in which I discuss them in Chapters 2 and 3.

military victories over the Syrian Greeks which finally resulted in complete liberation from the yoke of the Gentiles. In the words of one Maccabean historian, '[W]hat was forsaken in the wrath of the Almighty was restored again in all its glory when the great Lord became reconciled' (2 Macc. 5.20).

The balance of the book (Chapters 4 through 10) seeks to interpret the teachings and activities of Jesus against the defensive socio-cultural posture that characterized much of post-Maccabean Judaism. Chapter 4 serves as a methodological prolegomenon of sorts to the ensuing examination of Jesus in the Gospels. I first outline my approach to tradition history and then proceed to appeal for the admission to the hermeneutical process of what I call 'implicit cultural scripts', that is, cultural values and social codes not explicitly articulated in the texts themselves, but clearly operating behind the scenes as events unfolded in the ministry of Jesus. The chapter continues with a discussion of the new perspective on Second-Temple Judaism and Jewish soteriology, and it concludes with some observations about the implications of my methodology for the historical reliability of the canonical Gospels.

The three Chapters that follow (5, 6, and 7) examine Jesus' handling of sacred times, sacred space, and sacred food, respectively. In each case I argue from various passages in the Gospels that Jesus consistently relativized these important badges of Jewish ethnic solidarity. The sociological function of distinctions related to calendar, territory, and food suggests that, in challenging these vital identity markers, Jesus intentionally sought to subvert boundaries erected during the post-Maccabean era between sectarian and non-sectarian Judeans and, by extension, subtly to destabilize the most intractable social boundary of all—that which existed between Jew and Gentile. Jesus' behavior, in this regard, is to be interpreted in light of his conviction that a defining moment in salvation history had arrived in his life and ministry: 'The time is fulfilled, and the kingdom of God has come near; repent, and believe in the good news' (Mk 1.15). To summarize, conflicts with local leaders over Sabbath observance, temple polity, and exclusive table fellowship reveal a desire on Jesus' part to renegotiate the ethnic contours of the people of Yahweh in light of the inbreaking of the dominion of God.

Chapter 8 tackles the thorny problem of the apparent disconnect that obtains between Jesus' attitude toward Jewish identity markers, as illustrated in the Gospels, and the convictions and practices of his earliest post-Easter followers. The difficulty here cannot be easily dismissed. Those who were closest to Jesus seem to wrestle anew with matters of purity and boundaries, without any apparent knowledge of the precedent set by Jesus. The dilemma, however, is not an intractable one. Scholars are often misled here by an overly simplistic historiography that employs a singular explanatory trajectory of cause and effect, one which seeks to account for early Christian praxis solely on the basis of the historical Jesus. Such a perspective fails to take into consideration the multiplicity of factors that affected post-Easter convictions about purity and social boundaries. Particularly influential here was the persistent vitality of post-Maccabean nationalism, which strongly discouraged any propensity that the Jerusalem Christians might have had to follow in the footsteps of Jesus and play loose with badges of Jewish social identity. The chapter will consider other factors, as well, that served to reinforce this social conservatism among members of the Jesus movement in mid first-century Judea.

Chapter 9 turns to consider the positive aspect of Jesus' social program, namely, the organization of his followers as a family of surrogate siblings under the fatherhood of God. I expend some effort in the chapter to relate Jesus' teachings about the natural family—both positive and negative—to his vision for his disciples to function as a fictive kinship group. The intention here is to bring some balance to a scholarly discussion that has tended either to relegate Jesus and his earliest followers to the extreme margins of normal village and social life or, conversely, to domesticate the gospel traditions in search of a more family-friendly Jesus. I contend that we should assign priority to the surrogate family traditions, and then interpret the natural family passages accordingly. It was the combination of Jesus' relativization of traditional badges of Jewish identity, on the one hand, and the constitution of his group of followers as a surrogate family, on the other, which provided the ideological and symbolic foundation for the expansion of the Jesus movement beyond the boundaries of ethnic Judaism in the decades that followed. The surrogate family traditions in the Gospels are, therefore, central to Jesus' social agenda.

A final substantive Chapter considers Jesus functioning as an ethnic entrepreneur of sorts.[9] Anthropologists who study ethnic identity formation consistently emphasize the function of a 'shared past' to articulate and reinforce an ethnic group's sense of common destiny and collective identity. This shared

---

9. Through Chapter 9 I generally utilize a traditional socio-historical methodology, recently defined by Fuglseth, as involving 'description of a historical situation, primarily by taking over the terms from the historical actors themselves' (2005: 41). The discussion in Chapter 10 reflects, in contrast, the intentional employment of a social scientific model (ethnic identity formation), which I adopt as a heuristic device to help elucidate in more general terms the meaning of the evidence outlined in the previous chapters of the book. DeSilva helpfully distinguishes between social description, on the one hand, and the conscious employment of social-scientific models, on the other, as 'two modes in which social-scientific interpretation has proceeded' (2004: 120-24). The use of models has become an important methodological issue in social scientific biblical criticism. Helpful discussions of the benefits and pitfalls of employing modern models in the analysis of ancient texts and societies include Elliot (1993), Horrell (1999), and Fuglseth (2005: 38-43).

past typically consists of (a) a narrative of origins, related to the group's remote history, and (b) an interpretation of more recent group experiences designed to strengthen ethnic boundaries over against an opposing group of dominant foreigners. Judeans had in the Torah a compelling narrative of origins, and they possessed in the works of more recent Maccabean historians a potent ideology of ethnicity and boundary preservation. Given what we know about ethnic identity formation, anyone who sought to challenge or in some way reframe these defining stories and their respective values would be implicitly subverting the very contours of Judean ethnicity. Jesus, I suggest, intentionally reinterpreted the vital narratives of Israelite origins and more recent Maccabean history in terms of his own life and ministry, by the manner in which he dealt with symbols of purity and nationalism. Jesus' activities in this regard speak directly, therefore, to his convictions concerning the ethnic boundaries of the people of Yahweh. The book concludes with a chapter that briefly reviews the ground I have covered, and which offers some final methodological reflections from my insider's perspective as a professing Christian.

Chapter 1

BOUNDARIES AND CRISIS:
THE STORY OF A PARTICULAR PEOPLE OF GOD

> From the top of the crags I see him,
> from the hills I behold him;
> Here is a people living alone,
> and not reckoning itself among the nations!
>
> Numbers 23.9

Judeans living in the Roman world during the genesis of early Christianity distinguished themselves from other peoples of the empire through a number of practices that both insiders and outsiders regarded as distinctly Jewish.[1] Recognized marks of Jewish identity included male circumcision, adherence to the food laws prescribed in the Mosaic Law, and the observance of the Sabbath and various annual festivals. Judeans in Palestine also took great care to maintain geographical distinctions between sacred and profane space, particularly where Jerusalem and the temple were concerned, so that the temple came to serve as a vital symbol of Jewish national identity in the eyes of both Jews and Gentiles throughout the Roman East.

The present chapter examines these Jewish distinctives from several angles. I will first consider the manner in which Greek and Roman writers in the Hellenistic world described the Jews who lived among them. Whatever might be said about the variety of Judaisms that flourished during the Second-Temple period, outsiders viewed Judeans as a single entity and consistently characterized them with reference to the social boundary markers mentioned in the previous paragraph. After surveying the pagan perspective, the discussion turns to the Hebrew Scriptures briefly to consider the portrayals of these defining Jewish practices in biblical law and narrative. Old Testament writers were not as preoccupied with the sociological implications of purity as were Jews who wrote in the wake of the Maccabean

---

1. Debate continues over the appropriate term to use for the descendants of Abraham during the Second-Temple period, and no scholarly or literary consensus has yet to emerge (see Esler's case for 'Judean' [2003: 62-74], and Aymer's pointed response [2006: 485-86]). Since both 'Jew(ish)' and 'Judean' are presently stylistically acceptable, I will happily alternate rather indiscriminately between the two terms, much to the dismay, I am sure, of those who have a dog in this race.

crisis. Several Old Testament texts do, however, draw an explicit connection between (a) Israel's identity as the distinct people of Yahweh and (b) defining practices such as sabbath-keeping and adherence to levitical dietary laws. The Hebrew Scriptures thus contain sufficient raw materials for the much more extensive development of purity legislation which occurs during the Second-Temple period. The chapter concludes with a discussion of the threat to Jewish identity posed by the decrees of the Seleucid king Antiochus IV and the corresponding Maccabean response (167–164 BCE). In his efforts to constitute as 'one people' the various ethnic groups of his realm, Antiochus desecrated the Jewish temple and intentionally proscribed those very practices enjoined in the Torah which for generations had served to set apart the Jews as the people of Yahweh. Jewish resistance, as portrayed by Maccabean historians, led to the purification and rededication of the temple and ignited among Judeans a renewed concern to obey Torah legislation relating to sacred foods, sacred times, and sacred space.

1. *Boundaries in the Eyes of Non-Judeans*

As a prelude to our survey of Greco-Roman attitudes toward Jews in the Mediterranean world, we would do well to remind ourselves that religion in the ancient world was first and foremost an issue of cult and praxis, and only secondarily a system of theological convictions. This was true of Judaism, and it was true of pagan religion, as well. To be sure, Greco-Roman writers at times paused to reflect upon Jewish ideology, since ancient elites encountered in Israelite monotheism a genuine curiosity. Nevertheless, Jews were Jews in pagan eyes not principally because of their system of beliefs but, rather, because of the remarkable practices that set them apart from what Tacitus identifies as 'every other people' (*Hist.* 5.5). This reality will become immediately apparent in the texts cited below, where circumcision, sabbath-keeping, and exclusive table fellowship consistently surface as practices that define Jews over against other people groups in the empire.[2]

a. *Tacitus on the Jews*

As a prologue to his narrative of the Jewish War (66–70 CE), the esteemed Roman senator Tacitus introduces his readers to Rome's obdurate client

---

2. I am concerned in what follows with Jewish identity in the eyes of Greco-Romans, not with prevailing attitudes toward Judeans and things Jewish. There is some debate about the latter in the scholarly community. See the opposing conclusions of Gager (1983) and Schäfer (1997), who argue against and for the presence of Antijudaism, respectively, and the mediating position of Feldman (1993), who finds some Antijudaism among the masses but points to a benevolent government policy and a degree of admiration among elite intellectuals.

kingdom in the East (*Hist.* 5.2-5).³ Tacitus begins his account by relating various explanations of Judean origins which were circulating among his contemporaries, ultimately affirming the viewpoint held by 'most authors', namely, that the Jews had originated as a group of diseased persons expelled from Egypt in order to purify Pharaoh's kingdom of what was perceived to be a divine curse (*Hist.* 5.3). Tacitus then proceeds to trace two familiar Jewish identity markers—the dietary laws and Sabbath observance—to the Jews' experiences in Egypt. He introduces his examination of Jewish praxis at this point by highlighting the 'otherness' of the Jewish people:

> To establish his influence over this people for all time, Moses introduced new religious practices, quite opposed to those of all other religions. The Jews regard as profane all that we hold sacred; on the other hand, they permit all that we abhor (*Hist.* 5.4).

Among these 'new religious practices' Tacitus cites abstinence from pork, attributing the practice to the disease that infected the Jews in Egypt:

> They abstain from pork, in recollection of a plague, for the scab to which the animal is subject once afflicted them (*Hist.* 5.4).

Tacitus also traces Sabbath-keeping to Israel's formative years in Egypt, although for him some questions remain with respect to the specific details:

> They say that they first chose to rest on the seventh day because that day ended their toils; but after a time they were led by the charms of indolence to give over the seventh year as well to inactivity. Others say that this is done in honour of Saturn, whether it be that the primitive elements of their religion were given by the Idaeans, who, according to tradition, were expelled with Saturn and became the founders of the Jewish race, or is due to the fact that, of the seven planets that rule the fortunes of mankind, Saturn moves in the highest orbit and has the greatest potency; and that many of the heavenly bodies traverse their paths and courses in multiples of seven (*Hist.* 5.4).

The perception of the Jews as socially anomalous vividly colors the following text-segment, where our author begins to introduce a strongly (and regrettably) evaluative element into what has otherwise been a generally descriptive account of Jewish behaviors:

> Whatever their origin, these rites are maintained by their antiquity: the other customs of the Jews are base and abominable, and owe their persistence to their depravity. For the worst rascals among other peoples, renouncing their ancestral religions, always kept sending tribute and contributions to Jerusalem, thereby increasing the wealth of the Jews; again, the Jews are extremely loyal to one another, and always ready to show compassion, but toward every other people they feel only hate and enmity (*Hist.* 5.5).

---

3. The war formally ended c. 73/74 CE, when the fortress of Masada finally fell to the Romans.

Tacitus proceeds to identify exclusive table fellowship and the practice of strict endogamy as behaviors that distinguish Jews from the rest of humanity:

> They sit apart at meals, and they sleep apart, and although as a race, they are prone to lust, they abstain from intercourse with foreign women; yet among themselves nothing is unlawful (*Hist.* 5.5).

The covenant rite of circumcision, as well, functions to mark out the Jewish people as socially unique:

> They adopted circumcision to distinguish themselves from other peoples by this difference (*ut diversitate noscantur*) (*Hist.* 5.5).

Tacitus concludes his discussion of Jewish distinctives on a theological note, with a brief overview of 'their ideas of heavenly things', commenting in particular upon Jewish aniconic monotheism (*Hist.* 5.5).

Tacitus was but one in a long line of Greco-Roman observers who described Judeans by drawing attention to their particular socio-religious behaviors. The specific practices that Tacitus identifies had been noted by pagan writers for several centuries. Our survey will now proceed in a topical fashion. We will consider, in turn, comments from ancient authors about Jewish eating habits, Sabbath-keeping, and circumcision, behaviors that proved particularly defining for writers who sought to describe Judeans to their pagan contemporaries.

b. *Jewish Dietary Laws and Separate Table Fellowship*
During the first century BCE, in a high-profile trial in the Roman Forum, the skilled orator Cicero was prosecuting a rapacious provincial administrator, Verres, for crimes he had committed as governor of Sicily. A freedman named Caecilius, who was suspected by his Roman peers of Jewish practices, suddenly sought to thrust aside Verres' Sicilian accusers and denounce the defendant himself. Cicero, ever quick of wit, colorfully quipped, 'What has a Jew got to do with Verres?' Cicero's response tells us a lot about the common identification of abstinence from pork as a particularly Jewish behavior, since Plutarch, the narrator of the incident, informs his Greek readers that the term *verres* in Latin is a 'Roman word for a castrated porker' (*Cic.* 7.4). The public effectiveness of such a pun assumes, of course, a broad familiarity with Jewish eating habits on the part of those within earshot of Cicero in the Roman Forum that day.

Diodorus (1st cent. BCE) also mentions the food laws, and he explicitly connects them with Jewish social exclusivism. While narrating the exploits of the Seleucid king Antiochus VII Sidetes (138–129 BCE), Diodorus mentions a group of persons in the king's entourage who encouraged Antiochus to 'wipe out completely the race of the Jews, since they alone of all nations avoided dealings with any other people (ἀκοινωνήτους εἶναι τῆς πρὸς ἄλλο ἔθνος) and looked upon all men as their enemies'. The separation (ἀκοινωνία) in view relates in the context specifically to dietary practices, namely, Judean concern 'not to break bread with any other race (τὸ μηδενὶ ἄλλῳ ἔθνει τραπέζης κοινωνεῖν)' (Diodorus, *Hist.* 34-35.1.1-2).[4]

Strabo of Amaseia (ca. late 1st cent. BCE to 1st cent. CE) also remarks disparagingly about Jewish eating habits. Strabo praises Moses's original installation of imageless divine worship, but then proceeds to trace Jewish social distinctives, including both the food laws and circumcision, to a marked decline in religious practice which occurred after the death of Moses:

> [Moses's] successors for some time abided by the same course, acting righteously and being truly pious toward God; but afterwards, in the first place, superstitious men were appointed to the priesthood, and then tyrannical people; and from superstition arose abstinence from flesh, from which it is their custom to abstain even today, and circumcisions...and other observances of the kind (*Geog.* 16.2.37).

Jewish dietary scruples even attracted the interest of the philosophically inclined. Epictetus draws attention to a disagreement between Jews, Syrians, Egyptians, and Romans about 'whether the particular act of eating swine's flesh is holy or unholy' (*Diss.* 1.22.4). He finds the competing opinions mutually exclusive: 'I fancy, it is absolutely necessary, if the views of the Egyptians are right, that those of others are not right; if those of the Jews are well founded, that those of the others are not' (*Diss.* 1.11.12-13). Elsewhere, Plutarch devotes a whole section of a work to consider '[w]hether the Jews abstain from pork because of reverence or aversion for the pig' (*Quaest. conv.* 4.5.1-3). The former opinion led some to associate the pig directly with the Jewish cult: 'The Jew may worship his pig-god and clamour in the ears of high heaven' (Petronius, *Frag.* 37).

Finally, we have some interesting evidence from Seneca suggesting that the Jewish food laws played a rather indirect role in the dietary practices of the Roman philosopher himself. It seems that Seneca, for one reason or

---

4. Other references in Greco-Roman literature to Judean anti-social tendencies should probably also be traced back to issues of food and table, even where Jewish dietary laws are not specifically mentioned in the context. In Hecataeus of Abdera's otherwise positive assessment of the Jews (c. 300 BCE), he notes, 'The sacrifices [Moses] established differ from those of other nations, as does their way of living, for as a result of their own expulsion from Egypt he introduced an unsocial and intolerant mode of life (ἀπάνθρωπόν τινα καὶ μισόξενον βίον)' (cited in Diodorus, *Hist.* 40.3.4). According to Josephus, Manetho (3rd cent. BCE) claimed that Moses made it a law that the Jews 'should have intercourse with none save those of their own confederacy (συνάπτεσθαι δὲ μηδενὶ πλὴν τῶν συνομωμοσμένων)' (quoted by Josephus, *Ag. Ap.* 1.239). In each case Jewish eating habits are likely in view.

another, had for some time abstained from eating animal food. Certain political proceedings under the emperor Tiberius put an end to the philosopher's peculiar eating habits. Seneca informs us,

> The days of my youth coincided with the early part of the reign of Tiberius Caesar. Some foreign rites were at that time being inaugurated, and abstinence from certain kinds of animal food was set down as proof of interest in the strange cult. So at the request of my father...I returned to my previous habits (eating animal food) (*Ep.* 108.22).

Most scholars relate the events in view here to the persecution in Rome of Jewish and Egyptian practices, generally dated to 19 CE.[5] Seneca's father was apparently concerned that some might interpret his son's abstinence from meat as abstinence from pork, a distinctly Jewish practice currently suspect in the eyes of imperial authorities.

c. *Sabbath-keeping*
Sabbath observance also found its way into the comments of pagan writers who mention the Jews. The connection surfaces as early as the second century BCE, when Agatharchides of Cnidus observed,

> The people known as Jews, who inhabit the most strongly fortified of cities, called by the natives Jerusalem, have a custom of abstaining from work every seventh day; on those occasions they neither bear arms nor take any agricultural operations in hand, nor engage in any other form of public service, but pray with outstretched hands in the temples until the evening (quoted by Josephus, *Ag. Ap.* 1.209-11).

Dio Cassius similarly relates that the Jews 'dedicated to [God] the day called the day of Saturn, on which, among many other peculiar observances, they undertake no serious occupation' (*Hist.* 37.17.3). Like Tacitus, above, several voices trace Sabbath practice to the Jews' expulsion from Egypt. Pompeius Trogus (1st cent. BCE to 1st cent. CE) relates the following:

> Moyses...took possession of mount Sinai, on his arrival at which, after having suffered together with his followers, from a seven days' fast in the deserts of Arabia, he, for all time, consecrated the seventh day, which used to be called Sabbath by the custom of the nation, for a fast-day, because that day had ended at once their hunger and their wanderings (from Justin, *Epitoma historiarum philippicarum pompei trogi*, 2).[6]

---

5. Stern (1974: 1.434). Other Greco-Romans who make references to Jewish food laws include Apion (Josephus, *Ag. Ap.* 2.137), Erotianus, the glossator of Hippocrates (*Vocum hippocraticarum collectio cum fragmentis*, Fr. 33, *Morb. sacr.*, trans. Stern [1974: 1.446]), and the Roman emperor Caligula, who asked Philo and the embassy from Alexandria, 'Why do you abstain from pig's meat?' (Philo, *Leg.* 361).
6. A revised translation of J.S. Watson, cited by Stern (1974: 1.337-38).

Apion offers yet another twist on the story, based this time on a popular etymological interpretation of the term Sabbath. According to Josephus,

> [Apion] gives an astonishing and implausible explanation of the etymology of the word 'sabbath'! 'After a six days' march', he says, 'they developed tumours in the groin, and that was why, after safely reaching the country now called Judaea, they rested on the seventh day, and called that day *sabbaton*, preserving the Egyptian terminology; for disease of the groin in Egypt is called *sabbato*' (Josephus, *Ag. Ap.* 2.20-21).

The topic of Sabbath observance regularly appears in Greco-Roman literature when writers describe Judean military activities. The Jewish practice, early in the Second-Temple period, of refusing to fight on the Sabbath generated a number of comments on the part of ancient historians. Plutarch is representative:

> But the Jews, because it was the Sabbath day, sat in their places immovable, while the enemy were planting ladders against the walls and capturing the defences, and they did not get up, but remained there, fast bound in the toils of superstition as in one great net (Plutarch, *De superst.* 8).[7]

According to Augustine, Seneca (like Tacitus, above) found in the practice of Sabbath-keeping a reason to charge Judeans with idleness:

> Along with other superstitions of the civil theology Seneca also censures the sacred institutions of the Jews, especially the sabbath. He declares that their practice is inexpedient, because by introducing one day of rest in every seven they lose in idleness almost a seventh of their life, and by failing to act in times of urgency they often suffer loss (Augustine, *De civ. D.* 6.11).

Elsewhere, Seneca reflects an awareness of Jewish sabbath-keeping when he writes, 'But let us forbid lamps to be lighted on the Sabbath' (*Ep.* 95.47).

The utilization of the sabbath as a *topos* by satirists and poets constitutes perhaps the most convincing evidence for broad familiarity with this distinctly Jewish tradition throughout the ancient Mediterranean world.

---

[7] There is some question about which battle Plutarch has in view here. The Jews did not refrain from fighting on the Sabbath during the war with Rome, although the author may here be projecting early practices into a later encounter. Frontinus (c. 40–104 CE), a contemporary of the Flavians writing at the time of Domitian, makes a similar blunder:

> The deified Augustus Vespasian attacked the Jews on the day of Saturn, a day on which it is sinful for them to do any business, and defeated them (*Str.* 2.1.17, trans. Stern [1974: 1.510]).

Confusion aside, the association of sabbath-keeping with Jewish identity remains central to the thinking of both Plutarch and Frontinus, and that is the point in the present connection. On the subject of Jews taking up arms on the sabbath, see now Weiss's analysis of the sabbath in Josephus's works. Weiss questions whether Jews between the Maccabean era and the war with Rome regarded it permissible to fight on the sabbath (1998).

For example, Meleager, a Greek writer from the Hellenistic city of Gadara (c. 2nd–1st cent. BCE), wrote an epigram that reads: 'If thy lover is some Sabbath-keeper (σαββατικός) no great wonder! Love burns hot even on cold Sabbaths' (*Anthologia Graeca*, 5.160). The Roman writer Martial referred disparagingly to 'the stench...of the breath of fasting Sabbatarian women' (*Epigr.* 4.4). The Augustan era generated a plethora of references to Jewish Sabbath-keeping. Horace associates 'Sabbath' with 'the circumcised Jew' (*Sat.* 1.9.70). The poet Ovid twice refers to the Sabbath in *The Art of Love:* 'the seventh day that the Syrian Jew holds sacred'...'the seventh-day feast that the Syrian of Palestine observes' (*Ars am.* 1.76, 1.416), and uses the expression 'foreign sabbath' in yet another work (*Rem. am.* 219-20). Another Augustan era author pointedly remarks about 'the accursed day of Saturn' (Tibullus 1.18). Stern cites the various references to Sabbath-keeping in Augustan literature as evidence of 'the impression that the diffusion of Jewish customs made on Roman society'.[8] It was a significant impression, indeed.[9]

d. *Circumcision*

Ancient writers who were interested in Jewish history often speculated about the origin of circumcision. As early as the fifth century BCE, Herodotus had described Judeans as those who have 'learnt the custom [of circumcision] from the Egyptians' (*Hist.* 2.104.3). Diodorus (1st cent. BCE) also identified the Jews by their 'long-established institution' of circumcision, and informed his readers of the Egyptian origins of the rite, which, he claimed, was practiced by both the Colchi and the Jews:

> [T]he nation of the Colchi in Pontus and that of the Jews, which lies between Arabia and Syria, were founded as colonies by certain emigrants from their country; and this is the reason why it is a long-established institution among these two people to circumcise their male children, the custom having been brought over from Egypt (*Hist.* 1.28.2-3).

> And the proof which they offer of the Egyptian origin of this nation is the fact that the Colchi practise circumcision even as the Egyptians do, the custom continuing among the colonists sent out from Egypt as it also did in the case of the Jews (*Hist.* 1.55.5).

The nexus that exists between circumcision and Jewish identity is most apparent when ancient writers describe non-Jewish peoples who have converted—forcibly or otherwise—to Judaism. Timagenes (1st cent. BCE), a Roman rhetor whose work was known to Josephus through Strabo, discussed the extension of Jewish territorial boundaries under the Hasmoneans:

---

8. Stern (1974: 1.318).
9. For further discussion see the survey in Goldenberg (1979), and Doering (1999: 285-89).

> Strabo also testifies on the authority of Timagenes, writing as follows: 'This man [Aristobulus I, 104–103 BCE] was a kindly person and very serviceable to the Jews, for he acquired additional territory for them, and brought over to them a portion of the Ituraean nation, whom he joined to them by the bond of circumcision' (Josephus, *Ant.* 13.319).

Ptolemy the Historian (c. late 1st cent. BCE), cited by Ammonius, relates another such incident during the years of Hasmonean expansionism:

> Jews and Idumaeans differ, as Ptolemy states in the first book of the History of King Herod. Jews are those who are so by origin and nature. The Idumaeans, on the other hand, were not originally Jews, but Phoenicians and Syrians; having been subjugated by the Jews and having been forced to undergo circumcision, so as to be counted among the Jewish nation and keep the same customs, they were called Jews (*Historia Herodis*, cited by Ammonius, *Diff.* 243).[10]

The connection between circumcision (ἀναγκασθέντες περιτέμνεσθαι) and Jewish identity (ἐκλήθησαν Ἰουδαῖοι) could hardly be clearer.

Petronius (1st cent. CE), on his part, viewed circumcision as the fundamental mark of Judaism:

> The Jew may worship his pig-god and clamour in the ears of high heaven, but unless he also cuts back his foreskin with the knife, he shall go forth from the people and emigrate to Greek cities, and shall not tremble at the fasts of Sabbath imposed by the law (*Frag.* 37).

The citation nicely summarizes two advantages of Gentile life over against that of the Jews. Gentiles enjoy the freedom of a rather fluid set of social relations, and they are not bound to observe Jewish sacred times. One who converts to Judaism through the rite of circumcision, however, relinquishes both of these advantages. Elsewhere, Petronius twice associates circumcision with Judeans in the *Satyricon* (68.8; 102.14). Stern concludes that circumcision was, in the eyes of Petronius, the Jews' 'specific trait'.[11]

One could say the same of Martial.[12] In one epigram Martial decries 'the lecheries of the circumcised Jews' (*Epigr.* 7.30). Elsewhere he describes a Jewish actor who tried—and failed—to conceal the fact that he was circumcised (*Epigr.* 8.82).[13] In yet another piece Martial locks horns with

---

10. Trans. from Stern (1975: 1.356).

11. Stern (1974: 441).

12. Stern, in fact, does just that: 'It is the Jewish rite of circumcision that serves as the main target for the epigrammatist's wit' (1974: 1.521).

13. There was apparently some financial motivation for relinquishing one's Jewish identity in the wake of the destruction of the temple in 70 CE. Suetonius recounts the story of an elderly, non-practicing Jew who was stripped in court, in order to ascertain whether he was liable to the tax paid into the *fiscus iudaicus* (*Dom.* 12.2).

a Judean poet who had apparently made some disparaging remarks about Martial's literary ability. Four times in a few short lines, Martial refers to the Jew in ways that pointedly underscore the defining Jewish rite: 'circumcised poet...circumcised poet...circumcised poet...circumcised one' (*Epigr.* 11. 94). Other ancient writers who referred unsympathetically to the practice of circumcision include Horace (*Sat.* 1.9.70), Apion (Josephus, *Ag. Ap.* 2.137), Perseus (*Sat.* 5.180-84), and Strabo (*Geog.* 16.2.37).

e. *Summary*

The evidence is quite conclusive. Greco-Romans extensively and universally identified circumcision, Sabbath-keeping, and adherence to the levitical food laws as those practices that marked out Judeans as socially distinct from their pagan contemporaries.[14] The ancient geographer Strabo will serve us well as our final representative of the Greco-Roman perspective on Jews and Jewish identity. Josephus quotes Strabo's revealing ethnography of Cyrene and Egypt:

> There were four classes in the state of Cyrene; the first consisted of citizens, the second of farmers, the third of resident aliens (metics), the fourth of Jews... And it has come about that Cyrene, which had the same rulers as Egypt, has imitated it in many respects, particularly in notably encouraging and aiding the expansion of the organized groups of Jews, which observe the national Jewish laws (Josephus, *Ant.* 14.116).

For Strabo, as for our other ancient authors, Jews are clearly identifiable as a single social entity. They are simply those who 'observe the national Jewish laws' (τοῖς πατρίοις τῶν Ἰουδαίων νόμοις). And we need not wander far in our efforts to ascertain precisely what Jewish laws our author has in mind. For elsewhere Strabo clearly distinguishes Jews as those who 'abstain from flesh' and practice 'circumcisions' (*Geog.* 16.2.37). These vital markers of Jewish identity were apparently shared by nearly all Jews, regardless of their sectarian affiliations, for this is precisely how Judeans were identified by pagan detractors and admirers alike. As Theissen appropriately asserts, 'The ritual sign language of the Torah thus became the hallmark of Judaism,

---

14. Pagan writers also discuss the importance of the temple for Jewish identity, although Jerusalem and her temple were not immediately present in the social world of these writers as were Jewish practices like circumcision, Sabbath-keeping, and exclusive table fellowship. Strabo says the Jews 'honoured and revered [the temple mount] as a holy place' (*Geog.* 16.2.37; see also Polybius, who refers to 'the renown of the temple' [cited by Josephus, *Ant.* 12.136]; and Dio Cassius, who describes the Jewish temple as 'extremely large and beautiful' [*Hist.* 35.17.2]). We now have easy access to a compendium of Greek and Latin references to the Jerusalem temple, thanks to Hayward (1996).

which distinguished it from the surrounding world in a recognizable way'.[15] We will next consider the origins of these uniquely Jewish practices as outlined in the Hebrew Scriptures.

2. *Boundaries in the Hebrew Scriptures*

Judeans dwelling throughout the Roman Empire during the time of Jesus traced their origins back to the call of Abraham in the early chapters of Genesis:[16]

> 1 Now the LORD said to Abram, 'Go from your country and your kindred and your father's house to the land that I will show you. 2 I will make of you a great nation, and I will bless you, and make your name great, so that you will be a blessing. 3 I will bless those who bless you, and the one who curses you I will curse; and in you all the families of the earth shall be blessed' (Gen. 12.1-3).

From these seminal beginnings God's covenant with Abraham soon expanded to include promises of innumerable offspring and the possession of the land of Canaan (Gen. 15; 17.3-8; 22.16-18). According to the defining narratives of the Hebrew Scriptures, the hopes embedded in these texts found concrete fulfillment several centuries later, when Yahweh delivered a multitude of Abraham's descendants from bondage in Egypt, formally constituted the Israelites as his chosen people with the giving of the Law at Sinai, and, finally, led them into the promised land of Canaan after forty years of wandering in the wilderness (Exodus–Joshua). The ensuing story

---

15. Theissen (1998: 128). Deines is even more specific, outlining Jewish social identity in terms of the very practices I examine in this book:

> When Greek and Roman (and later Christian) authors wrote about Jews or Jewish religion, they and their readers associated concrete conceptions with it: at the visible level of 'practice' (which therefore was more readily perceptible to outsiders) were Sabbath, circumcision, food laws, and the temple cult (2001: 453).

A current trend in scholarship seeks to downplay Jewish distinctiveness. Cohen, for example, has recently asserted that 'Jews and Gentiles in antiquity were corporeally, visually, linguistically, and socially indistinguishable' (1999: 37). Someone should have told Dio Cassius. In his eyes Judeans were 'distinguished from the rest of mankind in practically every detail of life' (*Hist.* 37.17.1). The truth, of course, lies somewhere in between. See Duling's brief but judicious response to Cohen's perspective (2005: 136).

16. No attempt will be made to sort through various scholarly reconstructions of the tradition history of the passages I cite from the Hebrew Scriptures, and the corresponding implications of these source-critical hypotheses for the historical development of purity practices in ancient Israel. My concerns relate, instead, to the biblical resources available to post-Maccabean Judeans, who had the whole Old Testament, as we call it, at their disposal, and who utilized their sacred text in a pre-critical way to explain and justify behaviors deemed important in their own socio-historical setting.

of Israel is the story of a particular people of God surrounded (and ultimately conquered and ruled) by a number of hostile nations. The threat of assimilation and loss of national identity was an ever-present one, particularly during the exilic and postexilic periods.[17] These socio-political realities guaranteed that the notion of election—the conviction that Yahweh had chosen the descendants of Abraham as his covenant people—would serve as a unifying theme throughout the narrative of Israel's history as it unfolds in the Hebrew Scriptures.

Israel's election and social particularity find their roots in Israelite monotheism: the Mosaic Law intended that Yahweh's 'otherness', as a deity utterly unique among the Ancient Near Eastern pantheon of gods, be replicated in Israel's 'otherness', as a people of God standing alone in the midst of pagan idolatry. And Israel was expected to manifest her uniqueness among the nations in some decidedly observable ways. The book of Leviticus, for example, draws an explicit connection between the character of Yahweh and the otherness of his people, and insists that this connection be reflected in Israel's dietary practices. Yahweh instructs his people as follows:

> 22 'You shall keep all my statutes and all my ordinances, and observe them, so that the land to which I bring you to settle in may not vomit you out. 23 You shall not follow the practices of the nation that I am driving out before you. Because they did all these things, I abhorred them. 24 But I have said to you: "You shall inherit their land, and I will give it to you to possess, a land flowing with milk and honey. I am the Lord your God; I have separated you from the peoples. 25 You shall therefore make a distinction between the clean animal and the unclean, and between the unclean bird and the clean; you shall not bring abomination on yourselves by animal or by bird or by anything with which the ground teems, which I have set apart for you to hold unclean. 26 You shall be holy to me; for I the Lord am holy, and I have separated you from the other peoples to be mine"' (Lev. 20.22-26).[18]

The practice of eating only 'clean' foods—a practice designed ultimately to reflect the uniqueness of Israel's God: 'for I the LORD am holy' (v. 26)—was

---

17. A reality noted even by pagan writers: '...when [the Jews] became subject to foreign rule, as a result of their mingling with men of other nations (both under Persian rule and under that of the Macedonians who overthrew the Persians), many of their traditional practices were disturbed' (Diodorus, *Hist.* 40.3.8, citing Hecataeus of Abdera).

18. See Riches's helpful analysis of this passage (1982: 115-17). Riches notes that 'at least at the redactional stage, the sociological sense of such purity regulations was fully acknowledged and understood' (116). The food laws are elaborated upon in some detail in Leviticus 11, where, once again, we encounter the principle that the dietary statutes are intended to replicate and reflect Yahweh's and Israel's 'otherness' (vv. 44-45). Deuteronomy also contains a lengthy list of clean and unclean animals (14.3-21), this time right on the heels of a pointed divine assertion of Israel's social particularity: 'For you are a people holy to the Lord your God; it is you the Lord has chosen out of all the peoples on earth to be his people, his treasured possession' (Deut. 14.2).

but one of several visible ways in which Israel marked herself out as distinct from surrounding peoples. Additional expressions of Israel's otherness included the preservation of distinctions between sacred and profane times and between sacred and profane space. We will briefly consider each of these binary social constructs as they are articulated and developed in the Old Testament.

a. *Sacred and Profane Times*
The Hebrew Scriptures trace the origins of Israel's yearly calendar to the Sinaitic covenant. Sacred times for the Israelites included annual festivals, the sabbatical year, and the year of jubilee. As with most agrarian societies, the calendar closely followed the agricultural seasons. But in Israel's case, festivals which in other societies normally marked important changes in the natural cycle became, through Sinaitic legislation, directly tied to Israel's identity as the chosen people of Yahweh. The institution of the feast of Passover is a transparent example of this phenomenon. In this instance, the Mosaic Law historicizes the most important annual event among agrarian peoples—the celebration of the spring equinox—by redefining the festival as a celebration of Yahweh's great act of salvation in delivering Israel from bondage in Egypt.[19] The recurring high point in the yearly agricultural cycle is profoundly transformed into a striking reminder of a singular moment in history past when God constituted Israel as a people for his own possession by physically removing the Israelites from foreign domination. Israel's most sacred festival thus becomes an annual memorial to her otherness as the particular people of Yahweh.[20]

Then, of course, there was the Sabbath. The weekly Sabbath, unconnected to seasonal phenomena, was particularly amenable to theological interpretation. The Scriptures offer several reasons for Sabbath-keeping, including simply the interruption of normal day-to-day activities for the purpose of rest (Deut. 5.14-15). But the Law also relates the observance of the Sabbath to Israel's special covenantal relationship with Yahweh. Like the food laws, the Sabbath was intended to serve as a visible sign that God had set apart Israel for himself:

19. The festival was observed at the full moon of the first month of the vernal new year (Wise [1992: 237]).

20. The analysis obtains regardless of one's perspective on the historical origins of Passover. Ongoing questions concerning the development of the feast are not particularly relevant to the present project. I am concerned here not with the origins of Israel's religious practices but, rather, with the symbols that Second-Temple Judeans had available to them as they sought to reestablish and reconstruct the contours of Jewish identity in response to the crisis of Hellenization under Antiochus IV. The understanding of the feast of Passover outlined above had, of course, been deeply embedded in the written Torah for generations prior to the Maccabean revolt.

> 12 The LORD said to Moses: 13 You yourself are to speak to the Israelites: 'You shall keep my sabbaths, for this is a sign between me and you throughout your generations, given in order that you may know that I, the LORD, sanctify you. 14 You shall keep the sabbath, because it is holy for you; everyone who profanes it shall be put to death; whoever does any work on it shall be cut off from among the people. 15 Six days shall work be done, but the seventh day is a sabbath of solemn rest, holy to the LORD; whoever does any work on the sabbath day shall be put to death. 16 Therefore the Israelites shall keep the sabbath, observing the sabbath throughout their generations, as a perpetual covenant. 17 It is a sign forever between me and the people of Israel that in six days the LORD made heaven and earth, and on the seventh day he rested, and was refreshed' (Exod. 31.12-17).

Sabbath is more than a day of rest. It is a day that is 'holy'. To fail to observe the Sabbath is to risk being 'cut off from among the people' (v. 14).

The sociological implications of Sabbath legislation surface elsewhere in the Old Testament. During the postexilic period, for example, the relationship between Sabbath-keeping and Israel's socio-political identity constituted a central part of Nehemiah's reforms after his return from Babylon. Nehemiah 13 portrays the people of Israel separating themselves from 'all those of foreign descent' (v. 3). Specific reforms that follow include the removal of Tobiah the Ammonite from the temple precinct (vv. 4-8), the enforcement of a prohibition of intermarriage with foreigners (vv. 23-27), and careful attention to the proper observance of the Sabbath (vv. 15-22). In his efforts to lock foreign traders outside the gates of Jerusalem on the Sabbath day, moreover, Nehemiah's concern to preserve distinctions between sacred and profane times (Sabbath) intersects with yet another aspect of Israel's otherness vis-à-vis the nations: the practice of establishing territorial distinctions between sacred and profane space.[21]

b. *Sacred and Profane Space*
Yahweh's covenant with Abraham included a key territorial component—the promise of the land of Canaan:

> 18 On that day the LORD made a covenant with Abram, saying, 'To your descendants I give this land, from the river of Egypt to the great river, the river Euphrates, 19 the land of the Kenites, the Kenizzites, the Kadmonites, 20 the Hittites, the Perizzites, the Rephaim, 21 the Amorites, the Canaanites, the Girgashites, and the Jebusites' (Gen. 15.18-21).

Like the laws relating to food and calendar, the promise of the land was closely connected to Israel's otherness as a nation. Indeed, according to the

---

21. See Olyan (2004) for a discussion of purity and social boundaries in Ezra-Nehemiah.

author of Leviticus, Yahweh physically isolates Israel from foreign nations precisely by giving his people their own geographical space:

> 'But I have said to you: "You shall inherit their land, and I will give it to you to possess, a land flowing with milk and honey. I am the LORD your God; I have separated you from the peoples"' (Lev. 20.24).

Stories of the conquest and occupation of Canaan (Joshua), the establishment of the Davidic monarchy in Jerusalem (2 Samuel 5–7), and the erection of Solomon's temple on Yahweh's 'holy hill' (1 Kings 6–8; cf. Pss 2.6; 3.4; 15.1; 24.3; 43.3) encouraged Israel to develop a rather complex map of sacred and profane space, one centered, of course, on Jerusalem and her temple. Ps 137.5-6 pointedly highlights the preeminent place of Jerusalem on the Jewish map of territorial priorities:[22]

> 5 If I forget you, O Jerusalem,
>   let my right hand wither!
> 6 Let my tongue cling to the roof of my mouth,
>   if I do not remember you,
>   if I do not set Jerusalem
>   above my highest joy.

Later portions of the Old Testament exhibit the same concern to delineate between sacred and profane space. In his instructions for a postexilic temple, for example, the prophet Ezekiel writes the following:

> 1 When you allot the land as an inheritance, you shall set aside for the LORD a portion of the land as a holy district, twenty-five thousand cubits long and twenty thousand cubits wide; it shall be holy throughout its entire extent. 2 Of this, a square plot of five hundred by five hundred cubits shall be for the sanctuary, with fifty cubits for an open space around it. 3 In the holy district you shall measure off a section twenty-five thousand cubits long and ten

---

22. Schwartz singles out the territorial principle as the 'most salient' aspect of Jewish identity during the period of the Israelite monarchy (1992: 5-6). Examples abound. According to 1 Samuel, Saul, by causing David to flee the land of Israel, compromised David's 'share in the heritage of the Lord, saying, "Go, serve other gods"' (26.19). Exiled from Yahweh's territory, David fears that he will be driven 'away from the presence of the Lord' (26.20). Israel's sacred space later surfaces as an important bone of contention between Jeremiah and his opponents during the conflict with Babylon. As Schwartz perceptively observes,

> [T]he fact that the Assyrian army which conquered the north failed, miraculously (it seemed), to take Jerusalem (II Kings 19) certainly enhanced confidence in the belief that 'This is the Temple of the Lord, the Temple of the Lord, the Temple of the Lord' (Jeremiah 7.4) and, therefore, the impregnable capital of His land (1992: 6).

Yahweh's readiness to defend the temple in response to the pleas of a Torah-observant Israel would become a central point of ideology for multitudes of Second-Temple Judeans in the wake of the Maccabean revolt (see Chapter 2).

thousand wide, in which shall be the sanctuary, the most holy place. 4 It shall be a holy portion of the land; it shall be for the priests, who minister in the sanctuary and approach the LORD to minister to him; and it shall be both a place for their houses and a holy place for the sanctuary (Ezek. 45.1-4).

Passages like those cited above provided the basis for the later development of an increasingly detailed territoriality of sacred space, a perspective that would ultimately, by the time of Jesus, divide the earth into 'ten degrees of holiness' (*m. Kel.* 1.7-9).[23] The phrase 'holy land', familiar to us today, occurs only once in the Hebrew Scriptures (Zech. 2.12). In later generations the expression would become an increasingly popular one for the territory that God had given to Israel (Wis. 12.3; 2 Macc. 1.7; *Bib. Ant.* 19.10).

c. *Circumcision*

A final practice of social demarcation which finds itself deeply embedded in Israel's story is the covenant rite of circumcision. The Scriptures trace the rite back to Yahweh's covenant with Abraham:[24]

> 10 'This is my covenant, which you shall keep, between me and you and your offspring after you: Every male among you shall be circumcised. 11 You shall circumcise the flesh of your foreskins, and it shall be a sign of the covenant between me and you. 12 Throughout your generations every male among you shall be circumcised when he is eight days old, including the slave born in your house and the one bought with your money from any foreigner who is not of your offspring. 13 Both the slave born in your house and the one bought with your money must be circumcised. So shall my covenant be in your flesh an everlasting covenant. 14 Any uncircumcised male who is not circumcised in the flesh of his foreskin shall be cut off from his people; he has broken my covenant' (Gen. 17.10-14).

Circumcision was a vital symbol of Israel's otherness as the people of Yahweh among the nations of the ancient Near East. The connection between Israel's social identity and the rite of circumcision can be observed in the story of the defiling of Dinah by Shechem the Hivite (Genesis 34). When Hamor, Shechem's father, offers to the sons of Jacob the prospect of intermarriage and the sharing of the land, the Jacobites reply as follows:

> 15 'Only on this condition will we consent to you: that you will become as we are and every male among you be circumcised. 16 Then we will give our daughters to you, and we will take your daughters for ourselves, and we will live among you and become one people' (Gen. 34.15-16).

23. Note the informative study of purity and sacred space in the Priestly Code by Kawashima, who affirms that 'P's sense of purity and pollution rests on a well-defined spatial order' (2003: 379).

24. For a judicious treatment of the origin and significance of circumcision in Genesis 17, see Derouchie (2004: 182-89, and especially 182 n. 11, where the author emphasizes the 'exclusive significance' of the rite).

As it turns out, the offer is a ruse, but the function of circumcision as a badge of Israelite identity remains quite transparent. Israel can live together as 'one people' only with foreigners whose males are circumcised. The Hivites must agree to circumcision before they are permitted to intermarry with the people of God.

d. *Israel's Identity Markers as a Systemic Whole*

Though it has been helpful to examine each of Israel's boundary markers in turn, the Israelites themselves undoubtedly understood these defining social practices as a cultural gestalt, as behaviors that collectively articulated what it meant to be the particular people of God. The feast of Passover at once demonstrates the truth of this assertion. As noted above, Passover was the preeminent annual celebration of Israel's otherness as the chosen people of Yahweh, Israel's sacred time *par excellence*. But the celebration of Passover came to have a distinct territorial dimension, as well. Jews during the Second-Temple period would annually travel to God's holy city Jerusalem to observe Passover in obedience to the following legal statute:[25]

> 5 You are not permitted to offer the passover sacrifice within any of your towns that the LORD your God is giving you. 6 But at the place that the LORD your God will choose as a dwelling for his name, only there shall you offer the passover sacrifice, in the evening at sunset, the time of day when you departed from Egypt (Deut. 16.5-6).

Sacred time is thus to be celebrated in sacred space. And to this convergence of sacred time and space in the celebration of Passover we must add the important covenant symbol of circumcision, for a nexus also exists in the Scriptures between the rite of circumcision and Israel's holy festival—everyone who partakes of Passover must be circumcised. During the institution of the festival, the Lord instructs Moses,

> 'If an alien who resides with you wants to celebrate the passover to the LORD, all his males shall be circumcised; then he may draw near to celebrate it; he shall be regarded as a native of the land. But no uncircumcised person shall eat of it' (Exod. 12.48).[26]

---

25. It is not clear that Second-Temple Jews celebrated Passover only in Jerusalem. Saldarini has maintained as much (1984: 16), but there seems to be evidence for Judeans in the Diaspora observing the festival apart from the temple, for example, among the Elephantine garrison in Egypt (Oakman [2005: 7]).

26. The rite of circumcision intersects with Israel's concern to maintain distinctions between sacred and profane space in another important Old Testament narrative. In the early chapters of Joshua we discover that the new generation of Israelites who came out of the wilderness could not cross the Jordan to enter the land of promise until they were circumcised (Josh. 5.4-7).

Scholars are now arguing for a connection between Israel's various identity-related practices, even where such associations are not explicitly spelled out in the texts. See, for

The juxtaposition in the context of Passover of the themes of circumcision, sacred space, and sacred time demonstrates that the Israelites conceived of these defining symbols as a systemic whole, a socio-cultural 'package' of practices that served to mark out the descendants of Abraham as the particular people of God.

e. *A Concluding Note of Qualification*

The above discussion might give the impression that the Hebrew Scriptures are quite preoccupied with practices related to sacred food, sacred seasons, sacred space, and circumcision, particularly where issues of Israel's social identity are concerned. Such an impression would be somewhat misleading. Now it is certainly the case that the Old Testament texts cited above served as a perfectly adequate foundation for the erection of an elaborate edifice of purity legislation (oral and written) during the post-Maccabean era. But in order to appreciate the striking novelty of these later developments, it is important to recognize that such concerns do not occupy a particularly prominent place in the Hebrew Scriptures themselves. With the exception of the passages cited above (and, perhaps, the use of the pejorative expression 'uncircumcised' [ערל] in reference to the Philistines), these identity markers are seldom explicitly connected in the Old Testament with Israel's socio-cultural otherness as a particular people of God. All this would change, however, with the empire-building of the Macedonians and the Romans, and, particularly, with events that occurred during the reign of the Seleucid dynast Antiochus IV Epiphanes. It is to this defining era of Judean history that we now turn.

3. *The Crisis of Hellenization*

The end of Old Testament history finds once-exiled Judeans back in the land, now under Persian hegemony. After losing the northern tribes to an Assyrian invasion during the eighth century BCE, the southern kingdom of Judah had been sacked by the Babylonians in the early sixth century. A major upheaval in ancient Near Eastern politics opened the door for the first wave of Jews to return to Judea from captivity in Babylon. In 539 BCE, Cyrus, head of the Medo-Persian Empire, gained control of Babylon and immediately enacted a series of benevolent policies by which he sought to unite various subject peoples under Persian rule. Cyrus permitted Babylonian Jews, along with other deported nations, to return to their homeland. Judeans soon rebuilt

---

example, Kawashima's perceptive interpretation of the Year of Jubilee as a restoration to 'cosmic purity' of Israel's original territorial distribution, through the freeing of slaves and the return of ancestral property (2003). Here, sacred space and sacred time reinforce one another in a systematic and effective way.

their temple (completed c. 516 BCE), continued to return in groups from Babylon, and, finally, erected the walls of Jerusalem under the leadership of Nehemiah during the reign of the Persian king Artaxerxes I (c. 445 BCE).

The generations to follow saw Macedonian Greeks gain ascendancy over the Persians, as Alexander the Great defeated Darius III and the Persian royal army, first in Asia (333 BCE) and then outside of Baghdad (331 BCE). After an aborted foray eastward into India, Alexander returned to Babylon to consolidate his empire and plan for the future, only to have his hopes for further expansion end prematurely with his death at age thirty-two (323 BCE). Lacking a legitimate heir, a group of powerful contenders for the throne inaugurated a period of strife and chaos which ultimately resulted in a threefold division of Alexander's expansive realm. Antigonus took over those parts of the empire located in Macedonia, Greece, and Asia Minor. A second general, Seleucus, claimed for himself the eastern portion of Alexander's conquests, ultimately adding both Syria and Asia Minor to his kingdom, after various victories over Antigonus. Seleucus built Antioch on the Orontes to serve as the capital of the newly founded Syrian Greek empire. The third portion of Alexander's empire fell to Ptolemy I Soter, who established himself in Egypt in 305 BCE. From his capital at Alexandria, Ptolemy ruled over Egypt, Cyrene, Cyprus, and, for more than a century, over Judeans in Palestine.

Relations between the people of Yahweh and their Ptolemaic Greek rulers were generally positive in nature.[27] The Jews were permitted to govern their small temple state according to the provisions of the Torah, while Greek leaders in Alexandria administered and taxed the kingdom. Imperial power struggles in the eastern Mediterranean, however, cast an ominous shadow over the relative stability enjoyed by Judeans under Ptolemaic rule. Throughout much of the period the Ptolemies in Egypt competed with the Seleucids in the north for control of the East, with Judea awkwardly situated geographically between these warring empires. A decisive Syrian victory at the battle of Paneion in the early second century brought the Jews irreversibly under the hegemony of the Seleucids in Antioch. Shortly thereafter (190 BCE), the Seleucids themselves suffered a devastating defeat at the hands of the Romans, and relations between the Syrian Greeks and their remaining vassal peoples—especially the Jews—became increasingly strained. Deprived of income from wealthy portions of western Asia, and in need of money to indemnify Rome, Seleucid dynasts increasingly looked to dependent temple states in the east for much-needed financial resources. Antiochus III met his death attempting to plunder a famous Elamite temple,

---

27. From the Jewish side, see the *Letter of Aristeas*. Hecataeus of Abdera, who visited Egypt during the time of Ptolemy I, writes quite positively of the Jews (preserved in Diodorus, *Hist.* 40.3).

and his son Seleucus IV apparently tried unsuccessfully to appropriate money from the temple in Jerusalem—the first stage in the clash between the Seleucids and their Judean subjects.

Conflict between Jews and Greeks escalated exponentially under the rule of the next Syrian dynast, Antiochus IV Epiphanes (175–163 BCE). Rebuffed by the Romans in an attempt to annex Ptolemaic Egypt, and frustrated by factional intrigue and betrayal on the part of certain Judean elites, Antiochus proceeded to engage in a series of activities that guaranteed that his reign would become a watershed moment in Jewish history. To this day Antiochus IV is remembered by the Jews as the pagan king who desecrated the Jerusalem temple and proscribed socio-religious practices that for centuries had marked out Judeans as the particular people of Yahweh. The most important summary of Antiochus's edict of forced Hellenization is found in the first chapter of 1 Maccabees:

> 41 Then the king wrote to his whole kingdom that all should be one people, 42 and that all should give up their particular customs. 43 All the Gentiles accepted the command of the king. Many even from Israel gladly adopted his religion; they sacrificed to idols and profaned the sabbath. 44 And the king sent letters by messengers to Jerusalem and the towns of Judah; he directed them to follow customs strange to the land, 45 to forbid burnt offerings and sacrifices and drink offerings in the sanctuary, to profane sabbaths and festivals, 46 to defile the sanctuary and the priests, 47 to build altars and sacred precincts and shrines for idols, to sacrifice swine and other unclean animals, 48 and to leave their sons uncircumcised. They were to make themselves abominable by everything unclean and profane, 49 so that they would forget the law and change all the ordinances. 50 He added, 'And whoever does not obey the command of the king shall die' (1 Macc. 1.41-50).

The abuses reached their apex in the desecration of the temple in 167 BCE: 'Now on the fifteenth day of Chislev, in the one hundred forty-fifth year, they erected a desolating sacrilege on the altar of burnt offering' (1 Macc. 1.54).

The incomplete and polemical nature of our sources has generated a number of plausible reconstructions of events leading up to Antiochus's edict and the profanation of the temple. Scholars had traditionally interpreted texts like those cited above at face value, assigning to the godless Syrian king responsibility for the proscription of Jewish distinctives and the desecration of the temple. Students of the period now recognize the deeply ideological *tendenz* of the Maccabean accounts, and most scholars today, following the seminal contribution of Bickerman, trace the origins of the Antiochan persecution at least partly to the Jews.[28] The texts themselves

---

28. Aguilar refers to 'Syrian policies implemented through Judean supporters' (2000: 62). The thesis arguing that radical Hellenization had its beginnings in Jewish circles—and which views the imperial decree as a response to circumstances surround-

suggest Jewish complicity in the Hellenization project. Notice, for example, the brief comment in 1 Maccabees, above: 'Many even from Israel gladly adopted his religion; they sacrificed to idols and profaned the sabbath' (1 Macc. 1.43). 2 Maccabees is more adamant about Jewish involvement. It was not Antiochus but, rather, the Jewish high priest Jason who 'shifted his compatriots over to the Greek way of life' (2 Macc. 4.10). The author elaborates upon Jason's Hellenizing agenda as follows:

> 11 [H]e destroyed the lawful ways of living and introduced new customs contrary to the law. 12 He took delight in establishing a gymnasium right under the citadel, and he induced the noblest of the young men to wear the Greek hat. 13 There was such an extreme of Hellenization and increase in the adoption of foreign ways because of the surpassing wickedness of Jason, who was ungodly and no true high priest, 14 that the priests were no longer intent upon their service at the altar. Despising the sanctuary and neglecting the sacrifices, they hurried to take part in the unlawful proceedings in the wrestling arena after the signal for the discus-throwing, 15 disdaining the honors prized by their ancestors and putting the highest value upon Greek forms of prestige (2 Macc. 4.11-15).

To appreciate why Jewish priestly elites like Jason found Hellenism so attractive, we must return for a moment to the conquests of Alexander the Great some generations earlier.

The transition from Persian to Greek rule represented for the Jews of the Second-Temple period more than simply an exchange of Gentile overlords. Alexander and his followers brought with them a culture that would influence Jewish thinking and subsequent Jewish history in ways unimaginable during the late fourth century. Alexander inherited the leadership of a Greek world that could already boast centuries of history and cultural achievement. Homer's great epics, which served as the defining narratives for Greek identity in Alexander's day, had been in existence some five hundred years. Greek literature—drama, poetry, history, and romance—had an established pedigree, and Aristotle, Alexander's personal tutor, represented but a single branch of a lively philosophical tradition that could trace its roots back for generations. To this profound literary and philosophical heritage must be added Greek art, particularly sculpture, and, of course, Hellenistic religion. Religion for the Greeks was both civic and personal in orientation. Greek city-states continued to pay homage to the old gods of Mount Olympus, along with various local deities. Mystery religions appealed to the individual with their various rites of purification and initiation, offering, in some cases, a personal relationship with the deity and the promise of a blessed afterlife.

ing this Judean initiative—has seen considerable refinement over the years. See Bickerman (1937/1979); Tcherikover (1961); Hengel (1974); and Bringmann (1983). Grabbe provides a helpful summary of the history of the debate (1992a: 248-55).

The arrival of Alexander, and the ensuing establishment of the Ptolemaic and Seleucid kingdoms under the authority of his successors, meant that Hellenistic practices and ideals would now exist alongside the cultural values of indigenous peoples such as the Jews.[29] Among the most far-reaching achievements of Alexander and his followers in this regard was the colonization of the East by Macedonian and Greek veterans in cities established according to the pattern of the Greek model. For centuries Greeks had regarded the *polis* as the natural form of human social organization. Laid out in characteristic grid-like fashion, the typical Greek *polis* boasted a municipal office, a theater, an open agora, a stadium, a public water supply, and a gymnasium, along with numerous temples and altars dedicated to pagan deities. The gymnasium, in particular, served as a hub of social and intellectual life for male elites in the *polis*. Although the power of the *polis* to act in a totally independent manner was circumscribed in the imperial setting of Alexander and his successors, the Greek cities retained a degree of autonomy and, more importantly, continued to provide a fertile soil for the cultivation and propagation of Hellenic culture and values.

New cities were founded with exclusively Greek populations. Older cities were Hellenized and populated with Greeks, along with indigenous urbanites. By the Roman era, Judea was virtually surrounded by Greek cities, most of them thoroughly Hellenized during the Ptolemaic period. Gaza, for example, which served as a Macedonian garrison town from the time of its defeat after a two-month siege at the hands of Alexander the Great, is categorically designated as a 'Greek' city by Josephus (Josephus, *War* 2.97). Shortly after the siege of Gaza, Alexander visited Egypt, where his stay was interrupted when he was forced to respond to an uprising of the inhabitants of Samaria. He (or his commander Perdiccas) attacked Samaria and reestablished it as a Greek city with Macedonian colonists. Further north on the coast of Palestine, Ptolemy Philadelphus (285–246 BCE) refounded Acre as the thoroughly Hellenized Ptolemais. Regions east of the Jordan contained numerous Hellenistic settlements, including Philadelphia, Hippus, Gadara, Pella, and Dium. Plutarch probably exaggerates only somewhat when he ascribes to Alexander alone the creation of some seventy cities of this kind (*Alex.* 1.5).

The effect upon local peoples of the establishment by Alexander and his successors of these Greek centers of thought and culture cannot be overem-

---

29. It is probably overstatement to assert, with Emil Schürer, that '[it] was the grandiose plan of Alexander the Great to found a world empire that would be held together, not only by unity of government, but also by unity of language, customs and culture' (1973/1885: 143). A number of the cities founded by Alexander, and populated by Macedonian and Greek veterans, were intended primarily as garrisons. Cultural considerations were secondary, if present at all (Milns [1992: 147]). The result for local peoples, however, was much the same.

phasized. Indeed, it has now become quite clear that the Jewish high-priest Jason's Hellenizing agenda (above) specifically involved reconstituting Jerusalem as a Hellenistic *polis*:

> 9 In addition to this [Jason] promised to pay [Antiochus] one hundred fifty more if permission were given to establish by his authority a gymnasium and a body of youth for it, and to enroll the people of Jerusalem as citizens of Antioch. 10 When the king assented and Jason came to office, he at once shifted his compatriots over to the Greek way of life (2 Macc. 4.9-10).[30]

As we might imagine, not all were pleased with the attraction to Hellenism which characterized Jerusalem's priestly elites, even before the forceful intervention of Antiochus. Opposition to the Hellenization project only crystallized into organized military resistance, however, in response to the formal proscription of Torah-keeping which resulted from Antiochus's edict.

Jewish resistance erupted fervently in a small village in Judea named Modein, when agents of the Greek king attempted to force local residents to compromise their allegiance to Yahweh. Among the assembled village dignitaries was a family headed by an esteemed priest named Mattathias. Imperial officials first tried to get Mattathias to obey the king's orders by offering a sacrifice on a pagan altar. The aged priest adamantly refused:

> 19 'Even if all the nations that live under the rule of the king obey him, and have chosen to obey his commandments, everyone of them abandoning the religion of their ancestors, 20 I and my sons and my brothers will continue to live by the covenant of our ancestors. 21 Far be it from us to desert the law and the ordinances. 22 We will not obey the king's words by turning aside from our religion to the right hand or to the left' (1 Macc. 2.19-22).

A fellow-villager then came forward to sacrifice. Mattathias, righteously indignant, reacted in the tradition of Phineas, a faithful priest of an earlier generation who had turned away Yahweh's wrath from Israel by zealously killing a fellow-Israelite who had rebelled against the Lord (Num. 25.1-13):

> 24 When Mattathias saw it, he burned with zeal and his heart was stirred. He gave vent to righteous anger; he ran and killed him on the altar. 25 At the same time he killed the king's officer who was forcing them to sacrifice, and he tore down the altar. 26 Thus he burned with zeal for the law, just as Phinehas did against Zimri son of Salu (1 Macc. 2.24-26).

---

30. A newly published inscription, containing the texts of two letters from the Attalid king Eumenes II to the Phrygian community of Tyriaion, clarifies previously debated portions of the Greek text of 2 Maccabees. Kennell concludes his recent study of the parallels between 2 Macc. 4.7-15 and the letters from Eumenes with the categorical assertion that 'no reasonable doubt remains that Jason's intention was to transform Jerusalem into a *polis* along Greek lines' (Kennell [2005: 23]).

A line was drawn in the sand, and Mattathias now recognized that the damage done to relations between his family and Seleucid imperial authorities was irreversible:

> 27 Then Mattathias cried out in the town with a loud voice, saying: 'Let every one who is zealous for the law and supports the covenant come out with me!' 28 Then he and his sons fled to the hills and left all that they had in the town (1 Macc. 2.27-28).

The old priest's actions ignited a series of skirmishes and direct military encounters between the Seleucids and Mattathias's sons, which would go down in Jewish history as one of the noblest religious wars ever fought by the people of God. Three years after the desecration of the altar, Judas Maccabeus and his followers gained control of the temple precinct, purified the temple, and reinstituted Yahweh worship in accordance with the statutes of the Torah (164 BCE).[31]

Such are the broad contours of the history of the period, and it will not be necessary to decide here between competing reconstructions of events that unfolded as relations deteriorated between Antiochus IV and his Jewish subjects. Scholars will continue to debate the precise order of events and the respective degrees of complicity of the various players involved in the Hellenization project.[32] More germane to the present discussion are the par-

---

31. I employ throughout the traditional dates for the proscription of Jewish religious practices (167–164 BCE). Bringmann (1983: 15-28), followed by VanderKam (1987: 29), dates the rededication to December 165 BCE.

32. See Sievers's monograph (1990) on early Hasmonean history. Antiochus's motivation in the edict remains a mystery, so that Millar's observation of a generation ago still obtains: '[T]here seems to be no way of reaching an understanding of how Antiochus came to take a step so profoundly at variance with the normal assumptions of governance in his time' (1978: 17).

The motives of Mattathias and his sons, as well, are currently undergoing scholarly reevaluation. The traditional understanding identifies the Hasmoneans as champions of Jewish religious freedom who only later became entangled in the trappings of politics and power. Schwartz counters that the Maccabees' 'main concern at all periods was their own advancement' (1993: 309). Note also Nongbri's recent treatment of the revolt as political in motivation from the outset (2005). What distinguishes the Maccabees, in Nongbri's view, from other power hungry families, like the Oniads and Tobiads, is that the Hasmoneans successfully 'cast their actions as a defense of ancestral customs', in order to legitimate their authority (105).

I am not persuaded that we can accurately ascertain the original motivation of the Maccabean resistance movement. But Nongbri's point about the later legitimation of the Hasmonean venture is an important one, nonetheless. For whatever we might conclude about the events of 175–164 BCE, it was the success of the ensuing Maccabean historiographical enterprise—reflected in the widespread influence of documents like 1 and 2 Maccabees and *4 Maccabees*—that significantly contributed to the socio-cultural defensiveness of Judeans in Palestine under Roman rule some decades later.

ticular Jewish behaviors that found themselves at the center of the firestorm surrounding the king's edict (1 Macc. 1.45-48). It is crucial to recognize that the specific practices Antiochus proscribed were those now-familiar social identity markers that had served for centuries to mark out Judeans as Yahweh's chosen people: circumcision, and distinctions between sacred and profane space, times, and foods. These defining practices occupy a prominent place throughout the narratives of 1 and 2 Maccabees, as the authors proceed (after outlining Antiochus's edict) to portray imperial authorities torturing and murdering numbers of Jews who continued to circumcise their male infants and observe Old Testament dietary restrictions in defiance of the king's edict (1 Macc. 1.60-62; 2 Macc. 6.10; 6.18–7.42). What we see here in the Maccabean literature underscores an important historical reality with far-reaching implications for our understanding of the life of Jesus of Nazareth and the genesis of early Christianity—one of the key results of the Maccabean experience was a conspicuous change of attitude towards these vital badges of Jewish ethnic identity.

Compare, for example, the activities of the Judean Hellenizers (above) with the behaviors of Jews in the East two centuries later. We look in vain among Jewish leaders during the New Testament period for the kind of agenda championed by pre-Maccabean Jerusalem elites, such as the high-priest Jason and his followers, who played loose with Judaism's defining social practices. To be sure, the influence of Hellenic thought and culture was pervasive and permanent in many areas of life. This much has been indisputably established by a recent generation of New Testament scholars.[33] Faithfulness to the Jewish distinctives discussed above, however, was virtually universal among Judeans throughout the Roman Empire, and persons ready to abandon Jewish identity in favor of overt Hellenism stand out as exceptional among first-century Jews.[34]

33. Hengel (1974) remains the seminal work in this area.
34. Tiberius Julius Alexander, prefect of Judea (46–48 CE) and Egypt (68–69 CE) is a rare example (Josephus, *Ant.* 20.100-103), as are Dositheus of Alexandria, 'a Jew by birth who later changed his religion and apostasized from the ancestral traditions' (*3 Macc.* 1.3) and, also, perhaps, those whom Philo opposes as 'extreme allegorizers' (*Mig.* 89-93). Note, however, that these persons each abandoned their Jewish identity on Egyptian, not Palestinian, soil. And even here such behavior was exceptional. (On the Palestinian side, Josephus does charge John of Gischala with having 'unlawful food served at his table' and abrogating the 'rules of purity', but one wonders how much to make of this heated polemic against the author's bitter enemy [Josephus, *War* 7.264]). The great majority of Jews in the Diaspora remained faithful to their ethnic distinctives, as illustrated by the Greco-Roman take on Jewish identity discussed above. Thus, Philo—a highly Hellenized Alexandrian Jew who sought to discern the moral significance of the law through allegory, and who reinterpreted the commandments in philosophical terms—nevertheless insisted on the observance of boundary practices related to food and Sabbath (*Mig.* 89-93).

The change of attitude can be seen in Jewish literature penned during the post-Maccabean period. A number of writings of Palestinian provenance produced during and after the Maccabean crisis exhibit a distinct preoccupation with symbols of Jewish identity. Discussions about circumcision, the sanctity of the temple, and laws relating to food, festivals, and Sabbath abound in these texts. Such practices, moreover, are often explicitly associated with Israel's otherness, vis-à-vis the Gentiles, as the chosen people of God. For example, long before any 'gentiles' appear on the stage of Israelite history, the author of *Jubilees* depicts the patriarch Abraham exhorting his grandson Jacob as follows:

> 'Separate yourself from the gentiles, and do not eat with them, and do not perform deeds like theirs. And do not become associates of theirs. Because their deeds are defiled, and all of their ways are contaminated, and despicable, and abominable' (*Jub.* 22.16).

Works like *Jubilees* serve as helpful literary windows through which to view clearly the priorities and values of Judeans who produced and preserved these documents during the two centuries that followed the events of 167–164 BCE. Only against the background of the cultural values and social codes reflected in post-Maccabean literature can we properly contextualize Jesus' challenges to defining badges of Jewish identity, such as Sabbath, food, and the Jerusalem temple, as reflected in the gospel narratives. We turn now to examine a representative selection of these informing Second-Temple texts.

Documents articulating the perspectives of Jewish individuals and groups who lived in Palestine during the post-Maccabean period (c. 164 BCE to 70 CE) include the works of Josephus, the writings preserved at Qumran, early portions of the rabbinic corpus, as well as various texts from the Old Testament Apocrypha and Pseudepigrapha. Space limitations constrain the present project to a systematic exploration of seven selected works from the Apocrypha and Pseudepigrapha. The next two chapters examine in some detail 1–2 Maccabees, *4 Maccabees, Jubilees,* Pseudo-Philo's *Biblical Antiquities,* Judith, and the Additions to Esther.[35] For each document my analysis will highlight passages reflecting authorial preoccupation with these vital symbols of Jewish socio-political identity:

- Male circumcision
- Jerusalem and her temple
- Observation of levitical dietary laws
- Sabbath-keeping and the celebration of the annual festivals

---

35. Incidental excerpts from the works of Josephus and other Jewish writers surface later throughout the book.

Cultural practices arising from distinctions between sacred and profane space, times, and foods served, of course, to highlight an even more profound distinction, namely, that between sacred and profane people—the distinction between Second-Temple Judeans and their Gentile neighbors. We will therefore be particularly attentive in our literature survey to those passages that explicitly associate the purity practices outlined above with Jewish social identity.

Chapter 2

INTERPRETING RECENT HISTORY:
THE MACCABEAN THEOLOGICAL ENTERPRISE

> You shall keep my sabbaths and reverence my sanctuary: I am the Lord.
> Leviticus 19.30

> It is no light thing to show irreverence to the divine laws—a fact that later events will make clear.
> 2 Maccabees 4.17

The Maccabees and their supporters got more than they bargained for in their efforts to resist Syrian oppression and regain control of the Jerusalem temple. They ultimately won full independence from Seleucid political hegemony. In 146 BCE Simon was declared ethnarch and high-priest of the Jewish people, and Judeans entered a period of national sovereignty and territorial expansion that would last until Rome intervened and subjugated Judea in 63 BCE. It could hardly have been otherwise. With Rome pressing the Syrian Greeks from the west, and competing claimants to the throne fragmenting the Seleucid power base in Antioch, the currents of imperial history left Judeans relatively free to pursue their own political agenda for several generations.[1]

Jews in Palestine explained things otherwise. From their perspective Maccabean successes had little to do with the mundane events of imperial history. Rather, in concert with traditional Israelite historiography as reflected in the Hebrew Scriptures, Judeans sought explanation at the theological level for their victories over the Seleucid dynasty. It was God who had repulsed the Greeks. To restore and protect the sanctity of his temple Yahweh had intervened on behalf of his chosen people with 'appearances

---

1. The Hasmoneans were not alone in asserting their independence during this period of Seleucid instability. Fischer refers to 'continuous uprisings and strivings for independence throughout the Seleucid empire, particularly in the fringe areas' (1990: 13). It is crucial to distinguish actual political events and motivations surrounding the Maccabean revolt (to the degree that we can discern them) from later attempts on the part of the Hasmoneans to legitimate their authority. As Bickerman wrote long ago, documents like 1–2 Maccabees 'were produced in order to make history, not report it' (1937/1979: 4).

that came from heaven to those who fought bravely for Judaism' (2 Macc. 2.21). As Jewish thinkers sought theologically to account, however, for the various events that had transpired during the Maccabean crisis, they had some rather problematical explaining to do. For Yahweh's intervention on behalf of Jewish interests had been anything but consistent during the years of Seleucid rule.

At times, to be sure, God acted dramatically on Israel's behalf. During the priesthood of Onias III, for example, Yahweh was more than willing to defend his holy dwelling place. When Seleucus IV sent his agent, Heliodorus, to confiscate the temple treasury,

> the Sovereign of spirits and of all authority caused so great a manifestation that all who had been so bold as to accompany [Heliodorus] were astounded by the power of God, and became faint with terror (2 Macc. 3.24).

The author claims that a 'magnificently caparisoned horse' appeared from heaven with a rider armed with 'weapons of gold' (3.25). The theophanic horseman struck Heliodorus to the ground and deprived the Syrian emissary of 'any hope of recovery' (3.29). Only when the faithful high priest offered a sacrifice on his behalf did Heliodorus regain his strength. The humiliated imperial agent returned to Antioch empty-handed. The king, however, remained unwilling to relinquish his desire to confiscate the temple treasury. Seleucus asked Heliodorus whom else he might send to get the job done. Heliodorus was not at all optimistic about the prospects of plundering Yahweh's temple, no matter who the perpetrator might be:

> 38 'If you have any enemy or plotter against your government, send him there, for you will get him back thoroughly flogged, if he survives at all; for there is certainly some power of God about the place. 39 For he who has his dwelling in heaven watches over that place himself and brings it aid, and he strikes and destroys those who come to do it injury' (2 Macc. 3.38-39).

Unfortunately for the Jews, Heliodorus was only partially on target in his analysis. Yahweh had, indeed, watched over the temple and struck down the pagan aggressor on this occasion. Another attempt just a few years later, however, on the part of the next Seleucid dynast, Antiochus IV, encountered only silence from heaven. The author of 2 Maccabees informs us that Antiochus 'dared to enter the most holy temple in all the world', 'took the holy vessels with his polluted hands', and made off unharmed with 'eighteen hundred talents from the temple' (2 Macc. 5.15-16, 21).

The apparent inconsistency of Yahweh's response to an endangered people and temple cried out for explanation. Why had God forcefully repelled Heliodorus but left Antiochus unscathed to do as he wished? Maccabean historians found their solution in the vacillating commitment of the Jewish people to the Torah's badges of national identity. As long as Judeans remained true to injunctions related to the preservation of Jewish social particularity, 'the holy city was inhabited in unbroken peace', and God could be counted on to intervene when Judeans were threatened by Seleucid designs (2 Macc. 3.1). Compromises with Hellenism on the part of Jason and his followers elicited, in contrast, Yahweh's displeasure and corresponding judgment at the hands of Gentile oppressors like Antiochus IV. As one Maccabean historian concluded, 'It is no light thing to show irreverence to the divine laws' (2 Macc. 4.17).

Maccabean historiography sheds much light on the passionate commitment of post-Maccabean Judeans to preserve and reinforce traditional distinctions between sacred and profane times, space, and foods, along with the defining covenant symbol of circumcision. The stories contained in this literature continued to inspire Palestinian Jews in the generations to follow. With the coming of Rome, first-century Judeans were once again suffering under the heavy hand of Gentile imperial rule. Ongoing reflection upon the successes of the Maccabees could not help but convince Jesus' contemporaries that unwavering faithfulness to the socially defining behaviors enjoined in the Torah would be indispensable to any hope of liberation from Roman domination. It is important, therefore, to gain some familiarity with the Maccabean historical writings, in order fully to appreciate Jesus' approach to Jewish social particularity as outlined in the Gospels. The rest of the Chapter surveys 1 and 2 Maccabees and *4 Maccabees* in some detail. We will be attentive in these texts to matters related to Sabbath observance, circumcision, and the food laws, and we will be particularly sensitive to concerns on the part of the authors for the sanctity of Yahweh's holy temple.

1. *1 Maccabees*

1 Maccabees, written in Judea toward the close of the second century BCE, graphically portrays one writer's attitude toward the preservation of the Jewish way of life in the wake of the Maccabean crisis.[2] Concerns related to sacred space, sacred seasons, the dietary laws, and circumcision all find expression in this important narrative of Hasmonean history.

a. *Circumcision*
Circumcision became a defining issue near the beginning of the Maccabean conflict. Early in the narrative we read that Jewish Hellenizers 'removed the marks of circumcision' (1.15), and we are informed that Antiochus

---

2. Bar-Kochva dates 1 Maccabees to the reign of John Hyrcanus (135–104 BCE) (1989: 162-64). General consensus understands the narrative to be an official account of the years 175–135 BCE, written from the Hasmonean point of view. We know that the work enjoyed wide circulation in Jewish Palestine, since Josephus draws on 1 Maccabees some two centuries later, as the primary source for his account of the Maccabean period (*Ant.* 12.237-13.229; see Cohen [1979: 44-47]; Gafni [1989: 116-31]).

proscribed the practice and 'put to death the women who had their children circumcised, and their families and those who circumcised them' (1.48; 1.60-61). During the initial stages of the revolt that followed, the patriarch Mattathias and his friends 'forcibly circumcised all the uncircumcised boys that they found within the borders of Israel' (2.46).

b. *Sacred Space*

Concern for the temple as Israel's sacred space takes pride of place in 1 Maccabees, since the profanation of the temple constituted the low point in a series of actions which finally resulted in revolt on the part of more traditional Jews such as Mattathias and his family. 'To forbid burnt offerings and sacrifices and drink offerings' and 'to defile the sanctuary and the priests' were at the very heart of the king's Hellenizing agenda (1.45-46, 54).

Even before the 'desolating sacrilege' of 167 BCE, Antiochus and his emissaries had, in the eyes of the narrator, already profaned the temple on two separate occasions. Several years before the decree, the king 'arrogantly entered the sanctuary' and confiscated temple furnishings and utensils (1.21-23). Later a large force led by the king's 'chief collector of tribute' returned to Jerusalem, initiated a pogrom against the Jews in the city, and 'even defiled the sanctuary'. The Maccabean historian interjects an editorial lament: '[Jerusalem's] sanctuary became desolate as a desert' (1.29, 37, 39).

Not until the 'desolating sacrilege' of 167 BCE, however, does Jewish reaction to the desecration of the temple first find verbal expression among characters in the narrative itself. Here a lamentation is placed on the lips of Mattathias, which specifically highlights the horror of a defiled holy city and temple:

> 'Alas! Why was I born to see this...the ruin of the holy city...the sanctuary given over to aliens? Her temple has become like a man without honor...our holy place, our beauty, and our glory have been laid waste; the Gentiles have profaned it. Why should we live any longer?' (2.7-13).

The expressions 'our holy place, our beauty, and our glory', along with the explicitly articulated distinction between Judeans ('our...our...our...we') and their Syrian Greek oppressors ('aliens'...'the Gentiles'), pointedly testify to the centrality of the temple as a symbol of Jewish socio-religious identity.

The ensuing chapter finds Judas and his troops engaging a large Syrian force sent to crush the revolt (3.43-45). Here, too, territorial considerations occur in the same context as a self-conscious awareness of the distinction between 'our people' (v. 43) and 'the Gentiles' (v. 45). When the Judeans first hear of the approaching Greek army, they exhort one another, 'Let us...fight for our people and the sanctuary' (3.43). The narrator then intercedes with his own comments decrying the profanation of the temple: 'The sanctuary was trampled down, and the sons of aliens held the citadel; it was a lodging place for the Gentiles' (3.45). What follows is a poignant description of concerns shared among Maccabean sympathizers for the status of temple worship:

> They also brought the vestments of the priesthood and the first fruits and the tithes...and they cried aloud to Heaven, saying, 'What shall we do with these? Where shall we take them? Your sanctuary is trampled down and profaned, and your priests mourn in humiliation' (3.49-51).

The Syrians suffered defeat in this and several ensuing battles, and the temple mount, with the exception of the citadel, was finally in Maccabean hands. The first statement uttered by the victors in the narrative that follows reads, ' "Behold, our enemies are crushed; let us go up to cleanse the sanctuary and dedicate it" ' (4.36). The balance of the chapter details the purification and rededication of the temple and the joyous celebration that followed (4.37-59). Our narrator summarizes: 'There was very great joy among the people, and the disgrace brought by the Gentiles was removed' (v. 58).

Even after the story of the rededication of the temple, the narrative of 1 Maccabees continues to reflect authorial preoccupation with sacred space. Particularly informing is the fate of the Syrian general Nicanor, who threatens to burn down the temple unless Judas and his followers are delivered into his hands. The priests array themselves before the newly rededicated altar and temple and proceed to pray,

> 37 'You chose this house to be called by your name, and to be for your people a house of prayer and supplication. 38 Take vengeance on this man and on his army, and let them fall by the sword; remember their blasphemies, and let them live no longer' (7.37-38).

The prayer is answered in the affirmative; Nicanor is the first to die and his army is massacred so that 'not even one of them was left' (7.46).

The moral of the story of Nicanor's demise—that Gentiles who threaten Yahweh's dwelling place find themselves on the receiving end of divine retribution—is a recurring one in the literature. Even Jews who compromise their ancestral faith by profaning sacred space are not exempt. Sometime around 160 BCE, Alcimus, a Seleucid appointee to the high priesthood who was viewed with great suspicion by Maccabean sympathizers, also died as a direct result of an affront to the temple:

> 54 Alcimus gave orders to tear down the wall of the inner court of the sanctuary. He tore down the work of the prophets! 55 But he only began to tear it down, for at that time Alcimus was stricken and his work was hindered; his mouth was stopped and he was paralyzed, so that he could no longer say a word or give commands concerning his house. 56 And Alcimus died at that time in great agony (9.54-56).

The wall in question separated the Court of the Gentiles from the rest of the temple complex.

The remaining texts in 1 Maccabees which focus upon sacred space narrate portions of the rule of Simon, 'the great high priest and commander and leader of the Jews' (13.42). Immediately after his brother Jonathan is taken captive, but before Simon is formally installed as the nation's leader, he proclaims to his people, 'You yourselves know what great things I and my brothers and the house of my father have done for the laws and the sanctuary' (13.3).

In 1 Maccabees 14, Simon is extolled in a poetic text segment cited (or composed) by the narrator (14.4-15) and, again, on bronze tablets put upon 'pillars on Mount Zion' (14.27) by the Jewish people. The poetic passage characteristically focuses upon national independence (ἔθνος is repeated in the text, vv. 4, 6) and crescendos to a final affirmation of Simon's efforts on behalf of the temple: 'He made the sanctuary glorious, and added to the vessels of the sanctuary' (v. 15).[3]

The proclamation of gratitude erected on a stele by the people (14.27-45), which follows the poetic passage in the narrative, also emphasizes Simon's role in gaining Jewish independence and purging the temple of Gentile impurity:

> 29 Simon...and his brothers, exposed themselves to danger and resisted the enemies of their nation, in order that their sanctuary and the law might be preserved; and they brought great glory to their nation... 31 When their enemies decided to invade their country, and lay hands on their sanctuary, 32 then Simon rose up and fought for his nation... 36 In his days things prospered in his hands, so that the Gentiles were put out of the country, as were also those in the city of David in Jerusalem, who had built themselves a citadel from which they used to sally forth and defile the environs of the sanctuary, doing great damage to its purity (14.29, 31-32, 36).

Notice the connection here between the removal of Gentile occupation, national glory, and the defense of Israel's sacred space. For Simon and his contemporaries, to rise up and fight for one's nation meant repulsing any who dared 'lay hands on their sanctuary' (14.31).[4]

---

3. The first half of this citation—'He made the sanctuary glorious'—likely refers to Simon clearing out the last vestiges of Seleucid occupation from the citadel or, as our narrator expresses it in the immediately preceding context, '[Simon] removed uncleanness from it (the citadel)' (v. 7).

4. Nationalistic territorial ideology also manifests itself in 1 Maccabees in the descriptions of the conquests of the Hasmoneans and the corresponding enlargement of Judean territory. Specifically, the Old Testament notion of 'the land remaining' (to be conquered) became part and parcel of the Hasmonean ideology of territorial expansion (Freyne [2004: 77-80]). Freyne discusses Jonathan's engagement with the Seleucid dynast Demetrius II at Hamath (1 Macc. 11: 63-74) and concludes, 'What the northern

c. Sacred Times

Distinctions between sacred and profane times also occupy an important place in the symbolic universe of the author of 1 Maccabees. Among Antiochus's directives was an order to 'profane sabbaths and feasts' and thereby eliminate these uniquely Jewish practices. Initially in the conflict, the Jews refused to fight on the sabbath and 'so profane the sabbath day' (2.34). A slaughter at the hands of the king's forces encouraged Maccabean leadership to reconsider their position. Given the importance of the sabbath for Jewish identity, one can only imagine the heart-wrenching debate and discussion that was finally summarized in the following text segment:

> 40 And all said to their neighbors: 'If we all do as our kindred have done and refuse to fight with the Gentiles for our lives and for our ordinances, they will quickly destroy us from the earth'. 41 So they made this decision that day: 'Let us fight against anyone who comes to attack us on the sabbath day; let us not all die as our kindred died in their hiding places' (2.40-41).[5]

Antiochus's successors also recognized that sabbath and festivals were key components of Jewish socio-religious self-consciousness. As the hegemony of the Seleucid dynasty crumbled under Roman pressure, pretenders to the throne began to compete with one another to solicit favors from the Jews. Among the concessions Demetrius I (c. 152 BCE) offered 'the nation of the Jews' (10.25) was the right to observe '[a]ll the festivals and sabbaths and new moons and appointed days' (10.34). Finally, 1 Maccabees informs us of a new sacred time established to commemorate the rededication of the temple: the feast of Hanukkah (1 Macc. 4.59).

d. Sacred Food

Antiochus's decree, as related in 1 Maccabees, does not explicitly proscribe Jewish dietary laws. A more general command is found: '[The Jews] were to make themselves abominable by everything unclean and profane, so that they should forget the law and change all the ordinances' (1.48b-49). That this portion of the decree relates directly, however, to food injunctions in the Torah becomes patently clear when the author summarizes the response to Antiochus's program of forced Hellenization on the part of the faithful, a few verses later:

---

tribes had failed to accomplish [in the biblical narratives], Jonathan like a new Joshua, was achieving by military prowess in the name of reclaiming the allotted land' (79).

5. The *topos* of sabbath and warfare is a familiar one in the Maccabean literature and in the writings of Josephus (Josephus, *War* 1.145-47; 1.157-60; 2.517; *Ant.* 13.252; 14.237). The idea that the people of Yahweh should not fight on the sabbath never appears in the biblical stories of warfare during the time of the judges and pre-exilic kings. The subject became a vexing one, however, during the Second-Temple period (see Sanders [2000: 17]). Doering treats in some detail the conflicting evidence in the sources (1999: 537-65).

62 But many in Israel stood firm and were resolved in their hearts not to eat unclean food. 63 They chose to die rather than to be defiled by food or to profane the holy covenant; and they did die. 64 Very great wrath came upon Israel (1.62-64).

For our narrator, to 'profane the holy covenant' consists, preeminently, of eating food that was forbidden in the Torah and, therefore, defiling in the eyes of Yahweh.[6]

e. *Anti-Gentile* Tendenz *in 1 Maccabees*

A final aspect of 1 Maccabees serves further to underscore the sociological function of the identity markers discussed above. In an instructive treatment of the ideology and possible date of the work, Schwartz singles out as one of the more conspicuous features of 1 Maccabees the book's 'extreme hostility to gentiles'.[7] By 'gentiles', moreover, Schwartz refers not only to the Syrian Greeks, but to surrounding non-Judean peoples, as well. Simon's address to his followers prior to the attack of Tryphon pointedly illustrates the anti-Gentile *Tendenz* of 1 Maccabees:

> 3 'You yourselves know what great things my brothers and I and the house of my father have done for the laws and the sanctuary; you know also the wars and the difficulties that my brothers and I have seen. 4 By reason of this all my brothers have perished for the sake of Israel, and I alone am left. 5 And now, far be it from me to spare my life in any time of distress, for I am not better than my brothers. 6 But I will avenge my nation and the sanctuary and your wives and children, for all the nations have gathered together out of hatred to destroy us' (1 Macc. 13.3b-6).

Notice that it is not just the Syrian Greeks who have been at enmity with the Hasmoneans and their sympathizers during the years of war and hardship leading up to national independence. Simon charges 'all of the nations' (πάντα τὰ ἔθνη) with 'hatred' of the Jews (v. 6).[8] The narrative betrays this perspective from the outset. The opening chapter of 1 Maccabees describes in comprehensive terms the foreign peoples whom the Judean Hellenizers desire to emulate:

---

6. The conjunction 'or' in the expression 'to be defiled by food *or* to profane the holy covenant', in the above translation of 1.63, is unfortunate. The Greek conjunction, καί, is seldom, if ever, used in a disjunctive sense, and it is probably best to take it here as explicative: 'to be defiled by food *and so* profane the holy covenant'.

7. Schwartz (1991: 21).

8. Schwartz identifies Simon's speech as a 'programmatic expression' of the work's hostility to Gentiles: 'one of its purposes is to sum up the themes of the book' (1991: 21).

> In those days certain renegades came out from Israel and misled many, saying, 'Let us go and make a covenant with the Gentiles around us (τὰ ἔθνη ἐν κύκλῳ αὐτῶν), for since we separated from them many disasters have come upon us' (1.11).

The nations so described would include not only representatives of the Seleucid dynasty, but also Idumeans, Galileans, Samarians, Transjordanians, and other non-Judeans who lived in the surrounding areas. The anti-Gentile polemic surfaces throughout 1 Maccabees, so that the two passages cited above function together, as it were, as literary bookends to a work that has indiscriminately 'exaggerated or distorted the character of the hostility between Jews and gentiles'.[9] The author's seeming unawareness of the distinction between Greek and non-Greek Gentiles would render the exclusivist ideology of 1 Maccabees all the more accessible to Judeans who found themselves under Roman domination in the generations to come.

2. *2 Maccabees*

2 Maccabees is an abbreviated version of an extended narrative by Jason of Cyrene. The author (often referred to as an 'epitomizer') writes in a manner more overtly theological than is the case with 1 Maccabees, and provides more detail about the events leading up to the suppression of Jewish religion and about the resistance and martyrdoms which followed.[10] Van Henten emphasizes that the author of 2 Maccabees 'did not focus on an accurate reproduction of the events, but on the significance of these crucial events of the past for contemporary Jewish politics, religion, morality and self-understanding'.[11] The strongly ideological texture of 2 Maccabees renders the document all the more valuable for the present study, since the work colorfully illuminates the socio-religious priorities of the author and of post-Maccabean Judeans who found the work attractive. The survey that follows will briefly relate evidence for the author's concern with circumcision, and then proceed to focus more extensively upon 2 Maccabees' preoccupation with the sanctity of the temple, the proper observation of Sabbath and festivals, and the maintenance of the levitical food laws.

---

9. Schwartz (1991: 28).

10. Grabbe (1992a: 224). No attempt will be made to sort out the confused chronology of 2 Maccabees. I am concerned here with the ideological orientation of the author, not the historical reliability of the details of his narrative. For the latter, see the classic commentaries by Abel (1949) and Goldstein (1983a), as well as the important monograph by Doran (1981). Van Henten dates 2 Maccabees during the reign of John Hyrcanus (135/134–104 BCE) and asserts that, despite the fact that the document was originally written in Greek, 'It is obvious that 2 Maccabees is of Judean origin' (1997: 50-51).

11. Van Henten (1997: 25).

a. *Circumcision and Sacred Space*

Although the epitomizer who penned 2 Maccabees does not specifically describe the prohibition of circumcision as a part of Antiochus's decree, he provides more details than 1 Maccabees regarding the fate of those who refused to obey the edict:

> For example, two women were brought in for having circumcised their children. They publicly paraded them around the city, with their babies hanging at their breasts, and then hurled them down headlong from the wall (6.10).

More central to 2 Maccabees is the importance of Israel's sacred space. We first encounter these concerns in correspondence relayed by the author in the opening chapters, where the epitomizer cites two letters allegedly written to Jews in Alexandria in order to encourage them to celebrate Hanukkah like their compatriots in Palestine. A portion of the second letter draws, by way of analogy, upon a festal celebration at the time of Nehemiah. At one point in this feast, those gathered offer a prayer which closely connects the concept of a holy people with that of a holy place:

> 27 Gather together our scattered people, set free those who are slaves among the Gentiles, look on those who are rejected and despised, and let the Gentiles know that you are our God. 28 Punish those who oppress and are insolent with pride. 29 Plant your people in your holy place, as Moses promised (1.27-29).

The association of God's 'people' with a 'holy place' in this text-segment, thus linking Jewish social identity to territorial distinctions, is an overarching theme of 2 Maccabees.

After the two letters, the author introduces the abridgment of Jason of Cyrene's work which is to follow (2.19-32). Before he begins the narrative proper, however, the author feels compelled to offer his readers a brief summary, in list form, of what he will proceed to narrate in some detail as the work unfolds. Our epitomizer focuses particularly on circumstances relating to the Jewish temple. His catalogue of events begins as follows: 'The story of Judas Maccabeus and his brothers, and the purification of the great temple, and the dedication of the altar' (2.19).

True to his stated intentions, the author reflects upon the status of the temple throughout the body of the narrative proper (3.1–15.36), which begins with the delightful tale of the aborted attempt to desecrate the temple on the part of the Syrian representative Heliodorus. Sent by Seleucus IV to confiscate money from the temple treasury, Heliodorus first encountered the pious high priest, Onias, who desperately attempted to dissuade him, citing 'the holiness of the place' and 'the sanctity and inviolability of the temple which is honored throughout the whole world' (3.12). Onias's pleas had no effect, however, so the distressed populace then 'hurried out of their houses in crowds to make a general supplication because the holy place was about to be brought into dishonor' (3.18). We saw, above, how God responded to the prayers of the people, in the form of a theophanic horseman who struck Heliodorus to the ground. Throughout the account the author underscores the sacredness of Israel's holy temple. Even the pagan aggressor Heliodorus must ultimately acknowledge that 'there is certainly some power of God about the place' (3.38).

As the author proceeds to describe Antiochus's decree and the revolt of the Maccabees, events relating to the temple continue to occupy a prominent place in the narrative, and they are repeatedly and explicitly tied to issues of national identity. For example, the king's decree, as related in 2 Maccabees, compels the Jews 'to pollute the temple in Jerusalem and to call it the temple of Olympian Zeus' (6.2). The close association of the command to 'pollute the temple' with the phrase 'forsake the laws of their ancestors' in the verse immediately preceding (6.1) shows that the elimination of a key Jewish distinctive is directly in view in Antiochus's prohibition of traditional temple worship.

The same connection between Jewish sacred space and the 'ancestral way of life' emerges in a challenge offered by Judas to his soldiers, as they prepare to encounter Nicanor and his armies two chapters later. We read that Judas

> 16 exhorted them not to be frightened by the enemy and not to fear the great multitude of Gentiles who were wickedly coming against them, but to fight nobly, 17 keeping before their eyes the lawless outrage that the Gentiles had committed against the holy place, and the torture of the derided city, and besides, the overthrow of their ancestral way of life (8.16-17).

2 Maccabees 11.24-25 also combines concern for the sanctity of the temple with Israel's socio-religious identity. Antiochus V writes to his general Lysias after Judas had defeated the Syrian general and his armies. The king instructs Lysias as follows:

> 24 'We have heard that the Jews do not consent to our father's change to Greek customs but prefer their own way of living and ask that their own customs be allowed them. 25 Accordingly, since we choose that this nation also be free from disturbance, our decision is that their temple be restored to them and that they live according to the customs of their ancestors' (11.24-25).

The restoration of the temple cult is inextricably bound up with restoring the Jewish way of life 'according to the customs of their ancestors' (11.25).

A final illustration of the prominence of the temple occurs near the end of 2 Maccabees, when the author relates the response of Judas's army after Judas exhorted them to battle:

> 17 Encouraged by the words of Judas, so noble and so effective in arousing valor and awaking courage in the souls of the young, they determined not to carry on a campaign but to attack bravely, and to decide the matter by fighting hand to hand with all courage, because the city and the sanctuary and the temple were in danger. 18 Their concern for wives and children, and also for brothers and sisters and relatives, lay upon them less heavily; their greatest and first fear was for the consecrated sanctuary (15.17-18).

So sacred is the temple that even family relations become secondary when God's people are called upon to fight for Israel's sacred space.

b. *Sacred Times*

The epitomizer who produced 2 Maccabees (c. 1st cent. BCE) was particularly aware of the significance of sacred times to unify and identify Judeans of the Roman empire over against the Gentile majority. As is now recognized, the author's desire to establish the annual festival of Hanukkah (as it is now called) throughout the Jewish diaspora constitutes an important unifying element of an otherwise *mixtum compositum* consisting of two quoted letters (1.1–2.18), comments by the author (2.19-32; 15.37-39), along with an excerpt from a history by Jason of Cyrene (3.1–15.36).[12]

Sabbath-keeping, too, surfaces early in the narrative. Shortly before the king's decree, Antiochus sent Apollonius to Jerusalem, who 'waited until the holy sabbath day' to carry out his orders to massacre a number of resident Jews (5.25-26). Like the author of 1 Maccabees, our epitomizer includes in Antiochus's program of Hellenization the proscription of sabbath-keeping and the festal calendar (6.6). Here we are given more details, however, about those who resisted the king's decree. Certain Jews 'assembled in caves' to secretly observe the sabbath. Upon discovery they 'were all burned together, because their piety kept them from defending themselves, in view of their regard for that most holy day' (6.11).

A later passage finds victorious Judeans pursuing the fleeing remnants of the Syrian army. The pursuit ends prematurely, however, as the day wanes. The author explains:

> 26 It was the day before the sabbath, and for that reason they did not continue their pursuit. 27 When they had collected the arms of the enemy and stripped them of their spoils, they kept the sabbath, giving great praise and thanks to the Lord, who had preserved them for that day and allotted it to them as the beginning of mercy (8.26-27).

Several chapters later we encounter another passage in which Judas and his army cease hostilities on the sabbath (12.38). Here, as in the passage above, the Jews are now on the offensive and can safely refrain from warfare on their holy day.

---

12. Fischer (1992: 4.442).

A final sabbath text in 2 Maccabees finds Nicanor attempting to encourage a contingent of Judeans 'who were compelled to follow him' to fight against Judas on the seventh day. The enslaved Jewish mercenaries plea with Nicanor to 'show respect for the day that he who sees all things has honored and hallowed above other days'. Nicanor proceeds to insist, but the Jews stand their ground, and reply with a declaration that forms a fitting summary to our survey of sacred times in 2 Maccabees: 'It is the living Lord himself, the Sovereign in heaven, who ordered us to observe the seventh day' (15.1-5).

c. *Sacred Food*
Faithfulness to Old Testament food laws constitutes the defining act of piety for the author of 2 Maccabees. Early in the narrative Judas and his friends flee Jerusalem, for the first time, in the face of the attack of Apollonius. We are told that Judas

> ...got away to the wilderness, and kept himself and his companions alive in the mountains as wild animals do; they continued to live on what grew wild, so that they might not share in the defilement (5.27).

Shortly thereafter, Antiochus issued his decree, and our epitomizer relates the lengthy stories of the torture and martyrdoms of the aged Eleazar and a mother and her seven sons, who suffer the extreme penalty solely because they refused to eat pork (6.18–7.42). This text-segment has rightly been identified as central to the epitomizer's ideological agenda. The author of *4 Maccabees* later reworked and elevated the narrative to 'the crown of biblical martyrology'.[13] The stories are familiar and need not be repeated here, but their importance must not be underestimated. Traditions such as these, which situate sacred food at the very center of Jewish socio-religious identity, found wide reception and distribution throughout Jewish Palestine and the diaspora, and generated a cultural script that must inform our understanding of early Christian controversies relating to Jewish dietary laws and table fellowship.[14]

---

13. The quotation is from Fischer (1992: 4.442).

14. Van Henten's important work on the martyrs in 2 Maccabees and *4 Maccabees* should be consulted in this regard. The martyrdoms have undergone considerable adaptations prior to appearing in the form in which we have them in 2 Maccabees. Van Henten observes, 'This implies that the texts deal with issues of self-definition and Jewish identity in both the religious-cultural and the political spheres' (1997: 6). Van Henten finds a distinctly political element in 2 Maccabees 7, for example, where the brothers refer to the Jewish laws as 'the laws of our ancestors' (vv. 2, 37). He concludes, 'Thus, the laws of God are at the same time presented as the laws of a specific people. Apparently the Greek phrase οἱ πάτριοι νόμοι is part of a semantic field of terms referring to the Jewish people' (1997: 13-14).

A final passage explicitly correlates sacred food with Jewish ethnicity. I mentioned above a letter that Antiochus V wrote to Lysias after Judas had defeated the Syrian contingent and won religious freedom for his nation (11.24-25). The connection noted in that discussion—between sacred space and Jewish national identity—also applies to sacred food, as the ensuing context demonstrates. After our epitomizer finishes relating the contents of the king's letter to Lysias, he cites a second letter, this one addressed to the Jews themselves. Here, the newly permitted liberties, described only in general terms in the former letter, find specific expression in dietary practices, for Antiochus promises the Jews the freedom 'to enjoy their own food and laws, just as formerly' (11.31).

d. *Maccabean Ideology*

Our overview of 2 Maccabees would be incomplete without some observations about the ideological orientation of the author. More than a generation ago, Metzger asserted that the purpose of Jason (from whose work our author draws) was 'to interpret history theologically'.[15] Fischer has more recently cited the 'direct insights' 2 Maccabees gives us into 'the contemporary Judean understanding of history'.[16] For our purposes, it is important to discern an ideology—both tacitly assumed and explicitly articulated throughout the narrative of 2 Maccabees—which connects the preservation of Jewish socio-religious distinctives to national independence from Gentile occupation.

Responsibility for the initial sufferings and oppression of the Jews at the hand of Antiochus is laid at the feet of Jason and his Judean friends who placed 'the highest value upon Greek forms of prestige' and imitated Greek 'ways of living' (4.13-17). Correspondingly, the Maccabean victories that follow find explanation in a piety that willingly accepts martyrdom in order to faithfully obey the very laws proscribed by Antiochus. Scholars have, in fact, identified a Deuteronomistic scheme of sin and divine retribution in 2 Maccabees, which situates the faithfulness of Eleazar, the woman, and her seven sons as the crucial turning point of the narrative:

1. Blessing: Jerusalem during the priesthood of Onias III (3.1-40)
2. Sin: Hellenization of Jerusalem under Jason and Menelaus (4.1–5.10)
3. Punishment: Reprisals of Antiochus IV (5.11–6.17)
4. Turning point: Deaths of the martyrs and prayers of the people (6.18–8.4)
5. Judgment and salvation: The victories of Judas (8.5–15.36)[17]

---

15. Metzger (1977: 263).
16. Fischer (1992: 4.445).
17. Fischer (1992: 4.445), summarizing Doran (1981: 93-94, 110) and Nickelsburg (1981: 118). Van Henten suggests that before Judas can be assured of victory, the rela-

2. *Interpreting Recent History* 51

The theology outlined above finds vivid expression in a series of events related to the temple. Syrian leaders attempt to defile the Jews' sacred space several times in the course of the narrative of 2 Maccabees. As we saw above, however, their efforts meet with varying degrees of success, depending upon how faithful the Jews have been to their covenant with Yahweh at the time a particular Greek offense occurs.

It was during the period of great blessing (#1, above), for example, under the priesthood of Onias III, that Seleucus IV sent Heliodorus to confiscate money from the temple treasury (2 Maccabees 3). At that time, the reader is informed, 'the holy city was inhabited in unbroken peace and the laws were strictly observed because of the piety of the high priest Onias and his hatred of wickedness' (3.1). Given the author's Deuteronomistic interpretative framework, we are not surprised to discover that God supernaturally intervened on behalf of 'the holy place' (3.18), and Heliodorus was sent back to Antioch humiliated and empty-handed.[18]

Compare the experience of Heliodorus with a later attempt to defile the temple by Antiochus IV. As mentioned above, Antiochus encountered no divine opposition whatsoever, and he 'carried off eighteen hundred talents from the temple' (5.21). Why did God not intervene against Antiochus on behalf of his people like he did against Heliodorus? The narrator's explanation offers us significant insight into Maccabean ideology:

> 17 Antiochus...did not perceive that the Lord was angered for a little while because of the sins of those who lived in the city, and that this was the reason he was disregarding the holy place. 18 But if it had not happened that they were involved in many sins, this man would have been flogged and turned back from his rash act as soon as he came forward, just as Heliodorus had been, whom King Seleucus sent to inspect the treasury (5.17-18).

tionship between the Lord and his people, which had been ruptured by the defections of the Hellenizing party, had to be restored. The faithful activities of Eleazar and the mother and her seven sons—who refuse to eat pork and suffer martyrdom as a result—'fulfill the prerequisite need for restoring the bond' (1997: 27).

18. Haas somewhat misses the mark when he asserts, 'The central thesis of II Maccabees is that there is a direct relationship between the purity of the high Priest and the prosperity of Israel' (1990: 62). This is clearly the case for the incident surrounding Onias III and Heliodorus in 2 Maccabees 3, outlined above. For the work as a whole, however, we would have to expand Haas's 'purity of the high Priest' to include faithfulness to the Torah on the part of the populace in general. In his examination of the historiography of 2 Maccabees, Haas neglects to discuss the way in which the martyrdoms of Eleazar, the woman, and her seven sons function in the narrative. It is the refusal of these pious Jews to assent to the king's demands—not the purity of the high priest—that constitutes the turning point of the story, where Yahweh now, once again, undertakes to intervene on behalf of his people and temple (see the quotation from van Henten in the previous note).

The 'many sins', which resulted in the loss of God's protection and Antiochus's corresponding success in stealing temple monies, included preeminently the rejection of Jewish identity markers in favor of Greek social practices. The turn for the worse had begun when Jason bought the high priesthood from Antiochus, shortly after the humiliation of Heliodorus. In the previous chapter of 2 Maccabees our narrator had regrettably noted that Jason

> 11 destroyed the lawful ways of living and introduced new customs contrary to the law. 12 He took delight in establishing a gymnasium right under the citadel, and he induced the noblest of the young men to wear the Greek hat. 13 There was such an extreme of Hellenization and increase in the adoption of foreign ways because of the surpassing wickedness of Jason, who was ungodly and no true high priest, 14 that the priests were no longer intent upon their service at the altar. Despising the sanctuary and neglecting the sacrifices, they hurried to take part in the unlawful proceedings in the wrestling arena after the signal for the discus-throwing, 15 disdaining the honors prized by their ancestors and putting the highest value upon Greek forms of prestige (4.11-15).

Divine chastisement would inevitably result:

> 16 For this reason heavy disaster overtook them, and those whose ways of living they admired and wished to imitate completely became their enemies and punished them. 17 It is no light thing to show irreverence to the divine laws—a fact that later events will make clear (4.16-17).

It was, therefore, the 'extreme of Hellenization and increase in the adoption of foreign ways' (4.13) that explained why Antiochus, unlike Heliodorus, escaped unscathed with God's holy money.[19] Yahweh removes his divine protection from a people that plays loose with his covenant laws.

The story, however, is not over yet. Due to a change of attitude and behavior on the part of the Jews—epitomized in the tragic but faithful martyrdoms of Eleazar and the mother and her seven sons—the dynamic reverses yet again before the narrative concludes. In the persons of the faithful martyrs Israel has repented, and now God returns to defend the holy city and sanctuary. Thus, we find the Syrian king smitten with 'an incurable and unseen blow' because he had intended to 'make Jerusalem a cemetery of Jews' (9.4-5). Similarly, near the end of 2 Maccabees the Greek general Nicanor dies in battle because 'he stretched out his right hand toward the sanctuary' and threatened to 'level this shrine of God to the ground' (14.33). In 15.32, Judas publicly displays

---

19. The idea of a causal connection between Israel's disobedience, on the one hand, and the profanation of Yahweh's temple at the hands of a pagan nation, on the other, goes back at least to the time of the exile. Because of Israel's sin Yahweh proclaims, 'I will avert my face from them (invading foreign armies), so that they may profane my treasured place; the violent shall enter it, they shall profane it' (Ezek. 7.22).

Nicanor's severed head in the temple court, along with 'that profane man's arm, which had been boastfully stretched out against the holy house of the Almighty'.[20] These changes in God's response to offenses against his temple find their explanation in the theology of the author, who directly associates divine intervention on behalf of the Jews with the faithful keeping of the laws proscribed by Antiochus. In the words of our narrator, '[W]hat was forsaken in the wrath of the Almighty was restored again in all its glory when the great Lord became reconciled' (5.20).

Even foreigners must ultimately acknowledge the connection between Jewish national independence and faithfulness to the laws relating to sacred foods, times, and space. Upon his return to Antioch after a devastating defeat at the hands of Judas, Nicanor 'proclaimed that the Jews had a Defender, and that *therefore* the Jews were invulnerable, *because* they followed the laws ordained by him' (8.36; my italics). The author of 1 Maccabees had written, 'Pay back the Gentiles in full, and obey the commands of the law' (1 Macc. 2.68). For the epitomizer of 2 Maccabees, accomplishing the latter guarantees the success of the former.

The importance of these interpretations of Maccabean history for understanding the symbolic world of Jesus of Nazareth cannot be overestimated. Stephen Cummins recently surveyed the correspondence and continuity between Maccabean events and theology, on the one hand, and first-century Jewish nationalistic aspirations, on the other. The results confirm the ongoing influence of this remarkable period in later Second Temple history. Cummins (a) discerns a Maccabean element in early Pharisaism, (b) finds distinctly Maccabean echoes in portrayals of the Caligula episode and the Jewish response, and (c) traces the theme of Maccabean martyrdom in first-century Jewish texts and traditions. He concludes that 'the Maccabean period—not least the pivotal role of its martyr figures—was current as an inspirational living tradition readily at hand to a first-century Jew'.[21] A final piece of Maccabean history, *4 Maccabees*, further evidences the connection that was increasingly drawn in the minds of post-Maccabean Judeans between faithfulness to badges of Jewish identity and Yahweh's blessing upon his chosen people.

3. *4 Maccabees*

4 Maccabees retells the story of the martyrs in a way that colorfully illustrates the confluence of the two cultural streams of Hellenism and Judaism that typified Jewish thinking and praxis during the Second-Temple period.

---

20. On the ideological nature of the way in which the author chose to end his narrative in 2 Maccabees, see Doran (1999: 98-99).

21. Cummins (2001: 54, see 54-90).

The goal of the author, who is thoroughly acquainted with the popular Stoic and Platonic ethics of his day, is to demonstrate that 'devout reason is sovereign over the emotions' (1.1). He is primarily concerned, however, to argue the truth of his thesis as it relates to a particular aspect of Jewish life:

> 33 [H]ow is it that when we are attracted to forbidden foods we abstain from the pleasure to be had from them? Is it not because reason is able to rule over appetites? I for one think so. 34 Therefore when we crave seafood and fowl and animals and all sorts of foods that are forbidden to us by the law, we abstain because of domination by reason. 35 For the emotions of the appetites are restrained, checked by the temperate mind, and all the impulses of the body are bridled by reason (1.33-35).

The activities of Antiochus IV, of course, provided the ultimate challenge to the 'domination of reason' (v. 34, above) that enabled the Jews to abstain from forbidden foods:

> 26 [Antiochus] tried through torture to compel everyone in the nation to eat defiling foods and to renounce Judaism. 1 The tyrant Antiochus, sitting in state with his counselors on a certain high place, and with his armed soldiers standing around him, 2 ordered the guards to seize each and every Hebrew and to compel them to eat pork and food sacrificed to idols. 3 If any were not willing to eat defiling food, they were to be broken on the wheel and killed (4.26–5.3).

What follows in the text is a lengthy description of the torture and martyrdom of the Jewish heroes we encountered in 2 Maccabees (the aged Eleazar, and the mother and her seven sons)—a story now recast, however, in what could fairly be described as a 'Torah-ized Stoicism'. The author of *4 Maccabees* was deeply indebted to popular Hellenistic philosophy. But the 'reason' (λογισμός) that enables the Jewish martyrs to resist the temptation to eat swine's flesh is not merely reason as understood by the Stoics. It is, rather, a 'devout reason' (εὐσεβὴς λογισμός, 1.1), the kind of reason that has been trained in the law of God.[22]

The author of *4 Maccabees* has apparently utilized 2 Maccabees as a source, expanding and embellishing the stories of Eleazar and the seven young men in ways that particularly underscore the centrality of the food laws. The Eleazar narrative begins with a discussion between the protagonist and the Syrian king about the philosophical advisability of abstaining from pork. Antiochus offers his opinion at the outset:

> 6 'Before I begin to torture you, old man, I would advise you to save yourself by eating pork, 7 for I respect your age and your gray hairs. Although you have had them for so long a time, it does not seem to me that you are a philosopher when you observe the religion of the Jews' (5.6-7).

---

22. See the discussion in DeSilva (2002: 359-64). For a representative catalogue of Greek expressions and ideas in *4 Maccabees*, see Helyer (2002: 405-406).

2. Interpreting Recent History

Eleazar initially responds by answering the king's objections in philosophical terms. The law, Eleazar retorts, 'teaches us self-control, so that we master all pleasures and desires, and it also trains us in courage, so that we endure any suffering willingly'—the very virtues sought by the Greeks through philosophical inquiry (5.23). The aged hero then proceeds, however, to associate his refusal to eat pork more specifically with his relationship to Yahweh and his membership among the covenant people of God:

> 25 'Therefore we do not eat defiling food; for since we believe that the law was established by God, we know that in the nature of things the Creator of the world in giving us the law has shown sympathy toward us. 26 He has permitted us to eat what will be most suitable for our lives, but he has forbidden us to eat meats that would be contrary to this. 27 It would be tyrannical for you to compel us not only to transgress the law, but also to eat in such a way that you may deride us for eating defiling foods, which are most hateful to us. 28 But you shall have no such occasion to laugh at me, 29 nor will I transgress the sacred oaths of my ancestors concerning the keeping of the law, 30 not even if you gouge out my eyes and burn my entrails' (5.25-30).

After torturing Eleazar for some time in an attempt to force him to eat Gentile food, the king's retinue took pity on the old priest and tried to help him out of his dilemma by offering him some allowable meat. They whispered, '[S]ave yourself by pretending to eat pork'. Eleazar adamantly refused. Note carefully in the text the association of concerns for maintaining Jewish dietary regulations with the ethnic identifier 'the children of Abraham':

> 17 'Never may we, the children of Abraham, think so basely that out of cowardice we feign a role unbecoming to us! 18 For it would be irrational if having lived in accordance with truth up to old age and having maintained in accordance with law the reputation of such a life, we should now change our course 19 and ourselves become a pattern of impiety to the young by setting them an example in the eating of defiling food... 22 Therefore, O children of Abraham, die nobly for your religion!' (6.17-19, 22).

The narrator concludes by extolling Eleazar in a way that, again, combines a sanctified Stoicism with a focus on strict adherence to the dietary laws:

> 6 O priest, worthy of the priesthood, you neither defiled your sacred teeth nor profaned your stomach, which had room only for reverence and purity, by eating defiling foods. 7 O man in harmony with the law and philosopher of divine life! (7.6).

After Eleazar's death the drama intensifies:

> 2 For when the tyrant was conspicuously defeated in his first attempt, being unable to compel an aged man to eat defiling foods, then in violent rage he commanded that others of the Hebrew captives be brought, and that any who ate defiling food would be freed after eating, but if any were to refuse, they would be tortured even more cruelly (8.2).

The narrative continues with the gruesome torture and death of the mother and her seven sons. At the outset the author singles out the exchange of Jewish for Greek identity as the king's primary objective for the seven boys. Antiochus implores the young men,

> 7 'Trust me, then, and you will have positions of authority in my government if you will renounce the ancestral tradition of your national life (τὸν πάτριον ὑμῶν τῆς πολιτείας θεσμόν). 8 Enjoy your youth by adopting the Greek way of life (Ἑλληνικοῦ βίου) and by changing your manner of living' (8.7-8).

The seven will have no part of the king's offer, and they are tortured to death, each in turn, as they remain faithful to Jewish dietary restrictions. The expression 'eat defiling foods' occurs throughout the extended narrative (8.2, 12, 29; 11.16, 25; 13.2), as Antiochus and his officials repeatedly attempt to get the young men to consume the king's pork.

Although the author of *4 Maccabees* focuses primarily upon the dietary laws, other Jewish identity markers come into view in the narrative, as well. Circumcision enters the story as part of Antiochus's decree, where we read that certain 'women, because they had circumcised their sons, were thrown headlong from heights along with their infants, though they had known beforehand that they would suffer this' (4.25). The centrality of the temple as sacred space takes pride of place in the tale of the aborted attempt of King Seleucus to seize 'private funds' that had been deposited in the Jerusalem treasury. When Seleucus's agent, identified in *4 Maccabees* as Apollonius, arrived at the temple to confiscate the monies, he found that 'the priests together with women and children were imploring God in the temple to shield the holy place that was being treated so contemptuously' (4.9). The prayers are answered as the Syrian offender is supernaturally stopped in his tracks by 'angels on horseback with lightning flashing from their weapons' (4.10). Apollonius's reaction:

> 11 Then Apollonius fell down half dead in the temple area that was open to all, stretched out his hands toward heaven, and with tears begged the Hebrews to pray for him and propitiate the wrath of the heavenly army. 12 For he said that he had committed a sin deserving of death, and that if he were spared he would praise the blessedness of the holy place before all people (4.11-12).

The confusion of the name of the Syrian emissary—he is identified as Heliodorus in 2 Maccabees—suggests that the story circulated widely enough among Jews in the eastern empire to generate at least two alternative versions.

a. *Maccabean Ideology—Again*
Important for our purposes is the direct association in *4 Maccabees* of faithfulness to the Torah with Maccabean victories over the Syrian Greeks. We saw the ideology in play in 2 Maccabees, where a connection obtained

2. Interpreting Recent History

between (a) the faithfulness of the martyrs and (b) the ensuing victories of Judas culminating in the purification of the Temple in 164 BCE. *4 Maccabees* is even more explicit in this regard. The correlation between legal piety and national security first surfaces early in the narrative, before Jewish elites such as Jason and Menelaus had compromised with Hellenism. Our author describes the period as 'a time when our fathers were enjoying profound peace *because of their observance of the law* and were prospering' (3.20, my italics). Immediately following the statement is a striking illustration of this principle in action: the story of Apollonius's failed attempt to steal the monies in the treasury (see above). The author's theological perspective is quite transparent. As long as the Jews observed the law, their sacred space remained inviolable, such that even a Greek governor had to promise to 'praise the blessedness of the holy place before all people' (4.12).

Divine protection is soon compromised, however, when certain Jewish elites abandon their national customs for the values and practices of the Greeks:

> 19 Jason changed the nation's way of life and altered its form of government in complete violation of the law, 20 so that not only was a gymnasium constructed at the very citadel of our native land, but also the temple service was abolished. 21 *The divine justice was angered by these acts and caused Antiochus himself to make war on them* (4.19-21, my italics).

Our author could hardly draw a more direct connection between the Hellenizing agenda of Jason and God's orchestration of the ensuing pogrom of Antiochus.

The association of faithfulness to the law with the health of the nation next appears in the narrative as an expression of hope on the lips of the dying martyrs. Consider Eleazar's last words:

> 27 'You know, O God, that though I might have saved myself, I am dying in burning torments for the sake of the law. 28 Be merciful to your people, and let our punishment suffice for them. 29 Make my blood their purification, and take my life in exchange for theirs' (6.27-29).

The first brother's final charge is framed in similar terms:

> 23 'Imitate me, brothers', he said. 'Do not leave your post in my struggle or renounce our courageous family ties. 24 Fight the sacred and noble battle for religion. Thereby the just Providence of our ancestors may become merciful to our nation and take vengeance on the accursed tyrant' (9.23-24).

The martyrs' hopes are finally realized in the closing paragraphs of the narrative, where the author of *4 Maccabees* explicitly connects the deaths of the martyrs with the purification of the nation, and exhorts his readers to obey the Torah for that very reason:

> 20 These, then, who have been consecrated for the sake of God, are honored, not only with this honor, but also by the fact that *because of them* our enemies did not rule over our nation, 21 the tyrant was punished, and the homeland purified—they having become, as it were, a ransom for the sin of our nation. 22 And through the blood of those devout ones and their death as an atoning sacrifice, divine Providence preserved Israel that previously had been mistreated (17.20-22, my italics).
>
> 1 O Israelite children, offspring of the seed of Abraham, obey this law and exercise piety in every way, 2 knowing that devout reason is master of all emotions, not only of sufferings from within, but also of those from without. 3 Therefore those who gave over their bodies in suffering for the sake of religion were not only admired by mortals, but also were deemed worthy to share in a divine inheritance. 4 *Because of them* the nation gained peace, and by reviving observance of the law in the homeland they ravaged the enemy. 5 The tyrant Antiochus was both punished on earth and is being chastised after his death. Since in no way whatever was he able to compel the Israelites to become pagans and to abandon their ancestral customs, he left Jerusalem and marched against the Persians (18.1-5, my italics).

The author also links together the idea of national vindication with the activities of Eleazar and the woman and her sons in a suggested epitaph for the heroes:

> 8 Indeed it would be proper to inscribe on their tomb these words as a reminder to the people of our nation (τοῖς ἀπὸ τοῦ ἔθνους): 9 'Here lie buried an aged priest and an aged woman and seven sons, because of the violence of the tyrant who wished to destroy the way of life of the Hebrews (τὴν Ἑβραίων πολιτείαν). 10 They vindicated their nation (τὸ γένος), looking to God and enduring torture even to death' (17.8-10).

The author of *4 Maccabees* thus picked up and intentionally elaborated upon the Deuteronomistic theology he encountered in his source materials (2 Maccabees).

The probable date of *4 Maccabees* renders these causal links between dietary faithfulness and national security (as well as the narrative's general preoccupation with the food laws) particularly significant as background for understanding the early history of the Jesus movement. Recent scholarship, following arguments posed a generation ago by Elias Bickerman, dates *4 Maccabees* to the middle of the first century CE.[23] This suggests that the nationalistic ideology reflected in the narrative remained a vibrant one in the eastern Diaspora well into the early Christian era.

---

23. DeSilva (1998: 15-18) and (2002: 355-56). See also van Henten (1997: 74), Anderson (1985b: 533-34), and Bickerman (1976). Some time ago, Bickerman argued that the nomenclature used in *4 Maccabees* to refer to Syrian governors reflects Roman usage, suggesting a date between 18 and 55 CE (Bickerman [1945]). Anderson finds such reasoning 'very plausible' (1985b: 534).

In the case of *4 Maccabees*, moreover, Jewish nationalism flourished happily in concert with a distinctly Hellenized attitude towards Torah-keeping and biblical anthropology. This is an important piece of socio-cultural realia, given current scholarly emphasis upon the Hellenization of Judeans in the East during our period. Apparently, ideology and praxis related to the preservation of ethnic identity constituted one aspect of Jewish life that became relatively insulated from outside cultural influence during the post-Maccabean era. After the experiences of 167–164 BCE, the pagan presence in Palestine discouraged, rather than encouraged, compromise on these issues, even while Hellenization continued to make significant inroads into other areas of Judean thinking and behavior. The author of *4 Maccabees* was thus able to harness a decidedly Stoic anthropology in the service of an uncompromising approach to the social distinctives of his ancestral religion, and thereby craft an engaging narrative about the Maccabean era. The document usefully evidences the kind of selective Hellenization that occurred in Jewish Palestine during the late-Greek and early-Roman periods.[24]

4. *Conclusion*

The ideological orientation of the Maccabean literary corpus sheds much light upon the social world of first-century Palestine, and it readily accounts for the resistance of certain Jewish leaders to the way in which Jesus of Nazareth and his followers treated the central badges of Judean socio-religious identity. Jesus' observation about food, for example—'whatever goes into a person from outside cannot defile' (Mk 7.18)—would have generated not a little cognitive dissonance in the minds of persons familiar with the popular Macca-

---

24. Thus, Anderson's observation that *4 Maccabees* is characterized by 'an almost complete absorption in hellenistic modes of conceptualization' needs to be strongly qualified by the evidence I have cited for Jewish particularism in the document (Anderson [1985b: 533]).

The kind of selective Hellenization discussed above surfaces in a variety of connections. The Maccabean monarch Aristobulus I (104/103 BCE), for example, viewed himself as a 'philhellene' (Josephus, *Ant.* 13.318). Yet Aristobulus is remembered by Josephus for expanding the borders of Israel to the north, insisting on circumcision for any foreigners who wished to remain in the region (Josephus, *Ant.* 13.318). Gruen's observations, in this regard, are quite on the mark:

> Aristobulus within a short span of time at the helm developed the reputation of a prime benefactor to his native land and people. That such a man also proudly sported the label of 'philhellene'—indeed is referred to as such by Josephus in the same breath as he describes his benefactions for the Jews—speaks volumes. The historian found no inconsistency between the Hasmonean inclinations toward Hellenism and their championing of Jewish identity (Gruen [1998: 39]).

bean stories of the torturous martyrdoms of Eleazar, the mother, and her seven sons, faithful Jews who had died simply because they refused to eat pork. And for Torah observant Judeans whose ancestors had given their very lives and the lives of their own children to maintain the covenant rite of circumcision, it was surely nothing short of scandalous to hear reports that a former Pharisee was traveling the empire teaching that '[c]ircumcision is nothing, and uncircumcision is nothing' (1 Cor. 7.19).

Post-Maccabean Jews not only interpreted the events of recent history in ways that propagated expansionist views related to purity and nationalism.[25] They also recrafted and reinterpreted the Old Testament story of Israel's origins in a manner that served to reinforce Jewish social particularity in the context of a Gentile dominated world. The next chapter considers four representative documents: *Jubilees,* Pseudo-Philo's *Biblical Antiquities,* Judith, and the Additions to Esther. The authors of these engaging works found in the narratives of the Torah (and in the events of Israel's ensuing history, as related in later Old Testament books) ample resources to rewrite the account of Jewish origins so as to emphasize the importance of the defining social practices of circumcision, Sabbath observance, and exclusive table fellowship. We turn now to examine the genre of the rewritten Bible in search of further evidence for Jewish nationalism and boundary preservation during the post-Maccabean era.

---

25. Interpretations of recent Jewish history are not limited to the Maccabean documents surveyed above. Apocalyptic literature also treats the defining events of 167–164 BCE. Enoch's visions of the future, for example, include the revolt under Judas. The vision appears to portray suffering Judeans as 'sheep', the Syrian oppressors as unclean 'eagles, vultures, ravens, and kites' (see Lev. 11.13-14), and Judas Maccabeus as a great 'horned ram', to whom the rest of the sheep flock, and who gains victory over his Greek adversaries (*1 Enoch* 90.6-12).

Chapter 3

RECRAFTING ISRAEL'S STORY:
THE GENRE OF THE REWRITTEN BIBLE

> 'Separate yourself from the gentiles,
> and do not eat with them.'
>
> *Jubilees* 22.16

The genre of the rewritten Bible sought to modify and recast familiar stories from the Hebrew Scriptures in ways that more forcefully spoke to contemporary concerns. Authors representing this flourishing literary tradition typically included in their accounts of Israel's early history new materials intended to fill in perceived *lacunae* in the Old Testament narratives, and they eliminated portions of the biblical text that they deemed less relevant to their historiographical designs. In a number of instances, moreover, writers retained but significantly altered earlier stories to address current issues. Examples of the genre thus prove highly informative for understanding post-Maccabean Judaism, since the places in a narrative at which a writer departs from the Hebrew original give special insights into the author's agenda for his intended audience. The following survey will consider *Jubilees*, Pseudo-Philo's *Biblical Antiquities*, Judith, and the Additions to Esther. Each of these documents was written in the eastern Diaspora—the majority in Jewish Palestine—before the destruction of the Temple in 70 CE. As we might suspect, the works continue to attest to the intensified concern for purity and social boundary preservation which came to characterize much of Jewish life during the post-Maccabean period.

1. *Jubilees*

Jubilees is a haggadic expansion of portions of Genesis and the initial chapters of Exodus, purporting to contain information revealed by an angel to Moses on Sinai (see Exod. 24.18). The discovery of fragments at Qumran, and the comparison of the contents of the work with Qumran beliefs and practices, point to a pre-100 BCE date of composition.[1] The document's popularity at

---

1. Fragments of at least fourteen copies have been discovered at Qumran (Caves 1, 2, 3, 4, and 11), rendering *Jubilees* 'one of the most popular works to have emerged

Qumran might lead us to assume that *Jubilees* represents a rather narrow, sectarian outlook on purity and boundaries, an outlook which, in turn, would render the work less than useful as evidence for common Judaism during our period. Such an assumption would be decidedly off the mark. For despite certain similarities to Qumran ideology (for example, the use of a solar calendar), on a number of issues *Jubilees* reflects no discernable break with broader Judaism.[2] A careful reading of the work demonstrates that our author was generally preoccupied with preserving social boundaries between Jews and Gentiles—not with reinforcing distinctions between sectarian and non-sectarian Jews. I will briefly note some evidence along these lines.

Consider, first, the document's notable lack of emphasis upon exclusive table fellowship. The topic of purity and eating surfaces often in identifiably sectarian works from Qumran (1QS 6.2-5; 4Q514), and the community's meal practices remained distinctive among their contemporaries.[3] In contrast, the one explicit reference to separate table fellowship in *Jubilees* relates not to intra-Jewish sectarian divisions at mealtime but, rather, to the prohibition of sharing a table with Gentiles (*Jub.* 22.16).

The author's care to preserve the purity of the Abrahamic bloodline through strict endogamy points in the same direction. As with exclusive table fellowship, the goal here is to safeguard the social boundary between Jews and Gentiles, a boundary that would be compromised considerably, of course, should Judeans and non-Judeans intermarry. Compare the perspective of the author of *Jubilees* with the outlook of the Qumran sectarians, who, in contrast, 'understood membership in the holy people as a matter of merit, not of ancestry', since they 'viewed most Jews, together with all Gentiles, as children of darkness'.[4] General support for endogamous

---

from the eleven Qumran scroll caves' (Hempel [2000: 188]). *Jubilees* has also been identified as 'one of the most authoritative or 'biblical' texts at Qumran' (VanderKam [1992b: 648]). For an insightful analysis cataloguing four ways in which *Jubilees* seeks to convey its authority to it potential readers, see Najman (1999).

2. On the non-sectarian nature of *Jubilees*, Knibb should be consulted (1989: 16-17). See, also, Klawans, who fairly concludes that 'there is nothing particularly sectarian about the attitudes expressed in Jubilees toward impurity and sin' (2000: 46). It is increasingly recognized that the library at Qumran contains less sectarian than non-sectarian material, as evidenced in a recent attempt to classify the non-biblical materials that have come from the site (Dimante [1995]). It remains a challenge, of course, to identify halakhic practices—and related sociological concerns—common to the greater majority of Second-Temple Jews. Fortunately, earlier trends toward atomization (i.e. the identification of a variety of Judaisms, along with the assignment of texts to one group or another) are now balanced by a greater appreciation of a shared set of Jewish beliefs and practices (see Sanders [1992]).

3. Sanders (2000: 20-28).
4. Himmelfarb (2005: 130).

marriage practices thus situates *Jubilees*, once again, firmly in the world of common Judaism.

Finally, evidence for the popularity of the work outside of the Dead Sea community confirms the above analysis. An important recent comparison of *Jubilees* and Josephus's *Jewish Antiquities,* for example, has identified some forty-eight instances of 'parallel exegesis', twenty-eight of which are unique to the two works.[5] Josephus was apparently quite familiar with *Jubilees* or, at least, with numerous traditions that found their way into the document. These findings further support the evaluation of *Jubilees* as a non-sectarian work, and they underscore the widespread popularity of the document—and its profoundly exclusivist ideology—throughout the late Second-Temple period. We may reasonably view *Jubilees,* therefore, as representative of the perspective of a community of Hasidim, prior to the formal withdrawal of some members of the group to establish an isolated sect at Qumran.[6] A date between 170 and 140 BCE has recently been suggested.[7]

A mid-second century BCE date for *Jubilees* situates the book in a setting characterized by increasing preoccupation with symbols and practices related to Judean socio-ethnic identity. As Wintermute has asserted, 'Obedience to the Law is the central message of *Jubilees*'.[8] The legal piety in view here centers, however, around circumcision, sacred times, and sacred foods. Familiar to most scholars are the author's concerns with calendrical matters, and the document's preoccupation with the importance of Sabbath-keeping. Particularly notable is the considerable effort the author expends anachronistically to retroject back into the earliest chapters of Genesis Sabbath observation, circumcision, and other socially defining behaviors. Indeed, as we shall see below, God circumcised the angels when he created them, and they have been celebrating the Sabbath ever since.

a. *Circumcision*
Jubilees devotes particular attention to the rite of circumcision. Chapter 15 narrates the establishment of the covenant of circumcision with Abraham.

5. Halpern-Amaru (2001).
6. Wintermute (1985: 2.44).
7. Alleged allusions to Maccabean victories in the text have led Wintermute to suggest c. 161 BCE as the earliest date for the work (1985: 2.44). Some are not convinced, citing the absence of any mention of Antiochus's decree as indicating a pre-167 date (Goldstein [1983b]). The author's concern for the preservation of Jewish identity more generally assumes a historical setting for *Jubilees* when Judaism was on the defensive against Hellenistic ideas and practices. One can reasonably presuppose strong reservations to encroaching Hellenism on the part of a proto-Essene group of Judean Hasidim some years before Antiochus's decree, and a post-167 date for the work is not necessary for the present argument. VanderKam's 170–140 BCE dating for *Jubilees* can be adopted as a cautious but reasonable working hypothesis (1992a: 3.1030).
8. Wintermute (1985: 2.40).

Much of the storyline follows Genesis 17. The narrative concludes, however, with an excursus on the importance of circumcision, along with a prediction of future apostasy from the rite, each of which finds no parallel in the biblical account.[9] The author's elaboration upon the centrality of circumcision for Israel's identity warrants extended citation. The first text-segment reads as follows:

> This law is for all the eternal generations and…there is no passing a single day beyond eight days because it is an eternal ordinance ordained and written in the heavenly tablets. And anyone who is born whose own flesh is not circumcised on the eighth day is not from the sons of the covenant which the Lord made for Abraham since (he is) from the children of destruction. And there is therefore no sign upon him so that he might belong to the Lord… Because the nature of all of the angels of the presence and all of the angels of sanctification was thus from the day of their creation. And in the presence of the angels of the presence and the angels of sanctification he sanctified Israel so that they might be with him and with his holy angels (15.25-27).

The angels themselves were circumcised from creation. It is only appropriate, then, for Israel to be circumcised, so that they, too, might be with God and his holy angels.[10] The angelic messenger continues:

> And you command the sons of Israel and let them keep this sign of the covenant for their generations for an eternal ordinance. And they will not be uprooted from the land because the commandment was ordained for the covenant so that they might keep it forever for all of the children of Israel. For the Lord did not draw Ishmael and his sons and his brothers and Esau near himself, and he did not elect them because they are the sons of Abraham, for he knew them. But he chose Israel that they might be a people for himself. And he sanctified them and gathered them from all the sons of man because (there are) many nations and many people, and they all belong to him, but over all of them he caused spirits to rule so that they might lead them astray from following him. But over Israel he did not cause any angel or spirit rule because he alone is their ruler (15.28-32).

---

9. Much insight into the ideological agenda of the author can be gained by comparing *Jubilees* with source materials from the biblical account in Genesis. Monographs that have made substantial contributions in this regard include those at Endres (1987) and van Ruiten (2000).

10. The pronounced emphasis in the citation upon 'the eighth day' is characteristic of our author, who will draw upon the *topos* again to explain the choice of Isaac over Ishmael to inherit the promise. With Gen. 21.4, we learn in a later chapter of *Jubilees* that 'Abraham circumcised his son (Isaac) on the eighth day' (16.14a). Our author then adds an observation that goes beyond the Old Testament account: '[Isaac] was the first one circumcised according to the covenant which was ordained forever' (16.14b). The author's point is that Isaac was the first one circumcised on the eighth day. This, then, along with the elaboration on the importance of eighth-day circumcision in 15.25-27, above, explains why Isaac, not Ishmael, inherits the blessing. Isaac was eight days old when he was circumcised; Ishmael was circumcised at thirteen years of age (Gen. 17.25).

For the author of *Jubilees*, the covenant of circumcision has a profoundly sociological (even geographical) significance. The rite is inextricably linked both to Israel's election as God's people and to their hope of remaining in the land of promise.

The section concludes with a prediction of future apostasy from circumcision, a passage, again, unparalleled in Genesis. The sociological dimension ('they have made themselves like the gentiles to be removed and be uprooted from the land', v. 34) should be noted:

> And now I shall announce to you that the sons of Israel will deny this ordinance and they will not circumcise their sons according to all of this law because some of the flesh of their circumcision they will leave in the circumcision of their sons. And all of the sons of Beliar will leave their sons without circumcising just as they were born. And great wrath from the Lord will be upon the sons of Israel because they have left his covenant and have turned aside from his words. And they have provoked and blasphemed inasmuch as they have not done the ordinance of this law because they have made themselves like the gentiles to be removed and be uprooted from the land (15.33-34).

b. *Sacred Space*

Jubilees also focuses upon the identification and preservation of the Torah's territorial distinctions. As with circumcision (above), our author alters the Old Testament narratives in some rather creative ways in order to underscore the significance of Israel's sacred space. The work begins with a passage predicting that Israel will one day forsake the Lord, after they have settled in the land of promise. The author quotes God as saying that his people will 'forget all of my commandments...and they will walk after the Gentiles and after the defilement of their shame' (1.9). The speaker (God) then elaborates upon this general prediction with the specific acts of apostasy here in view. Practices relating to sacred space and sacred seasons stand decidedly at the forefront of the narrator's mind:

> ...they will walk after the gentiles and after their defilement and shame. And they will serve their gods...and many will be destroyed...because they have forsaken my ordinances and my commandments and the feasts of my covenant and my sabbaths and my sacred place, which I sanctified for myself among them, and my tabernacle and my sanctuary, which I sanctified for myself in the midst of the land...they will err concerning new moons, sabbaths, festivals, *Jubilees*, and ordinances (1.9b-10, 14).

Notice that the worship of pagan deities described in the passage—a passage which sets the tone for the narrative, since it occurs at the beginning of the book—relates exclusively to issues of sacred space and sacred seasons, and it has profound implications for Jewish social particularity. To compromise these vital badges of Jewish social identity is, in the view of the author, to 'walk after the gentiles and after their defilement and shame' (1.9b).

Sacred space later receives striking emphasis in a narrative unique to *Jubilees*, in which the author locates the conceptual origins of levitical injunctions relating to purification after childbirth (Lev. 12.2-5) in the earlier account of creation. The Torah stipulated that a woman could not 'come into the sanctuary' until she had completed 'the days of her purification' (Lev. 12.4). *Jubilees* establishes a precedent for this legislation in the story of Adam and Eve who, according our author, had to wait forty and eighty days, respectively, after they were created, to enter the garden of Eden. The purification ritual in Leviticus assumes a distinction between sacred and profane space, which depends, in turn, upon the existence of Israel's localized sacred tabernacle. There is, of course, no tabernacle in the creation account in Genesis 2, and thus no sacred space for Adam and Eve to enter after their days of 'purification'. *Jubilees* resourcefully overcomes this difficulty by identifying the garden of Eden as God's sacred space during the pre-Sinaitic period—Eden is 'more holy than any land' (*Jub*. 3.12).[11] Eve's introduction into the garden by God's angelic assistants, and the corresponding holiness of Eden, is thus described as follows:

> And when she finished those eighty days, we brought her into the garden of Eden because it is more holy than any land. And every tree which is planted in it is holy (*Jub*. 3.12; see v. 9 for the introduction of Adam into Eden).

The experience of the first couple is then used to explain later levitical purity legislation relating to childbirth:

> Therefore the ordinances of these days were ordained for anyone who bears a male or female that she might not touch anything holy and she might not enter the sanctuary until these days are completed for a male or female (3.13-14).

The ensuing chapter continues the theme of Eden as Yahweh's sacred space. The following text identifies Eden as one of four holy places:

> For the Lord has four (sacred) places upon the earth: the garden of Eden [see earlier] and the mountain of the East and this mountain which you are upon today, Mount Sinai, and Mount Zion, which will be sanctified in the new creation for the sanctification of all the earth (4.26).[12]

Later, when Noah divides the land between his sons, Shem, Ham, and Japheth, the idea of Eden as a sacred locale surfaces again in the narrative:

---

11. There is some precedent for such a conception in the Hebrew Scriptures. The book of Ezekiel identifies Eden as 'the garden of God' (28.13; 31.9).

12. Eden, Sinai, and Zion will be familiar to most readers. The 'mountain of the East' represents the mountain on which Enoch offers incense to the Lord in the preceding narrative (4.24-25). On all this see now van Ruiten (1999: 63-94).

> And [Noah] knew that the garden of Eden was the holy of holies and the dwelling of the Lord. And Mount Sinai (was) in the midst of the desert and Mount Zion (was) in the midst of the navel of the earth. The three of these places were created as holy places, one facing the other (8.19).[13]

We must pause here to appreciate the creativity of our author in view of his historical agenda and sociological convictions. The Genesis account contains no explicit ideology of sacred versus profane space. The raw materials for such a project are present, however, in the identification of Eden as a distinctive geographical locale (Gen. 2.8-14), in the ensuing expulsion of Adam and Eve from the garden (3.23-24), and in the table of the nations outlined in Genesis 10. The author of *Jubilees* has adapted this raw material and creatively (and anachronistically) reworked the Genesis accounts to include the important symbolic dichotomy of sacred versus profane space, which is so characteristic of both levitical and, especially, post-Maccabean sensibilities.

Jubilees 8–10, which chronicles the post-deluge dividing of the land, seeks persuasively to legitimize Israel's claim to Canaan. A tactic now familiar to the reader—moving later realities into earlier times—is again adopted by the author, who moves the description of the boundaries of the land, first encountered in Genesis 15, back into ch. 10, before the Bible has made reference to any Canaanite in the land. VanderKam summarizes the author's purpose:

> Shem, the ancestor of the Israelites, is the favorite of his father and the overwhelming winner in the cartographic sweepstakes… Not only is he holy; his inheritance encompasses the most sacred spots on earth, including the 'holy of holies'. Shem's patrimony was twice reduced: once through the generosity of several of his sons (the Madai case) and once through thievery (the Canaan affair)… It is evident that the writer has decided to make the table of nations address, among other concerns, primarily the problem of who really owned Canaan.[14]

---

13. The idea of Jerusalem as 'the navel of the earth' is first attested in *Jubilees* and is likely intended as polemical in view of Greek geography, which identified Delphi as 'the *omphalos* of the world' (Alexander [1997: 147-58]). See Tilly's thorough investigation (2002).

14. VanderKam (1994: 46-69). The settlement of the lands of the earth by Noah's sons and their descendents receives extensive elaboration at the hands of our author. This material includes a Noahic curse upon anyone who violates boundaries and seizes another's land (9.14-15), along with the unlawful seizure of a portion of Shem's land by Ham's son, Canaan (10.29-34). The latter story was included in *Jubilees*, as Wintermute aptly notes, 'in order to prove that any contemporary claim to [the promised land] was illegitimate' (1985: 2.37). Sacred space was apparently a pressing issue for the author of *Jubilees*.

Interestingly enough, *Jubilees*' 'ideological attempt to put the nations in their places' confines the Greeks to their islands, assigning them no land in Asia Minor or farther east. Greek occupation of Palestine, a historical reality at the time *Jubilees* was written, provides the most satisfying explanation of this polemic.[15]

c. *Sacred Times*
Of all the symbols of Jewish social identity, concern to distinguish between sacred and profane times singularly drives the ideology of *Jubilees*. The earliest Hebrew description of the work reads as follows: 'The book of the divisions of the times according to their jubilees and their weeks'. Wintermute elaborates:

> The author believed that there was a theological value inherent in certain special times. Unlike modern man, he did not limit himself to the *quantitative* measuring or counting of days from an arbitrary starting point. For him, the days were also to be divided on a *qualitative* scale with respect to their sanctity. Some days were sacred and others profane.[16]

Alongside Wintermute's 'theological value' it is appropriate to emphasize a sociological value inherent in sacred times, as well. For the author of *Jubilees* viewed faithfulness to the calendar as vital to the preservation of Israel's identity, as evidenced by his treatment of Sabbath and the festivals throughout the narrative.

Like circumcision and purification after childbirth, the author of *Jubilees* anachronistically writes Sabbath-keeping back into the creation account of Genesis 1.[17] The result is a striking excursus upon the centrality of Sabbath

---

[15] The quote is from VanderKam (1994).

[16] Wintermute (1985: 2.38, author's italics).

[17] The perspective of *Jubilees* contrasts sharply, in this regard, with that of the early postexilic period, where the institution of the Sabbath continues to be associated with the giving of the Law at Sinai. See, for example, the recounting of Israel's history in Nehemiah 9:

> 'You came down also upon Mount Sinai, and spoke with them from heaven, and gave them right ordinances and true laws, good statutes and commandments, and you made known your holy sabbath to them and gave them commandments and statutes and a law through your servant Moses' (Neh. 9.13-14).

The kind of anachronism which reads a distinction between Israel and the Gentiles back into pre-Sinaitic stories in Genesis abounds in *Jubilees*. In his rewrite of the Adam and Even narrative (Genesis 3), for example, the author interjects the following commentary on the origin of clothing (Gen. 3.21): 'Therefore it is commanded in the heavenly tablets to all who will know the judgment of the Law that they should cover their shame and they should not be uncovered as the gentiles are uncovered' (*Jub.* 3.31). There are, of course, no Jews or Gentiles in the Genesis 3 narrative. The reference may be a polemical one, directed to Hellenized Jews who joined Greeks exercising nude in the gymnasium (2 Macc. 4.12-14).

for the people of God. The discussion begins with the institution of the Sabbath among the angels:

> And he gave us [the angels] a great sign, the sabbath day, so that we might work six days and observe a sabbath from all work on the seventh day. And he told us—all of the angels of the presence and all of the angels of sanctification, these two great kinds—that we might keep the sabbath with him in heaven and on earth (2.17-18).

The discussion continues with the importance of Sabbath as a social identity marker:

> And he said to us, 'Behold I shall separate for myself a people from among all the nations. And they will also keep the sabbath. And I will sanctify them for myself, and I will bless them. Just as I have sanctified and shall sanctify the sabbath day for myself thus shall I bless them. And they will be my people and I will be their God. And I have chosen the seed of Jacob from among all that I have seen. And I have recorded him as my firstborn son, and have sanctified him for myself forever and ever. And I will make known to them the sabbath day so that they might observe therein a sabbath from all work' (2.19-20).

The conclusion which follows underscores both the celestial observation of the Sabbath on the part of the angelic host and the special application of this sacred day to the nation Israel:

As most have recognized, the emphasis in *Jubilees* upon Sabbath, festivals, and circumcision is to be explained as a response to the inroads of Hellenization. The author's fondness for pushing the dates of these practices (as well as Israel's election) back into the creation account, however, has elicited a more nuanced explanation. Some time ago, Bickerman (1937/1979: 83-88), Hengel (1974: 1.299-301), and Goldstein (1976: 199-200) postulated a theology among certain Jerusalem elites which understood Sinaitic law—legislating distinctive practices for Israel and separation from the seven nations native to the promised land—as a later innovation. The 'covenant with the Gentiles', referred to in 1 Macc. 1.11, would then reflect the desire of this party to reform Judaism by going back to a time long ago in biblical history when Jew and Gentile were not separated as the law required. There is some evidence among non-Judean writers for the conception of a 'pure Mosaic cult—with a spiritual, aniconic notion of God, but also without the separatist rites like circumcision, the sabbath commandment and the food laws' (Theissen [1998: 130-31]). Thus, Strabo charges not Moses but, rather, 'superstitious men' who followed him with devising laws relating to food and circumcision (*Geog.* 16.2.37). VanderKam suggests that the author of *Jubilees* directly challenged this primitivist theology by purposefully retrojecting Israel's election, Sabbath law, and other Jewish distinctives back into the Genesis 1 creation account:

> Rituals such as sabbath celebration, circumcision, sacrifices, and festivals...had been practiced from the beginning. In other words, true religion was detailed and separatist and had always been so. Sabbath-keeping and Israel's election *out of* the nations dated from the time of creation (VanderKam [1994/2000: 521, author's italics]).

> On this day we kept the sabbath in heaven before it was made known to any human to keep the sabbath thereon upon the earth. The Creator of all blessed it, but he did not sanctify any people or nations to keep the sabbath thereon with the sole exception of Israel. He granted to them alone that they might eat and drink and keep the sabbath thereon upon the earth. And the Creator of all, who created this day for a blessing and sanctification and glory, blessed it more than all days (2.30-32).[18]

It is hardly surprising that VanderKam summarizes his careful study of *Jubilees* 2 with the assertion that 'the writer envelops the creation in words about the sabbath'.[19] Indeed, one could argue that the theme of Sabbath-keeping forms an *inclusio* for *Jubilees* as a whole, since the emphasis upon Sabbath early in the narrative finds an echo in an extensive Sabbath exhortation which serves as the conclusion to the book (50.1-13).[20]

Our author's preoccupation with sacred seasons finds vivid expression in his adamant insistence upon a solar, as opposed to a lunar, calendar. Only Sabbaths and feasts celebrated according to the former are legitimate. A

---

18. The emphasis upon the Sabbath as uniquely Israel's apparently found expression among the rabbis, as well. The Mishnah makes mention of a *Habdalah* ('separation') prayer that offered thanks for separation between the holy and the profane, particularly where the Sabbath was concerned (*m. Ber.* 5.2, 8.5). Instone-Brewer dates the traditions securely to the pre-70 CE schools disputes (2004: 67, 87). Although the Mishnah does not preserve the actual contents of the prayer, a tenth-century version of the *Habdalah* reads as follows:

> Blessed art Thou, O Lord, our God, King of the Universe! Who hast made a separation between what is holy and what is profane; between light and darkness; between Israel and the other nations; between the seventh day and the six days of creation. Blessed are Thou who hast separated the holy from the profane. (Instone-Brewer cites Saadya's tenth-century text of the *Habdalah* [2004: 67 n. 26]).

The similarities between the *Habdalah* and *Jubilees* 2 (above) are quite transparent. Instone-Brewer thinks that the application of the concept of separation to 'Israel and the nations' may have been present in some form in the first-century version of the *Habdalah,* referred to in the Mishnah (Instone-Brewer [2004: 67]).

19. VanderKam (1994/2000: 505). A parallel to *Jubilees* occurs in the Qumran Sabbath Songs, which also portray an angelic priesthood in heaven observing the Sabbath (4QShirShabb) (Sturcke [2005: 68]).

20. Other sacred times familiar from sinaitic law appear in the author's account of creation. In Genesis account, the sun and moon are intended simply 'to separate the day from the night' and 'for signs and for seasons and for days and years' (1.14). The author of *Jubilees* feels the need to be more specific: 'And the Lord set the sun as a great sign upon the earth for days, sabbaths, months, feast (days), years, sabbaths of years, jubilees, and for all of the (appointed) times of the years' (2.9). In contrast to Gen. 1.14-19, where both sun and moon are mentioned, here only the sun determines the sacred calendar, a reflection of *Jubilees*' adamant apologetic for a 364-day solar calendar. See Rietz (2005) for social and cosmic dimensions of the calendrical dispute in post-Maccabean Judaism.

key passage dealing with the 364-day calendar occurs in *Jubilees* 6. I will refrain from discussing the various technicalities associated with competing calendars in early Judaism.[21] More important for our purposes are the author's general admonitions to his readers to observe these sacred times (6.32-35) and his corresponding regret that some will continue to insist upon a lunar calendar:

> And there will be those who will examine the moon diligently because it will corrupt the (appointed) times and it will advance from year to year ten days. Therefore, the years will come to them as they corrupt and make a day of testimony a reproach and a profane day a festival, and they will mix up everything, a holy day (as) profaned and a profane (one) for a holy day, because they will set awry the months and sabbaths and feasts and jubilees (6.36-37).

The fear that the disobedient will 'mix up everything' aptly summarizes the concerns of persons like the author of *Jubilees*, for whom distinctions between sacred and profane space, times and food constituted non-negotiable symbols of social identity. In the present connection, 'everything' clearly includes not only the distinction between sacred and profane seasons but, more importantly, the social distinction symbolized by the proper observation of these festivals—the distinction between Jew and Gentile. For in the immediately preceding context, our author pointedly warns his readers that to ignore the 364-day calendar is 'to forget the feasts of the covenant and walk in the feasts of the gentiles' (6.35).

d. *Sacred Food*

Given the above survey, a general absence of expressed concern for Judean dietary practices in *Jubilees* is rather surprising. One passage, however, unequivocally articulates the author's convictions along these lines, and the text can serve as a summary statement for the thrust of *Jubilees* as a whole. In the context, Abraham exhorts his grandson Jacob as follows:

> 'Separate yourself from the gentiles, and do not eat with them, and do not perform deeds like theirs. And do not become associates of theirs. Because their deeds are defiled, and all of their ways are contaminated, and despicable, and abominable' (22.16).

---

21. See the works of VanderKam and the references cited there (1979; 1981). VanderKam postulates a conflict during the post-Maccabean period between conservative Judeans, who championed the traditional solar calendar, and more progressive Jews, who favored a 354-day lunisolar system first imposed by the Seleucids in 167 BCE. The theory continues to be refined (Daise [2005]; Eshel [2005]). Those who have challenged VanderKam's reconstruction include Davies (1983) and Stern (2001: 28-31). On this see also Beckwith (1997).

The prohibition against table fellowship with the Gentiles assumes as its background, of course, the Jewish dietary laws. The text reflects concerns that are contemporary to the author, however, and quite irrelevant to the biblical account of Abraham and his immediate descendants.[22]

e. Intermarriage

As we have seen, our author's preoccupation with the various symbols of Jewish identity has a marked sociological component—the identification and preservation of Jews, versus Gentiles, as the people of Yahweh. This distinction between sacred and profane people finds explicit expression in the prohibitions of intermarriage in *Jubilees*.[23] At two places in the Genesis account, our author significantly expands the Old Testament narrative, in order to interject extended warnings about intermarriage with Gentiles.[24]

Genesis 27.46–28.2, for example, portrays Rebekah and Isaac arranging to send Jacob to find a wife from among their own extended patrilineal kinship group. *Jubilees* cites these three verses from Genesis almost verbatim (*Jub.* 27.8-9). Earlier in the text, however, we encounter an extended dialogue between Rebekah and Jacob about the evils of intermarriage with the Canaanites, which finds no parallel in Genesis (*Jub.* 25.1-10). In response to his mother's exhortation, Jacob assures Rebekah that he has not even 'been thinking about taking...a wife from the daughters of Canaan' (25.4).

The Genesis 34 story of Dinah and the Shechemites also provided the author of *Jubilees* with an opportunity to warn against intermarriage. Here is an excerpt from an extended warning passage (30.7-17) which, again, is absent from the biblical account:

> And you, Moses, command the children of Israel and exhort them not to give any of their daughters to the gentiles and not to take for their sons any of the daughters of the gentiles because that is contemptible before the Lord.

---

22. Wintermute (1985: 2.98 n. 'd').

23. Kvanvig identifies the idea of transgressing 'the forbidden border of sexuality' as 'the central theme of Jubilees' (2005: 76-77). The story of the Watchers is paradigmatic in this regard: 'the Watchers could be seen as outsiders taking women belonging to the human family as the insiders, or the Watchers could be seen as insiders, belonging to the heavenly realm, defiling themselves with human woman as outsiders' (78). The former perspective is analogous to the rape of Dinah (*Jubilees* 30), where foreign men take an Israelite woman; the latter to the danger (emphasized throughout *Jubilees*) of Israelite men taking foreign wives (78).

24. On the prohibition of intermarriage and its relationship to the expansion of narratives about women in *Jubilees*, see Halpern-Amaru (1999). Halpern-Amaru argues that prohibitions of intermarriage reflect 'an apprehension that is more concerned with being the assimilator than with becoming assimilated', and suggests that our author disallowed conversion to Judaism in any form—'only descent from a woman who carries the appropriate genealogical credentials' qualifies one to be identified as a member of the chosen people (1999: 159, 155).

Therefore I have written for you in the words of the law all of the deeds of the Shechemites which they did against Dinah and how the sons of Jacob spoke, saying, 'We will not give our daughter to a man who is uncircumcised because that is a reproach to us'. And it is a reproach to Israel, to those who give and those who take any of the daughters of the gentile nations because it is a defilement and it is contemptible to Israel. And Israel will not be cleansed from this defilement if there is in it a woman from the daughters of the gentiles or one who has given any of his daughters to a man who is from any of the gentiles (30.11-14).

2. *Pseudo-Philo*

Pseudo-Philo's *Biblical Antiquities* serves as our second example of the genre of the rewritten Bible. The work, extant in Latin, is believed to have been written in Hebrew, in first-century Palestine, most likely before the destruction of the temple in 70 CE.[25] *Biblical Antiquities* traces Israel's history from Adam to David, and we will not be surprised to discover that the post-Maccabean location of the author generated a great deal of concern in the document for the preservation of Jewish identity in the context of Roman occupation.

a. *Sacred Space*

Pseudo-Philo is particularly concerned to safeguard distinctions between sacred and profane space, in ways that go well beyond the Old Testament narratives. The *Tendenz* first appears in the story of the tower of Babel (*Biblical Antiquities* 6–7), where the author retrojects Abraham back into the narrative from Genesis 12. Abraham (here Abram) refuses to take part in the plan to build the tower. God judges those who did, and he blesses Abraham for his obedience as follows:

> 'And before all of these I will choose my servant Abram, and I will bring him out from their land and will bring him into the land upon which my eye has looked from old, when all those inhabiting the earth sinned in my sight and I

---

25. See Murphy (1993) for a solid monograph-length treatment of *Biblical Antiquities*. Harrington (1988) should be consulted for a general overview of an important decade of research. Jacobson (1996) argues for a post-70 CE date but his arguments have not proved wholly convincing (see Hayward [1997: 365-66] and Adler [1998: 160], both of whom argue for a pre-70 date). Feldman has recently published a series of articles comparing *Biblical Antiquities*' treatment of various biblical narratives with the approach of Josephus, Philo, and the rabbinic traditions (2001; 2002a; 2002b; 2003a; 2003b). Begg has produced a similar collection of articles, in which he compares Pseudo-Philo's use of the OT with that of Josephus (1996; 1997a; 1997b; 2000). See, too, Fisk's monograph on Pseudo-Philo's use of the Hebrew Scriptures (2001). Fisk focuses especially upon the rather idiosyncratic reordering of materials related to the wilderness wanderings and the conquest of Canaan (*Bib. Ant.* 12–24).

brought the water of the flood and I did not destroy it but preserved that land. For neither did the springs of my wrath burst forth in it, nor did my water of destruction descend on it. For there will I have my servant Abram dwell and will establish my covenant with him and will bless his seed and be lord for him as God forever' (*Bib. Ant.* 7.4).

The promise of the land, highlighted above, is a theme wholly missing from the Babel narrative in Genesis 11. Nor does Abram appear in the biblical version of the story. Notice, as well, the presence of an interesting bit of information which is also absent from the Hebrew Scriptures: it did not rain on the promised land during the great flood. The idea surfaces again in later rabbinic works, and apparently originated during the Second-Temple period, when Judeans were increasingly sensitive to the 'otherness' of Israel's sacred space.[26]

Later in the work, the author significantly expands the biblical materials treating the death of Moses. Again the issue of the land of Israel as sacred space enters the picture. The narrator informs us that before Moses died he was shown not only the promised land (Deut. 34.1-4), but also

> the place from which the clouds draw up water to water the whole earth...and the place in the firmament from which only the holy land drinks (*Bib. Ant.* 19.10).

Even the sources of rain water in the firmament are divided into two portions, one for the nations and one for Israel, respectively.

Territorial concerns also emerge in the author's recasting of the conquest narratives, but now the focus narrows to Jerusalem as Israel's particular place of worship. Some familiarity with a memorable story from the book of Joshua will help us to appreciate Pseudo-Philo's creative approach to the Hebrew Scriptures at this point in the biblical storyline. Joshua 22 portrays Reuben, Gad, and the half-tribe of Manasseh erecting an altar east of the Jordan. The western tribes are initially troubled, for they are under the erroneous impression that the altar is intended as a cult site to compete with the tabernacle. The eastern settlers assure their fellow Israelites that this is not the case. The altar was erected

> 28 not for burnt offerings, nor for sacrifice, but to be a witness between us and you. 29 Far be it from us that we should rebel against the LORD, and turn away this day from following the LORD by building an altar for burnt offering, grain offering, or sacrifice, other than the altar of the LORD our God that stands before his tabernacle! (Josh. 22.28b-29)

As it turns out the altar was built solely to memorialize the unity of the eastern and western tribes as God's chosen people. When the tribes to the

---

26. The idea that it did not rain in Israel during the flood is also attested in *b. Zeb* 113a and *Cant. R.* 1.15.

west of the Jordan realize this, they are satisfied, and the altar remains in place (22.30-34).

As is apparent from the above summary of the altar incident, concern for sacred space already plays a role in the Old Testament version of the story. In Pseudo-Philo, however, the issue becomes much more pronounced, for here the eastern tribes do, indeed, appoint priests and offer sacrifices on their altar, in marked contrast to the biblical account (*Bib. Ant.* 22.1-2). Joshua chastises the easterners, who finally (again in direct contrast to the Old Testament), 'went and destroyed the altar' (22.7). The author proceeds to utilize this reframing of Joshua 22 as a point of departure for a lengthy excursus on the proper place for sacrifice, a digression paralleled nowhere in the Hebrew text of Joshua. The conclusion to this excursus is representative of a much longer text-segment that cannot be cited here in full:

> For until the house of the Lord was built in Jerusalem and sacrifice offered on the new altar, the people were not prohibited from offering sacrifice there, because the Thummim and Urim revealed all things in Shiloh. And until the ark was placed in the sanctuary of the Lord by Solomon, they were offering sacrifice there until that day (*Bib. Ant.* 22.9).

The next chapter of Pseudo-Philo continues to relate the idea of sacred space to Israel's otherness as the people of Yahweh, with a statement that is also missing in Joshua. God informs the people,

> 'And now, if you listen to your fathers...your land will be renowned over all the earth, and your seed special among all the peoples, who will say, "Behold a faithful people! Because they believed in the Lord, therefore the Lord freed them and planted them"' (23.12).

The texts cited above amply attest to Pseudo-Philo's preoccupation with Jewish territoriality, whether the sacred space in view consists of the holy land in general or, more narrowly, the tabernacle, Jerusalem, and her temple.

b. *God's Election of Israel*
The identification of Israel's descendents as 'special among all the peoples' (see *Bib. Ant.* 23.12, immediately above) reflects a pronounced emphasis throughout Pseudo-Philo upon God's election of the Jewish people.[27] In

---

27. Reinmuth (1997) carefully compares *Biblical Antiquities* 1–8 with parallels in Genesis, and he proceeds to identify Israel's election in Abraham as the central thread running through the narrative. The theme persists throughout the work, as illustrated by the fact that the excerpts I cite in this regard each come from later portions of Pseudo-Philo.

Social anthropologists identify a 'myth of ethnic election' as a notable—but by no means ubiquitous—intensification of the 'myth of remote origins' that is normally shared by members of an ethnic group. The idea of election seems to be particularly important for the long-term survival of an ethnic group (Smith [1992]). See Chapter 10 for further discussion.

various places the author adds a number of such statements to the Old Testament narratives of Israel's history. During the period of the judges, for example, God informs Israel, 'Behold I have chosen one people from every tribe of the earth, and I said that my glory would reside in this world with it' (30.2). Similarly, before killing Sisera, Jael prays

> 'And now be mindful, Lord, of when you assigned every tribe or race to the earth. Did you not choose Israel alone and liken it to no animal except to the ram that goes before and leads the flock?' (31.5).

Later Gideon has trouble reconciling Israel's election with oppression at hands of the Midianites. He asks, 'The Lord has chosen Israel alone before all the peoples of the earth?' The angel of the Lord, in turn, explains the oppression as due to Israel's sin, but adds that God 'will have mercy, as no one else has mercy, on the race of Israel' (35.1-3). The emphasis on Israel's election surfaces yet again in the Jephthah narrative, this time in conjunction with a reference to the promised land. The people pray,

> 'Look, Lord, upon the people that you have chosen, and may you not destroy the vine that your right hand has planted, in order that this nation, which you have had from the beginning and always preferred and for which you made dwelling places and brought into the land you promised, may be for you an inheritance; and may you not hand us over before those who hate you, Lord' (39.7).

The excerpts cited above appear nowhere in the biblical stories on which these rewritten narratives are based. This tells us much about the worldview of the first-century CE author of *Biblical Antiquities*, an outlook pointedly articulated in a comment placed in the mouth of the Old Testament figure Amram, Moses's father:

> 'It will sooner happen that this age will be ended forever or the world will sink into the immeasurable deep or the heart of the abyss will touch the stars than that the race of the sons of Israel will be ended' (*Bib. Ant.* 9.3).

One suspects our author would have had more than a little problem with Paul's sweeping assertions in Galatians, where he insists, 'There is no longer Jew or Greek, there is no longer slave or free, there is no longer male and female; for all of you are one in Christ Jesus. And if you belong to Christ, then you are Abraham's offspring, heirs according to the promise' (Gal. 3.28-29).

c. *Circumcision and Sabbath*

The familiar identity markers of circumcision and Sabbath observance also come to the foreground of the narrative of Pseudo-Philo. The author intentionally interjects the issue of circumcision into the Old Testament story of the discovery of the baby Moses by Pharaoh's daughter:

> [Moses] was born in the covenant of God and the covenant of the flesh... And when [Pharaoh's daughter] saw the boy and while she was looking upon the covenant (that is, the covenant of the flesh), she said, 'It is one of the Hebrew children' (9.13-15).

The author of *Biblical Antiquities* apparently wants his readers to understand that Moses was born circumcised. The idea comes into view again in late rabbinic literature, and it somewhat parallels the creation account in *Jubilees*, where the angels of God's presence are said to be circumcised.[28]

The identity marker of Sabbath observance is elevated to a position of extreme importance when, during a purging of the nation, a group of Israelites who 'profaned the sabbaths of the Lord' receive the same punishment—death by fire—as some who had eaten the flesh of their own children (25.13). At another place in Pseudo-Philo the transgression of the Sabbath commandment is added to a passage in Judges which recounts the sin of an Israelite named Micah (Judges 17). The Lord is speaking:

> 'And I commanded them to keep the sabbath, and they agreed to keep it holy... And the day of the sabbath that they agreed to keep, they have done abominable things on it' (*Bib. Ant.* 44.6-7).

Additions like these serve to underscore the significance of the Sabbath for the author of this reinterpretation of Hebrew history.

d. *Intermarriage*

Finally, the author of *Biblical Antiquities* forcefully presses his exclusivist social agenda by means of his unmitigated abhorrence of intermarriage.[29] The theme materializes throughout the narrative.[30] The Levite's concubine, who is ravaged in the regrettable story of Judges 19, receives the abuse, according to our author, 'because she had transgressed against her man once when she committed sin with the Amalekites, and on account of this the Lord God delivered her into the hands of sinners' (*Bib. Ant.* 45.3). Tamar's intent in having sexual relations with her father-in-law Judah 'was not fornication'. Rather, she was 'unwilling to separate from the sons of Israel'.

---

28. The rabbinic references include *b. Sot* 12a and *Exod. Rab.* 1.24. For the circumcision of the angels see *Jub.* 15.25-27.

29. Social anthropologists emphasize the importance of endogamy for the preservation of ethnic boundaries. Enloe thus refers to the study of the phenomenon of intermarriage as 'the 'bottom line' of ethnicity' (Enloe [1980: 354]).

30. DesCamp (1997) argues that a woman authored *Biblical Antiquities*, based on the polemic against intermarriage. The suggestion is intriguing but the evidence is insufficient to either support or refute such a proposal. Pseudo-Philo is not the only work that discourages intermarriage during the period.

The words that follow, placed in the mouth of Tamar, plainly betray the particularistic orientation of their post-Maccabean author: 'It is better for me to die for having intercourse with my father-in-law than to have intercourse with a gentile' (9.5). A final text advocating social separation frames the issue in terms of the Deuteronomistic theology we saw evidenced in other Second-Temple literature. As Israel is about to enter the promised land, Balaam counsels Balak, king of Moab,

> 'Come and let us plan what you should do to them. Pick out the beautiful women who are among us and in Midian, and station them naked and adorned with gold and precious stones before them. And when they see them and lie with them, they will sin against their Lord and fall into your hands; for otherwise you cannot fight against them' (18.13).

The message is clear. An Israel that mixes with foreigners forfeits the divine protection afforded by her covenant God. But a people of Yahweh that preserves its ethnic identity will ultimately triumph over a Gentile oppressor.

3. *Judith*

Judith is another Second-Temple work reflecting Jewish preoccupation with the Torah's dietary legislation. Of Palestinian provenance and dated to the Hasmonean period, this delightful piece of historical fiction depicts a pious widow, Judith, delivering her people from the threat of Gentile domination.[31] The work contains allusions to events that occurred over the course of some five centuries of Israel's history.[32] Cowley neatly summarized the author's methodology nearly a century ago: 'Details of history provide the raw materials for a fictional story'.[33] Judith thus qualifies, albeit somewhat loosely, for the genre of the rewritten Bible, even though the work is formally framed as a novelistic romance. The food laws come into play at several points in the story, and they become thematically

---

31. For dating and provenance see Helyer (2002: 167-68); deSilva (2002: 90-92); Moore (1985: 50-70); and van Henten (1995: 244). Baslez attempts to be more precise, seeing in the details of the military imagery an allusion to Seleucid campaigns in the mid-second century BCE and, specifically, to the battle of Beth Zacharias, at which Judas lost his life, in 162 BCE (2004). Craven (2003) surveys the approaches to the book of Judith adopted by scholars throughout most of the twentieth century (1913–2001).

32. See Nickelsburg for allusions in Judith to various Old Testament events and characters (1981: 152 n. 10). Van Henten's study of the phenomenon is even more detailed. He concludes that the author portrays Judith as a parallel to Moses, in the service of Hasmonean ideology (Van Henten [1995]).

33. Cowley (1913: 246).

central to the ruse Judith perpetrates on Holofernes, the pagan general who attempts to destroy Israel.[34]

The story begins with a plot to wipe out the inhabitants of Judea, conceived by the Assyrian king, Nebuchadnezzar.[35] As Nebuchadnezzar's chief general, Holofernes, approaches Israel, he inquires of the Ammonite leader Achior about the strength and fortification of the Jewish army. Achior's response reiterates the Deuteronomistic schema of sin-and-vulnerability versus faithfulness-and-security, which runs throughout the Hebrew Scriptures and much of Second-Temple literature:

> 20 'So now, my master and lord, if there is any oversight in this people and they sin against their God and we find out their offense, then we can go up and defeat them. 21 But if they are not a guilty nation, then let my lord pass them by; for their Lord and God will defend them, and we shall become the laughingstock of the whole world' (5.20-21).

Holofernes responds negatively, dismissing Achior's admonition until, that is, he hears precisely the same advice from the Jewish protagonist Judith, who now takes center stage for the balance of the tale.

In preparation for her encounter with Holofernes, Judith had arrayed herself in her finest clothing and, with the blessing of her Jewish elders, had

---

34. Other Jewish identity markers also find their way into the narrative. For example, among Judith's acts of piety is the careful observance of the Jewish calendar:

> She fasted all the days of her widowhood, except the day before the sabbath and the sabbath itself, the day before the new moon and the day of the new moon, and the festivals and days of rejoicing of the house of Israel (8.6).

Israel's sacred space also receives attention at several points in the story. The temple becomes symbolic of the nation as a whole, in a prayer in which Judith informs God,

> '[The Assyrians] intend to defile your sanctuary, and to pollute the tabernacle where your glorious name resides, and…have planned cruel things against your covenant, and against your sacred house, and against Mount Zion, and against the house your children possess' (9.8, 13).

Judith's entreaty echoes an earlier prayer in the narrative, where the people implored 'the God of Israel not to give up…the sanctuary to be profaned and desecrated to the malicious joy of the Gentiles' (4.12). The defining rite of circumcision even finds its way into this story of the pious woman Judith, when Achior, the Ammonite leader, 'saw all that the God of Israel had done' and 'was circumcised, and joined the house of Israel' (14.10). It is the dietary laws, however, that take pride of place in the narrative. As Duran recently noted, 'The story is exceptionally concerned, in fact, with keeping kosher' (Duran 2005: 119).

35. The historical confusion associating Nebuchadnezzar with the Assyrians is one of several indications that the author intentionally crafted the work as a piece of historical fiction, since Nebuchadnezzar's historical role as king of Babylon would have been well known from the biblical account (deSilva [2002: 94]). Those who argue that the 'errors' in the narrative are intentional include Craven (1983) and van Henten (1995).

pretended to flee from the besieged town of Bethulia in order to defect to the Assyrian camp (Judith 10). When Judith arrived, Holofernes, immediately overwhelmed by our heroine's beauty, listened once again—this time responsively—to Israel's theology of divine protection. Judith informed him,

> 9 'Now as for Achior's speech in your council, we have heard his words, for the people of Bethulia spared him and he told them all he had said to you. 10 Therefore, lord and master, do not disregard what he said, but keep it in your mind, for it is true. Indeed our nation cannot be punished, nor can the sword prevail against them, unless they sin against their God' (11.9-10).

Judith proceeds deceitfully to assure Holofernes that the Jews of Bethulia are, indeed, about to compromise their safety by engaging in such a sin. The sin in view just happens to be that of eating food forbidden by the Torah:

> 11 'But now, in order that my lord may not be defeated and his purpose frustrated, death will fall upon them, for a sin has overtaken them by which they are about to provoke their God to anger when they do what is wrong. 12 Since their food supply is exhausted and their water has almost given out, they have planned to kill their livestock and have determined to use all that God by his laws has forbidden them to eat. 13 They have decided to consume the first fruits of the grain and the tithes of the wine and oil, which they had consecrated and set aside for the priests who minister in the presence of our God in Jerusalem—things it is not lawful for any of the people even to touch with their hands. 14 Since even the people in Jerusalem have been doing this, they have sent messengers there in order to bring back permission from the council of the elders. 15 When the response reaches them and they act upon it, on that very day they will be handed over to you to be destroyed' (11.11-14).

As the story unfolds, Judith increasingly gains the confidence of Holofernes, all the while taking care herself to remain faithful to the very practices that she claims her fellow-residents of Bethulia are about to disavow. At a strategic point in the narrative, Holofernes sends for Judith and orders his lieutenants 'to set a table for her with some of his own delicacies, and with some of his own wine to drink'. Judith refuses the general's food:

> 2 'I cannot partake of them, or it will be an offense; but I will have enough with the things I brought with me'. 3 Holofernes said to her, 'If your supply runs out, where can we get you more of the same? For none of your people are here with us'. 4 Judith replied, 'As surely as you live, my lord, your servant will not use up the supplies I have with me before the Lord carries out by my hand what he has determined' (12.2-4).

As Duran has recently remarked, 'Judith is nothing if not boundary-conscious'.[36]

---

36. Duran (2005: 120).

For several consecutive evenings Judith leaves her tent to pray and bathe at the spring in the camp. In this way, the author informs us, 'she returned purified and stayed in the tent until she ate her food toward evening' (12.9). The story reaches its climax when Judith pretends to seduce a drunken Holofernes, decapitates him, and flees back to her home in Bethulia with his severed head in a bag (12.10–13.10).[37] The author specifically identifies the bag in which the Gentile general's bloody head was placed as Judith's 'food bag' (13.10). The entire work is characterized by irony, intentional ambiguities, and double entendres, so it is likely that the author intended this jarring juxtaposition of purity with impurity to symbolize a causal connection between Judith's faithfulness to the food laws and her triumph over the Assyrian general.[38] As the story concludes, Holofernes's forces are routed, and the Jews proceed to plunder the Assyrian camp for a full month (14.1–15.7).

a. *Reframing Deuteronomistic Ideology*
The centrality of Jewish dietary laws to the narrative of Judith must not be overlooked. As deSilva aptly notes, the theology of the book is a familiar one: 'Judith tells the story of a contest between the dominant Gentiles, with their claims about the gods, and the God of Israel—a prominent dynamic that runs throughout the history of Israel from the exodus through the Second-Temple period'.[39] In Judith, however, this 'basic theology of Deuteronomistic history', as deSilva properly labels it, is framed in terms particular to the author's social location as a post-Maccabean Jew of Palestinian provenance. In order to fully appreciate this, it will prove helpful first to consider briefly Israel's theology of sin, judgment, and repentance, as understood by the authors of the Hebrew Scriptures.

Old Testament expressions of Deuteronomistic ideology consistently portray Israel suffering the loss of God's protection—and corresponding punishment at the hands of the nations—because the Israelites worshipped foreign gods. Psalm 106 serves as a representative overview of Israel's experiences in this regard. When the Israelites entered the promised land,

---

37. See deSilva (2006) for a culturally sensitive reading of Judith's behavior—behavior that strikes Euro-American readers as 'morally reprehensible at worst and morally ambiguous at best' (deSilva [2006: 55]). Judeans who heard or read the story would have evaluated the 'Lies, Seduction, and Murder' perpetrated by the heroine in positive terms, as culturally appropriate strategies utilized in defense of Judith's own honor, the honor of her people, and the honor of Yahweh (the words in quotation marks are taken from the title of deSilva's essay).

38. On irony, ambiguity, and double entendre in Judith, see deSilva (2002: 89-90) and, especially, the extended discussion in Moore (1985: 78-84).

39. DeSilva (2002: 85). Davies also identified the theology of Judith as Deuteronomistic: 'if Israel keeps the divine law it is inviolate; only if it sins can it be overcome by foreign nations' (2001: 117).

> 34 They did not destroy the peoples,
>   as the LORD commanded them,
> 35 but they mingled with the nations
>   and learned to do as they did.
> 36 They served their idols,
>   which became a snare to them.
> 37 They sacrificed their sons
>   and their daughters to the demons;
> 38 they poured out innocent blood,
>   the blood of their sons and daughters,
>   whom they sacrificed to the idols of Canaan;
>   and the land was polluted with blood.
> 39 Thus they became unclean by their acts,
>   and prostituted themselves in their doings (Ps 106.34-39).

The result of Israel's apostasy was the displeasure of Yahweh and the discipline of Israel at the hands of her enemies:

> 40 Then the anger of the LORD was kindled against his people,
>   and he abhorred his heritage;
> 41 he gave them into the hand of the nations,
>   so that those who hated them ruled over them.
> 42 Their enemies oppressed them,
>   and they were brought into subjection under their power.
> 43 Many times he delivered them,
>   but they were rebellious in their purposes,
>   and were brought low through their iniquity (Ps 106.40-43).

The above connection between cultic compromise and divine displeasure surfaces throughout the Hebrew Scriptures, particularly in the historical narratives. In addition to the worship of foreign gods, moreover, Israel also suffers under God's judgment because of social injustice, a theme more prominent in the prophets. The following passage from Amos is illustrative:

> 4 Hear this, you that trample on the needy,
>   and bring to ruin the poor of the land,
> 5 saying, 'When will the new moon be over
>   so that we may sell grain;
>   and the sabbath,
>   so that we may offer wheat for sale?
>   We will make the ephah small and the shekel great,
>   and practice deceit with false balances,
> 6 buying the poor for silver
>   and the needy for a pair of sandals,
>   and selling the sweepings of the wheat'.
> 7 The LORD has sworn by the pride of Jacob:
>   Surely I will never forget any of their deeds.

> 8 Shall not the land tremble on this account,
> and everyone mourn who lives in it,
> and all of it rise like the Nile,
> and be tossed about and sink again, like the Nile of Egypt?
> (Amos 8.4-8).

Idolatry and social injustice thus constitute the primary sins that elicit God's judgment, as described in Old Testament literature. As Yahweh said to Israel through the prophet Ezekiel, 'You have become guilty by the blood that you have shed, and defiled by the idols that you have made' (22.4). It is highly informative, in this regard, to note that, in spite of extensive legislation in Leviticus regarding sacred and profane food, the Hebrew Scriptures almost never cite the eating of unclean food, or the consumption by commoners of food reserved for the priesthood, as reasons for Yahweh's displeasure with Israel.[40] The food laws simply do not figure in the biblical theology of sin, judgment, repentance, and restoration.

Compare, in contrast, the book of Judith, where obedience and disobedience to the Torah's dietary laws are highlighted as the particular behaviors that elicit God's blessing and judgment, respectively. The Old Testament Deuteronomistic framework has been preserved, but the focus of covenant faithfulness has subtly shifted. When Judith deceitfully informs Holofernes that the Jews will sin and forfeit God's protection, neither idolatry nor social injustice are in view. Rather, consuming 'all that God by his laws has forbidden them to eat' is the transgression that will render the Jews vulnerable to Holofernes' attack (11.12). Faithfulness to the food laws,

---

40. The Torah does order the people to remove from their number individual Israelites who disobey certain regulations related to purity of food (Lev. 7.20-27). Only Isa. 65.1-7, however, explicitly relates the practice of eating 'swine's flesh' (v. 4) to Yahweh's displeasure with the nation as a whole, and this passage lacks the corresponding judgment of Israel at the hands of a foreign power (compare Ps 106.41-42, above). Disobedience to the food laws thus occupies no place of any significance in the Old Testament theology of sin, judgment, repentance, and restoration, outlined above. (Interestingly enough, the eating of unclean food is mentioned on occasion not as a cause for judgment but, rather, as part of the punishment for Israel's idolatrous practices. Because the Israelites have forsaken Yahweh, they will eat unclean food where they are dispersed among foreign nations [Ezek. 4.13; Hos. 9.3]).

Neglect of Sabbath observance, on the other hand, is connected in the Hebrew Scriptures to divine chastisement on a number of occasions (Lev. 26.1-45; Neh. 13.17-18; Jer. 17.19-27). Josephus picks up and elaborates on this theme. As Weiss observes,

> It is significant for our purposes to note that after idolatry, which all Jews would agree is the most grievous of sins, Josephus singles out the breaking of the Sabbath as the one that most seriously threatens the Jewish community (1998: 384).

Elsewhere in the essay Weiss asserts, 'Josephus considers the Sabbath a barometer of piety and describes Sabbath observance as if it were a label with which to tag people' (1998: 381).

in contrast, guarantees deliverance from a Gentile threat, as evidenced by Judith's concern for purity of diet in preparation for her great act of heroism which results in the salvation of the Jewish nation. For the author of Judith, then, the eating of prohibited food has apparently displaced idolatry and social injustice as the fundamental sin that has the potential to compromise Israel's national security. And maintaining a sacred diet correspondingly guarantees a faithful Jew victory over a Gentile adversary. Such a perspective is to be traced to our author's experience as a Judean dwelling in post-Maccabean Palestine, where a Gentile presence and a corresponding concern for the preservation of Jewish identity constantly informed the realities of daily life.[41]

4. *Additions to Esther*

The Additions to Esther will serve as a final illustration of the way in which post-Maccabean Judeans augmented their sacred traditions in order to address the pressing needs of their own generation. The Greek version of Esther contains six portions of text not found in the Masoretic Text, along with other minor variations which, together, reflect the Hasmonean milieu of the first and second centuries BCE.[42] Jerome removed the Additions and placed them after Esther 10.3, at the end of the canonical Esther, with the result that the passages are now traditionally identified as 10.4–16.24. The enumeration is misleading, however, since the blocks of material are properly interspersed in the LXX at various points in the narrative. The contents of the Additions may be briefly summarized as follows, listed in the order in which they appear in the Greek text:

> Addition A (11.2–12.6—appears before Esther 1.1)—Relates a dream of Mordecai in which he see two dragons fighting each other amidst characteristic apocalyptic imagery. 'The righteous nation' is threatened, until 'as though from a tiny spring, there came a great river, with abundant water; light came, and the sun rose, and the lowly were exalted and consumed those held in honor' (11.10-12).[43]

> Addition B (13.1-7—appears after Esther 3.13)—Purports to relate the text of the king's edict, dictated by Haman.

---

41. Helyer interprets the focus on food and ritual purity in Judith as evidence of a proto-Pharisaic outlook (2002: 170-71). The practices he cites, however, were not exclusively Pharisaic. Fasting, concern for purity of food, and ritual washing attest more generally to the expansionist approach to purity that increasingly characterized much of Second-Temple Judaism in the wake of the Maccabean revolt.

42. DeSilva (2002: 116-18); Collins (2000: 110-11); and Bickerman (1944: 346-47).

43. English translations of the Additions are taken from the RSV.

Addition C (13.8–14.19—appears after Esther 4.17)—Contains the prayers of Mordecai and Esther in preparation for Esther's daring entrance unbidden into the king's court.

Addition D (15.1-16—replaces Esther 5.1-2 in MT)—Consists of a dramatically extended narrative of Esther's entrance into Artaxerxes's throne room.

Addition E (16.1-24—appears after Esther 8.12)—Provides the text of the edict in which the king rescinds his previous order.

Addition F (10.4–11.1—added to the end of the MT)—Offers an interpretation of Mordecai's original dream, and reinterprets the meaning of 'lots' (Heb. *purim*) for the reader.

The textual history of the Additions presents a set of thorny problems that inevitably render conclusions about date and provenance somewhat tentative.[44] Scholars have reached a degree of consensus, however, in tracing four of the Additions (A, C, D, F) to a Palestinian Semitic *Vorlage,* contemporary with the book of Judith (c. 2nd cent. BCE), and in identifying the remaining text-segments (B, E) as Greek originals, likely originating in Alexandria a century later (c. 1st cent. BCE).[45]

Mordecai's dream, in particular, speaks to a specific scenario that helps us date Addition A and, by extension, the rest of the Hebrew originals (C, D, F). Gardner has persuasively identified the warring dragons in the dream as the Ptolemaic and Seleucid empires, who threaten 'the nation of the righteousness'. The Jews are 'troubled' and 'they feared the evils that threatened them, and were ready to perish' because of the edict of Antiochus which proscribed Jewish religious praxis (11.6-9). The stream that becomes a river represents, in turn, the successful development of the Maccabean revolt (v. 10).[46] As Collins has appropriately noted of the Additions as a whole, 'The rigid division between Israel and the nations and the exaggerated emphasis on the separatist piety of Esther may be taken to reflect the Hasmonean milieu in which the translation was made'.[47] It remains to examine the evidence for this separatist outlook, as illustrated in the Additions themselves.

The edict of the king, related in Addition B, may be helpfully compared with an English translation of the MT original. The underlined text highlights the expansion of the original:

---

44. Moore has given much attention to the origin of the Additions (1973, 1977: 163-67). For a brief but informative history of scholarship on the issue, see now deSilva (2002: 114-16).
45. Moore (1973: 384); Martin (1975).
46. Gardner (1984).
47. Collins (2000: 111-12).

Esther 3.8	Addition B—13.3-5
Then Haman said to King Ahasuerus, 'There is a certain people scattered and separated among the peoples in all the provinces of your kingdom; their laws are different from those of every other people, and they do not keep the king's laws, so that it is not appropriate for the king to tolerate them'.	'Haman...pointed out to us that among all the nations in the world there is scattered a certain <u>hostile</u> people, who have laws contrary to those of every nation and continually disregard the ordinances of kings, <u>so that the unifying of the kingdom that we honorably intend cannot be brought about. We understand that this people, and it alone, stands constantly in opposition to every nation, perversely following a strange manner of life and laws, and is ill-disposed to our government, doing all the harm they can so that our kingdom may not attain stability</u>'.

The expanded text underscores the function of the Torah as a vehicle enforcing boundaries that preserve Jewish identity in the midst of a dominant Gentile culture. The pagan reaction to Torah-keeping is not a positive one, for Jewish particularism, the edict asserts, is incompatible with 'the unifying of the kingdom that we so honorably intend' (13.4). The sentiment brings to mind the goal of Antiochus's directive, as related in 1 Maccabees: 'Then the king wrote to his whole kingdom that all should be one people, and that all should give up their particular customs' (1.41-42). In each case it is the Jewish law that obstructs any attempt to unify the respective empires, and the parallel between these two texts serves as yet another indication that the author of Addition B composed his edict in the midst of post-Maccabean tensions between Jews and Gentiles.

The prayers of the protagonists found in Addition C similarly highlight Judean particularism—and Jew-Gentile antipathy—in ways foreign to the canonical Esther. The book of Esther is remarkable among Old Testament literary works for the absence in the text of any reference to God, or to Israel as Yahweh's particular people. Addition C seeks effectively to remedy this perceived deficiency. In striking contrast to the language of the canonical Esther, Mordecai prays,

> 'O Lord God and King, God of Abraham, spare thy people...the inheritance that has been thine from the beginning. Do not neglect thy portion, which thou didst redeem for thyself out of the land of Egypt' (13.15-16).

3. *Recrafting Israel's Story*

Esther's own prayer in the verses that follow echoes the theme of Israel as God's chosen people, adding to the mix a profoundly anti-Gentile outlook that includes pointed references to several fundamental Jewish identity markers:

> 'Ever since I was born I have heard in the tribe of my family that thou, O Lord, didst take Israel out of all the nations, and our fathers from among all their ancestors, for an everlasting inheritance…thou knowest that I hate the splendor of the wicked and abhor the bed of the uncircumcised and of any alien. Thou knowest my necessity—that I abhor the sign of my proud position, which is upon my head on the days when I appear in public. I abhor it like a menstruous rag, and I do not wear it on the days when I am at leisure. And thy servant has not eaten at Haman's table, and I have not honored the king's feast or drunk the wine of libations' (14.5, 15-17).

In harmony with the general contours of Maccabean ideology, the Esther of Addition C trusts that her piety with respect to Jewish particularism will gain her favor in the eyes of God when she approaches Artaxerxes to intercede for her people. The reader had, in fact, been prepared in advance for the emphasis upon Jewish identity markers in Esther's prayer. Earlier in the Greek version of the text, Mordecai instructed Esther to 'fear God and keep his laws', and the reader is told that, after entering the king's harem, Esther 'did not change her mode of life' (2.20), information wholly lacking from the Masoretic Text.[48]

As a final illustration of the post-Maccabean *tendenz* of the Additions to Esther, compare the explanation of the origin of the title 'Purim' for the newly instituted festival as related by the two parallel texts:

Esther 9.24-28	*Addition F—10.7-13*
24 Haman son of Hammedatha the Agagite, the enemy of all the Jews, had plotted against the Jews to destroy them, and had cast Pur—that is 'the lot'—to crush and destroy them; 25 but when Esther came before the king, he gave orders in writing that the wicked plot that he had devised against the Jews should come upon his own head, and that he and his sons should be hanged on the gallows. 26 Therefore these days are called	[Mordecai recalling his dream:] 7 'The two dragons are Haman and myself. 8 The nations are those gathered to destroy the name of the Jews. 9 And my nation, this is Israel, who cried out to God and were saved… 10 For this purpose [God] made two lots, one for the people of God and one for all the nations. 11 And these two lots came to the hour and moment and day of decision

---

48. Esther's comment in 14.17 is particularly revealing: 'And thy servant has not eaten at Haman's table, and I have not honored the king's feast or drunk the wine of libations'. As Blomberg notes (2005: 69), following Moore (1977: 212), Esther's assertion here contrasts directly with what is implied in the MT, where the king provides Esther 'with her cosmetic treatments and her portion of food' (2.9).

Purim, from the word Pur... 28 These days should be remembered and kept throughout every generation, in every family, province, and city; and these days of Purim should never fall into disuse among the Jews, nor should the commemoration of these days cease among their descendants.	before God and among all the nations. 12 And God remembered his people and vindicated his inheritance. 13 So they will observe these days in the month of Adar, on the fourteenth and fifteenth of that month, with an assembly and joy and gladness before God, from generation to generation for ever among his people Israel'.

The canonical Esther traces 'Purim' to the lot Haman had cast against the Jews. Addition F reframes the explanation in terms of God's broad historical intentions for Israel versus the nations, thus emphasizing, once again, God's oversight and care for his particular people. In the words of deSilva, 'The Purim festival is thus presented in such a way as emphasizes not only timely deliverance from disaster but also the fundamental difference between, and separation of, Jew and Gentile in the plan of God'.[49]

5. Conclusion

Our formal survey of Second-Temple literature is now complete, although I will cite additional works at various places in the chapters to follow. We have examined in some detail (a) several defining accounts of recent Jewish experiences (1–2, *4 Maccabees*), (b) three pieces of literature seeking to recast stories from Israel's distant past in terms relevant to current issues and challenges (*Jubilees*, Pseudo-Philo's *Biblical Antiquities*, the Additions to Esther), and (c) a delightful romance that utilized persons and events from some five centuries of Judean history in order to underscore the importance of *kashrut* for Israel's national security (Judith). It has become quite clear that the authors of these documents intentionally crafted their stories in such a way as to address pressing concerns of Jewish life which surfaced in the wake of the Maccabean experience with Antiochus IV and the Syrian Greeks. The events of 167–164 BCE apparently made Judeans highly sensitive to the threat to Israel's socio-religious identity posed by foreign occupation. Thinking Jews thus became deeply concerned with the preservation of social boundaries between Jews and Gentiles, as evidenced by a preoccupation in the literature with practices related to sacred times, sacred space, and sacred food, along with the covenant rite of circumcision.

We now turn to consider the teachings and activities of Jesus of Nazareth against the background of Jewish nationalism reflected in post-Maccabean

---

49. DeSilva (2002: 112).

literature. Anyone who sought to initiate a renewal movement among first-century Judeans had to come to terms with the powerful currents of Maccabean ideology that flowed through the socio-religious value system of the day. Jesus was no exception in this regard, and we are not surprised to find him dealing directly with vital national symbols of Sabbath, food, and temple. Jesus handled these badges of identity in ways, however, that deeply troubled many of his Jewish contemporaries, and the convictions of the authors surveyed in this and the previous chapter help us to see why this was the case. Persons steeped in a post-Maccabean ideology of purity and nationalism, and who lived their daily lives under the menacing shadow of Roman occupation, could hardly abide with a charismatic leader who played loose with the defining symbols of Judean ethnicity. Conflict between Jesus and scribal authorities was inevitable. For Jesus, however, God had begun a new chapter in the story of his people, and it was now time to renegotiate social boundaries that had defined the people of Yahweh for generations.

Chapter 4

JESUS AND JEWISH NATIONALISM:
ISSUES OF APPROACH AND METHODOLOGY

> In discussion of the historical Jesus nothing is free from
> wishes and interest, not even skepticism.
>
> *Theissen and Merz*

To attempt to understand the aims of Jesus is to grapple with one of the most studied and hotly debated areas of historical research, where even a modicum of relative neutrality proves to be a rather elusive goal. As Wright pointedly observes, 'Few people, faced with the uncomfortable fact that Jesus did not after all underwrite their favourite project or programme, are prepared to say "so much the worse for Jesus" '.[1] We will not be surprised, then, to discover that more than a few recent (and not-so-recent) lives of Jesus rather conveniently align themselves with the values of those who have produced them, thus confirming Schweitzer's timeless maxim of a century ago: 'There is no historical task which so reveals a man's true self as the writing of a life of Jesus'.[2]

The trend is not wholly regrettable, since a number of these reconstructions contain lasting insights that continue to inform our work in the area.[3]

---

1. Wright (1992: 102).
2. Schweitzer (1906/2001: 6). The rather trendy Jesus championed by certain North American scholars is a case in point. As Theissen has quipped, the non-eschatological Jesus who tends to emerge from such a minimalist database 'seems to have more Californian than Galilean local colouring' (1998: 11). The humorous barb from a German scholar strikes this native Californian as dangerously close to the truth.

The phenomenon is hardly limited to Jesus research. Historical reconstruction in general inevitably struggles to retain a reasonable degree of objectivity. Smith puts it rather bluntly: 'Historians usually find what they are looking for—a fact that makes me uneasy' (1973: 96).

3. I have learned a great deal, for example, from the writings of Crossan (1991), with whose methodologies (some of them) and conclusions (nearly all of them) I tend to disagree. McKnight's recent discussion of 'the problem of modernization' of Jesus should be consulted (2004: 150-53). As McKnight aptly notes, the modernization of Jesus 'began with the earliest Christians and can be seen in the (redactional) editing of the evangelists' (150).

The personal investment that, for better or for worse, characterizes the work of most New Testament scholars does, however, oblige an author offering a new interpretation of Jesus of Nazareth to assist his or her readers by clarifying key issues of methodology and historiography that underlie such a study. I thought it would prove helpful, in this regard, to devote a chapter to several such matters, matters that will serve as essential guidelines for my interaction with the Gospels later in the book. The discussion that follows treats four issues of methodology: I will (1) discuss in general terms my evaluation of the historical reliability of the Gospels, (2) consider more narrowly tradition history as it relates specifically to the project at hand, (3) offer some comments on the use of implicit cultural scripts in the hermeneutical process, and, finally, (4) interact with recent developments in the study of Jewish soteriology, with special focus on the relationship between boundary preservation and what has traditionally been referred to as Jewish legalism. A brief conclusion to the chapter will attempt to draw together these key issues of method and background.

1. *The Canonical Gospels and the Jesus of History: An Overview*

I related my optimism about the integrity of the Gospels in the Introduction, and I believe such an approach makes good historical sense.[4] As Wright has correctly observed, the cost of dicing up the gospel traditions in the service of a simple hypothesis about Jesus has been a 'resultant complexity of the picture of the church and its creative activity and traditions'.[5] Such complexity should make us a bit suspicious about the whole enterprise at the outset, given the noticeable lack of creativity that obtains in the extra-gospel evidence we do possess for the way in which the traditions about Jesus were passed along in earliest Christianity. I have in mind here Paul's letters and the book of Acts, where we find next to no appeal to Jesus traditions—invented or otherwise—in the service of controversy or catechetical concerns. Nor do the canonical Gospels themselves provide much evidence for wholesale early church creativity where Jesus is concerned, since the Gospels are revealingly silent on a number of matters that became significant areas of debate in the early church.

We may add to the above considerations the recent findings of Larry Hurtado and Richard Bauckham, two British scholars whose work, though unrelated,

---

4. I am not particularly impressed by the potential of documents such as the *Gospel of Thomas* and the *Gospel of Peter* to enhance our understanding of the historical Jesus. Although these texts likely contain some vestigial evidence for the life and ministry of Jesus, the additional data, properly interpreted, does not appear appreciably to alter the image of Jesus portrayed in the canonical Gospels.

5. Wright (1992: 101).

confirms a relatively conservative handling of the Jesus traditions among the earliest Christians. Hurtado's expansive monograph on the worship of Jesus in Jewish Christianity takes pride of place here. The study effectively challenges a long-held scholarly paradigm that has attributed the image of Jesus in the Gospels to the Hellenizing tendencies of creative Christian tradents in the decades following Jesus' earthly ministry. Hurtado instead traces a decidedly high Christology to Jewish-Christian circles in the earliest years of the movement. Devotion to Jesus as divine, and the practice of establishing communities of followers organized around what Hurtado calls a binitarian form of worship, 'erupted suddenly and quickly, not gradually and late, among first-century circles of followers'.[6] What this means for the present project is that we can no longer summarily consign the Christology of the canonical Gospels to the creative activities of later church tradents. To be sure, individual gospel pericopes will still need to be authenticated on a case-by-case basis. Hurtado's findings suggest, however, that we should readily embrace as broadly historical the general picture of Jesus presented in the gospel accounts.

Similarly encouraging, in this regard, are Bauckham's analysis of the gospel audiences and his study of the importance of eyewitness testimony among the early Christians.[7] For several generations, scholars have approached the documents assuming that they tell us as much about the early church (the gospel audience) as they do about the historical Jesus (the putative subject).[8] Bultmann had insisted that attention to the former should take priority in any attempt to reconstruct the life of Jesus: 'Only after we have obtained such a historical picture of the community are we in a position to attempt to reconstruct the picture of Jesus and of his preaching'.[9] The rise of redaction criticism encouraged the next generation of scholars to focus more narrowly upon the creative activity of specific, localized groups of Jesus' post-Easter followers. Many interpreters became convinced that each Gospel was written for a specific church or group of churches, and much recent work has sought to elucidate the social contours and theological convictions of the so-called Matthean, Markan, Lukan, and Johannine communities.[10]

---

6. Hurtado (2003: 650).
7. Bauckham (1998a) and (2006), respectively.
8. Classic along these lines is Bultmann's assertion that the controversy narratives in the Gospels originated 'in the apologetic and polemic of the Palestinian church'. Bultmann viewed the stories as 'imaginary scenes', created by the early Christians to illustrate 'in some concrete occasion a principle which the church ascribed to Jesus' (1963: 40-41). As a result, for Bultmann the Gospels reveal much more about the post-Easter church than they do about the historical Jesus.
9. Bultmann (1926: 341). Bultmann, of course, was highly pessimistic about finding anything of substance in the Gospels about the life and ministry of the historical Jesus.
10. Representative reconstructions include Orton on Matthew (1989), Kee on Mark (1977), Esler on Luke (and Acts) (1987), and Brown on John (1979).

Scholarly reflection about the gospel audiences has undergone somewhat of a paradigm shift in recent years, however, and the hypothesis that associates the Gospels with the specific needs of localized Jesus communities now appears, in retrospect, 'not just flawed or one-sided but simply wrong'.[11] Bauckham's critique of the whole enterprise has demonstrated, instead, that 'the Gospels were written for general circulation around the churches and so envisaged a very general Christian audience. Their implied readership is not specific but indefinite: any and every Christian community in the late-first-century Roman Empire'.[12]

Genre criticism confirms Bauckham's findings concerning the evangelists' audiences. A scholarly consensus of sorts has formed around the classification of the Gospels as expressions of ancient biography (Greek: βίοι; Latin: *vitae*), indicating that the Gospels were written primarily to relate the life of a person.[13] Matters of literary genre speak broadly, in turn, to our understanding of the authorship, the intended audience, and the content of the Gospels. And here it is important to note that the identification of the Gospels as forms of Greco-Roman biography coheres remarkably well with Bauckham's conclusions concerning the nature of the gospel audiences. Burridge summarizes:

> The essentially person-centered nature of biography reminds us that *bioi* are works by people for people about people. The *content* of the works concerns the subject of Jesus [not the needs of the church]; the *author* is a particular writer [not a community] with a view of Jesus he wishes to communicate; and the intended *audience* is more likely to include various groups and individuals across the Mediterranean world interested in Jesus [not a local Christian community], probably both inside and outside the churches.[14]

None of the above, of course, offers any wholesale guarantee of the historical reliability of the gospel traditions. We may still expect 'a particular writer', addressing 'a very general Christian audience', to press a theological agenda by the way in which he frames his distinct story of Jesus. Recent developments relating to audience, authorship, and the content of the Gospels do suggest, however, (*contra* Bultmann and his followers) that we can expect the Gospels to tell us more about Jesus than they tell us about the concerns of the early church. This is important. For although we must

---

11. Watson (1998: 195).
12. Bauckham (1998b: 1). Bauckham's collection of essays on the topic should be consulted (1998a). Especially perceptive is Watson's analysis of the theological and sociological origins of current scholarly interest in the *Sitze im Leben* of the evangelists and their respective communities (Watson [1998; more extensively, 1997]).
13. Talbert (1977); Aune (1987, 1988); Burridge (1992).
14. Burridge (1998: 144, author's italics). The bracketed portions are mine, and are intended to bring out the threefold contrast reflected in Burridge's extended discussion.

certainly allow for the *Tendenz* of the individual evangelists, the identification of the Gospels as *bioi*, intentionally presenting Jesus to a broad, indiscriminate audience, should, I think, encourage a more optimistic evaluation of the traditions about Jesus which the authors of the canonical Gospels have chosen to include in their respective accounts.

It remains to offer some brief comments about eyewitness testimony. Here, again, Bauckham has moved the discussion forward significantly, in a wide-ranging and detailed work which draws extensively upon both canonical and non-canonical literature to underscore the importance of eyewitness testimony among early Christian tradents during the first two centuries of church history.[15] The evidence Bauckham adduces decisively undermines the foundational form-critical assumption that the Gospels consist of anonymous traditions, collectively passed on through many stages of oral transmission. And Bauckham's findings leave little room for the kind of early church creativity postulated by scholars who take a minimalist perspective on the historical reliability of the Gospels.

These variegated discoveries related to early Christian worship, the audiences of the Gospels, and eyewitness testimony among Jesus' followers converge strongly to favor a conservative traditioning process on the part of the early Christians. We can be quite confident, then, that we have in the canonical Gospels four relatively trustworthy portraits of Jesus of Nazareth. What this means for the present undertaking is that I will engage the biblical text with a degree of historical optimism uncharacteristic of some research in the field.

2. *Tradition History and a* Gesamtbild *of the Historical Jesus*

Two trends, in particular, will characterize my tradition-historical approach to the Gospels, both of which find expression in an important recent study by Theissen and Winter.[16] The first trend, which can be traced throughout 'third quest' research, displaces the criterion of dissimilarity from its preeminent position as the methodological basis for historical Jesus research in favor of a broader principle identified (and carefully articulated) by Theissen and Winter as the criterion of historical plausibility.[17] A second recent trend in Jesus studies privileges a deductive, as opposed to an inductive, point of

---

15. Bauckham's treatment will likely become a landmark work in the study of gospel origins (2006).

16. The study was originally published in German (Theissen and Winter [1997]) and was later translated into English (2002). I will cite the English version. See also Theissen (1996).

17. Theissen's criterion of historical plausibility has been warmly embraced by (among others) Freyne (2004: 12) and Dunn (2005: chapter 3).

departure in Jesus research, postulating at the outset a *Gesamtbild* (holistic picture) of Jesus, which is then tested against the particular evidence of the gospel texts. Each trend finds specific application in the project at hand.

a. *The Quest for Historical Plausibility*
Theissen and Winter's criterion of historical plausibility encompasses the following considerations (subcriteria), which address Jesus' relationship to early Christianity and Judaism, respectively:

Jesus and Christianity The Plausibility of Historical Effects	*Opposition to Traditional Bias* Elements within the Jesus tradition that contrast with the interests of the early Christian sources are likely to be historical	*Coherence of Sources* Independent sources that agree on some aspect of Jesus' life or teaching are more likely to be historical than isolated traditions
Jesus and Judaism The Plausibility of Historical Context	*Contextual Appropriateness* What Jesus intended and said must be compatible with the Judaism of the first half of the first century in Galilee	*Contextual Distinctiveness* Jesus will exhibit a degree of individual recognizability that gives him a particular social identity

Satisfying Theissen and Winter's fourfold criterion of historical plausibility proves to be a daunting task for scholars of all persuasions. In what follows I consider the viability of my project in view of the demands of the subcriteria outlined in the chart above.[18]

We begin with the relationship of Jesus to Judaism. Theissen and Winter's approach makes room here for both continuity and discontinuity. A historically plausible Jesus must both (a) answer to his Jewish origins and (b) exhibit a degree of 'individual recognizability' that gives him 'a particular social identity' in his broader cultural environment.[19] The distinctiveness of Jesus poses no problem for my thesis. My challenge will be to demonstrate that a rather anomalous Jesus—who subverts Jewish particularism at a time when most of his contemporaries are emphasizing practices that reinforce ethnic boundaries—nevertheless functions in a historically plausible way in

---

18. Although I have made every attempt accurately to summarize and interact with Theissen and Winter's approach, the authors nuance and expand upon the four subcriteria outlined in the chart above in ways that cannot be addressed (or adequately represented) in the concise treatment that follows. Theissen and Winter further divide the criterion of coherence of sources, for example, into three related subcriteria: 'cross-section evidence', 'genre constancy', and 'multiple attestation' (2002: 178-79, 235-39). In the interest of brevity I have treated the criterion in a singular, but inevitably more simplistic, fashion. See the authors' extended discussion (2002: 172-212).

19. Theissen and Winter (2002: 211; 184-88).

his socio-religious context.[20] It will be profitable, therefore, first to consider Theissen and Winter's subcriterion of contextual appropriateness.

Contextual Appropriateness—Although the Jesus of the Gospels stands out from his contemporaries in a variety of ways, we note at the outset that Jesus is hardly unique in addressing practices related to purity and boundary preservation. Such matters preoccupied many of his fellow-Judeans. Fervent convictions about the relative importance of Jerusalem and her temple, Sabbath observation, and purity at table surface in a variety of our sources, representing a disparate number of groups and individuals throughout the Second-Temple period. In dealing with long held distinctions between sacred and profane times, places, and food, then, Jesus grappled with issues at the heart of Judaism during our period. To be sure, Jesus adopted a non-traditional perspective on these matters, a perspective which deeply troubled numbers of his contemporaries. But even here we encounter occasional commonalities. Leaders of the community at Qumran went even farther than Jesus, for example, in their critique of temple polity and administration.[21]

Theissen and Winter find it helpful to distinguish between Jesus' teaching and his behavior, where the criterion of contextual appropriateness is concerned. Consider, for example, the familiar dominical pronouncement about purity at table: 'It is not what goes into the mouth that defiles a person, but it is what comes out of the mouth that defiles' (Mt. 15.11).[22] The assertion profoundly undermines the distinction between clean and unclean food, and, as I will argue later, should not be interpreted as simply prioritizing internal over external purity. The saying occurs, however, in the indicative mood, with only limited comments (still in the indicative) regarding its application in the surrounding context (Mt. 15.20). As Theissen and Winter perceptively observe,

> One can have consistent reservations in principle with regard to an objectively based distinction between clean and unclean things—and nonetheless observe the purity rules, whether as a matter of accommodation, out of respect for valid traditions, or because one interprets them spiritually. In

---

20. Holtzmann's comment from nearly a century ago still applies: 'A genius who is not rooted in his own time and homeland cannot effect a transformation in his time' (1911: 408; trans. Boring in Theissen and Winter [2002: 274]).

21. The adoption of what was perceived to be a pagan calendar (CD 6.18-19) and the exclusion of the Zadokite priestly line (CD 4.3) rendered the temple utterly defiled in the eyes of leaders at Qumran (CD 5.6-7; 1QpHab 12.7-9) (Murphy-O'Connor [2000: 49 n. 24]).

22. I will contend in Chapter 7 for the priority of the Matthean version (over Mk 7.15). Neither version simply prioritizes internal purity over external purity. Theissen and Winter are quite on target to see here a more 'fundamental skepticism of the distinction between clean and unclean things' (2002: 181).

Judaism the decisive thing is not what ideas one has in principle, but what one concretely does!²³

The distinction between ideas and behavior is an important one. For although Jesus appears conceptually to dismantle the categories of clean and unclean food in the pronouncement recorded in Mt. 15.11, never do the Gospels portray Jesus formally dining with Gentiles or otherwise compromising levitical purity at table. The teaching is distinctive. Jesus' behavior, however, coheres well with the practices of many of his Jewish contemporaries. The same could be said for his attendance at synagogue on the Sabbath, and for his presence at the temple in Jerusalem during major Jewish festivals.

Recent scholarship in the field of ethnic identity theory helps further to situate Jesus squarely in his social environment. The contextual appropriateness of his subversive treatment of sacred space, sacred times, and sacred food, as illustrated in the canonical Gospels, becomes increasingly apparent when we view the purity-related activities of Jesus and his contemporaries as parallel projects in the ongoing construction of Jewish ethnicity. As I will demonstrate in a later chapter (Chapter 10), Jesus was not the only one who tried to redraw the ethnic contours of the people of God. Pharisees and others in post-Maccabean Roman Palestine also sought to reinterpret Israel's heritage in the service of their own social agendas. It is certainly the case that Jesus and the Pharisees entertained markedly different ideas about the social boundaries that ought to result from such an undertaking. The two movements, however, were actively engaged in similar reconstructive projects, and this is a significant point of resonance between Jesus and his broader Jewish context. Indeed, it was precisely the intelligibility of Jesus' actions, in this regard, that elicited so much animosity from Pharisees and others who opposed his boundary-breaking agenda.

Contextual Distinctiveness—The 'individual recognizability' of Jesus comes to the forefront often in the pages that follow.²⁴ The combination of (a) a general optimism regarding the reliability of the gospel traditions and (b) a preference for an anomalous Jesus, rather than an anomalous Jesus movement—both of which characterize my discussion of the

---

23. Theissen and Winter (2002: 181). As Theissen notes in an earlier work, Jesus' indicative becomes an imperative in the post-Easter church, where Peter is commanded to 'kill and eat' (Acts 10.13). A 'gnomic maxim' has now given birth to a 'concrete rule of behaviour' (Theissen [1999: 32]).

24. Theissen's and Winter's understanding of Jesus' individuality provides a refreshing alternative to extremes that either efface Jesus' historical particularity in the service of dogmatic theology or, conversely, obscure Jesus' special contribution to the genesis of early Christianity by appeal to historical analogies and related lines of development: 'Jesus' singularity consists in a singular combination of Jewish traditions as well as in the fact that his words and deeds represent a unique stage in the development that leads from Judaism to Christianity' (2002: 244).

Gospels in the next three chapters—generates a picture of Jesus which readily satisfies the subcriterion of contextual distinctiveness. Specifically, for all the commonalities he shared with his peers in ideology and behavior, Jesus consistently questioned and destabilized institutions and practices that had for generations encouraged the preservation of sacred times, sacred space, and sacred food. This marks out Jesus as relatively distinct from those around him in his overall treatment of matters related to Jewish ethnicity and boundary preservation. So much for Jesus and his Jewish context.

The relationship between Jesus, the gospel traditions, and the early church proves more problematic. On the positive side, we find Jesus' non-traditional approach to purity attested across a broad base of early Christian source materials, so that satisfying the subcriterion of coherence of sources will not prove particularly difficult. It will be otherwise, however, with the criterion of opposition to traditional bias. Here a boundary-breaking Jesus harmonizes rather too easily with a Gentile-friendly church, thus directly supporting—rather than opposing—tendencies observable in the church during the first two generations of early Christianity. This reality, along with the apparent lack of knowledge about Jesus' indifference to purity among leaders in the Jerusalem church who had interacted with him during his lifetime, will pose no small problem to my thesis.

Coherence of Sources—We need not labor long here. Jesus' counter-cultural treatment of Jewish identity markers surfaces in a number of independent sources. We encounter Sabbath controversies, for example, in the triple tradition (Mk 2.23–3.6 and parallels), in the Gospel of John (5.1-17), and in Luke's special material (13.10-17; 14.1-6). Sayings related to the destruction of the temple are even more widely attested, occurring, again, in the triple tradition (Mk 13.2 and par.), in Matthew's and Mark's versions of both the trial scene (Mk 14.57-58; Mt. 26.60-61) and the crucifixion (Mk 15.29-30; Mt. 27.40), in John's Gospel (2.19), and in Acts (6.13-14). The anti-temple rhetoric coheres well, moreover, with Jesus' action in the temple court, an event attested in the triple tradition and in John. The theme of open table fellowship similarly 'permeates every layer of the Synoptic tradition'.[25] We could thus make a reasonable case for the historicity of Jesus' iconoclastic treatment of any one of several defining symbols of Jewish particularism. Taken together the activities and teaching outlined above generate a coherent picture of Jesus as one who consistently challenged the contours of Jewish ethnicity, as understood and championed by numbers of his more conservative contemporaries.

---

25. Blomberg (2005: 20). Blomberg cites texts from (a) the triple tradition (Mk 2.13-17 par.; 6.30-44 par.; 8.1-10 par.), (b) the Q material (Mt. 11.19 par.; 8.11-12 par.), and (c) material unique to Luke (7.36-50; 10.38-42; 11.37-54; 14.1-24; 19.1-10).

Opposition to Traditional Bias—This subcriterion represents part of Theissen and Winter's attempt to rehabilitate and refine the much maligned criterion of dissimilarity.[26] Significant for our purposes is the fact that the authors utilize their renewed criterion—now identified as the criterion of 'opposition to traditional bias'—in a positive (confirming) function and not a negative (excluding) function.[27] I take this to mean that the criterion continues to mark out as historically probable those materials in the Jesus tradition that go against clearly demonstrable tendencies in the church, *but that the criterion as reframed by Theissen and Winter no longer necessarily excludes materials in the Gospels that happen to cohere with early church convictions and practices.* The latter qualification is an important one, for it leaves a whole plethora of potentially authentic materials in the database (including Jesus' attitude towards Jewish exclusivism) to be evaluated using other tools of historical analysis. In the present connection this means that the happy coherence between (a) a boundary-breaking Jesus who consistently challenges Jewish nationalism and (b) an expanding Gentile mission will not, in and of itself, necessitate dismissing the relevant gospel texts as unhistorical.

A further consideration, however, seriously complicates the matter and has the potential to render my thesis significantly less persuasive. For it is not only the agreement between Jesus and the Gentile church on issues of purity and nationalism which tends to engender a degree of historical skepticism towards the idea of a boundary-breaking Jesus. More problematic is the fact that our earliest evidence for the church's position on Jewish particularism finds Jesus' followers quite unaware that their Messiah ever challenged the traditional badges of Jewish identity to begin with. The disconnect is quite obvious and generates a glaring *non sequitur*. The leaders in the Jerusalem church who had most direct access to the historical Jesus appear to struggle

---

26. The criterion, traditionally conceived, dealt with double dissimilarity, interpreting Jesus against the backgrounds of Judaism and early Christianity, respectively. Theissen and Winter's criterion of opposition to traditional bias addresses solely the latter relationship. The authors have reframed the other half of the criterion—Jesus as dissimilar to Judaism—as their criterion of contextual distinctiveness (see above).

27. Scholars have consistently critiqued the negative (excluding) function of the criterion of double dissimilarity for (a) its tendency to generate an unacceptably peculiar Jesus, unconnected to Judaism and effectively unrelated to the movement he initiated, and (b) its uncritical assumption that our knowledge of Judaism and the early church is such that we can accurately identify that which is distinct about Jesus (Cullmann [1961: 141-43]; Marxsen [1969: 15]; Kee [1970: 264-65]; Jeremias [1971: 2]; Gager [1974: 257]; Dahl [1976: 168-72]; Schillebeeckx [1979: 92-94]; Harvey [1982: 6-10]; Sanders [1985: 16]; Gnilka [1997: 20]; along with a host of others cited in Theissen and Winter [2002: 261-316]). See Theissen and Winter's historical survey of various attempts to refine the criterion of double dissimilarity in order to downplay its potentially excluding tendencies (2002: 124-36).

anew with issues of purity and boundaries, without recourse to the teachings or convictions of their founder. How could this be so, if Jesus challenged the familiar markers of Jewish ethnicity, as indicated in the gospel narratives?

The difficulties here cannot be minimized, but neither, in my view, are they insurmountable. The complexities of the matter are such that I have devoted a whole chapter to the historical plausibility of a boundary-breaking Jesus in light of activities in the post-Easter church. I refer the reader there (Chapter 8) for a detailed treatment of the apparent disconnect between Jesus and his earliest followers on issues of boundaries and nationalism, a disconnect that finds reasonable explanation in the reaction of the broader Jewish populace to political and religious challenges confronting Judeans in the East during the 30s-50s of the common era.

b. *Crafting a* Gesamtbild *of the Historical Jesus*
A second recent trend that will characterize my treatment of the Gospels privileges a deductive methodology—one which intentionally moves from a holistic picture of the historical Jesus to the details of the gospel traditions—over an inductive approach that builds from isolated traditions towards a comprehensive depiction of Jesus. Advances in our understanding of historical method strongly suggest that the kind of naïve empiricism often associated with a purely inductive approach to the Gospels represents an ideological fallacy. Again, citing Theissen and Winter:

> Methodologically, judgments about the authenticity of individual traditions by no means stand at the beginning of the effort to reconstruct a historical picture of Jesus, as though we could then inductively piece together a comprehensive picture. It is rather the case that judgments about individual traditions are dependent on a comprehensive picture of Jesus, however vague and open this picture may be.[28]

Wright's monograph, *Jesus and the Victory of God*, is, perhaps, the classic example of a deductive approach consciously adopted, but the method has found strong support among other Jesus scholars, and among philosophers of history, as well—and for good reason, given our understanding of how language and behavior function in human communication and interaction.[29]

---

28. Theissen and Winter (2002: 201). And again: 'All judgments about the authenticity or inauthenticity of individual Jesus traditions are determined by more or less explicit comprehensive pictures of the life of Jesus, which are examined in the course of every individual decision' (211-12).

29. Wright (1996: 131-33). As McKnight perceptively observes, 'Wright's case is built by way of "explanation" of a given historical datum (a saying, an action) within the "story" (Judaism's, Jesus') previously established' (2004: 161). See also the comments of philosopher C.S. Evans, who similarly maintains that 'it is impossible to determine which individual sayings or pericopes are authentic in isolation from broader theories' (1999: 187).

It has become increasingly apparent, in this regard, that words and deeds cannot be abstracted from the interpretative socio-cultural matrices in which they occur. This reality characterizes our daily lives, and the phenomenon inevitably informs our interaction with ancient texts like the Gospels. The idea that we can devise criteria that will somehow enable us objectively to separate history from later tradition, and then utilize these 'facts' to generate an accurate picture of the historical Jesus, thus proves to be a positivist illusion. Kazen explains:

> We cannot deal with Jesus' words in isolation from possible contexts, from other words or from some sort of picture of his person. The same is true of the acts of Jesus. The historicity of a certain act is judged differently depending on how that act is interpreted, i.e. what sense is given to it; and interpretation is dependent on the interpreter's total picture. Thus it is more fruitful to discuss the authenticity of a *Gesamtbild* than of separate words and deeds.[30]

This is not to say that just any *Gesamtbild* (comprehensive picture) of Jesus will do.[31] In the historical process the interpreter's image of Jesus must be informed by individual gospel traditions. Those traditions, however, will at the same time be interpreted in light of the total picture. It is this latter point that I am emphasizing in the present connection.[32] Furthermore, both the interpretations of specific texts and the postulated *Gesamtbild* of Jesus will, in turn, answer to the fourfold criterion of historical plausibility outlined above.

The portrait of Jesus in the pages to follow does not aspire to comprehensiveness, in that I treat but a single aspect of Jesus' life and ministry, namely, Jesus' redefinition of the socio-ethnic boundaries of the people of God in view of the eschatological inbreaking of the kingdom age.[33] Within the confines of my project, though, I will generally proceed deductively, from Jesus to text, so to speak. That is, I will assume throughout that Jesus functioned as an ethnic entrepreneur of sorts, deconstructing Jewish ethnicity by subverting various badges of Jewish identity, as he

---

30. Kazen (2002: 29-30)

31. According to Theissen and Winter, 'These comprehensive pictures derive in part from the sources, in part from the history of research, in part from prescholarly engagement with the Christian tradition' (2002: 212).

32. Scholars speak, in this regard, of a hermeneutical circle that inevitably highlights the element of interpretation on both counts (Kazen [2002: 35]; Theissen and Winter [2002: 201]).

33. What follows is decidedly not a holistic portrait of Jesus of Nazareth, nor should it be interpreted as such. My intention, rather, is to explore in some detail what I consider to be one very significant aspect of Jesus' life and ministry. Much of importance will inevitably be left unaddressed. I generally ignore, for example, that which the New Testament authors found most noteworthy about Jesus, namely, his crucifixion, burial, and resurrection (1 Cor. 15.1-8).

simultaneously redefined the social contours of the people of God in terms of surrogate kinship. Individual pericopes will, in turn, be interpreted in light of this modest but clearly articulated *Gesamtbild*, with the result, I trust, that both the gospel narratives and the aims of Jesus will be mutually illuminated.[34]

3. *Behind the Scenes: Cultural Scripts and Gospel Interpretation*

A third issue of methodology relates to the use of socio-cultural background materials to interpret the gospel narratives. I find in the Sabbath controversies between Jesus and the Pharisees, in the action in the temple during the final week of Jesus' life, and in Jesus' open table fellowship a desire on Jesus' part to renegotiate the social boundaries of the people of God in light of the arriving reign of Yahweh. My seminary students, however, have been somewhat ambivalent about the whole enterprise. They are quite impressed by the compelling evidence from the post-Maccabean period which underscores the sociological function of sacred times, sacred space, and sacred food (along with the covenant rite of circumcision) to delineate the boundaries of the Jewish people in the context of Roman occupation. The background materials presented in the previous chapters tend to persuade. When students turn to the Gospels, however, many are often perplexed by my analysis, for they do not see Jesus reconstructing social boundaries in the text itself. Jesus is simply performing a compassionate healing on the Sabbath; or cleansing the temple of spiritual or financial corruption; or extending hospitality to 'sinners and tax-collectors' at mealtime. Jesus deconstructs Jewish nationalism? My students just do not see it in the Bible.

The problem here is a hermeneutic which is so text-based that it tends to ignore social codes and cultural scripts that are shared—but seldom articulated—by authors far removed from the world of today's Euro-American readers. For various reasons, Protestant students of the Bible have historically emphasized the perspicuity of Scripture, the priesthood of all believers, and a grammatical-historical approach to the text on the part of the individual interpreter which looks for the plain sense of the passage. At the popular level evangelicals challenge persons in our churches not to take what they hear at face value but, rather, to read the Bible for themselves to see what it truly means. The implication is that an individual with the right

---

34. I find myself attracted to the 'moderately positivistic' methodology adopted by Schwartz in a recent survey of early Jewish history (2004: 2). As Millar approvingly observes in a review of Schwartz's work, such an approach means 'that the available evidence has to be taken seriously, but that it is not, and cannot be, a simple mirror of reality, and always requires interpretation, which itself is impossible without some hypothesis, or hermeneutical model' (2006: 140).

attitude—and the right Spirit—can effectively discern the plain meaning of the biblical text. All the more so if the person happens to be a scholar who reads Hebrew or Greek.

Without dismissing the considerable benefits of such a hermeneutic, we need to come to grips with its potential pitfalls which, in my view, are twofold: (1) a suspicion of anything not explicitly specified in the text that might contribute to our understanding of the author's intended meaning, and (2) the unconscious substitution of the interpreter's own cultural values for those that characterized the world in which the text was produced.[35] Unfortunately, taken together these pitfalls threaten to derail the whole exegetical process. With respect to the issue of cultural sensitivity, we can be thankful that the expansion of the scholarly guild in recent decades to include persons from a variety of social locations has forcefully called to account those of us of any background who would continue unknowingly to privilege our own cultural perspectives in the process of biblical exegesis. Competing interpretations from persons of different ethnicities, genders, and socio-economic backgrounds now compel us humbly to acknowledge our own perspectival baggage and to seek, alternatively, to read the Bible against the socio-cultural background of Mediterranean antiquity. For this we can all be grateful.

By way of illustration, some time ago a pair of South African scholars compared the ways in which two disparate social groups interpreted the narrative of the rich man who approaches Jesus to inquire, 'Good Teacher, what must I do to inherit eternal life?' (Mk 10.17-22). One reading group consisted of relatively affluent South African Anglicans. The second group was made up of 'pre-critical readers. . .poor and oppressed'.[36] The results of the study are rather enlightening. For the upper-class Anglicans, Mk 10.17-22 was simply a story about individual sin. The rich man valued his wealth more than following Jesus. Readers from economically marginalized backgrounds interpreted the passage quite differently. They concluded that Jesus' dialogue partner had probably obtained his wealth by exploiting others. Individual sin did not go unnoticed by these readers. But the man's wealth was not seen as merely a personal barrier between him and God, an 'idol' of some sort. Rather, the rich man's sin consisted of the misuse

---

35. The latter pitfall inevitably compromises much of our cross-cultural communication. Rohrbaugh summarizes:

> [S]tudies of cross-cultural communication indicate that when the familiar guideposts that allow people to proceed without conscious thought are missing, as they are in many cross-cultural situations, people tend to rather quickly substitute markers from their own culture. They assume that their own ways are normal, natural, and right and therefore project their own sense of things onto the situation as a simple means of finding their way (Rohrbaugh [2007: 5]).

36. Draper and West (1989: 42-43). See also West (1993).

of his wealth in his relationships with others (especially the poor).[37] The disadvantaged readers cited in the study, moreover, interpreted the passage to be addressing structural evils, as well as the individual sin of the rich young man. They surmised that

> there might have been social structures which produced wealth for the man and poverty for the people, in the same way that the social system of apartheid empowered white South Africans to become wealthy and pushed black South Africans into poverty. So even if the man had worked for his property and or had inherited his wealth, he was still part of a sinful social structure.[38]

Affluent Anglicans, on their part, drew none of these insights from the text.

I now introduce my seminary course on exegesis in the Gospels by presenting these two competing interpretations of Mk 10.17-22 (without identifying the respective reading communities). I then ask the class, 'Which interpretation most faithfully represents the author's intention?' Students almost invariably side with the upper-class Anglicans—persons who, as we might suspect, more closely share their own socio-economic background. The point in the present connection is not to adjudicate between these alternative interpretations of Mark 10, although, as I have argued elsewhere, I suspect that our pre-critical readers are closer to the truth on this one.[39] Here I simply wish to underscore the fact that one's social location has much to do with the way in which one interprets the gospel narratives.

I am no longer surprised to discover, moreover, that the primary objection my students raise against the pre-critical reading of Mk 10.17-22 described above, is that they find no evidence for interpersonal sin or institutional evil in the passage itself. Equipped with a solely text-based hermeneutic, and lacking the sophistication to read the New Testament against the background of Mediterranean cultural values and agrarian economic realities, students

---

37. Disadvantaged readers were particularly sensitive to the fact that the commandments which Jesus selectively cites from the Decalogue have nothing to do with idolatry and everything to do with interpersonal relations (West [1993]). In contrast, Euro-Western scholars have traditionally employed a great deal of creativity in their efforts to read the first commandment of the Decalogue into the pericope. Schmithals, for example, attempts to draw a connection between 'der Eine' of v. 18 (εἷς) and 'das Eine' of v. 21 (ἕν), in order to argue that the man's difficulty is not with the second table of the Decalogue but, rather, 'mit dem ersten Gebot' (1979: 453). Compare Cranfield's assertion that Jesus is here 'particularly concerned with the First Commandment' (1959: 330). It is quite evident, however, that Second-Temple Jews clearly distinguished between (a) statutes of the Decalogue governing relations between humans and God and (b) those governing relations among people (see Philo, *Heres* 168; 171-73, *Spec. leg.* 2.63; Josephus, *Ant.* 7.356, 374, 384; 8.280, 300, 394; 9.236; and the discussion in Sanders [1992:.192-94]).
38. West (1993: 176-77).
39. Hellerman (2000b).

unwittingly import radical individualism, capitalist economic structures, and, in many cases, Pauline soteriology into the passage, thus concluding, with a host of Western interpreters, that Jesus is addressing an individual who is attempting to earn God's favor, and whose wealth has somehow become an idol separating him from his God.[40]

The alternative to reading the Gospels through our own cultural lenses is, of course, to become familiar with and appropriate the social values and cultural cues that made sense of life for Jesus and his contemporaries. The problem we face in this regard is that much of the cultural information necessary to properly interpret the Gospels, or any ancient documents for that matter, is implicitly encoded—rather than explicitly articulated—in the texts themselves. A brief look at culture from the perspective of the social sciences will demonstrate why this is the case. Geertz has helpfully defined culture as

> an historically transmitted pattern of meanings embodied in symbols, a system of inherited conceptions expressed in symbolic forms by means of which men communicate, perpetuate, and develop their knowledge about and attitudes toward life.[41]

Now while anthropologists will continue to quibble over an acceptable definition of an all-encompassing term like 'culture', it can hardly be denied that a key part of the cultural matrix of any society is what Samuel has described as 'informal knowledge', that is, 'the knowledge that is *implicit* in our daily activities, in the collection of techniques, information, and ways of behaving that we use to carry on the business of living'.[42]

Samuel's point is that much of the 'informal knowledge' that generates behavioral patterns in a given society will never be explicitly articulated in

---

40. It is not only second-year seminary students who struggle along these lines. Cranfield's understanding of Mk 10.21 reveals the extent to which highly trained Western commentators will go to import Pauline soteriology into the text:

> [Mk 10.21] does not mean that selling one's goods and giving the proceeds to the poor is a meritorious act that will *earn* treasure in heaven; for the reward is God's undeserved gift to those who are willing to receive it. But trust, willingness to accept God's gift as a gift, cannot help but show itself by outward tokens. Jesus by commanding the man to show the tokens which are the outward expression of faith is really appealing to him to have faith (1959: 330).

And Cranfield is hardly alone. Sariola goes so far as to find in Mk 10.17-21 the teaching that salvation is 'eine Gabe und Gnade Gottes', and that 'alle Menschen böse sind' (1990: 174-75). Similarly, Pesch remarks disparagingly of 'das Leistung-Lohn-Denken des Mannes', and refers to the rich man's regrettable lack of 'unbedingtes Gottvertrauen, die Basis wirklich sozialer Praxis' (1980: 141). Pesch's 'Gottvertrauen', however, is nowhere explicitly mentioned in the text, while the 'Leistung-Lohn' connection surfaces throughout the pericope, primarily on the lips of Jesus (vv. 17, 19, 21, 28-30).

41. Geertz (1973: 89).
42. Samuel (1990: 5-6, my italics).

the context of day-to-day social interaction, or in written communication, *precisely because it is already shared by the culture's participants*. This is especially true of traditional peoples for whom cultural cues and social norms tend to remain relatively static and unchanging for generations. The idea of implicit informal knowledge will prove somewhat less familiar, however, to modern Western readers. As Malina notes, 'Multiple [cultural] scripts can be and are the rule in complex, immigrant societies such as the US'.[43] And it is not only the multiplicity of various matrices of behavioral expectations that complicates social relations in our culture. The rapid rate of change characteristic of life in the modern West also adds complexity to the cultural mix. American society therefore demands a relatively explicit articulation of various social norms, in order to assist persons of different backgrounds satisfactorily to negotiate their way through life. Thus, to cite a rather mundane but revealing example, there are hundreds of signs posted all around the small Southern California beach community where I live informing residents and non-residents alike where they can and cannot walk their dogs and park their cars.

Things were quite different for the world of the New Testament. Cultural scripts defining norms for persons in Mediterranean antiquity were by comparison much more uniform, and they had remained in place, in many cases, for hundreds of years. The result is that much 'informal knowledge', to adopt Samuel's expression, above, could be—and, indeed, most often was—left unexpressed in the course of social interaction. And what was true of social interaction in general in the ancient world was particularly the case for linguistic communication, be it oral or written. Language, as Malina has observed, transmits 'a hidden load of shared assumptions, a collective and shared set of interpretations of reality that make up the culture of a particular group'.[44] The challenge of biblical interpretation, then, is to

---

43. Malina (1986: 31).

44. Malina (1986: 2). Speech act theorists particularly emphasize the importance of shared knowledge, beliefs, and presumptions for the communication process. Bach and Harnish call this shared knowledge 'mutual contextual beliefs' (MCBs) (1979: 5-6). As Botha enjoins, '[I]t is extremely important to be well versed in the cultural context of the utterances or discourse, that is, the mutual contextual beliefs (MCBs)' (1991: 77).

Social scientists make a distinction, in this regard, between 'low context' societies, like the modern West, and 'high context' societies, such as those that populated the ancient Mediterranean basin. The former communicate in ways—and produce texts—that spell out matters in great detail. High context cultures, in contrast, leave a lot more to the imagination, precisely because they can assume so much in the way of shared cultural knowledge on the part of the readers/auditors (Hall [1976: 91-101]; 1983 [59-77]; on this see Malina [1991]; Neyrey [1994: 81]; and Rohrbaugh [2007: 8-10]). As Rohrbaugh rightly observes, '[T]he difference between these two types of societies is not in the importance of context, but rather in whether the speaker can presume that the listener knows the context ahead of time and does not need it spelled out' (2007: 8).

trade one's own 'hidden load of shared assumptions' and 'interpretations of reality' for those that characterized the world of the text—whether or not those social values and cultural scripts appear overtly in the text of the Bible itself. Indeed, given the conservative nature of the first-century Mediterranean world, we will hardly expect the biblical authors to explicitly articulate the 'informal knowledge' and 'shared assumptions' common to a social world that they—and their readers—knew so very well.

The examination of the documents in the previous chapters constitutes my attempt to elucidate certain key cultural scripts relating to Jewish identity, which were in play in the Roman East during the post-Maccabean periods of Jewish independence and ensuing Roman domination. I trust that the evidence has satisfactorily demonstrated the function of various purity practices to mark off social boundaries between Judeans and non-Judeans, boundaries that had become increasingly strategic in the wake of the Syrian proscription of circumcision, Sabbath-keeping, and levitical dietary practices under the Hellenistic monarch Antiochus IV (167–164 BCE). Perhaps even more crucial was the ideology underlying these practices. Popular interpretations of Maccabean history had reinforced the conviction among Judeans that Yahweh intervenes on behalf of a people who faithfully preserve their social distinctives, and that persons who play loose with the familiar markers of Jewish ethnicity seriously compromise Israel's relationship with God and, by extension, her national integrity. This, I submit, is the socio-cultural background which must be brought to bear in order fully to appreciate Jesus of Nazareth's perspective on these vital badges of Jewish identity in the Gospels. And for reasons outlined above, cultural scripts of post-Maccabean purity and nationalism will seldom find explicit expression in the biblical texts themselves. They will in every case, however, be actively operating behind the scenes of the narrative. Of this we can be assured, for so it is with traditional peoples and their shared informal knowledge. It remains to be seen just how much these background materials illuminate Jesus' activities as related in the canonical Gospels. But first I must offer some observations concerning a final fundamental matter of methodology, one related to the current debate surrounding the nature of Second-Temple Jewish soteriology.

4. *Nationalism, Legalism, and the Not-So-New Perspective*

In has been three decades now since Sanders's book *Paul and Palestinian Judaism* launched what one writer has called 'a Copernican revolution in Pauline studies'.[45] At thirty years of age, the 'New Perspective' (NP), as

---

45. Sanders (1977). The words in quotes come from Hagner (1993: 111), whose essay provides a helpful overview and an insightful critique of recent (to 1992) streams of

it has been dubbed, is no longer new, but the massive bibliography that has accumulated on the subject since the publication of Sanders's book in 1977 attests to its ongoing importance for New Testament interpretation. Sanders's monograph was primarily concerned with Jewish soteriology as it related to the individual. The burden of *Paul and Palestinian Judaism* was to demonstrate that Judaism was not a religion of meritorious works-righteousness. To account for the preoccupation with law-keeping that characterizes much of the literature, Sanders distinguished between 'getting in' and 'staying in' the covenant. He placed the careful observation of the commandments of the Torah firmly in the latter category, and labeled the resulting soteriological perspective 'covenantal nomism'. The expression pointedly highlights what Sanders saw to be an inter-relationship between divine initiative (covenantal) and human response (nomism) in ancient Judaism:

> [C]ovenantal nomism is the view that one's place in God's plan is established on the basis of the covenant and that the covenant requires as the proper response of man his obedience to its commandments, while providing means of atonement for transgression.[46]

Any law-centeredness observable in Judaism must therefore be understood to have functioned within the context of prior elective grace.[47]

A reevaluation of Second-Temple Jewish soteriology called for a new understanding of Paul, thus the expression 'New Perspective'.[48] In the

---

Pauline scholarship. The expression 'New Perspective' appears to have been coined by Dunn, who used it as a title for his Manson Memorial Lecture at the University of Manchester in 1982 (Hagner [1993: 111]; Dunn [1990: 183-214]). Useful introductions to the New Perspective and its critics include Thompson (2002), Westerholm (2003), and Smith (2005). See, too, the extensive bibliography at http://www.thepaulpage.com/ (as of May 1, 2005).

As has been noted, Sanders's perspective on Judaism had been anticipated by a number of his scholarly predecessors. *Paul and Palestinian Judaism* was, however, the first attempt during the post-Holocaust era to challenge traditional caricatures of Judaism as a legalistic religion. 'It was', as Hagner observes, 'a point whose time had come' (1993: 112).

46. Sanders (1977: 75).

47. In Sanders' view both 'election and ultimately salvation are considered to be by God's mercy rather than human achievement' (Sanders [1977: 422]). Theissen crisply summarizes Sanders's perspective:

> By election, God has made the people [of Israel] his own possession—in the fundamental acts of the making of the covenant, the call of Abraham, the exodus and the lawgiving at Sinai. The Torah was given so that the people could remain in the covenant—not to create it by fulfilling the commandments (1998: 126).

48. Dunn capsulizes well the dilemma that Sanders's monograph created for Pauline scholarship: 'If the Judaism of Paul's day also gave such a place to divine election, atonement and forgiveness, then what was Paul objecting to?' (2005: 7).

alleged absence of a legalistic Judaism, Paul, it was thought, must be resisting something other than the idea that a person merits acceptance with God by successfully observing the statutes of the Torah.[49] Perhaps the most fruitful attempt to revisit Paul's attitude towards the law reframes the debate in sociological terms. Accordingly, Paul's foundational concern in the dispute revolves not around the deeds an individual must do to 'get in', or even 'stay in', the covenant.[50] At issue, rather, is the social identity of the people of God in the eschatological era of the Spirit, where Gentiles are now admitted to the company of the faithful and the familiar badges of Jewish particularism no longer carry any soteriological freight. The focus of the discussion has thus shifted from '*how* one gets in' to '*who* gets in', or, more precisely, to the way in which the resulting multi-ethnic social entity—the Christian *ekklesia*—is to be distinguished from the rest of humanity.

When Paul resists the idea of basing one's salvation upon doing 'the works of the law', then, he opposes not legalism but, rather, national-ethnic pride. Dunn, a major proponent of the position, defines the expression 'works of the law' as

> precisely the phrase chosen by Paul (as either already familiar to his readers or self-evident to them in its significance), by which Paul denotes those obligations prescribed by the law which show the individual concerned to belong to the law, which mark out the practitioner as a member of the people of the law, the covenant people, the Jewish nation.[51]

Another advocate of the NP frames the issue in more colorful terms:

> The 'works of the Torah' were not a legalist's ladder, up which one climbed to earn the divine favour, but were the badges that one wore as the marks of identity, of belonging to the chosen people in the present, and hence the all-important signs, to oneself and one's neighbours, that one belonged to the company who would be vindicated when the covenant god acted to redeem his people.[52]

---

49. Sanders, in fact, insists that such a conception is wholly foreign to Paul: 'The supposed objection to Jewish self-righteousness is as absent from Paul's letters as self-righteousness itself is from Jewish literature' (1983: 156).

50. Sanders's analysis, framed as it is in individualistic terms, is not broad enough to allow for the collective and eschatological orientation of Paul's approach. Witherington notes:

> Sanders is reacting against the still ongoing effects of Luther's analysis of Galatians and Romans and the stereotypes of early Judaism that that analysis produced. It is ironic then that he himself is indebted to that same sort of soteriological analysis in that he chooses to frame the discussion in terms of 'getting in' and 'staying in' (Witherington 2005: 45).

51. Dunn (1990: 219-20).

52. Wright (1992: 238). Paul correspondingly critiques the 'relentless pursuit of national, ethnic, and territorial identity' which characterized the worldview of his non-Messianist Jewish contemporaries (Wright [1997: 84]).

What Paul refuses to entertain, then, in his epistles, is not legalism, traditionally understood. Rather, Paul challenges the soteriological assurance that his Jewish contemporaries found in their ethnic identity as the descendants of Abraham, an identity tangibly expressed in the socially defining practices of Jewish particularism discussed elsewhere in this book. The debate about circumcision that permeates the letter to the Galatians is an example of just this sort of conflict between Paul and those who opposed his law-free gospel. Individual self-confidence remains a point of contention between Paul and his adversaries, but the confidence in view ultimately relates to one's socio-ethnic identity, not to one's personal achievements as a Torah-observant Jew.

a. *Evaluating the New Perspective*
As Hagner noted over a decade ago, 'The real test of the new perspective on Paul is how well it can explain all the pertinent texts'.[53] Here the results have been somewhat mixed. Those who have revisited Second-Temple texts addressing the issue of individual salvation are not universally persuaded that Sanders's 'covenantal nomism' should be embraced without qualification as a reflection of normative Jewish soteriology.[54] Scholars have raised similar concerns about the NP's understanding of the biblical materials. No one has expended more effort to interpret the Pauline corpus against the background of Jewish nationalism than Dunn, and the readings he has proposed have, indeed, shed light on certain passages in Paul's letters.[55] Many of us, however, remain unconvinced that Paul's phrase 'works of the law' can in every case be interpreted to refer solely to badges of Jewish identity.[56] Paul seems to move beyond the law understood in a nationalistic sense, for example, in Romans 3, where we find his celebrated categorical assertion of the universal sinfulness of Jew and Gentile. Efforts to shoehorn

---

53. Hagner (1993: 128).
54. See Carson (2001). Philo of Alexandria, for example, appears to be attempting to correct some kind of merit theology among Jews in Alexandria during the first century (*De sacr.* 54-57). Schreiner finds significant evidence for legalism in post-biblical Jewish literature (1993: 114-21). Schreiner, however, resists defining legalism as a reliance upon human achievement to the exclusion of God's elective grace (or, for Christians, God's provision in Christ). Rather, legalism is the conviction that humans must contribute, in any way, to their soteriological destiny (thus adding to what God has done) (1993: 94-95). By way of example, the 'other gospel' of Paul's opponents in Galatia made room for both Christ's redemptive work and obedience to the Torah. This more nuanced definition of legalism is an important refinement, one which moves the debate ahead considerably.
55. For examples of Dunn's work in this connection see the essays in Dunn (1990) and his Romans commentary (1988a; 1988b).
56. The exchange between Cranfield (1991) and Dunn (1992b) highlights some of the salient issues. See also Witherington (2005: 52-55).

the concluding statement of Paul's argument into the glass slipper of Jewish nationalism simply do not persuade. Paul asserts, 'For through the works of the law no human being will be justified before him, for through the law comes the knowledge of sin' (3.20). How 'the knowledge of sin' could come through the law understood in narrowly nationalistic terms has not been adequately explained by any of the proponents of the NP.[57] It appears that there remains a place for legalism—and the corresponding Pauline response—among the various soteriological expressions of Second-Temple Jewish thought.[58]

This is a book about Jesus and not a book about Paul, however, so I must leave the ongoing firestorm surrounding Paul's theology to others who are better equipped to enter the fray. The brief excursus has been necessary due to the importance of certain issues raised in the debate about Paul and the law for understanding the aims of Jesus, who was, of course, part of the same Jewish world as the apostle to the Gentiles. Readers will surely note the connection between the NP's nationalistic interpretation of Judaism (above) and the evidence and arguments presented in the first portion of this book. I remain indebted to Dunn and Wright for driving me deep into post-Maccabean literature to confirm the intense preoccupation with social exclusivism—and Jewish identity markers—which characterized Judean thought and praxis in the Roman East.

The sociological insights of Dunn and others will, I believe, prove to be the most lasting and fruitful contributions of NP scholarship to the broader field of biblical studies, provided that our awareness of Jewish nationalism takes its rightful place in the hermeneutical toolbox alongside other aspects of Second-Temple Judaism and is not pressed reductionistically to explain every soteriological passage in the New Testament. This is an important qualification. The present project, which deals with ethnic boundaries and the social organization of the people of God, will necessarily focus almost exclusively upon the sociological function of the Torah. Yet preoccupation with law-keeping during our period cannot be reduced wholly to boundary preservation. Jewish nationalism is only one aspect, for example, of Paul's

---

57. In a similar vein, Thurén argues, I think correctly, that the boasting excluded in Rom. 3.27 (a thesis Paul expands in Romans 4), involves not just the possession of the law (Jewish national privilege) but, also, compliance with it (2000: 166-71). Dunn's reading of Galatians 3 proves similarly problematic. As Kim observes, 'A mere correction of the Jews' "wrong understanding of the law" can hardly be said to be redemption from the curse of the law that pronounces upon their not "abiding by all that has been written in the book of the law to do it"' (2001: 133).

58. New Perspective proponents are increasingly bringing more balance to the discussion. Longenecker, for example, may be counted among those who have embraced the New Perspective, but he sees Paul expanding his criticism of 'ethnocentric covenantalism' to include, in places, a challenge to legalism (1991: 213-14).

problem with the law. As Witherington rightly insists, Paul's treatment must be interpreted in view of his broader understanding of the inbreaking of the eschatological age in the Christ event. For Paul, the law has served its purpose and is now simply obsolete. Under this overarching salvation-historical rubric Paul can, in retrospect, identify a number of problems with the law, as he considers the *pro tempore* era of the Mosaic covenant. They include: (1) the effect of the law on fallen human beings, (2) the law's inability to give life and power, and, finally, (3) the law's sociological function dividing Jews from Gentiles.[59] The first two issues have dominated the discussion for generations, whereas the third has been almost wholly ignored. The NP has now helped us to appreciate the social implications of Torah observation, so that even Hagner, a traditionalist who is convinced that 'Copernicus and his followers are taking us down the wrong path', acknowledges the truth of the NP's central affirmation: 'Now it can hardly be denied that Dunn's fundamental point is true. The law does play a socially determinative role in its boundary markers separating Jew from Gentile'.[60] It is this sociological function of the law in post-Maccabean Judaism which forms the backdrop for the discussion in the chapters to follow, as we turn to the Gospels and interpret Jesus' trenchant critiques of Sabbath-keeping, sacred space, and sectarian table practices against the background of Jewish social particularity.

b. *Nationalism and Legalism in Second-Temple Judaism*
An important challenge facing those of us who assume the presence of both nationalism and legalism among Second-Temple Judeans is that of ascertaining just how these two factors functioned in relationship with one another. I will summarize my perspective with two statements which will receive some elaboration in the paragraphs to follow:

1. Nationalism is to be understood as a dominant motivation fueling the marked preoccupation with Torah-keeping that characterized the post-Maccabean period.
2. Nationalism naturally—but not necessarily—generated legalistic tendencies among certain Second-Temple Jews.

My survey of post-Maccabean writings was designed to underscore the viability of the first assertion. The statement is also corroborated by early rabbinic literature, where we discover, for example, that the Mishnah's halakhah contains a disproportionately large amount of material specifically addressing practices that are in some way related to the boundary markers of sacred times, sacred space, and sacred food. Two of the Mishnah's six

---

59. Witherington (2005: 54).
60. Hagner (1993: 126).

Divisions (*Sedarim*), *Moed* and *Tohoroth*, are wholly devoted to sacred times and ritual purity, respectively, and directives for proper temple polity surface elsewhere throughout the work.[61] I find it quite reasonable, therefore, to conclude that boundary preservation constituted a primary motivation for the expansionist approach to purity and Torah observance reflected in the behaviors and convictions of numbers of post-Maccabean Judeans.

It remains to offer a few comments about the origins of Jewish legalism. The first relates to the definition of the term itself. Legalism traditionally conceived—the legalism that Sanders disavows as wholly uncharacteristic of Jewish soteriology—may broadly be understood as the weighing of an individual's good deeds against his or her bad deeds, in order to merit God's salvific favor. Sanders finds Bultmann's view of rabbinic soteriology representative of the outlook of the New Testament scholarly guild as a whole. Sanders summarizes Bultmann as follows:

> The legalistic conception of man's relation to God led to the view that at the judgment all of one's works would be counted and weighed, the verdict on a man's fate being determined by the balance of merits and demerits.[62]

I believe that Sanders is generally on target to dismiss such an outlook as unhistorical. Our sources will not allow us to establish as the touchstone of Jewish personal eschatology the mechanical weighing of good against bad deeds, and the above perspective wholly excludes from the soteriological equation the pervasive and defining belief in Yahweh's gracious election of Israel, a conviction which characterized much Second-Temple Jewish thinking.

Nevertheless, as I remarked earlier, I do not think we can entirely eliminate the idea of meritorious works from certain strains of Jewish soteriology. If I am correct, however, to identify boundary keeping as a primary motivation for Judaism's preoccupation with the law (above), then the notion of merit will have to be nuanced accordingly. A better definition of legalism (for which I will now substitute, instead, the more neutral expression 'meritorious nomism') will thus retain clearly in view both the idea of personal merit and the nationalistic impulse that generated the intense focus on Torah observation which marked life in post-Maccabean Jewish Palestine.[63]

---

61. Nearly a century ago Montefiore summarized the general trajectory of rabbinic halakhah as follows: 'The compulsion of the Law was chiefly felt in two directions—the Sabbath and food' (1914: 32).

62. Sanders (1977: 45). Sanders find the same view, in only slightly varied form, in the works of Weber, Bousset, Billerbeck, Rössler, Becker, Jaubert, and others (1977: 36-54).

63. As Bird has recently noted, the term 'legalism' (a) presupposes a religion devoid of grace, (b) is associated in popular circles with hypocritical attention to legal minutia, and (c) finds no semantic equivalent in Second-Temple literature (2005: 58).

Accordingly, I will use meritorious nomism in what follows to describe *the sense of pride and personal accomplishment that dominated the outlook of certain individuals who believed that their efforts to maintain their Jewish social distinctives (a) earned them special favor in the eyes of Yahweh, (b) rendered them somehow superior to less observant Jews—and, especially, to the Gentiles—around them, and, when push came to shove, (c) took priority over the apparently more mundane social and physical needs of persons in their villages and synagogues.*[64] Such an understanding of Jewish merit theology has, I think, much to commend it. It eliminates from the equation the mechanical counting of good and bad deeds, which characterized the traditional view, but it factors in a robust awareness of Israel's election and identity as the chosen people of Yahweh. Finally, it offers some explanation for the apparent insensitivity to human need on the part of certain Jewish leaders whom we encounter in the Gospels and in other Second-Temple Jewish literature.

As indicated by the label itself, moreover, my understanding of meritorious nomism retains from the traditional view the notion of personal merit. This, in turn, encourages us to consider the connection between the sense of pride and personal accomplishment associated with the occasional expressions of merit theology observable in Jewish thought and praxis, on the one hand, and Israel's overarching program of purity and nationalism, on the other. Just how are we to understand the relationship between personal merit and boundary preservation?

That an emphasis on boundary markers did not necessarily entail meritorious nomism can be demonstrated most convincingly from the writings of the Qumran community. It has been widely acknowledged that the covenanters at the Dead Sea were even stricter than the Pharisees in their concern to separate themselves from Gentiles and from those whom they deemed apostate Jews. The degree to which members of the community exercised personal discipline in the practice of Qumran *halakah* renders the anthropology—and corresponding soteriology—of the following excerpts from the Dead Sea Scrolls rather striking:

> Who is able to bear thy glory,
> and what then is he,
> the son of man among thy marvelous works;
> what shall one born of woman be accounted before thee?
> As for him, he was kneaded from dust,

---

64. Any such definition must, of course, remain provisional. Defining 'legalism' has, in fact, been an important aspect of recent work on the New Testament and ancient Judaism (Westerholm [2003: 332-33]). Many scholars attracted to the New Perspective appear, however, to see merit theology and nationalism as mutually exclusive alternatives. I believe we need to keep both in view and to attempt to discern the relationship between them.

and the food of worms his portion.
He is an emission of spittle, a cut-off bit of clay,
and his desire is for the dust.
What will clay reply, a thing formed by hand?
What counsel will it understand?
But as for me, my justification belongs to God,
and in his hand is the blamelessness of my conduct
together with the uprightness of my heart;
and in his righteousness my transgression will be wiped out.
(1QH^a 1; see also 1QH 15.18-20)

As for me, I belong to wicked humanity, to the assembly of perverse flesh; my iniquities and rebellion and sin together with the iniquity of my heart belong to the assembly doomed to worms, the assembly of men who walk in darkness. For is man the master of his way? No, men cannot establish their steps, for their justification belongs to God and from His hand comes perfection of way... And I, if I stagger, God's mercies are my salvation forever; and if I stumble because of the sin of the flesh, my justification is the righteousness of God which exists forever... He has caused me to approach by His mercy and by His favours He will bring my justification. He has justified me by His true justice and by His immense goodness He will pardon all my iniquities (1QS 11.9-14).

I have been intrigued over the years to watch my Protestant students struggle to wrap their conceptual arms around the idea that certain members of a Jewish purity sect (Qumran) were somehow able to combine (a) a super-Pharisaic concern for legal precision and social exclusivity with (b) a Pauline-like view of the inability of human beings to get right with God apart from God's gracious intervention on their behalf.[65] For Jesus' contemporaries law and grace were apparently not mutually exclusive categories. Nationalism did not necessarily entail notions of pride and personal merit. This is yet another important insight produced by recent studies of the Second-Temple Period.

How then are we to account for the presence of merit theology in Jewish thinking and praxis? I suggest that, although not a *necessary* corollary of

---

65. As Dunn reflects, commenting upon his own first encounter, in the late 1960s, with 1QS 11: 'The text was so *Pauline* in character and emphasis!' (2005: 4, author's italics). Bockmuehl summarizes: 'The community combined a strong sense of the sinfulness of all humanity with a belief in divine grace to the believer as the only means of salvation' (2001: 413). To be sure, this represents somewhat of an oversimplification of Qumran soteriology, and Bockmuehl himself cautions against dogmatism with respect to a singular 'Qumran pattern of religion', given the complexity and apparent diachronic development of the group's theology as reflected in the Scrolls (2001: 381-83). Nevertheless, on any fair reading of the evidence it would be erroneous to characterize Essene soteriology as one of meritorious works-righteousness. See Falk (2001: 25-34) for a recent discussion of the *Hodayot* and their relationship to Sanders's covenantal nomism.

nationalism, convictions of personal merit nonetheless surfaced at times as a *natural* consequence of the intense focus upon halakhic regulations which characterized the period—regulations that, again, were preeminently concerned with socially defining practices such as Sabbath-keeping and sectarian table fellowship. I use the term *natural* intentionally, since the above assertion assumes some basic realities about the nature of human beings and the nature of human institutions, common-sense realities too often ignored in the sometimes artificial process of historical analysis.

First, some observations about human nature. It cannot be denied that the nationalistic agenda outlined in the previous chapters involved a marked preoccupation with Torah observance, and Sanders's covenantal nomism has received some much needed correction in this regard. As Gundry has rightly maintained, the NP 'has not succeeded in relating the law to elective grace in a way that materially scales down preoccupation with legal interpretation, extension, application, and observance'. Whether we situate Torah-keeping under the rubric of 'getting in' or 'staying in', it remains the case that during our period the law is 'searched, pulled, stretched, and applied. The rabbis start building a fence around it in order that people may not even come close to breaking it'.[66]

The boundary-building enterprise that has come to be known as Jewish nationalism thus involved a great deal of careful attention to halakhic behavioral priorities, 'a preoccupation which by its very nature makes for human insecurity and thus prepares a promising ground for the nurture of legalistic tendencies'.[67] Common sense argues for a natural connection between the meticulous observance of the law and a corresponding sense of personal accomplishment, that is, between nationalism and meritorious nomism. We should not be surprised, then, to find persons in the world of Jesus and Paul who felt that their considerable efforts to maintain Jewish social distinctives would earn them affirmation at the eschatological court of Yahweh—all of this against the best understanding of their faith at the theoretical level, a faith that was predicated from the beginning of Israel's history upon the gracious intervention of Yahweh to deliver his people from Egyptian slavery. So much for human nature.

66. Gundry (1985: 6-7).

67. Hagner (1993: 118). The Torah itself, after all, required that Israel obey the law (Lev. 18.5; Deut. 4.1). And whatever we might say of the role of such obedience as an *entrance* requirement to the people of God, the recent works of Yinger (1999) and Gathercole (2002) demonstrate that obedience is 'the *sine qua non* of a favorable verdict on the day of judgment' (Garlington [2005: 30]; see also Rom. 2.6-10). The historically situated contextualization of this biblical outlook during the post-Maccabean period—represented by the intense focus upon Torah observance as a boundary-keeping enterprise—would seem to provide a natural setting for development of a sense of personal merit among those so inclined.

The inertia characteristic of human institutions will be transparent to most anyone belonging to a religious congregation that has been in existence for more than a generation or two. In contexts like these the relative purity of the initial motivation of the founders tends to give way over the years to a sense of entitlement and privilege on the part of second and third generation members who have inherited the movement. To be sure, such a scenario represents an oversimplification of what is invariably a highly complex process, but one can hardly deny the calcification that exists among certain members of older religious establishments who have traded the dynamics of the Spirit for the external behavioral trappings of an increasingly merit-oriented approach to the faith. As Hagner correctly maintains, 'There have been many instances where the experience of Christian congregations substantiates this'.[68] Other individuals (and movements), of course, will resist this institutional inertia and somehow remain faithful to the original motivation of the movement. It is important to note, in this regard, that the Pharisees and other sectarian movements that arose out of the Maccabean period had been in existence for well over a hundred years by the first century CE, more than enough time for considerable calcification to set in. As we sift through the evidence for life in first-century Roman Palestine, we will expect, therefore, to come across persons who 'trusted in themselves that they were righteous and regarded others with contempt' (Lk. 18.9). And, given the complexity of human society, we will not be surprised to encounter other Judeans who, like the author of the Qumran texts cited above, passionately observed purity halakhah with a robust awareness of their own spiritual poverty and their corresponding need for the 'righteousness of God'.

c. *Nationalism, Meritorious Nomism, and the Historical Jesus*
The relationship between nationalism and meritorious nomism outlined above generates a useful set of parameters for understanding the activities of Jesus in the Gospels. Once we admit into the historical equation a merit-oriented strain of Jewish soteriology, along with a considerable degree of institutional calcification, we will no longer be compelled to relegate Jesus' trenchant critique of the Pharisees and the priestly elite to the creativity of later church tradents trying to work through their own conflicts with local Jewish leadership. On the contrary, we will expect a prophetic figure like Jesus to challenge perceived corruption and abuse on the part of Judean leaders. After all, Jesus was hardly alone in this regard, as illustrated by the criticism of the priestly aristocracy found in a number of Second Temple documents. Leaders of religious renewal movements often encounter as their most determined adversaries persons who have become 'stuck' in the

---

68. Hagner (1993: 119).

behavioral trappings of a more traditional approach to their faith. It will be no different for Jesus and certain leaders among the Pharisees.

The inclination among some in the guild to overlook evidence for corruption among Jewish leaders during the Second-Temple Period in one sense parallels concerted efforts by many of the same scholars to exclude the idea of merit from our understanding of Jewish soteriology. Both tendencies stem, at least in part, from a heightened sensitivity to the role that negative caricatures of ancient Judaism have played in nurturing anti-Semitism in Euro-Western history. Such sensitivity is, of course, eminently commendable until, that is, it downplays, obscures, or excludes material from our sources which portrays Judaism or her leaders in what we might deem to be a less-than-positive light. As Hagner insightfully observes, in the context of our post-holocaust *Zeitgeist*, the NP was 'a point whose time had come', and we can be grateful for the positive aspects of Second-Temple Judaism that have been emphasized in recent scholarship.[69] Some thirty years have passed, however, since the publication of Sanders's influential monograph, and the time has now come to allow the pendulum of scholarly debate to settle securely between the unacceptable extremes of anti-Jewish caricature, at the one end, and overly enthusiastic idealization, at the other, in order to make room at the table for all of our evidence for ancient Jewish praxis and ideology. On a fair reading, such evidence attests, in my view, to the occasional presence among Second-Temple Judeans of both meritorious nomism and institutional calcification, and both should be allowed to inform our interpretations of Jesus' activities in the gospel narratives.[70]

69. Hagner (1993: 112).
70. Ironically, proponents of various permutations of the New Perspective—many of whom have sought intentionally to distance themselves from the anti-Judaism associated with a 'legalistic' interpretation of Second-Temple Jewish soteriology—are now charged by others with perpetuating the same anti-Judaism by 'opposing Paul's inclusive gospel to "Jewish exclusivism"' (Elliott [2005: 245]). In the words of Horsley, paradigms that assume a Jewish exclusivism conform to 'the theologically determined metanarrative of the field, the replacement of the overly political and particularistic religion "Judaism" by the purely spiritual and universal religion "Christianity"' (Horsley [1998: 154]).

By way of response, first of all, Horsley's broad-brush assertion is only half-right, at best, since it is increasingly difficult to find any scholarly treatment that depoliticizes Jesus or Paul to the point where early Christianity becomes a 'religion' that is 'purely spiritual'. More to the point, it seems to me that these representatives of what might broadly be labeled the new historicism are simply replacing a 'theologically determined metanarrative of the field' (to adopt Horsley's phrase) with a competing metanarrative, one no longer theologically determined but now driven, instead, by the liberal Euro-Western social values that characterize much of academia in the post-Shoah era in which we live.

The heart of Elliott's analysis of the New Perspective, in this regard, is to be found in the four observations he makes under the rubric *A Critical Assessment* (2005: 245-47).

It must be emphasized, however, that the critiques of bad religion and bad leadership we encounter in the Gospels were decidedly secondary to Jesus' overarching objectives. To be sure, given Jesus' subversive social agenda, conflict with the Pharisees and others in positions of authority was inevitable, as we will see in the following chapters. Debates with Jewish leadership over what has traditionally been referred to as legalistic religion were not, however, central to Jesus' program. The days of utilizing the perceived abuses of medieval Catholicism as the primary foil against which to interpret Jesus' conflicts with Pharisaic leadership and praxis are, thankfully, now behind us.[71] Just as we must view Jewish merit theology as a regrettable but very real by-product of an overarching preoccupation with boundary preservation, so also should we view Jesus' critiques of scribal authority as the inevitable but secondary fallout of a more sweeping sociopolitical agenda. Jesus was not just challenging meritorious nomism. He was championing a whole new way of defining the people of Yahweh in the context of foreign domination. Conflict with the Pharisees and other religious authorities was inevitable.

Once we embrace nationalism as a primary motivation for the noticeable fixation upon law-keeping that characterized early Judaism, moreover, the differences between the aims of Jesus and the designs of other Jewish renewal groups become increasingly acute. Jesus was not simply offering

---

Not surprisingly, two of the critiques relate not directly to Second-Temple Judaism at all but, rather, to issues of discourse and historiography. Elliott asserts that a particularistic view of Judaism is 'stereotypical and prejudicial' (Observation #2), and he wonders why interpreters persist in assuming Paul found something wrong with Judaism to begin with (Observation #4). Neither observation sheds any light on the activities of Jesus and the early Christians. It is important, of course, to seek to discern both the sources and the effects of our ideological constructs, and there is something to be said for the kind of self-examination and self-criticism that characterizes the works of writers like Elliott and others who seek to situate NT scholarship in its own historical context (see also Kelley [2002]; Eisenbaum [2005]; Gaston [2005]; Nanos [2005]; and, for the historical Jesus, the important collection of essays edited by Kloppenborg and Marshall [2005]). Much more helpful in my view, however, are the other two observations Elliott makes—particularly his challenge to New Perspective scholars 'to meet the standard set by Sanders for documenting the prevalence of Jewish 'exclusivism' in Paul's day' (2005: 245). Here I believe Elliott is right on target. For when all is said and done, it is only by examining evidence from the period itself that we can hope to adjudicate between the competing metanarratives that determine the trajectory of the various 'perspectives' of NT scholarship. Chapters 2 and 3 of this book are intended as a small contribution toward this end, and I will leave it to my readers to evaluate the degree to which the evidence I cite attests to the vitality of Jewish exclusivism in post-Maccabean Palestine.

71. McKnight's observations reflect a growing consensus among New Testament scholars: 'Reformation theology needs to answer to Jesus, not Jesus to it. Jesus did not talk about earning salvation; he talked about what covenant members are obliged to do (or strive to do) if they wish to be faithful' (1999: 34).

another way to maintain Jewish particularity in the highly Hellenized world of Roman Palestine. Here is where a sectarian analysis that identifies early Christianity as just another form of Judaism loses some of its explanatory power. Unlike the Pharisees, Sadducees, and Essenes, the movement started by Jesus of Nazareth ultimately transcended the boundaries of normative Judaism by relativizing those marks of national identity which characterized the lives of Judeans of every stripe during the Second-Temple Period. Any satisfactory explanation of this anomalous phenomenon must begin with the activities of the historical Jesus. I intend in the chapters that follow to locate in the ministry of Jesus the symbolic and ideological foundations for the parting of the ways between Judaism and what was to become early Christianity, a social trajectory established, in my view, by the manner in which Jesus attended to Jewish distinctives of sacred time, sacred space, and sacred foods.[72]

5. *Conclusion*

It will prove useful here briefly to pull together the themes of the Chapter and consider how the methodological observations offered above regarding Jewish nationalism, on the one hand, and the presence of implicit cultural scripts, on the other, might inform the thorny issue of tradition history. I will draw upon Jesus' Sabbath controversies with the Jewish leaders as a test case, in order to anticipate some of the findings in the chapters to follow.

Apart from an appreciation for the phenomenon of implicitly shared cultural information, along with an acute awareness of the persistent strain of Maccabean ideology permeating much of first-century Judaism, it has been rather easy to dismiss the Sabbath controversies as just more evidence for early church creativity. Gentile Christians conflicted with Messianist Jews in the church over whether Sabbath observance should continue to

---

72. The phrase 'parting of the ways' comes from Dunn's book of the same title (1991). He used the plural, *Partings of the Ways*. Recent scholarship has understood the relationship between the Jesus movement and Judaism to be more complex than previously assumed (Lieu [1994]; Becker and Reed [2003]; Boyarin [2004]), and it is likely the case that the split was not 'early and decisive' (Buell [2005: 4]). The two groups certainly shared much in common at the level of daily living; note, for example, their mutual rejection of a number of Greco-Roman social practices. But only a most extreme revisionist perspective would seek to efface all substantive differences between the two movements—differences that were observed by the ancients themselves. Thus, as Judge has recently noted, among the Romans Christianity was never confused with Judaism (1994). As Riches asserts, moreover, 'Admission of Gentiles to the Christian *ecclesiai* without circumcision was the surest sign that these new groups were not Jewish' (2000: 3).

demarcate the people of God under the new covenant, and the debates between Jesus and the Pharisees in the Gospels represent the literary fruit of just such a conflict in early Christianity. Or so it is assumed.

It has been particularly easy to make this argument with a passage like Mk 3.1-6, for example, when nationalism is factored out of the mix, the Sabbath healing is interpreted solely as an act of compassion performed for the benefit of a suffering individual, and the conflict with the Pharisees is reduced to an intra-Jewish halakhic dispute. Such a reading renders the intense reaction of Jesus' opponents—'The Pharisees went out and immediately conspired with the Herodians against him, how to destroy him' (Mk 3.6)—intolerably unreasonable in the context, and the whole scenario (or, at least, v. 6) is relegated to the resourceful creativity of the early Christians, and with some justification. After all, who would plot to kill a healer who did something good for a fellow human being, in accordance with one among several competing halakhic positions on Sabbath observance? As Sanders asserts, '[I]t is incredible that Pharisees or anyone else would seek to put Jesus to death for the event described in Mk 3.1-6'.[73]

The argument tends to persuade, until the background materials canvassed in the previous chapters are brought to bear on the narrative, and we interpret the healing in light of Jesus' overarching program of deconstructing Jewish nationalism (my suggested *Gesamtbild*). Only then do we begin to grasp the reality that, in the synagogue encounter (Mk 3.1-6), Jesus performed a compassionate act of healing, *which at the same time intentionally destabilized a vital symbol of Jewish national identity*. Suddenly the historical plausibility of the severe response of the Pharisees and the Herodians in Mk 3.6 increases considerably.[74]

---

73. Sanders (1990: 6-23). See also Bultmann (1963: 52), Schweizer (1970: 74), Kuhn (1971: 19-21), Gnilka (1978: 1.126), Lührmann (1987: 66), Sariola (1990: 94), and Loader (2002: 46), each of whom assign v. 6 to Markan redaction, although not, in every case, for the reasons outlined above.

74. It is not only the reaction of the Pharisees and Herodians in Mk 3.6 which gains a degree of plausibility in view of the background materials canvassed in the previous Chapters (Chapters 2 and 3). In his sophisticated refinement of the criteria of authenticity traditionally employed in Jesus research, Meier identifies as historically probable those materials in the tradition which serve to explain the rejection and execution of Jesus by Jewish and Roman authorities (1991: 167-95). Jesus' destabilizing approach to sacred times, sacred space, and sacred food would appear to fit here rather nicely. Official opposition to the treatment of Jewish identity markers surfaces early in Jesus' ministry, in the Sabbath controversies (Mk 2.23–3.6) and in the scribal criticism of Jesus' open table fellowship (Mk 2.16). The resistance reaches its climax in the response to Jesus' action in the temple during the last week of his life (Mk 11.15-33). Given the persistence of Maccabean national ideology among Jesus' contemporaries (on this see Chapter 8), we may reasonably trace a good deal of the opposition Jesus encountered throughout his public ministry to his pointed rejection of boundary-oriented symbols

At this point one might object that the issue of Jewish nationalism is explicitly articulated nowhere in the biblical text. The story simply portrays Jesus healing an individual on the Sabbath. This, however, is precisely where a solely text-based hermeneutic must give way to a more nuanced understanding of the manner in which implicit cultural scenarios operate behind the scenes of social discourse in traditional societies like the one in which Jesus lived and ministered. Given the extensive evidence for Jewish nationalism during the Second-Temple period, and the corresponding preoccupation with the boundary-preserving symbol of Sabbath-keeping, we can reasonably assume that Jesus' opponents interpreted the Sabbath healings as a profound threat to their social priorities as Torah-observant Jews. Too much was at stake for Pharisees and other scribal authorities to continue to allow an increasingly popular public figure miraculously to authenticate his destabilizing approach toward this key badge of Jewish ethnicity.[75] Add to the mix later evidence from early Christianity, where the trajectory established by Jesus' embryonic relativization of Torah-based boundaries ultimately reached its logical conclusion in a law-free gospel, and the result is a narrative (Mk 3.1-6) that makes good historical sense as evidence for the life and ministry of Jesus of Nazareth.[76] We now turn directly to the Gospels to consider Jesus' approach to these familiar marks of Jewish social identity.

---

and practices. This, in turn, has significant implications for the historical authenticity of related traditions in the Gospels.

75. Guelich's observation that the 'root of the conflict goes to Jesus' claim of authority' is accurate but too general—authority over what? Guelich maintains that Jesus came into mortal conflict with the religious authorities 'over the right to forgive sin and the use of the sabbath, two issues that have to do with God's prerogatives alone' (1989: 133). So far, so good, but it seems a bit anti-climactic for the series of controversy stories in Mk 2.1–3.6 to crescendo in an attempt on Jesus' life which results from a simple Sabbath healing. The claim to forgive sins in the previous chapter would seem to offer more convincing justification for a reaction like that of the Pharisees and the Herodians in 3.6. Unless, of course, cultural scripts of post-Maccabean nationalism and boundary preservation were playing vibrantly in the background, as I argue above, in which case the intensity of the reaction of Jesus' opponents to the Sabbath healing makes good historical sense.

76. Bits of social realia explicitly articulated in the text itself confirm the historical integrity of the account. As Theissen and Merz have noted, the mention of the 'Herodians' in Mk 3.6 'suggests a historical deposit' in the narrative (1998: 233-34). Casey has recently marshaled an impressive argument for the historicity of Mk 3.1-6 (including the reaction of the Pharisees and Herodians in the final verse) apart from direct appeal to the kind of post-Maccabean nationalism which I draw upon above (1998: 190-92).

Chapter 5

JESUS AND SACRED TIMES

'This man is not from God, for he does not observe the sabbath.'
John 9.16

Sometime during the middle of the second century BCE, an anonymous Jewish author rewrote the narrative of Genesis 1 in such a way as to affirm that God had established Sabbath-keeping among the angels at the beginning of creation. The angelic narrator is especially concerned to emphasize the sociological function of the Sabbath, a practice designed to serve a vital badge of identity for Israel, the particular people of God:

> On this day we kept the sabbath in heaven before it was made known to any human to keep the sabbath thereon upon the earth. The Creator of all blessed it, but he did not sanctify any people or nations to keep the sabbath thereon with the sole exception of Israel. He granted to them alone that they might eat and drink and keep the sabbath thereon upon the earth. And the Creator of all, who created this day for a blessing and sanctification and glory, blessed it more than all days (*Jub.* 2.30-32).

The general directive to 'keep the sabbath' had to be worked out, of course, in the practical realities of daily life, and the Hebrew Scriptures offered little in the way of specifics to facilitate the process.[1] The result during the post-Maccabean period was the creation, in certain scribal circles, of a considerable body of oral tradition regarding the Sabbath, as well as detailed instructions for the proper observance of annual festivals on the Jewish calendar.[2] Sabbath law, as ultimately codified in the Mishnah at the end of the second century CE, delineated some thirty-nine 'classes of work', the last of which was particularly comprehensive: 'taking anything from one place

---

1. The Old Testament does contain several illustrations of sabbath prohibitions (Exod. 16.22-30; 34.21; 35.2-3; Num. 15.32-36; Neh. 10.31; 13.15-22; Jer. 17.21-22), and *Jubilees* gives a more detailed list (*Jub.* 50.6-13).
2. An accessible insider's catalogue of Jewish sacred times during our period can be found in Philo (*Spec. leg.* 2.41-222). Philo enumerates and analyzes 'all the feasts which are recorded in the law' (*Spec. leg.* 2.41). Not included are Hanukkah and Purim, which are not found in the Pentateuch.

to another' (*m. Shab.* 7.2). These categories of work were, in turn, elaborated upon in the context of specific life situations, and the ensuing legislation became so detailed as to specify, for example, what kind of knots a person was allowed or forbidden to tie on the Sabbath (*m. Shab.* 15.1-2).[3]

Compare the increasingly detailed legislative trajectory summarized above with the viewpoint of an influential Jew writing to a mixed Jewish-Gentile congregation of Messianists in Rome during the first century CE: 'Some judge one day to be better than another, while others judge all days to be alike. Let all be fully convinced in their own minds' (Rom. 14.5). Paul of Tarsus, and those who shared his view of reality, summarily dismissed the observance of Jewish holy days as irrelevant to their socio-religious identity. The Sabbath, the festivals, and new moons were 'only a shadow of what [was] to come, but the substance belongs to Christ' (Col. 2.16-17; see Gal. 4.10). The relativization of the sacred calendar formed a key part of early Christianity's attempt to reconstruct the ethnic contours of the people of God in the Greco-Roman world, and tendencies along these lines already appear in embryonic form in the activities of Jesus of Nazareth.[4]

1. *Jesus and Sabbath*

Readers of the four Gospels will be immediately familiar with Sabbath controversies involving Jesus and his adversaries.[5] The triple tradition (material common to Matthew–Mark–Luke) contains a pair of pericopes in which Jesus engages in conflict over the issue with Jewish leaders (Mt. 12.1-14; Mk 2.23–3.6; Lk. 6.1-11). Luke relates two additional Sabbath narratives not found elsewhere in the Gospels (13.10-17; 14.1-6), and John's Gospel

---

3. Although the detailed codification of Sabbath law reflected in the Mishnah dates to the end of the second century, it is reasonable to assume that the material represents in principle the approach to Sabbath taken by Pharisees at the time of Jesus. The Essenes offered a still more rigorous interpretation of the law of the Sabbath (CD 10.14–11.18), which even proscribed giving help to a birthing animal or to an animal—or a human—that had fallen into a pit (CD 11.13-14).

4. The Jesus movement, of course, soon constructed its own sacred calendar, beginning with the practice of worship on the first day of the week. Treatments of the development include Rordorf (1962), Bacchiocchi (1977), Carson (1982), Beckwith (1996), Snyder (1999: 119-28), Mayer-Haas (2003), and Sturcke (2005). The close association of the Jewish calendar with Jewish ethnic solidarity meant that the early Christians had finally to dispense with Jewish sacred times, in order to redefine the contours of the people of God as a multi-ethnic surrogate family.

5. Jesus' treatment of the Sabbath warrants special attention, since (a) only the Sabbath among Israel's sacred times is mentioned in the Decalogue, and (b) the Sabbath commandment is the one statute of the Ten not reiterated in some form in the New Testament.

also portrays Jesus offending Jewish leaders by healing on the Sabbath (5.1-18, cf. 7.21-24; 9.1-16). The emphasis on Sabbath in the Gospels attests both to the importance of the practice for first-century Judeans and to Jesus' exceptional attitude toward this fundamental symbol of Jewish identity. Most familiar are the pair of stories found in all three Synoptics, and I will consider Mark's version of each in some detail. First, however, a brief word about approach and methodology is in order.

It has been common for those treating the topic of Jesus and the Sabbath to seek to discern, in some absolute sense, whether or not Jesus 'broke' the Sabbath commandment.[6] I find this approach to the matter unhelpful and ultimately rather distracting. The quest for a categorical answer to such a question seems doomed to failure at the outset, because of conflicting opinions among Jesus' contemporaries about the precise application of Old Testament Sabbath legislation to the realities of daily life. Behavior that contravened Sabbath law in the eyes of a group of strict sectarians, for example, may have been wholly acceptable among Judeans who took a more liberal approach to the seventh day.

A more profitable approach to Jesus and the Sabbath seeks, instead, to discern (a) the general *degree* to which Jesus challenged the convictions of his contemporaries about Sabbath observance and (b) the *significance* of such behavior in the socio-cultural setting in which Jesus found himself. Here I think that our sources allow for some meaningful observations, and I have framed my discussion of Jesus and the Sabbath accordingly.

a. *Mark 2.23-28*

The first of the two Sabbath pericopes in Mark's Gospel reads as follows:

> 23 One sabbath he was going through the grainfields; and as they made their way his disciples began to pluck heads of grain. 24 The Pharisees said to him, 'Look, why are they doing what is not lawful on the sabbath?' 25 And he said to them, 'Have you never read what David did when he and his companions were hungry and in need of food? 26 He entered the house of God, when Abiathar was high priest, and ate the bread of the Presence, which it is not lawful for any but the priests to eat, and he gave some to his companions'. 27 Then he said to them, 'The sabbath was made for humankind, and not humankind for the sabbath; 28 so the Son of Man is lord even of the sabbath' (Mk 2.23-28).

---

6. Rordorf, for example, asserts that Jesus 'repeatedly' broke the Sabbath (1962: 67). Theissen and Merz find in the Sabbath healings a 'breach of the Sabbath', 'a clear transgression of the letter of the Torah' (1998: 368, 370; similarly Gundry [1993: 141] and Banks [1975: 114 n. 2]). I am not convinced that the evidence warrants such sweeping assertions, though I do appreciate the authors' sensitivity to the degree to which Jesus challenged current Sabbath praxis.

The passage has elicited a variety of comments occasioned by a number of thorny interpretative issues in the narrative.[7] For our purposes, it is important to highlight the extent to which Jesus challenges Sabbath law as understood by his contemporaries. Many assume that in Mk 2.23-28 Jesus criticizes only a non-humanitarian tendency characteristic of Pharisaic tradition and praxis,[8] or, somewhat more broadly, that Jesus rejects a halakhic position held by a small minority of 'strict Jews'.[9] Now one can hardly eliminate a humanitarian element from the story, since Jesus states that David and his companions were 'hungry and in need of food', and he explicitly describes the Sabbath as 'made for humankind'.[10] And it may, indeed, be the case that we are dealing here with an intra-Jewish halakhic dispute, as Crossley and others have recently maintained.[11] The paucity of evidence renders any conclusion on the matter provisional, however, and the discussion that follows will take a different approach. I will contend that Jesus' position in Mk 2.23-28 transcends limited criticism of sectarian halakhah to call into question what was likely a more widely accepted interpretation of biblical Sabbath law. Several considerations support such an understanding.

The first consideration relates to the alleged illegality of plucking grain on the Sabbath. The prohibition of plucking grain represents more than an example of narrow Pharisaic halakhah. It constitutes a wholly reasonable application of biblical Sabbath law and would likely have been understood as such not only by the Pharisees but by numbers of Jesus' contemporaries. The disciples' behavior (v. 23) finds explanation in Deut. 23.25, where the Torah permits the Israelites to pluck the ears of their neighbors' standing grain, provided they use only their hands and not a sickle. Similarly, one could eat his fill of grapes from a neighbor's vineyard but not gather grapes in a sack or container for later consumption or profit (Deut. 23.24).[12] The

7. Crossley should be consulted on the historicity of the incident related in Mk 2.23-28 (2004: 164-66). Crossley effectively counters Sanders's arguments against tracing the conflict back to the historical Jesus (Sanders [1985: 264-66]). He concludes, 'There are no sound objections to the argument that Mk 2.23-28 reflects an event in the ministry of the historical Jesus' (Crossley [2004: 166]). Casey is similarly optimistic in this regard (1998: 145-151).

8. For example, Moo (1984: 7-9).

9. Crossley (2004: 161).

10. Matthew's version includes an additional saying of a humanitarian nature: 'But if you had known what this means, "I desire mercy and not sacrifice", you would not have condemned the guiltless' (Mt. 12.7, citing Hos. 6.6).

11. Casey (1998: 146-50), Loader (2002: 33-35), and Crossley (2004: 162-72) offer the most reasoned and sophisticated interpretations of Jesus' position as a limited challenge to sectarian halakhah.

12. Casey identifies the disciples' activity somewhat more narrowly as an expression of *Peah*, 'a conventional institution, part of the social security system of ancient Israel'

question at hand is whether such behavior, clearly legal six days per week, violates the command to rest on the Sabbath.[13] Loader thinks not: 'There is no law or law interpretation known to us which Jesus' disciples would be contravening'.[14] Nothing specific, perhaps, but the general tenor of both the Torah and later scribal interpretation seem to point in such a direction. It is important to remember that Judeans had to apply the broad statutes of the Hebrew Scriptures to the specific exigencies of daily life. Some applications were, of course, more self-evident than others. In the present case, Exod. 34.21 expressly forbids harvesting on the Sabbath (expanded in the Mishnah to include 'reaping, binding sheaves, threshing, winnowing, cleansing crops' [*m. Shab.* 7.2]), and it seems only reasonable to view plucking grain, as permitted in Deuteronomy 23 (above), as a form of harvesting.

But there is more. Should the injunction against harvesting on the Sabbath (Exod. 34.21) prove somehow ambiguous or otherwise insufficient for disallowing the disciples' behavior, a biblical analogy lay close at hand to confirm the illegality of plucking grain on the Sabbath in the mind of

(1998: 141). *Peah* had to do with unharvested crops left for the poor, in the present case the unharvested border of a field along which the disciples 'made their way' (Mk 2.23). Scriptural texts include Lev. 19.9-10 and Deut. 26.12-13. The institution is well summarized by Instone-Brewer (2004: 121).

13. As Loader properly notes, other legal matters, such as traveling beyond the Sabbath's limit, stealing, or making a path on the Sabbath, are nowhere at issue in the narrative (2002: 33). Kiilunen's suggestion—that only day laborers were allowed to glean in the first century, and that the transgression thus constituted petty theft—is unconvincing (Kiilunen [1985: 209]).

14. Loader (2002: 52). He is technically correct where the Torah and Mishnah are concerned. The Mishnah relates a debate about how often each day the poor should be allowed to glean a field, but the text makes no mention of the Sabbath (*m. Peah* 4.5). Although admittedly an argument from silence, I suspect that it was simply assumed by the Tannaim that the gathering of grain was prohibited on the Sabbath. Catchpole's observations about the nature of rabbinic halakhah prove insightful at this point:

> [T]he discussions they record may be theoretical and sometimes even playful. To use a contemporary analogy, they may belong more to the to-and-fro exchange of ideas in a seminar than to the self-conscious decisions of a synod. Their usefulness is not so much in the rulings they lay down as in the evidence they provide of long-lasting cultural assumptions (Catchpole [2006: 71]).

Although I suspect that Catchpole has somewhat overemphasized the informality of the rabbinic debates, his comments are generally quite on the mark. What this means in the present connection is that it may be rather beside the point to seek after a specific mishnaic text to underscore the alleged illegality of the disciples' behavior. Our focus, rather, should be upon the general preoccupation with Sabbath observation which characterizes tannaitic literature (Catchpole's 'long-lasting cultural assumptions'), a preoccupation that would seem to assume from the outset the impropriety of an activity like gleaning grain on the Sabbath.

anyone familiar with the account of Israel's liberation from Egypt. For forty years in the wilderness God fed his people with 'bread from heaven' (Exodus 16). Sabbath legislation intersected with God's gracious provision, moreover, in a very specific way. The Israelites were instructed not to gather manna on the Sabbath. Moses explained,

> 23 This is what the LORD has commanded: 'Tomorrow is a day of solemn rest, a holy sabbath to the LORD' ... 26 Six days you shall gather it; but on the seventh day, which is a sabbath, there will be none' (Exod. 16.23, 26).

To compensate, the Israelites were to gather a double-portion the day before the Sabbath, half of which God would preserve unspoiled for nourishment on their Sabbath day of rest. The narrative concludes with a description of some disobedient Israelites who attempted unsuccessfully to gather manna on the Sabbath despite Moses's admonitions. Yahweh's response is pointed and memorable: 'How long will you refuse to keep my commandments and instructions?' (Exod. 16.28).

The manna narrative in Exodus 16 happens to be the first passage in the Torah in which the noun 'Sabbath' (שבת) occurs, anticipating, as it does, the formal legislation of the Decalogue some four chapters later (Exod. 20.8-11).[15] The story represents one of only a handful of Old Testament texts, moreover, which directly apply Sabbath law to specific life situations. One might assume from these two considerations that Exodus 16 would gain for itself a position of preeminence among the various strands of biblical teaching about Israel's day of rest, and that the prohibition of gathering manna on the Sabbath would serve as a ready precedent for disallowing the plucking of grain on the seventh day, as well. Unfortunately, no surviving text from our period draws such a connection. This may simply be due, however, to the limited nature of our evidence for current Sabbath convictions and practices. What we do know is that numbers of post-Maccabean Judeans expended considerable amounts of energy in their efforts to preserve distinctions between sacred and profane times. And they grounded their various prescriptions for acceptable Sabbath behavior in

---

15. The author of the creation story in Genesis employs, instead, the expression 'the seventh day' (ביום השליעה) (Gen. 2.1-3; 3×) to denote the day on which God 'rested' (the homophonic verb שבת is used here [Gen. 2.2-3, 2×]). Sturcke explains: 'Although the Sabbath is not named—thus avoiding the implication that God *kept* the Sabbath—the basis for its later observance is clearly laid: "Elohim blessed the seventh day by setting it apart" (v. 3)' (2005: 38-39). The connection between Israel's Sabbath and 'the seventh day' of creation finally becomes explicit in Exod. 20.11. (There are also a few references to the 'seventh day' of the Feast of Unleavened Bread [Exod. 12.15-16; 13.6], but here, as in the creation account, the context does not explicitly connect the expression to the Sabbath, or to later Sabbath legislation.)

their interpretations of relevant passages from the Hebrew Scriptures.[16] It strikes me as counterintuitive, in this regard, to imagine that Jesus' contemporaries might have overlooked a foundational Sabbath narrative like Exodus 16, as they sought to remain faithful to the practice in their own socio-cultural situation. And once Exodus 16 is brought to bear on the issue of the Sabbath, an analogy between the gathering of manna and the plucking of grain lies close at hand.

Given the prohibition of harvesting on the Sabbath (Exod. 34.21), along with the analogy of the manna legislation as described in Exodus 16, it seems fair to conclude that Second-Temple Judeans familiar with the Torah would naturally assume that plucking grain conflicted with biblical injunctions which disallowed work on the Sabbath. Limited evidence in fact portrays various Judeans coming to precisely this conclusion. Thus, Philo of Alexandria writes of the Sabbath, 'For it is not permitted to cut any shoot or branch, or even a leaf, or to pluck any fruit whatsoever' (Philo, *Vit. Mos.* 2.22). Note also CD 10.22-23:

> No one is to eat on the Sabbath day except what has been prepared; and from what is lost in the field […] he should not eat, nor should he drink except of what there is in the camp.[17]

Later rabbis recorded similar convictions (*y. Shab.* 7.2; *t. Shab.* 9.17). We can also include here a possible hint of such an outlook in *Jub.* 2.29-30, along with more direct evidence (for the Pharisees) from our passage in Mk 2.24. Crossley classifies these texts rather narrowly as the halakhic traditions of certain 'strict Jews'.[18] For reasons stated above, I find here, instead, a

---

16. Sanders has appropriately emphasized the necessary connection that obtained in rabbinic thinking between halakhah and the biblical materials:

> The purpose of halakhah is to determine whether or not a biblical passage does in fact constitute a commandment, if there is any doubt; to establish the application of a biblical commandment; to define its precise scope and meaning; and to determine precisely what must be done in order to fulfill it (1977: 76).

17. The translation is from Crossley, who asserts, '[T]his surely must imply a prohibition of plucking' (2004: 161). Casey translates the text differently but comes to a similar conclusion (1998: 148). See, also, Schiffman (1975: 98-101).

18. Crossley (2004: 161). Crossley apparently assumes that the Sabbath practices of these 'strict Jews' had little impact upon broader Jewish society. In the case of the Pharisees I suspect we should grant more credence than has traditionally been the case to Josephus's insistence that the sect exercised a considerable degree of influence among the people at large (Josephus, *Ant.* 13.298, 401; 18.14; Josephus, *War* 2.166), and it is refreshing to see some scholars moving in precisely this direction. Thus Catchpole reasonably concludes that the Pharisees

> were not just talking to themselves about how the will of God should be defined. Rather, they had a programme for the nation. That programme they set about communicating. It seems that many Jews, while not joining Pharisaic fellowships, nevertheless respected Pharisaic rulings (Catchpole [2006: 192]).

sensible application of the biblical legislation prohibiting agricultural work on the Sabbath.[19] For Jesus to defend his disciples' behavior in this regard is to call into question what would likely have been a broadly accepted understanding of Sabbath law—not merely Pharisaic halakhah—in light of the inbreaking of the kingdom of God.

The example of David which Jesus cites in response to the Pharisees points in the same direction. Even allowing for humanitarian considerations, what is highlighted in the text is the illegality of David's act—an illegality explicitly paralleled with the illegality of the disciples' behavior (v. 24: ὃ οὐκ ἔξεστιν...; v. 26: οὓς οὐκ ἔξεστιν). As Sturcke rightly observes, 'Jesus appears to concede that something illegal has happened' in the disciples' behavior.[20] Crossley recognizes this, but his understanding of the conflict as an intra-Jewish halakhic dispute necessitates that he interpret the parallel somewhat unevenly:

> [I]f the Pharisees accept that David broke a biblical law then they should find acceptable the actions of Jesus' disciples, even if they are in opposition to a certain [Pharisaic] *interpretation* of biblical law.[21]

This is certainly possible, and we cannot be dogmatic here. Yet as Gundry properly asserts, a straightforward reading of the parallel more directly implies that Jesus' disciples are 'indeed breaking the Sabbath just as David and his companions broke the law concerning the loaves of the presentation'.[22] More

---

Scholars increasingly view the Pharisees as but one (intensive) expression of an expansionist approach to purity and boundaries that characterized Judaism as a whole during our period (see Chapter 7). To be sure, many of the Pharisees' purity practices proved impractical for non-sectarian sympathizers in the broader Jewish community. But surely not all of them. The prohibition of gleaning grain on the Sabbath, for example, was likely a portion of Pharisaic halakhah that an admiring populace could not only esteem, but easily and readily emulate.

19. Banks overstates the case, however, when he describes the disciples' behavior as 'an act which unquestionably violated all current practice of the sabbath laws' (1975: 114 n. 2). We cannot be this categorical in our conclusions on the matter, because we do not know what constituted 'all current practice of sabbath laws'.

20. Sturcke (2005: 149).

21. Crossley (2004: 163, my italics). Similarly, Hooker: 'If David and his companions could break the command of the torah, how much more can Jesus and his companions dispense with the regulations *surrounding* the law' (2000: 119-20, author's italics).

22. Gundry (1993: 141). I would take issue here with Gundry's categorical expression, 'breaking the Sabbath', since I do not think we have an absolute standard against which to assess the behavior of the disciples which Jesus affirms. Otherwise, I think Gundry is quite on target (a) to take the parallel at face value, as he does, and (b) to assume that more than Pharisaic halakhah is at stake in the encounter.

Loader disagrees, reading the text, instead, in humanitarian terms: 'The argument is not: David broke the law, therefore so can I; but need justified David's breaking of the law; i.e. another principle of Torah overrode the law that only priests should eat the

seems to be at stake in the dispute over the disciples' behavior than Pharisaic halakhah.

Jesus' description of the episode contains information lacking in the Old Testament account, moreover, which reinforces this impression. Among the added material:

(1) David enters 'the house of God'. The 'house of God' is not mentioned in the Old Testament account (1 Sam. 21.1-9).

(2) Abiathar is identified as 'high priest'. The Old Testament account refers to Ahimelech, who is identified as simply a 'priest'.[23]

(3) David 'ate the bread of the Presence', by implication, in the house of God, and gave some to his companions. Neither the consumption of the holy bread nor the sharing with the companions is mentioned in 1 Samuel 21.[24]

Jesus has elaborated upon the biblical episode of David and the shewbread, and he has done so in such a way as to emphasize the fact that David transgressed well-known purity legislation relating to the tabernacle and the bread of Presence.[25] The pointed appeal to such an exceptional biblical narrative makes the most sense if we assume that Jesus viewed his disciples' behavior, like David's, as a transgression of a reasonable interpretation of biblical legislation and not merely as a breach of Pharisaic halakhah.[26] The

shewbread' (2002: 34-35). Loader concludes that Jesus does not reject Sabbath law as such (34).

23. The reason for the reference to Abiathar instead of Ahimelech need not detain us here. See Daube (1972/73: 6), Derrett (1977: 92), and Kiilunen (1985: 200) for various explanations of the discrepancy.

24. The inclusion of the companions may simply reflect an alternative text available to Jesus and his contemporaries. Casey emends the MT based on the reading of 4Q52 (frg. 7, line 17) (1998: 152). See the discussion in Cross and Parry (1997: 69).

25. As noted by Westerholm (1978: 98-99). At another level, I believe that Wright is generally on target to find in the David story 'a kingdom-parallel in an essentially kingdom case' (1996: 393). It is difficult to deny such a connection between David and Jesus, both true kings who will in due time be vindicated by Yahweh, and I will comment below on the salvation-historical aspects of Jesus' activities in the Sabbath controversies. Wright is off-base, however, wholly to exclude legal considerations from Jesus' appeal to the David narrative in Mk 2.25-26. The parallel between the disciples' behavior, on the one hand, and the unlawful action of David, on the other, must not be overlooked.

26. It is possible that the story of David and the showbread brought to mind a more recent compromise of purity where the Jerusalem temple was concerned. Josephus relates the regrettable behavior of the Roman general Pompey, when he conquered Jerusalem, stormed the temple compound, and insisted on entering the holy structure itself, in 63 BCE:

affirmation of such behavior, in turn, raises profound questions about the place and function of Sabbath observance in the context of Jesus' vision for a renewed people of God.

The concluding pronouncement that 'the Son of Man is lord even of the sabbath' (v. 28) further supports this explanation of the conflict. Jesus' statement constitutes the interpretative crux of the passage and has occasioned a variety of readings. Given its syntactical connection (as a result clause) with the assertion in the previous verse, it would make good sense to interpret ὁ υἱὸς τοῦ ἀνθρώπου as a circumlocution equivalent to ἄνθρωπος in v. 27 (2×).²⁷ The idea would be that the Sabbath was created for humankind, with the result that humankind is 'lord even of the sabbath', and the statement

> And not light was the sin committed against the sanctuary, which before that time had never been entered or seen. For Pompey and not a few of his men went into it and saw what it was unlawful for any but the high priests to see. (Josephus, *Ant.* 14.71-72)

Two parallels occur between Jesus' story of David (Mk 2.25-26) and Josephus's account of Pompey, neither of which are found in the MT of 1 Samuel 21. First, Josephus and Jesus both mention the office of high priest, a reference missing from the Old Testament original. Also in contrast to 1 Samuel—which emphasizes that David was 'alone' when he approached the priest (1 Sam. 21.1) and says nothing about David entering the temple structure—our story is framed in such a way as to imply that David entered the temple, ate the holy bread, and that he did so in the company of a group of 'companions' (Mk 2.25-26). In similar fashion, Josephus claims that Pompey entered the sanctuary, and that he did so with 'not a few of his men'.

Would the manner in which Jesus retold the David incident have stirred up in the minds of those present memories of Pompey's activities in the temple in 63 BCE? We can only speculate, but the parallels are intriguing. And the collective memory of Pompey's offense was certainly alive and well in certain circles in first-century Palestine. The author of the *Psalms of Solomon* (1st cent. CE), for example, alludes to Pompey's activities in the East in various passages (2.1-2, 26-29; 8.16-18; 17.12), ultimately attributing the Roman general's ignominious demise to divine chastisement:

> And I did not wait long until God showed me his insolence pierced on the mountains of Egypt, more despised than the smallest thing on earth and sea. His body was carried about on the waves in much shame, and there was no one to bury (him), for he (God) had despised him with contempt (*Pss. Sol.* 2.26-27).

Given the parallels between Mk 2.25-26 and Josephus's narrative, along with the enduring memory of Pompey's offense, as reflected in contemporary literature, it is quite possible that the way in which Jesus retold the 1 Samuel narrative subtly elicited in the minds of his hearers unpleasant memories of Pompey's brazen intrusion into Yahweh's sacred space. This, in turn, would only have served further to underscore the illegality of David's activities and, according to the parallel (v. 24: ὃ οὐκ ἔξεστιν... in v. 26: οὓς οὐκ ἔξεστιν), the disciples' behavior, as well.

27. The origin of the saying in v. 27 has occasioned a good bit of speculation. Compare R. Simeon b. Menasya, *Mekhilta* 109b on Exod. 31.14: 'The sabbath was given to you, not you to the sabbath' (Witherington [1994: 162]). Crossan views the asssertion as a general saying that was later appropriated by the Jesus tradition (1983: 78-85).

would lack any titular self-referential connotation on the lips of Jesus. This understanding, which fits the syntax and nicely reinforces a decidedly humanitarian interpretation of the text, nevertheless stumbles on several accounts.

One is led to wonder at the outset, for example, why the text substitutes for the simple term ἄνθρωπος (2× in v. 27) the more opaque idiom ὁ υἱὸς τοῦ ἀνθρώπου (v. 28), if both expressions are intended to refer to 'humankind' in general. We could, of course, view the change of terminology as a characteristic example of stylistic variation. But the identification in the verse of 'the Son of Man' as 'lord even of the sabbath' becomes problematic on such a reading, for, as Gundry notes, κύριος is too strong an expression to denote the relationship between an ordinary human being and the Sabbath.[28] The change from ἄνθρωπος (v. 27) to ὁ υἱὸς τοῦ ἀνθρώπου (v. 28) is best taken, therefore, to signal a change in referent, from humankind to Jesus. Still more damaging to the view that interprets ὁ υἱὸς τοῦ ἀνθρώπου in Mk 2.28 in generic terms is Mark's use of 'Son of man' earlier in the chapter, where the expression more transparently refers not to humankind in general but to Jesus himself:

> 10 'But so that you may know that the Son of Man has authority on earth to forgive sins'—he said to the paralytic—11 'I say to you, stand up, take your mat and go to your home' (Mk 2.10-11).

The emphasis upon authority in this passage—a conceptual parallel to the idea of lordship in 2.28—encourages us to interpret the phrase 'Son of man' to refer to Jesus in both 2.10 and 2.28.[29]

---

28. Gundry (1993: 144).

29. To identify Jesus as 'the Son of man' in the text still leaves unaddressed the extensive and complex scholarly debate over the expression ὁ υἱὸς τοῦ ἀνθρώπου and its meaning in the present context. And the resulting connection between v. 27 and v. 28 remains problematic on this interpretation. For to deduce from the humanitarian purpose of the Sabbath (v. 27) that Jesus is 'Lord of the sabbath' (v. 28)—whatever the meaning of 'Son of man'—cries out for further elucidation.

See Davies and Allison for a helpful summary of the ὁ υἱὸς τοῦ ἀνθρώπου debate (1991: 43-53), and Burkett for a thorough history of scholarship from the patristic period to the end of the twentieth century (1999). With a number of scholars I see ὁ υἱὸς τοῦ ἀνθρώπου used most often in the Gospels as a title for Jesus, which at times intentionally alludes to the son of man figure in Dan. 7.13-14, particularly at places where ideas of power and authority are at issue in the narrative (likely here in Mk 2.10, 28). For the association of 'son of man' with Daniel 7, see Witherington (1990: 233-62). The use of the phrase to refer to humanity in general also finds limited expression in the Gospels (possibly, for example, in Mt. 12.32; par. Lk. 12.10). Scholarship is divided over whether to interpret ὁ υἱὸς τοῦ ἀνθρώπου in Mk 2.10 and 2.28 in titular or generic terms. As Burkett has recently maintained, common (titular) usage and not exceptional (generic) usage should inform decisions concerning debatable texts, and it is preferable,

The statement under consideration identifies the Son of man (Jesus) as 'lord *even* of the sabbath'. The conjunction picks up on the reference to the authority of the Son of man to forgive sins in 2.10, and the NRSV is probably correct to assign to καί an ascensive force.[30] The concluding verse thus further underscores the viability of my understanding of the passage, since Jesus' lofty assertion would be overkill in the context of a debate over Pharisaic halakhah, but functions nicely as a dominical pronouncement summarizing the overall thrust of a narrative with more far-reaching implications: 'The Son of man is lord *even* of the sabbath'.[31] That is, the Sabbath—a defining symbol of Jewish identity which finds its origins in the Decalogue itself—offers the ultimate test of Jesus' authority over socio-religious practice, and Jesus passes with flying colors. The Son of man is lord of the Sabbath, just as (καί) the Son of man has authority on earth to forgive sins (2.10).

b. *Mark 3.1-6*

The second of our two controversy stories in the triple tradition similarly highlights the troubling nature of Jesus' attitude toward the Sabbath in the eyes of his adversaries (here Pharisees and Herodians):

> 1 Again he entered the synagogue, and a man was there who had a withered hand. 2 They watched him to see whether he would cure him on the sabbath, so that they might accuse him. 3 And he said to the man who had the withered hand, 'Come forward'. 4 Then he said to them, 'Is it lawful to do good or

therefore, to understand ὁ υἱὸς τοῦ ἀνθρώπου as a title in both occurrences in Mark 2 (Burkett [1999: 96]). Unlike Burkett, however, I would trace this titular usage back to Jesus himself.

It remains to discern the connection between (a) the assertion of the humanitarian purpose of the Sabbath (v. 27) and (b) the ὥστε-clause that identifies Jesus as its Lord (v. 28), a logical conundrum that cannot be ameliorated by assuming, against normal Marcan usage, that the ὥστε-clause is somehow loosely connected to the pericope as a whole (Gundry 1993: 147). Gundry finds the key to the connection in both meanings of the phrase 'Son of man', mentioned above. The generic usage ('son of man' for 'humankind') preserves a linguistic/conceptual connection between vv. 27 and 28: 'if the Sabbath came into being on account of human beings, then it came into being on account of me' (1993: 145). The Danielic allusion elicits a further, exegetical, deduction: 'but since I am no ordinary human being, but the figure like a son of man in Dan. 7.13, I am more than a beneficiary of the Sabbath. I am also its Lord, who can let my disciples break the Sabbath' (145). Similarly, and a bit more succinctly, Taylor: '[T]he thought is that, since the Sabbath was made for man, He who is man's Lord and Representative has authority to determine its laws and use' (1966/1981: 219).

30. This is certainly preferable to Crossan, who interprets the conjunction to signify that Jesus' authority over the Sabbath is 'just barely achieved' (1983: 80).

31. Both the forward position of the anarthrous κύριος (immediately after the conjunction ὥστε) and the καί that occurs before τοῦ σαββάτου highlight the notion of authority in the pronouncement (Gundry [1993: 143])

to do harm on the sabbath, to save life or to kill?' But they were silent. 5 He looked around at them with anger; he was grieved at their hardness of heart and said to the man, 'Stretch out your hand'. He stretched it out, and his hand was restored. 6 The Pharisees went out and immediately conspired with the Herodians against him, how to destroy him (Mk 3.1-6).

Commentators have traditionally interpreted Jesus' behavior in the encounter as a challenge to a rigid Pharisaic legalism that placed the good of Sabbath-keeping above the good of restoring a man's withered hand.[32] The healing then serves as a shining illustration of the humanitarian purpose for the Sabbath allegedly emphasized in the previous pericope. As with our first controversy story (above), however, Jesus' behavior appears to be motivated by more than the incidental needs of a suffering individual.

In contrast to Mk 2.23-28, where the Pharisees initiated the interaction with Jesus, here Jesus himself elicits controversy by calling the man with the withered hand into the midst of the synagogue crowd (3.3). It is not implausible to suppose that Jesus has come into contact with the man before and has intentionally chosen this moment to perform the healing. The intentionality in the encounter can hardly be disputed. As an examination of the healing narratives in the Gospels demonstrates, it is not Jesus' normal practice to seek out persons in need. Rather, Jesus heals those who take the initiative to come to him. Sabbath healings form a striking exception to this pattern, however, for they generally portray Jesus as the one who initiates contact with individuals who need healing (Mk 3.3; Lk. 13.12, 14.4; Jn 5.6).[33]

According to Mark's narrative, moreover, Jesus has already visited the synagogue in Capernaum on at least one occasion (1.21), and he is said to have 'returned to Capernaum' in 2.1. No indication of a change of venue for Jesus' activities has been given since. Finally, the pericope immediately following our story finds Jesus departing 'to the sea', beside which Capernaum was located (3.7). The evidence has led a number of commentators to conclude that the encounter in 3.1-6 occurred at the synagogue in Capernaum (as also suggested by πάλιν in 3.1). This is not an insignificant bit of social realia. Gehring has recently identified Capernaum as *'the* residence for Jesus', and the Gospels agree in portraying the town as a center for Jesus' life and ministry.[34] If this reconstruction is accurate, it is not unreasonable

32. Cranfield (1959: 125); Schweizer (1970: 75-76); Gnilka (1978: 1.127).
33. Rhoads, Dewey, and Michie (1999: 108).
34. Gehring (2004: 36, author's italics). See also France (2002: 149); Gundry (1993: 149). The traditions situating Jesus' ministry in Capernaum rest upon a secure historical foundation (Theissen [1998: 166-67]; Catchpole [2006: 62]). Gehring should be consulted for a careful, optimistic evaluation of the evidence identifying Peter's house as Jesus' residence and base of operations in Capernaum (2004: 35-42; also note the summary in Charlesworth [1988: 109-15]). Capernaum had a certain strategic importance and was

to suppose that Jesus, having spent much time in Capernaum, was already familiar with the man's condition, a supposition that would render Jesus' choice to heal the man in the synagogue on the Sabbath highly intentional and deliberately provocative.

Jesus presses his agenda further by posing a pair of challenging questions: 'Is it lawful to do good or to do harm on the sabbath, to save life or to kill?' Abstracted from the context of the encounter the questions are innocent enough. The answer to the first was self-evident. Of course it was lawful to do good on the Sabbath (and, even more obviously, unlawful to do evil), since Sabbath-keeping itself was good, unless a greater good demanded temporarily setting aside the observance of the Sabbath. The second question probes further into the latter issue. Just how does one determine which greater good would permit Sabbath-breaking? Jesus offers two options, 'to save a life or to kill'. 'To kill' was certainly illegal, not only on the Sabbath, but on the other six days, as well.[35] Saving a life, however, just happened to be the one legitimate reason held in certain scribal circles for breaking the Sabbath: 'whenever there is doubt whether life is in danger this overrides the Sabbath' (*m. Yoma* 8.6). Jesus' adversaries were in full agreement that it was permissible to save a life on the Sabbath.[36] In the present context, however, Jesus highlights this key Sabbath guideline from Pharisaic oral tradition in order to set the stage for a wholesale redefinition of the guideline as the story unfolds. What renders Jesus' allusion controversial here is that the man whom Jesus has called forth is not in a life-threatening situation. He is crippled, not dying, and therefore not a candidate for the setting aside of Sabbath law.[37]

---

likely flourishing economically during the time of Jesus. Population estimates range from a conservative 1,000 or so (Loffreda [1993: 18]) to as high as 25,000 residents (Kee [1989], cited by Reed [1992: 1-19]). Meyers and Strange estimate 12-15,000 (1981: 58). Josephus extols the beauty and agricultural wealth of the region (Josephus, *War* 3.516-19).

35. Some see here an echo of a halakhic debate about the application of Sabbath law during a time of war. During the Maccabean period, pious Jews decided to defend themselves on the Sabbath, after numbers had been massacred while refusing to do so (1 Macc. 2.41; Josephus, *Ant.* 12.272-77) (see Theissen [1998: 234] and Casey [1998: 182]).

36. As Casey maintains, 'Jesus' argument makes sense only if we suppose that this principle was already accepted by the Pharisees' (1998: 182).

37. Casey (1998: 182). This, in turn, explains the silence of Jesus' adversaries. To affirm the lawfulness of doing evil or taking a life is, of course, unthinkable. But to affirm the opposite—ἀγαθὸν ποιῆσαι...ψυχὴν σῶσαι—would be to play into Jesus' hand and only underscore the impending healing as an acceptable reinterpretation of 'saving a life'. Mark's statement 'But they were silent' is to be taken as an indication that Jesus has shamed his interlocuters in a culture in which verbal jousting between males in a public setting had the potential profoundly to affect the honor of the respective

By his act of healing in response to his own question (3.4-5) Jesus thus proceeds to redefine the contents of 'to do good' and 'to save a life' in terms of healing the crippled man. But this only serves to raise a further question: how does healing a man with a withered hand qualify as 'to save a life'? Guelich's response is insightful:

> The answer lies in the implicit claim of Jesus' ministry as depicted in the previous controversy narratives. Healing the sick, forgiving the sinner, sharing a table with toll collectors and sinners, feasting rather than fasting, and his authority over the sabbath—all point to an implicit claim of something special in his work. The claim is summarized in 1.14-15. Jesus was announcing the coming of God's sovereign rule in history, the 'fulfillment of time', the dawn of the day of salvation as promised in the scriptures (cf. 1.1-3). Jesus was not only healing a crippled hand, he was bringing wholeness and a new life in relationship with God befitting the age of salvation. In this sense, he was 'saving a life'.[38]

Jesus' redefinition of 'saving a life' to include the restoration of a suffering individual's paralyzed hand is thus to be situated in the context of the eschatological moment at which it occurs: 'The time is fulfilled and the kingdom of God has come near' (1.15).[39]

Of note in this connection is the association in certain circles of Sabbath imagery with the eschatological day of salvation. In an important survey of the theological import of the Sabbath day, the Sabbath year, and the year of Jubilee in the Hebrew Scriptures, Shead aptly notes that 'the institution of the sabbath day had an eschatological edge from the first'.[40] Second-Temple literature attests to the persistence of this view of the seventh day. The *Life of Adam and Eve*, for example, portrays Seth mourning the death of his

---

participants. This aspect of Jesus' various interactions with the Jewish leaders—and the antagonism such behavior generated in an agonistic society—should not be missed (see Hellerman [2000]). Kahl highlights the irony of the account, in which Jesus' understanding of Sabbath leads to life, while that of the Pharisees and Herodians leads to death—in the healing Jesus proceeds to 'save life'; his opponents, in contrast, try to 'destroy' Jesus in the final verse of the pericope (1998: 316; Casey argues similarly [1998: 183]).

38. Guelich (1989: 140). It is common to read the Sabbath healings in terms of the presence of the kingdom of God in Jesus. Thus, Kahl concludes his study of the passage by observing,

> Jesu ganzes Wirken war getragen von der Gewissheit, dass das Reich Gottes seit Johannes dem Täufer schon verborgen und für Eingeweihte sichtbar angebrochen ist— mit Jesus als ersten neuen Menschen. Jesu Zeit ist Sabbatzeit (Kahl [1998: 334]).

39. The English expression 'was restored' translates the term ἀπεκατεστάθη. It is interesting to note that two of the occurrences of this rare New Testament verb are found in an explicitly eschatological context (Mt. 17.11; Mk 9.12; Acts 1.6) (Guelich [1989: 137]).

40. Shead (2002: 19). Nikiprowetzky writes, 'The Sabbath rest prefigures the banquet that the righteous will celebrate in the kingdom of God' (2000: 3, my translation).

father Adam. The archangel Michael charges him not to mourn beyond the sixth day, 'because the seventh day bears the sign of the resurrection and the rest of the age to come' (*Adam and Eve* 60.1; see Heb. 4.9).[41]

The eschatological orientation of the Sabbath in Jewish thinking helpfully informs our understanding of Jesus' healings and his approach to the sacred day in general. The Sabbath, as a symbol of the dawn of the eschaton, likely represented for Jesus the ideal time to restore a suffering individual to wholeness. Guelich is quite on target, then, to explain Jesus' redefinition of 'saving a life' in terms of kingdom eschatology. I must insist, however, that for Jesus the 'coming of God's sovereign rule in history' (to adopt Guelich's expression, above) also had a decidedly corporate dimension, one which included as part of its program the reconstruction of the social identity of God's people. This, in turn, leads us to consider two alternative readings of the scene that unfolds between Jesus and his Pharisaic and Herodian opponents in Mk 3.1-6.

Based on (a) information provided by the narrative itself, (b) convictions relating to Sabbath-keeping which were in play in first-century Palestine, and (c) the background in oral tradition cited above (*m. Yoma* 8.6), we might imagine either of two possible scripts being played out in the course of the narrative:

> *Scenario 1*—Jesus is dealing in the encounter with Pharisees who have lost their sense of relational solidarity with—and sympathy for—their fellow-human beings and who, therefore, insist on their own, unbiblical, brand of Sabbath-keeping to the exclusion of a compassionate act of healing on Jesus' part. By healing the crippled man Jesus, in turn, sets human need above *halakhic* concerns, thus restoring God's original design for the Sabbath in view of the eschatological moment in salvation history.
>
> *Scenario 2*—Jesus is dealing with a group of Pharisees whose socialization into a scribal culture immersed in post-Maccabean ideology has convinced them that hope for divine intervention on Israel's behalf—and the corresponding end of Gentile domination—lies in maintaining those socio-religious boundaries for which their ancestors had sacrificed their very lives. In harmony with the determination of Maccabean freedom fighters to fight on the Sabbath only if their lives were in jeopardy, Pharisees and their sympathizers guard the Sabbath consistently, unless a life-threatening situation demands otherwise. In the present case, no such situation obtains, and sentiments like those expressed in the synagogue ruler's assertion in Lk. 13.14 would seem to constitute a wholly reasonable compromise: 'There are six days on which work ought to be done; come on those days and be cured, and not on the sabbath day'. Jesus could simply wait until sundown to heal the man. The Sabbath would be preserved and the man's need would be met. Jesus, however, has something

---

41. On the eschatological context of the idea of Sabbath rest in Hebrews, see Weiss (1996). He also treats, in less detail, the way in which Sabbath was understood by Philo, Paul, and the author of the Gospel of John.

else in mind. He deliberately and provocatively restores the man's arm on the Sabbath in the presence of all. And in the context of this second scenario, the healing can only be interpreted as a challenge, however embryonic, to post-Maccabean nationalistic ideology and, therefore, to the function of Sabbath as a non-negotiable identity marker for the people of God.

The two scenarios are intentionally somewhat artificial, and they do not exhaust the possibilities for interpreting the passage. Nor are they mutually exclusive. I am quite happy to admit the presence of a humanitarian element among Jesus' intentions, however secondary it might be to his salvation-historical designs. And we would probably do well to view the Pharisees' lack of compassion as a real but regrettable by-product of an exclusivist socio-religious agenda. It is this broader socio-religious agenda, however—reflected in the second of the two scenarios outlined above—which should take pride of place in our interpretation of Mk 3.1-6. According to this understanding, Jesus' purpose in the encounter is not simply to restore the original intent of the Sabbath in view of the dawn of the end of the age. As in the previous pericope (2.23-28), Jesus' behavior raises questions which destabilize the very function of the practice and which, by extension, lay the groundwork for a future time when Sabbath observance will no longer serve as an identity marker for an ethnic people of God.

In summary, given the historical and ideological background related in the previous chapters, it seems reasonable to conclude that the intentional provocation of conflict with the tradents of oral Sabbath law reflects Jesus' profound dissatisfaction with a central aspect of post-Maccabean ideology, namely, the meticulous concern to maintain distinctions between sacred and profane times—distinctions designed to mark out the descendants of Abraham as the particular people of God. In the words of Wright, 'now that the moment for fulfillment had come, it was time to relativize those god-given markers of Israel's distinctiveness'.[42]

c. *The Literary Context of Mark 2.23–3.6*
It will be helpful to conclude our examination of the two Sabbath controversy stories by considering their placement in the overall progression of the Marcan account, a progression that I take generally to reflect the order of the events as they occurred in the life of the historical Jesus.[43] Most scholars

42. Wright (1996: 389). As France has observed, Mk 2.27 and 3.4, taken together, establish 'a positive approach to sabbath observance which is in principle so elastic that it will be hard to rule out any act which is not in itself unacceptable. Certainly, it leaves no scope for building a fence around the sabbath law' (2002: 150).

43. Scholars are much more optimistic about the historicity of the Markan framework than they were during the earlier days of form criticism. Stanton, for example, finds the overall structure and individual narratives of Mark to be closely intertwined, and deduces that 'the framework of Mark emerges with strong claims to historicity' (1975: 15).

identify the healing narrative (3.1-6) as the last in a cycle of controversy stories that began in 2.1.[44] Kingsbury enumerates five such stories in the cycle:[45]

(1) The healing of the paralytic, with Jesus' scandalous assertion that the Son of man has authority to forgive sin (2.1-10)

(2) Jesus' table fellowship with toll collectors and sinners (2.15-17)

(3) The failure of Jesus' disciples to fast in accordance with Pharisaic practice (2.18-22)

(4) The plucking of grain on the Sabbath (2.23-28)

(5) The healing of the crippled man on the Sabbath (3.1-6)

Conflict between Jesus and his adversaries reaches a crescendo in the Sabbath controversies, which occur at the end of the cycle.[46] This can be seen most clearly in the increasingly hostile reactions of the various antagonists as the five-fold cycle progresses:

Controversy	Adversaries	Reaction
1. Healing of the paralytic	'some of the scribes'	[questioning in their hearts] '"Why does this man speak like this? He is blaspheming! Who can forgive sins but God alone?"'
2. Table fellowship with sinners	'the scribes of the Pharisees'	[spoken to the disciples] '"Why does he eat with tax collectors and sinners?"'
3. Failure to fast	'people'	[spoken to Jesus] '"Why do John's disciples and the disciples of the Pharisees fast, but your disciples do not fast?"'

44. Guelich (1989: 133); Gundry (1993: 6); Taylor (1966/1981: 91). France sees the cycle concluding at 3.6 but understands it to have begun at 1.40 (2002: 13). Dunn's arguments for the coherence of 2.1–3.6 as a pre-Markan unit should also be consulted (1990), although he identifies the unit as a group of individual Jesus traditions later brought together by Christians in 'a Hellenistic-Jewish Christian life-setting' during 'the tunnel period between Jesus and Paul' (1990: 28, 12).

45. Kingsbury (1989: 70-72).

46. In Gundry's view the cycle deals more with Jesus' authority than with controversy (1993: 6). The distinction is unnecessary, however, since the two ideas are closely related. When Jesus presses his authority as God's kingdom agent, controversy inevitably erupts.

| 4. Plucking grain on the Sabbath | 'The Pharisees' | [spoken to Jesus] '"Look, why are they doing what is not lawful on the sabbath?"' |
| 5. Healing on the Sabbath | 'Pharisees and Herodians' | 'The Pharisees went out and immediately conspired with the Herodians against him, how to destroy him'. |

Not until the fourth controversy in the cycle do the Jewish leaders themselves directly address Jesus, and only in the final story do they conspire to kill him. It is not accidental that these last two pericopes happen to be the Sabbath controversy stories in the cycle. A characteristic legal procedure, moreover, attested elsewhere in Jewish literature, traverses the two pericopes. The question in 2.24, 'Why are they doing what is not lawful on the sabbath?' amounts to a warning the violation of which (in the final story in the cycle) will lead to a capital charge (implicit) and the plot against Jesus (3.6). The adversaries' watching (3.2) appears to confirm the presence of this legal progression.[47]

Jewish leaders had legal justification for putting to death a Sabbath-breaker: 'Six days shall work be done, but on the seventh day you shall have a holy sabbath of solemn rest to the Lord; whoever does any work on it shall be put to death' (Exod. 35.2). We should not, however, interpret the reaction of the Pharisees and Herodians in Mk 3.6 solely as a dispassionate exercise in the application of biblical law. Post-Maccabean nationalistic sentiments surely served as the necessary contextual catalyst for the apparent attempt to enforce Exod. 35.2 in the legal procedure outlined above. The marked escalation, at this point in the narrative, of conflict between Jesus and his opponents is thus to be explained by the pervasive presence, behind the text, of the cultural scripts relating to purity and nationalism outlined in the first part of this book. For Jesus' adversaries, Sabbath observance functioned as a critical marker of Jewish identity in the context of Gentile hegemony. Jesus' challenges to the very foundations of this defining social practice serve to explain the vociferous opposition that his behavior elicited from Jewish scribal leaders.

d. *Luke 13.10-17*
Luke's special material contains two additional Sabbath narratives, the most memorable of which is a synagogue healing of 'a woman with a spirit that had crippled her for eighteen years' (Lk. 13.10-17). The story is characterized by a decidedly humanitarian emphasis that reaches its climax in a

---

47. The procedure moved from warning to capital charge to execution, and was apparently designed to determine whether or not a violation was deliberate. On the role of the warning see *m. Sanh.* 5.1, 7.8; *m. Mak.* 1.8-9 (Gundry [1993: 146]).

scathing dominical rebuke: 'You hypocrites! Does not each of you on the sabbath untie his ox or his donkey from the manger, and lead it away to give it water?' (v. 15). As the encounter concludes, however, Jesus describes the woman's predicament in a way that transcends the incidental nature of the healing. His second and final rhetorical question would have generated considerable dissonance in the minds of adversaries steeped in a post-Maccabean nationalistic ideology: 'And ought not this woman, a daughter of Abraham whom Satan bound for eighteen long years, be set free from this bondage on the sabbath day?' (v. 16). The juxtaposition of the expressions 'daughter of Abraham', 'Satan', and 'sabbath' should not be missed. It was precisely the descendants of Abraham who were preoccupied with preserving Sabbath observance as a mark of identity as the chosen people of God. In the words of the synagogue leader, 'There are six days on which work ought to be done; come on those days and be cured, and not on the sabbath day' (v. 14). Yet Jesus pointedly identifies the Sabbath as the day, *par excellence,* for 'a daughter of Abraham' to be healed.[48] The reference to the woman being bound by Satan explains why, by situating the healing, once again, in its proper eschatological context. Notice the previous use of the term 'Satan' in Lk. 11.18-20:

> 18 'If Satan also is divided against himself, how will his kingdom stand?—for you say that I cast out the demons by Beelzebul. 19 Now if I cast out the demons by Beelzebul, by whom do your exorcists cast them out? Therefore they will be your judges. 20 But if it is by the finger of God that I cast out the demons, then the kingdom of God has come to you.'

As is the case in the Sabbath controversies in the triple tradition, so it is here. The dominion of God has arrived in the person of Jesus, Satan is on the retreat, and the children of Abraham will now enjoy a completely different relationship with the Sabbath and other sacred times on the Jewish calendar. The turn of the eschatological moment demands a whole new approach to the social identity of the people of God.[49]

e. *Jesus and the Sabbath: Some Final Reflections*
We encounter yet another Sabbath debate between Jesus and a group of 'lawyers and Pharisees' later in Luke's Gospel (14.1-6), and the Gospel of John contains two additional independent Sabbath conflict narratives

---

48. The idea that '[t]he Sabbath was for Jesus precisely the day on which the healing sovereignty of God should be expressed in deeds' is an increasingly common one in the scholarly literature (Sturcke [2005: 141]; see, too, Kahl [1998]). Turner (1982: 107) offers a dissenting opinion.

49. The connection between the defeat of Satan and the time of eschatological renewal surfaces a number of times in Jewish literature (*1 En.* 55.4; *Jub.* 23.29; *T. Simeon* 6.6; *T. Judah* 25.3; *T. Moses* 10.1).

(Jn 5.1-18, cf. 7.21-24; and 9.1-16). A detailed examination of these texts is beyond the scope of this project. Scholars will continue to quibble over the interpretation of this or that phrase in the controversy stories, and I hardly expect my readers to concur in every detail with the analysis of the passages examined above. What cannot be denied, however, is the pervasive presence of these Sabbath conflict stories across the various strands of the gospel tradition.[50] As Guelich has properly noted, 'as far as the gospel tradition goes, the one recurring charge against [Jesus] was his transgression of the sabbath'.[51] And the charge was so serious in the eyes of Jesus' opponents that they conspired to put him to death (Mk 3.6).

Why was this the case? It has traditionally been argued that Jesus was driven by a compassionate desire to restore Sabbath-keeping to its original design, in view of the dawn of the eschatological age of blessing—this in contrast to an impersonal, casuistic orientation toward the practice, which resulted from halakhic positions adopted by adversarial scribes and Pharisees. Now one can hardly dismiss the marked humanitarian emphasis that characterizes the controversies and still remain faithful to the text, for Jesus compassionately responds to individual human need in nearly all of these encounters, much to the consternation of his apparently uncaring opponents. That (a) Jesus does so intentionally and repeatedly on the Sabbath,[52] however, and that (b) his behavior elicits such intense opposition from his opponents demands an explanation that goes beyond the postulation of a humanitarian or Sabbath restorationist agenda on Jesus' part, even under the rubric of an inaugurated eschatology. Restorationist explanations, taken in isolation, tend to divorce the conflicts from the post-Maccabean socio-historical milieu in which they occurred, and, as a result, they particularly labor to explain the intensity of the opposition to Jesus' Sabbath activities. This is an important consideration. For if the issue were simply that of compassion for human beings versus the alternative halakhic convictions of a minority of 'strict Jews', would Jesus' opponents really have plotted to take his life? One suspects that the stakes were much higher for the Jewish leaders who responded so passionately to the Sabbath healings.[53]

---

50. My approach here parallels Dunn's methodological strategy of 'looking at the broad picture, focusing on *the characteristic motifs and emphases* of the Jesus tradition, rather than making findings overly dependent on individual items of the tradition' (2003: 882, author's emphasis).

51. Guelich (1989: 128).

52. Theissen's observation is an important one: 'in no instance is the sick person in acute danger: all could have been healed the following day' (1998: 367).

53. As Sanders remarks, 'The halakic material especially tends to deal with relatively minor details, with areas where there are problems. In it the Rabbis, as it were, are skirmishing on the borders of their religion' (1977: 235). Yet something of much greater consequence than a mere skirmish over 'minor details' on the 'borders of

A more satisfying explanation for the ubiquitous presence of conflict over the Sabbath in the ministry of Jesus—and, particularly, for the severity of the reaction of his adversaries—is to be found in the profound collision of worldviews that occurred between Jesus and his opponents. Pharisees and others steeped in Maccabean ideology lived in the lingering twilight of a glorious day of national independence, an era in the not-too-distant past when their ancestors had broken free of Gentile hegemony in a very specific way: 'by reviving observance of the law in the homeland they ravaged the enemy' (*4 Macc.* 18.4). Such observance, of course, included preeminently the preservation of that vital social identity marker of Sabbath-keeping.[54] According to post-Maccabean nationalistic sensibilities, then, to play loose with the Sabbath, as Jesus was perceived to have done, was to invite God's displeasure and, therefore, to run the risk that Judeans would remain subject to the evils of pagan oppression. To rigorously guard the Sabbath, in contrast, fueled hope that Yahweh would intervene on behalf of ethnic Israel and throw off the Gentile yoke, in short, that the Jews would once again become 'invulnerable, *because* they followed the laws ordained by him' (2 Macc. 8.36, my italics). As a later rabbinic text relates, 'If Israel were to keep two Sabbaths according to the rules, they would immediately be redeemed' (*b. Shab.* 118b).[55]

Jesus, too, was vitally interested in the intervention of God on behalf of his people. In his view, however, the anticipated hour of Yahweh's intervention had already arrived, and the dominion of God was now at hand. God's program, moreover, would not involve the political exaltation of ethnic Israel at the expense of imperial occupiers and oppressors. Nor would it involve the passionate preservation of traditional indicators of Jewish social identity. Rather, Israel would begin to fulfill her vocation to be a light to the Gentiles, and socio-religious boundaries that had marked out the particular people of God for centuries would now need to be systematically redefined. Read against the background of such a collision of worldviews, Jesus' persistent violations of current convictions about the Sabbath—and the severe opposition he encountered as a result—find satisfactory explanation. Jesus' vision for the social reconstruction of the people of God during the dawning of the kingdom age could only provoke determined resistance from a scribal leadership steeped in the values and behavioral priorities of exclusivist post-Maccabean ideology.

---

religion' appears to be at issue in the Sabbath controversies between Jesus and his opponents.

54. Sturcke refers to a 'fierce loyalty to the Sabbath in the time of the Maccabees' (2005: 78).

55. As Barnett reasonably maintains, the sentiments reflected in this citation from the Babylonian Talmud were 'probably current in the time of Jesus' (1999: 139).

2. Jesus and the Jewish Festivals

The Gospels also portray Jesus taking a non-traditional approach to the annual festivals, celebrations that, like Sabbath-keeping, reminded Judeans of their special status as the people of Yahweh. Readers will be immediately familiar with Jesus' reinterpretation of Passover in terms of his own life and ministry, for the story of Jesus' last meal with his disciples appears in all three Synoptics and also in the Gospel of John. The fourth Gospel is most explicit in presenting Jesus as 'the fulfiller of the meaning of the Feasts of Israel'.[56] Jewish feasts that appear in John include Tabernacles (Booths), Hanukkah (Dedication), and Passover. In the case of Tabernacles, Jesus intentionally draws upon the two major symbols of the festival, water and light, in a self-referential way, thus proclaiming that the messianic hopes associated with the feast have found their fulfillment in him (Jn 7.37-39; 8.12).

The balance of the chapter will consider Jesus' treatment of Tabernacles and Passover against the background of the two festivals as they were celebrated—and increasingly nationalized—by Jesus' contemporaries. As was the case with the Sabbath (above), the intense concern for the preservation of sacred times which characterized post-Maccabean Judaism left its mark on the festivals, as well, and this was particularly so for Tabernacles and Passover. Literary evidence demonstrates, for example, that numbers of persons who reflected upon Booths and Passover in the wake of the Maccabean crisis did so specifically in terms of Jewish national identity and boundary preservation. Jews and Gentiles alike rewrote the story of the origins of the Judean people (the Exodus account of the first Passover), and at least two important Jewish texts connect the feast of Tabernacles to Jewish social identity in ways that depart significantly from the understanding of Booths in the Hebrew Scriptures.

And then there were the celebrations themselves. The gathering together of tremendous crowds of pilgrims in Jerusalem for the annual feasts only served to amplify the already volatile nationalistic sentiments associated with Booths and Passover, resulting on occasion in deadly confrontation with Roman occupying forces. It will prove illuminating, then, to consider Jesus' reinterpretation of Booths and Passover—with its implications for

---

56. Beasley-Murray (1999: lix). References to Jewish festivals in John include 2.13, 5.1, 6.4, 7.2 (encompassing all of 7.1–10.21), 10.22, and the Passion narrative. Moloney draws attention to the way in which the various portions of John 5.1–10.42 are united by their connection with the feasts. Temporal indicators 'lead the reader from Jesus' presence at one Jewish feast after another': 5.1 (Μετὰ ταῦτα; the Sabbath [weekly]); 6.1 (Μετὰ ταῦτα; Passover [Spring]); 7.1 (Καὶ μετὰ ταῦτα; Tabernacles [Fall]); 10.22 ('Εγένετο τότε; Dedication [Winter]) (Moloney [2002: 159]).

the corresponding revisioning of the social orientation of God's people in relation to the non-Jewish world—against this social and literary background. We begin with the feast of Tabernacles.

a. *The Feast of Tabernacles and Jewish National Identity*

Tabernacles finds its literary origins in the Torah, where the institution of the feast is connected with the Israelites' deliverance from Egyptian bondage and their constitution as the people of Yahweh at Sinai.[57] Several passages from the Torah offer instructions for the observation of Israel's annual festivals.[58] Leviticus 23 outlines the institution of the feasts during the giving of the law at Sinai:

> 1 The LORD spoke to Moses, saying: 2 'Speak to the people of Israel and say to them: "These are the appointed festivals of the LORD that you shall proclaim as holy convocations, my appointed festivals"' (23.1-2).

Instructions relating specifically to the feast of Booths appear later in the chapter:

> 33 The LORD spoke to Moses, saying: 34 'Speak to the people of Israel, saying: "On the fifteenth day of this seventh month, and lasting seven days, there shall be the festival of booths to the LORD. 35 The first day shall be a holy convocation; you shall not work at your occupations. 36 Seven days you shall present the LORD'S offerings by fire; on the eighth day you shall observe a holy convocation and present the LORD'S offerings by fire; it is a solemn assembly; you shall not work at your occupations"' (23.33-36).

Yahweh intends the festival to serve as a reminder of Israel's deliverance from Egypt and God's provision in the wilderness:

> 42 'You shall live in booths for seven days; all that are citizens in Israel shall live in booths, 43 so that your generations may know that I made the people of Israel live in booths when I brought them out of the land of Egypt: I am the LORD your God' (23.42-43).

---

57. I use the terms 'Tabernacles' and 'Booths' interchangeably to refer to the festival.

58. It would take us far afield to discuss the origins of the Jewish festivals. We may assume that Second-Temple Judeans traced the origin of Booths to the giving of the Law at Sinai, as outlined in the Torah. For a representative scholarly reconstruction of the development of the feast see Rubenstein (1995: 13-30) and the literature cited there. Moloney offers an abbreviated version (2002). He understands Tabernacles to have originated as an agricultural harvest feast that was later 'historicized and associated with God's care and guidance during the wilderness experience of the exodus'. The booths which the celebrants erected at Tabernacles to recall the wandering in the wilderness were originally temporary dwellings which sheltered those who attended the fall harvest (Moloney [2002: 156]).

The daily sacrifices enjoined in Lev. 23.36 (above) are elaborated upon in some detail in Numbers 29, a second Torah passage that focuses upon Israel's sacred feasts (for Booths, see Num. 29.12-38). Instructions relating to the festival also appear in Deuteronomy, which adds a territorial component to the annual celebrations:

> 'Three times a year all your males shall appear before the LORD your God at the place that he will choose: at the festival of unleavened bread, at the festival of weeks, and at the festival of booths' (Deut. 16.16).

The festival of Tabernacles fades somewhat from the Old Testament narrative, only to surface again during the postexilic period.[59] As the author of Nehemiah explains,

> All the assembly of those who had returned from the captivity made booths and lived in them; for from the days of Jeshua son of Nun to that day the people of Israel had not done so. And there was very great rejoicing (Neh. 8.17).

Zechariah 14 is our final Old Testament text highlighting the feast of Tabernacles.[60] The passage would prove to be a treasure house of symbolism for the celebration of the festival in later Jewish history, and it will be crucial for our understanding of Jesus' reinterpretation of Booths, as related in the Gospel of John. The author of Zechariah narrates a series of eschatological events that include the oppression of Jerusalem by the nations (vv. 1-2), the appearance of Yahweh to fight on behalf of his people (vv. 3-4), and Yahweh's ultimate victory over his enemies (vv. 5-15). The narrative concludes, rather curiously, with instructions relating to the annual celebration of Tabernacles by all survivors of the eschatological conflict, Jew and Gentile alike:

> 16 Then all who survive of the nations that have come against Jerusalem shall go up year after year to worship the King, the LORD of hosts, and to keep the festival of booths. 17 If any of the families of the earth do not go up to Jerusalem to worship the King, the LORD of hosts, there will be

---

59. But see 2 Chron. 8.13, where Booths is mentioned in passing, as part of the annual calendar observed under Solomon. Whatever might be said of the fate of the feast during the pre-exilic monarchy, it is quite clear that Judeans during the Greek and Roman periods faithfully observed Tabernacles. The festival was apparently so sacred that during a siege of Jerusalem under John Hyrcanus, Antiochus VII agreed to cease hostilities for seven days so that the inhabitants could celebrate the feast (Josephus, *Ant.* 13.242-43).

60. Various reconstructions of the literary history of Zechariah need not detain us here. Most scholars who view the document as a composite work still trace Zechariah 14 back as far as the late fifth or early fourth century BCE (Hanson [1975: 400]; Schaefer [1993b]; Meyers and Meyers [1993: 26-28]). Post-Maccabean Jews would therefore have been familiar with a version of the text similar in content to our MT.

no rain upon them. 18 And if the family of Egypt do not go up and present themselves, then on them shall come the plague that the LORD inflicts on the nations that do not go up to keep the festival of booths. 19 Such shall be the punishment of Egypt and the punishment of all the nations that do not go up to keep the festival of booths. 20 On that day there shall be inscribed on the bells of the horses, 'Holy to the LORD'. And the cooking pots in the house of the LORD shall be as holy as the bowls in front of the altar; 21 and every cooking pot in Jerusalem and Judah shall be sacred to the LORD of hosts, so that all who sacrifice may come and use them to boil the flesh of the sacrifice. And there shall no longer be traders in the house of the LORD of hosts on that day (14.16-21).

Two features of Zechariah 14 later surface as important symbols of the feast of Tabernacles in both the Mishnah and in John's gospel narrative. The first is the image of light in the text. The eschatological era, during which all the nations will observe the festival (v. 16), will be a time characterized by perpetual daylight: 'And there shall be continuous day (it is known to the LORD), not day and not night, for at evening time there shall be light' (v. 7). Zechariah proceeds to utilize the life-sustaining commodity of water as a second symbol of the promised time of blessing. The association of 'rain' with the proper observance of Booths can be seen in v. 17, above. Earlier in the chapter, the author had written, 'On that day living waters shall flow out from Jerusalem, half of them to the eastern sea and half of them to the western sea; it shall continue in summer as in winter' (v. 8). The verse immediately following explicitly connects the abundance of water with the future reign of Yahweh: 'And the LORD will become king over all the earth; on that day the LORD will be one and his name one' (v. 9).[61]

The central symbols of light and water take on a profoundly dramatic character during the celebration of Booths later in Jewish history, as illustrated by the extended instructions for the proper observation of the feast which are included in the Mishnah.[62] According to the compiler of tractate

---

61. Rubenstein curiously asserts, 'Those who celebrated Sukkot annually at the temple probably experienced no eschatological longings'. The focus was limited to 'the past harvest season and the fertility of the upcoming year' (1995: 50). Booths, as presented in Zechariah, however, is distinctly eschatological and messianic in orientation (Schaefer [1993a: 223-32]), as Rubenstein himself acknowledges (1995: 50). The idealized picture in Zechariah surely influenced sentiments surrounding the feast as it was celebrated during the Second-Temple period (Bergler [1998: 153-55]). Moloney properly maintains that the water-pouring rite, and the feast itself, involved the 'public celebration of messianic expectation' (2002: 157-58).

62. The degree to which traditions in the Mishnah can be used to reconstruct various aspects of the Second-Temple era remains a perplexing issue. Neusner, who pioneered work in this area, has not been optimistic (Neusner [1981: 14-22]). Recent scholarship sees a bit more continuity between our period and the early rabbinic era. A halakhic document from Qumran, known as 4QMMT, for example, portrays a dispute between

5. Jesus and Sacred Times

Sukkah, two arresting rituals dominated the celebration of Booths, rituals which involved Zechariah's symbols of water and light, respectively. Each of the seven days of the festival involved a formal willow procession, which led worshippers from a nearby town into the temple complex and culminated in a dramatic water-pouring rite (*m. Suk.* 4.5–5.1). The compiler summarizes: 'He who has not seen the joy of the water-drawing has not seen joy in his whole lifetime' (*m. Suk.* 5.1). The statement likely alludes to Isa. 12.3: 'With joy you will draw water from the wells of salvation'.[63] Light imagery

---

the Qumran group and its opponents which coheres closely with debates between Sadducees and Pharisees as related in the Mishnah. See the discussion in Rubenstein (1995: 104-105) and the sources cited there. Baumgarten (1992) should be consulted for additional evidence from Qumran corroborating the reliability of the Mishnah as a source for pre-70 Judaism. Instone-Brewer has recently summed up a generation of work on dating the rabbinic materials, helpfully outlining his own methodology, as well (2004: 28-40).

Rubenstein specifically discusses the value of the Mishnaic traditions for reconstructing events at the feast of Booths while the temple was still standing. The treatment is a judicious one, which concludes on a cautiously positive note: 'Given the general agreement with extra-rabbinic sources, it seems that the rabbinic materials [related to Sukkot] acquire a presumptive plausibility once the obvious historiographic tendencies are filtered out' (1995: 160). Epstein is even more optimistic, asserting that the fourth and fifth chapters of the tractate *Sukkah*, which describe the festal rituals, were 'essentially redacted during the time of the temple' (cited by Rubenstein [1995: 106], who prefers a date 'soon after the destruction' [106]). Keener traces the establishment of the water pouring ceremony to 'Maccabean times' (2003: 1.722). A souvenir amphorisk from Cyprus dated to the Second-Temple period appears to evoke the ceremony. It was likely brought to the island by a Diaspora pilgrim who had attended the feast (Engle [1977]).

63. We can be relatively confident that the practices at Booths reflected in the Mishnah go back at least to the time of Jesus some two centuries earlier. The symbolism of the water-pouring rite at Tabernacles would be even more pronounced, however, if we could trace later, post-Mishnaic Jewish traditions back to the first century CE. The traditions in view associate the Water Gate in the temple (through which entered the daily willow procession described above) with Ezekiel's 'south side' of the temple, where 'water was coming out' (Ezek. 47.2). The Ezekiel text is then interpreted in connection with the eschatological river of 'living waters' mentioned in Zech. 14.8 (see *t. Suk.* 3.3-9). Grigsby suggests that 'Jesus' audience, perhaps just having passed through the Water Gate, would quite naturally relate the Nazarene's phrase, 'rivers of living water', to those eschatological waters foretold by Ezekiel and Zechariah' (1986: 106). A later portion of the same chapter of the Tosefta identifies the wilderness water miracle (Exod. 17.1-7; Num. 20.8-13) as a typological forerunner of the water-pouring ceremony at Booths (*t. Suk.* 3.11-12).

It is interesting to note that the liturgy prescribed for the festival in the Babylonian Talmud (*b. Meg.* 31a) includes the reading of Zechariah 14. Older tannaitic sources also associate the text with the feast of Booths (*t. Suk.* 3.18, quoting Zech. 14.17-18 in connection with the festival). The practice of reading Zechariah at the festival likely goes back much earlier, given the emphasis in the Mishnah on Zechariah's two key symbols of water and light, as outlined above. Keener thus judges the reading of Zechariah 14 also played a central part in the celebration of Tabernacles. The perpetual daylight of Zechariah's account of the feast (14.7) found vivid expression in the illumination of four enormous candelabras that were set up in the Court of Women on the evening of the first day of the feast. The effect was such that 'there was not one courtyard in Jerusalem that did not reflect the light' (*m. Suk.* 5.3; see 5.2-4).

Western readers will need to employ no little creative imagination in order properly to appreciate the dramatic power of an event like Tabernacles. Due to a variety of influences, both pietistic and sociopolitical, Christianity in the West has increasingly framed itself in highly individualistic and subjective terms. As a result, modern Euro-Americans tend to view religion as a private and personal enterprise, unrelated to life in the public arena. Such a conception of religion, however, poses no small obstacle to properly appreciating the impact of a celebration like Tabernacles, since Judaism's annual festivals were decidedly public and collective in nature.

The social and sensory experiences generated by public religious festivals in the ancient world were, in fact, more akin to our contemporary rock festivals or major sporting events than to a weekly church or synagogue experience. This would have been particularly the case for Booths. For as Rubenstein maintains, 'While the Jerusalem temple stood Sukkot was the preeminent festival and primary pilgrimage'.[64] At Tabernacles thousands

at Tabernacles during our period 'intrinsically likely' (2003: 1.725). The connection suggests a conservative preservation in later rabbinic works of earlier traditions relating to the feast of Tabernacles, a conservatism not untypical where practices of a liturgical nature are concerned.

Factoring in the traditions from the Tosefta, we may surmise that the significance of the water-pouring rite at Booths was, thus, quite complex, encompassing elements past, present, and future. Most basic was the agricultural component. Water was a highly uncertain commodity in ancient Palestine, and we should not be surprised to find Tabernacles continuing to reflect its origins as an agricultural festival, as evidenced by the association of the feast with God's provision of rain (see Zech. 14.17, above, and Ps.-Philo, *Bib. Ant.* 13.7). The rite looked backwards, as well, however, to God's care for Israel in the wilderness, when the people were in danger of perishing from thirst (Exodus 17). Finally, water came to be connected in the feast with the eschatological blessings of the kingdom of God, when living water would flow from Jerusalem (Zech. 14.8; Isa. 12.2; Ezek. 47.1-12). As Beasley-Murray aptly notes of the daily water-pouring rite outlined above, 'The associations of the ceremony with the salvation of God, past, present, and future were accordingly evident to the people at the festival' (Beasley-Murray [1999: 114]).

64. Rubenstein (1995: 1); similarly, Moloney, who calls Tabernacles 'the most popular of the three pilgrimage feasts' (2002: 156). The singling out of Booths, in this regard, is well attested in our sources. Josephus identifies Booths as 'the holiest and greatest feast' (*Ant.* 8.100). Tabernacles was distinguished from its sister festivals even in the Hebrew Scriptures, as illustrated by the fact that Deuteronomy 31 designates the feast as the occasion for the septennial assembly ritual when the entire people gather together for the reading of the Torah (Deut. 31.10-13) (Rubenstein [1995: 15]).

of pilgrims gathered in and around Jerusalem for the feast, erecting their booths both outside the city and in the outer courts of the temple itself. And not only was Tabernacles the most popular of the yearly festivals, it was also the only annual gathering involving celebrations that lasted throughout the night. We must keep this in mind as we consider the ability of an event like Tabernacles to stir emotions and incite nationalistic fervor among the multitudes gathered together in the holy city of Jerusalem. As mentioned above, moreover, the function of Tabernacles as a symbol of Jewish nationalism appears to have become increasingly pronounced in certain literary circles during the Second-Temple period. Two streams of tradition point in this direction.

b. *Booths and Hanukkah in 2 Maccabees*
The first indication comes from the Maccabean corpus. Maccabean literature associates Booths not only with the exodus from Egypt, but also with the purification of the temple in 164 BCE, thus drawing an explicit connection between deliverance from pagan oppression under the Maccabees and escape from Egyptian bondage during the exodus. 2 Maccabees begins with the citation of a letter from a group of Jerusalem Jews to 'their Jewish kindred in Egypt'. The letter specifically associates Tabernacles with Hanukkah by referring to the latter as 'the festival of booths in the month of Chislev' (2 Macc. 1.9).[65] A second letter, this one purportedly written in 164 BCE to 'Aristobulus, who is of the family of the anointed priests, teacher of King Ptolemy, and to the Jews in Egypt' (1.10), contains the following instruction, again presenting the newly inaugurated dedicatory feast as a 'festival of booths':[66]

> Since on the twenty-fifth day of Chislev we shall celebrate the purification of the temple, we thought it necessary to notify you, in order that you also may celebrate the festival of booths and the festival of the fire given when Nehemiah, who built the temple and the altar, offered sacrifices (1.18).

---

65. VanderKam does not think that 2 Maccabees (1.9, 18) actually names Hanukkah 'Tabernacles', since the Greek reads τὰς ἡμέρας τῆς σκηνοπηγίας. This contrasts with the LXX where the term 'feast' (ἑορτή) generally appears in connection with σκηνοπηγία (1987: 32-33). As Daise observes, though, Esther 9.26-31 consistently refers to the feast of Purim as the 'days [of] Purim' (2005: 125; see also τὰς ἡμέρας τῶν ἀζύμων [Acts 20.6]). It seems fair, then, to translate τὰς ἡμέρας τῆς σκηνοπηγίας in 2 Maccabees (with the NRSV) as 'the festival of booths'. Rubenstein explains the terminology as follows:

> Apparently the festival was known by several names for some years until the title 'Hanukka' (Dedication) became dominant: Josephus calls the festival 'Lights' (*phota*), while the letters at the beginning of 2 Maccabees employ 'Purification', and 'Sukkot in the month of Kislev' (1995: 60).

66. On the dates of the two letters, the latter of which is believed to be (at least partially) a forgery, see Goldstein (1983a: 164) and Rubenstein (1995: 57-58).

The author further presses his agenda along these lines in yet another passage that directly connects Tabernacles with the purification of the temple by Judas and his followers in 164 BCE. The narrative of 2 Maccabees reaches its climax in the tenth chapter, where the Jewish protagonists gain control of the temple precinct and proceed to celebrate the purification of the once-defiled sanctuary. The festivities are described as follows:

> 6 They celebrated it for eight days with rejoicing, in the manner of the festival of booths, remembering how not long before, during the festival of booths, they had been wandering in the mountains and caves like wild animals. 7 Therefore, carrying ivy-wreathed wands and beautiful branches and also fronds of palm, they offered hymns of thanksgiving to him who had given success to the purifying of his own holy place. 8 They decreed by public edict, ratified by vote, that the whole nation of the Jews should observe these days every year (2 Macc. 10.6-8).

The rededication of the temple, the reader is informed, was celebrated 'in the manner of the festival of booths' (v. 6). The text also suggests a conceptual link in the celebrants' minds between Israel's wandering in the wilderness after the exodus, on the one hand, and the displacement of faithful Jews from their villages, 'wandering in the mountains and caves', during the early Maccabean era, on the other (v. 6). Additionally, the 'wands', 'branches', and 'fronds of palm', along with the 'hymns of thanksgiving' (v. 7), recall the daily willow procession that formed the heart of the celebration of Booths during our period. Finally, the Maccabean victors celebrated their festival of rededication 'with rejoicing' (v. 6), an attitude explicitly associated with Booths in a number of Jewish writings (Lev. 23.40; Deut. 16.14; *Jub.* 16.20-21, 25, 27, 29, 31; Josephus, *Ant.* 3.244-45; *m. Suk.* 4.1, 8; 5.6). It is quite clear that, according to 2 Maccabees, the feast of Dedication (Hanukkah) was initially patterned after Booths.[67]

The association of the two festivals during the Maccabean period has elicited a variety of explanations.[68] Particularly informative are the parallels Rubenstein and others have noted between (a) the dedication of the first temple by Solomon, (b) the rededication of the altar upon the return from exile during the sixth century, and (c) the rededication, again, under the Maccabees in 164 BCE. It seems that Booths is somehow linked with each of these dedicatory celebrations. Josephus, for example, explicitly connects

---

67. The celebration of Hanukkah according to the pattern of Tabernacles may not have been universally embraced. Daise has recently suggested that the Qumran community polemicized against the Maccabean observation of a Booths-like festival in Kislev, based on concerns that Jewish feasts should not be 'delayed' from their 'appointed times' (1QS 1.14) (Daise [2005]).

68. For the relationship between Hanukkah and Tabernacles, the works of Rankin (1930), Abel (1946), Nodet (1986), and VanderKam (1987) should be consulted.

the festival with the dedication of Solomon's temple (*Ant.* 8.100), and we learn from Ezra 3.1-6 that Sukkot inaugurated the reintroduction of both the yearly festal cycle and the daily sacrifices in Jerusalem, when Judean leaders returned from Babylonian captivity:

> 1 When the seventh month came, and the Israelites were in the towns, the people gathered together in Jerusalem. 2 Then Jeshua son of Jozadak, with his fellow priests, and Zerubbabel son of Shealtiel with his kin set out to build the altar of the God of Israel, to offer burnt offerings on it, as prescribed in the law of Moses the man of God. 3 They set up the altar on its foundation, because they were in dread of the neighboring peoples, and they offered burnt offerings upon it to the LORD, morning and evening. 4 And they kept the festival of booths, as prescribed, and offered the daily burnt offerings by number according to the ordinance, as required for each day, 5 and after that the regular burnt offerings, the offerings at the new moon and at all the sacred festivals of the LORD, and the offerings of everyone who made a freewill offering to the LORD. 6 From the first day of the seventh month they began to offer burnt offerings to the LORD (Ezra 3.1-6a).

The celebration of Booths at the dedication of the first temple and, again, at the initiation of the cult upon return from exile serves to explain the association of Booths with Hanukkah, when the temple altar was dedicated, once again, in 164 BCE.[69] Unique to this third dedicatory enterprise, however, was the establishment by the Hasmoneans and their supporters of Hanukkah as a new annual celebration, separate from Booths on the Jewish calendar.

The connection between Booths and Hanukkah during the post-Maccabean period would only have served to reinforce another, more prominent, commonality shared by the two festivals: each celebration reminded Judeans of a watershed moment in Israel's history when Yahweh intervened on behalf of his people to liberate them from the yoke of foreign domination. Given the symbolism shared by the two festivals, it is not unreasonable to suppose that Hanukkah and Tabernacles became, in some sense, mutually reinforcing dramatic memorials of post-Maccabean nationalistic ideology, by bringing to mind God's deliverance from pagan oppression in both the recent (the Maccabean revolt) and distant (the Exodus) past.[70]

---

69. Rubenstein carefully considers the association of Booths with the three dedicatory festivals (1995: 18-19, 59-62). Josephus relates the following about the dedication under Solomon: 'At this same time happened to fall the festival of Sukkot which is considered especially sacred and important by the Hebrews' (*Ant.* 8.100; on this see VanderKam [1987: 33]).

70. Problematic here is the degree to which the portrayal in 2 Maccabees corresponds with actual events surrounding the purification of the temple. Goldstein argues in some detail for the intentional association of Hanukkah with the feast of Booths by Judas himself in 164 BCE (1976: 274-80). Though differing in details, VanderKam (1987:

c. *The Feast of Booths in* Jubilees

The book of *Jubilees* provides a second line of evidence for the intentional association of Tabernacles with Jewish exclusivism during our period. Earlier we noted a tendency whereby the author of *Jubilees* anachronistically retrojects the practices of Sabbath and circumcision, along with distinctions between sacred and profane space, back into the earliest chapters of Genesis. In the case of Booths, we find the institution of the feast displaced from Sinai to the birth of Isaac centuries earlier.[71] The author appropriately portrays Abraham, the progenitor of ethnic Israel, as the first person in history to celebrate the feast of Tabernacles, in joyful response to the birth of Isaac and an angelic visitation:[72]

> And he built there an altar to the Lord who delivered him and who made him rejoice in the land of his sojourn. And he celebrated a feast of rejoicing in this month, seven days, near the altar which he built by the Well of the Oath. And he built booths for himself and for his servants on that festival. And he first observed the feast of booths on the earth (*Jub.* 16.20-21).

In the near context of this citation the author is quite concerned to distinguish between foreigners, on the one hand, and Abraham and Isaac as God's holy seed, on the other. During Abraham's seven-day celebration of the feast, the narrator assures us that

> there was no alien with him or any who were not circumcised. And he blessed his Creator who created him in his generation because by his will he created

---

32-34) and Ulfgard (1998: 183-85) are also relatively optimistic about the accuracy of 2 Maccabees on this point. Rubenstein charges such a perspective (specifically, Goldstein's reconstruction) with confusing 'history with historiography', and maintains instead that the connection between Sukkot and Hanukkah was, for the most part, created by Jason, as he wrote 2 Maccabees. The connection is nowhere reflected, for example, in 1 Maccabees (1995: 62 n. 73).

Even if Rubenstein is correct, we nevertheless possess in 2 Maccabees a popular document that would have encouraged its broad readership to associate Hanukkah with Booths. The later use of 2 Maccabees as a source for both *3* and *4 Maccabees* testifies to the enduring and widespread popularity of Jason's work. As Rubenstein notes, moreover, the description of Hanukkah as 'Sukkot in the month of Kislev' (2 Macc. 1.9) predates Jason's creative literary activity in the final redaction of the work (Rubenstein 1995: 61-62). The letter that includes the verse (1.9) has, in fact, been securely dated to 124 BCE (Bickerman [1933]). Thus, others before Jason had apparently associated Booths with Hanukkah, a reasonable connection given the celebration of Booths at the earlier dedicatory festivals under Solomon and Ezra.

71. There is some indication in *Jubilees* 32 that Jacob, too, celebrated Booths (Rubenstein [1995: 55-56]).

72. The portrayal in *Jubilees* of Abraham as the first to celebrate Tabernacles suggests a link between Jesus' proclamations at the feast in (Jn 7.37-39; 8.12) and the heated dialogue about Abrahamic descent which immediately follows in Jn 8.33-58. Moloney (2002: 160, 164-67), following Coloe (1999), argues for just such a connection.

him, for he knew and he perceived that from him there would be a righteous planting for eternal generations and a holy seed from him so that he might be like the one who made everything (16.25b-26).

One can appreciate the intensified concern for Jewish separatism that arose in the wake of the Maccabean crisis by comparing the *Jubilees* account with Zechariah's treatment of Tabernacles earlier in the Second-Temple period (see above). For Zechariah, all 'the families of the earth', including Egypt, join the Jews in their eschatological celebration of the feast.[73] The prophet thus finds in Tabernacles an occasion to include, rather than exclude, foreigners. The author of *Jubilees*, in contrast, utilizes his narrative of the institution of the feast as a vehicle for emphasizing Jewish particularism. When Abraham observed Booths, we are told, 'there was no alien with him or any who were not circumcised' (16.25b, above).

Even more pointed are the comments emphasizing God's choice of Isaac, which appear in the portion of the narrative immediately preceding the patriarch's inauguration of Tabernacles:

[the angel announced to Abraham that] through Isaac a name and seed would be named for him. And all of the seed of his sons would become nations. And they would be counted with the nations. But from the sons of Isaac one would become a holy seed and he would not be counted among the nations because he would become the portion of the Most High and all his seed would fall (by lot) into that which God will rule so that he might become a people (belonging) to the Lord, a (special) possession from all people, and so that he might become a kingdom of priests and a holy people (16.17-19).

From Isaac alone will come a 'holy seed', 'a people (belonging) to the Lord', a progeny that 'would not be counted among the nations'. Abraham's other sons, in contrast, will generate offspring all of whom will be 'counted with

---

73. Bergler contrasts the universalistic portrayal of Sukkot in Zechariah 14 with the traditional understanding of Passover as symbolic of Yahweh's exclusive choice of Israel:

Während Pessach Israels besondere Erwählung thematisiert, soll Sukkot das heilsuniversalistische, die Welt mit dem Gottesvolk in Jerusalem vereinende Fest der Endzeit werden! (1998: 154).

Evidence from 2 Maccabees and *Jubilees* suggests that the universalistic orientation of Booths in Zechariah 14 received little emphasis during the post-Maccabean era. The feast was instead interpreted, like Passover, in stridently nationalistic terms. The tendency persists well beyond the watershed years of the first Jewish revolt. Bergler finds in the Bar Kochba letters a markedly nationalistic understanding of Booths, which associated the festival with Hanukkah, as in 2 Maccabees (1998: 191). Bar Kochba in turn becomes 'ein Streiter für jüdische Friehet und Religion nach dem Vorbild eines Judas Makkabäus' (188). All of this attests, once again, to the perseverance and resilience of Maccabean nationalistic ideology throughout many decades of Judean history post-164 BCE.

the nations'. And it is precisely in response to this angelic announcement that Abraham 'first observed the feast of booths on the earth' (16.21; cf. 20-31). The association in *Jubilees* of the feast of Tabernacles with Israel's identity as the chosen people of Yahweh could hardly be more pronounced. We are now prepared to appreciate Jesus' interpretation of Booths in terms of his own agenda for the renewal of Israel under the dominion of Yahweh.

d. *Jesus and Tabernacles*
Jesus' treatment of the Feast of Booths becomes central to the narrative of John's Gospel in chapters 7-8. The meaning of the text has unfortunately been obscured by the insertion of the pericope of the adulterous woman (7.53–8.11), a story that originally formed no part of John's gospel. With the pericope removed, the progression of the storyline over the course of the two chapters becomes quite transparent.[74] Equally clear is the connection between Jesus' striking public pronouncements at the feast and the Jewish background to Tabernacles discussed above.

The story begins with Jesus going up to the feast in Jerusalem in private, after rejecting his brothers' encouragement to travel to Judea openly in order to show himself 'to the world' (7.1-10). 'About the middle of the feast' (v. 14) Jesus enters the temple complex, however, and begins to teach in a public setting. Even before his appearance Jesus had become a topic of debate among celebrants at the feast (vv. 11-12), and his public instruction now elicits an immediate reaction from 'the Jews', who marvel at the untaught teacher's erudition (v. 15). Jesus responds by highlighting a theme reiterated throughout John 7–8, namely, the idea that he derives his legitimacy from the Father who has sent him (vv. 16-18, cf. 28-29; 8.16-19).

The narrative proceeds with some observations from Jesus about a previous Sabbath healing (vv. 19-24; for the healing see Jn 5.1-9), observations likely intended as an allusion to the feast of Tabernacles. Jesus' claim in 7.21 to have performed one work (ἓν ἔργον ἐποίησα) calls to mind the theme of doing the work of God which characterized the narrative of

---

74. We would expect Jesus to attend the annual feasts, and the details of the story comport well with what we know about Booths during the Second-Temple period. Accordingly, Wenham includes various aspects of the account in John 7–8 in his representative catalogue of 'all sorts of things in the Gospel that are historically plausible, given what we know of first-century Palestine' (1998: 8). Also attesting to the general historicity of the narrative is the way in which Booths was generally ignored in early Christian literature, while Passover was emphasized as the preeminent Jewish festival that found its fulfillment in Christ—this in spite of the fact that Tabernacles was apparently the more popular of the two feasts during the Second-Temple period (on which see Smith [1962–63: 130, 141]). The narrative in John 7–8 thus goes against the grain of observable literary and theological tendencies in the tradition, and this, in turn, encourages us to trace the general contours of the account back to the historical Jesus.

the Sabbath healing two chapters earlier in John's gospel: 'My Father is still working, and I also am working' (5.17). The ποιέω word group occurs throughout John 5 in direct or indirect reference to the healing (5.11, 15, 16, 19 [4×], 20, 29).[75]

Compare the Mishnah, where we read that during the ceremony of the candle-lighting at Tabernacles, 'Men of piety and good works used to dance before them [the candelabras] with burning torches in their hands, singing songs and praises' (*m. Suk.* 5.4). Evidence from elsewhere in the Mishnah suggests that the expression 'Men of piety and good works' represents a particular class of persons and may refer specifically to workers of miracles. Hanini ben Dosa, for example, is included among a group of persons identified as 'men of good deeds' (*m. Sot.* 9.15). Another tractate describes Hanini ben Dosa as follows:

> They tell of R. Hanini b. Dosa that he used to pray over the sick and say, 'This one will live', or 'This one will die'. They said to him, 'How knowest thou?' He replied, 'If my prayer is fluent in my mouth I know that he is accepted; and if it is not I know that he is rejected' (*m. Ber.* 5.5).

By insisting that his Sabbath healing represented a work of God, Jesus may be intentionally including himself among the 'men of piety and good works', workers of miracles who are thereby qualified to play a special role in the candelabra ceremony at Tabernacles.

As our story in John 7 continues, Jesus' comments about the Sabbath healing generate more debate among the Jews about Jesus' origins, interspersed with yet more teaching from Jesus himself (vv. 25-36). Finally, Jesus makes an explicit connection between his own ministry and the feast of Tabernacles. The two climactic pronouncements occur as the week-long festival draws to a close:

> 37 On the last day of the festival, the great day, while Jesus was standing there, he cried out, 'Let anyone who is thirsty come to me, 38 and let the one who believes in me drink. As the scripture has said, "Out of the believer's heart shall flow rivers of living water"'. 39 Now he said this about the Spirit, which believers in him were to receive; for as yet there was no Spirit, because Jesus was not yet glorified (7.37-39).

> 12 Again Jesus spoke to them, saying, 'I am the light of the world. Whoever follows me will never walk in darkness but will have the light of life' (8.12).

Given the background to Tabernacles outlined above, the connection between Jesus' proclamations and the water-pouring and candelabra rites of

---

75. Ensor's careful analysis of the language of Jesus in John encourages a degree of optimism concerning the historicity of Jesus' claim in John 5 to do his Father's 'work' (1996).

the feast are quite transparent.⁷⁶ In such a setting the promise to provide 'rivers of living water' (7.38), and the claim to be 'the light of the world' (8.12), would have made a profound impression upon those within earshot. Jesus essentially asserts that the Jewish feast of Tabernacles now finds fulfillment in him.⁷⁷ The claim is simply astounding.

e. *The Feast of Passover and Jewish National Identity*
The feast of Passover memorialized Yahweh's act of salvation on Israel's behalf, when God delivered the descendants of Abraham from Egyptian bondage and established them as his own through the giving of the Law at Sinai. The Torah's account of the exodus soon positioned itself as the defining story of Israel's origins as a people, and references to God's great act of deliverance appear throughout the Hebrew Scriptures. During the Second-Temple period pilgrims gathered annually to celebrate the festival in Jerusalem, where Passover became a dramatic annual reminder to participants of their distinctive identity as the people of Yahweh. The two central themes of the feast—deliverance from foreign domination and the establishment of Israel as a sovereign people—proved increasingly problematic, however, in the context of imperial hegemony. By the time of

---

76. Those who treat the imagery of water and light in John include Culpepper (1983: 190-95) and Koester (1995: 141-206). See, too, Jones's monograph-length treatment of water as a symbol in the Fourth Gospel (1997). The symbolism is multivalent, and Koester rightly finds in 'living water' an image pointing to several aspects of Jesus' identity. The association of water with wisdom and the Law, in both the Hebrew Scriptures and the Targums, for example, encourages us to interpret Jesus' saying in 7.37-38, at one level, as 'an invitation to partake of divine wisdom', thus positioning Jesus over against contemporary legal tradition as the true source of the wisdom of Yahweh (1995: 175; Cory, too, emphasizes the wisdom background to the Tabernacles narrative [1997]; see also Keener's discussion of the image of water in 4.10-11, 13-14 [2003: 1.603-604], and Lindars on the same text [1982: 183-84]). Koester also finds in the expression 'living water' images of Jesus as prophet and Messiah (175-77; with Moloney [2002: 161]). Koester appropriately concludes his discussion of water imagery in John 7 by returning to the setting of the proclamation in the context of the feast of Booths: 'Jesus' invitation to come and drink from him shows that the hopes of the festival are fulfilled in him' (178). It is Jesus as the fulfillment of Tabernacles—and the corresponding relativization of this sacred time on Israel's festal calendar—that is the point in the present connection.

77. I refer the reader to the commentaries for treatments of interpretational problems surrounding Jn 7.37b-38, a notorious crux in the Greek text (Brown [1966: 320-23]; Barrett [1978: 326-39]; Lindars [1982: 298-99]; Schnackenburg [1987: 2.152-56]; Carson [1991: 323-26]; and Keener [2003: 1.730]). The conclusions one comes to here have little bearing on the arguments outlined above. The same can be said for the debate about whether Booths was a seven-day or an eight-day feast, on which see, among others, Lindars (1982: 298), Grigsby (1986: 102-105), Schaefer (1993a: 180), and Beasley-Murray (1999: 114).

Jesus, annual gatherings of tens of thousands of Jews, celebrating deliverance from Egyptian oppression under the watchful oversight of their Roman occupiers, inevitably generated a volatile and potentially explosive situation during Passover week in Jerusalem. It is in this context that Jesus of Nazareth redefines the feast of Passover in terms of his own ministry and, particularly, in terms of his impending crucifixion.

f. *Passover in the Hebrew Scriptures*
The story of Israel's deliverance from captivity in Egypt through the agency of Moses will be familiar to most readers. Extensive scholarly debates about the tradition history of the Old Testament texts, and various related attempts to explain the origins of Israel's Passover celebration, can be set aside as not directly relevant to the project at hand. Jesus' contemporaries drew their understanding of the exodus from the stories as they appear in the completed Torah, so a brief reminder of the biblical origins of the feast will suffice in the present connection.

The institution of Passover is presented in detail in Exodus 11–13, where Yahweh unleashes a final plague upon the Egyptians, resulting in the death of the firstborn of all non-Israelites, human and animal. After giving the Israelites specific guidelines to protect them from the plague (Exod. 12.1-13), Yahweh proceeds to provide instructions for the annual observation of the feast of Passover:

> 14 'This day shall be a day of remembrance for you. You shall celebrate it as a festival to the LORD; throughout your generations you shall observe it as a perpetual ordinance. 15 Seven days you shall eat unleavened bread; on the first day you shall remove leaven from your houses, for whoever eats leavened bread from the first day until the seventh day shall be cut off from Israel. 16 On the first day you shall hold a solemn assembly, and on the seventh day a solemn assembly; no work shall be done on those days; only what everyone must eat, that alone may be prepared by you. 17 You shall observe the festival of unleavened bread, for on this very day I brought your companies out of the land of Egypt: you shall observe this day throughout your generations as a perpetual ordinance. 18 In the first month, from the evening of the fourteenth day until the evening of the twenty-first day, you shall eat unleavened bread. 19 For seven days no leaven shall be found in your houses; for whoever eats what is leavened shall be cut off from the congregation of Israel, whether an alien or a native of the land. 20 You shall eat nothing leavened; in all your settlements you shall eat unleavened bread' (12.14-20).

Passover became a yearly celebration of the physical removal of the Israelites from the land of Egypt, and of their liberation from their Egyptian taskmasters. This alone would have sufficed to remind celebrants of their distinctive identity as God's chosen people. Explicit statements to this effect, however, in the defining narratives of Exodus 11–13, further encouraged such an outlook. For example, when Moses confronts Pharaoh with a warning about the final plague, he promises that every firstborn in the land of Egypt will die. Israel, in contrast, will be totally spared: 'not a dog shall growl at any of the Israelites—not at people, not at animals'. The reason Moses offers: 'so that you may know that the LORD makes *a distinction between Egypt and Israel*' (Exod. 11.7, my italics). The uniqueness of Israel is again emphasized in additional instructions given by Yahweh for the observation of the feast:

> 43 The LORD said to Moses and Aaron: 'This is the ordinance for the passover: no foreigner shall eat of it, 44 but any slave who has been purchased may eat of it after he has been circumcised; 45 no bound or hired servant may eat of it. 46 It shall be eaten in one house; you shall not take any of the animal outside the house, and you shall not break any of its bones. 47 The whole congregation of Israel shall celebrate it. 48 If an alien who resides with you wants to celebrate the passover to the LORD, all his males shall be circumcised; then he may draw near to celebrate it; he shall be regarded as a native of the land. But no uncircumcised person shall eat of it; 49 there shall be one law for the native and for the alien who resides among you' (12.43-49).

The inclusion of stipulations concerning the covenant badge of circumcision served further to underscore the sociological function of the Passover celebration as a dramatic symbol of Israel's otherness as the people of Yahweh.

g. *Passover in the Second-Temple Period*
The works of Josephus constitute a key source of information about the observation of Passover during the Second-Temple period. I will limit my examination to two aspects of Josephus's presentation which particularly highlight the function of the feast to distinguish between Israel and the nations. First, we learn from Josephus that both Jews and Gentiles traced Israel's origins to the exodus experience in Egypt, an experience later memorialized in the feast of Passover. This interest in the exodus account generated a rather vigorous literary exchange, moreover, which found Judeans and Gentiles sharply contending for the 'truth' about Jewish origins. Judeans, of course, defended the Torah's account of early Israelite history, while pagans significantly modified the biblical story in ways that portrayed Jewish origins in less than flattering terms.[78] Secondly, Josephus's narrative of recent Jewish history repeatedly illustrates the volatile nature of the annual celebration of Passover in Jerusalem during the Roman period. On more than one occasion violence erupted in the capital between celebrants and those charged with keeping the peace. The preoccupation with

---

78. Collins refers to the exchange as 'competitive historiography' (2000: 33).

5. *Jesus and Sacred Times* 161

Passover and Jewish origins in ancient literature, combined with heightened tensions during the annual celebration of the feast in Jerusalem, present an instructive socio-historical context for Jesus of Nazareth's redefinition of the central symbols of Passover in terms of his own life and ministry in the gospel narratives.

The debate between Judeans and pagans over Israelite origins supplies the agenda for Josephus's treatise *Against Apion,* where our author is determined

> to convict our detractors of malignity and deliberate falsehood, to correct the ignorance of others, and to instruct all who desire to know the truth concerning the antiquity of our race (*Ag. Ap.* 1.3).

The 'truth' for Josephus has already been told, of course, in the Torah's book of Exodus (1.40). In the course of his defense of the Jewish account, however, Josephus grapples with various 'scurrilous and mendacious statements' of pagan writers, each of which he takes great pains to refute. The number and ingenuity of Josephus's interlocutors attest to a rather robust interest in Jewish origins and Jewish identity among pagan elites during the first century of the common era.

The most persistent pagan reconstruction of the exodus associated the Israelites with 'a crowd of Egyptian lepers and others, who for various maladies were condemned, as [Manetho] asserts, to banishment from the country' (*Ag. Ap.* 1.229). Assorted versions of the story appeared in the writings of Manetho, Charemon, Lysimachus, and, of course, 'Apion the grammarian', Josephus's primary dialogue partner. Josephus seeks systematically to expose the inconsistencies of these accounts and to demonstrate the implausibility of their explanations of his Israelite heritage. Our author had his work cut out for him, however, since the pagan spin on the book of Exodus had secured quite a foothold in the Roman world. Tacitus, for example, cites as majority opinion among his contemporaries the popular notion that Judeans had originated as a group of diseased persons expelled from Egypt in order to purify Pharaoh's kingdom (*Hist.* 5.3).

We need not treat in detail the various renderings of the story of Jewish origins which were passed on in the writings of Greek and Latin authors.[79] It will suffice to note that the ubiquitous presence of these lively debates vividly attests to a persistent interest in Jewish identity among Judeans and pagans alike in the Roman world. This literary scuffle for the 'truth' about Jewish history centered, moreover, around the story of the Israel-

---

79. A brief overview of the pagan accounts of the exodus can be found in Gruen (2005: 32-34). Gruen downplays the anti-Judaism that characterizes these stories as they are related in *Contra Apionem*; but he (rightly) stops short of identifying the tales as Josephan fabrication.

ites' departure from Egypt, the defining narrative that was memorialized among Judeans in the annual feast of Passover. The exodus account—and, we may surmise, the feast of Passover—thus became closely associated, in the minds of Jews and Gentiles alike, with Jewish identity and social particularism. Accordingly, a number of the Greek and Latin treatments of the passover story include in their accounts speculation about the origins of Jewish ethnic badges like sacred food and Sabbath observance (see Chapter 1). The festival of Passover, however, and that which it symbolized, generated more than simply a war of words between literate Jews and pagans. During the Roman period the annual celebration of the feast in Jerusalem became a platform for expressions of nationalistic fervor, which at times resulted in violent confrontation between Herodian or Roman authorities and Jewish celebrants in the capital.

Judea's Gentile overlords were well aware of the potential of Passover to exacerbate nationalistic pride and unrest among the multitudes who gathered in Jerusalem to celebrate the festival. According to Josephus, Roman governors typically assembled a contingent of soldiers on the porticoes of the temple during the week of Passover 'so as to quell any uprising that might occur' (Josephus, *Ant.* 20.106-107). On at least one occasion the precautionary measure encouraged, rather than discouraged, riotous behavior on the part of the people. Josephus narrates the events as follows:

> The usual crowd had assembled at Jerusalem for the feast of the unleavened bread, and the Roman cohort had taken up its position on the roof of the portico of the temple; for a body of men invariably mounts guard at the feasts, to prevent disorders arising from such a concourse of people. Thereupon one of the soldiers, raising his robe, stooped in an indecent attitude, so as to turn his backside to the Jews, and made a noise in keeping with his posture. Enraged at this insult, the whole multitude with loud cries called upon Cumanus to punish the soldier; some of the more hot-headed young men and seditious persons in the crowd started a fight, and, picking up stones, hurled them at the troops (Josephus, *War* 2.224-26; cf. *Ant.* 20.106-12).

Violence escalated between Roman forces and the celebrants, and the prefect Cumanus swiftly brought more troops into the temple area. The results were tragic:

> These troops pouring into the porticoes, the Jews were seized with irresistible panic and turned to fly from the temple and make their escape into the town. But such violence was used as they pressed round the exits that they were trodden under foot and crushed to death by one another; upwards of thirty thousand perished, and the feast was turned into mourning for the whole nation and for every household into lamentation (Josephus, *War* 2.226-27).

Other disturbances at Passover included a violent confrontation between worshippers and the forces of the Herodian client-king Archelaus in 4 BCE (Josephus, *Ant.* 17.213; Josephus, *War* 2.10), and a debacle with a group of

Samaritans who 'threw human bones about in the porticoes and the entire temple' in 9 CE (Josephus, *Ant.* 18.29). Later, during the middle of the first century, while tensions steadily increased between Jewish peasants and Roman prefects, the Jews utilized the Passover gathering of 66 CE to lodge a mass protest before Cestius Gallus, governor of Syria, against the treatment they were receiving at the hands of the Roman prefect Florus (Josephus, *War* 2.280).

The feast of Passover thus served as a forceful symbol to Jews and pagans alike of the distinctive nature of the Jewish people. The lively literary exchange outlined above confirms the presence during the first century of widespread fascination with things Jewish. More specifically, the debate reveals a desire on the part of certain pagan elites to delegitimize Jewish particularism by recasting in a negative light the story of Israel's origins as the chosen people of God. On the Jewish side, repeated outbreaks of violence at Passover in Jerusalem, fueled by a 'lust for revolution' (Josephus, *Ant.* 20.109), attest to the ability of the annual festival to stir up memories of a time in history past when Yahweh made 'a distinction between Egypt and Israel' by delivering his people from pagan oppression (Exod. 11.7). As Catchpole notes, 'While the liturgy of the festival celebration caused the families of Israel to speak about one gentile nation, Egypt, what they could not but see watching them suspiciously at this season above all others was another gentile power, Rome'.[80] The feast of Passover, and all that it symbolized, would have demanded the attention of anyone in first-century Roman Palestine who sought to renegotiate Israel's ethnic boundaries, and Jesus of Nazareth's treatment of Passover has considerable implications for his vision for the social organization of those who would become his followers.

h. *Jesus and Passover*

The feast of Passover and the aims of Jesus intersect most profoundly at Jesus' last meal with his disciples.[81] The Last Supper presents a number of historical problems that are beyond the purview of this project.[82] In the

---

80. Catchpole (1996: 172).

81. For a sober discussion of the various viewpoints regarding the historicity of the Last Supper see Klawans (2002: 3-7), who situates the general outlines of the tradition, particularly as reflected in Paul (1 Cor. 11.23-26), 'within a plausible first-century Jewish context' (7). Those who share Klawans's optimism include Sanders (1985: 107), Chilton (1994: 46-74; 2000: 250-54), Wright (1996: 554-63), Theissen and Merz (1998: 423-26), and Fredriksen (1999: 117-19, 241-42). Casey argues persuasively for the historicity of Mark's account (1998: 219-52; see the summary on p. 250). Rejecting the Last Supper traditions as unhistorical are the minimalist treatments of Mack (1988: 271-78, 298-304), Crossan (1991: 360-67), and the Jesus Seminar (Funk [1993: 117-18, 387-88; 1998: 139-42]).

82. I am not persuaded by attempts to disassociate the Last Supper from the Passover meal (Taylor [1966/1981: 543, 663]; Anderson [1976: 308-309]; Hooker [1991: 338];

present connection I simply wish briefly to consider how Jesus' revisioning of the central symbols of the sacred meal relates to his understanding of the people of God under the New Covenant. By transforming the salvation imagery associated with Israel's exodus from Egypt into symbols of his own saving death, Jesus has, once again, relativized a sacred moment on Israel's calendar, one which, as we have seen, served as a forceful annual reminder to the children of Abraham of their distinctive social identity as Yahweh's chosen people in the midst of a Gentile dominated world.

The following chart outlines some of the parallels between the Passover meal and the Last Supper, and elucidates the manner in which Jesus reconfigured various aspects of Passover in view of his own life and ministry:[83]

Passover	*The Last Supper*
God remembered his covenant	A new covenant is enacted
Ritual washing	Washing disciples feet
Slavery in Egypt	[Slavery to sin?]
Deliverance from Egypt	Forgiveness of sins

and Theissen and Merz [1998: 426]). The connection between Jesus' last meal and Passover was transparently clear to the authors of the Synoptic Gospels (Mk 14.12-17; Mt. 26.17-19; Lk. 22.7-13), and there are good reasons for taking the biblical perspective at face value (with Stein [1992: 446] and Casey [1998: 229, 236-37]; Jeremias's classic treatment [1966] of the meal as a celebration of Passover should also be consulted).

Theissen and Merz have recently offered two 'intrinsic' improbabilities that they believe mitigate against the view that Jesus' last meal was a Passover celebration: (a) the meal would have been an annual one later in the church, and (b) Jesus shared the meal with his disciples, not with his family, as would have been the norm for Passover (1998: 426). Here I would counter that (a) Jesus purposely detached the commemorative meal from Passover's place on the Jewish calendar, as part of his efforts to relativize calendrical symbols of Jewish nationalism (see below); and that (b) Jesus did, in fact, share the meal with 'family', since the disciples constituted the core of a new, surrogate kinship group that Jesus was forming around himself (see Chapter 9).

I have also chosen not to address the thorny chronological problems involved in relating John's account to that of the Synoptics. One's view on the issue does not, in the final analysis, compromise the association of the Last Supper with the Passover meal. Even on John's chronology, which situates Jesus' death before the Passover meal, one could interpret the meal with the disciples proleptically in terms of Passover. For a brief overview, and direction to the relevant literature, see now Routledge (2002: 205-206). B. Smith's ambitious attempt to reinterpret the Johannine account to harmonize with the Synoptics should also be consulted (1991).

83. The chart is taken from Stein (1992: 447), significantly augmented with information gleaned from Routledge (2002: 209-20).

Haggadah explaining significance of the evening and the elements of the meal	Explanation of significance of bread and cup
Unleavened Bread	Body of Christ
Blood of the Passover lamb	Blood of Christ
Call for annual celebration	Call for continual celebration

In redefining salvation—and the traditional symbols of Passover—in terms of his own 'body' and 'blood' (Mk 14.22, 24), Jesus essentially evacuates the ritual meal of its association with the deliverance of the Israelites from Egypt and their formal constitution at Sinai as God's chosen people. No longer would Jesus' followers celebrate Passover as a yearly memorial of the liberation and establishment of the descendants of Abraham as the national people of Yahweh. They would instead celebrate the Lord's Supper as a reminder of Jesus' death on their behalf and of the establishment thereby of a new covenant people of God.

Anthropologists single out an ethnic group's story of origins—here the exodus account as symbolized in Passover—as a foundational component of the group's social identity (see Chapter 10). One can hardly imagine a more radical and bold reconfiguration of Israel's story of origins than Jesus of Nazareth's reinterpretation of Passover in terms of his own life and ministry. Particularly important, in this regard, is the way in which Jesus apparently severed the connection between the meal that he instituted and the place of Passover on the Jewish calendar. As demonstrated in previous chapters, calendrical distinctions between sacred and profane times served as tangible badges of identity distinguishing Jews from Gentiles in the Roman world. Had Jesus wished to preserve these boundaries, while at the same time replacing Passover and all that it symbolized with the Lord's Supper, it would have made much sense for him to establish the Supper as an annual celebration, on Nissan 14, in lieu of Passover.

Evidence suggests, however, that Jesus had no such interest in preserving this high holy day on the Jewish calendar for his followers. For in the early church the Lord's Supper was almost immediately separated from Passover on the calendar, and it was celebrated far more frequently than once a year. The Supper was held weekly (Acts 20.7; 1 Cor. 16.2) and even daily (Acts 2.46-47). The New Testament, in fact, prescribes no rate of frequency. Jesus' instructions during the Last Supper constitute the best explanation for this phenomenon. In this regard, it is proper to read Jesus' statement, 'Do this, as often as you drink it, in remembrance of me' (1 Cor. 11.25; cf. Lk. 22.19) as an abbreviation of a more extensive *haggadah* in which Jesus intentionally disassociated the Lord's Supper from the annual position that Passover had occupied on the Jewish calendar.

3. Conclusion

The significance of the reconfiguration of Booths and Passover, the two high points on the annual festal calendar, should be easy to grasp at this juncture. Jesus' handling of the Jewish festivals corresponds precisely to his approach to the Sabbath, as outlined in some detail earlier in the chapter. According to Israel's story of origins in the book of Exodus, Yahweh had commanded the descendants of Abraham to observe each of these sacred times, when he formally constituted them as his people through the giving of the law at Sinai. Sabbath and festivals were thus inextricably associated in the minds of Jesus' contemporaries with Israel's origins and identity as a sovereign nation. During the post-Maccabean period these distinctions between sacred and profane times increasingly served as a fundamental rallying point for the preservation of Jewish identity in the context of Roman occupation. Festivals such as Booths and Passover were progressively nationalized, and preoccupation with Sabbath observation became something of a cottage industry among scribes and others who were determined to preserve their Jewish social distinctives. The manner in which Jesus consistently challenged these essential calendrical symbols would one day provide his followers with the ideological raw materials to construct a social vision for a people of God who would transcend the boundaries of Jewish ethnicity, who would be free to 'judge all days to be alike', and who would summarily relegate post-Maccabean preoccupation with distinctions between sacred and profane times to salvation history past, as but 'a shadow' of things to come (Rom. 14.5; Col. 2.17).[84]

---

84. I am hardly the only one to connect Jesus' attitude toward the festal calendar with the later convictions and practices of his followers. Snyder describes Jesus as a 'calendric anarchist' and observes that 'the Jesus tradition kept the disdain for the Jewish calendar' (1999: 122).

Chapter 6

JESUS AND SACRED SPACE

> 'He who has not seen the temple in its full splendour has never seen a beautiful building.'
>
> *b. Suk.* 51b; *b. B. Bat.* 4a
>
> 'I tell you, something greater than the temple is here.'
>
> Matthew 12.6

On July 19, 390 BCE, the Gauls sacked Rome and set building after building ablaze for several days, until the city was half ruined. After the heroic Roman dictator Marcus Furius Camillus had finally expelled the Gauls from the city, the populace, encouraged by the tribunes, favored abandoning the ruins entirely and migrating some ten miles north, to the newly won city of Veii. Camillus and the senate, however, would have no part of it. The victorious general's speech swiftly reversed the tide of public opinion:

> 'We have a city founded with all due rites of auspice and augury; not a stone of her streets but is permeated by our sense of the divine; for our annual sacrifices not the days only are fixed but the places too, where they may be performed: men of Rome, would you desert your gods—the tutelary spirits which guard your families, and those the nation prays to as its saviours?' (Livy 5.52.2-3).

The people were easily persuaded and Rome was rebuilt.[1] We should have expected as much. Ancestral connections between a people, their religion, and sacred space are deeply embedded in the collective memories of persons in traditional societies.[2] This was the case for Rome and the descendents of

---

1. The story is essentially a legend that the Romans accepted as history as early as the second century BCE. Livy, for example, from whom the above citation has been taken, honored Camillus's death, some twenty-five years after the Gallic invasion, with a laudatory obituary, declaring him the second founder of Rome (after Romulus) (Champlin [2003: 196-97]).

2. For the intersection of space and religion in Roman ideology, see Price (1996). On Odysseus and his sense of belonging to Ithaca, see Riches (2000: 8-9). The Jews were unusual among ancient Mediterranean peoples in having only one cult site. Among the Greeks, for example, each city had its own patron deity and its own temple. Jews had a single god with a single temple. This reality served sociologically to unite Judeans across

168   *Jesus and the People of God*

Romulus. And it was also the case for the descendants of Abraham with their holy land and their temple in Jerusalem.

1. *Territoriality and the Cultic Topography of the Jerusalem Temple*

It is helpful to consider the idea of sacred space under the broader rubric of territoriality. Cultural anthropologists have given much attention in recent decades to the function of territoriality among social groups. Sack characterizes it as follows:

> Territoriality will be defined as the attempt by an individual or group to affect, influence, or control people, phenomena, and relationships, by delimiting and asserting control over a geographic area.[3]

Note, in particular, the social component of territoriality, as outlined in the above definition. Such attempts 'to affect, influence, or control people, phenomena, and relationships' typically manifest themselves in three ways: (1) classification of places, (2) communication of this classification, and (3) control of the places so classified. As we might expect, the strategies related to territoriality become actualized in culturally specific beliefs and social practices.

Second-Temple Judeans boasted a highly elaborate system of classification where sacred space was concerned, and much energy was expended to communicate and preserve this map of territorial purity in the context of foreign occupation. The Mishnah outlines 'ten degrees of holiness', in a passage that warrants extended citation:

> The Land of Israel is holier than any other land. Wherein lies its holiness? In that from it they may bring the *Omer*, the Firstfruits, and the Two Loaves, which they may not bring from any other land.
>   The walled cities [of the Land of Israel] are still more holy, in that they must send forth the lepers from their midst; moreover they may carry around

---

the empire (Bohak [1999]). See Kugel for the increased association among Judeans of a sacred people with sacred space during the Second-Temple period. Kugel attributes such changes to 'the problems of self-definition inherent in the geopolitics of postexilic Judea' (1996: 28).

   3. Sack (1986: 19). See also R. Taylor (1988) and Cresswell (1996). Jackson and Henrie's definition of sacred space is representative:

> [T]hat portion of the earth's surface which is recognised by individuals or groups as worthy of devotion, loyalty or esteem. Sacred space is sharply distinguished from the non-sacred or profane world around it. Sacred space does not exist naturally, but is assigned sanctity as man defines, limits and characterises it through his culture, experience and goals (1983: 94).

For Jewish conceptions of sacred space, consult now Kunin (1998), noting, however, that Kunin's structuralist anthropological approach tends to neglect the importance of primary source data from ancient literature and archaeology.

a corpse therein wheresoever they will, but once it is gone forth [from the city] they may not bring it back.

Within the wall [of Jerusalem] is still more holy, for there [only] they may eat the Lesser Holy Things and the Second Tithe. The Temple Mount is still more holy, for no man or woman that has a flux, no menstruant, and no woman after childbirth may enter therein. The Rampart is still more holy, for no gentiles and none that have contracted uncleanness from a corpse may enter therein. The Court of the Women is still more holy, for none that had immersed himself the selfsame day [because of uncleanness] may enter therein, yet none would thereby become liable to a Sin-offering. The Court of the Israelites is still more holy, for none whose atonement is yet incomplete may enter therein, and they would thereby become liable to a Sin-offering. The Court of Priests is still more holy, for Israelites may not enter therein save only when they must perform the laying on of hands, slaughtering, and waving.

Between the Porch and the Altar is still more holy, for none that has a blemish or whose hair is unloosed may enter there. The Sanctuary is still more holy, for none may enter therein with hands and feet unwashed. The Holy of Holies is still more holy, for none may enter therein save only the High Priest on the Day of Atonement at the time of the [Temple-] service (*m. Kel.* 1.6-9).[4]

Religious authorities communicated this highly structured map of sacred space to their contemporaries in a variety of ways. Exposure to the Torah and scribal tradition in the home and the synagogue surely contributed much toward solidifying Jewish convictions concerning sacred space, particularly where Jerusalem and the temple were concerned. First-hand experiences of those who were able to attend the annual festivals in the capital likely proved even more effective in socializing young Judeans to embrace Judaism's 'ten degrees of [territorial] holiness' and to appreciate the significance of the temple for God's chosen people.[5]

Imagine, for example, the indelible impression left upon the mind of a young girl who accompanies her parents to Jerusalem for the first time, to offer a sacrifice on one of the high holy days of the Jewish calendar. Approaching the temple mount from afar, our young pilgrim is deeply

---

4. The connection between sacred space and sacred people is a recurring theme in the Mishnah (see, for example, *m. Ohal.* 18.7; *m. Hag.* 1.1).

5. The importance of the temple as the central Jewish institution of our period is reflected in its multitude of functions. In addition to serving as an administrative center and Judaism's cult site, the temple acted, according to Fuglseth,

> almost like a national bank and storage depot. It was a meeting place for the Sanhedrin, i.e. the civil and religious governing body, it served the function of study and teaching of the Law, the function of repository of funds and, in times of siege, the function of a citadel (2005: 118).

The temple also served, of course, as the territorial rallying point for annual festivals such as Sukkot and Passover (see the previous Chapter).

moved as she views first-hand the imposing physical symbol of her people's national identity. Josephus expounds on the external beauty of Herod's temple as follows:

> The exterior of the building wanted nothing that could astound either mind or eye. For, being covered on all sides with massive plates of gold, the sun was no sooner up than it radiated so fiery a flash that persons straining to look at it were compelled to avert their eyes, as from the solar rays. To approaching strangers it appeared from a distance like a snow-clad mountain; for all that was not overlaid with gold was of purest white (Josephus, *War* 5.222-23).

After making proper provisions for ceremonial purity, and spending the night in Jerusalem, the girl and her family ascend the temple mount early the following day and enter the expansive outer courtyard through a gate in the southern wall.[6] As she catches her first glimpse of the various components of the temple complex, our young Jewish pilgrim is suddenly confronted with a tangible expression, in stone and masonry, of the sacred spatial boundaries outlined in the Mishnah, above. She is also immediately struck by the fact that these various demarcations of sacred space—visibly manifest in the layout of the temple and powerfully dramatized in the sacrificial cult—correspond precisely to different classes of persons along a sacred-profane continuum. As can be seen in the citation from the Mishnah, permanent divisions between specific classes of persons (female/male, male/priest, priest/high-priest), and temporary distinctions that resulted from various kinds of impurity (menstruation, childbirth), delimited the 'territory' that a given person was permitted to frequent in and around the temple courts. The temple effectively functioned as 'a map for social relations'.[7]

The girl and her family would next traverse what was arguably the most important boundary line in the classification of Jewish sacred space, one decorated with an explicit series of warnings posted for the benefit of those whom it sought to exclude. I have in mind the rampart that separated the Court of the Gentiles from the inner courts and the temple structure itself, an imposing physical barricade marked with a series of pointed and unambiguous 'No Trespassing' signs. Josephus describes the rampart as 'a stone

---

6. Excavations near the temple mount, which have uncovered a large number of ritual baths (*miqwaoth*), speak directly to the issue of purification in association with a visit to the temple. Regev suggests that the baths attest to a 'special purity practice related to the Temple cult: an extra-purification of an already ritually pure person, before the entrance to the sacred domains of the Temple' (2005: 194). Regev is likely accurate in his assessment. For the whole priestly purity system of Israel seems designed to protect the holiness of the temple (Houston [1993: 245]), and it is quite clear that this cultic territoriality, as we might label it, became increasingly pronounced during the post-Maccabean period.

7. Fuglseth (2005: 118).

balustrade, three cubits high and of exquisite workmanship'. He proceeds to note,

> [I]n this at regular intervals stood slabs giving warning, some in Greek, others in Latin characters, of the law of purification, to wit that no foreigner was permitted to enter the holy place, for so the second enclosure of the temple was called (Josephus, *War* 5.194; see *Ant.* 15.417).

Archaeologists have unearthed two of Josephus's 'slabs', one fragmentary, the other virtually complete. Both are inscribed in Greek. The temple warning inscription reads as follows:

> No foreign-born person [ΑΛΛΟΓΕΝΗ] is to enter the protective enclosure around the temple; whoever does will have only himself to blame for the death that follows.[8]

As our young Jewish girl and her family cross this sacred boundary they are solemnly reminded in a most impressive way of their special status as descendants of Abraham.

Because of her gender our young pilgrim's journey has come to an end. After leaving foreigners behind, by crossing the balustrade that separates Jews from Gentiles, the youngster goes no further. She now remains in the Court of Women, watching from afar with her mother and sisters, as her father, accompanied by her brothers, enters the Court of the Israelites and, with the assistance of a Levite, reaches over the parapet into the Court of the Priests and slaughters the family's sacrificial victim.[9]

The drama is now complete. Family members retrace their steps across the boundaries demarcating varying degrees of territorial holiness, they leave the temple mount, and they return to their place of lodging somewhere in the expanse of greater Jerusalem. In the context of such an experience it would not take long for a Jewish young person to learn his or her place on the map of territorial purity in first-century Jerusalem. A festival or two would surely suffice.

The sociological significance of Jewish territoriality should not be missed. The warning inscription, along with the Mishnah's carefully articulated 'ten degrees of holiness', underscore the connection that obtained between sacred space and Jewish particularism, a connection that surfaced repeatedly in the writings of post-Maccabean authors surveyed in an earlier portion of this book.[10] As the evidence demonstrates, the increasing pre-

---

8. The translation is from Hanson and Oakman (1998: 140).
9. I am indebted to Sanders (1992: 112-14) for this imaginative scenario, though I have altered it significantly to emphasize distinctions between sacred and profane space.
10. Judeans found other ways to map out sacred space besides the model reflected in the Mishnah. *Jubilees,* as we saw, located the holy of holies in Eden, situated Zion in the 'midst

occupation with spatial demarcation which characterized post-Maccabean Jewish ideology was energized by a decidedly nationalistic agenda, with the result that distinctions between sacred and profane space were inextricably linked to corresponding distinctions between sacred and profane persons. To challenge the contours of Jewish territorialism, then, was to call into question related sociological distinctions between various classes of persons—distinctions that had come to determine the way in which the people of Yahweh defined themselves in the context of foreign occupation. We will now consider Jesus' prophecy of the destruction of the temple, his action in the temple courtyard, and his encounter with a Samaritan woman against this socio-historical background.

2. Predictions of the Temple's Destruction

References to the destruction of the Jerusalem temple are deeply embedded in the Jesus tradition.[11] The first occurs during Passion Week, before Jesus is arrested:

> 1 As he came out of the temple, one of his disciples said to him, 'Look, Teacher, what large stones and what large buildings!' 2 Then Jesus asked him, 'Do you see these great buildings? Not one stone will be left here upon another; all will be thrown down' (Mk 13.1-2).

of the navel of the earth', and identified Sinai as the third of three 'holy places' (8.19). The result is a map of sacred space that differs markedly from the 'ten degrees of holiness' outlined above. Riches has recently made much of this variety in Jewish approaches to the construction of sacred space (2000: 24-37). In connection with the present project I should like to underscore the following: (1) Differences aside, the mapping of sacred space reflected in *Jubilees* served much the same particularistic agenda as the Mishnah's temple-centered demarcations cited above (see, also, Magness [2002: 127-29] on the mapping of pure and impure space at Qumran). As Riches himself notes, the conscious adaptation of Ionian geography, combined with the intentional displacement of the 'navel' of the earth from Delphi to Zion, 'affirms that Israel's story is the central story of the world' (2000: 26). (2) *Jubilees'* vision of 'a triangle of three holy places' remained just that—a vision put forth in a creative and imaginative literary work, which had little connection with the actual topography of Roman Palestine. The Mishnah's tenfold territorial demarcation, in contrast, found expression in the physical layout of the land of Israel, the location of Jerusalem, and, especially, in the various portions of the temple structure itself. For Judeans in Palestine, life was actually lived—and social distinctions were vividly reinforced—in the context of this particular construction of Jewish sacred space, as illustrated by the recreated experience of our young pilgrim, outlined above.

11. The various premonitions and prophecies of the temple's destruction are summarized in Evans (1995). See Evans (2001) and the works he cites for arguments in favor of the historicity of Jesus' prediction (Evans [2001: 295, 298]; note also Dunn [2000: 4-5] and Edwards [2002: 388 n. 9]). Schlosser finds in Jesus' statements not the observations of an astute student of the times but, rather, the predictions of an eschatological prophet who envisions a day when 'le Temple ne sera plus car Dieu sera tout, en tous' (1990: 414).

Jesus' accusers proceed to reframe the prediction in terms of a threat at Jesus' trial before the Jewish leaders:

> 57 Some stood up and gave false testimony against him, saying, 58 'We heard him say, "I will destroy this temple that is made with hands, and in three days I will build another, not made with hands"' (Mk 14.57-58; par. Mt. 26.60-61).

The theme surfaces yet again during the crucifixion:

> 29 Those who passed by derided him, shaking their heads and saying, 'Aha! You who would destroy the temple and build it in three days, 30 save yourself, and come down from the cross!' (Mk 15.29-30; par. Mt. 27.40)

The tradition persisted, for Jesus' alleged threat to destroy the temple becomes an important bit of evidence in the condemnation of Stephen, early in the narrative of Acts:

> 13 They set up false witnesses who said, 'This man never stops saying things against this holy place and the law; 14 for we have heard him say that this Jesus of Nazareth will destroy this place and will change the customs that Moses handed on to us' (Acts 6.13-14).

And then there is John's version, theologically rich and more difficult to situate historically, since it is found near the beginning of John's narrative of Jesus' public ministry:

> 18 The Jews then said to him, 'What sign can you show us for doing this?' 19 Jesus answered them, 'Destroy this temple, and in three days I will raise it up'. 20 The Jews then said, 'This temple has been under construction for forty-six years, and will you raise it up in three days?' 21 But he was speaking of the temple of his body. 22 After he was raised from the dead, his disciples remembered that he had said this; and they believed the scripture and the word that Jesus had spoken (Jn 2.18-22).

Whole books have been written on the tradition history of these passages, and I will make no attempt here to revisit the debate. I cite the texts simply to emphasize the central role that Jesus' attitude toward the temple played during his life and ministry, as evidenced by the interest of the Gospel writers. Indeed, given the physical magnificence of Herod's massive project, and the centrality of the temple to Jewish nationalistic aspirations, it would be hard to imagine the leader of a first-century Jewish renewal movement failing to address the issue of the dwelling place of Yahweh in his efforts to articulate a vision for his followers. As the above passages indicate, Jesus does not disappoint in this regard, and his attitude toward the temple sheds much light upon Jesus' convictions about the distinctions between sacred and profane space which were etched into the socio-territorial map of post-Maccabean Judaism.

The association of the temple with Jewish identity has been amply demonstrated from the extra-biblical literature surveyed in previous chapters. A number of these authors wrote in the context of Maccabean expansionism, several generations before the time of Jesus, but it is quite evident that the cultural scripts and social codes reflected in these documents actively informed the worldview of first-century Judeans decades later. This is particularly the case where the centrality of Jerusalem and the temple are concerned. The Feast of Dedication (Hanukkah), for example, provided Jesus' contemporaries with a stirring annual reminder of the purification of the temple in 164 BCE, and of the ensuing military victories that ultimately garnered for the Maccabees and their followers independence from Syrian Greek hegemony.

Josephus's detailed narrative of the war with Rome further underscores the capacity of the temple to continue to function as an inspiring symbol for Jewish national aspirations, well out into the first century of the common era (66–70 CE). From the Jewish side, the final act determining the inevitability of war was the cessation of daily sacrifices for the welfare of the empire in 66 CE:

> Eleazar, son of Ananias the high-priest, a very daring youth, then holding the position of captain, persuaded those who officiated in the Temple services to accept no gift or sacrifice from a foreigner. This action laid the foundation for war with the Romans, for the sacrifices offered on behalf of that nation and the emperor were in consequence rejected (Josephus, *War* 2.409).[12]

And Jewish rebels chose the temple mount as the place to make their final stand against the Romans in the years that followed. The location of this concentration of Jewish resistance is primarily to be explained by the strategic position of the holy site, and by the fact that the Romans had ravaged much of Galilee and the countryside of Judea by 69–70 CE. Displaced peasants had nowhere else to flee. But more than pragmatics was involved. Pious Jews genuinely believed that God inhabited the temple, and many clung to the hope that the structure 'would yet be saved by Him who dwelt therein' (Josephus, *War* 5.459). Surely Yahweh would intercede on their behalf and grant them victory over their Roman adversaries, as they took their stand on his sacred temple mount.

Various charismatic figures fanned the flames of such expectations by promising divine deliverance during the extended siege. Josephus brands these self-proclaimed prophets as charlatans, and he charges them with complicity in the death of his fellow Jews at the hands of the Romans. We can be confident, however, that Josephus's narrative paints a reasonably

---

12. The incident was 'the first action connected with the revolt which was independently undertaken by the Jews and expressed public rejection of the Romans' (McLaren [1991: 169, see 169-72]).

accurate picture of the expectations of the masses, as they looked to Yahweh to intervene on behalf of his people and his sacred temple:

> [A large number of Jews] owed their destruction to a false prophet, who had on that day proclaimed to the people in the city that God commanded them to go up to the temple court, to receive there the tokens of their deliverance. Numerous prophets, indeed, were at this period suborned by the tyrants to delude the people, by bidding them await help from God, in order that desertions might be checked and that those who were above fear and precaution might be encouraged by hope. In adversity man is quickly persuaded; but when the deceiver actually pictures release from prevailing horrors, then the sufferer wholly abandons himself to expectation (Josephus, *War* 6.285-87).

Indeed, the Jewish people had a vibrant historical precedent to affirm their 'hope' and 'expectation' that God would intervene on their behalf. According to Maccabean historiography Yahweh had mightily aided the ancestral heroes of those who were now surrounded by the Romans, when Judas and his army defeated the Syrian Greeks and rededicated the temple in 164 BCE. Maccabean ideology thus offered much encouragement to those who took their final stand in the temple complex in 70 CE: 'For he who has his dwelling in heaven watches over that place himself and brings it aid, and he strikes and destroys those who come to do it injury' (2 Macc. 3.39).[13]

Hope for divine intervention proved fruitless in 70 CE, however, as the Romans forced their way into the temple complex and brutally suppressed every vestige of Jewish resistance. The mopping-up operation of the Roman general Titus, after he had conquered his Jewish adversaries, reveals a sensitivity to Jewish territorialism on the Roman side. Titus was apparently well aware of the symbolic importance of Jerusalem and her temple for Jewish national identity. After totally defeating the Jews ('the army now having no victims either for slaughter or plunder' [Josephus, *War* 7.1]), and burning Jerusalem and the sanctuary proper (Josephus, *War* 6.250-66), one would think that the Roman general's task would have been complete. Titus apparently felt the need, however, to undertake further territorial deconstruction. Josephus informs us that

> Caesar ordered the whole city and the temple to be razed to the ground... All the rest of the wall encompassing the city was so completely leveled to the ground as to leave future visitors to the spot no ground for believing that it had ever been inhabited (Josephus, *War* 7.1-4).[14]

---

13. Elsewhere 2 Maccabees refers to 'appearances that came from heaven to those who fought bravely for Judaism' (2.21). Thus, Schwartz, writing about the temple during the siege, observes that 'it was theologically reasonable (although in fact suicidal) to suppose that it 'would be saved by Him who resides in it' (*BJ* 5.459)' (1992: 34-35). Apparently, less successful encounters with pagan aggressors in history past—the sieges of the Babylonians and Pompey come to mind—were easily forgotten.

14. Josephus's attempt to excuse Titus from responsibility for the burning of the

The best explanation for Titus's decision to utterly destroy Jerusalem and her temple lies in the Roman general's appreciation of the potential for these tangible territorial badges of Jewish identity to inspire revolutionary sentiments. Josephus, in fact, directly appends to the above description a comment that seems to point to just such a consideration on Titus's part: 'Such was the end to which the frenzy of revolutionaries brought Jerusalem, that splendid city of worldwide renown' (Josephus, *War* 7.4). To stamp out, once and for all, aspirations for Jewish independence, Titus felt compelled to eradicate every trace of Jerusalem and her temple. So strong was the connection in Jewish ideology between sacred space and national identity.[15]

The carrying out of Titus's orders likely occupied a considerable amount of time, perhaps even years. The project was a daunting one and was never completed in its entirety. It is not hard to see why. Herod's massive rebuilding of the temple had involved hundreds of workers laboring for decades, and the task was still incomplete at the time of Jesus, some fifty years after it had begun. Excavations now give us an idea of the magnitude of the task involved in the construction—and destruction—of such an edifice. Herod had enlarged the temple precincts to encompass a thirty-five acre enclosure equivalent to the square footage of some twelve football fields. The vertical dimensions of the complex were equally impressive. The southeast corner of the retaining wall stretched nearly fifteen stories from the Kidron Valley below. Josephus claims that the stones used in the walls were forty cubits in length. He exaggerates only slightly. Stones found north of Wilson's arch measure 42 ft × 11 × 14 and weigh more than a million pounds. The greater temple structure exceeded in size any other temple in the ancient world.[16] Little wonder that one of Jesus' disciples was sufficiently awed by the edifice to cry out, 'Look, Teacher, what large stones and what large buildings!' (Mk 13.1).

The buildings were, indeed, as impressive as the stones that supported them.[17] The magnificence of the complex renders Jesus' response to the disciple's exclamation all the more striking: 'Do you see these great buildings? Not one stone will be left here upon another; all will be thrown down' (Mk 13.2). Evans's commentary on the verse is quite on the mark:

---

sanctuary proper (Josephus, *War* 6.250-66) makes for entertaining reading but is hardly credible. It is in Josephus's interest to exonerate his patron, and the author's *tendenz*, in this regard, is never more apparent than it is in this portion of his narrative.

15. Keener explains the transfer of the temple tax along similar lines: 'Probably partly because the Romans found revolutionary potential in such ethnic ties of geographical loyalty, they eventually diverted the didrachma tax once used for the temple's upkeep' (2003: 1.615).

16. Edwards (2002: 387).

17. Josephus describes the temple extensively in his *Jewish War* (5.184-247) and *Antiquities* (15.391-402).

Jesus' prophecy is so stunning because it was occasioned by the disciple's admiration of the massive stones and large, impressive buildings. Such sturdy stonework and impressive architecture surely inspired a sense of permanence, not impending catastrophe.[18]

I would only add that the sense of permanence to which Evans refers would certainly have extended, in the minds of Jesus' contemporaries, to a confidence in the permanence of that which the temple symbolized, namely, the identity of Abraham's offspring as the particular people of Yahweh. Social anthropologists underscore the power of symbols, in this regard—especially visual ones—to 'reach and trigger' the 'nonrational core' of national identity among members of an ethnic group.[19] Schwartz thus speaks about a 'conjunction of holy race and holy place', and his categorical assertion about the problematic nature of the temple as a national symbol in the context of Roman occupation bears repeating in the present connection:

> *The central problem of the Second-Temple period was the contradiction between the existence of the Temple in Jerusalem, which seemed to be the palace of a sovereign in the capital of his state, and the fact of foreign sovereignty.*[20]

Understood in concert with the manner in which Jesus relativized other symbols of Jewish national identity, the prediction of the temple's destruction points to a desire on Jesus' part to renegotiate the boundary between Israel and the nations, a desire expressed most dramatically in Jesus' action in the temple court, as narrated in Mk 11.15-18.

3. Jesus' Action in the Temple

Few gospel stories have attracted as much attention in recent years as Jesus' action in the temple, an event related, in various forms, by all four evangelists (Mt. 21.12-13; Mk 11.15-18; Lk. 19.45-46; Jn 2.14-17). I will focus here upon Mark's version:

> 15 Then they came to Jerusalem. And he entered the temple and began to drive out those who were selling and those who were buying in the temple, and he overturned the tables of the money changers and the seats of those who sold doves; 16 and he would not allow anyone to carry anything through the temple. 17 He was teaching and saying, 'Is it not written,
> "My house shall be called a house of prayer for all the nations"?
> But you have made it a den of robbers.'
> 18 And when the chief priests and the scribes heard it, they kept looking for a way to kill him; for they were afraid of him, because the whole crowd was spellbound by his teaching (Mk 11.15-18).

18. Evans (2001: 299).
19. Connor (1994: 205).
20. Schwartz (1992: 9-10, author's italics).

As has rightly been acknowledged, the narrative is of great consequence for understanding the aims of Jesus and the immediate reasons for his crucifixion. The history of scholarship on the temple incident, however, is quite complex and replete with nuanced and often conflicting interpretations of a number of aspects of the account. At the risk of oversimplification, reconstructions of Jesus' intentions can be divided into two basic categories:[21]

1. *Reform*—Jesus intended to challenge practices that he deemed incongruent with Yahweh's intentions for temple polity and the function of the sacrificial system.[22]

2. *Destruction*—Jesus' action was symbolic and portended the destruction of the temple.

Restorationist (*Reform*) readings dominated the scholarly landscape until the publication of Sanders's volume, *Jesus and Judaism*, in 1985. Sanders summarized his interpretation as follows:

> [W]e conclude that Jesus publicly predicted or threatened the destruction of the temple, that the statement was shaped by his expectation of the arrival of the eschaton, that he probably also expected a new temple to be given by God from heaven, and that he made a demonstration which prophetically symbolized the coming event.[23]

The final statement in the quotation pertains to Jesus' action in the temple. Like Israel's prophets, who often acted out their verbal predictions in symbolically colorful ways, Jesus' behavior constituted the dramatic enactment of convictions reflected in statements made elsewhere, where Jesus explicitly predicted the destruction of the temple. Sanders wholly excludes the reform of current practices from Jesus' intentions: 'I think we should drop the discussion of Jesus' action as one concerned with purifying the worship

---

21. For a succinct but thorough survey of the 'bewildering variety' of scholarly explanations of the temple action see Wedderburn (2006: 2-5), who similarly divides into two broad categories the various interpretations of Jesus' action: (1) a 'cleansing' of some sort; (2) a prophetic sign symbolizing the temple's destruction. Ådna (2000: 334-430) and Metzdorf (2003: 182-242) should be consulted for much more extensive overviews of scholarship. Not addressed in my discussion, above, is the view that the story has been created by the evangelists or their sources and has, therefore, no claim to authenticity in the life of the historical Jesus. The position is held by Mack (1988: 291-92); Buchanan (1991); Miller (1991); and Seeley (1993; 2000).

22. I have purposely avoided the traditional expression 'cleansing'. The term has the potential to be quite ambiguous, since the priests were those charged with maintaining the cultic purity of the temple, and Jesus was not a priest (Betz [1997: 459]). Expressions such as 'restoration' or 'reform' more accurately describe the critique of temple polity reflected in viewpoint #1, above.

23. Sanders (1985: 75).

of God... He did not wish to purify the temple, either of dishonest trading or of trading in contrast to 'pure' worship'.[24]

Sanders's seminal contribution has engendered a lively and prolific discussion in the literature, and for this we remain in his debt. The strength of the reading lies in the coherence that results between the temple action, as understood by Sanders, and Jesus' prediction of the destruction of the sacred site, discussed above. In the final analysis, however, the interpretation fails fully to persuade.[25] I believe Sanders is correct to find in Jesus' behavior a symbolic prediction of the temple's destruction, and I will return to this idea below. But Sanders is wrong to exclude from the incident a critique of current temple administration. As I will seek to demonstrate, it was Jesus' profound distaste for what he perceived to be a corrupt and socially exclusive temple polity which elicited the threat of destruction symbolized by his striking action in the temple court.

Much of the dispute revolves around the highly debated tradition history of the pericope, and one's interpretation of the incident inevitably turns upon his or her view of the authenticity of various portions of Mk 11.15-18. It is difficult, for example, to exclude some kind of critique of current temple polity on Jesus' part, if one views the teaching in v. 17 as historical. For this reason Sanders must assign the verse to the creation of later church tradents who, in his view, wish to downplay Jesus' predictions of the temple's destruction and instead portray the temple action in reformist terms. Others are more optimistic about tracing nearly all of the narrative back to the historical Jesus, and it is this perspective on the tradition history of the text which I will adopt in the present connection.[26]

A portion of the Old Testament citation which Sanders dismisses as unhistorical in fact supports his assertion that Jesus intended his action in the temple to symbolize its coming destruction. The excerpt in view (Mk 11.17b) comes from Jer. 7.11: 'Has this house, which is called by my name,

---

24. Sanders (1985: 68, 75). Sanders does not think Jesus rejected the sacrificial system as such. Rather, Jesus likely envisioned a new eschatological temple to replace Herod's temple that was to be destroyed (1985: 75).

25. See Evans (1989b) for a persuasive critique of Sanders's view.

26. Paesler surveys in some detail the various viewpoints surrounding the historicity of Jesus' Old Testament citations in Mk 11.17 (1999: 234-45). Those who take a positive view of the quotations include Bauckham (1988: 81-83), Evans (1989a; 1989b; 1993: 107 n. 48), Wright (1996: 418-20), Betz (1997), and, especially, Casey (1997: 316-19). Theissen (1991: 261) and Marcus (1992: 450-52) reject the authenticity of the citations and locate their *Sitz em Leben* later, during the Jewish War. But see Crossley's critique of this position (2004: 72).

As Catchpole insightfully notes, public explanations consistently accompany the commonly cited analogies to Jesus' symbolic prophetic action among the Hebrew prophets (Isa. 20.1-6; Jer. 19.1-9, 11-15; 27.1-15; Ezek. 12.1-16). We should expect the same of Jesus' action in the temple (Catchpole [2006: 265]).

become a den of robbers in your sight? You know, I too am watching, says the LORD'. Consider the ensuing context of Jeremiah's prophecy:

> 12 Go now to my place that was in Shiloh, where I made my name dwell at first, and see what I did to it for the wickedness of my people Israel. 13 And now, because you have done all these things, says the LORD, and when I spoke to you persistently, you did not listen, and when I called you, you did not answer, 14 therefore I will do to the house that is called by my name, in which you trust, and to the place that I gave to you and to your ancestors, just what I did to Shiloh (Jer. 7.12-14).

Shiloh was one of the places where the tabernacle and the ark of the covenant had been located before the building of a permanent temple structure in Jerusalem (Judg. 18.31). Shiloh ultimately became a ruin, abandoned by God, due to the disobedience of the Israelites (see Ps 78.60). Jeremiah, of course, draws upon the Shiloh tradition as he threatens Jerusalem and her temple with impending doom at the hands of the Babylonians. If Jesus intended his listeners to make the connection between Jer. 7.11 and its ensuing context, he may, indeed, have implicitly threatened the destruction of the temple.[27] The correlation of the thrust of Jeremiah 7 with the meaning of Jesus' symbolic action, as understood by Sanders, suggests that this was precisely the case.

It remains to determine why Jesus viewed the temple in such negative terms, and here is where certain aspects of a restorationist reading of the text prove quite illuminating. Given popular dissatisfaction with priestly leaders and current temple polity, amply documented for our period, we do well to assume with the traditional understanding that Jesus in Mk 11.15-16 is deeply troubled by abusive or otherwise unacceptable practices on the part of those who controlled temple activities.[28] Even among commentators

---

27. Supporting the assumption that Jesus expected his audience to make this connection is an allusion to Jeremiah 7 made by another Jesus, a certain 'son of Ananias', who predicted the destruction of Jerusalem and the temple at the Feast of Booths in 62 CE: 'A voice from the east, a voice from the west, a voice from the four winds; a voice against Jerusalem and the sanctuary, a voice against the bridegroom and the bride, a voice against all the people!' (Josephus, *War* 6.301; see Jer. 7.34).

Jesus himself may have explicitly made the connection between Jer. 7.11 and the ensuing Shiloh imagery in Jeremiah's prophecy. The excerpts from Isaiah and Jeremiah, as presented in Mk 11.17, surely represent an abbreviated summary of more extensive teaching and interpretation of the temple action on Jesus' part. It is not improbable that Jesus further expounded upon the meaning of these Old Testament excerpts, and he may have done so by drawing attention to their broader literary contexts in the Hebrew Scriptures.

28. Evans cites a number of traditions lamenting priestly corruption, offering ample evidence for widespread reservations about current temple polity (1989a; 1992; see Betz's comments in this regard [1997: 460]). Schwartz's Hebrew University dissertation

6. *Jesus and Sacred Space*

who take a restorationist view of the incident, however, Jesus' actions have elicited a variety of interpretations, for it is no easy task to identify the import of the specific practices that Jesus disallows. Any reconstruction of current temple administration, and of Jesus' corresponding intentions, must therefore remain somewhat tentative. Several considerations, however, point us in a direction that coheres quite well with the attitudes of Jesus toward sacred space and Jewish nationalism evidenced elsewhere in the Gospels.

The citation of Isa. 56.7 provides the most immediate window through which to consider what might have motivated Jesus symbolically to threaten the destruction of the temple: 'My house shall be called a house of prayer for all the nations' (Mk 11.17a). The Old Testament context is highly illuminating:

> 6 And the foreigners who join themselves to the LORD,
>   to minister to him, to love the name of the LORD,
>   and to be his servants,
> all who keep the sabbath, and do not profane it,
>   and hold fast my covenant—
> 7 these I will bring to my holy mountain,
>   and make them joyful in my house of prayer;
> their burnt offerings and their sacrifices
>   will be accepted on my altar;
> for my house shall be called a house of prayer
>   for all peoples (Isa. 56.6-7).

The portion of the text Jesus quotes (56.7c) functions in the context of Isaiah as the conclusion to a striking eschatological discourse in which the prophet envisions a day when 'foreigners' will join the descendants of Abraham worshipping and sacrificing to Yahweh in the Jerusalem temple. Given Jesus' citation of this summary statement, it is reasonable to conclude (a) that Jesus sought (in some terms) the realization of Isaiah's vision and (b) that his behavior in the temple courtyard expressed his displeasure with those aspects of current practice which, in his view, conflicted with the prophecy. But can we be more specific? Which aspects of Isaiah's vision were being compromised, and how do these relate to Jesus' actions in the temple?

We begin with the money changers. Jacob Neusner has recently applied his noteworthy erudition as a rabbinics scholar to identifying the function of the money changers in Herod's temple. Two texts from the Mishnah and the Tosefta, respectively, shed much light on the issue. The Mishnah reads as follows:

---

also includes a number of these sources (1979: 14-35). The Roman period, in particular, saw an escalation in criticism of the ruling priesthood's morality (Schwartz [1992: 39]).

> On the 15th thereof (Adar, before Nisan) the tables [of the money-changers] were set up in the provinces; and on the 25th thereof they were set up in the temple. After they were set up in the temple they began to exact pledges (of those who had not paid). From whom did they exact pledges? From levites, Israelites, proselytes, and freed slaves, but not from women, slaves, or minors (*m. Sheq.* 1.3).

> Although they have said, 'They do not exact pledges from women, slaves, or minors', if they paid the Shekel it is accepted of them; but if a gentile or a Samaritan paid the Shekel it is not accepted of them (*m. Sheq.* 1.5).

The Tosefta expounds upon the teachings of the Mishnah:

> A. *Once they were set up in the temple, they began to exact pledges from those who had not yet paid [M. Sheqalim 1.3C].*
> B. They exact pledges from Israelites for their sheqels, so that the public offerings might be made [paid for] by using their funds.
> C. This is like a man who got a sore on his foot, and the doctor has to force it and cut off his flesh so as to heal him. Thus did the Holy One, blessed be he, exact a pledge from Israelites for the payment of their sheqels, so that the public offerings might be made out of their funds.
> D. For public offerings appease and effect atonement between Israel and their father in heaven.
> E. Likewise we find of the heave-offering of sheqels which the Israelites paid in the wilderness, as it is said, 'And you shall take the atonement money from the people of Israel and shall appoint it for the service of the tent of meeting, that it may bring the people of Israel to remembrance before the Lord, so as to make atonement for yourselves' (Exod. 30.16) (*t. Sheq.* 1.6).[29]

The money changers thus exchanged diverse coinage for the shekels required for the temple tax, a tax which, in turn, provided for the daily public offerings on behalf of the people.[30] The offering, however, and the tax that supported it, related only to ethnic Jews and proselytes. Neusner summarizes the above excerpts from rabbinic literature as follows:

---

29. The Mishnah translation, as elsewhere, is Danby's. The translation of the Tosefta is from Neusner (1989: 288). Neusner is convinced of a 'wide circulation in the first century' of the convictions reflected in these early rabbinic texts (1989: 289). Richardson concurs (2004: 245).

30. I am assuming throughout the necessity of the service provided by the money changers and those who traded in sacrificial animals (Sanders 1985: 65; Neusner 1989: 289; Richardson 2004: 243). Jesus was not opposed to these activities as such. Nor do I think that Jesus' action was directed against the use of Tyrian coinage with its pagan symbols (Richardson [1992]; Murphy-O'Connor [2000]). As Richardson himself notes, there is 'no explicit evidence' that Judeans viewed the Tyrian coinage in negative terms (1992: 518). See the critique in Wedderburn (2006: 2 n. 5).

6. *Jesus and Sacred Space* 183

The explicit explanation of the payment of the half-sheqel, therefore, is that it allowed all Israelites to participate in the provision of the daily whole-offering, which accomplished atonement for sin on behalf of the holy people as a whole. That explains why gentiles and Samaritans may not pay the sheqel, while women, slaves, or minor Israelites may do so. *For gentiles and Samaritans do not form part of 'Israel', and therefore are unaffected by the expiation accomplished by the daily whole offering.*[31]

For our purposes it is important to note that the exclusion of Gentiles and Samaritans from participation in the atoning sacrifices of the temple flies in the face of the portion of Isaiah 56 which immediately precedes the excerpt cited by Jesus in Mk 11.17:

> their (foreigners') burnt offerings and their sacrifices
>   will be accepted on my altar;
> for my house shall be called a house of prayer
>   for all peoples (Isa. 56.7b-c).

Isaiah envisions a day when the offerings of 'foreigners' will be accepted by Yahweh on the altar of his temple.[32] In Jesus' day 'foreigners' were, in contrast, excluded from participation in the daily sacrifices, and the role of the money changers in the temple was central to these daily offerings on behalf of ethnic Israel.[33] I suspect, then, that we should explain the debacle with the money changers by assuming that Jesus was angered by this incongruity between Isaiah's vision and current practice. It is interesting, in this regard, that the word translated 'foreigner' in Isaiah 56 is the same word used to refer to Gentiles in the Greek versions of the warning inscription

---

31. Neusner (1989: 289, my italics). From here on I wholly depart from Neusner's ensuing interpretation of the temple action. Neusner utilizes the rabbinic background to interpret Jesus' action in a rather iconoclastic and ultimately unpersuasive way. He joins Sanders in seeing the destruction of the temple symbolized in Jesus' action. For Neusner, though, there will be no replacement temple, and the symbolism is more specific. The turning over of the tables of the money changers points to the exchange of the daily whole-offering at the temple for the Eucharistic table of Jesus: 'one table overturned, another table set up in place, and both for the same purpose of atonement and expiation of sin' (290). Neusner's proposal, though homiletically attractive, has not been warmly embraced (see Buchanan [1991: 285]; and Casey [1997: 322]).

32. In both the MT and the LXX, the statement is closely tied to what follows (the portion of the text Jesus cites):

> their burnt offerings and their sacrifices
>   will be accepted on my altar;
> for (MT: כִּי; LXX: γάρ) my house shall be called a house of prayer
>   for all peoples. (Isa. 56.7)

33. Consult Schwartz (1992: 102-16) for a careful study of sacrifices by Gentiles during the Second-Temple period.

which graced the rampart of the temple (ἀλλογενής, LXX Isa. 56.3, 6). This leads us, then, to a further consideration, namely, the location of Jesus' striking action among the various portions of sacred real estate that defined the temple complex.[34]

Given the reference to the 'house of prayer for all nations', the setting for the incident can be none other than the Court of the Gentiles, the outermost court of the temple, which 'was open to all, foreigners included' (Josephus, *Ag. Ap.* 2.103). The irony of money-changers making provisions in the Court of the Gentiles for daily offerings that effected expiation for Jews alone must not be missed. The location of the activity may, in fact, have been somewhat recent. It has been suggested that Jesus' actions were motivated by the policies of Caiaphas who, driven by financial and political considerations, moved the selling of sacrificial animals and the exchanging of money into the temple courtyard for the first time in 30 CE.[35] Such specificity, date-wise, remains highly conjectural, and it is unnecessary, in any case.[36] The location of the money-changing and trade in animals remains relatively novel, since Herod's rebuilding program involved the dramatic expansion of the Court of the Gentiles, as well as the addition of surrounding porticoes, which are the obvious place for the kind of trading reflected in Mk 11.15.[37] This back-

---

34. Sanders asserts, wrongly I think, that the Court of the Gentiles 'should be seen as coincidental and not determinative for the meaning of the event' (Sanders 1985: 68). My argument throughout depends upon an analysis of Jesus' own interpretation of his temple action in Mk 11.17, a text Sanders excludes from consideration as non-historical. The inevitable result is two markedly different assessments of the relative importance of the Gentiles to Jesus' temple action. See Davies for a reading of the text which properly gives weight to the significance of the location of the events in the Court of the Gentiles (1974: 350-51). Older commentators who understood Jesus to be expressing concern for the Gentiles include Lightfoot (1950: 60-65) and Jeremias (1982/1958).

35. Eppstein (1964).

36. See Evans's reservations (1989b: 266-67), and Wedderburn's discussion of Eppstein's proposal (2006: 11-13).

37. Casey (1997: 309). Ancient Mediterranean cultures—socially and religiously conservative, and slow to embrace any alteration of long-held traditions—would tend to view as innovative any change occurring in recent generations. In the present connection, modifications of temple polity which resulted from Herod's rebuilding program would continue to qualify as 'relatively novel' during the time of Jesus. Betz's analysis of Herod's temple, as an act of monumentalization which mimicked Augustus's building agenda in Rome, may be profitably consulted in this connection (1997: 462-65). With respect to the novelty of the Herodian project, Betz remarks,

> There was no denying it: the old cult had been abolished with Zerubbabel's Temple. The new Temple had acquired new functions: It was now Herod's Temple, a divine manifestation of Herodian legitimacy (15 §425), built to his 'eternal remembrance' (15 §380)...the Temple cult thus politicized and commercialized... (Betz [1997: 465, citing Josephus, *Ant.* 15.267-425 throughout]).

ground, along with the forcefulness of Jesus' actions and the citation of Isa. 56.7, suggest that Jesus was troubled by more than monetary extortion or other financial abuses on the part of those overseeing the buying and selling of sacrificial animals. He likely wanted the whole operation removed from the Court of the Gentiles.[38] It was the relationship of the Gentiles to Yahweh that was at the forefront of Jesus' mind.

A related passage from the Hebrew Scriptures supports this understanding. Zechariah 14.21b asserts that 'there shall no longer be traders in the house of the LORD of hosts on that day'. The statement occurs in a prophecy that portrays all of the nations going up to Jerusalem to celebrate the Feast of Booths. The text thus corresponds thematically with Isaiah 56 in its emphasis upon the inclusion of Gentiles in Jewish temple worship. Jesus does not directly cite Zechariah 14, however, and we must exercise caution in utilizing the prophecy to shed light on his temple action. As noted in the previous chapter, though, the text was central to the Feast of Tabernacles during the time of Jesus, and was likely read aloud in a public setting during the celebration of the festival. Zechariah 14 may have been more immediately familiar to Jesus' audience, therefore, than some modern writers want to assume.[39] It is not implausible to surmise that onlookers made a connection between Jesus' driving out of the traders and Zechariah's prophecy, given the public use of the text at Booths and the thematic connection between Zechariah 14 and the Isaianic passage that Jesus did choose to cite.

Consider, as well, Mark's observation that Jesus 'would not allow anyone to carry anything through the temple' (v. 16). As Casey notes, the prohibition coheres entirely with the removal of the traders in that it 'defends the sacred space of the house of God'.[40] It does so, however, in a rather subver-

---

Josephus claims that the populace responded positively to the new temple (*Ant.* 15.421). Yet, as we know from the activities of John the Baptist, Jesus, and Qumran, such feelings were hardly universal.

38. So Casey (1997: 309-10). I am not under the illusion that Jesus effectively stopped the money changing or the trade necessary for temple activities. Nor was he ultimately successful in his efforts to forbid 'anyone to carry anything through the temple' (v. 16). Jesus' actions likely resulted in but a brief—yet notable—interruption of the daily routine in the Court of the Gentiles during Passover week. Here, then, I agree with Sanders that Jesus' gesture was 'intended to make a point rather than to have a concrete result; that is, [onlookers] would have seen the action as symbolic' (Sanders 1985: 70).

39. Seeley, for example, 'doubts that this snippet from Zechariah by itself had so much clarity and familiarity during Jesus' day that he could be motivated by it and then rely on it to create the proper context of interpretation' (1993: 268). Those who argue in favor of a connection between the temple action and Zech. 14.21b include Roth (1960), Evans (1989b: 252), and Paesler (1999: 248).

40. Casey (1997: 310). Betz surmises that people were using the temple area 'as a shortcut for getting from one side of town to the other' (1997: 457). For a prohibition of

sive way, given the function of the rampart that kept Gentiles out of Jewish space in the temple complex (see above). Josephus informs us, in an interesting parallel to Mk 11.16, that 'no vessel whatever might be carried into the temple' (*Ag. Ap.* 2.106). In Josephus it is the Holy Place of the temple building proper which is in view, as the ensuing context demonstrates. In our narrative Jesus essentially extends this prohibition from the sanctuary proper out into the Court of the Gentiles. In doing so, Jesus emphasizes the sacredness of the Court and, thereby, pointedly undermines current conceptions of sacred space—conceptions that had established markedly different degrees of territorial holiness on opposite sides of the balustrade that separated Jew from Gentile in the Jerusalem temple.

It remains briefly to reconsider the second portion of the Old Testament citation in Mk 11.17: 'But you have made it a den of robbers'. As we saw above, the ensuing context of Jeremiah 7 strongly suggests that Jesus had the destruction of the temple in view in his citation of the text, and this coheres nicely with the symbolic import of the temple action, as correctly understood by Sanders. Here I wish to consider what the phrase 'den of robbers' might contribute to our understanding of the particular abuses that elicited Jesus' displeasure with current temple polity in the first place.

Many have sought to interpret 'den of robbers' against the preceding context of Jeremiah 7, which contains an extended denouncement of a number of practices that offended Yahweh:

> 5 'For if you truly amend your ways and your doings, if you truly act justly one with another, 6 if you do not oppress the alien, the orphan, and the widow, or shed innocent blood in this place, and if you do not go after other gods to your own hurt, 7 then I will dwell with you in this place, in the land that I gave of old to your ancestors forever and ever. 8 Here you are, trusting in deceptive words to no avail. 9 Will you steal, murder, commit adultery, swear falsely, make offerings to Baal, and go after other gods that you have not known, 10 and then come and stand before me in this house, which is called by my name, and say, "We are safe!"—only to go on doing all these abominations? 11 Has this house, which is called by my name, become a den of robbers in your sight? You know, I too am watching', says the LORD (Jer. 7.5-11).

Commentators have traditionally assumed that Jesus cited Jer. 7.11 to censure unfair trading practices occurring in the temple courtyard under the approval of high-priestly families who likely profited from such activities.[41] The assumption is supported by the presence, in the context of Jeremiah 7, above, of comments about oppression and theft (vv. 6, 9).

---

such behavior see *m. Ber.* 9.5 (Instone-Brewer also connects Mk 11.16 to this passage in the Mishnah [2004: 94]).

41. See, for example, Gundry (1993: 644-45) and Crossley (2004: 69). There is some evidence in the sources. Simon ben Gamaliel (c. 10–80 CE) was critical of what he perceived to be the exorbitant price of doves (*m. Ker.* 1.7).

A problem with this view relates to the term translated 'robbers' in Mk 11.17 (λῃστής), a word that refers not to swindlers or cheats but, rather, to brigands. The lexical objection proves to be a non-issue, however, for, as Evans appropriately notes, 'the citation of this prophetic text is more rhetorical than it is descriptive of what actually was going on'.[42] The first-century *Targum of Jeremiah*, for example, substitutes for the Hebrew text's 'den of robbers' the broader expression 'synagogue of the wicked', attesting to the lack of specificity with which Jesus' contemporaries often interpreted such phrases.[43] The point is simply that of temple corruption in general. Jesus is not implying that the Jewish leaders were actually operating as brigands. He is simply utilizing a familiar and colorful image to rebuke temple authorities for unacceptable behavior that remains unspecified in the image itself. This, however, opens up the possibility of tying the phrase 'den of robbers' not only to economic oppression, but to any number of abuses currently perpetrated by high-priestly elites who controlled temple polity.

To what temple corruption, then, is Jesus referring? It may well be the case that economic realities are in view, as a cursory reading of the incident might imply.[44] Yet, as demonstrated above, the citation of Isa. 56.7 (Mk 11.17a) suggests that Jesus' action against the money changers and the traffic in sacrificial animals was motivated by a desire to sanctify the Court of the Gentiles and thereby challenge current conceptions of sacred space, rather than by indignation at financial abuse on the part of the temple administration. And, as it turns out, the quotation of Jer. 7.11 likely points in the same direction. The context of the Old Testament passage, generally taken to favor an economic interpretation of Jesus' action in the temple court, can just as reasonably be cited in support of a socio-territorial understanding of the incident, since Jeremiah includes, at the very the beginning of his catalog of admonitions, a warning not to 'oppress the alien' (Jer. 7.6).

I suggest, then, that the corruption of temple activities referenced in the phrase 'den of robbers' points not to economic abuse at all but, rather, to perceived violations of God's intentions with respect to Gentile inclusion in the worship of Yahweh, as outlined in Isaiah 56.[45] According to this reading, Jesus accuses Jewish priestly leaders of criminally undermining the proper worship of Yahweh on the part of foreigners by defiling the Court of the

42. Evans (1989b: 268).
43. Hayward (1987: 70-71 n. 4). Hayward dates the *Tg. Jer.* to 'during, or slightly before, the first century AD' (1987: 38).
44. Evans thus offers evidence that 'the temple establishment of the first century was viewed by some Jews as corrupt and, specifically, guilty of robbery' (1993: 108). See also Evans (1989a).
45. Similarly, Bergler: 'die Charakterisierung "Räuberhöhle" die bisher dort geübte jüdische Exklusivität geisselt' (1998: 164).

Gentiles with commerce and money changing—this at the very moment in salvation history when Yahweh was working to fulfill Isaiah's vision. Jesus' action in the temple, in turn, symbolizes the destruction of the edifice that will result from continued resistance to God's kingdom program. The temple action (Mk 11.15-16), then, and Jesus' Old Testament quotations (v. 17) lend themselves to a single coherent interpretation.[46] The dominion of God is at hand, and the eschatological day foreseen by the prophet Isaiah has come to pass. It is now time to renegotiate the boundaries of Jewish territoriality which had excluded Gentiles from access to Yahweh in the Jerusalem temple.

As Betz has recently observed, '[I]n regard to the historical Jesus' own motivation for performing the [temple] act we can, with reason, discuss a number of options, none of them conclusively provable, but some of them highly probable'.[47] Given the complexities surrounding the interpretation of Mk 11.15-18, the details of the above analysis must remain somewhat conjectural, and I do not expect my readers to concur with my exegetical judgments at every turn. Nevertheless, I find it 'highly probable' (to adopt Betz's expression)—based upon Jesus' own interpretation of his temple action, as related in Mk 11.17—that Jesus offered a scathing critique of the way in which Gentiles were being marginalized by temple authorities, and that he warned of the destruction of the temple in view of such abuses. Jesus' forceful symbolic action in the Court of the Gentiles during his final week in Jerusalem thus constituted a direct affront to a stridently nationalistic polity on the part of temple authorities and, by extension, to the temple's function as the preeminent tangible symbol of Jewish identity in the Roman world.

4. *Neither on This Mountain Nor in Jerusalem*

In 35 CE a self-proclaimed prophet led an uprising of 'the Samaritan nation' against Roman rule. Josephus relates the following details:

---

46. As Wedderburn has recently emphasized, restorationist readings, on the one hand, and interpretations of Jesus' action as symbolizing the temple's impending destruction, on the other, are not mutually exclusive alternatives:

> As long as Jesus neither cleansed all evil from the cult nor really expected that the high-priestly authorities would repent and mend their ways, the threat and indeed expectation of judgement remained. The cleansing remained symbolic, an act that, like so many prophetic acts before it, would go unheeded and would therefore be followed by the disaster that the prophet foresaw... In other words, Jesus' action would be better described as warning of the need for cleansing *and* threatening destruction if that were not done (Wedderburn [2006: 14], author's italics).

Wedderburn, however, does not view the marginalization of Gentiles as a central target of Jesus' critique of temple polity.

47. Betz (1997: 456).

The Samaritan nation too was not exempt from disturbance. For a man who made light of mendacity and in all his designs catered to the mob, rallied them, bidding them to go in a body with him to Mount Gerizim, which in their belief is the most sacred of mountains. He assured them that on their arrival he would show them the sacred vessels which were buried there, where Moses had deposited them. His hearers, viewing this tale as plausible, appeared in arms. They posted themselves in a certain village named Tirathana, and, as they planned to climb the mountain in a great multitude, they welcomed to their ranks the new arrivals who kept coming (*Ant.* 18.85-86).

The ill-fated adventure was short-lived, for Pilate swiftly intercepted the Samaritan throng, killed 'the firstcomers' and 'the principal leaders', and put the rest of the pilgrims to flight.[48] For our purposes the colorful incident dramatically underscores the importance of Mount Gerizim for the Samaritans, who viewed the site—in contrast to the temple mount in Jerusalem—as 'the most sacred of mountains'.[49]

The Jewish–Samaritan debate over the proper place to worship Yahweh surfaces in early Christian literature in a familiar text in John's Gospel, where Jesus' approach to sacred space, and his corresponding attitude toward Jewish social boundaries, manifest themselves most transparently in an encounter with a Samaritan woman at the well of Jacob (John 4).[50] The story finds Jesus, weary during a journey from Judea to

---

48. The surviving Samaritans, in turn, lodged a protest with Vitellus, proconsul of Syria, and the debacle ultimately resulted in Pilate's recall to Rome (Josephus, *Ant.* 18.88-89). A generation later Samaritans took their stand to oppose the Romans not in Jerusalem but on Gerizim. Those who refused to surrender were slaughtered at the sacred site (Josephus, *War* 3.307-15).

49. Theissen appropriately finds in the actions of the Samaritan prophet an underlying anti-Judean polemic—the incident constitutes an attempt 'to demonstrate the sanctity of [Gerizim] over against the Jerusalem temple' (1998: 179). Elsewhere in his writings Josephus twice describes Alexandrian Jews and Samaritans quarreling over which temple is right for the worship of God (*Ant.* 12.10; 13.74-79). Although the dating of these events is problematic, Josephus's interest does show that by his time the dispute between Jews and Samaritans over sacred space had spread to the Diaspora (Hakola [2005: 104]).

50. Scholars have been reluctant to trace much of Jn 4.4-42 to the historical Jesus (Brown [1979: 36]; Lindars [1982: 176]; Wyckoff [2005: 90]). Matthew portrays Jesus forbidding the disciples to enter any Samaritan town (Mt. 10.5), and Luke has Samaritan villagers rejecting Jesus (Lk. 9.52-55). Our passage is also characteristically Johannine in theology, vocabulary, and literary style.

Even Meier, however, who is 'wary' of finding a particular event in the life of Jesus behind the story, nevertheless acknowledges that the passage is well-informed throughout about Samaritans, and about Jewish-Samaritan relations (2001: 548; see Keener [2003: 1.587]). And whatever we make of the positive response of the Samaritans to Jesus' preaching (vv. 39-41; the idea of a mission to the Samaritans in Jesus' ministry

Galilee, resting at a well outside of the Samaritan town of Sychar (vv. 1-6). The theme of sacred space manifests itself early in the narrative, when the author locates Sychar 'near the plot of ground that Jacob had given to his son Joseph' (v. 5). The connection between the patriarchs and Shechem (now in Samaritan territory) can be traced back to the Hebrew Scriptures. According to Genesis 33, Jacob bought a plot of land from the Shechemites (v. 19), where he proceeded to build an altar (v. 20). As a result, the field at Shechem became 'the oldest part of the Holy Land to belong to the Israelites by right of purchase'.[51] Now, however, Jacob's well lies in Samaritan territory (Jn 4.4-5), and the Jewish patriarch has been co-opted by the Samaritans as 'our father Jacob' (v. 12).[52] The connection between ancestry and territory, which will move to the forefront of the narrative at the climax of the dialogue (vv. 20-21), has, therefore, already become a key subtext in our story. As the narrative continues, a woman

'strains credulity' according to Lindars [1982: 175]), the interaction with the woman at the well has a strong claim to historical authenticity. As Blomberg asserts, '[Jesus'] refusal to be put off by his conversation partner because of her gender, ethnicity, and moral reputation meshes perfectly with that strand of synoptic tradition almost universally acknowledged as authentic—Jesus as a friend who eats with outcasts and notorious sinners' (2001: 100; with Keener [2003: 1.587]). Thus Neyrey finds Jesus' treatment of the woman a match for his 'radical inclusivity' elsewhere (1994). More specifically, Jesus' behavior coheres well with what we know about his attitude toward Samaritans from Luke's special material (Lk. 10.29-37; 17.11-19), and it accords with his convictions about sacred space, as reflected elsewhere in the gospel traditions. Finally, the lack of references to Samaritans in the New Testament epistles may further encourage us to affirm the presence of a genuinely Palestinian tradition in John 4 (Keener [2003: 1.588]).

51. Lindars (1982: 179).

52. Later Samaritan traditions identified Mt Gerizim as the place where Jacob had his vision of a ladder extending from heaven to earth (Gen. 28.10-18). Note the pronounced emphasis on sacred space in the Genesis account of Jacob's dream:

> 16 Then Jacob woke from his sleep and said, 'Surely the LORD is in this place—and I did not know it!' 17 And he was afraid, and said, 'How awesome is this place! This is none other than the house of God, and this is the gate of heaven'. 18 So Jacob rose early in the morning, and he took the stone that he had put under his head and set it up for a pillar and poured oil on the top of it. (Gen. 28.16-18)

Samaritan traditions situating the dream at Gerizim are late, but the use of the story to validate a particular location for worship goes back at least as far as the book of *Jubilees*, which insists that the place where Jacob had his vision is '*not* the place' for a permanent cult site (*Jub.* 32.22). For the Samaritan traditions linking the Jacob story to Gerizim, see Neyrey (1979: 427-28, citing *Memar Marqah* II.10), who concludes that 'Jacob is certainly a factor in a northern and Samaritan tradition which asserted that Mt Gerizim is the legitimate place of worship' (428). Late Jewish traditions, in turn, used the Jacob narratives to validate their conviction that Jerusalem was the proper place for the cult (428-29).

6. Jesus and Sacred Space

from Samaria approaches to draw water from the well, and Jesus requests a drink (vv. 7-8). The woman's response is symptomatic of pronounced ethnic strife that had characterized relations between Jews and Samaritans throughout much of the Second-Temple period: ' "How is it that you, a Jew, ask a drink of me, a woman of Samaria?" (Jews do not share things in common with Samaritans)' (v. 9).

a. *Jews and Samaritans in Context*

The history of the struggle between Jews and Samaritans significantly informs our understanding of the ways in which religion, ethnicity, and territoriality intersect one another in traditional societies such as those that populated first-century Palestine. According to the Jewish account, Samaritans were not related to Abraham, but descended, instead, from colonists brought into the region by the Assyrians from other peoples they had conquered (2 Kings 17; Josephus, *Ant.* 9.277-91). Samaritans, as we might imagine, told a different story in order to legitimize their Israelite origins. They insisted that they were the direct descendents of persons from the tribes of Ephraim and Manasseh who survived the destruction of the Northern Kingdom by Shalmaneser V in 722 BCE (or Sargon II in 721 BCE).[53]

b. *The Jewish Explanation of Samaritan Origins*

Jesus' contemporaries found in the Old Testament books of Ezra and Nehemiah the earliest evidence for Jewish-Samaritan relations during our period, and from the outset the relations were less than cordial.[54] Early in the postexilic era Jews excluded Samaritans from participation in the worship of Yahweh in Jerusalem:

---

53. Current debates about the historicity of the two accounts are irrelevant in the present connection, since I am interested here in the tension generated by these competing ethnographies and not their relative historical worth (see Purvis [1992: 918]; Anderson [1992: 941]). Recent scholarship tends to regard both the Jewish and Samaritan accounts of Samaritan origins as tendentious. Consult Meier's careful survey, and the bibliography he provides (2001: 535-49; note also Crown [1984, 1989] and Hjelm [2000]).

54. Josephus, for example, links the Samaritans of his own day (a) to the descendents of the pagans settled in the north by the Assyrians in 722 BCE (*Ant.* 9.277-91) and (b) to Ezra and Nehemiah's political opponents in the north during the early postexilic period (*Ant.* 11.19-30, 84-119). Neither connection finds solid support in the Hebrew Scriptures, however, and Josephus's reconstruction is thus to be evaluated as 'good propaganda' but 'bad history' (Meier [2001: 536]). Nevertheless, as Meier proceeds to observe, 'that Samaritans were the main source of opposition [to Ezra and Nehemiah] is how Jews and Christians of a later date came to read and tell the story' (538). It is this (Jewish) emic conception of Samaritan origins and Jewish-Samaritan relations which is of concern in the present connection, and this is why I have adopted the Jewish perspective in the paragraphs that follow.

> 1 When the adversaries of Judah and Benjamin heard that the returned exiles were building a temple to the LORD, the God of Israel, 2 they approached Zerubbabel and the heads of families and said to them, 'Let us build with you, for we worship your God as you do, and we have been sacrificing to him ever since the days of King Esar-haddon of Assyria who brought us here'. 3 But Zerubbabel, Jeshua, and the rest of the heads of families in Israel said to them, 'You shall have no part with us in building a house to our God; but we alone will build to the LORD, the God of Israel, as King Cyrus of Persia has commanded us' (Ezra 4.1-3).

The rebuffed Samaritans, in turn, opposed Jewish efforts to rebuild the temple:

> 4 Then the people of the land discouraged the people of Judah, and made them afraid to build, 5 and they bribed officials to frustrate their plan throughout the reign of King Cyrus of Persia and until the reign of King Darius of Persia (Ezra 4.4-5).

After some delay, the Jews received permission from Darius I to complete their work on the sanctuary (c. 520 BCE), but several generations later discord between the two peoples erupted once again, when Sanballat, governor of Samaria, attempted to thwart Nehemiah's plan to rebuild the walls of Jerusalem (c. 444 BCE). The alliance formed by the Samaritan governor attests to the political orientation of the struggle:

> 7 But when Sanballat and Tobiah and the Arabs and the Ammonites and the Ashdodites heard that the repairing of the walls of Jerusalem was going forward and the gaps were beginning to be closed, they were very angry, 8 and all plotted together to come and fight against Jerusalem and to cause confusion in it (Neh. 4.7-8).

Efforts to halt the fortification of the Jewish capital proved unsuccessful, but animosity between Jews and Samaritans persisted, and relations further deteriorated during the Greek period.

c. *Jews and Samaritans during the Greek and Roman Periods*
After initially supporting the Greek presence in the East by contributing a significant contingent of troops to Alexander's Egyptian campaign, Samaria revolted against Macedonian rule, and Alexander and his generals destroyed the city and rebuilt it as a Hellenistic *polis*. A portion of the disenfranchised citizenry apparently moved to nearby Shechem and erected a Samaritan temple on Mt Gerizim. Our earliest extant Judean assessment of the Samaritans during the Greek period is less than affirming. The book of Ben Sira (c. 180 BCE) relegates those who dwell in Shechem to a lower status than Israel's traditional enemies, the Philistines and the Edomites:

> 25 Two nations my soul detests,
>   and the third is not even a people:
> 26 Those who live in Seir, and the Philistines,
>   and the foolish people that live in Shechem (Sir. 50.25-26).

Jewish disdain for Samaritans, who in Ben Sira's view are 'not even a people', would prove disastrous for both Samaria and Shechem after the Jews gained their independence from the Seleucid empire during the second century BCE.

Upon the death of the Syrian dynast Antiochus VII Sidetes, John Hyrcanus seized upon the opportunity to expand his territory northward and secure the region between Judea and Galilee. According to Josephus, the Jewish priest-king captured

> Shechem and Garizein and the Cuthean nation, which lives near the temple built after the model of the sanctuary at Jerusalem, which Alexander permitted their governor Sanaballetes to build...this temple was laid to waste (*Ant.* 13.255-57).[55]

The destruction of the Samaritan sanctuary on Mt Gerizim (128 BCE) and the town of Shechem (107 BCE) is indicative of the fact that, in addition to disputes about ancestral origins, Jews and Samaritans vigorously contended for legitimacy where sacred space was concerned.[56]

---

55. Josephus designates the Samaritans as 'Cutheans' (*Ant.* 9.290) because this was one of the foreign nations brought to Israel by the Assyrians from other lands in 722 BCE. Archaeological evidence for the kind of temple Josephus describes ('built after the model of the sanctuary at Jerusalem') was lacking until just recently, leading Anderson to suggest that the structure may have been 'a more modest tabernacle' (1992: 942). Such an assessment must now be revised in view of recent excavations that have uncovered a sanctuary at Gerizim exhibiting monumental architecture and a sacrificial cult as early as the first half of the fifth century BCE. The structure was massively rebuilt and expanded during the Hellenistic period (Magen [1990, 1993, 2000]).

56. Hyrcanus's destruction of Shechem and the cult site 'crystallized the disputes about the legitimate priesthood and the true "sacred space" ' (Weiss [1994: 253]). From a strictly military perspective, Hyrcanus had good reason to destroy the walls of the recently fortified Hellenistic *polis* of Samaria in 107 BCE (Purvis [1992: 919]). Strategic considerations do not, however, suffice to explain the sack of Shechem and, especially, the destruction of the Samaritan sanctuary on Gerizim, actions best understood as expressions of the ongoing Jewish-Samaritan dispute over the proper place to worship Yahweh.

Dexinger thinks it was the marginalization of the Zadokites, when Jonathan usurped the priesthood in 152 BCE, which 'confirmed the priesthood on Mount Gerizim as well as the priests who had moved to Qumran in their opposition to Jerusalem' (1981: 102). The effect of the Hasmonean priesthood on Qumran is a reasonable deduction. Recent excavations at Gerizim, however, suggest that the Samaritan priesthood had been confirmed for many generations prior to the mid-second century BCE. Bones of goats, sheep, cattle,

The debate over the proper cult site had a long history. Both groups maintained a decidedly territorial outlook on worship and sacrifice in their respective attempts to remain faithful to a key injunction found in the Torah: 'But you shall seek the place that the LORD your God will choose out of all your tribes as his habitation to put his name there' (Deut. 12.5). Jews and Samaritans differed, however, on the precise location of that sacred place. Drawing upon the history of David and Solomon, as narrated in 2 Samuel and 1 Kings, Judeans naturally identified Jerusalem as the location Moses had in mind. After all, according to the Scriptures Yahweh himself had authorized Solomon to build the temple in Jerusalem. The site thus acquired lasting significance in Jewish eyes, as reflected in the building of the second temple in Jerusalem under Zerubbabel and its Herodian expansion several centuries later.

In contrast to the Jews, Samaritans recognized as authoritative only the Pentateuch among the Hebrew Scriptures, and their own textual tradition rendered Deut. 12.5 in such a way as to suggest that God had already chosen his sacred place by the time the Torah was completed: 'seek the place the LORD your God *has chosen*'.[57] As a result, Samaritans searched through the Pentateuch to find God's intended location. According to the Torah, Mt Gerizim was the place where the blessings were pronounced over the people of Yahweh after they entered Canaan (Deut. 11.29-30; 27.12), and Abraham had first sacrificed to God in the promised land at Shechem (Gen. 12.6-7). In the Samaritan Pentateuch (Deut. 27.3-4), moreover, Gerizim, not Ebal as in the MT, is identified as the place for an altar to be built upon arrival in the promised land.[58] Samaritans naturally concluded that Mt Gerizim was 'the place' Yahweh had chosen. So sacred was the cult site at Mt Gerizim, in fact, that Samaritans continued to offer sacrifices and conduct other rites on the mountain even after the loss of the sanctuary proper in 128 BCE. These territorial convictions, along with the devastation of the sacred cult site at the hands of John Hyrcanus, guaranteed that animosity between Jews and Samaritans would only escalate in the decades to come.

Political realities never afforded the Samaritans an occasion to respond in kind and raze the Jerusalem temple to the ground, as Hyrcanus had done to the Samaritan temple at Gerizim. A number of Samaritans did, however, take advantage of an opportunity to defile Jewish sacred space in a way that disrupted a most important annual celebration on the Jewish calendar. The incident occurred while Coponius was prefect of Judea (6–10 CE). Josephus relates:

and doves (likely offered as sacrifices in the cult) found at Gerizim have been dated to the early fifth century BCE (Magen [2000: 111]).

57. Carson (1991: 222, author's italics).

58. It is entirely possible that Gerizim was the original reading, and that it was changed to Ebal through 'anti-Samaritan motives' (Beasley-Murray [1999: 61]).

When the Festival of Unleavened Bread, which we call Passover, was going on, the priests were accustomed to throw open the gates of the temple after midnight. This time, when the gates were first opened, some Samaritans, who had secretly entered Jerusalem, began to scatter human bones in the porticoes and throughout the temple. As a result the priests, although they had previously observed no such custom, excluded everyone from the temple, in addition to taking other measures for the greater protection of the temple (*Ant.* 18.29-30).

Relations between Jews and Samaritans remained tense, and occasionally erupted in violence, until the destruction of the Jerusalem temple in 70 CE.[59]

d. *The Ethnic Dimension of the Conflict*
Debate and conflict over issues of descent and sacred space may be seen as evidence of a much more foundational point of contention between Jews and Samaritans, one related to ethnic identity and social boundaries. According to social scientists, ethnic identity typically includes both a mythological and a territorial component. Hutchinson and Smith, for example, include in their catalogue of eight cultural characteristics associated with ethnic identity (1) a myth of common ancestry and (2) a link with a homeland.[60] Esler has recently identified these characteristics, 'ancestry and territory', as the two most significant cultural indicia of shared ethnicity.[61] The fact that Jews and Samaritans contended with one another over these very issues encourages us to evaluate the conflict between the two groups in ethnic terms.

A people's 'territory' can, of course, refer to a geographical entity as large as one's homeland or as small as a carefully delineated section of one's cult site, such as the Court of the Israelites in the Jerusalem temple. For Jews and Samaritans, the territorial point of contention lay in between these two extremes, since it centered around the proper location for the worship of Yahweh within the boundaries of Old Testament Israel. 'Myth of common ancestry' points to the fact that ethnic groups generally rally around a narrative of shared descent, typically from a common ancestor, whether or not such a blood relationship actually exists.[62] At issue in the struggle between Judeans and Samaritans was the story of Samaritan ancestry. Samaritans insisted upon a shared Israelite descent. Judeans rejected the claim, and these conflicting stories, along with differences over sacred space, inevitably resulted in robust social boundaries between the two ethnic groups—thus

---

59. In 52 CE Samaritans massacred a contingent of Galilean pilgrims (Josephus, *Ant.* 20.118; Josephus, *War* 2.232-46). See McLaren (1991: 131-39).
60. Hutchinson and Smith (1996: 6-7).
61. Esler (2003: 44).
62. See the discussion in Esler (2003: 41-44).

the parenthetical comment in Jn 4.9, 'Jews do not share things in common with Samaritans'.⁶³

It has been the trend in some scholarly circles, however, to downplay ethnic discord between Jews and Samaritans, by highlighting possible indications of accord and cooperation between the two groups.⁶⁴ Fewell and Phillips draw upon just such a revisionist reading of Jewish–Samaritan relations further to challenge agendas which they perceive might be operating behind the traditional view: 'This stereotyping of Jewish–Samaritan relationships can serve partisan Christian interests to present Jesus as the boundary breaker who better than anyone else rises above cultural, ethnic, and religious differences'.⁶⁵

My response is twofold, relating to the Samaritans and Jesus, respectively. First of all, the 'stereotyping of Jewish–Samaritan relationships' to which the authors refer is not stereotyping at all, but likely represents the majority view of Jews and Samaritans alike in Palestine during the Second-Temple period. Limited evidence demonstrating that Jewish–Samaritan relations were not 'uniformly antagonistic'⁶⁶ fails to controvert a larger and more representative body of data which supports the traditional view. No set of human relations is uniform in the complex world of social interaction, and exceptions do not undermine reasoned conclusions derived from prevailing evidence to the contrary. Secondly, despite how out of fashion such a notion has become in certain scholarly circles, it remains self-evident to many of us that the enduring memories of Jesus of Nazareth are to be traced, at least in part, to the fact that he genuinely was a 'boundary breaker who better than anyone else [rose] above cultural, ethnic, and religious differences' (Fewell and Philips, above). John 4 is, after all, hardly the only gospel text that portrays Jesus in this light.

Much to be preferred, therefore, is Neyrey's reading of our passage, a reading that allows ancient cultural values and social codes relating to gender and space—rather than contemporary scholarly concerns about discourse

---

63. The explanation is lacking in some textual witnesses (ℵ* and the Western text) but well attested in the papyri. The RSV translates the statement 'Jews have no dealings with Samaritans', a view supported by Lindars (1982: 181). The immediate context, in which Jesus has no utensil or vessel with which to draw water (v. 11), supports the NRSV's more narrow understanding of the debated term συγχρῶνται, an interpretation which assumes that Jews will not use Samaritan utensils because of considerations of purity (Daube [1950]; Coggins [1975: 139]; Meier [2001: 603 n. 178]). Given the connection between purity, table fellowship, and social relations in Second-Temple Judaism, the debate over the two interpretations of συγχρῶνται may end up in much the same place, assuming we do not press the RSV's 'no dealings' too far.

64. Maccini (1994: 44-45); Fewell and Phillips (1997: 24 n. 5).

65. Fewell and Phillips (1997: 24 n. 5).

66. Fewell and Phillips (1997: 24 n. 5).

and power—to control the interpretation of the narrative. As Neyrey rightly concludes: 'According to cultural expectations, [the Samaritan woman] represents the quintessential deviant (non-Jew, unclean, shameless, even sinner); but in her transformation, she exemplifies the radical inclusivity of Jesus' circle'.[67] In his encounter with the Samaritan woman at the well of Jacob, then, Jesus relativizes competing territorial convictions that had contributed to ethnic strife between Jews and Samaritans, and he subverts related cultural codes by ignoring the social boundary that had been firmly established between the two groups.[68] We continue now with our narrative in John 4.[69]

e. *Jesus and the Relativization of Sacred Space*
It is understandable, given the above background, that the Samaritan woman was shocked when Jesus, a Jewish male, requested water from her. Jesus responded to her surprise as follows:

> 'If you knew the gift of God, and who it is that is saying to you, "Give me a drink", you would have asked him, and he would have given you living water' (v. 10).

There follows a discussion in which Jesus draws upon the image of physical water to dialogue with the woman about the 'living water' that he offers (vv. 11-14). In the course of the interaction the woman mentions 'our ancestor Jacob, who gave us the well' (v. 12), a reference which takes up and reiterates themes of ethnicity and sacred space which had dominated the opening verses of the narrative.[70]

An important intertext colors the story of Jesus and the Samaritan woman, one which would have functioned effectively to remind Jesus' earliest followers, who passed on this tradition, of the importance of proper descent and

---

67. Neyrey (1994: 77).

68. Keener helpfully identifies three barriers crossed by Jesus in the encounter: a moral barrier imposed by the woman's apparent behavior, a gender barrier, and the socioethnic barrier erected through centuries of Jewish–Samaritan strife and prejudice (2003: 1.585). As Keener rightly notes, the most intractable of these was the social boundary between Jews and Samaritans (1.598).

69. I have intentionally omitted later rabbinic evidence for Jewish–Samaritan relations, where a less than positive perspective continued to prevail. Most of the passages are quite late and of questionable value for reconstructing Samaritanism of Jesus' day. Keener cites a number of these traditions (2003: 1.599-600, 612-13).

70. For sacred space as a theme in the introduction to the story of the woman at the well in John 4, see the earlier discussion of the phrase 'near the plot of ground that Jacob had given to his son Joseph' (v. 5). The surface structure of verses 4-9 resonates with references to ancestry and ethnic relations: 'Samaria' (v. 4); 'Samaritan city', 'Jacob', 'Joseph', (v. 5); 'Jacob's well', (v. 6); 'Samaritan woman' (vv. 7, 9); 'Jew', 'Samaria', 'Jews', 'Samaritans' (v. 9).

endogamous matrimony for maintaining the purity of the Israelite bloodline. For some time scholars have noted allusions in the narrative to cross-gender well scenes from the Hebrew Scriptures.[71] The reference to 'Jacob's well' (v. 6) recalls, for example, another well in Mesopotamia, where Jacob met Rachel and provided water for her (Gen. 29.10).[72] Our story is particularly marked with parallels from Genesis 24, in which Abraham's servant procures a wife for Isaac. The meeting between Jesus and the woman of Samaria thus exhibits 'the characteristics of a courtship scene' and 'invites the reader to expect a significant union between Jesus and this woman before the narrative ends'.[73] The result in the present story is not a literal marriage, of course, but a union that takes place when the woman and her fellow Samaritans respond in faith to Jesus.[74]

We should recall here the manner in which Second-Temple authors appropriated, reworked, and expanded upon these courtship scenes in the Hebrew Scriptures in order to encourage strict endogamy where marital relations were concerned. As noted in Chapter 3, the author of *Jubilees* significantly reframed the Jacob courtship narrative from Genesis 28–29. In the Old Testament account, Isaac charges Jacob not to marry 'one of the Canaanite women' (Gen. 28.6). The author of *Jubilees* builds upon this theme, as he portrays Jacob assuring his mother that he has not even 'been thinking about taking...a wife from the daughters of Canaan' (25.4). Pseudo-Philo's *Biblical Antiquities* betrays a similar preoccupation with the purity of the Jewish bloodline. Although not spoken in the context of a cross-gender well scene, Tamar's exclamation is representative of the author's convictions about sexual relations between Jews and Gentiles: 'It is better for me to die for having intercourse with my father-in-law than to have intercourse with a gentile' (9.5). For readers and hearers immersed in the social world of post-Maccabean Judaism, where intermarriage with non-Judeans was strongly discouraged and, indeed, in some cases abhorred, the intertextual allusions to these Old Testament well scenes in John 4 would have served strongly to reinforce the emphasis on descent and ethnicity which is explicitly articulated in the surface structure of the narrative itself.

All of this, of course, renders Jesus' behavior all the more anomalous, for Jesus courts not an honorable Jewish maiden at the well, but a Samaritan

---

71. Bonneau (1973); Neyrey (1979: 425-26); Carmichael (1980); Alter (1981: 51-52); Staley (1988: 100); Botha (1991: 110-11); Eslinger (1993); and Jones (1997: 91-92). Lindars (1982: 179-80) and Okure (1988: 90-91), however, reject such allusions.

72. The story in Exodus 2 of Moses meeting his wife Zipporah at a well in Midian also comes to mind. Moses, like Jesus, sat by a well (Exod. 2.15; Jn 4.6) (Bonneau [1973: 1255]).

73. Jones (1997: 92).

74. Jones (1997: 92).

woman of questionable moral background. The resulting dissonance in John 4 between text and intertext is considerable. Botha elaborates: 'The intertext is used here to create intolerable expectations' for the implied readers, since they 'are now confronted with a situation in which the outcome is the liason between the male and female involved, which is unthinkable in this situation'.[75] This intentional portrayal of Jesus courting a Samaritan—which ultimately results in a spiritual union that proves profoundly more encompassing than a simple contract marriage between two families—pointedly destabilizes the ethnic boundary between Jews and Samaritans and thus comports well with Jesus' relativization of Jewish and Samaritan sacred space in the verses to follow.

Returning to the story, the interaction continues with the woman requesting the water Jesus offers, but it becomes immediately clear to the reader that she has yet to make the distinction between physical water and the living water to which Jesus refers (v. 15). At this point the narrative changes abruptly, as Jesus instructs the woman to depart and return with her husband (v. 16). The woman replies that she has no husband, and Jesus proceeds to reveal personal information about the woman's marital history, which, in turn, causes her to say, 'Sir, I see that you are a prophet' (vv. 17-19).[76] The Samaritan woman then raises the contentious issue of the proper place to worship God:

> 'Our ancestors worshiped on this mountain, but you say that the place where people must worship is in Jerusalem' (v. 20).

The statement refers, of course, to the ongoing debate between Jews and Samaritans about the place Yahweh had chosen for sacrificial worship. Jesus' response to the woman's assertion reveals much about his convictions concerning sacred space. Heard against the backdrop of post-Maccabean Jewish territoriality and the Samaritan schism, Jesus' answer could only

---

75. Botha (1991: 113).

76. The woman's insight is to be compared with Nicodemus's attitude in the previous chapter (Smith [1999: 109]). Although at times confused, the woman is otherwise an equal partner in the dialogue, and finally comes to faith in Jesus. Nicodemus, on the other hand, never wholly grasps what Jesus says to him, and he contributes less and less to the dialogue as the narrative unfolds. For the numerous points of (presumably intentional) contrast between Nicodemus and the Samaritan woman in the two narratives, see Francis (1988). Jones further notes that Nicodemus comes to Jesus 'by night' (3.1), the Samaritan woman 'about noon' (4.6) (1997: 97). Hakola sees in the contrast a broader theme at work: 'The whole story illustrates, therefore, how Jesus moves away from the Jews to non-Jews who welcome him. The narrator's remark that the Jews do not deal with the Samaritans adds irony to the story (v. 9): a representative of Jesus' own nation failed to receive Jesus, while those despised by the Jews accept him' (2005: 96). For a close reading of the dialogue between Jesus and the woman, as it unfolds from vv. 7-18, see now Giblin's analysis (1999).

strike his dialogue partner as utterly counter-intuitive.[77] It is a reply which perfectly coheres, however, with Jesus' culturally subversive behavior in crossing social boundaries to interact with the Samaritan woman in the first place:[78]

> 21 'Woman, believe me, the hour is coming when you will worship the Father neither on this mountain nor in Jerusalem. 22 You worship what you do not know; we worship what we know, for salvation is from the Jews. 23 But the hour is coming, and is now here, when the true worshipers will worship the Father in spirit and truth, for the Father seeks such as these to worship him. 24 God is spirit, and those who worship him must worship in spirit and truth' (vv. 21-24).[79]

Not surprisingly, Jesus, a Jew, affirms the Jewish interpretation of salvation history and, by implication, of Samaritan origins (v. 22).[80] We would expect

---

77. Scholars have become increasingly reluctant in recent years to use the term 'schism' in reference to Jewish–Samaritan relations (Coggins [1975: 162-65]; Meier [2001: 541-42]). Although it is, indeed, the case that one cannot point to a 'definitive moment of schism' in the history of relations between the two groups (Meier [2001: 541]), the term remains helpful when used in an ethnic, rather than a strictly religious, sense. Meier's emphasis upon the Samaritans as a religious group naturally leads him, with recent scholarship, to emphasize what Samaritans and Jews had in common ideologically, as co-heirs of Israelite tradition. Recent social scientific work in the area of ethnicity, however, suggests a more substantive breach between the two groups than Meier wants to allow, a breach that accords well with the evidence from our sources, cited above. As we have seen, Samaritans and Jews contended over two key cultural indicia of ethnicity—territory and ancestry, so we can fairly characterize the fallout between the two groups as a schism from the perspective of ethnic relations. The issue remains a complicated one, however, since anthropologists also identify shared religion as a contributing factor to ethnic solidarity (Hutchinson and Smith [1996: 6-7]). Jews and Samaritans, of course, had much in common in this area, as Meier appropriately notes (2001: 541-42).

78. Gundry-Volf thus refers to the 'barrier-breaking significance' of Jesus' request in v. 7 (1995: 510).

79. The introductory imperative of v. 21, 'Woman, believe me' (πίστευέ μοι, γύναι), is variously interpreted. Many regard it as an asseverative comparable to the more frequent 'truly, truly, I say to you' (Barrett [1978: 236]; Lindars [1982: 188]). I am attracted to Jones's suggestion that the construction is more forceful: 'More than a mere asseverative, the imperative calls for a faith response' (1997: 103).

80. Hakola (2005: 105-106). Jesus clearly asserts that 'the Jewish side was correct on the matter of salvation history' (Keener [2003: 1.610]). Some have seized upon the affirmation of Jewish worship as a corrective to other passages in John that are open to anti-Jewish interpretations, as if Jesus here asserts the ongoing value of Judaism for early Christianity (Mussner [1979: 51]; Thyen [1980: 169]; Söding [2000: 21-41]; Van Belle [2001: 400]). As the conjunction ἀλλά at the beginning of the next verse indicates, however, the affirmation of Jewish versus Samaritan worship in v. 22 is subordinated in the narrative to an overarching temporal distinction between the era before Jesus' coming and that which has begun with his arrival. This distinction, in turn, relativizes the

him also to affirm the corresponding legitimacy of Jerusalem as Israel's sacred space, thus confirming the two primary cultural indicia of ethnicity which reinforced social boundaries between Jews and Samaritans. In verse 21, however, Jesus completely relativizes the position of Jerusalem (and, for the Samaritans, Gerizim) on the territorial map of sacred space, thus summarily dismissing a key component of Jewish (and Samaritan) ethnic identity.[81] Neyrey summarizes the implications of Jesus' behavior as follows:

> By Jesus' dealings with the Samaritans, which we are told are contrary to custom (4.9), and by the de-classification of both Judean and Samaritan temples, we learn that there is no 'holy land', no sacred turf, and thus no chosen place. Classification of space, then, replicates classification of people.[82]

For Jesus, 'The hour is coming, and now is here' (v. 23),[83] and, once again, we find Jesus seizing the eschatological moment to deconstruct symbols

---

sacred space of both Jews and Samaritans, by consigning territorially situated worship to a previous era in salvation history (Hakola [2005: 107-108, 111-12]; Keener [2003: 1.611]). (Haenchen's relegation of verse 22 to later 'ecclesiastical redaction' [a view that goes back to Bultmann], however, is completely unnecessary [1984: 222]).

81. As Hakola insightfully observes, 'Jesus' mention of 'the Father' [vv. 21, 23] undermines the earlier appeals to many fathers' (see v. 20, 'our ancestors') (2005: 100). The subversion of patriarchy, which characterizes Jesus' approach to family relations at various places in the Gospels, is a vital aspect of his reconfiguration of ethnic boundaries, as I will demonstrate when I consider the relationship between ancestry and ethnicity in some detail in a later Chapter.

82. Neyrey (2002a: 65). Fuglseth reads v. 21 not as an ideological rejection of the temple institution but, rather, as a simple reflection of the temple's destruction, 'without any ideological message' (2005: 181). Such a position is wholly untenable, since the supposition that Jesus relativizes sacred space in the proclamation is corroborated by his crossing of ethnic boundaries to interact with the Samaritan woman in the first place. Synder's observation, that 'spaces have been eliminated in favor of a universal reality', is more on target (1999: 48). See also Swanson (1994).

There are some Greco-Roman analogies to Jesus' relativization of sacred space, although they lack the corresponding ethnic component noted by Neyrey in the quotation cited above. Philosophers and prophets critiqued territorial worship devoid of moral and relational integrity (Talbert [1993: 337-40] cites Xenophon, *Mem.* 1.3.1-3; Plato, *Alc.* 2.149E; Persius, *Sat.* 2.69-75; Amos 5.21-24; Hos. 6.6). Some philosophers 'reconceptualized' sacred space, turning philosophy into a genuine cultic activity (Talbert [1993: 340-46] references Seneca, *Ep.* 41; Apollonius of Tyana, *On Sacrifices* frg. in Eusebius, *Praep. ev.* 4.12-13; Apollonius of Tyana, *Ep.* 26; Porphyry, *On Abstinence* frg. in Eusebius, *Praep. ev.* 4.11; Philo, *Prob.* 75). It is, however, the ethnic corollary to Jesus' critique of sacred space which renders the statement in Jn 4.21-24 exceptional, particularly in a Jewish context. As Keener aptly concludes, 'In its most dramatic divergence from traditional Jewish expectations' John 4 'speaks of a worship in the Spirit that ultimately transcends ethnic allegiances' (2003: 1.617).

83. The statement 'The hour is coming, and now is here' (v. 23) may reflect both the time of Jesus' ministry ('is coming') and the post-resurrection perspective of the author ('is now') (Smith [1999: 116]).

of Jewish national identity, and thereby undermine social boundaries that separated the descendants of Abraham from other ethnic groups during the post-Maccabean era of Jewish history.

5. *Summary: Jesus and Sacred Space*

'Do you not know that you are God's temple and that God's Spirit dwells in you?' So wrote Paul of Tarsus to a fledgling Jesus community on the Grecian peninsula during the middle of the first century CE (1 Cor. 3.16). The sentiments are remarkable in view of the way in which Paul's Jewish compatriots tenaciously preserved their territorial map of sacred and profane space during the post-Maccabean era of Roman imperial hegemony. Yet for Paul, and for those who shared his outlook, there was now 'no longer Jew or Greek', since Jesus had 'made us both one and...broken down in his flesh the dividing wall of hostility by abolishing the law of commandments' (Gal. 3.28; Eph. 2.14-15, ESV). Notice, once again, that the Pauline perspective assumes a close connection between territoriality and ethnic relations. In Paul's case, however, the vital nexus between sacred space and social identity which characterized post-Maccabean Judaism has been turned on its head. Paul's disavowal of Jewish identity as a prerequisite for membership in the people of God has necessitated, as its corollary, the relativization of Jewish conceptions of sacred and profane space. Or, to put it a bit differently, 'fixed sacred space' becomes 'fluid sacred space', as the locus of God's dwelling place moves from a permanent geo-political location (the Jerusalem temple) to the 'mobile and portable' *ekklesia* of God.[84]

The road was a long one, however, from the Mishnah's 'ten degrees of holiness' to the convictions about sacred space held by those who shared Paul's vision for an ethnically inclusive people of Yahweh. As argued in the pages above, it seems quite apparent that Jesus of Nazareth laid the groundwork for such a journey, when he began to challenge long-held territorial conceptions during his pre-Easter ministry in Roman Palestine. Jesus' attitude toward the Jerusalem temple, as evidenced by both his words and his actions, and his encounter with the Samaritan woman at the well of Jacob, reveal a perspective on sacred space which differs markedly from that of the great majority of Jesus' Jewish contemporaries.[85] Jesus' outlook

---

84. On the distinction between 'fixed' and 'fluid' sacred space, see Neyrey (2002a: 62-63, 66) who draws upon Malina (1986: 31-38).

85. Space constraints have limited my discussion to treatments of (a) Jesus' predictions of the temple's destruction, (b) the action in the temple, and (c) the encounter with the Samaritan woman. Much additional evidence has been adduced for Jesus' program of 'de-territorialization' (see Riches [2000] on Mark and Matthew. The expression

in this regard must be related, moreover, to his view of social relations, and we should explain Jesus' relativization of the territorial map of post-Maccabean Judaism in the same way as we explain his attitude toward the Jewish calendar. In each case, Jesus intentionally subverts symbols of Jewish particularism which had helped define Israel's social boundaries for generations. The legacy left by Jesus would well serve the ensuing agenda of persons like Paul who sought more directly to challenge the soteriological efficacy of Jewish identity, in order to reconstitute the people of God as a multi-ethnic, surrogate family.

in quotations is taken from Riches [2000: 254]). Freyne, for example, interprets the absence of any reference to 'Zion' in the Jesus traditions as a rejection by Jesus of the 'Hasmonean-style militarism' that was popularly associated with the term (2004: 116).

Chapter 7

JESUS AND SACRED FOOD

> 'To prevent our being perverted by contact with others or by mixing with bad influences God hedged us in on all sides with strict observances connected with meat and drink and touch and hearing and sight, after the manner of the Law'.
>
> *Letter of Aristeas* 142

Sometime during our period (c. 1st cent. BCE–1st cent. CE), a Jewish writer encountered an intriguing bit of social realia as he worked his way through the Joseph cycle in the book of Genesis: 'Pharaoh gave Joseph the name Zaphenath-paneah; and he gave him Asenath daughter of Potiphera, priest of On, as his wife' (Gen. 41.45). The brief statement receives little elaboration in the Old Testament, leaving the reader completely in the dark about the relationship between Joseph and Asenath. The lacuna apparently led our Second-Temple Jewish author to utilize the verse as a point of departure to craft a full-length story about Joseph and his Egyptian bride. The result is a delightful romance that portrays the pagan priest's daughter as an archetypical Jewish proselyte.

As the story begins, Aseneth wants nothing to do with Joseph, whom she summarily dismisses as a common Hebrew shepherd.[1] Until, that is, Aseneth actually sees Joseph for the first time, all decked out in his royal finery. Then she is immediately and utterly love-struck:

> Aseneth saw Joseph on his chariot and was strongly cut (to the heart), and her soul was crushed, and her knees were paralyzed, and her entire body trembled, and she was filled with great fear (*Jos. Asen.* 6.1).

The ensuing narrative traces the pilgrimage of Aseneth, as she eagerly disowns Egyptian religion to embrace the worship of Yahweh and finally marry Joseph.

Joseph, on his part, is pictured in the tale as a faithful Hebrew who 'never ate with the Egyptians, for this was an abomination to him' (7.1). The image forms quite a contrast with a related piece of social realia

---

1. Asenath (Gen. 41.45) is spelled 'Aseneth' in the Second-Temple romance.

found in the Joseph cycle in Genesis, where it is the Egyptians—not the Hebrews—who find such table fellowship offensive: 'the Egyptians could not eat with the Hebrews, for that is an abomination to the Egyptians' (Gen. 43.32). The striking reversal of the Old Testament account directly betrays the ideological orientation of the author, for whom Jews, not Gentiles, are those who are to be concerned with maintaining a pure table. *Joseph and Aseneth*, as the work has been titled, is laced throughout with the writer's contemporary Jewish convictions. Given the importance of the food laws to Jewish identity during the Second-Temple period, we are hardly surprised to find the adoption of Jewish dietary practices functioning as a key aspect of Aseneth's conversion to Judaism.

The theme surfaces throughout the narrative. Two prayers of confession, for example, serve as bookends to the engaging saga of Aseneth's spiritual and social metamorphosis. Both prayers underscore the centrality to the author's agenda of Jewish purity and social separation. During her initial period of repentance, Aseneth confesses as follows: 'My mouth is defiled from the sacrifices of the idols and from the tables of the gods of the Egyptians' (12.5). Later in the work, after her conversion to Judaism is complete and she is now married to Joseph, Aseneth reflects back upon her pagan past and prays a second time:

> 'I have sinned, Lord, I have sinned; before you I have sinned much. And I have worshipped strange gods who were without number, and eaten bread from their sacrifices. I have sinned, Lord, I have sinned; before you I have sinned much. Bread of strangulation I have eaten, and a cup of insidiousness I have drunk from the table of death' (21.13-14).

The author apparently felt he needed still more material in his narrative to underscore the importance of the food laws for a convert to Judaism, for elsewhere he paints a colorful image of our heroine throwing her Egyptian food out of a window:

> And Aseneth took her royal dinner and the fatlings and the fish and the flesh of the heifer and all the sacrifices of her gods and the vessels of their wine of libation and threw everything through the window looking north, and gave everything to the strange dogs. For Aseneth said to herself, 'By no means must my dogs eat from my dinner and from the sacrifice of idols, but let the strange dogs eat those' (10.13).

Foodstuffs tainted with pagan idolatry are apparently unfit even for the household pets of a truly sincere convert to Judaism! Given this emphasis upon proper Jewish table fellowship, the reader is hardly surprised to discover that the first thing Joseph and Aseneth do, after the heroine cleans her cupboards and is reintroduced to Joseph as a converted proselyte, is to share a meal together:

> And Aseneth said to Joseph, 'Come, my Lord, and enter our house, because I have prepared our house and made a great dinner...' And after this they ate and drank and celebrated (20.1, 8).

Aseneth, the ideal Jewish convert, abandons unclean food and embraces the Torah's dietary laws, in order to share a table with her newly won Jewish husband. The author's convictions concerning diet and social relations could not be more transparent.[2] And he is hardly alone, in this regard, among his post-Maccabean Jewish contemporaries.

1. *Food, Social Relations, and Jewish Sectarianism*

The study of table fellowship in the Roman world has become something of a cottage industry among New Testament scholars in recent years. Eating occupies pride of place among social activities in every society, but for traditional peoples, such as those inhabiting the ancient Mediterranean basin, mealtime served as a crucial vehicle for reinforcing systems of social stratification, and for preserving boundaries between various ethnic and social groups. Scholars have emphasized the connection between food and social relations for some time. Klosinski, who used anthropological studies of table fellowship to interpret the meals in the Gospel of Mark, observed, 'Eating is a behavior which symbolizes feelings and relationships, mediates social status and power, and expresses the boundaries of group identity'.[3] Feeley-Harnik put it even more succinctly: 'food is commonly one of the principal ways in which differences among social groups are marked'.[4]

It is helpful to think of meals in the Mediterranean world marking differences among social groups in two ways, relating to the social hierarchy and to ethnicity, respectively. As an advanced agrarian culture, the Roman world exhibited a profound degree of social stratification in every corner of society, and putting people in their places at mealtime served as one of the primary means of publicly reinforcing the relational hierarchy. The result was that persons were seated (and sometimes fed) at table accord-

---

2. The conclusion to Evans's recent analysis of *Joseph and Aseneth* is quite on the mark: 'From these statements one is left with the impression that the change of lifestyle, not least the change of diet, plays a vital role in the redemption of Aseneth. God's grace is the presupposition, to be sure, but apart from wholesale adoption of Jewish food and purity laws, the conversion of Aseneth could not have taken place' (Evans [2001b: 66]).

3. Klosinski (1988: 58).

4. Feeley-Harnik (1981: 10). Snyder's discussion of food and meals is informative and insightful (1999: 129-74). He notes, 'While [Jewish] dietary regulations may be defended for environmental, health, or theological reasons, in fact, they define a people and prevent the crossing of boundaries' (148).

ing to social status. The phenomenon manifested itself at the Roman table and could also be observed among Essenes living at Qumran.[5] Mealtime thus became a living parable for the social verticality that characterized the various people-groups of the Mediterranean world. This was the primary way in which table fellowship served to fortify the social status quo. But there was also a horizontal dimension. I refer here to the potential of the table to reinforce boundaries between distinct ethnic groups.[6] Jewish antipathy toward dining with Gentiles will be most familiar along these lines, but the practice can be found among the Romans, as well. According to Suetonius, for example, Julius Caesar fed his Greek and Roman acquaintances in two separate dining halls (Suetonius, *Iul.* 48).

Jesus of Nazareth challenged both of these functions of table fellowship. His criticism of the marked verticality of his social world, which found characteristic expression in the incessant competition among males for honor and social dominance, is deeply embedded in the teaching tradition (Mk 9.33-37; 10.42-45; Lk. 18.9-14), and Jesus at times drew upon the eating practices of his contemporaries to highlight his radically alternative approach to social relations:

> 24 A dispute also arose among them as to which one of them was to be regarded as the greatest. 25 But he said to them, 'The kings of the Gentiles lord it over them; and those in authority over them are called benefactors. 26 But not so with you; rather the greatest among you must become like the youngest, and the leader like one who serves. 27 For who is greater, the one who is at the table or the one who serves? Is it not the one at the table? But I am among you as one who serves' (Lk. 22.24-27; cf. 14.7-11).

In view of texts like these Bartchy understands Jesus' 'non-hierarchical table fellowship as a central strategy in his announcement and redefinition of the inbreaking rule of God'.[7]

Jesus also subverted the manner in which table praxis among Jews in Roman Palestine functioned to reinforce boundaries horizontally, between broader social groups, and it is this aspect of Jesus' attitude toward table fellowship that is of interest in the present connection. Indeed, it can be fairly argued that Jesus' behavior established a trajectory along these lines

---

5. For an extensive discussion of Roman social values, including a look at the way in which the social hierarchy manifested itself at mealtime, see Hellerman (2005: 3-63).

6. Some anthropologists see a strong connection between table fellowship and ethnicity. Nash, for example, lists '*commensality*' as one among a 'trinity of boundary markers and mechanisms' that constitute 'the deep or basic structure of ethnic group differentiation' (Nash's other two markers are kinship and a common cult). Sharing meals together indicates 'a kind of equality, peership, and the promise of future kinship links stemming from the intimate acts of dining together, only one step removed from the intimacy of bedding together' (Nash [1989: 10-11, author's italics]).

7. Bartchy (1992: 796).

which would find his followers welcoming Gentiles to the table of Yahweh's eschatological banquet not too many years after his death and resurrection. From what we can tell, however, Jesus himself did not eat with Gentiles, and some background is in order at this point properly to set the stage for the discussion of the gospel materials in the pages to follow.

Students of the New Testament are now quite familiar with Mary Douglas's work in comprehending the significance of ancient Israelite laws of purity. Douglas argues for a connection between heightened concerns for purity among individuals, on the one hand, and threats to the social body, on the other. In the case of ancient Israel, 'The threatened boundaries of their body politic' is 'mirrored in their care for the integrity, unity and purity of the physical body'.[8] Included in this 'care' are laws relating to marriage, childbirth, sexual activities, and Old Testament dietary distinctions between clean and unclean animals. The intensification of Jewish preoccupation with purity and table fellowship during the post-Maccabean era would seem to confirm Douglas's theory, though I have encountered significant resistance to this interpretation of Jewish purity among members of the anthropological community. In the final analysis, however, we are not dependent upon anthropological models to underscore the relationship between Jewish purity and social boundaries during our period, because the connection is manifestly present in the ancient sources themselves. I expended considerable effort in earlier chapters documenting the relationship between Jewish identity and sacred food. Antipathy to dining with Gentiles characterized Jewish table practice throughout the Roman world, and this behavior contributed significantly toward establishing a robust social boundary between the two groups—a reality widely recognized by Jews and Gentiles alike.[9]

Indispensable to a proper understanding of Jesus' approach to table, however, are the intensification of the food laws and the corresponding establishment of social boundaries *among Jews themselves* in Palestine during the period of Roman occupation. The Pharisees and Essenes represent two groups in particular who refrained from table fellowship with certain of their fellow Jews.[10] We have no evidence for interaction between

---

8. Douglas (1966: 24).

9. Esler (1987: 76-86) effectively rebuts opinions to the contrary (Dunn [1983: 23]; Wilson [1983: 70]).

10. Debates between the schools of Shammai and Hillel usefully illustrate how minor differences in halakhah could serve to demarcate table boundaries. A tradition in the Mishnah portrays the schools debating about the timing of a special blessing given during the Sabbath meal. Hillelites placed the Sabbath blessing before the blessing over the wine; Shammaites insisted on blessing the wine first (*m. Ber.* 8.1). Disputes such as these concerning blessings and other details of table praxis (see *m. Ber.* 8.2-8) suggest that members of the two schools 'often ate in groups, but rarely together' (Instone-Brewer [2004: 84]).

Jesus and the Essenes, so I will limit my focus to the program of the Pharisees, whom the Gospels portray as Jesus' primary opponents.

a. *The Pharisees and Purity at Table*

Unfortunately, we know much less about the Pharisees than we would like, for, as Keck has remarked, '[T]he quest of the historical Pharisees is even more complex and controversial than the quest of the historical Jesus'.[11] Our sources are tendentious and sometimes mutually contradictory, and we may never reach consensus on certain issues in the discussion, such as the relationship between the Pharisees of Jesus' day and the *haberim* ('Associates') of the Mishnah.[12] Of some help in clarifying one key point of contention, though, has been the debate between Neusner and Sanders over the relative importance of food and table praxis for the Pharisees' program. Neusner summarizes his perspective as follows:

> [T]he Pharisees (whatever else they were) were primarily a society for table-fellowship, the high point of their life as a group. The laws of table-fellowship predominate in the Houses-disputes, as they ought to—three-fourths of all pericopae—and correspond to the legal agenda of the Pharisees according to the Synoptic stories.[13]

Sanders objects to the strong emphasis that Neusner places upon purity among first-century Pharisees.[14] Two lines of evidence for Pharisaic preoccupation with food and purity, however, suggest that Neusner has the best of this one.

First, as Neusner has repeatedly emphasized (see above), pre-70 CE rabbinic traditions attributed to the houses of Hillel and Shammai are replete with details concerning the purchase, preparation, and consumption of food.[15] To be sure, debate will continue over the relative value of specific traditions in these early rabbinic texts for reconstructing the beliefs and practices of the Pharisees of Jesus' day, and Neusner has almost certainly

---

11. Keck (2000: 34).

12. Whatever the relation of the *haberim* to the Pharisees, traditions describing the Associates in the Mishnah usefully illustrate how the multiplication of halakhic regulations inevitably generated social boundaries between various groups of Jews—and not only at mealtime. Concerns about eating properly tithed food, for example, discouraged Associates from selling produce to non-Associates, and purchasing from a non-Associate was limited to dry produce only. Nor could an Associate lodge with a commoner (*m. Dem.* 2.3a). According to Instone-Brewer, such regulations (which he dates with some degree of confidence to pre-70 CE) tended to produce 'ghettos of carefully observant Jews who bought and sold [and, of course, dined] only among themselves' (2004: 178).

13. Neusner (1992: 152).

14. For Neusner's perspective see Neusner (1971 and 1973a/b). The debate can be traced through Sanders (1990) and Neusner (1991, 1992).

15. Neusner (1973b: 86; 1971).

underestimated the political influence of the sect during the Roman period.[16] The general agreement of the Gospels with the purity agenda of the Pharisees as outlined in the Mishnah should encourage some optimism, however, where the issue of table fellowship is concerned. It is hardly coincidental, in this regard, that Sanders, who downplays matters of food and purity, brackets out the evidence from the Gospels in his reconstruction of Pharisaic priorities. Such a move is methodologically questionable, at the very least, since the Gospels constitute a second (and legitimate) source of evidence for seeing purity at table as central to the Pharisees' concerns.

As Dunn has recently noted, of the several criticisms of Jesus attributed in the Gospels to the Pharisees, four relate to food, eating, or table fellowship: 'eating with the religiously unacceptable', 'feasting rather than fasting', 'plucking grain', and 'eating with defiled hands'.[17] The last criticism is particularly informative. A comparison of Mk 7.3-4 (cited below) with passages from the Mishnah dealing with ritual purity, food preparation, and consumption generates a rather monochromatic picture of the Pharisees. Even a minimalist reconstruction of the program of the first-century Pharisees should include, therefore, a vital concern for purity of food and exclusive table fellowship.[18] It remains to consider more closely the significance of such preoccupation on the part of Jesus' Pharisaic opponents.

It has traditionally been assumed that the Pharisees' program was motivated by a desire to extend the holiness of the temple and priesthood throughout the whole land, according to Exod. 19.5-6:

16. See Hengel and Deines (1995) for evidence of continued Pharisaic involvement in the formal political arena. The general distinction between 'politics and piety', while a useful heuristic device, remains problematic, since religion was not a separate institution in antiquity but was, instead, embedded in politics and kinship. Groups like the Pharisees inevitably made strong political statements by the ways in which they practiced and promoted their ancestral religion. Theissen summarizes:

> The Pharisees whom we meet in the Hasmonean period as a political and religious group which goes on the offensive, now adopt a defensive strategy to protect Jewish identity against the political and cultural supremacy of foreigners. So they do not make a change 'from politics to piety' but rather alter their strategy. They are always both a religious and a political factor at the same time (1998: 229).

We should not be surprised, then, to find Pharisees, once again, exercising more overt political authority, when (along with the priestly aristocracy) they began to fill the power vacuum left by the expulsion of the Romans at the beginning of the Jewish revolt. The three Pharisees who constituted the majority of a four-person delegation to Galilee early in the revolt thus speak forcefully to the reality of Pharisaic influence in politics during the first century (Josephus, *Vita* 197).

17. Dunn (2003: 600).

18. Thus Klawans (2000: 108) soundly rejects Sanders's contention that the Pharisees did not eat ordinary food in a state of ritual purity.

5 'Now therefore, if you obey my voice and keep my covenant, you shall be my treasured possession out of all the peoples. Indeed, the whole earth is mine, 6 but you shall be for me a priestly kingdom and a holy nation. These are the words that you shall speak to the Israelites.'

Neusner refined this perspective in his influential book, *From Politics to Piety*, suggesting that the Pharisees viewed their tables as surrogates for the temple altar, and that they sought to eat their meals in a state of priestly purity throughout the calendar year:

> The Pharisees held that even outside the temple, in one's own home, the laws of ritual purity were to be followed in the only circumstances in which they might apply, namely, at the table. Therefore, one must eat secular food (ordinary, everyday meals) in a state of ritual purity as if one were a temple priest.[19]

Neusner's linking of Pharisaic practice with cultic purity has not gone unchallenged. Regev, for example, cites some rather persuasive evidence to support his assertion that 'the "acting like a priest" theory cannot fully explain the comprehensive phenomenon of non-priestly purity'.[20]

Fortunately the argument here does not depend upon the connection Neusner draws between lay purity and the priesthood. For whatever we make of the Pharisees' motivation, much evidence exists for the practice of purity on the part of a broad cross-section of the Jewish population of Roman Palestine at the time of Jesus.[21] The Pharisees' praxis at table can simply be viewed as an intensification of such behavior, apart from any etiological association with the temple cult. More important for our purposes are the sociological ramifications of the Pharisees' program, an aspect of purity which Regev, in my view, somewhat underemphasizes. As Bartchy accurately notes, Pharisaic purity inevitably involved 'a special focus on the purity of one's everyday food and of one's companions at every meal'.[22] Food had to be properly prepared and tithed, and eating was done in a

---

19. Neusner (1973a: 83). The linking of Pharisaic practice with cultic purity is also reflected in the work of Alon (1977: 190-234) and has become 'a regular fixture in scholarship—indeed a datum of Ancient Jewish Introduction' (Poirier [1996: 219]). For a more nuanced expression of the view see Deines's ground-breaking treatment of Pharisaism (1997; summarized in Deines [2001]).

20. Regev (2000: 186); see also Poirier (1996; 2003). Kazen suggests that '[i]t would perhaps be better to drop the discussion about living or eating "like priests" ' (2002: 69).

21. Regev (2000: 177-86). At the other extreme, Maccoby's recent book-length attempt to argue that '[t]he vast majority of Jews were not expected to be in a state of ritual purity except at festival times, when they entered the Temple area' simply does not convince (Maccoby [1999]).

22. Bartchy (1992: 796).

state of ritual purity. The behavior assigned to the Pharisees in Mark 7 is representative:

> 3 For the Pharisees, and all the Jews, do not eat unless they thoroughly wash their hands, thus observing the tradition of the elders; 4 and they do not eat anything from the market unless they wash it; and there are also many other traditions that they observe, the washing of cups, pots, and bronze kettles (Mk 7.3-4).

Inevitably excluded from table were persons unwilling or unable to eat their food in the state of purity which such a program demanded—thus the Pharisees' concerns about the table manners of Jesus: 'Why does he eat with tax collectors and sinners?' (Mk 2.16).

Also of importance in understanding the Pharisees' critique of Jesus' radically contrary approach to table is the seriousness with which Second Temple sectarian groups took their respective halakhic prescriptions. Those of us socialized to embrace Euro-American values of tolerance and religious pluralism will struggle properly to appreciate just how much was at stake in these Jewish debates over the correct application of the Torah to the exigencies of daily life. As Dunn rightly observes, '[W]here particular religious practices are integral to a group's identity, even 'minor gestures' can become make or break points of division'.[23] In the words of another pair of scholars, 'In such instances, differences in interpretation and disputes about law are raised to the level of absolute truth and falsehood and have as their consequences salvation and damnation'.[24] Thus the Pharisees of John's Gospel assert, 'But this crowd, which does not know the law—they are accursed' (Jn 7.49).[25]

---

23. Dunn (2003: 267).

24. Kraft and Nickelsburg (1986: 18). See, for example, the curse of the *minim* in the twelfth of the Eighteen Benedictions, a portion of which reads, 'For the apostates let there be no hope, and may *minim* instantly perish' (Babylonian version, cited by Instone-Brewer [2004: 104]). From an extended analysis of a rabbinic tradition describing the origin of the curse (*b. Ber.* 28b.f.), Instone-Brewer dates the curse to pre-70 CE and outlines a rather persuasive case that identifies the *minim* as 'the Sadducees of Temple times' (2004: 108-11). The Sadducees, on their part, proceeded to insert *Perushim* into the curse, in order to marginalize the Pharisees (114-15).

25. Elliott attempts to interpret Jewish sectarianism as a reaction *against* the idea of identity focused on ethnic Israel. Sectarianism in his view constitutes 'a protest movement that expressed itself in *nonnationalistic* terms' (2000: 353). On one level Elliott is technically correct, of course, since, by definition, sects like the Pharisees included among their number only a subset of those persons who by virtue of their Abrahamic patriline belonged to the broader population of ethnic Israel. Such an approach fails to give sufficient weight, however, to the manner in which these groups constructed their worldview—a worldview which invariably identified group insiders as the true remnant of *national* Israel. Qumran thus thought of itself as 'the congregation of Israel' (1Q28a [1QSa] 1.1). Jewish sectarianism is best understood, then, not as a protest against

Much of the Pharisees' halakhah dealt with food and related matters of purity, so it is likely that the table served as the primary place where this boundary between a renewed Israel, as envisioned by the Pharisees, and unobservant outsiders was tangibly expressed. We know that this was the case for Jesus and for the covenanters at Qumran, since each group viewed their daily meals as 'a foretaste of the eschatological banquet in the presence of the royal Messiah'.[26] It is not unreasonable to suppose that table fellowship functioned similarly among the Pharisees.[27]

All of this renders Jesus' behavior at mealtime highly informative for ascertaining just where Jesus established the boundary between insiders and outsiders in light of the inbreaking of the dominion of God through his public ministry. By inviting tax collectors, 'sinners', and others excluded from a renewed Israel by Pharisees and Essenes alike, Jesus essentially redrew the boundary to include all of the descendants of Abraham among the eschatological people of Yahweh. This much can be easily demonstrated from the gospel accounts. Certain statements of Jesus, however, appear even more radical in their implications, as they seem to subvert another, much more intractable, social boundary at table, namely, the boundary between Jew and Gentile. We will consider each of these aspects of Jesus' approach to table fellowship in turn.

2. *Dismantling Intra-Jewish Boundaries*

Jesus developed a scandalous reputation for sharing meals with fellow-Jews of every social and ritual stripe:[28]

---

nationalism but, rather, as an intensification of ethnic boundary concerns, as '*a focusing of the national hope on the devout of Israel*' (Dunn [2005: 60] author's italics).

26. Dunn (2003: 603). This is pretty standard fare among Jesus scholars. Thus Chilton observes of Jesus and his followers, 'Each meal was a proleptic celebration of God's kingdom' (1996: 86). Jesus' table praxis represented the 'realization of the coming Kingdom of God' (Becker [1998: 160-61]).

Much evidence obtains for the notion of an eschatological banquet in Second-Temple literature. Blomberg's survey is thorough and judicious (2005: 65-86). *1 En.* 62.13-14, for example, envisions the 'elect' dining with the 'Son of Man', presumably at an eschatological meal of some sort. The concept finds its origins in the Hebrews Scriptures, in a passage that is likely the single most influential text for the later development of the idea in Judaism and early Christianity: 'On this mountain the Lord of hosts will make for all peoples a feast of rich food, a feast of well-aged wines, of rich food filled with marrow, of well-aged wines strained clear' (Isa. 25.6, on which see Miller [1995]). Psalm 36.7-9 may also have contributed to the notion of a messianic banquet: 'All people…feast on the abundance of your house' (Blomberg [2005: 50-51]).

27. Not all would agree with this observation (Sanders [1977: 152-55]). I will return to the matter, below, in my treatment of Lk. 7.36-50 (see n. 44).

28. Karris's quip—that Jesus was killed because of the way he ate—has become somewhat of a classic in the ongoing discussion of Jesus and table fellowship (1985: 70).

> 18 'For John came neither eating nor drinking, and they say, 'He has a demon'; 19 the Son of Man came eating and drinking, and they say, 'Look, a glutton and a drunkard, a friend of tax collectors and sinners!' Yet wisdom is vindicated by her deeds' (Mt. 11.18-19; par. Lk. 7.33-34).[29]

The criticism is reiterated in various layers of the gospel tradition:

> 15 And as he sat at dinner in Levi's house, many tax collectors and sinners were also sitting with Jesus and his disciples—for there were many who followed him. 16 When the scribes of the Pharisees saw that he was eating with sinners and tax collectors, they said to his disciples, 'Why does he eat with tax collectors and sinners?' 17 When Jesus heard this, he said to them, 'Those who are well have no need of a physician, but those who are sick; I have come to call not the righteous but sinners' (Mk 2.15-17; par. Mt. 9.9-13; Lk 5.29-32).[30]

> 1 Now all the tax collectors and sinners were coming near to listen to him. 2 And the Pharisees and the scribes were grumbling and saying, 'This fellow welcomes sinners and eats with them' (Lk. 15.1-2).

The two texts above introduce the Pharisees as frontline critics of Jesus' behavior. Given our understanding of the socio-religious function of table fellowship among the Pharisees (above), we may surmise that by eating with 'tax collectors and sinners' Jesus effectively repositions the boundary that defined the people of Yahweh, so as to include any descendant of Abraham who will embrace his program for Israel's renewal—irrespective of his or her state of ritual purity. In perfect accord, then, with his subversive approach to sacred times and sacred space, Jesus, by practicing open table fellowship, once again renegotiates the way in which Yahweh's people will be identified in the context of the newly inaugurated kingdom of God.

a. *Inviting Jesus to Dinner*
The Gospel of Luke relates a story that vividly highlights Jesus' radically inclusive approach to table fellowship. Jesus receives an invitation to dine

---

29. See Bartchy's arguments for the reliability of this tradition from the synoptic sayings source (1992: 797). Jesus' table fellowship with tax gatherers and sinners is an aspect of his ministry the historicity of which is 'supported by all the standard criteria of authenticity' (Catchpole [2006: 78]; see Blomberg [2005: 20-31]). A minority viewpoint locates the practice in the creative activity of the evangelists (most notably, D.E. Smith [1987; 2003]).

30. Dunn insightfully comments on the passage as follows:

> However freely creative individuals or groups may have been with regard to the Jesus-tradition, no attempt has been made here to include Gentiles within the 'sinners', and no attempt made to show Jesus at this point eating with Gentiles (Dunn [1990: 19-20]).

This, of course, suggests a conservative preservation of the materials in Mk 2.15-17.

with a Pharisee named Simon (Lk. 7.36-50).[31] Luke informs us that Jesus 'went into the Pharisee's house and took his place at the table' (v. 36), a bit of social realia that is surely intended by the author to draw the reader's attention to issues of purity and table fellowship, which will serve as a key subtext for the balance of the narrative. The plot of the story turns on the intrusion into Simon's dinner party of a 'woman in the city' who is identified in the text as a 'sinner' (v. 37). Jesus welcomes the woman's lavish attention, as she washes Jesus' feet with her own tears and anoints them with oil (v. 38).[32] Simon, of course, has no room at his table for such a person, and he surmises that if Jesus were truly a prophet, he would know 'who and what kind of woman this is who is touching him—that she is a sinner' (v. 39).

Simon's identification of the woman as a 'sinner' (v. 39) must be understood against the way in which the term was used by various writers and sectarian groups to marginalize non-members as outsiders. Scholars have generally been too eager in seeking for the word 'sinner' some absolute referent, thereby ignoring the rhetorical function of the term in its Second Temple context. Jeremias, for example, identified 'sinners' as 'a specific

---

31. The tradition history of Lk. 7.36-50 is complicated by the parallel account in Mk 14.3-9 (cf. Mt. 26.6-13, and Jn 12.1-8), where the setting is not Galilee but, rather, Bethany, near the end of Jesus' life. The basic question relates to whether Luke's version and the versions of the other evangelists represent (a) two forms of one story, or (b) two distinct stories having similarities that can be accounted for by cross-fertilization at the level of oral tradition. The above analysis proceeds on the latter assumption and reflects a corresponding optimism about the historical integrity of Luke's account. Those who argue for two distinct anointing stories include Marshall (1978: 306), Witherington (1984: 110-11), Bock (1994: 689-91), and Blomberg (2005: 131). See, also, the list of supporters for the two story view in Holst (1976: 435 n. 2), though the author himself is not among them. Gundry (1993: 809-10) and Bock (1994: 689-91) helpfully enumerate the similarities and differences between the two accounts. Bock resists Marshall's suggestion that the two stories influenced one another during the oral traditioning process (1994: 691), and he may be correct. As Blomberg notes, the only unusual features that Mark and Luke have in common are the name of the host (Simon) and the use of an 'alabaster jar of ointment' (1987: 147). Simon was an extremely common name (Plummer [1896/1975: 209] notes some ten or eleven Simons in the New Testament, and about twenty in Josephus), and the phrase describing the perfume is stereotypical, so neither parallel carries much weight.

32. Instone-Brewer remarks at some length about the likely impurity of the woman's oil and the implications of the anointing for Jesus' ensuing ritual status. He suggests that Simon and his guests 'were probably thinking about this issue among all the other issues of *impurity* which this event provoked' (Instone-Brewer [2004: 387], author's italics). Instone-Brewer is undoubtedly correct. We get a glimpse of Galilean convictions about pure versus impure oil in Josephus's narrative of his experience in the north during the early part of the Jewish revolt. During a food shortage in Caesarea Philippi the Jewish inhabitants of the city were willing to pay an exorbitant price for 'pure oil. . .lest they should be driven to violate their legal ordinances by resort to Grecian oil' (*Vita* 74–75).

term for those engaged in despised trades' and included them among 'the *'ammē hā-'āreṣ* (people of the land), the uneducated, the ignorant, whose *religious* ignorance and *moral* behaviour stood in the way of their access to salvation, according to the convictions of the time'.[33] Recent scholarship has strongly resisted this definition, preferring instead to see in 'sinners' a reference to 'the wicked', 'deliberate and unrepentant transgressors of the law'.[34] The interpretation represents somewhat of an improvement over Jeremias's definition, in that it coheres well with the consistent use of the term in the Old Testament, where a 'sinner' is one who breaks, or fails to observe, the injunctions of the Torah. The view remains problematic, however, since various Second Temple religious groups adamantly disagreed about precisely what the law required. As we saw above, moreover, these halakhic differences often became determinative for establishing boundaries between insiders and outsiders according to a given group's conception of the true people of Yahweh. In such a social context 'sinner' becomes a malleable term that can be applied by members of a sectarian group to anyone whose conduct they view as incompatible with their own group norms. As Dunn summarizes, 'The unavoidable conclusion for such a group is that others are 'sinners' because they fail to observe the doctrine or praxis which is of such self-definitional significance for the group'.[35] Malina relates this rhetorical use of the term specifically to differences over ritual purity: 'When viewed through the prism of the prevailing purity system, the dissident is seen clearly as outside the realm of what is holy and exclusive to the group'.[36]

From Simon's perspective in the Lukan narrative, then, the woman is a 'sinner', at least in part, because she is apparently in a state of ritual impurity which renders her presence in Simon's home wholly unacceptable according to Pharisaic scruples related to food and table fellowship. This is not to exclude a moral component from the mix, for the narrator, not just Simon,

---

33. Jeremias (1971: 109-12).
34. Sanders (1985: 177-80). Similarly, Meier (1994: 149, 211-12; 2001: 28-29) and Crossan and Reed (2001: 119).
35. Dunn (2003: 529; cf. 528-32). I am depending on Dunn throughout for the discussion of the term 'sinner'. By way of example, see *m. Sheb.* 9.9, which labels as 'sinners' those persons who fail to adhere to detailed halakhah related to the buying and selling of foodstuffs during the Sabbath Year. Catchpole comes to similar conclusions based on the use of 'sinner(s)' in the *Psalms of Solomon*. Commenting on the label in the Gospels, he notes,

> There must be the strong suspicion that the most important feature of a sinner is that, viewed from the perspective of a sectarian or special interest group, s/he is not 'one of us…' So in all talk of the so-called sinners we have to bear in mind that the issue is probably the drawing of a line around the authentic people of God, or the defining of the boundary of that people *on the basis of Pharisaic convictions* (Catchpole [2006: 81] author's italics).

36. Malina (2001: 60).

labels the woman a 'sinner' (v. 37).[37] The forgiving of her 'many' sins in vv. 47-48 also points in this direction, and a number of commentators have plausibly suggested that the woman was a prostitute.[38] Whatever might have been the moral state of the woman, however, we can be assured that she was ritually unfit for table fellowship with Simon and his guests, as well.[39] Both the setting of the narrative—at table in the home of a Pharisee—and

---

37. As Méndez-Moratalla remarks, 'sinner' takes on a somewhat different connotation depending on who uses the term in Luke. Of 7.36-50, he notes: 'That the woman is a sinner is a picture that Luke provides (7.37), the Pharisee accentuates (7.39), and Jesus implicitly endorses (7.47)' (2004: 106).

38. Bovon (1991: 383); York (1991: 122 n. 3); Nolland (1989: 353, 360); Marshall (1978: 308). Bock is less certain and offers several alternatives (1994: 695). Corley suggests that the woman may have been 'a lower-class working woman or freedwoman who may have earned her freedom by prostituting herself' (1993: 124). See also Reid, who offers a number of options for the woman's status and background (1995: 43).

39. The relationship between sin and impurity has only recently begun to receive the attention it deserves. The most important treatments are Klawans (2000) and Kazen (2002). Different Jewish groups, it seems, related moral defilement to ritual impurity in different ways. At Qumran the two categories were 'melded into a single conception of defilement, which had both ritual and moral ramifications' (Klawans 2000: 90). A person who was morally impure was viewed as ritually defiling, and vice-versa. Among the Tannaim, in contrast, the two categories of moral defilement and ritual defilement remained distinct, so that an immoral person did not render another Jew ritually impure.

The kind of compartmentalization Klawans claims for the tannaim, however, would not necessarily have characterized general expansionist purity practices at the time of Jesus (Kazen [2002: 216-19]). In Kazen's view, the perspective of Qumran, which collapsed ritual and moral defilement into a single category, was not anomalous but, rather, represented an extreme point along a 'moral trajectory' that variously related bodily impurity to sinful behavior. Kazen thus posits '*some* sort of interaction or link between sin and bodily impurity both in popular belief and among Essenes as well as among Pharisees' (2002: 219, author's italics).

This blurring of moral and ritual categories would have been particularly acute at mealtime. For although we might intuitively interpret the levitical dietary regulations in terms of ritual purity, the outright prohibition of eating certain foods functions 'more like a moral defilement than a ritual one' (Klawans [2000: 32]). The moral component would have been decidedly reinforced during our period by Maccabean historiography, which so closely connected the maintenance of the dietary laws to God's blessing upon the Jewish nation.

For Simon and his Jewish contemporaries, therefore, the line between moral and ritual purity at table was likely a tenuous one, at best. At any rate, a woman who lived a life that was morally questionable according to village standards would surely be excluded from a dinner like Simon's (Westerholm [1992: 131]), whatever her ritual status. The woman's blatant indifference to Pharisaic conventions of purity, exhibited in her behavior toward Jesus, would only have reinforced Simon's assumption that the woman had no claim to a place at the table of Yahweh's holy remnant. Given the social function of Pharisaic table fellowship, for Jesus to affirm such a person's presence at Simon's meal is to say volumes about his vision for a socially inclusive eschatological people of God.

Simon's comment about the woman 'touching' Jesus (v. 39) argue in favor of seeing Pharisaic convictions concerning ritual purity as meaningful for understanding the import of Jesus' counter-cultural behavior in the story.[40] We continue now with the Lukan narrative.

By way of response to Simon's concerns (v. 39), Jesus tells his host a parable that he will proceed to interpret in such a way as utterly to invert the cultural values and social codes by which Pharisees made sense of their relational world:[41]

> 40 Jesus spoke up and said to him, 'Simon, I have something to say to you'. 'Teacher', he replied, 'Speak.' 41 'A certain creditor had two debtors; one owed five hundred denarii, and the other fifty. 42 When they could not pay, he canceled the debts for both of them. Now which of them will love him more?' 43 Simon answered, 'I suppose the one for whom he canceled the greater debt'. And Jesus said to him, 'You have judged rightly' (vv. 40-43).

Simon's half-hearted answer has set him up for a pointed and wholly unexpected rebuke. At this point in the narrative Jesus has already tacitly affirmed the woman's presence at the table by warmly receiving her efforts on his behalf (v. 38). Now Jesus goes so far as to identify the woman—not Simon—as the one who has proven to be the true host at the meal:

> 44 Then turning toward the woman, he said to Simon, 'Do you see this woman? I entered your house; you gave me no water for my feet, but she has bathed my feet with her tears and dried them with her hair. 45 You gave me no kiss, but from the time I came in she has not stopped kissing my feet. 46 You did not anoint my head with oil, but she has anointed my feet with ointment' (vv. 44-46).[42]

---

40. Méndez-Moratalla (2004: 104-105). Kazen, too, argues for the presence of purity concerns in Luke's narrative from 'the impropriety of the woman touching Jesus' and from the setting of the encounter at a meal. Simon's invitation 'could be taken to imply that the Pharisee regarded Jesus as trustworthy in matters of purity. The incident with the woman touching Jesus would then prove the Pharisee's expectation to be false, and risk defiling not only Jesus, but the food and drink' (2002: 137-38, cf. 138 n. 268). Bock (1994: 697) and Plummer (1896/1975: 211) offer the present tense of ἅπτεται as evidence that ongoing contact with Jesus is in view in Simon's comment in v. 39. See, as well, the comments about the potential impurity of the anointing oil, above (footnote 32).

41. Blomberg mounts a reasonable defense of the authenticity of the parable in its present context (1990: 184-85).

42. 'Seeing' (v. 44, 'Do you see this woman?') is a common Lukan metaphor, describing the enlightened perspective of those who embrace the kingdom (Méndez-Moratalla [2004: 117]). Green thus sees Jesus' question here as 'an invitation to enlightenment' (1997: 312). I take it as ironic. Jesus' point in the question is that Simon assuredly has not 'seen' the woman as Jesus has seen her.

Luke's grammar is specifically framed, moreover, to emphasize the woman as an example whom Jesus extols. The demonstrative pronoun ταύτην (v. 44) is picked up

The irony is almost deafening given the cultural scripts that defined roles and circumscribed social behavior at such an event. As the host of a Pharisaic meal, Simon would have been the one responsible to maintain a guest list that insured a degree of table purity appropriate to the scruples of his sect.[43] As we saw above, moreover, the resulting social boundaries would, in turn, symbolize the host's (and his guests') conception of the true people of Yahweh. It is therefore part of Simon's function, as host of the meal, to fashion around his table a living parable, so to speak, of the holy remnant of a renewed Israel. In this social microcosm of the people of God, Simon the Pharisee determines who is in and who is out.[44]

Or does he? It just so happens that Jesus singles out not Simon but the uninvited 'sinner' as the truly honorable host at the event, affirming the woman's hospitable gestures even as she blatantly defied every ideal of Pharisaic table purity. According to Jesus' reconstruction of the roles at Simon's table, then, it is the sinful woman who, by usurping Simon's position as the host of the meal, earns the right symbolically to redefine

---

three times with αὕτη (vv. 44, 45, 46) in reference to the woman, while Simon gets only the second person singular inflection of the verb throughout the threefold comparison (Arlandson [1997: 161]).

43. Thus the dismay of another Pharisee who invited Jesus to share a meal: 'While he was speaking, a Pharisee invited him to dine with him; so he went in and took his place at the table. The Pharisee was amazed to see that he did not first wash before dinner' (Lk. 11.37-38). Not only was the host responsible for the guest list. According to Plutarch, the host was responsible for arranging the placement of the guests at the meal, as well (*Mor.* 1.615D). See Neyrey on the role of the host at table in the Mediterranean world (1991: 364).

44. Sanders, in contrast, finds "not a shred of evidence" for the notion that the Pharisees were a soteriologically exclusive sect like the Essenes (1977: 155). He would almost certainly take issue, therefore, with my interpretation of Lk. 7.36-50. As we saw earlier in the chapter, however, Sanders assumes (in contrast to Neusner and others) that the Pharisees were not particularly concerned with purity of food and table. Such a perspective coheres nicely, in turn, with the conviction that the Pharisees were not, in fact, a sectarian movement analogous to the Essenes at Qumran.

In my view, Sanders is wide of the mark on both counts, as persuasively argued by Dunn (1988c and, more briefly, 1992a: 257-60). Pharisaic preoccupation with purity of food and table, as evidenced in the Mishnah and the Gospels, coupled with the eschatological orientation of table fellowship at Qumran (and among Jesus and his followers), would seem to imply some kind of remnant theology on the part of the Pharisees, an ideology which likely found expression at mealtime. (Note, for example, the exclamation of a guest at another Pharisaic dinner party, narrated in Luke 14: "Blessed is anyone who will eat bread in the kingdom of God!" [v. 15]). Jesus, at any rate, seems to assume as much in our passage, when he (a) identifies the uninvited woman as the true host of the meal, and (b) pronounces her "forgiven"—a status that assures her a place among the eschatological people of God. Much more seems to be at stake at Simon's table, therefore, than would be the case at a simple social gathering.

the boundaries of the eschatological people of God.[45] And in the story's conclusion Jesus pointedly affirms the map of persons that results from this repositioning of social boundaries, when he points to the woman's 'great love' as evidence that she has been a forgiven guest at God's banquet table all along:[46]

> 47 Therefore, I tell you, her sins, which were many, have been forgiven; hence she has shown great love. But the one to whom little is forgiven, loves little'. 48 Then he said to her, 'Your sins are forgiven'. 49 But those who were at the table with him began to say among themselves, 'Who is this who even forgives sins?' 50 And he said to the woman, 'Your faith has saved you; go in peace' (vv. 47-50).

A notorious 'sinner' has intruded into a Pharisee's house. She has boldly joined those gathered around Simon's table, and she has ostensibly defiled the guest of honor by repeatedly touching him with hands that are ritually

---

45. 'The one who had sought to be a host of Jesus is thus shown to be less hospitable than the sinful woman of the city: she is the truly hospitable one in the story' (York [1991: 124]). Some have maintained, in contrast, that Simon lacked nothing in the basic hospitality owed to a guest like Jesus. Thus, Fitzmyer: Simon's 'omissions should not be emphasized as signs of impoliteness' [1981: 691]; see Marshall [1978: 311]). However, given (a) the meal setting of the event, (b) Simon's role as host, and (c) the comparison Jesus draws between Simon and the woman, it can fairly be argued that Jesus is identifying the woman as the one who has proved to be the true host at the meal. As Méndez-Moratalla rightly affirms, '[T]he attentions the intruding woman offers to Jesus come closer to those expected of a host than those of Simon the Pharisee' (2004: 118). So also Resseguie, who claims that Simon omits customary amenities for his guest (1991: 145). Bailey, who sees in Simon's behavior toward Jesus a host who intentionally insults his guest, lists the following as the usual order of events when welcoming a guest into one's home in such a setting: (1) the kiss of greeting; (2) the washing of the feet of the guest; and (3) the anointing of the head with oil (1980: 7-8). The parallels with the woman's behavior in our passage are significant.

The third of the three obligations which Simon neglected may be particularly revealing given rabbinic aversion to the practice. A tradition from the Tosefta suggests that the normal practice of anointing the head with perfumed oil was disdained by pre-70 CE rabbis (*t. Ber.* 5.29). Jesus, however, reminds Simon that to offer the anointing 'was part of natural hospitality, as was a kiss and foot washing' (Instone-Brewer [2004: 91], who dates the tradition firmly to our period).

46. With most commentators I assume that the woman's approach, and Jesus' parable and explanation, presuppose a prior experience of forgiveness. Forgiveness generates the woman's love and not the reverse. Nolland suggests that Lk. 7.29-30 'may encourage us to view the woman as coming to Jesus to express gratitude to him for the forgiveness already proleptically bestowed on her by John (cf. at 3.3)' (1989: 354; see also Green [1997: 313] and Bock [1994: 705]). Méndez-Moratalla, in contrast, understands the forgiveness to be bestowed in Jesus' pronouncement at the banquet (2004: 110, 124-25). See his extended discussion of the debated relationship between love and forgiveness in the passage (119-21).

impure. All of this Jesus defines as an act of 'faith' (v. 50). In his affirmation of the woman's behavior Jesus has turned Simon's symbolic universe on its head by effectively redrawing the boundary line between the people of God and those whom the Pharisees and others had marginalized as 'sinners'. This repositioning of food-related identity markers to include all of Jesus' fellow Jews in his program for Israel's renewal is well-attested in the gospel accounts. As Jesus elsewhere proclaimed to those who objected to his fellowship with the notorious tax collector Zacchaeus, 'Today salvation has come to this house, because he too is a son of Abraham' (Lk. 19.9). It remains to be considered whether Jesus envisioned extending the horizons of God's eschatological banquet to include Gentiles at the table.

3. *Table Fellowship with Gentiles*

We have no evidence of Jesus formally dining with Gentiles, and certain passages seem to indicate an intentional restriction of Jesus' mission to the descendants of Abraham. The mission instructions to the disciples in Matthew 10 are illustrative: 'Go nowhere among the Gentiles, and enter no town of the Samaritans' (v. 5). So is Jesus' initial reaction to the request of the Syrophoenician woman (Mk 7.27; par. Mt. 15.24). For several reasons, however, we should hesitate to assume that Jesus wholly excluded Gentiles from his kingdom program.

During his ministry Jesus did interact with Gentiles, both fulfilling their requests and affirming their faith. His response to the request of a Roman centurion who had asked Jesus to heal a slave is the classic example of such affirmation: 'I tell you, not even in Israel have I found such faith' (Lk. 7.9; par. Mt. 8.10). Jesus' predecessor, John, had pointedly cautioned against the widespread tendency to base soteriological confidence solely on Abrahamic descent: 'Do not presume to say to yourselves, "We have Abraham as our ancestor"; for I tell you, God is able from these stones to raise up children to Abraham' (Mt. 3.9; par. Lk. 3.8). Related warnings imply that Gentiles might fare even better than Jews in the court of God's justice at the end of the age:

> 20 Then he began to reproach the cities in which most of his deeds of power had been done, because they did not repent. 21 'Woe to you, Chorazin! Woe to you, Bethsaida! For if the deeds of power done in you had been done in Tyre and Sidon, they would have repented long ago in sackcloth and ashes. 22 But I tell you, on the day of judgment it will be more tolerable for Tyre and Sidon than for you' (Mt. 11.20-22; par. Lk. 10.13-14; see also Mt. 12.41; par. Lk. 11.32).

As we have seen, moreover, Jesus interpreted his temple action by citing Isa. 56.7 (Mk 11.17), a text that looked forward to the inclusion of 'foreigners' among worshippers at the Jerusalem temple at the end of the age.

The Isaianic text is representative of 'a strong strand of Jewish expectation' which anticipated Gentiles joining Israel in the worship of Yahweh on Zion.[47] The gospel passages cited above suggest that Jesus himself shared this hope. Can we now in any way connect Jesus' openness to Gentiles with his praxis at table? There is some evidence that may point in this direction.

a. *Matthew 8.11-12 and Luke 13.28-29*

Among recurring emphases in the teaching of Jesus is the theme of eschatological reversal, evidenced most memorably in the collection of beatitudes (Mt. 5.3-12; par. Lk. 6.20-23). Other examples of reversal include the image of children as those who typify kingdom persons, the woes to the Jewish cities (cited above), and the following warning passage, which identifies the participants at the eschatological kingdom banquet:

> 11 'I tell you, many will come from east and west and will eat with Abraham and Isaac and Jacob in the kingdom of heaven, 12 while the heirs of the kingdom will be thrown into the outer darkness, where there will be weeping and gnashing of teeth' (Mt. 8.11-12; par. Lk. 13.28-29).

Jesus' assertion draws upon passages from the Hebrew Scriptures which anticipate the return of Israel's exiles to their homeland, such as Isa. 43.5-6:

> 5 Do not fear, for I am with you;
>   I will bring your offspring from the east,
>   and from the west I will gather you;
> 6 I will say to the north, 'Give them up',
>   and to the south, 'Do not withhold;
> bring my sons from far away
>   and my daughters from the end of the earth'.

The promise, as it occurs in both the Old Testament (Ps 107.3; Isa. 49.12; Jer. 3.18) and in later Jewish literature (Bar. 4.36-37; 5.5), relates not to Gentiles but to ethnic Israel. It is the dispersion of Israel which will be gathered together at Zion from the four corners of the earth. There is some question, though, as to whether Jesus has not reinterpreted the promise to refer to the future ingathering of 'the eschatological pilgrims from the nations', also a familiar Old Testament theme (see Isa. 25.6-9).[48] If so, then

---

47. Dunn (2003: 538). One could add to the database of Gentile-friendly traditions the programmatic proclamation in the synagogue at Nazareth, where Jesus pointedly refers to the ministries of the prophets Elijah and Elisha to non-Israelites (a Sidonian widow and a Syrian general, respectively) (Lk. 4.25-27).

48. So Dunn (2003: 415). Stuhlmacher, too, cites Mt. 8.11-12 in his discussion of 'the pilgrimage of the nations to Zion which Jesus had looked ahead to' (2000: 30). See also H. Stettler (2004: 158-59). Sanders, in contrast, assigns Mt. 8.12 to Matthean redaction and interprets the remaining saying in terms of the return of the Jewish dispersion men-

we have Gentiles at the eschatological table of Yahweh, an image which, at the very least, would have generated considerable dissonance among Jesus' listeners, given contemporary Jewish preoccupation with the vital identity marker of separate table fellowship.

Both Matthew and Luke appear to have interpreted Jesus' words to refer to Gentiles. In Luke's case, the above saying occurs in the context of a dialogue with an anonymous questioner while Jesus is on his way to Jerusalem:

> 22 Jesus went through one town and village after another, teaching as he made his way to Jerusalem. 23 Someone asked him, 'Lord, will only a few be saved?' He said to them, 24 'Strive to enter through the narrow door; for many, I tell you, will try to enter and will not be able. 25 When once the owner of the house has got up and shut the door, and you begin to stand outside and to knock at the door, saying, "Lord, open to us", then in reply he will say to you, "I do not know where you come from". 26 Then you will begin to say, "We ate and drank with you, and you taught in our streets". 27 But he will say, "I do not know where you come from; go away from me, all you evildoers!" 28 There will be weeping and gnashing of teeth when you see Abraham and Isaac and Jacob and all the prophets in the kingdom of God, and you yourselves thrown out. 29 Then people will come from east and west, from north and south, and will eat in the kingdom of God' (Lk. 13.22-29).

The text contrasts those who will come 'from east and west, from north and south' (v. 29) with 'you yourselves' (v. 28; cf. 'you', vv. 25, 26), that is, Jesus' fellow-Jews, whom he encounters during his travels 'through one village after another' (v. 22). The implication, then, may be that the former are Gentiles.[49]

Matthew is even more transparent in this regard, since he appends the warning directly to Jesus' exclamation at the faith of the pagan centurion:

> 10 When Jesus heard him, he was amazed and said to those who followed him, 'Truly I tell you, in no one in Israel have I found such faith. 11 I tell you, many will come from east and west and will eat with Abraham and Isaac and

tioned above (1985: 219-20). Sanders finally attributes to Jesus 'no explicit viewpoint at all' on the Gentiles (221).

49. Marshall: 'The subject of the verse (v. 29) is of course the gentiles' (1978: 568; also Wilson [1973: 33]; Morris [1992: 195]; and Freyne [2004: 12-13]). Nolland disagrees. He sees Luke's version as reflecting an original reference solely to the dispersion of Israel (1993: 735). Yet as Keener observes, no one questioned whether or not Jews as a whole outside Palestine would inherit the kingdom. Diaspora Judaism, therefore, would make little sense rhetorically as a surprising example of inclusion in the context of the theme of eschatological reversal (Keener [1999: 270]). Keener is commenting here about Matthew's version of the saying (*contra* the minority viewpoint of Davies and Allison [1991: 27-28], who see only Judeans in Jesus' pronouncement), but his observations could be equally applied to the Lukan version.

Jacob in the kingdom of heaven, 12 while the heirs of the kingdom will be thrown into the outer darkness, where there will be weeping and gnashing of teeth' (Mt. 8.10-12).[50]

Understanding the pilgrims from afar to be Gentiles coheres well with other Jew–Gentile reversal passages (cited above) which, for example, portray Tyre and Sidon faring better than Chorazin and Bethsaida at the end of the age (Mt.11.20-22; par. Lk. 10.13-14), and Nineveh triumphing in judgment over 'this generation' (Mt.12.41; par. Lk. 11.32).

b. *Luke 14.1-24*

Another Lukan narrative appears to paint a similar picture of initially uninvited Gentiles replacing Jews at the kingdom table. The story occurs in Luke 14, in a series of interactions between Jesus and persons eating together in 'the house of a leader of the Pharisees' on the Sabbath (Lk. 14.1). During the course of the narrative Jesus first performs a Sabbath healing (vv. 2-6). He then challenges the social hierarchy so characteristic of table fellowship in the Mediterranean world (vv. 7-11). In what follows Jesus turns his attention directly to his host, instructing him about the kinds of persons he should invite to a dinner party (vv. 12-14). At this point, one of the guests at the table exclaims, 'Blessed is anyone who will eat bread in the kingdom of God!' (v. 15). Jesus replies with yet another striking parable of eschatological reversal:

> 16 Then Jesus said to him, 'Someone gave a great dinner and invited many. 17 At the time for the dinner he sent his slave to say to those who had been invited, "Come; for everything is ready now". 18 But they all alike began to make excuses. The first said to him, "I have bought a piece of land, and I must go out and see it; please accept my regrets". 19 Another said, "I have bought five yoke of oxen, and I am going to try them out; please accept my regrets". 20 Another said, "I have just been married, and therefore I cannot come". 21 So the slave returned and reported this to his master. Then the owner of the house became angry and said to his slave, "Go out at once into the streets and lanes of the town and bring in the poor, the crippled, the blind, and the lame" ' (Lk. 14.16-21).

In the parable, every last one of those initially invited excuses himself from the 'great dinner'. The host orders them to be replaced with 'the poor, the crippled, the blind, and the lame' (v. 21). The list appears to have been framed with ritual purity in view, and a contrast with eating practices at Qumran may be intended. The covenanters at Qumran were even more strict than the Pharisees in excluding the ritually impure from their table. Specifically identified as unclean is anyone 'paralysed in his feet or hands, or lame,

---

50. Marshall thinks the linking of the text in question with the story of the centurion's slave in Matthew's version may be original, although the saying may have formerly preceded the story (1978: 564).

or blind, or deaf, or dumb, or smitten in his flesh with a visible blemish' (1Q28a [1QSa] 2.3-10).[51] The list echoes Lev. 21.17-24 and thereby reflects the self-understanding of the Essenes at Qumran as a priestly community. Notice, in the present connection, the parallel with what we find in Lk. 14.21, above. It is not unreasonable to suppose that Jesus gave the exhortation with Qumran practices directly in view.[52] Assuming this to be the case, we here find Jesus, once again, expanding the boundaries of table fellowship to include certain Judeans who, for reasons of impurity, had been excluded from table by sectarian halakhah.

Jesus' parable, however, is not yet complete. The Lukan narrative goes on to include yet another group of persons at the 'great dinner', persons who may be taken to symbolize non-Judean guests:

> 22 'And the slave said, "Sir, what you ordered has been done, and there is still room". 23 Then the master said to the slave, "Go out into the roads and lanes, and compel people to come in, so that my house may be filled. 24 For I tell you, none of those who were invited will taste my dinner" ' (vv. 22-24).

The parable does not explicitly include representatives from other nations among the invited guests, but the allusion to Gentile participants seems reasonably clear. The contextual juxtaposition of the command to indiscriminately fill the house (v. 23) with the host's assertion that 'none of those who were invited will taste my dinner' suggests an eschatological reversal whereby Gentiles join marginalized unclean Jews at the table of Yahweh.[53]

---

51. The quotation is from Dunn (2003: 604).

52. Dunn (1992a) analyzes the various terms in Luke, Leviticus, and the DSS in some detail.

53. According to Marshall, the last group 'can most plausibly be identified as gentiles'. Marshall proceeds to argue for the authenticity of the second invitation in the life of Jesus: 'it is far from certain that Luke has expanded the original parable here' (1978: 590). Others, however, assign the second invitation (v. 23) to Lukan redaction, in view of Luke's interest in the twofold spread of the Gospel to Jews and Gentiles (York [1991: 143]; see Jeremias [1963: 64]).

Braun offers an alternative, socio-economic interpretation of Lk. 14.16-24, which excludes entirely considerations of purity and ethnicity (1995: 62-97). According to his reading, the host invites first his peer elites (vv. 16-17), then the urban poor (v. 21), and, finally, 'para-urban' persons 'who lived close to the city precincts...but not within the city walls because the nature of their business was too naturally noxious, socially odious or religiously suspect' (v. 23) (1995: 93). Each invitation in the story thus utilizes 'spatial language for a socially locative rather than for an ethnic-identifying purpose', and Gentiles are therefore nowhere explicitly in view (1995: 89). Braun fails to consider the Qumran parallel (see above), however, which encourages us to identify the second group of invited guests as Jews who were deemed impure according to Essene halakhah, rather than (with Braun) as the more general 'urban poor' (81-88). This, in turn, renders the interpretation of the final group (v. 23) as Gentiles a wholly reasonable one.

c. *The Feedings in the Wilderness*

Scholars are increasingly considering the implications of the feedings in the wilderness for Jesus' attitude towards food and social boundaries.[54] Both the feeding of the five thousand (Mk 6.30-44 and par.) and the feeding of the four thousand (Mk 8.1-10 and par.) occur in geographical settings that wholly preclude the possibility of maintaining Pharisaic standards of purity. The wide cross-section of social classes inevitably represented by the crowds, the lack of guest lists or formal seating plans of any sort, and the absence of any facilities for handwashing or other cleansing rites guarantee in both feedings a radically inclusive approach to 'table' on Jesus' part. Jesus' lack of concern for sectarian boundaries is therefore patently clear. As Poon observes of the first feeding, 'The good news of God's unconditional acceptance of sinners is materially fulfilled by Jesus' table fellowship with all kinds of "undesirables" without regard to the meal conventions of the Pharisees'.[55] The five thousand fed by Jesus in the first story are Jews, not Gentiles, so that the undermining of social boundaries reflected in the event applies solely to boundaries that had been erected between sectarian and non-sectarian Jews.

The second wilderness feeding (Mk 8.1-10) appears, however, to expand Jesus' boundary-breaking activities to include Gentiles among those who feast upon the messianic abundance of loaves and fishes.[56] Several hints in the text suggest as much. The setting of the event, in Gentile territory east of the Sea of Galilee, assumes the presence of Gentiles in an ethnically mixed gathering.[57] The way in which Mark describes the surplus food points in the same direction. After the first feeding (Mk 6.43), the disciples gathered up twelve basketfuls of bread. Here, as the narrative of the second feeding concludes (8.8), they pick up seven basketfuls. According to Blomberg, the former is a standard Jewish number, possibly alluding to the twelve tribes of Israel; 'seven' is, in contrast, the common number for universal realities.

---

54. I am depending for much of what follows upon Blomberg's judicious treatment of the wilderness feedings (2005: 103-12). With the author of Mark, I take the two accounts (6.30-44 and 8.1-10) to represent two different events in the life of the historical Jesus (see Edwards [2002: 228]; France [2002: 307]; and Blomberg [2005: 109]).

55. Poon (2003: 226), commenting on Luke's version of the feeding of the five thousand (Lk. 9.10-17). On this see Bartchy, who commented in similar fashion about the story more than a decade earlier. As Bartchy notes, moreover, the feeding of the five thousand is the only miracle tradition recounted in all four Gospels (1992: 798).

56. Many understand the feedings to foreshadow the eschatological messianic banquet (for example, Lane [1974: 232-33]; Overman [1996: 218-19]; Keener [1999: 402]; Edwards [2002: 191-92]; and Poon [2003: 226]). Others (also) interpret the feedings in terms of the Eucharist, a view I find less persuasive. See the discussion in Blomberg (2005: 103-107).

57. The NRSV's 'have come from a great distance' (Mk 8.3) translates a Greek phrase that is nearly identical to an expression used in the LXX to refer to non-Israelites (Josh. 9.6) (Twelftree [1999: 81]).

Finally, the terms used for basket in the two texts refer to 'Jewish lunch bags and common Gentile shopping baskets, respectively'.[58] As Witherington reasonably concludes, 'The emphasis in Mark 8 is quite clearly on Jesus feeding Gentiles, though of course the audience is mixed since it also involves some disciples'.[59]

This is not to interpret the feeding of the four thousand as a formal dinner at which Jesus dines with Gentiles. The setting is completely informal, and Jesus does not partake of Gentile food. Indeed, the text does not explicitly portray Jesus eating at all. Nevertheless, the image of a Jewish messianic figure sharing his disciples' food (implied in v. 5) with Gentiles remains a culturally dissonant one according to Second-Temple Jewish social sensibilities, and we should not underestimate the ability of a story like this to reinforce and legitimize the agenda of Paul and others who later sought to expand the boundaries of the people of God to include non-Judeans. Guelich accurately notes, in this regard, that the feeding of the four thousand 'bears witness to the breaking down of the boundaries between Jews and Gentiles rooted in Jesus' ministry'.[60]

By way of summary, then, although he himself did not formally eat with Gentiles, we may fairly interpret the above passages to suggest that Jesus envisioned a day when Jews and Gentiles would, indeed, share the same table in the kingdom of God. Supporting such a conclusion are the other proclamations of eschatological reversal, which lack reference to table fellowship, but which explicitly identify Gentiles among those favored by Yahweh at the end of the age (Mt. 11.20-22; par. Lk. 10.13-14; Mt. 12.41; par. Lk. 11.32). Finally, Jesus almost certainly laid the ideological foundation for future table fellowship between Jews and Gentiles in a debate with the Pharisees about ritual hand-washing, as related in Mark 7 and Matthew 15.

4. *'He Declared All Foods Clean'*

A discussion of Jesus and table purity would be incomplete apart from careful consideration of perhaps the most important passage elucidating Jesus' attitudes toward Pharisaic halakhah. I refer to the extended narrative

---

58. Blomberg (2005: 110: also Twelftree [1999: 81]).

59. Witherington (2001: 236). One might wonder just how much of the Gentile-related imagery in Mk 8.1-10 can fairly be traced back to the event itself. I find it reasonable to suppose that Mark knew of a feeding of a mixed crowd which occurred in Gentile territory, and that this historical bedrock is reflected in the geographical data provided in 8.10 ('he got into the boat with his disciples and went to the district of Dalmanutha'), which suggests that the feeding occurred on the east side of the Sea of Galilee (see the parallel in Mt. 15.39, and the observations of Blomberg [2005: 109-10]). We may assume, then, that the evangelist (or his source) framed the balance of the account (including, perhaps, the symbolic numbers) with this historical reality in view.

60. Guelich (1989: 409).

of Mk 7.1-23 (par. Mt. 15.1-20), where, according to the author's interpretation, Jesus 'declared all foods clean' (v. 19).[61] The sweeping statement would seem to trump all arguments against Jewish–Gentile table fellowship. What was apparently self-evident to Mark, however, was hardly transparent to Jesus' earliest followers in the post-Easter community in Jerusalem, and the Markan text has become somewhat of a lightning rod for the ongoing debate over Jesus and purity.[62] The bibliography on the topic continues to expand, running the gamut from books dealing broadly with Jesus and the law, to specific treatments of the perspectives of the individual evangelists, to technical monographs focusing specifically on Mark 7.[63] To offer even a brief survey of the various proposals for the tradition history or interpretation of Mk 7.1-23 would be hopelessly distracting in the present connection. In what follows, I will briefly examine the relationship between the parallel gospel accounts, and then discuss the way in which I believe the text contributes to our understanding of Jesus and the Jewish food laws.

As the story begins, Jesus interacts with a group of Pharisees and scribes who are upset that the disciples eat with unwashed hands (Mk 7.1-5). Here we see reflected, once again, Jesus' indifference to ritual purity where Pharisaic table scruples are concerned.[64] In his ensuing message to the crowds (vv. 14-16) and to the disciples (vv. 17-23), however, Jesus' agenda seems to move beyond a critique of Pharisaic halakhah to question the validity of the broader categories of pure and impure food, as such.[65] A comparison of the text in Mark with its Matthean parallel clarifies the differences between the two accounts. Key points of divergence are marked for emphasis:

61. Manuscript evidence strongly supports the retention of the masculine καθαρίζων, against Malina's attempt to argue in favor of the poorly attested καθάριζον (1988: 22-23).

62. Thus Chilton pointedly remarks, after comparing Mark's comment in 7.19c with the story of the Jerusalem Council in Acts 15, 'Not even the liberal Jesus is up to denying the laws of *kashrut*, only to have his own brother invoke them afresh' (2003: 359).

63. Berger (1972); Hübner (1973); Banks (1975); Westerholm (1978); Booth (1986); Vouga (1988); Sanders (1990); Svartvik (2000); Loader (2002); Kazen (2002); Rudolph (2002).

64. Sanders's skepticism about Pharisaic concern for purity of hands before 70 CE is unwarranted (Sanders [1985: 185-86, 264-65]), as Dunn maintains (Dunn [2003: 571-72]). See also Gundry (1993: 358-59), Tomson (1988), and, most persuasively, Kazen (2002: 81-85).

65. Gundry's summary of the chapter is on the mark:

Since the Pharisees and scribes have not asked about unclean foods, but about unclean hands (see vv 1-5), Jesus' saying [v. 15] marks a progression from the question *how* to eat to the question *what* to eat. The progression is a natural one…and entails shifting from a question about the oral law of the elders to a question about the written law of the Old Testament (1993: 354; similarly, Hurtado [1989: 111-12]; Rudolph [2002] disagrees).

Matthew 15.10-20	Mark 7.14-23
10 Then he called the crowd to him and said to them, 'Listen and understand: 11 *it is not what goes into the mouth that defiles a person, but it is what comes out of the mouth that defiles'.* 12 Then the disciples approached and said to him, 'Do you know that the Pharisees took offense when they heard what you said?' 13 He answered, 'Every plant that my heavenly Father has not planted will be uprooted. 14 Let them alone; they are blind guides of the blind. And if one blind person guides another, both will fall into a pit'. 15 But Peter said to him, 'Explain this parable to us'. 16 Then he said, 'Are you also still without understanding? 17 *Do you not see that whatever goes into the mouth enters the stomach, and goes out into the sewer?* 18 But what comes out of the mouth proceeds from the heart, and this is what defiles. 19 For out of the heart come evil intentions, murder, adultery, fornication, theft, false witness, slander. 20 These are what defile a person, *but to eat with unwashed hands does not defile'.*	14 Then he called the crowd again and said to them, 'Listen to me, all of you, and understand: 15 *there is nothing outside a person that by going in can defile, but the things that come out are what defile'.* 17 When he had left the crowd and entered the house, his disciples asked him about the parable. 18 He said to them, 'Then do you also fail to understand? *Do you not see that whatever goes into a person from outside cannot defile,* 19 *since it enters, not the heart but the stomach, and goes out into the sewer?'* (*Thus he declared all foods clean.*) 20 And he said, 'It is what comes out of a person that defiles. 21 For it is from within, from the human heart, that evil intentions come: fornication, theft, murder, 22 adultery, avarice, wickedness, deceit, licentiousness, envy, slander, pride, folly. 23 All these evil things come from within, and they defile a person'.

Numerous scholars, assuming Markan priority, believe that Mark has retained Jesus' teaching in the pericope.[66] Matthew, in turn, ameliorates his source (Mark) in such a way as to allow room for levitical food concerns for an audience of Jewish Messianists who still hold the Torah's purity laws in high esteem. This reconstruction of the tradition history of Jesus' teaching runs aground in the eyes of many, however, on the rocky shore of subsequent Christian history. As Dunn suggests, commenting on Mark's version of the story,

> [I]f Jesus had spoken so clearly and decisively on the subject it becomes difficult to see how Peter could ever have been recorded as saying subse-

---

66. Among others, Taylor (1966/1981: 342-43); Pesch (1980: 383); Gnilka (1997: 215-16); Houlden (1983: 63); Becker (1998: 304-308); and Theissen and Merz (1998: 365-67).

quently, 'I have never eaten anything common or unclean' (Acts 10.14; 11.8), or why the issue of food laws could have become so divisive in earliest Christianity.[67]

Dunn offers an alternative reconstruction of the sources behind Matthew and Mark. He postulates an oral traditioning process whereby Matthew is no longer dependent solely upon Mark as a source for the pericope but has at his disposal, as well, another stream of tradition that goes back to the same teaching of Jesus. Aware of this alternative tradition, Matthew, Dunn surmises, would have recognized features that had been added by Mark (or by the stream of tradition Mark utilized), and would have felt free to omit them accordingly. Matthew's form thus represents the way in which the teaching was related in Jewish Christian contexts, Mark's in Gentile or mixed churches.[68] The above reconstruction would leave Matthew's version as the one most accurately representing Jesus' actual teaching in a first-century Palestinian Jewish setting. It is, after all, the more Jewish of the two.

Dunn's approach to the tradition history of the texts is appealing in that it factors into the mix the robust oral tradition that we know existed among the earliest followers of Jesus. This is an important methodological improvement over source-critical theories that focus narrowly and artificially on written sources alone. I am not convinced, however, that Dunn has solved the thorny historical problem that he has placed at the feet of those who would trace Mark's version back to the historical Jesus (see the quote above). Matthew's account is, in fact, more potentially subversive of biblical purity legislation than Dunn seems to assume.

Let us suppose for a moment that Matthew's version of the pericope does, indeed, more closely reflect Jesus' teaching. What can we say from this text about Jesus and the food laws? At minimum, Jesus rejects Pharisaic purity standards, thus, once again, implicitly repositioning the identity marker of sacred food at the boundary between Jews and Gentiles, rather than at the boundary between Jews who maintain sectarian standards of ritual purity and Jews who do not. This much is clear, for Matthew's version ends on precisely this note: 'to eat with unwashed hands does not defile' (v. 20).[69]

Jesus' direct challenge to Pharisaic halakhah, however, is pregnant with implications for his attitude toward the current convictions of the broader Judean populace relating to issues of food and levitical purity. Students of

---

67. Dunn (2003: 574), echoing the views of Sanders (1985: 266-68), Vermes (1993: 25-26), Fredriksen (1999: 108), and Harvey (1982: 39-41).

68. Dunn (1990: 44-55; 2003: 575); Kazen agrees with Dunn's reconstruction (2002: 228).

69. Thus, Loader says Matthew's version is 'concerned with deprecating Pharisaic interpretation of purity laws' (2002: 212).

post-Maccabean Judaism have become increasingly aware of the close connection that existed between purity as practiced by groups like the Pharisees and Essenes, on the one hand, and the similar but less intensified behaviors that characterized the general Jewish population of Roman Palestine, on the other. Material remains, in particular, plainly attest to concerns of non-sectarian Jews for ritual purity in both Judea and Galilee during the post-Maccabean era. Archaeological evidence for a preoccupation with ritual purity on the part of the common people, apart from the temple, includes (a) vessels made of chalk or soft limestone, which were deemed impervious to impurity (*m. Kel.* 10.1), (b) hundreds of Jewish ritual immersion pools (*miqwaoth*), excavated in private homes and public settings, and (c) a notable lack of pork bones among eating remains in Jewish settlements during the period.[70] In view of the wedge often driven by scholars between the practices of sectarian and non-sectarian Jews,[71] we would do well seriously to consider the common-sense assertion that Dunn puts forth in the course of an important discussion of Jesus and purity:

> [T]he emphasis on purity which has been seen as distinctive of the Jewish 'sects', particularly the Pharisees and Essenes, should be seen not so much as distinctive, rather as an exaggeration or reinforcement or expansion of the purity concerns which characterized what Sanders calls 'common Judaism'.[72]

Viewing sectarian praxis as the extension of an expansionist approach to ritual purity which characterized the general population during the post-Maccabean era sheds much light on Jesus' evaluation of Pharisaic practices. To challenge the distinct practices of a group like the Pharisees in such a context is to speak to the broader issue of purity in general, and suddenly the

---

70. The ubiquitous presence of the immersion pools, in particular, suggests that the *miqwaoth* were used by a broad cross-section of the population, not just by members of sectarian groups like the Pharisees. At Gezer, for example, stepped pools were added to the houses after the takeover and repopulation of the site by the Maccabees (Reich [1981: 48-52]). Numerous stone-cut cups, bowls, and jugs, found in several recently excavated sites, point in a similar direction. Recent work at the well-preserved site of Yodafat in Galilee, for example, has unearthed widespread material evidence for concern for ritual purity and the avoidance of impurity in everyday utensils (Richardson [2000: 68-69]). On all this, see Reed (2000: 43-51) and, especially, Kazen (2002: 72-88), who argues persuasively for an 'expansionist purity practice in Second-Temple Judaism' (72). Deines's important work on the stone vessels should also be consulted (1993). It is therefore 'no longer possible to argue that only one group—Pharisees, for example—were concerned with ritual purity' (Richardson [2000: 69]).

71. Neusner's exclamation—'as if the masses kept the purity laws!'—is illustrative (1986: 54). Sanders's pointed riposte—'as if he knows that they did not'—is quite on the mark (1992: 229).

72. Dunn (2002: 453-54).

ideological chasm between the rejection of Pharisaic halakhah in Mt. 15.20 (and elsewhere in the Jesus traditions) and Mark's observation that Jesus 'declared all foods clean' (7.19) narrows considerably.

But there is more. Implied even in Matthew's version is Mark's sweeping assertion that nothing entering the body from without can defile (Mk 7.18)—an assertion that struggles to remain within the narrow confines of sectarian debate over the proper interpretation of the Torah. We know this to be the case because Matthew's Jesus affirms a clear distinction between 'whatever goes into the mouth'—obviously to be understood as food in the context—and 'what comes out of the mouth' (vv. 11, 17-18).[73] The latter, he specifically avows, is 'what defiles' (v. 18; cf. v. 11b). It is surely but a short step to conclude from this (with Mark) that 'whatever goes into a person from the outside *cannot* defile' (Mk 7.18).[74]

The differences between the two accounts thus prove to be matters of style and emphasis rather than matters of substance.[75] The most significant disparity actually consists of divergent—but equally legitimate—applications of the categorical antithesis between what goes into the mouth and what comes out, an antithesis which occurs in both gospel narratives.[76] Matthew applies

---

73. Matthew has added 'mouth' in v. 11 and vv. 17-18, thus making even clearer than Mark the reference to food (Loader [2002: 214]). On the historical authenticity of the saying, as expressed in Mk 7.15 and Mt. 15.11, see Klawans (2000: 146-47) and Wright (1996: 397). The contrast between the inside and the outside, along with the emphasis on purity of heart, is deeply embedded in the Jesus tradition (Mt. 5.8; 23.25; par. Lk. 11.39; *Gos. Thom.* 89), in continuity with similar themes from the Hebrew Scriptures (Deut. 10.16; Jer. 4.4, 9.25-26; Ezek. 44.9; cf. 1QpHab 11.13; 1QS 5.5).

There is a trend among some to downplay or even eliminate from the story the question of the levitical food laws, as such. Thus, for Booth the issue is not one of food *per se*, but of communicable impurity that could contaminate food (1986: 205-10). Svartvik, as well, frames the matter not in terms of the food laws, but in terms of food contaminated by bodily impurity, through unwashed hands (2000: 370). Although the text certainly begins on this note (Mk 7.1-5; par. Mt. 15.1-2), it is hard to imagine a first-century Judean not hearing an implicit challenge to Old Testament *kashrut* in Jesus' categorical pronouncement later in the pericope (Mk 7.15; par. Mt. 15.11).

74. We should not make too much of Mark's 'can' and 'cannot' language (vv. 15 and 18, respectively) to begin with. Elsewhere Mark uses 'cannot' terminology unambiguously simply to connote 'does not'. In Mk 2.19, for example, reads, Jesus asks, 'The wedding guests cannot (μὴ δύνανται) fast while the bridegroom is with them, can they?' What is meant here, of course, is that guests typically 'do not' fast in such a situation. Mark 9.39 and 10.26 may reflect similar usage (Catchpole [2006: 200]).

75. Crossan and Reed significantly overstate the differences in the accounts when they claim that Matthew and Mark 'pull the historical Jesus in opposite directions on the subject of food purity and impurity' (Crossan [2001: 132]).

76. Although one cannot be dogmatic here, I am inclined (with Theissen [1998: 366] and Gundry [1993: 365]) to take the contrast between 'what goes into the mouth' and 'what comes out of the mouth' as antithetical and not merely relative (Meyer [1979:

7. Jesus and Sacred Food 233

the antithesis of vv. 11, 17-18 to the circumscribed confines of Pharisaic halakhah. Mark and his tradents draw out its full and logical implications in a Gentile Christian context in which those implications would have become increasingly transparent: 'Thus he declared all foods clean' (v. 19).[77] This is not to argue, of course, that Jesus explicitly abrogated the food laws during his earthly ministry, or that Jesus himself ate with Gentiles. It is simply to point out that the DNA of Jewish–Gentile table fellowship is present in embryonic form, so to speak, in Jesus' teaching on food and purity in Matthew 15/Mark 7, whichever version we take to be more original.[78]

149]; Dunn [1990: 51]; Klawans [2000: 147]; Hooker [2000: 120]; Loader [2002: 215]; and Kazen [2002: 63, 65-67]). Proponents of the latter view appropriately cite the prioritization of justice and mercy over cult in the Hebrew Scriptures as evidence for a 'Semitic idiom of dialectical negation', an idiom which, in turn, encourages us to read the antithesis in Mt. 15.11 (par. Mk 7.15) not 'as an "either…or", but rather with the force of "more important than"' (Dunn [1990: 51]; Marcus [2000: 453]; see Rudolph [2002: 297-98]).

The grammar, however, in both Matthew and Mark, resists attempts to soften the language by arguing for a relative degree of difference between the two statements, that is, that defilement from within is worse than defilement from without. It is the absolute denial of defilement from without in Mk 7.15, for example, that leads Räisänen to relegate the text to early church traditioning. Räisänen correctly recognizes that 'the sweeping οὐδέν and the strengthening δύναται' stand in the way of interpreting Mk 7.15 only in terms of relative degree (1982: 94 n. 41; cf. Gundry [1993: 365]). With respect to Matthew, the similarly antithetical grammar in 15.11 (οὐ…ἀλλά) differs markedly from the language of Mt. 23.23, for example, where a relative degree of emphasis seems to be in view.

In Matthew's account, moreover, the antithetical interpretation of the saying finds further support in Jesus' application of the pronouncement in the concluding verses of the pericope (15.18-20). For although Matthew's Jesus proceeds to limit the application of the pronouncement of v. 11 to the sphere Pharisaic halakhah, he does so in a decidedly antithetical way. That is, Jesus does not conclude by suggesting that what 'proceeds from the heart' is somehow 'more important than' (see Dunn, above) eating with unwashed hands (vv. 18-20). In harmony with the explicit antithesis reflected in the grammar of v. 11, Jesus categorically and unequivocally asserts, 'to eat with unwashed hands does not defile' (v. 20).

77. Some interpret Jesus' instructions to his disciples in Luke 10 along the same lines as Mark 7:

> 7 'Remain in the same house, eating and drinking whatever they provide, for the laborer deserves to be paid. Do not move about from house to house. 8 Whenever you enter a town and its people welcome you, eat what is set before you'. (Lk. 10.7-8)

Thus Theissen and Merz remark that 'the disciples may accept any food that is offered them—regardless of whether it is clean or unclean, tithed or not tithed' (1998: 366). Jesus, however, explicitly frames the food-related instructions in Luke 10 in terms of a laborer's wages, so an interpretation of the text in relation to purity must remain conjectural.

78. On the historical probability of a Palestinian Jew taking such a position on food

5. Summary: Jesus and Sacred Food

Jesus' approach to table fellowship falls generally in line with his attitude toward the identity markers of sacred space and sacred times. In challenging the passion with which many of his fellow Jews engaged in these practices in the post-Maccabean milieu of first-century Judea and Galilee, Jesus encouraged his followers to reconsider the social contours of the people of God in the kingdom age. In the case of sacred food, moreover, we have observed some further subtleties. It is quite clear that Jesus did not, in his own eating practices, ingest pork or any other food explicitly prohibited in the Torah. Nor, from what we can tell, did he dine with Gentiles, although the feeding of the four thousand in Gentile territory borders on such behavior (Mk 8.1-10). Jesus' treatment of sacred food thus differs somewhat from his treatment of sacred times, where, for example, Jesus unequivocally affirmed his disciples' violation of what appears to be a reasonable interpretation of the Torah prohibition of work on the Sabbath (Mk 2.23-28).

In the case of food, it is helpful to distinguish between Jesus' behavior at table, on the one hand, and his teaching, on the other. Jesus lived in a social context in which the identity marker of sacred food had been extended and elaborated upon in such a way as to generate practices that excluded not only Gentiles but also great numbers of Judeans from the tables of sectarian groups such as the Pharisees and the members of the separatist community at Qumran. Jesus, in contrast, consistently shared meals with persons ('tax collectors and sinners') who had been marginalized by the various purity sects. In doing so, he essentially redefined the boundaries of God's people to include any and all descendants of Abraham who would become his followers. This much is clear about Jesus' behavior at table.

In his teaching, however, Jesus seems to have moved beyond sectarian concerns to relativize the exclusive table fellowship that separated Jews from Gentiles—a practice that had defined the people of God for centuries in the Mediterranean world in both Jewish and pagan eyes. Sayings and parables of eschatological reversal portray Gentiles replacing Jesus' Jewish contemporaries at the banquet table of Yahweh (Mt. 8.11-12; Lk. 14.16-24). Post-Easter events would soon lead Jesus' followers to believe that they were already experiencing the inbreaking of the kingdom age (Acts 2),

---

and purity, see now the discussion in Theissen and Merz. Assuming Markan priority, they trace the more radical logion in Mk 7.15 back to the historical Jesus, and nevertheless conclude from Jewish analogies that 'radical thoughts on the question of purity are not inconceivable in Palestine' (1998: 366). Those who, like Dunn (and myself), find Matthew's version to be the more original will be even more persuaded by Theissen and Merz's case for the historical probability of a first-century Jew adopting an unsympathetic stance toward purity.

and such convictions apparently encouraged some Christians to turn Jesus' teaching about the future eschatological banquet into a present reality around their tables. Jesus' categorical antithesis between 'what goes into the mouth' and 'what comes out of the mouth' (Mt. 15.11), coupled with the emphatic assertion that the latter is 'what defiles' (15.18), apparently provided further ideological foundation for just such a development, for a significant portion of the Jesus movement ultimately concluded that Jesus had essentially 'declared all foods clean' (Mk 7.19c).

Cultural anthropologists talk about the 'redundancy' of social systems, whereby distinct activities function in parallel to reinforce common values and convictions, generally in a markedly conservative way.[79] As we saw in our survey of Second-Temple Jewish literature, post-Maccabean preoccupation with sacred times, sacred space, and sacred food were all united in the service of a single social agenda—the preservation of Jewish identity in the context of Roman occupation and oppression. We have observed in the practices and teachings of Jesus a corresponding redundancy. By playing loose with contemporary convictions concerning Sabbath-keeping, the sanctity of Jerusalem and her temple, and food-related purity, Jesus consistently challenged the ways in which his fellow-Jews sought to define themselves over against the empire's Gentile majority. Jesus complemented his deconstruction of post-Maccabean Jewish nationalism, moreover, with the creation of an alternative model for the social organization of the people of Yahweh, and we are now prepared to consider Jesus' establishment of his followers as a (potentially multi-ethnic) surrogate kinship group. First, however, we must grapple with the thorny issue of the apparent discontinuity that obtains between Jesus' approach to Jewish identity markers, on the one hand, and the convictions of his earliest followers in the post-Easter church, on the other.

---

79. Neyrey (1991: 387).

Chapter 8

JESUS AND HIS EARLIEST FOLLOWERS:
ANTICIPATING OBJECTIONS

> But Peter said, 'By no means, Lord; for I have never eaten anything that is profane or unclean'.
>
> Acts 10.14

It is now time to wrestle with what I anticipate will be the main objections to the portrayal of Jesus outlined in the previous chapters. The most challenging of these relates to the apparent disconnect that exists between Jesus' deconstruction of Jewish nationalism, as evidenced in the Gospels, and the convictions of his earliest followers in the post-Easter church in Jerusalem. Sanders has succinctly summarized the resulting dilemma that confronts the student of early Christian history:

> Here the great *fact* is that Jesus' followers did not know that he had directly opposed the law, and in particular they did not know him to have opposed the laws governing *Sabbath, food, and purity*.[1]

Sanders's observation is not an insignificant one. How could Jesus' own disciples have failed to grasp such a central aspect of his life and ministry? If Jesus actually relativized the laws of purity, as the Gospels suggest he did, the debate at the Jerusalem Council in Acts 15 over terms for including Gentiles among the people of God becomes historically inexplicable. Peter's interaction with Cornelius (Acts 10–11), and his behavior later at Antioch (Gal. 2), would also be rendered rather curious, to say the least, if Jesus, whom Peter had followed for some three years, challenged Jewish

---

1. Sanders (1985: 325). See also Catchpole, who rejects the historicity of traditions portraying Jesus at odds with the food laws because such passages betray his '*criterion of plausible historical continuity*: a tradition must lead straightforwardly towards later securely established historical events' (Catchpole [2006: 59] author's italics). Sanders, Fredriksen (1999: 209), and Catchpole (2006: 230) find the same unacceptable discontinuity between Jesus' allegedly negative attitude toward the Temple, as portrayed in the Gospels, and the pro-Temple stance of the post-Easter Jerusalem Christians. Again, in the words of Sanders, 'If [Jesus] actually explicitly opposed one of the main institutions of Judaism, he kept it secret from his disciples' (Sanders [1985: 67]).

particularism in the ways in which I have argued in the preceding pages. Or so the argument goes.[2]

A second objection centers on certain texts in the Gospels in which Jesus appears actually to affirm Jewish laws of purity. Mark 1.44 is often cited in this connection. After healing a leper Jesus tells the man to observe the ritual law of cleansing: 'See that you say nothing to anyone; but go, show yourself to the priest, and offer for your cleansing what Moses commanded, as a testimony to them'.[3] Jesus also seems to uphold practices of ritual purity in the course of a series of woes against the Pharisees in Matthew 23. Notice the final assertion in v. 23:

> 'Woe to you, scribes and Pharisees, hypocrites! For you tithe mint, dill, and cummin, and have neglected the weightier matters of the law: justice and mercy and faith. It is these you ought to have practiced without neglecting the others' (Mt. 23.23; par. Lk. 11.42).

Scholars who find themselves persuaded by the above objections understandably find it difficult to imagine a Jesus who takes an adversarial position toward the defining badges of Jewish identity.

---

2. It is possible that some persons in the Jerusalem church did embrace Jesus' program and proceed to play loose with purity and boundaries. The most promising evidence along these lines surfaces in connection with Stephen's martyrdom. According to Luke, Stephen's adversaries 'secretly instigated some men to say, "We have heard him speak blasphemous words against Moses and God" ' (Acts 6.11). Others, identified by the narrator as 'false witnesses' (v. 12), assert, 'This man never stops saying things against this holy place and the law; for we have heard him say that this Jesus of Nazareth will destroy this place and will change the customs that Moses handed on to us' (vv. 13-14). Given the comment about 'false witnesses', one wonders just how much to make of all this, although Stephen's comments in the ensuing narrative do appear to confirm at least the portion of the charge related to the temple (7.48-50). Hengel has made the most of this data, maintaining that the Hellenistic wing of the Jerusalem church served as the bridge, ideologically, between Jesus and Paul, by means of its 'criticism of the ritual law and the cult' (1983: 29, see 25-29). Hurtado, following Hill (1992), effectively challenges this common scholarly paradigm, which assumes a hard and fast distinction between Hellenist and Hebrew believers in the early Jesus movement in Jerusalem (Hurtado [2003: 211-14]).

Whatever we conclude concerning Stephen and the Hellenists, it remains the case that the apostles themselves, who had interacted for extended periods of time with the historical Jesus, exhibit little awareness of their mentor's boundary-breaking agenda in the narrative in Acts (though see the citation of the promise to Abraham in Peter's speech in Acts 3.25: 'And in your descendants all the families of the earth shall be blessed'). When Peter finally does come to terms with what the Holy Spirit is doing (by means of the vision related in Acts 10), he exclaims, 'God [not Jesus] has shown me that I should not call anyone profane or unclean' (Acts 10.28). The Jerusalem Council also addresses the issue of Gentile inclusion without appealing to any precedent that might have been set by Jesus (Acts 15).

3. Booth (1986: 102-103).

Those who adopt such a perspective generally take one of two approaches to the gospel materials that portray Jesus challenging practices related to sacred times, sacred space, and the levitical dietary laws. The simplest solution relegates such texts to the creative activity of the early church, where the problem of Gentile inclusion and Jewish–Gentile relations first becomes acute.[4] An apparent historical conundrum is thereby eliminated, but at too great a cost to the gospel traditions, in my view. Commentators who are more optimistic about the authenticity of the passages in which Jesus subverts symbols of Jewish identity, but who nevertheless remain troubled by the apparent incongruity that results between Jesus and the early church, tend to argue for a relative, rather than an absolute, approach to Sabbath, temple, and food on Jesus' part. That is, Jesus, like Israel's prophets before him (Isa. 1.1-17, 58.1-14; Jer. 7.21-23; Hos. 6.4-6; Amos 5.21-27), polemicized against ritual that was devoid of relational integrity and morality—not against ritual purity as such.[5] For those who adopt this approach, Mt. 23.23 (above) accurately represents Jesus' outlook towards purity, and the more radical pericopes are interpreted accordingly.

The balance of this Chapter responds to these objections. With respect to the gospel passages in which Jesus appears to affirm Jewish purity, I will maintain that the extensive evidence cited in the previous chapters for Jesus' relativization of markers of Jewish identity should take priority over the comparatively limited amount of data portraying Jesus as an advocate of Jewish particularism. Hermeneutical common sense encourages us to interpret the latter texts in the light of the former, and not *vice versa*. I will devote more attention in what follows to the thorny problem of historical continuity between Jesus and the post-Easter church. I will argue in some detail that the lack of clarity in the church on issues such as Sabbath-keeping, *kashrut*, and Jewish-Gentile relations finds reasonable explanation in a combination of factors that would have obviated any facile abrogation of purity on the part of the early Christians: (1) the persistent presence of Maccabean ideology in a historical context of increasing tension between Judeans and their Roman occupiers during the years in question (30s–50s CE); (2) the solely Jewish make-up of the early Jesus communities throughout the first post-Easter decade; (3) the embryonic nature of Jesus' teachings about purity, which rendered his sayings and deeds susceptible to a variety of applications in the context of later community life; and, finally, (4) popular, biblically-based Jewish eschatological expectations, which anticipated the purification and restoration of national Israel.

---

4. See, for example, Räisänen on Mk 7.15 (1982: 86-88; 1986: 209-301).

5. Kruse (1954); Meyer (1979: 149). This is the basic conclusion of Loader, who claims that 'Jesus gave priority to ethical behaviour and attitude over cultic and ritual law, but without surrendering the latter' (Loader [2002: 518]).

It is the natural tendency of human beings to resist, rather than embrace, radical alterations of their social institutions, particularly where ethnic identity is concerned, and given the fact that Jesus' closest disciples struggled to get on board with various aspects of his program during his earthly ministry, any one of the above factors would likely have given some pause to a wholesale renegotiation of the socio-ethnic boundaries of the people of God on the part of the earliest Judean believers. Taken together these considerations virtually guaranteed a rather messy and often painful transition from *ethnos* to *oikos*, as the increasingly multi-ethnic movement that was to become Christianity struggled to add Gentiles to what was originally a Jewish renewal group led by a Palestinian Jewish Messiah.

1. *A Purity-Friendly Jesus?*

Any fair treatment of Jesus and post-Maccabean nationalism must include in its analysis those passages that portray Jesus apparently affirming various aspects of Jewish purity. It will prove helpful, in this regard, first to consider Jesus' own involvement in purification practices, a subject about which the Gospels are strangely silent. Fredriksen insists that Jesus observed purity regulations like any other first-century Palestinian Jew. While acknowledging the inferential nature of her argument, she nevertheless maintains that 'the loudness of this silence in this instance gives the measure of our own *un*familiarity with and distance from the ancient world'.[6] Perhaps so, but I remain unconvinced. Fredriksen, perhaps more than any other New Testament scholar, has sought to situate Jesus in his own socio-religious milieu, and she argues her case with an impressive and engaging erudition. I suspect, however, that most of us will continue to find it preferable methodologically to draw our understanding of Jesus from the explicit evidence that we do possess in the gospel narratives. And here, as Kazen observes in a useful critique of Fredriksen's position, 'There are almost no hints that Jesus took any interest in purification practices'.[7]

It is instructive to compare the silence of the Gospels about Jesus' own purification practices with the behaviors of other Jews whose activities are described in extended narratives from the period. In contrast to the evangelists, the authors of several of the stories cited in earlier chapters

---

6. Fredriksen (1999: 206; author's italics); so, too, Loader (2002: 520).
7. Kazen (2002: 250). Fredriksen's assumption that Jesus faithfully engaged in rites of purification, while a sensible conjecture historically, nevertheless conflicts with Jesus' treatment of sacred times, sacred space, and sacred food, as illustrated in the Gospels. When these texts are taken seriously as a legitimate point of departure for ascertaining his attitude towards purity, the silence of the Gospels about Jesus' own purification practices finds adequate explanation, thus leading us reasonably to assume, with Kazen, that Jesus was, at best, indifferent to impurity (Kazen [2002]).

(1–2, *4 Maccabees*, Judith, *Joseph and Aseneth*, *Jubilees*) have a good deal to say about their protagonists' efforts to keep ritually pure. Clearly these writers did not think that such behaviors could simply be left to the inferences of their readers. Dunn elaborates with respect to the food laws:

> Of the stories of Jewish heroes and heroines which must have fed popular piety wherever they were read, we might note how consistently they were portrayed as prospering precisely because of their loyalty to the food laws and refusal to eat the food of the Gentiles.[8]

All of this, in turn, renders the silence of the Gospels potentially illuminating for evaluating Jesus' attitude toward Judean rites of purification. Apparently Jesus truly was indifferent to purity.

We turn now to those passages in which Jesus seems to affirm the purity practices of others. It is crucial at the outset to note that the extensive testimony of the Gospels to Jesus' relativization of the markers of Jewish identity outweighs evidence to the contrary and should be given priority in ascertaining Jesus' attitudes towards Jewish particularism. Some of the alleged data cited in support of a purity-friendly Jesus, moreover, fails to persuade upon closer examination. The exhortation to the healed leper—'go, show yourself to the priest, and offer for your cleansing what Moses commanded, as a testimony to them' (Mk 1.44)—is a case in point. Given Jesus' familiar practice of restoring marginalized persons to normal village relations, Gundry is probably correct to suggest that Jesus intends here 'to insure the ex-leper's reentry into normal social life, not to take a theological position on ritual law'.[9]

Matthew 23.23 appears more directly to reflect a positive attitude to Pharisaic purity on Jesus' part, but the incidental aside which concludes the saying—'It is these you ought to have practiced without neglecting the others'—should not be adopted as the defining lens through which to interpret the many gospel passages in which Jesus seems to play loose with purity and thereby destabilize Jewish ethnic boundaries. For the view

---

8. Dunn (2003: 275); citing Dan. 1.3-16, 10.3; Tob. 1.10-13; Jdt. 12.2, 6-9, 19; Add Esth. 14.17; 1 Macc. 1.62-63; *Jos. Asen.* 7.1, 8.5 (275 n. 97).

9. Gundry (1993: 365). As Loader notes of the healing, 'The effect must still be formally certified in accordance with the provisions of Torah and the man declared clean so that he can reenter the community' (2002: 23). For the practice of restoring the socially marginalized, see, for example, Jesus' instruction to the Gerasene demoniac in Mk 5.19: 'Go home to your friends, and tell them how much the Lord has done for you, and what mercy he has shown you'. Another common alternative interprets the phrase 'as a testimony to them' negatively, as a critique, rather than an affirmation, of the temple and its leaders (H. Stettler [2004: 166]). This, however, assumes a degree of antagonism between Jesus and the temple authorities, an antagonism for which the reader has not been prepared by Mark's narrative (Loader [2002: 22]). Consult Loader (19-25) for an extended discussion of the scholarship on the passage.

that Jesus simply prioritizes moral purity over ritual purity runs aground elsewhere. Such an approach does not set well, for example, with Jesus' categorical pronouncement about food (Mt. 15.11; par. Mk 7.15), nor does it work for Jesus' treatment of Sabbath observance in Mk 2.23–3.6. In each instance it seems that Jesus has come close to subverting a vital aspect of the Mosaic law, as demonstrated in the treatment of the passages earlier in the discussion.

Two obvious but crucial realities must remain in view in any reconstruction of Jesus' perspective on Jewish national identity: (1) Jesus was Jewish, and (2) Jesus functioned as the key salvation-historical figure bridging the old covenant with the new. We will expect Jesus, as a Jew living under the old covenant, to abstain from pork, and we will not be surprised to find him frequenting the synagogue on the Sabbath, attending the annual festivals in Jerusalem, and even occasionally granting an affirmative nod to the purity practices of his contemporaries through an incidental aside like the one recorded in Mt. 23.23.[10] To expect otherwise would be to ask Jesus to 'shed his skin', so to speak, that is, to become such an anomalous iconoclast that he would have appealed to no one among his Jewish contemporaries in first-century Palestine.

It may even be the case that Jesus himself struggled fully to embrace the implications of what Yahweh was doing through his life and ministry. Jesus, after all, operated in the same post-Maccabean setting as his earliest followers in the Jerusalem church (see below). The socio-cultural pressures to conform would have been considerable. Loader, in fact, finds evidence of an initial reluctance on Jesus' part when faced with traditional Jewish boundaries—a reluctance that, in each case, is overcome, but which may nevertheless be indicative of 'Jesus and his own struggles on the issues'.[11]

None of this, however, seriously compromises the picture of Jesus painted in the previous chapters. For Jesus not only lived as a Jew under the old covenant. He also inaugurated the new. And as the inaugurator of a new

10. This observation would also apply to evidence that is often put forth to demonstrate that Jesus had a positive view towards the temple (e.g. Mk 12.41-44, par. Lk. 21.1-4). Ådna situates teachings like these in their proper place in the unfolding of the drama of salvation history. They reflect the way in which Jesus viewed the temple functioning during the transitional stage of his earthly ministry, that is, 'ehe der Kairos der eschatologischen Erfüllung des Tempel gekommen ist' (Ådna [2000: 439]).

11. Loader cites as evidence Jesus' initial responses to three unclean persons who approached him: the leper (Mk 1.40-45), the woman with the flow of blood (Mk 5.25-34), and the Syrophoenician woman (Mk 7.24-30) (2002: 520). The latter text most clearly supports Loader's assumption (see Freyne's reasoned discussion of the historical plausibility of the encounter [2004: 89-90]). Marcus's interpretation of the encounter with the Syrophoenician woman as a story about 'the transcendence of Jewish particularism' seems to erroneously identify as the central theme of the narrative what is in fact a rather reluctant response to the woman on Jesus' part (Marcus [2000: 468]).

covenant, Jesus apparently understood a key part of his mission to consist of relativizing the socio-ethnic boundaries that had defined God's people for centuries. So he steadily undermined time-honored distinctions between sacred and profane times, space, and foods. This aspect of Jesus' ministry is deeply embedded in the gospel traditions. It remains to consider the manner in which the early church remembered and contextualized Jesus' potentially boundary-breaking teachings and activities.

2. *Jesus, Jewish Identity, and the Post-Easter Church*

The gist of my response to those who have difficulty imagining the early church debating issues of Jewish particularism, given the Jesus of the canonical Gospels, may be summarized as follows: history is not nearly as neat and linear as many of us in the scholarly guild would make it out to be. For every cause and (expected) effect, we will often uncover a counter-cause or two, bringing in tow their own counter-effects and working behind the scenes to confound and complicate historical analysis. Only in the artificial world of the historian's study, therefore, will Jesus' teachings and activities constitute the sole source of influence on early Christian beliefs and behaviors, and only in such a context will we consequently expect the Jesus of the Gospels to generate a group of followers who perfectly understood the need to relativize identity markers like food and Sabbath, and who were ready to do so the minute Gentiles came knocking on the door of the *ekklesia*. It would be delightful, indeed, if historical analysis could count on such a singular trajectory of cause-and-effect in assessing the relationship between Jesus and his earliest followers. Unfortunately, such is not the case, and in actuality a multiplicity of factors, historical and sociological, played into early Christian attitudes towards purity and boundaries.[12] And most of these factors worked distinctly against the grain of the trajectory Jesus had set in his desire to renegotiate the ethnic contours of the people of Yahweh in light of God's kingdom reign. We will consider several of these realities in turn.

3. *Factor #1: Roman Abuses and the Persistence of Maccabean Ideology*

If Maccabean historiography taught first-century Judeans anything at all, it taught them that the proper response to Roman occupation and oppression was to preserve their Jewish distinctives, if necessary, to the point of death. God had, after all, rewarded a previous generation of faithful Jews—a number of whom had paid the ultimate price to maintain a kosher diet

---

12. This is appropriately emphasized by Theissen and Winter, who assume a causal —but reject what they label a 'monocausal'—connection between Jesus and early Christianity (2002: 188-89).

and continue to circumcise their male babies—with a series of stunning victories over a pagan colonial power, victories which ultimately issued in national independence and the control of a kingdom that rivaled the size of David's. Now Judeans again found themselves under the heavy hand of a Gentile empire. And a string of Roman blunders and abuses that had begun with Pompey's profanation of the temple in 63 BCE only reinforced Jewish convictions that foreign occupation acutely endangered the socio-religious integrity of the particular people of God. In such a setting it is only reasonable to suppose that Jesus' contemporaries would hearken back to the glorious years of the Maccabees, in the hope that they, like their ancestors, might throw off the Gentile yoke through uncompromising faithfulness to the sacred socio-religious badges of covenant loyalty. Much evidence, in fact, points to a persistent tradition of Maccabean ideology flourishing in first-century Palestine, a tradition that would have effectively discouraged a community of Jewish messianists in Jerusalem, c. 30–50 CE, from emulating their founder in pushing the envelope on issues of purity and social relations. Jesus, after all, got himself crucified for doing so.

a. *The Persistent Influence of Maccabean Historiography*
A strong case can be made for the vibrant presence of post-Maccabean nationalistic ideology among Judeans in the East during the time of Jesus. The widespread influence of the Maccabean historical corpus (1–2, *4 Maccabees*) forcefully attests to an enduring interest in events of the mid-second century BCE. We can confidently assume that the reconstruction of Deuteronomistic theology represented in these works indelibly marked the worldview of those who were exposed to the inspiring tales of Yahweh's intervention on Israel's behalf during the glory years of the first Hasmoneans. Josephus utilized 1 Maccabees, for example, as the main source for his narration of the period from the Hasmonean uprising until the days of Simon in his *Jewish Antiquities*.[13] The lasting appeal of 2 Maccabees—a text in which Deuteronomistic theology is most pointedly brought to bear on events of the Maccabean era—explains the use of the document by two later authors, who drew upon 2 Maccabees to compose *3 Maccabees* and *4 Maccabees*, respectively.[14] The ongoing popularity of these works supports Deines's identification of 1 and 2 Maccabees as expressions of 'mainstream "Common Judaism"'.[15]

Also attesting to the enduring appeal of the Maccabean narratives, and to the persistence of idealized memories of Hasmonean hegemony, is what

13. Gafni (1989: 116); deSilva (2002: 265).
14. DeSilva (2002: 307, 355).
15. Deines (2001: 479). One could say the same of *Jubilees*. See Chapter 3 for evidence for the popularity of *Jubilees* and its use as a source by Josephus.

Williams has recently described as 'the mainly Maccabean onomasticon' that was in use in Palestine during the late Hellenistic and early Roman periods.[16] The names of the Hasmonean heroes proved extremely popular among Jewish families during the post-Maccabean era.[17] Six of the nine most popular male names (Mattathias, John, Simon, Judas, Eleazar and Jonathan), and the three most popular female names (Mary, Salome, and Shelamzion), had all belonged to members of the Hasmonean family. The Palestinian onomasticon differs markedly, moreover, from the various Jewish names identified from inscriptions from Greco-Roman Egypt, where Hasmonean names (except for Eleazar) are conspicuously absent. This contrast, in turn, further underscores the pervasive nationalistic mood that characterized the post-Maccabean Palestinian environment in which Jesus of Nazareth lived and ministered.[18]

And Maccabean historiography contributed to the perpetuation of nationalistic ideology in another vital way. DeSilva relates,

> Perhaps one of the more obvious signs of the influence of 2 Maccabees (together with 1 Maccabees) is the gradual acceptance of Hanukkah into the calendar of Jewish festivals (see Jn 10.22, where this is one of the festivals included in John's presentation of Jesus as the fulfillment of all those things celebrated in the liturgical cycle). The feast does not owe its existence to these documents, but the literary celebration and promulgation of the festal story would certainly have supported and encouraged its acceptance.[19]

We must not miss the significance of adding a new festival to the annual series of national feasts that had been on the Jewish calendar for centuries. Persons in societies like those that populated the ancient Mediterranean world are seldom open to innovation where traditional religious practices are concerned. This would have been particularly true of Judeans, whose sacred calendar had been preserved in written form in the Hebrew Scriptures for generations. The acceptance of Hanukkah into the yearly festal cycle is best explained by ongoing interest in the story of Judas and the rededication of the

---

16. Williams (2005: 27).
17. See Williams (1995: 106-109) and Ilan (2002: 6-8).
18. Bauckham (2006: 73-74). Bauckham also identifies two other widely attested names, Joshua and Menahem, as those which, along with the Hasmonean names, 'were popular because of their association with the nationalistic religious expectations of national deliverance and restoration by God' (2006: 77).

As an aside, it is of no small consequence to note that the names found in the four Gospels 'could not possibly have resulted from the addition of names to the traditions outside Jewish Palestine', since the gospel data corresponds directly with naming practices in Palestine, not the Diaspora, thus further attesting to the origins of the gospel stories as genuine Palestinian traditions (Bauckham [2006: 84, 73-74]).

19. DeSilva (2002: 278).

temple in 164 BCE.[20] Maccabean literature likely served as a primary vehicle for nurturing such interest. Once Hanukkah found a place on the calendar, the celebration itself renewed the memories of the Maccabean years on an annual basis for Jews who gathered in Jerusalem for the festival, continually reminding celebrants that God intervenes on behalf of a people who remain faithful to the covenant badges of circumcision, Sabbath observance, and levitical food. Maccabean literature and the feast of Hanukkah thus worked in tandem mutually to reinforce in the minds of first-century Judeans the honor to be gained by persons who tenaciously preserved their marks of Jewish particularism in the context of Gentile occupation and oppression.

b. *Zeal for Yahweh*
Dunn traces a tradition of 'zeal' throughout the history of the Jewish people, a tradition that closely associated Israel's otherness vis-à-vis the surrounding nations with a significant aspect of the character of Yahweh. The theme finds its conceptual roots in the Hebrew Scriptures, which portray Yahweh as 'a jealous God' (אל קנא) who will tolerate no compromise with foreign gods on the part of his people. So central, in fact, is the idea to the Torah's understanding of the nature of God, that the zeal or jealousy of Yahweh can serve as the primary theological foundation for the defining ethical charges related in the Decalogue:

> 4 You shall not make for yourself an idol, whether in the form of anything that is in heaven above, or that is on the earth beneath, or that is in the water under the earth. 5 You shall not bow down to them or worship them; for I the LORD your God am a jealous God, punishing children for the iniquity of parents, to the third and the fourth generation of those who reject me, 6 but showing steadfast love to the thousandth generation of those who love me and keep my commandments (Exod. 20.4-6; see Deut. 4.24; 5.9; 6.15).

The zeal *of* Yahweh was replicated (or, perhaps more accurately, reciprocated) in a zeal *for* Yahweh on the part of his people, who were expected to maintain a pure and pagan-free cult. Due to the influence of the Maccabean histories and other Second-Temple documents, the 'zeal' tradition persisted as an informing ideological and behavioral construct well out into the first century of the common era.[21] It was a tradition, moreover, which strongly discouraged compromise on the part of the faithful, where matters related to purity and social identity were concerned.

Judeans found 'zeal for the Lord' exemplified in a number of Old Testament stories, where various Israelite heroes acted dramatically in defense

---

20. On which see VanderKam (1987).
21. I am indebted to Dunn for much of what follows (2005: 354-55). Other treatments of the theme include Donaldson (1989) and, more extensively, Seland (1995). Meier offers a good summary, as well (2001: 205-208).

of the nation's socio-religious distinctives. Second-Temple writers, in turn, generously laced their narratives with the *topos*, as they patterned the behaviors of their own protagonists after the activities of Israel's zealous heroes of old. The story of the rape of Dinah, for example, and the ensuing response of Dinah's brothers, who slaughtered the Shechemites, plays a part in Judith's prayer for success in the ruse against Holofernes. Judith informs God of her desire to avenge Israel after the manner of Simeon and Levi, 'who burned with zeal for you and abhorred the pollution of their blood' (Jdt. 9.4; see also *Jub.* 30.8-18). Phinehas, especially, secured for himself a permanent place in Israel's folk memory, as one who proved himself 'zealous for his God', when he killed a fellow Israelite and his Midianite paramour who were sharing a tent in the camp of Yahweh. The OT narrative explicitly connects the jealousy of Yahweh for his people with the zeal of Phinehas for the preservation of pure Yahwehism:

> 10 The LORD spoke to Moses, saying: 11 'Phinehas son of Eleazar, son of Aaron the priest, has turned back my wrath from the Israelites by manifesting such zeal among them on my behalf that in my jealousy I did not consume the Israelites. 12 Therefore say, "I hereby grant him my covenant of peace. 13 It shall be for him and for his descendants after him a covenant of perpetual priesthood, because he was zealous for his God, and made atonement for the Israelites"' (Num. 25.10-14).

Phinehas is later remembered both in Sirach and in 1 Maccabees and *4 Maccabees*. 'Zeal' terminology surfaces in each account (Sir. 45.23-24; 1 Macc. 2.54; *4 Macc.* 18.12). Elijah, too, is extolled in Second-Temple literature for his 'zeal' in defending Yahwehism, presumably when he slaughtered 450 prophets of a syncretistic Baal cult championed by Ahab and Jezebel in Wadi Kishon (1 Kings 18; see Sir. 48.1-3; 1 Macc. 2.58).

Most important for our purposes is the portrayal of the instigation of the Maccabean revolt itself as an archetypical expression of 'zeal for the law', the epitome of covenant loyalty. The aged Mattathias triggered the revolt when he killed both the Syrian official who sought to force his village to commit idolatry and a fellow Jew who had come forth to obey the pagan mandate. The parallels with the Phinehas affair are transparent, and the Maccabean historian's ensuing commentary on Mattathias's behavior has 'zeal' written all over it:

> 26 Thus he burned with zeal for the law, just as Phinehas did against Zimri son of Salu. 27 Then Mattathias cried out in the town with a loud voice, saying: 'Let every one who is zealous for the law and supports the covenant come out with me!' (1 Macc. 2.26-27).

Dunn helpfully teases out of the above narratives 'three striking features of "zeal" thus understood'.[22] First, in each of these incidents the protago-

---

22. Dunn (2005: 355).

nist exhibits an unconditional commitment to preserve the purity of Israel's socio-religious otherness in the face of perceived compromise or defilement. Israel's identity as the set-apart people of a jealous God thus surfaces consistently as the central ideological bedrock of both (a) Second-Temple stories of persons who exhibited 'zeal for God' (Judith and Mattathias) and (b) the Old Testament narratives after which these later stories are patterned. Second, the above heroes of the faith all resorted to violent measures in service of their zeal for Yahweh. Simeon and Levi, Phinehas, Elijah, Judith, and Mattathias each killed their adversaries in defense of Israel's religious purity. Finally, our protagonists not only directed their zeal against foreigners who threatened Israel's socio-religious integrity. Fellow Jews (and Israelites) who were judged to have compromised their covenant with Yahweh found themselves on the receiving end of 'zeal for the Lord' in these enduring and influential narratives, as well. Thus Phinehas slew 'Zimri son of Salu, head of an ancestral house belonging to the Simeonites' (Num. 25.14). And Mattathias killed 'a Jew' who 'came forward in the sight of all to offer sacrifice on the altar in Modein, according to the king's command' (1 Macc. 2.23). What we have here, in summary, are occasions of violence exercised in the service of Jewish nationalism—extreme expressions of covenant loyalty directed towards Judeans and Gentiles alike. Such was the tradition of 'zeal' that defined religious fidelity for certain representatives of post-Maccabean Judaism.

The question is whether the perspective that identified 'zeal' for Yahweh and his law as the epitome of covenant loyalty—with its concomitant potential for the exercise of extreme measures in the service of boundary preservation—persisted out into the first century CE, while the post-Easter church was establishing itself in Jerusalem. The answer is near at hand. The apostle Paul twice informs us of his pre-Christian zeal for Judaism, and in both instances he directly relates the theme of 'zeal' to his role as a 'persecutor of the church' (Phil. 3.6; Gal. 1.14). As Dunn appropriately concludes, 'Paul the persecutor undoubtedly saw himself as a "zealot" in the tradition of Phinehas and the Maccabees'.[23] And Paul was hardly unique in this regard. All of this, of course, would have strongly discouraged the Jerusalem Christians from embracing Jesus' counter-cultural approach toward purity and nationalism.

c. *The Desolating Sacrilege*
Also to be considered in this connection is a striking expression occurring in 1 Maccabees, which continued for several generations to trigger memories of the desecration of the temple altar by Antiochus IV in 167 BCE. The expression occurs in 1 Macc. 1.54, at the climax of the author's description of Syrian suppression of Jewish socio-religious practices:

---

23. Dunn (2005: 356).

'Now on the fifteenth day of Chislev, in the one hundred forty-fifth year, they erected a *desolating sacrilege* (LXX: βδέλυγμα ἐρημώσεως) on the altar of burnt offering'. The reference is to the transformation of the altar before the temple structure into a pagan altar on which swine were sacrificed (Josephus, *Ant.* 12.253). The author of Daniel used the identical expression once in reference to Antiochus's activities and twice again, elsewhere in his prophecy, to describe a later eschatological desecration of the temple altar:

> Forces sent by him [Antiochus IV] shall occupy and profane the temple and fortress. They shall abolish the regular burnt offering and set up *the abomination that makes desolate* (LXX: βδέλυγμα ἐρημώσεως) (Dan. 11.31).

> From the time that the regular burnt offering is taken away and *the abomination that desolates* (LXX: βδέλυγμα τῆς ἐρημώσεως) is set up, there shall be one thousand two hundred ninety days (Dan. 12.11; see also 9.27).

Jesus draws upon the same imagery in his great eschatological discourse, as recorded in Mark 13: 'But when you see the *desolating sacrilege* (βδέλυγμα τῆς ἐρημώσεως) set up where it ought not to be (let the reader understand), then those in Judea must flee to the mountains' (Mk 13.14). Theissen's observations about the text are quite on the mark:

> The expression 'desolating sacrilege' is a cipher to be decoded, as the address to the readers indicates. It is thus legitimate to regard the expression as a *terminus technicus* meant to remind us of some particular thing. The only thing that fits is the establishment of the cult of Zeus Olympios in 168–67 BCE.[24]

To describe a future desecration of the Jerusalem temple, Jesus thus employs an expression that needs no explanation, since it strongly resonates with the enduring memories of the threat to Israel's sacred space during the Maccabean era.[25] The command in the verse to 'flee to the mountains' (Mk 13.14) may also have been influenced by Maccabean literature, for we read that Mattathias and his sons 'fled to the hills' (1 Macc. 2.28) and that others who defied the decrees of Antiochus 'had been wandering in the mountains and caves like wild animals' (2 Macc. 10.6). The way in which Jesus framed portions of his eschatological discourse therefore plainly demonstrates that the profanation of the temple at the hands of Antiochus IV remained a vibrant part of the collective memory of Judeans in Palestine during the first century of the common era.[26]

---

24. Theissen (1991: 159-60). I am indebted to Theissen for a number of the insights that follow.

25. For the way in which the passages from Daniel would have been understood during the Roman period, see Crossley (2004: 27-29).

26. Theissen (1991: 158).

d. *The Caligula Affair*

Maccabean sentiments were profoundly aroused in yet another way during the first post-Easter decades, this time from the Roman side. A historical event occurred in 40 CE, which would have brought directly to mind the sufferings under Antiochus IV, and which almost certainly left its imprint on the way in which the early church responded to Jesus' relativization of distinctions between sacred and profane space. I refer here to Gaius Caligula's proposal to set up his own statue in the Jerusalem temple and thus transform the Jews' most sacred space into a sanctuary of Zeus Epiphanes Gaius.[27] The response of the Jews to Caligula's plan was immediate and widespread. Judeans held mass demonstrations on the plain of Phoenicia in May of 40 CE and refused to sow their fields the following October. Meanwhile, Petronius, the proconsular governor charged with the task of installing the statue in the temple, proved more sober than his emperor, for he intentionally delayed the project and soon appealed to Caligula to call off the plan entirely. Sometime just before Gaius's death in January of 41 CE, the emperor rescinded the order, and the conflict came to a close. By this time, however, the threat had lingered for the better part of a year and had provoked renewed concern for the sanctity of the temple, which was, of course, the primary tangible symbol of Jewish socio-religious identity.

Caligula's threat, moreover, could not have helped but bring to mind the activities of Antiochus IV, for the parallels between the affair in 167 BCE and the debacle of 40 CE are quite remarkable.[28] In both cases, a self-deifying imperial leader sought to turn the Jewish temple into a pagan sanctuary. And in both cases, interestingly enough, Judean zeal in dismantling a pagan altar played a central role in events related to the temple. In 167 BCE, the aged priest Mattathias ignited the Maccabean revolt when he tore down one of Antiochus's pagan altars in the Jewish town of Modein (1 Macc. 2.25). A similar incident, perhaps directly inspired by memories of Mattathias's act of pious zeal, triggered Caligula's order in 40 CE. Once again, Jews tore down a pagan altar in what was perceived to be Jewish territory, this time in a city only 35 kilometers from Modein.[29] Philo relates the incident as follows:

---

27. Philo (*Leg.* 347). Extended accounts of the statue incident can be found in Josephus (*Ant.* 18.261-308; Josephus, *War* 2.184-203) and Philo (*Leg.* 207-333). The sources agree in the main on the general outline of events, but they differ considerably on certain key details. Important scholarly reconstructions include Smallwood (1970) and McLaren (1991: 114-26).

28. For years scholars have noted parallels between the activities of Gaius and Antiochus IV. Townsend suggested nearly a century ago that 'we might call [Caligula] the Second Brilliant Madman' (1913: 2.653).

29. Theissen remarks, 'The Jews of Jamnia probably had his [Mattathias's] example in mind when they destroyed the pagan (imperial?) altar, because Modein is only 35 kilometers away from Jamnia. In that area the memory of the uprising would not have faded so quickly' (1991: 158).

> Jamneia, one of the most populous cities of Judaea, is inhabited by a mixture of people, the majority being Jews with some others of alien races, intruders for mischief from the dwellers in adjacent countries. These people being new settlers have made themselves a pest and a nuisance to those who are in a sense indigenous by perpetually subverting some part of the institutions of the Jews. Hearing from travellers visiting them how earnestly Gaius was pressing his deification and the extreme hostility which he felt towards the whole Jewish race, they thought that a fit opportunity of attacking them had fallen their way. Accordingly they erected an extemporized altar of the commonest material with the clay moulded into bricks, merely as a plan to injure their neighbours, for they knew that they [the Jews] would not allow their customs to be subverted, as indeed it turned out. For, when they saw it and felt it intolerable that the sanctity which truly belongs to the Holy Land should be destroyed, they met together and pulled it down (*Leg.* 200-202).

By way of response, the local Roman procurator at Jamnia, Herennius Capito, sent an exaggerated report to the emperor, which resulted in Gaius's order to Petronius to install an imperial statue in the temple in Jerusalem (*Leg.* 200-207).

Roman leaders had good reason to be deeply troubled about Jewish behavior at Jamnia. The city had passed from Herodian control to the Roman imperial family through inheritance and, as mentioned above, was currently governed by an imperial procurator. The Jews tolerated imperial temples in Caesarea Maritima and Sebaste, and would likely have been expected to do the same in the emperor's own territory at Jamnia. To be factored in, as well, were recent occurrences in Roman Egypt, where the erection of imperial images in Jewish synagogues ignited fiery conflict between Jews and pagans in Alexandria (Philo, *In Flacc.* 41). Rome likely viewed the relatively concurrent Jewish protests in Alexandria and Palestine as organized resistance against the emperor. Swift and sharp reaction to the Jamnia incident was only to be expected. The unfortunate timing, during Gaius's principate, simply meant that the Roman reaction took the form of a colossal political blunder, instead of a wise and judicious response that might have emanated from a more sober imperial administration.

Judeans, of course, saw things differently. Pagan activities in both Egypt and Palestine constituted a blatant affront to Jewish religious sensibilities, and Gaius's order concerning the statue irredeemably confirmed Jewish convictions that their way of life faced a fundamental and unacceptable challenge from the non-Jewish world, particularly where the sanctity of the temple was concerned. Given the nature of Caligula's designs, and the episode at Jamnia, it must have appeared to the Jews that the events of 167 BCE were repeating themselves all over again, this time at the hands of a Roman emperor whose 'propensity to self-deification' surely seemed chillingly similar to that of the Syrian Greek despot of generations ago.³⁰ The inevitable result was 'a crisis of fierce religious nationalism unparallel since Antiochus's assault on Judaism two centuries earlier'.³¹

At this defining juncture in history, the Gospels had not yet been written, but we can be assured that the Jesus traditions later used by the four evangelists were actively circulating among Christians in Jewish Palestine. Theissen has argued from parallels between Mark 13 and the Caligula episode that the synoptic apocalypse was composed in 40 CE, just before word came that Gaius had rescinded his order.³² I am not convinced that the text was created *ex nihilo* with Caligula's intentions in view, but it does appear that the way in which a key portion of Jesus' prophecy was transmitted was, indeed, influenced by Gaius's directive. One of the more interesting observations Theissen makes along these lines relates to the gender of the participle ἑστηκότα ('set up') that modifies the expression 'desolating sacrilege' (τὸ βδέλυγμα τῆς ἐρημώσεως) in Mk 13.14. The participle is masculine, where we would expect the neuter ἑστός to agree with the gender of βδέλυγμα. As Theissen notes, the construction in its present form is something like saying in English, 'the thing *who* stands where it should not stand'. The wording of the verse could very well have been influenced by the Caligula incident. Theissen elaborates,

> The *constructio ad sensum* leads us to suspect that the 'desolating sacrilege' represents a person. The emperor's statue is both: as lifeless matter, it is neuter (a βδέλυγμα), but as the image of the emperor it is a person. In addition, the participle 'standing' is ideally chosen to represent a statue.³³

While the evidence must remain somewhat less than conclusive, it does appear that the early Christian tradents who handled the teachings that were later included in the synoptic apocalypse saw in Gaius's plan to desecrate the temple the fulfillment of Jesus' prophecy. They then framed the Greek version of the tradition accordingly, a version later utilized by Mark.

---

30. The phrase in quotations is from Theissen (1991: 145). Crossley finds 'distinct echoes' of the Maccabean crisis in Josephus's and Philo's retelling of the Caligula crisis: (a) like the Maccabean martyrs, Jews were prepared to die for their traditions during the Caligula crisis (Philo, *Leg.* 117, 196; Josephus, *Ant.* 18.265, 271); (b) a threat of Jewish rebellion (recalling the Maccabean revolt) is present throughout the Caligula account (*Leg.* 226; *Ant.* 18.261-64); (c) Josephus refers to the 'madness' of Caligula's intentions (μανία, *Ant.* 18.277), a reference analogous to Polybius's labeling of Antiochus as 'mad' (Ἐπαμανής, *Hist.* 26.1) (Crossley [2004: 30]).

31. Barnett (1999: 242).

32. Theissen is not the first to make the connection between Mark 13 and the Caligula crisis. See, for example, Torrey (1941: 1-40) and Zuntz (1984: 47-71). More recently, Crossley has discussed the Caligula background to Mark 13 in some detail (2004: 29-37).

33. Theissen (1991: 160).

The fuel thrown on the fire of Jewish particularism by Caligula's aborted attempt to put his statue in the temple, and the way in which the incident hearkened back to the events of 167 BCE, must be taken into account in any attempt to ascertain why the Jerusalem Christians might have been a bit slow to get with Jesus' program of relativizing the fundamental badges of Jewish identity. Already, during the 30s CE, Jewish messianists were suspect where commitment to the temple was concerned. Jesus' saying about the destruction of the edifice circulated widely among his first followers, and Stephen had been stoned, at least in part, for a less-than-desirable attitude toward the centrality of Israel's most sacred space (Acts 7). Now the temple was suddenly threatened with desecration at the hands of a Roman despot who reminded Judeans all too much of the notorious Antiochus IV of Maccabean lore. It appears, moreover (see on Mk 13.14, above), that Palestinian Christians saw in Caligula's decree and the ensuing Jewish protest the irreversible first steps toward the fulfillment of Jesus' memorable prophecy of the temple's destruction. Such an outlook would have strongly discouraged Jewish messianists from resisting Caligula's designs.[34] This is an important point. For the reaction of the broader Jewish populace was, of course, precisely the opposite—non-messianist Judeans were prepared to fight to the death, if necessary, in order to defend the sacred site (Philo, *Leg.* 117, 196; Josephus, *Ant.* 18.265, 271).

Tensions between messianist and non-messianist Jews would likely have been considerable, therefore, and Theissen's incisive reflections about the tenuous position of Palestinian Christians in the aftermath of the crisis are quite on the mark:

> We can guess what a difficult situation ensued for those Christians after the surprising rescue of the temple. The aggressions aroused among the people against the Romans in the crisis year 40 could only be expressed in a muted manner against the rulers of the land, especially since a leading Roman official [Petronius] had evaded the command to desecrate the temple. It was all the more likely that the pent-up tensions would be vented on a group of outsiders who disassociated themselves from the temple and circulated ambiguous sayings about its destruction.[35]

The popularity of Maccabean historiography may have contributed directly to such animosity. Given that first-century Judeans saw in Caligula's plan a repeat of the pogrom under Antiochus IV, it is quite possible that Torah-observant Judeans correspondingly cast the early Christians in the role of Jason and his philhellene followers during the Greek period. Theissen and Merz are generally on target to interpret both early Christianity and Jason's

---

34. I have drawn here upon Taylor's insightful discussion of the social and historical setting of Palestinian Christianity during the 40s CE (1996).

35. Theissen (1991: 174).

Hellenizing agenda as attempts to form 'a universalist Judaism without separatist rites'. Jesus' early followers could very well have 'reminded many Jews of the failed Hellenistic reform and therefore provoked bitter resistance'.[36]

Christians therefore provided an opportune target for the nationalistic frustrations of their Jewish compatriots, and we are not surprised to encounter shortly after the Caligula crisis, when Agrippa I was in control of Judea and Samaria, a persecution directed against some of the highest-ranking members of the Jerusalem congregation. James, the son of Zebedee, suffered martyrdom, and Peter barely escaped a similar fate (Acts 12). According to the narrative in Acts, moreover, the populace responded quite positively to Agrippa's actions against the church leaders, thus confirming the postulation (above) of a severe fallout between messianist and non-messianist Jews in the wake of the Caligula debacle.[37] As Theissen concludes, 'Anyone who maintained a reserved attitude toward the temple, in the face of God's obvious intervention on its behalf, could get into a fatal situation'.[38]

---

36. Theissen and Merz (1998: 131). Certain Judeans took a public stand against the inroads of Hellenism long before the crisis under Caligula. For example, Herod ran into opposition as he attempted to introduce pagan athletic contests and spectacles in a theater or an amphitheater (Josephus, *Ant.* 15.267-91). The Jewish reaction to images later proved even stronger (*Ant.* 17.149-54; 18.55-59) (Witherington [1994: 119]).

37. Note the markedly different attitude of the Jewish populace toward the nascent Jesus movement before the Caligula affair, when, according to the author of Acts, the church enjoyed 'the goodwill of all the people' (Acts 2.47).

38. Theissen (1991: 174). The early Christians' attitude toward the temple is a point of contention in the scholarly community. Ådna, who has recently devoted much energy to the topic, understands the atoning death of Jesus to have replaced the temple cult in the views and practices of both the Jerusalem congregation and Paul (1993; 1999; 2000). In Ådna's view, the first Christians in Jerusalem may have frequented the temple as a place to preach and pray (1999: 470; see Acts 2.46; 5.42), but it is highly unlikely that they participated in the propitiatory sacrifices (1993: 554-55). Fuglseth, following Dunn (1991: 95), argues for more variety along these lines. Perspectives on the temple among the first followers of Jesus ranged from antagonistic, to indifferent, to supportive (Fuglseth [2005: 128-36]).

I think that Fuglseth has over-interpreted the evidence for actual involvement in the temple cult on the part of the early Christians, much of which is ambiguous at best. The same could be said of Klawans, who addresses the post-Easter role of the temple in the course of his treatment of the Last Supper (2002). I see a continuum, in this regard, which runs from (a) explicit challenges to the temple as an institution, at one end, to (b) tacit indifference to temple and cult, at the other. Among those post-Easter Jerusalem believers who adopted the latter approach, we may suppose a limited involvement with certain temple rituals (Acts 21.17-26). I find it questionable, however, categorically to infer from Acts 2 that the Jerusalem church performed 'Jewish sacrificial rituals', and to assume from the use of sacrificial imagery in his letters that Paul regarded the temple cult as 'proper and *effective*' (Klawans [2002: 14-15, see 11-12], my italics). The fact that Jerusalem leaders like 'Peter and John' (Acts 4.1-22) and 'the apostles' (5.17-39)

Increased concern among Judeans in the early 40s CE for the integrity of Israel's sacred space surely overflowed onto other aspects of Jewish identity, as well, given the way in which the Caligula affair stirred up memories of the pogrom under Antiochus IV. The pointed reminder of the faithfulness of the Maccabean martyrs to uphold Torah injunctions relating to circumcision, Sabbath observance, and a levitical diet would have encouraged a heightened sensitivity to any compromises in these areas, as well.

The effect of the Caligula crisis upon mid-first century Jews, whose worldview was profoundly influenced by the collective memories of Hasmonean history (as outlined in 1–2 Maccabees and *4 Maccabees*), must be factored into any reasonable explanation of the attitude of Jesus' post-Easter followers toward practices related to purity and boundaries. In a socio-religious context that awakened memories of the glory years of the early Hasmoneans at every turn—and which extolled violent expressions of Maccabean ideology as the epitome of 'zeal for the Lord' (see above)—it is hardly surprising that members of the Jerusalem Jesus movement hesitated fully to embrace their founder's program for the relativization of key symbols of Jewish identity and the renegotiation of the socio-ethnic boundaries of the people of God. The currents of history were flowing much too fast in the opposite direction.[39]

4. *Factor #2: The Jewish Make-up of the Post-Easter Church*

Other considerations can be addressed more concisely. The most obvious of these is the Jewish make-up of the church during the first decade of its existence. Until the inclusion of Gentiles in the Jesus community at Antioch compelled the church to wrestle with the ethnic contours of the Christian *ekklesia*, there would have been little motivation for the first Jewish Christians to afford much consideration to Jesus' relativization of Jewish identity markers. Peter's response to the heavenly vision in Acts 10.14—'By no means, Lord; for I have never eaten anything that is profane or unclean'—is hardly surprising. Until he encountered the work of God in the lives of Gentiles like Cornelius, and until he later journeyed to Antioch and found himself among members of a Jesus community who were not ethnic Jews, Peter would have had no occasion to share a table with Gentiles. The longer

---

conflicted with temple authorities suggests a less-than-supportive stance toward the cult on their part. And Paul's interpretation of the death of Jesus seems to leave little room in his worldview for the continuing efficacy of the temple sacrifices (Rom. 3.21-26; 5.9-10; 1 Cor. 15.3).

39. The transition after the death of Herod Agrippa I (44 CE) to direct Roman administration in Judea also exacerbated Jewish nationalistic sentiments, as illustrated by the tax revolt that occurred under the procuratorship of Tiberius Alexander (c. 46–48 CE; Josephus, *Ant.* 20.102).

the Jewish messianists constituted the sole expression of the post-Easter Jesus movement, the more their Torah-based approach to social boundaries would have confirmed and established itself as normative among persons who had kept the law for generations and who, at this point in their pilgrimage under the new covenant, had no pressing reasons to do otherwise.[40]

5. *Factor #3: The Nature of Jesus' Teachings*

A third factor affecting the way in which the church handled Jesus' teachings on purity and nationalism relates to the character of the teachings themselves.[41] Nowhere in the gospel record does Jesus explicitly instruct his disciples to disregard the socio-ethnic boundaries of the Jewish people in order to admit Gentiles to the new community.[42] Even those few sayings

---

40. A burgeoning Gentile mission would eventually force the issue. Dunn summarizes:

> It was evidently the success of that mission which brought to the surface the question of whether justification by faith in Christ Jesus was in any way or degree dependent on observance of the law, on doing the works of the law, on adopting a characteristically Jewish way of life (2005: 37).

I estimate an interval of approximately ten years, between the passion in 30 CE and Peter's interaction with Cornelius c. 40 CE (Acts 10.1–11.18), before the Jerusalem church had to wrestle at all with conditions for Gentile inclusion. And not until nearly a decade later (49 CE) did the issue become significant enough to generate formal discussion and decisions on the part of the congregation's leaders (Acts 15.1-29). The incident at Antioch (Gal. 2.11-14), which Dunn offers as 'the first major dispute on the issue of food laws', was likely a key catalyst in moving the debate forward (2005: 180).

41. Wright remarks, in this regard, about Jesus' 'cryptic and coded riddles and stories', 'cryptic and subversive wisdom' (Wright [1996: 591, 606]).

42. It is possible that Jesus spoke more transparently in private than in public about issues of purity and boundaries. Perhaps some of this private instruction to the disciples (see Mk 4.10-11) was handed down as oral tradition that never found its way into the canonical Gospels. Jesus' pronouncement about the uselessness of physical circumcision, found in the *Gospel of Thomas* (53), may be an example of just such a teaching.

I wonder, however, just how widespread such traditions actually were. We should expect Mark, in particular, to have found it in his interest to include Jesus traditions clearly abrogating Jewish boundary markers, had such traditions been circulating at the time he wrote his Gospel. It is Mark, after all, who enthusiastically interprets Jesus' enigmatic saying about food in precisely such terms (7.19), yet he must do so in an editorial aside, apparently having no access (even from the teaching of Peter [Eusebius, *H.E.* 3.39.15]) to such a categorical statement on the part of Jesus himself. In the case of the food pronouncement, moreover, both Matthew and Mark do, in fact, give us a glimpse into the kind of insider information given to the disciples about such issues (Mt. 15.12-20; Mk 7.17-23). And what we have remains somewhat ambiguous and open to alternative applications in disparate social settings, as argued above. I am indebted to my colleague, Dr Alan Hultberg, for stimulating my thinking along these lines, although he will, perhaps, be less than persuaded by my conclusion.

that directly promote a ministry to 'all nations' (Mt. 28.19-20) were most likely interpreted in the early church in accordance with various texts in the Hebrew Scriptures which portray non-Jews worshipping in Jewish fashion at the temple in Jerusalem. The perspective on Gentile inclusion related in Acts 15 is illustrative: 'It is necessary for them to be circumcised and ordered to keep the law of Moses' (Acts 15.4; see v. 1). It is certainly the case that Jesus laid the symbolic foundation for the dismantling of ethnic boundaries in the later church by means of his unsympathetic stance towards the vital covenant symbols of sacred times, sacred space, and sacred food. This much has been demonstrated in the chapters above. Jesus' teachings and actions regarding purity were at times somewhat ambiguous, however, and their embryonic form inevitably left them open to a variety of interpretations.[43]

We saw this phenomenon reflected in our comparison of Mark 7 and Matthew 15 (Chapter 7). Jesus' categorical assertion—'it is not what goes into the mouth that defiles a person' (Mt. 15.11)—lent itself to divergent applications, depending on whether the primary social context of the tradents was Jewish or Gentile. Thus, Matthew's Jesus concludes his teaching in the pericope with a summary statement that leaves the assertion in v. 11 safely within the sphere of Jewish ethnic identity, but distinctly outside of a sectarian redefinition of that identity: 'to eat with unwashed hands does not defile' (Mt. 15.20). Mark, however, who crafted his Gospel in a Gentile setting, extends the potential trajectory of Jesus' programmatic statement to its logical conclusion, in an arresting editorial aside: 'Thus he declared all foods clean' (7.19).[44] The malleability of Jesus' original assertion rendered either interpretation a reasonable one, and we can perhaps imagine other applications, as well, as sayings like these were contextualized at different times and places along the gradual social trajectory from *ethnos* to *oikos* that would define Christian history for several generations post-Easter.[45]

---

43. Thus, even much later, in the fourth century CE, when Jesus' teaching on Jewish boundary markers as we have it in the canonical Gospels circulated widely, the church still wrestled with the issue of Gentiles voluntarily observing Jewish law, as evidenced from John Chrysostom's diatribes against Jews (Simon [1986: 306-38]). Apparently the teachings of Jesus about purity in the Synoptic Gospels were not as clear to his followers as Sanders and others assume that they would have been. See Rudolph for the persistence of food-related purity concerns among Gentile and Jewish Christians alike during the Patristic period (2002: 301-202).

44. I find myself attracted to Rudolph's suggestion that Mark added his editorial note for the benefit of his Gentile audience, in order to 'construct a theological basis for the Acts 15 food law exemption [or, perhaps, for Paul's view of sacred food, as evidenced in Rom. 14.14] in the teachings of Jesus' (2002: 304).

45. As mentioned in a note in the previous Chapter (n. 76), scholarship is currently divided over whether Jesus framed the contrast between 'what goes into the mouth' and 'what comes out of the mouth' (Mt. 15.11) in antithetical (potentially abrogating levitical purity) or relative (prioritizing moral over ritual purity) terms. I suspect that the

Consider, as well, the two parables of eschatological reversal related in Lk. 13.28-29 and 14.15-24. It is not completely clear here that Jesus envisions Gentiles reclining around Yahweh's kingdom table at the end of the age. Jews—and Jews alone—may be in view, although the way in which each text is framed easily allows for the more expansive interpretation (see Chapter 7). This lack of clarity almost certainly encouraged alternative readings of these parables of reversal, readings that corresponded, again, to the different social contexts in which Jesus' post-Easter followers found themselves. In Lk. 13.28-29, for example, those who come 'from east and west, from north and south' to recline at the eschatological banquet with Abraham, Isaac, and Jacob can be understood to represent either Jews or Gentiles. The parallel in Matthew removes the ambiguity by associating the dominical pronouncement with the healing of a pagan centurion's servant (Mt. 8.5-12). Matthew thereby makes the allusion to Gentiles quite transparent.

Briefly to cite a final example, we may assume that the symbolic nature of the temple action rendered it susceptible to a variety of explanations, as well, especially if the plethora of conflicting interpretations of the event offered by modern scholars—*quot homines, tot sententiae*—is any indication of the ambiguity of Jesus' behavior that day in the Court of the Gentiles.[46]

6. *Factor #4: Jewish Eschatological Expectations*

Prophecies in the Hebrew Scriptures which appear to outline a distinctly geopolitical future for the nation of Israel would also have compromised the ability of Jesus' disciples fully to grasp the implications of their mentor's

---

divergence of opinion on the issue among contemporary exegetes betrays an inherent ambiguity in the dominical pronouncement itself. With some risk of anachronism, we might almost imagine that Matthew (along with the post-Easter Jewish messianists in Jerusalem) defended a relative interpretation of Jesus' saying, while Gentile Christians like Mark read the explicitly antithetical grammar (reflected in the surface structure of the saying) to imply the end of levitical purity where food was concerned. At any rate, given the lively debate among contemporary scholars about the meaning of Jesus' striking assertion, it only makes sense to assume that the early Christians found the ambiguous pronouncement amenable to a variety of applications in the context of community life, and this is the point in the present connection.

Finally, we must not lose sight of the fact that the logion in Mk 7.15 formulates no instructions concerning specific behavior, and therefore does not necessarily exclude the practice of *kashrut* out of respect for tradition or in order to avoid scandal. 'Mk 7.15 is therefore rightly regarded as an 'enigmatic saying' (as a παραβολή, 7.17), and there is controversy over its interpretation' (Theissen and Merz [1998: 366-67]).

46. I have taken the Latin expression (very loosely paraphrased, 'there are as many interpretations as there are interpreters') from Wedderburn's recent treatment of Jesus' temple action (2006: 5).

attitude toward purity and boundaries.[47] Israel's prophetic traditions are complex and variegated, but several common themes emerge repeatedly in the writings of the Old Testament prophets. Two familiar ideas, in particular, would have done much to discourage any creativity among the Jerusalem Christians where badges of Jewish ethnicity were concerned. I have in mind here the recurring predictions of (a) a future purging of Israel to produce a righteous remnant for the Lord, followed by (b) the reconstitution of a regathered Israel as a sovereign nation under the dominion of Yahweh in Zion.

The future purification of a remnant is central to the book of Zechariah, a work which, as we have seen, was quite familiar to Jesus and his contemporaries through its use at the Feast of Booths:

> 1 On that day a fountain shall be opened for the house of David and the inhabitants of Jerusalem, to cleanse them from sin and impurity. 2 On that day, says the Lord of hosts, I will cut off the names of the idols from the land, so that they shall be remembered no more; and also I will remove from the land the prophets and the unclean spirit... 8 In the whole land, says the Lord, two-thirds shall be cut off and perish, and one-third shall be left alive. 9 And I will put this third into the fire, refine them as one refines silver, and test them as gold is tested. They will call on my name, and I will answer them (Zech. 13.1-2, 8-9).

The theme surfaces again in Malachi (with special focus on the temple leaders), where the prophet predicts that a 'messenger of the covenant', who is like 'a refiner's fire and like fullers' soap', 'will purify the descendants of Levi and refine them like gold and silver, until they present offerings to the Lord in righteousness' (3.1-3). The prophet Hosea also looks forward to a day when the Lord will purge a faithless Israel, and here an ensuing restoration involves the rule of a Davidic Messiah. Hosea's extended predictions of the purification and restoration of the nation are summarized in the following excerpt:

> 4 For the Israelites shall remain many days without king or prince, without sacrifice or pillar, without ephod or teraphim. 5 Afterward the Israelites shall return and seek the Lord their God, and David their king; they shall come in awe to the Lord and to his goodness in the latter days (3.4-5).

As in Hosea, forewarnings of a purging of the nation are often accompanied in the literature by promises of future restoration, so that the expectation that national Israel would one day be reestablished as Yahweh's sovereign people in Zion frequently comes into view in the Old Testament prophetic works. The book of Zechariah is, again, representative:

---

47. I am grateful to a dear friend and colleague, Dr Walt Russell, for the insights that follow in this section of the chapter.

> 3 Thus says the Lord: I will return to Zion, and will dwell in the midst of Jerusalem; Jerusalem shall be called the faithful city, and the mountain of the Lord of hosts shall be called the holy mountain. 4 Thus says the Lord of hosts: Old men and old women shall again sit in the streets of Jerusalem, each with staff in hand because of their great age. 5 And the streets of the city shall be full of boys and girls playing in its streets. 6 Thus says the Lord of hosts: Even though it seems impossible to the remnant of this people in these days, should it also seem impossible to me, says the Lord of hosts? 7 Thus says the Lord of hosts: I will save my people from the east country and from the west country; 8 and I will bring them to live in Jerusalem. They shall be my people and I will be their God, in faithfulness and in righteousness (8.3-8; see also 14.8-11).

Comparable predictions surface repeatedly throughout the prophetic writings (Isa. 40.1-11; 49.8-21; 51.1-16; 52.1-12; Hos. 14.4-8; Joel 2.18-32; Mic. 2.12-13; Zeph. 3.9-20).

This twofold prophetic expectation of the purging and restoration of national Israel apparently encouraged Jesus' earliest followers initially to interpret his messianic vocation accordingly. Such tendencies manifest themselves in several early Christian texts. John the Baptizer, for example, conceived of the Messiah's ministry precisely in terms of the purification of the nation: 'His winnowing fork is in his hand, and he will clear his threshing floor and will gather his wheat into the granary; but the chaff he will burn with unquenchable fire' (Mt. 3.12). It seems that Jesus did not meet John's expectations, in this regard, and we may reasonably take the Baptizer's ensuing lack of clarity concerning Jesus' identity (Mt. 11.2-3) as representative of the outlook of numbers of Jesus' earliest followers who struggled to harmonize their Messiah's innovative program with traditional expectations regarding Israel's future. The apostles themselves betray the pervasive influence of the second part of the twofold prophetic program outlined above—namely, national restoration—when they ask Jesus, 'Lord, is this the time when you will restore the kingdom to Israel?' (Acts 1.6). The idea that 'the kingdom' and ethnic 'Israel' might not be coterminous entities in Jesus' agenda would be quickly lost on persons who held such convictions.

It is interesting, in this regard, that Peter, in his first sermon (Acts 2.17-21), cites Joel 2.28-32a, in order to situate in the context of salvation history the activity of the Holy Spirit at Pentecost. As it happens, the portion of the text which Peter quotes is sandwiched in Joel's prophecy between dramatic predictions of the future restoration and exaltation of Israel as a sovereign nation (Joel 2.21-27, 32b). It is not unlikely, then, that Peter interpreted Jesus' messianic vocation through the lens of the twofold purification-and-restoration schema outlined above. Though it involves some degree of speculation, I suspect that the Jerusalem apostles had seen in Jesus' atoning death the promised purification of the nation, and that they now looked anxiously forward to the fulfillment of what they perceived to be the second half of the prophetic program, namely, the restoration of national Israel under the reign of Yahweh in Jerusalem. Such sentiments would decidedly not have encouraged the Jerusalem Christians to get on board with Jesus' subversive approach to purity and boundaries.

7. *Some Related Evidence: The Case of Paul*

Some early Christians did play loose with purity and boundaries, of course, when the fledgling movement began to reach out to Gentiles during the late 40s and early 50s CE. We may pause for a moment at this juncture to wonder what motivated them to do so, if Jesus himself had done nothing during his earthly ministry to encourage such behavior. Paul of Tarsus is the figure most closely associated with the mission to the Gentiles, so it will prove profitable briefly to consider the origins of Paul's Torah-free Gospel. What we will encounter in Paul is an apostle who was apparently well aware of Jesus' socially expansive program, and whose mission setting allowed for the actualization of Jesus' boundary breaking agenda in ways that Peter's ministry to the Jews in Judea did not.

Scholars have been generally hesitant to trace Paul's liberal approach to purity and social boundaries back to Jesus of Nazareth. A basic tenet of form criticism contends that Christians of Paul's generation had little interest in the Jesus of history. Rather, communication from the risen Lord to the post-Easter church, mediated by early Christian prophets, provided direction for congregational life. It is further alleged that the distinction between the Jesus of history and the risen Lord of the church is, in fact, anachronistic when applied to primitive Christianity. The early Christians blurred these categories, as evidenced by the way in which they situated the prophetic sayings of the risen Lord in narrative frameworks purporting to reflect the ministry of the historical Jesus. Bauckham summarizes the fundamental hypothesis of the tradition critical enterprise as follows:

> This contemporary Jesus addressed the community through the Christian prophets, whose words were often incorporated in the Gospel traditions and came to be attributed in the Gospels to the pre-Easter Jesus.[48]

Such a schema hardly encourages much historical optimism where Jesus' purity-related activities in the Gospels are concerned: It was the risen Jesus of post-Easter Gentile Christianity who authenticated and legitimated Paul's Torah-free Gospel. The historical Jesus had championed no such agenda.

---

48. Bauckham (2006: 245).

It would take us far afield directly to interact with the form-critical program, and it would be redundant, as well. Nearly all the contentions of classical form criticism have now been refuted, and there is little to be gained by reviewing the discussion here.[49] Instead, I will briefly assess what information we do possess from Paul's letters for the way in which the apostle to the Gentiles handled the Jesus traditions. The evidence effectively puts the lie to the basic assumptions of form criticism (where Paul is concerned, at any rate). More importantly, for our purposes, it strongly suggests that Paul's convictions about purity and boundaries found their genesis not in post-Easter saying(s) of the risen Christ but, rather, in the teachings and activities of the historical Jesus.

Several considerations encourage us to trace the embryonic origins of Paul's Law-free Gospel to the pre-Easter Jesus.[50] First of all, it is quite clear from his use of technical terminology about the receiving and passing on of tradition (παραλαμβάνω/παραδίδωμι) that Paul understood himself to be involved in a formal traditioning process (1 Cor. 11.2, 23; 15.1, 3; Gal. 1.9). As Gerhardsson has observed, such activity involved the careful passing on of tradition from one person to the next—not in the sense of merely communicating it, but in the sense of assuring that both the tradent and the receiver of the tradition 'possess[ed] it'.[51]

In Paul's case, we can be quite confident that he received his traditions about Jesus directly from the Jerusalem apostles.[52] Paul himself tells us, for example, that he spent two weeks in Jerusalem with Peter, and he relates this information in an epistolary context in which it is hardly in Paul's interest to invoke his dependence upon those who had become apostles before him (Gal. 1.18). Bauckham reasonably presumes that 'Paul was becoming thoroughly informed of the Jesus traditions as formulated by the Twelve, learning them from the leader of the Twelve, Peter'.[53] We will return to this important insight below.

---

49. See Bauckham's discussion for a useful overview of recent developments in the field (2006: 241-51; see, also, the literature he cites). Bauckham notes:

> It is a curious fact that nearly all the contentions of the early form critics have by now been convincingly refuted, but the general picture of the process of oral transmission that the form critics pioneered still governs the way most New Testament scholars think (242).

To reflect in Kuhnian terms, one has to wonder just how much anomaly the form-critical paradigm can endure before it finally gives way to a more historically viable alternative.

50. I am indebted to Bauckham for much of what follows (Bauckham [2006: 264-71]).

51. Gerhardsson (1991: 306).

52. There have been other suggestions but none is convincing (Bauckham [2006: 265-66]).

53. Bauckham (2006: 266).

Secondly, Paul unequivocally distinguishes in his letters between what he understood to be traditions of the earthly Jesus and his own instruction as an apostle. The teaching on marriage and divorce in 1 Corinthians 7 is most informative, in this regard. Paul initially appeals to the historical Jesus, as the source of his general teaching about divorce (vv. 10-11): 'not I but the Lord' (v. 10; see also 1 Cor. 9.14). When he proceeds more narrowly to discuss the special situation of a marriage between a believer and an unbeliever, however, Paul makes it clear that he has no tradition on the matter from Jesus. He must base his instruction on his own apostolic authority: 'I and not the Lord' (v. 12).

Finally, Paul refers, again, to 'the Lord' as his source of tradition in 1 Corinthians 11, in a passage in which he intentionally includes the technical terminology mentioned above:

> 23 For I received (παρέλαβον) from the Lord what I also handed on (παρέδωκα) to you, that the Lord Jesus on the night when he was betrayed took a loaf of bread, 24 and when he had given thanks, he broke it and said, 'This is my body that is for you. Do this in remembrance of me'. 25 In the same way he took the cup also, after supper, saying, 'This cup is the new covenant in my blood. Do this, as often as you drink it, in remembrance of me' (1 Cor. 11.23-25).

The passage is the only unit of Jesus tradition which Paul quotes at length and, as such, it serves as a revealing test-case for Paul's activities as an early Christian tradent. For at least two reasons we may eliminate from the outset the supposition that Paul received the tradition he relates in 1 Cor. 11.23-25 directly from the exalted Lord. First, as we saw above, the references earlier in the letter to information Paul possessed from 'the Lord' all refer to teachings of the historical Jesus. Secondly, the version of the Last Supper tradition which Paul cites in 1 Corinthians 11 is verbally quite close to Lk. 22.19-20. Literary dependence of some sort is highly unlikely,[54] so it is most reasonable to assume that Paul and Luke each drew upon an oral tradition that had been quite closely memorized. What all this implies about Paul's role in the traditioning process is illuminating, to say the least. Bauckham elaborates:

> [Paul] envisages a chain of transmission that *begins from Jesus himself* and passes through intermediaries to Paul himself, who has already passed it on to the Corinthians when he first established their church. The intermediaries are surely, again, the Jerusalem apostles, and this part of the passion traditions will have been part of what Paul learned (in the strong sense of learning a tradition such that he could later recite it) from Peter during that significant fortnight in Jerusalem.[55]

---

54. Paul had no access to Luke's Gospel, and Luke appears not to have been influenced in his Gospel by Paul's letters.

55. Bauckham (2006: 268, author's italics). This model of the traditioning process

What we see in each of the above examples is a Paul who is highly concerned to ground the traditions he attributes to 'the Lord' in his letters not in revelation imparted by the risen Christ but, rather, in the teachings and activities of the historical Jesus of Nazareth. It remains to apply this insight to Paul's inclusive approach to purity and boundaries, an approach which permeates his letters and ultimately defines his Gospel to the Gentiles.

Those who relegate Jesus' boundary-breaking activities in the Gospels to the creative work of early church tradents must assume that Paul—who is clearly concerned to root the non-negotiables of his Gospel in Jesus traditions that he had received from Peter and others (1 Cor. 15.1-5)—intentionally departs from what he has learned about Jesus' approach to the social identity of the people of God, strikes out completely on his own, and addresses this defining community issue in an utterly novel and radical way. This is certainly possible. But it is historically probable? Would the apostolic leadership in Jerusalem, moreover, have blessed such an endeavor (Gal. 2.7-10)?

I think not. More reasonable is the supposition that Peter's instruction to Paul included reflections about Jesus' subversive approach to purity and boundaries, and that it was precisely this aspect of the Jesus tradition that led Paul, in the apposite context of his Gentile mission, to extend to its logical conclusion the trajectory established by the historical Jesus.[56] Two distinct social settings, then, guaranteed that the teachings and activities of Jesus would be contextualized in different ways in Jewish and Gentile churches, respectively—a reality that was apparently clear from the outset to both Peter and Paul: 'I had been entrusted with the gospel for the uncircumcised, just as Peter had been entrusted with the gospel for the circumcised' (Gal. 2.7).

8. *Conclusion*

In light of the above discussion the statement of Sanders cited at the beginning of the chapter—'Jesus' followers did not know that he had directly

---

is hardly unique to Paul. Papias (Eusebius, *Hist. eccl.* 3.39.3-4), Irenaeus (Eusebius, *Hist. eccl.* 5.20.4-7), and Clement of Alexandria (Eusebius, *Hist. eccl.* 2.1.4)—to name but three Christian leaders—assumed a similar approach to the receiving and passing on of the Jesus traditions. In each of these cases, moreover, individual tradents are explicitly named as the intermediary sources of the traditions. In contrast, as Bauckham notes, nowhere in early church literature is a local Christian community identified as the source of a tradition about Jesus (2006: 293-97).

56. See the positive assessment of H. Stettler, in this regard, who finds evidence in Paul's letters that he and his circle were well aware of Jesus' approach to the Sabbath, and that the church knew of the sweeping pronouncement about food in Mk 7.15. She notes, 'Rom. 14,14 (cf. 14,20 and Tit. 1,15) is still best explained as a reference to this saying of Jesus' (2004: 170; in agreement with Westerholm [1978: 81-82]).

opposed the law, and in particular they did not know him to have opposed the laws governing *Sabbath, food, and purity*'—cries out for qualification.[57] Given the embryonic nature of Jesus' teachings and activities with respect to Jewish particularism, what his followers 'knew', in this regard, would have varied considerably according to their social location. In Judea—where Maccabean ideology enjoyed a lively literary enterprise, where volatile annual festivals like Hanukkah and Passover dramatically revived memories of an independent Israel, and where the primary tangible symbol of national Judaism barely escaped profanation by a self-deifying Roman emperor in 40 CE— Jewish Christians would have been understandably cautious about extending to its logical conclusion the social trajectory established by Jesus. Nor did they particularly have reason to do so, given the monochromatic ethnic make-up of the Jerusalem community. Where elements of Jesus' program did break through in Judea, moreover, as in the case of certain branches of the church that appear to have disassociated themselves from unqualified commitment to the temple, resistance was severe from non-messianist Judeans of more traditional sensibilities (Acts 6.13; 7.48-60; 12.1-4).

Other members of the Jesus movement soon operated in the context of a Gentile mission, and for them the implications of Jesus' attitude toward badges of Jewish identity proved more far-reaching. Christian leaders such as Mark and Paul apparently 'knew' quite well, in retrospect, that Jesus' devaluation of Sabbath-keeping, territorial distinctions, and sectarian eating habits ultimately pointed to an epochal transformation of the people of God from Israel as *ethnos* under the old covenant to the Christian *ekklesia* as a multi-ethnic surrogate family under the new covenant. We now turn to examine the positive component of Jesus' social vision for his movement, a vision which united his followers together in community as a fictive kinship group.

57. Sanders (1985: 325).

Chapter 9

JESUS' VISION FOR A FAMILY OF GOD

> 'Whoever does the will of God is my brother and sister and mother'.
>
> Mark 3.35

Jesus' dealings with family lie at the heart of his vision for the people of Yahweh during the inbreaking of the rule of God, and I will now situate the establishment of his community of followers as a surrogate kinship group in the broader context of Jesus' social aims. Jesus' critique of Jewish particularity and the formation of his group as a fictive Mediterranean family are best understood as two aspects of the same social program. In his challenges to contemporary values and practices relating to Sabbath, temple, and dietary laws, Jesus begins to deconstruct the idea of God's people as a localized *ethnos* that had prevailed since Sinai, in order to reconstruct the social identity of the people of God in terms of surrogate family. This, in turn, sets the stage for Pentecost and the Gentile mission to follow, when persons from every nation will become 'children of God through faith in Christ Jesus' (Gal. 3.26).

The family traditions in the Gospels are somewhat perplexing, however, since Jesus gave his followers some rather mixed messages about kinship and family loyalty. In a number of texts he plays quite loose with family values, in some cases scandalously so. Other traditions portray Jesus warmly affirming Jewish family ties. Kinship language found in yet a third category of texts no longer relates to the natural family at all but, rather, to the surrogate family of followers Jesus gathers around himself. The latter group of passages is of particular interest here, since the gospel sayings that include references to surrogate kinship vividly reflect the constructive side of Jesus' social agenda. The fictive family teachings, however, must be read in connection with Jesus' corresponding attitude towards natural family relations, since the way in which we interpret the various family texts relative to one another significantly informs our understanding of discipleship, family loyalty, and Jesus' vision for community under the new covenant.

In what follows I will outline the basic values and priorities that characterized family relations in the Mediterranean world, and then survey the family texts in the Gospels in an attempt to prioritize their various emphases in relation to one another. The gospel traditions that attend to natural and surrogate family relations constitute an indispensable part of Jesus' contribution toward the transformation of national Israel into the multi-ethnic fictive kinship group that was to constitute the Christian *ekklesia*.

1. *Mediterranean Family Values*

We cannot fully appreciate Jesus' teachings about family until we gain some understanding of kinship structure and family relations as Jesus and his contemporaries experienced them.[1] Perhaps the most counterintuitive aspect of ancient Mediterranean kinship, from a Western point of view, has to do with the family relationships that people valued the most. In Euro-American culture, a person's spouse ideally functions as (a) her central locus of relational loyalty and (b) her main source of emotional and material support. Correspondingly, most Westerners expect their closest relational bond within a given generation to be the bond of marriage, and we build our families around that marriage relationship. What is so familiar to Euro-Americans, however, was not true of ancient society, where family was structured not around marriage but was, instead, based on blood.

In the New Testament world, a person viewed as family those persons with whom he shared a common patriline—a bloodline traced from generation to generation solely through the male line. Due to the patrilineal nature of Mediterranean kinship, only a father could pass family membership down to the next generation. A mother could not. A male therefore regarded as immediate family (a) his father (from whom he had received his blood), (b) his brothers and sisters (with whom he shared his blood), and (c) offspring of both genders (to whom he passed on his blood). Females, like males, viewed fathers and siblings as consanguine. Since, however, a mother could not pass on membership in her patriline to the next generation, her children technically belonged not to her family but, rather, to the patriline of her husband. And because a husband and wife had different fathers—and therefore belonged to different patrilines—married persons in the world of the New Testament generally expressed primary relational allegiance not to a spouse but, rather, to members of their family of origin. Marriages were contracted with a view to enhancing the honor or wealth of the extended patrilineal kinship group. The relational satisfaction of the couple involved was seldom a key consideration.

---

1. The pages that follow summarize the much more detailed study of Mediterranean family systems, and the church as a surrogate family, in Hellerman (2001). The definitive study of Paul's sibling terminology is now Aasgaard (2004). See also Burke (2003) on kinship metaphors in 1 Thessalonians. Harland (2005) has recently made a good case for the presence of surrogate family relations in non-Christian associations of the Greek East. The early Christians were apparently not unique in this regard.

9. *Jesus' Vision for a Family of God*

This blood-based orientation to kinship, therefore, directly informed the nature of family relationships. Among persons belonging to the same generation in the world of Mediterranean antiquity, the closest family tie was not the contractual relationship between a husband and wife. It was the blood relationship between siblings. As is now generally recognized by students of ancient family systems, the tightest unit of loyalty and affection in the New Testament world was the consanguine group of brothers and sisters. The emotional bonding modern Westerners expect as a mark of a healthy husband-and-wife relationship was ideally to characterize relations between siblings. As one Jewish writer exclaimed, 'If I do not love my brother, whom shall I love?' (*Jub.* 35.22).[2]

Passages extolling the virtue of sibling solidarity abound in ancient literature. A colorful excerpt from the Jewish book of *Jubilees* vividly reflects ancient convictions concerning the solidarity—and inviolability—of the sibling bond. The anonymous author of this second-century BCE rewrite of the book of Genesis portrays the patriarch Isaac offering a final charge to Jacob and Esau:

> Among yourselves, my sons, be loving of your brothers as a man loves himself, with each man seeking for his brother what is good for him...and each one will love his brother with compassion and righteousness and no one will desire evil for his brother from now and forever all the days of your lives so that you will prosper in all your deeds and not be destroyed.

The passage concludes with some severe consequences for someone who dares betray a brother:

> And if either of you seeks evil against his brother, know that hereafter each one who seeks evil against his brother will fall into his (God's) hands and be uprooted from the land of the living and his seed will be destroyed from under heaven. And on the day of turmoil and execration and indignation and wrath, (then) with devouring burning fire just as he burned Sodom so too he will burn up his land and his city and everything which will be his...and he

---

2. Sibling solidarity was, of course, an ideal that was often compromised in the messy world of day-to-day social interaction. Endogamous marriage, for example, rendered real-life family relations somewhat more complicated than might be deduced from the above overview of lineage kinship structure. Spouses who were also first cousins—a common situation in Jewish antiquity—would share the same patriline beginning with their grandfather's generation. Nor was it unusual for a friend to displace a sibling as an individual's most important affective relationship. None of this, however, undermines the power of sibling terminology to connote relational solidarity at its best in the minds of ancient Mediterranean persons. Thus Plutarch opines: 'even if we feel an equal affection for a friend, we should always be careful to reserve for a brother the first place' (*De frat. amor.* 491B). See Hellerman (2001) for numerous examples of sibling solidarity in practice, and sibling language employed as rhetoric, among the early Christians, c. 50–250 CE.

will not be written on high in the Book of Life... I am exhorting you, my sons, according to the judgment which will come upon the man who desires to harm his brother (*Jub.* 36.4-11).

The Bible also bears witness to this enduring cultural value. Jesus, for example, places the act of leaving one's siblings at the forefront of the relational sacrifices made by some of his followers:

> 28 Peter began to say to him, 'Look, we have left everything and followed you'. 29 Jesus said, 'Truly I tell you, there is no one who has left house or *brothers or sisters* or mother or father or children or fields, for my sake and for the sake of the good news, 30 who will not receive a hundredfold now in this age—houses, *brothers and sisters,* mothers and children, and fields with persecutions—and in the age to come eternal life' (Mk 10.28-30, my italics).

The same priority is reflected somewhat differently in a passage from Matthew. In Mt. 10.21, Jesus lists the inevitable relational chaos that will result from his call to radical discipleship. Since the most important relationship in Jesus' world is the bond between blood brothers, it only follows that discord between siblings constitutes the worst family tragedy imaginable. This is precisely what we find at the beginning of Jesus' list: 'Brother will betray brother to death, and a father his child, and children will rise against parents and have them put to death'. It might help to recall, at this point, the numerous Old Testament narratives that describe various incidents of brother betrayal (Cain and Abel, Jacob and Esau, Joseph and his brothers, and so on). Such stories captured the imagination of their readers precisely because ancient persons felt so strongly about the need for harmony among siblings. Sentiments such as these, then, provide the background for interpreting the family language found in the Gospels, whether that language applies to the realm of the natural family or to Jesus' surrogate family of followers.

Sibling solidarity, as the ancients understood it, naturally included a whole host of relational expectations and responsibilities for brothers and sisters in the context of daily life. In order to appreciate Jesus' social vision for his followers, it will help briefly to review some of these expectations through the matrix of the surrogate church family as illustrated in the New Testament. New Testament writings exhibit a constellation of relational ideals and behaviors that find their origins in the natural family values of the patrilineal kinship group. For example, siblings shared material resources with one another, and a person's brothers and sisters provided the first line of defense against the ever-present threat of economic hardship (Acts 2.43-47; 1 Jn 3.17). To fail to share in times of need was to betray a brother after the analogy of Cain (1 Jn 3.10-17). Brothers and sisters also challenged one another to take responsibility for actions which were inappropriate among persons who viewed themselves as family (Mt. 18.15-20). Siblings were, nevertheless, expected to restore a genuinely repentant brother to normal family relations (Mt. 18.21-35).

The world of the New Testament was a social environment, moreover, in which males generally sought revenge for every interpersonal affront or injustice, in order to defend their (and their family's) public honor—except in dealings with siblings, where honor was always extended but never defended (Rom. 12.10). It was a shameful thing, therefore, for a brother to seek compensation for some real or perceived fraternal offense through litigation in the public courts. As Paul admonished the family of God at Corinth, 'The very fact that you have lawsuits among you means you have been completely defeated already. Why not rather be wronged? Why not rather be cheated? Instead, you yourselves cheat and do wrong, and you do this to your brothers' (1 Cor. 6.7-8).[3]

Finally, siblings in antiquity enjoyed a strong sense of emotional bonding. In the New Testament, we see this most clearly in the connections that Paul experienced with his brothers and sisters in the family of God. Paul claims, for example, that the Philippians hold Paul in their 'heart'.[4] He longs for them all 'with the compassion of Christ Jesus' (1.7-8). Later in the letter he exhorts, 'Therefore, my brothers and sisters, whom I love and long for, my joy and crown, stand firm in the Lord in this way, my beloved' (4.1). At another point in his ministry, Paul sent Timothy to Thessalonica to inquire about the well being of the church he had recently established. Later, when he received Timothy's good report, Paul was so overjoyed that he could hardly contain himself in his reply to this young congregation. The emotional bonding Paul experienced with his siblings in the faith is patently clear:

> 6 Timothy has just now come to us from you, and has brought us the good news of your faith and love. He has told us also that you always remember us kindly and long to see us—just as we long to see you. 7 For this reason, brothers and sisters, during all our distress and persecution we have been encouraged about you through your faith. 8 For we now live, if you continue to stand firm in the Lord (1 Thess. 3.6-8).

All of the above corresponds, interestingly enough, to modern genetic research. Social scientists have identified a direct correlation between altruistic behavior among relatives, on the one hand, and the number of genes shared by these persons, on the other. Siblings share more of the genetic

---

3. I have cited the NIV here. The NRSV unfortunately conceals Paul's family rhetoric in the passage by repeatedly translating ἀδελφοί as 'believers'.

4. The paraphrase represents the NRSV's interpretation of τὸ ἔχειν με ἐν τῇ καρδίᾳ ὑμᾶς. Equally plausible is the idea that Paul has the Philippians in his heart (NIV and most other versions). The point in the present connection remains the same on either reading.

code than any persons of the same generation (50%), and they typically exhibit a closer relational bond, where altruistic behavior is concerned, than any other family relation. The New Testament metaphor of 'brothers and sisters in Christ' thus resonates in any social setting, but the image proved particularly compelling to ancient Mediterranean persons, whose culture had institutionalized consanguinity by means of its lineage kinship structure. It is hardly incidental, then, that Jesus chose the sibling bond—'you are all brothers' (Mt. 23.8)—to define the quality of relationships he envisioned for his community of followers.[5] Jesus intended sibling solidarity, as understood by the ancients, to constitute the heart of the relational values and behavioral priorities that would characterize life together among a renewed people of Yahweh. We turn now to the family passages in the gospel traditions, in order to better appreciate the constructive side of Jesus' social vision.

2. *Jesus and Family: Readjusting the Pendulum*

In an important monograph about Jesus, Dunn has recently challenged a noticeable trend in the scholarly community which privileges the more radical texts in the Gospels to the near exclusion of the family-friendly traditions.[6] The trend Dunn seeks to refute has generated a Jesus who lives on the margins of normal peasant life and who, to various degrees, challenges his followers to adopt a similar lifestyle.[7] Related is a tendency in some circles to see the community of Jesus and his disciples as a fictive family whose members no longer exercise any loyalty whatsoever to their natural family relations.[8] In the words of one writer, 'Blood relationships are devalued in Jesus' idea of the family; his real family is the family of God'.[9] Another commentator asserts even more categorically, 'All genetic, familial and sex distinctions are eradicated in this new concept of family'.[10] Such reconstructions of the earliest Jesus movement encourage us to come to grips with some persistent themes in the gospel traditions, and this is certainly in their favor. As Dunn maintains, however, these views of discipleship are in need of qualification and cannot be embraced in the stark terms outlined above.[11]

---

5. The translation of the phrase from Mt. 23.8 is my own. The NRSV's rendition—'you are all students'—is hopelessly misleading.
6. Dunn (2003: 598-99).
7. Most prominently, Theissen (1992a; 1992b) and Crossan (1991). See also Gnilka (1997: 169).
8. Hammerton-Kelly (1979: 101-102); Funk and Hoover (1993: 197-99).
9. Funk (1996: 197-99).
10. Kee, treating Mark's Gospel (1977: 109).
11. Dunn (2003: 593).

Consider, for example, Mk 1.29-31, which finds Peter at home with his mother-in-law, and also Peter's later travels with his wife (1 Cor. 9.5). This, we must recall, is the same Peter who had 'left everything' to follow Jesus (Mk 10.28).[12] Jesus, on his part, is remembered to have placed a high priority upon filial loyalty by drawing attention to the command to honor father and mother in the Decalogue (Mk 7.9-13; Mt. 15.3-6). The teachings on divorce are also markedly pro-family, again finding their validation in Israel's sacred Torah (Mk 10.2-9; par. Mt. 19.3-9). Also of a positive nature are the familiar texts in which Jesus welcomes children (Mk 10.13-16 and pars.). As Dunn reasonably asserts, any reconstruction of Jesus' view of family which defines discipleship as a wholesale transfer of loyalty from the natural family to Jesus' surrogate family fails to persuade. It will not do to ignore these family-friendly texts. Nor do I find it acceptable simply to relegate these passages to the alleged domesticating tendencies of later church tradents. We must instead seek satisfactorily to account for both the positive and negative streams of tradition relating to family in the Gospels by considering their function relative to one another.

The degrees of loyalty that Jesus' followers retained toward their natural families undoubtedly varied from person to person, depending primarily upon the reaction to Jesus' call to discipleship on the part of a disciple's blood relations. In cases where whole households converted, family solidarity was not compromised and was likely even enhanced. The three siblings, Mary, Martha, and Lazarus, may serve as an example (Lk. 10.38-42; Jn 11). A commitment to follow Jesus on the part of only a single family member, however, could very well divide 'father against son and son against father' (Lk. 12.53), or father against daughter, and daughter against father, as the early third-century text *Passion of Perpetua* so graphically reveals.[13]

The relationship of Jesus and his followers to normal village life also benefits from some careful nuancing. Jesus did travel from place to place. In that sense he had 'nowhere to lay his head' (Mt. 8.20; Lk. 9.58) and was, to some degree, a 'wandering charismatic'. What we see of Paul's life points in the same direction, and evidence for itinerant prophets and evangelists surfaces later in Christian history, as well (*Didache* 4). In each case, though, some crucial qualifications are in order. Jesus made a home in Capernaum (Mk 1.21; 2.1; 3.20; Mt. 4.13; 9.1, see 11.23; Lk. 10.15), and had among his followers numbers of persons who remained connected to normal village life. Paul, as well, settled in various locations for significant portions of time (Acts 18.11 [Corinth]; Acts 20.31 [Ephesus])

---

12. Peter had apparently not left quite 'everything', in the sense some scholars wish to believe, since he still had a boat to fish from some time later, if we can trust the Johannine account (Jn 21.3).
13. See Hellerman (2001: 169-72).

and established local Jesus communities throughout the eastern Roman Empire. And the thrust of the relevant text in the *Didache* is to provide guidelines for the treatment of itinerant figures on the part of the majority of believers who remained in local congregations. The picture, in each case, is of a small minority of persons who (a) engage in an itinerant lifestyle, who (b) rely on the support of local Jesus communities to facilitate their ministries, and who, in the case of Jesus and Paul, (c) spend a great deal of time themselves in these local settings.[14] We must therefore balance the socio-culturally anomalous texts with passages that show a continuing attachment to village and family life on the part of the great majority of Jesus' followers. But we must be careful in doing so. The family-friendly traditions cited above still, in my view, tell less than half the story, and here is where I think Dunn has overstated his case.

3. *Jesus and Family: Adjusting the Pendulum Back Again*

In his otherwise commendable effort to bring some balance to the discussion, Dunn has decidedly undervalued the more radical traditions in the Gospels. He not only fails to appreciate the subversive thrust of such passages in view of the familial loyalty expected of those who belonged to the patrilineal kinship groups of the Mediterranean world. Dunn also neglects sufficiently to take into account the numerous instances of surrogate family language occurring through the gospel narratives. An examination of some of the family passages in the Gospels will help us to see that this is clearly the case.

a. *Not So Family-Friendly Texts*
Jesus strongly emphasized the Gospel's potential irrevocably to undermine family unity and to divide family members one against the other. Consider the following passage:

> 34 'Do not think that I have come to bring peace to the earth; I have not come to bring peace, but a sword.
> 35 For I have come to set a man against his father,
>   and a daughter against her mother,
>   and a daughter-in-law against her mother-in-law;
> 36 and one's foes will be members of one's own household.
> 37 Whoever loves father or mother more than me is not worthy of me; and whoever loves son or daughter more than me is not worthy of me; 38 and whoever does not take up the cross and follow me is not worthy of me' (Mt. 10.34-38).

---

14. Essene practice is somewhat analogous if we are to trust the testimony of Josephus (Josephus, *War* 2.124-27).

9. *Jesus' Vision for a Family of God* 273

Luke's version of the final two verses is even more troubling. Notice the change in the language. Instead of defining an unworthy disciple as one who 'loves his father or mother more than me', in Luke's parallel a person must 'hate' his relatives in order to qualify as a follower of Jesus:

> 25 Now large crowds were traveling with him; and he turned and said to them, 26 'Whoever comes to me and does not hate father and mother, wife and children, brothers and sisters, yes, and even life itself, cannot be my disciple. 27 Whoever does not carry the cross and follow me cannot be my disciple' (Lk. 14.25-27).[15]

Older scholarship typically sought to ameliorate Luke's harsh language by suggesting that 'hate' in the text carries a semantic connotation of 'love less'.[16] Recent treatments of the passage generally reject such attempts to blunt the force of the hatred terminology in the saying.[17] Jacobson has recently placed the text-segment in its proper socio-historical context:

> Especially shocking is the first [relation] to be mentioned, the father. To be sure, one was to honour both father and mother but Jewish families, like most other Mediterranean families, were strongly patriarchal. Filial obedience was expected. The penalty for the 'stubborn and rebellious son' was death by stoning (Deut. 21.18-21), though it is not likely this penalty was ever imposed. Q 14.26 is not just radical; it would have been profoundly offensive.[18]

I purposely included the last verse of each passage in my citations above (Mt. 10.38 and Lk. 14.27) to emphasize the fact that the challenge Jesus puts forth in these texts is not a peripheral one, applying only to radical itinerants among Jesus' followers. Both Matthew and Luke connect the problematic family sayings with Jesus' classic statement about the demands of discipleship: 'Whoever does not carry the cross and follow me cannot be my disciple' (Matthew: 'is not worthy of me'). Those who handed down

---

15. Scholars almost universally trace the Lukan 'hate' terminology back to the historical Jesus, an assumption confirmed by the parallels in the *Gospel of Thomas* (55, 101) (Becker [1998: 309-10]; Davies and Allison [1991: 221]).

16. Manson (1949: 131); Hammerton-Kelly (1979: 66). Dunn affirms the interpretation: 'Matthew's rendition may convey the principal point adequately, even if it loses the shock value of the 'hate' language' (2003: 594). If 'hate' transparently meant 'love less', however, one wonders why Matthew would have taken the trouble to soften the tradition. Perhaps Jesus himself spoke the two versions on separate occasions, an attractive and wholly reasonable option given the centrality of the notion to Jesus' concept of discipleship (see further, above).

17. For example, Nolland (1993: 763). Jacobson claims that 'hate' here probably does not mean 'dislike intensely' but, rather, 'sever one's relationship with' the family (1995: 362, 364). Compare Marshall, who reads in the 'hate' language the idea of renunciation, drawing for background upon the Hebrew root שׂנא, which has the sense 'to leave aside, abandon' (1978: 592).

18. Jacobson (1995: 362-63).

the gospel traditions clearly viewed cutting loose with family loyalty as an indispensable part of what it meant to follow Jesus. Family strife and division are an anticipated result. We can confidently trace this perspective on social relations back to Jesus himself.

The same sentiment finds expression in narrative form in the calling of the four fishermen near the beginning of Mark's Gospel:

> 16 As Jesus passed along the Sea of Galilee, he saw Simon and his brother Andrew casting a net into the sea—for they were fishermen. 17 And Jesus said to them, 'Follow me and I will make you fish for people'. 18 And immediately they left their nets and followed him. 19 As he went a little farther, he saw James son of Zebedee and his brother John, who were in their boat mending the nets. 20 Immediately he called them; and they left their father Zebedee in the boat with the hired men, and followed him (Mk 1.16-20).

Mark's primary agenda here is to highlight Jesus' irresistible authority, but we must not miss the unorthodox response of the four fishermen, who apparently leave family and livelihood behind to follow Jesus. The placement of the pericope in Mark's narrative should also be noted. Immediately preceding the story of the calling of the fishermen the reader encounters the following programmatic statement:

> 14 Now after John was arrested, Jesus came to Galilee, proclaiming the good news of God, 15 and saying, 'The time is fulfilled, and the kingdom of God has come near; repent, and believe in the good news' (Mk 1.14-15).

Verses 14-15 and 16-20 are, of course, to be read together. The behavior of Simon, Andrew, James, and John is intended to illustrate the proper response to Jesus' message in Mk 1.14-15. Apparently, leaving one's father and following Jesus constitutes for Mark a paradigmatic example of what it means to 'repent, and believe in the good news'.[19] It is reasonable to assume that Mark faithfully relates the values of Jesus himself, in this regard, as well.

Even more scandalous, given the patriarchal orientation of the Mediterranean family, is the discipleship tradition preserved in Mt. 8.21-22 (par. Lk. 9.59-60):

> 21 Another of his disciples said to him, 'Lord, first let me go and bury my father'. 22 But Jesus said to him, 'Follow me, and let the dead bury their own dead'.[20]

---

19. See Barton (1994: 61-67) on the passage. Barton rightly sees texts like these functioning 'not only as models of discipleship in the period of Jesus' earthly ministry, but also as models for missionary discipleship in the period after Easter' (1994: 62).

20. Directly following his own version of the saying (Lk. 9.59-60), Luke relates a somewhat similar encounter with yet another would be disciple:

> 61 Another said, 'I will follow you, Lord; but let me first say farewell to those at my home'. 62 Jesus said to him, 'No one who puts a hand to the plow and looks back is fit for the kingdom of God' (Lk. 9.61-62).

There is some debate about whether the potential disciple's father has recently died, a secondary burial is in view, or the father is perhaps still alive. The conclusion one reaches on the matter is relatively inconsequential in the present connection, though, since the counter-cultural thrust of the saying is preserved on any account.[21] Notice the particular family relationship at stake in Jesus' exhortation. The relationship between father and son constituted the most inviolable obligatory bond between generations in the ancient family, and filial loyalty was tantamount to loyalty to one's family god(s).[22] Jesus' challenge to the inquiring disciple simply stands alone in the literature. There are no true parallels to this scandalous saying in the Greco-Roman world.[23] Wright is therefore quite on target to characterize the statement as 'quite frankly, outrageous', and to conclude, moreover, that '[the] only explanation for Jesus' astonishing command is that he envisaged loyalty to himself and his kingdom-movement as creating an alternative family'.[24] We turn now to consider Jesus' vision for this surrogate family of disciples.

b. *Surrogate Family Traditions*

Passages that portray Jesus reconstituting his followers as a surrogate family are profitably read alongside the traditions discussed above. Not only did Jesus teach his potential followers to reconsider their loyalty to their families. He modeled this kind of behavior in his own natural family relations:

> 31 Then his mother and his brothers came; and standing outside, they sent to him and called him. 32 A crowd was sitting around him; and they said to him, 'Your mother and your brothers and sisters are outside, asking for you'.

---

21. For the various interpretations of the passage see Klemm (1969–70); Kingsbury (1988); McCane (1990); and, most recently, Catchpole, who helpfully outlines the relevant background materials (2006: 64-65). McCane interprets the request of the would be follower of Jesus to refer to secondary burial. McCane claims it was a common practice to remove a corpse from its original place of burial after approximately one year (during which the flesh would decompose), in order to move the bones to their permanent burial site. Secondary burial is what is meant when the Bible speaks of someone being 'gathered to his people' (cf. Gen. 25.8). On this interpretation, as McCane himself observes, the saying of Jesus remains highly offensive to Judean familial piety. Jacobson appropriately adds, 'Indeed, since secondary burial is an expression of kinship with the dead, the demand to sever that kinship would be all the more offensive' (1995: 362-63).

22. Jewish texts extolling filial piety, and the responsibility of children to bury their parents, include the *Letter of Aristeas* (228), Josephus (*Ag. Ap.* 2.205-206), Sirach (3.6-8, 12-15), and Tobit (4.3-4; 6.14-15).

23. Hengel (1981: 8-15). Accordingly, we find no entry under Mt. 8.21-22 in an important compendium of Hellenistic parallels to New Testament literature (Boring [1995]).

24. Wright (1996: 401).

> 33 And he replied, 'Who are my mother and my brothers?' 34 And looking at those who sat around him, he said, 'Here are my mother and my brothers! 35 Whoever does the will of God is my brother and sister and mother' (Mk 3.31-35; pars. Mt. 12.46-50; Lk. 8.19-21).[25]

The passage has received appropriate attention from social historians and commentators concerned to highlight the radically counter-cultural nature of Jesus' statements.[26] It will suffice to observe that the community Jesus envisions (one which, indeed, he assumes is already gathering around him) constitutes a surrogate kinship group, where membership depends upon obedience to God and not upon one's patriline. Moreover, according to the example publicly provided by Jesus himself, membership in this fictive family demands a degree of group loyalty which transcends a disciple's natural family ties. The passage prepares the reader for Mk 6.1-6, where Jesus and his mission are essentially rejected by his own villagers. These themes reappear throughout the Gospel accounts.

Elsewhere in Mark, for example, a prominent character in the narrative discovers that his new fictive family is intended to provide for his material and relational needs in a manner identical to the very Mediterranean kin group he had left in order to become a follower of Jesus:

> 28 Peter began to say to him, 'Look, we have left everything and followed you'. 29 Jesus said, 'Truly I tell you, there is no one who has left house or brothers or sisters or mother or father or children or fields, for my sake and for the sake of the good news, 30 who will not receive a hundredfold now in this age—houses, brothers and sisters, mothers and children, and fields with persecutions—and in the age to come eternal life' (Mk 10.28-30).

According to the most straightforward reading of the saying, Jesus here assumes his followers will relate to one another according to the standards of solidarity shared by families in Mediterranean antiquity. Jesus promises Peter, who (in some sense) left his own family to follow him, that Peter will (a) enjoy kinship-like relationships with others who have made such a sacrifice ('brothers and sisters, mothers and children') and (b) find life's necessary physical resources—such as shelter ('houses') and food ('fields')—in the context of the new community. Other images in Mark that assume a surrogate

---

25. The return to Nazareth in Mk 6.1-3 (par. Mt. 13.54-56) suggests that Jesus may have maintained ongoing relations of some kind with his natural family. I owe this insight to Dr Michael Wilkins, a friend and colleague in NT studies.

26. McVann (1993: 70-73); Malina and Rohrbaugh (1992: 201-203, cf., 100-101); Gundry (1993: 178); Crossan (1973); Barton (1994: 67-86). Efforts to explain the text as a reflection of hostility between Gentile churches, represented here by Mark's community, and Jesus' family (especially James), who remain in positions of leadership in Jerusalem, do not convince (Trocmé [1975: 130-37; Crossan [1973: 112]). See Barton's judicious evaluation of this perspective (1994: 83-85).

9. *Jesus' Vision for a Family of God*

family model for Jesus' community of followers include Jesus sharing Passover with his disciples (since Passover was traditionally a family event during the Second-Temple Period) (Mk 14.12-26), and Joseph of Arimathea providing for Jesus' burial (a kinship responsibility) (Mk 15.43; see Mt. 8.21).[27]

4. *Surrogate Family Language in the Gospel of Matthew*

'Requirements for discipleship and the constitution of the community of Jesus' followers that became the church dominate Matthew's gospel as they do no other.'[28] So writes Baptist commentator Blomberg, and the evaluation is mirrored in the assessments of New Testament scholars of all confessional persuasions. Matthew, more than any of the other evangelists, exhibits a noticeable preoccupation with the contours of the community that Jesus began to establish during his three-year ministry in Roman Palestine. And for Matthew's Jesus, that community is constituted as a kinship group of surrogate siblings with God as Father of the family.[29]

The first Gospel contains much in the way of kinship terminology. The idea that God functions as the surrogate father of Jesus' community will be immediately familiar to anyone who has read through the Gospel of Matthew. The term (πατήρ) is used metaphorically forty-four times in the narrative. Some texts portray God as uniquely Jesus' father (3.17; 10.32-33; 11.25-27). Other uses of 'father' are applied to God as he relates to Jesus' followers. The following text is representative: 'And call no one your father on earth, for you have one Father—the one in heaven' (23.9). The fatherhood of God has direct implications, moreover, for the way in which Jesus' followers are to interact with one another. As Barton observes,

---

27. Argued in some detail in Hellerman (2001: 64-90).
28. Blomberg (1992: 32-33). More pointedly, Barton notes in Matthew 'a powerful thrust of the kinship idea in the direction of ecclesiology, via the notion of followers of Jesus as a brotherhood' (1994: 217). On kinship language in Matthew, see also Saldarini (1994: 90-94) and Riches (2000: 209-25).
29. The discussion that follows emphasizes only the constructive side of Jesus' social program—the constitution of his followers as a surrogate family—as portrayed in the first Gospel. For an examination of the way in which Jesus deconstructs Jewish ethnic identity in Matthew, see Riches (2000: 181-261). Riches treats kinship and sacred space in some detail in his insightful study. With respect to Jewish territorialism, he maintains that in Matthew 'theology is de-territorialised and attachment to Land and Temple replaced by attachment to the person of Jesus' (254). Natural kinship experiences a similar fate, so that family status is no longer relevant to true discipleship. Riches finally concludes that 'Matthew metaphoricises ethnicity' (319). None of this, I might add, is unique to Matthew, as demonstrated by the analysis of the gospel materials in the previous chapters (chs. 5-7). It is therefore reasonable to trace both the constructive and deconstructive aspects of the social agenda of Matthew's Jesus back to Jesus of Nazareth himself (on this see below, n. 32).

The strong emphasis on the fatherhood of God in the First Gospel, with its christological corollary of Jesus as the divine Son of God, provides a profound theological basis for an ecclesiology centred on the idea of brotherhood and of the church as the true, spiritual kindred of Jesus.[30]

We will not be surprised, therefore, to discover that sibling terminology is central to Jesus' conception of his followers as a surrogate family in Matthew. The word 'brother' (ἀδελφός) arguably represents the defining metaphor for interpersonal relations in the group.

Eighteen times in the course of Jesus' teachings 'brother' is used to refer to the fictive siblings who belong to Jesus' nascent community.[31] Matthew 18 pointedly exemplifies the way in which sibling solidarity informs Jesus' designs for social interaction among his followers:

> 15 'If another *member of the church* sins against you, go and point out the fault when the two of you are alone. If the member listens to you, you have regained *that one*. 16 But if you are not listened to, take one or two others along with you, so that every word may be confirmed by the evidence of two or three witnesses. 17 If the member refuses to listen to them, tell it to the church; and if the offender refuses to listen even to the church, let such a one be to you as a Gentile and a tax collector. 18 Truly I tell you, whatever you bind on earth will be bound in heaven, and whatever you loose on earth will be loosed in heaven...' 21 Then Peter came and said to him, 'Lord, if another *member of the church* sins against me, how often should I forgive? As many as seven times?' 22 Jesus said to him, 'Not seven times, but, I tell you, seventy-seven times' (15-18, 21-22, my italics).[32]

The relational expectations reflected in the passage are patently transparent and need no elaboration. The NRSV translators have in this case, however,

---

30. Barton (1994: 180).

31. 5.22 (4×), 5.47, 7.3-5 (3×), 12.49-50 (3×), 18.15 (2×), 18.21, 18.35, 23.8, 25.40, 28.10.

32. Regrettably, the historicity of the so-called ἐκκλησία texts (Mt. 16.17-19 and 18.17) remains highly suspect in the scholarly community (see, among others, Luz [1991]). I suspect that much of the problem here relates to a tendency unconsciously to read later church institutional structure back into the term ἐκκλησία. The expression in Hellenistic Greek often simply meant an 'assembly', as was also the case with the underlying Aramaic קהל. The assertion of Albright and Mann of a generation ago still holds true: 'A Messiah without a Messianic Community would have been unthinkable to any Jew' (1971: 195). It was certainly unthinkable to the author of the *Psalms of Solomon*, who anticipates that the Messiah will 'gather a holy people, whom he will lead in righteousness' (17.26).

For Mt. 18.15-17, analogies can be found for the testimony of two witnesses in the Hebrew Scriptures (Deut. 17.6; 19.15), at Qumran (CD 9; 1QS 5-6), and in Josephus (*Life* 49; *Ant.* 4.219). Overman's assertion—'Matthew took the wisdom of this advice from his forbearers [*sic*] in the Hebrew Bible and applied it to his own community' (1996: 269)—could just as reasonably be said of Jesus himself.

9. *Jesus' Vision for a Family of God*

profoundly obscured Jesus' message and robbed it of much of its rhetorical energy. The sibling term 'brother' (ἀδελφός) appears three times in the Greek text of the passage (four, if we include v. 35, which concludes the pericope). In each case (represented by the italicized phrases in the above citation), the NRSV translators have chosen to render the term with English expressions totally devoid of any kinship connotation.[33] This is unfortunate. For in view of the centrality of sibling relations in the social world of Jesus and his followers, it is not insignificant that Jesus repeatedly draws upon 'brother' terminology here to frame his ethic of interpersonal accountability and bountiful forgiveness. The 'church' of Jesus (ἐκκλησία, v. 17) is, in most practical, relational terms, a society of surrogate siblings (ἀδελφός, vv. 15 [2×], 21, 35).

a. *Surrogate Family in the Sermon on the Mount*
Nowhere is this idea more clearly articulated than in the Sermon on the Mount (SM), and a special appreciation can be gained for the importance of family solidarity to Jesus' conception of community through a brief look at the use of kinship language in this magnificent ethical treatise.[34] The emphasis upon interpersonal behavior in the SM is quite obvious to anyone familiar with the contents of the discourse. What must be highlighted in the present connection is the family orientation of Jesus' admonitions concerning human relations.[35]

---

33. The intentions of the translators are commendable, the results less so. The term ἀδελφός, literally 'brother', was often used generically in Greek to include in its purview both genders. The NRSV, sensitive to this lexical reality, elsewhere attempts to bring it to the attention of the English reader (see 'brother and sister', 5.22-24). Due, however, to the awkwardness of repeating in English the words 'brother(s) and sister(s)', the translators commonly substitute alternative expressions such as 'neighbor' (7.3-5) or 'believer' (1 Cor. 6.5-6). The problem, of course, is that such expressions remove the family metaphor—along with its powerful rhetorical edge and associated behavioral expectations—from the English text.

34. The bibliography on the SM is immense. Recent scholarly treatments include Guelich (1982), Schnackenburg (1995), and Allison (1999). For a history of interpretation see Kissinger (1975) and Carter (1994). Betz's magisterial commentary on the SM is an indispensable scholarly resource (1995).

35. Gnilka described Matthew's community as a 'brotherhood' some years ago (1963: 51). Overman emphasizes the point in a brief discussion of ἀδελφός in the SM:

> Matthew's use of this term suggests his community is a fictive family. The metaphor of family, and *adelphoi* in particular, captures the ideal nature of the relationships and commitment which Matthew sought to engender within his church. Matthew, through his instruction, encouragement, and his particular presentation of Jesus and his message, hoped to foster a family that withstands the competition and conflict with those powers and leaders opposed to the community. The Sermon on the Mount plays a pivotal role in Matthew's attempt to achieve these ends (1996: 74-75).

Family imagery enters the SM as early as the Beatitudes (5.3-12), where we find the phrases 'inherit the earth' (v. 5) and 'children of God' (v. 9). A block of teaching which appears later in the chapter is more explicitly family focused:

> 21 'You have heard that it was said to those of ancient times, "You shall not murder'; and 'whoever murders shall be liable to judgment". 22 But I say to you that if you are angry with a brother or sister (ἀδελφός), you will be liable to judgment; and if you insult a brother or sister (ἀδελφός), you will be liable to the council; and if you say, "You fool", you will be liable to the hell of fire. 23 So when you are offering your gift at the altar, if you remember that your brother or sister (ἀδελφός) has something against you, 24 leave your gift there before the altar and go; first be reconciled to your brother or sister (ἀδελφός), and then come and offer your gift' (5.21-24).

In each occurrence, as indicated above, the NRSV translators accurately gloss the Greek sibling term ἀδελφός with an acceptable English equivalent. Such is not the case, unfortunately, for another important passage from the SM:

> 3 'Why do you see the speck in your neighbor's (ἀδελφός) eye, but do not notice the log in your own eye? 4 Or how can you say to your neighbor (ἀδελφός), "Let me take the speck out of your eye", while the log is in your own eye? 5 You hypocrite, first take the log out of your own eye, and then you will see clearly to take the speck out of your neighbor's (ἀδελφός) eye' (7.3-5).

Once again the translators have obscured Jesus' family language, this time using the term 'neighbor' for ἀδελφός. The unfortunate choice of words effectively transfers Jesus' admonition from the realm of family to another

---

Overman's comments are generally on the mark, but I strongly question his assumption that the surrogate family idea represents Matthew's—rather than Jesus'—social agenda. To be sure, Matthew uses ἀδελφός in a fictive sense much more often than Mark or Luke, and it is certainly possible to trace some of these occurrences to Matthean redaction. Yet, as Overman recognizes, surrogate sibling terminology occurs elsewhere in the gospel tradition and is, therefore, hardly unique to Matthew (Mk 3.34; Lk. 6.42, 8.21; see also Mk 10.28-29, which Overman fails to mention) (1996: 74).

With respect to the family language found in Matthew's version of the SM, it is important to note that Lk. 6.41-42—which parallels Mt. 7.3-5 (cited below)—contains more occurrences of ἀδελφός (4 versus 3) than Matthew's version of the teaching. Luke also mirrors Matthew's surrogate kinship language in another portion of the SM discussed below (Mt. 7.9-11; par. Lk. 11.11-13). This data clearly attests to the presence of the family construct in the double tradition utilized by the two evangelists, an emphasis that can reasonably be traced back to the historical Jesus. The most we can say, then, about Matthean redaction is that, in the use of surrogate family language in his special material, Matthew has faithfully extended and elaborated upon the social vision of Jesus himself.

9. *Jesus' Vision for a Family of God*

social context and, thereby, frames Jesus' ethic in markedly different terms. No longer in view is the bond (brotherhood) which ideally claimed the highest degree of interpersonal allegiance in antiquity. A secondary locus of loyalty—one's relationship with one's 'neighbor'—has been substituted instead. And expectations for the two social bonds were quite different, as illustrated by Ben Sira's order of relational priorities:

> I take pleasure in three things, and they are beautiful in the sight of God and of mortals: agreement among brothers and sisters, friendship among neighbors, and a wife and a husband who live in harmony (Sir. 25.1).

'Friendship among neighbors' is important in an agrarian setting, but it must ultimately take second place to sibling loyalty, for as Plutarch similarly asserts: 'even if we feel an equal affection for a friend, we should always be careful to reserve for a brother the first place' (*De frat. amor.* 491B).

Fortunately, the NRSV consistently retains in English the surrogate father imagery which appears in the Greek text of the SM. References to God as Father occur throughout the discourse (5.16, 45, 48; 6.1, 4, 6 [2×], 8, 9, 14, 15, 18 [2×], 26, 32; 7.11, 21). For Jesus, moreover, the father metaphor, like the sibling idea discussed above, carries with it a constellation of tangible, relational realities. The following text is illustrative:

> 9 Is there anyone among you who, if your child asks for bread, will give a stone? 10 Or if the child asks for a fish, will give a snake? 11 If you then, who are evil, know how to give good gifts to your children, how much more will your Father in heaven give good things to those who ask him! (7.9-11)

Because God is the father of Jesus' followers, he can be counted on to deal with his children according to the commonly understood values of fatherhood in Mediterranean antiquity.

A final text from the SM combines the sibling and father metaphors in a manner which I find strikingly innovative, and which renders Jesus' teaching at this point decidedly anomalous given its social setting. The exhortations in the passage also speak strongly to issues of boundary preservation, which occupied our attention throughout much of the discussion in the earlier chapters of the book. The text reads as follows:

> 43 'You have heard that it was said, "You shall love your neighbor and hate your enemy". 44 But I say to you, Love your enemies and pray for those who persecute you, 45 so that you may be children of your Father in heaven; for he makes his sun rise on the evil and on the good, and sends rain on the righteous and on the unrighteous. 46 For if you love those who love you, what reward do you have? Do not even the tax collectors do the same? 47 And if you greet only your brothers and sisters, what more are you doing than others? Do not even the Gentiles do the same? 48 Be perfect, therefore, as your heavenly Father is perfect' (5.43-48).

Notice the paternal ('children of your Father in heaven') and sibling ('brothers and sisters') imagery in the passage (vv. 45, 47-48). In this case, however, Jesus moves beyond the subject of in-group relations (compare 5.21-24; 7.3-5, above) and now proceeds to challenge his followers concerning their dealings with those outside the surrogate family of faith.

The text in view concludes the section of the SM commonly known as the Antitheses, so called because in this section Jesus purposely contrasts his teachings with (or elaborates upon) a series of six convictions which, Jesus assumes, reflect the moral values of his audience. The opening point of comparison for each of the first five antitheses (vv. 21-42) can be found in the Hebrew Scriptures. Thus, 'You shall not murder' (5.21) comes directly from Exod. 20.13. The same is the case for the first half of Jesus' introductory quotation in the text we are presently examining: 'You shall love your neighbor' (v. 43a; see Lev. 19.18). The command 'hate your enemy' (v. 43b), however, appears nowhere in the Old Testament. Commentators debate whether the sentiment can be inferred from certain OT passages (see Deut. 23.3-6; 25.17-19; Ps 139.21), but such speculation is quite unnecessary given the polarization of various Jewish groups—not to mention the Jewish–Gentile divide—in first-century Palestine.

The discovery of the Dead Sea Scrolls has provided us with a colorful, if regrettable, example of a group whose members were explicitly encouraged to hate those who did not belong to their number. The Community Rule, the central treatise enumerating ethical norms for the Qumran settlers, required that group members

> love all the sons of light [the community's self-designation], each according to his lot in God's design, and hate all the sons of darkness, each according to his guilt in God's vengeance (1QS 1.10).[36]

Although the community which produced the Scrolls was geographically removed from Jewish Palestine, some evidence exists for sympathizers in Judean villages, as well as for an Essene settlement in Jerusalem itself. Perhaps Jesus assumed that his audience was familiar with Essene convictions through avenues such as these.[37] More generally, however, it is rather

---

36. Vermes (1995: 70).

37. Charlesworth, following Schubert (1957: 120) and Yadin (1985: 241-42), finds in our passage a direct challenge to Essene theology (Charlesworth [1992: 24]).

The relationship between the Essenes and the early Jesus movement remains shrouded in speculation. The New Testament is strangely silent about the sect. On the identification of the Dead Sea community as an Essene settlement, see Schiffman (1994: 78-81, 103-105). As Collins observes, 'The assumption that Qumran was an Essene settlement remains the most economical way to account for the evidence' (1992: 625). The settlers at Qumran, however, were not the only Essenes. Philo and Josephus describe Essenes in Judean villages and cities, and the Damascus Document (found at Qumran but known earlier from a manuscript uncovered at the turn of the century in the Cairo Genizah),

typical for individuals in strong-group cultures to adhere to one ethical norm in relation to persons in their own social group, while displaying other values toward those deemed outsiders. Jesus may not have had the Essenes in view at all in his admonition. The introductory love–hate citation (v. 43) may simply serve as a pointed intensification of a commonly accepted cultural value.

Jesus, however, will have nothing to do with a twofold love-hate ethic. He encourages his followers instead to love and pray for their enemies and persecutors. I find this highly innovative, for Jesus here summarily rejects a pivotal value of his social world—disdain for those outside one's group—and challenges the members of his nascent family to exercise the same love toward outsiders as they would be expected naturally to exhibit toward members of their surrogate kinship group. Such behavior, Jesus maintains, finds its logic in the Father's love for all (5.45).

The command to love one's enemies has particular application in the present connection. Although Jesus may not have had Qumran's ethic solely in view, the excerpt from the Community Rule, cited above, helpfully elucidates two important aspects of the broader socio-cultural background that should inform our interpretation of Jesus' exhortations in Mt. 5.43-48. First of all, first-century Judeans of sectarian affiliation tended to identify as their 'enemies' persons who did not belong to their group. Secondly, sectarian insiders generally viewed group outsiders as standing beyond the boundaries of the covenant remnant of Israel. The Essenes at Qumran are illustrative on both counts. The community emphasized an insider-outsider distinction between 'the sons of light' and 'the sons of darkness', and covenanters were to 'love' the former group and 'hate' the latter. While the terminology is harsh and unattested elsewhere (except for Mt. 5.43), the Essenes were probably not alone in their social outlook, as Jesus' admonition in the SM suggests. Disdain for those outside one's group is a common feature of strong-group cultures, one that likely found ample opportunity for expression among Judeans who were influenced by the pervasive strains of social exclusivism that marked life in Palestine during the post-Maccabean era.

Jesus, in contrast, desires that members of his newly constituted faith family 'love' group outsiders. In the challenge to his followers to love their enemies, then, Jesus does not simply address issues of interpersonal animosity between isolated individuals, though such matters can reason-

provides rules for Essenes located in 'the towns of Israel' who, unlike those at Qumran, may 'take a wife and beget children' (CD 12.19, 7.6-7).

The first four decades of the Jesus movement in Judea coincided with the final years of the existence of the Dead Sea community (c. 30–70 CE). This has occasioned much speculation concerning the possibility of contact between the communities. See, on this, Riesner, for example, who has argued from archaeological discoveries that the center of the original Jerusalem Christian community was located on the southwest hill of Jerusalem, not far from what was called the Gate of the Essenes (1985).

ably be included under the extended rubric of the striking exhortation. More to the point, Jesus here challenges in-group attitudes and behaviors that had perpetuated rivalry and hostility between various groups of Jews and, by extension, between Judeans and Gentiles, as well.[38] In calling his listeners to love their enemies, therefore, Jesus once again subtly subverts boundaries that had been drawn by various Judean sectarian movements in their attempts narrowly to define the social contours of the true people of Yahweh—boundaries which replicated in miniature the more intractable and enduring social chasm that for generations had divided Jews and Gentiles in the Greco-Roman world.[39]

Here, moreover, it appears that Jesus' boundary-breaking activities have come full circle. For the teaching reflected in Mt. 5.43-48 potentially destabilizes even the social integrity of Jesus' own group, should his followers fall short of his ideals and somehow seek to replicate the values of the dominant culture by erecting impermeable boundaries between themselves and those who resist their vision for a multi-ethnic family of God. As our text so powerfully reveals, Jesus intended his disciples to function as an *inclusive* family, always ready to extend hospitality to even the most recalcitrant outsider—a truly alternative social vision in a relational world where in-group loyalties reigned supreme, and where 'love' was reserved for persons of similar ethnicity, background, and religious conviction.

b. *The Sermon on the Mount as a Community Charter*
We conclude our look at the SM with a consideration of the relative density of kinship terminology in this portion of Matthew's Gospel. The chart below highlights the fact that Jesus' great ethical treatise in Matthew 5–7 contains a disproportionate amount of surrogate kinship terminology vis-à-vis the rest of the Gospel:

	'Father' ($\pi\alpha\tau\acute{\eta}\rho$) surrogate usage	'brother/sister' ($\dot{\alpha}\delta\epsilon\lambda\varphi\acute{o}\varsigma$) surrogate usage
Gospel of Matthew	44×	18×
Sermon on the Mount	17×	8×

38. Ruzer's contention that 'the enemies here are not simply insufficiently pious or even shamefully sinful persons whom one may resent, but real 'hard-core' enemies, those who hurt one physically or rob one of his possessions' (2004: 194, agreeing with Gundry [1994: 96]) fails properly to take into consideration the group orientation of ancient Mediterranean society, an outlook graphically illustrated by the parallel to Mt. 5.43 in 1QS 1.10, where a contrast between insiders and outsiders is clearly in view.

39. Riches, in fact, thinks Jesus has non-Jews specifically in view here in the expression 'enemies' (1982: 134).

The density of family language at this point in Matthew's narrative is hardly accidental. Note the reflections of Roger Keesing, a cultural anthropologist specializing in the study of kinship:

> In many societies, kin terms are apparently used only rarely. A common pattern seems to be to refer to a person's kinship relation to you not in everyday conversation, but in situations when that person is violating the norms of kinship; or in situations when you are trying to manipulate him (lend me a dollar, brother...). Use of kin terms often turns out to be a political strategy, not an everyday social nicety.[40]

Keesing's observations encourage us to draw an informative connection between (a) the disproportionate amount of family language uncovered in the SM and (b) the ethical orientation of the treatise. Specifically, Jesus in the SM extensively utilizes the kinship metaphor as (to adopt Keesing's terminology) 'a political strategy', that is, to challenge his followers to treat one another like siblings in a Mediterranean family according to the ethics outlined in the course of the Sermon. It is important to note from the above discussion, therefore, that Jesus has in view in the SM a community of persons, not a cluster of unrelated individuals. The SM is not intended primarily as a template to adopt in the pursuit of personal sanctification.[41] Rather, in the SM Jesus is concerned to engender interpersonal behavior appropriate for Mediterranean siblings in his newly forming community.[42] The Sermon on the Mount, then, is an ethical charter for the family of God that Jesus established during his brief ministry in first-century Palestine.

5. *Some Concluding Thoughts*

How, then, are we to conceive of the relationship between the family-friendly texts mentioned earlier in the chapter and the more radical traditions outlined above? As a point of departure, it will not do to return to the views of a generation or two ago and privilege the positive natural family sayings to the detriment of the more subversive streams of tradition. Dunn's recent attempt to revive such a perspective—by attempting to relegate the above evidence, text by text, to 'Jesus' rhetoric', 'shock tactics' (Lk. 14.26),

---

40. Keesing (1975: 126).

41. Thus Blomberg: 'Jesus' ethical teachings were never intended either to be legislated by civil governments or to be used merely as personal guidelines for individual lifestyles' (1999: 31-32).

42. 'The Sermon on the Mount can rightly be called a constitution for the Matthean community. Like a constitution the Sermon provided in broad outline the nature of membership and life in the community' (Overman [1996: 104]). See also Cahill (1987) and Bailey (1993). Blomberg sees the SM as 'a manifesto for what would become known as the church' (2004: 3).

'Mark's tendentious presentation' (Mk 3.31-35), or 'simply an encouragement to those for whom discipleship did involve such a breach' of family relations (Mk 10.29-30)—fails to persuade.[43] Particularly revealing is Dunn's characterization of Jesus' striking comment in Mk 3.35 ('Whoever does the will of God is my brother and sister and mother') as simply 'a vivid repartee on a particular occasion'.[44] The surrogate family texts surveyed above speak forcefully against reading the saying as an incidental aside. There is simply too much evidence to the contrary. The data also effectively rebuts attempts to dismiss these traditions as after-the-fact constructions of the early church, designed to comfort adherents to the Jesus movement who had experienced alienation from their natural families. The widespread occurrence of surrogate kinship terminology in the Gospels and in other early Christian literature suggests, instead, that Jesus truly intended for his followers to function in their social relations like siblings in a Mediterranean family, and we must find a way to relate this aspect of the tradition to the more family-friendly texts that Dunn has chosen to emphasize.

I suggest with recent scholarship that we assign priority to the more challenging traditions without, however, failing to appreciate the importance of natural family solidarity for Jesus' social vision. With respect to the former group of passages, Jesus' surrogate family instructions in the Gospels and the negative family texts, such as Lk. 14.26 and Mt. 8.22, must be read together. Jesus would not have chosen 'family' as the central social metaphor for his community had he not consciously intended to elicit a profound degree of tension in his followers' minds between loyalty to their natural families, on the one hand, and loyalty to the newfound family of surrogate siblings, on the other. Conceptions of kinship solidarity in Mediterranean antiquity assure us that this was the case. The surrogate family texts and the passages predicting division in the natural family thus go hand-in-hand.[45]

---

43. Dunn (2003: 594, 596 [n. 234], 597).
44. Dunn (2003: 596). Riches is much more on target on this one:

> Of course it is possible to read 3.35, 'Whoever does the will of God is my brother, and sister, and mother', as simply affirming the overriding importance of doing the will of God: family ties must take second place to that. But this does not quite get to the heart of the matter. Mark is attempting to identify the defining characteristics of his group. And these do not lie in ties of kinship, of family relationships, or in descent from Abraham, but in doing the will of God as taught by Jesus. Fictive ties replace natural ties *as definitive of group membership* (Riches 2000: 77, author's italics).

45. Similarly, Barton consistently connects the subordination of natural family ties to 'a new solidarity bound together by ties of discipleship' in his analysis of the family traditions in Mark and Matthew (1994: 96). I find myself generally in agreement with the concluding sentence to Barton's monograph: '[D]iscipleship is understood as a priority of the kingdom of God which relativizes all other ties of allegiance and makes possible access to a new solidarity, the eschatological family of 'brothers, sisters and mothers' who do the will of God' (1994: 225).

Relating the fictive kinship texts to the anti-family traditions also helps us not to lose sight of the corporate nature of discipleship. Dunn is certainly correct to assert that Jesus intended in the more subversive anti-family sayings to call his followers to 'unqualified commitment' 'in the face of eschatological crisis'.[46] That commitment, however, was not merely personal allegiance to Jesus as an engaging teacher, a charismatic prophet, or messianic king—that is, to Jesus as an individual. Jesus' call to discipleship had a decidedly corporate dimension. It involved 'unqualified commitment' to a new set of family relations.

We could perhaps interpret Jesus' demands in individualistic terms, if sayings like Lk. 14.26, which play loose with natural family relations, were not complemented by numerous passages in which Jesus refers to his followers as a surrogate family. Taken together these two strands of tradition virtually guarantee that when Jesus challenged his disciples to follow him, he intended this personal allegiance to be actualized in the disciples' loyalty to a new kinship group. To become a follower of Jesus was to become a brother or sister in Jesus' family of surrogate siblings. And Jesus expected loyalty to this faith family to take precedence over loyalty to a disciple's natural family, if and when the two conflicted and choices had to be made. The fictive family construct represented for Jesus the heart of his social vision for a renewed Israel.

With respect, finally, to the family-friendly traditions, we can unreservedly acknowledge that, wherever possible, Jesus encouraged ongoing loyalty to natural family relations on the part of his followers, as Dunn has appropriately reminded us. Surrogate family loyalty and natural family loyalty were not necessarily mutually exclusive expressions of relational solidarity for those who belonged to the Jesus movement. An ideal and not uncommon situation, we might surmise, would see the conversion of a whole household, with the disciple's natural family embedded in, and serving the mission of, the dominant surrogate family of faith. Here there would be no conflict of loyalties. Where conflict arose, however, the faith family was to become the primary locus of relational solidarity. The positioning of natural family solidarity under the overarching rubric of loyalty to the surrogate church family in fact characterized the Jesus movement well out into the first two centuries of the common era, and it provides the best explanation for the apparently conflicting strains of family traditions in the Gospels. It remains, finally, to consider Jesus' social agenda, and particularly his approach to family relations, against the background of current studies in ethnicity and the construction of ethnic identity.

---

46. Dunn (2003: 594).

Chapter 10

JESUS AS AN ETHNIC ENTREPRENEUR

'Do not presume to say to yourselves, 'We have Abraham as our ancestor'; for I tell you, God is able from these stones to raise up children to Abraham'.

Matthew 3.9

Ethnic differentiation is 'a ubiquitous feature of human sociability, and hence of all human societies'.[1] We gain much insight when we examine Jesus' activities in the light of recent anthropological thinking about the construction of ethnic identity. By challenging post-Maccabean Jewish nationalism, and organizing his followers as a surrogate family, Jesus functioned as a kind of 'ethnic entrepreneur', subverting and reconstructing various symbols of Judean identity, in order to reengineer the social contours of God's people in a way that would one day transcend the boundaries of ethnic Israel.[2] In what follows I will survey a number of definitions of 'ethnicity' and 'ethnic group'.[3] Virtually all who work in the field of ethnic studies identify common historical experiences and some sense of shared ancestry as fundamental features of ethnic identity. Eller has offered a helpful threefold typology of the 'shared past' that characterizes the ethnic worldview, and I will adopt his outline, below, as a heuristic device to elucidate the social aims of Jesus in the context of Second-Temple Judaism.

The discussion will also emphasize that ethnicity is a highly malleable reality that varies over time, due to the ever changing social context in

---

1. Jenkins (1997: 46).
2. The expression 'ethnic entrepreneur' is from Eller (1999: 15), who appears to have picked it up from Kasfir (1979: 370). I am indebted to Eller for much of the discussion of ethnic identity which follows. The study of ethnicity and ethnic conflict has blossomed in recent years, and NT scholars have now begun to utilize promising insights from the field for the study of early Christianity (Brett [1996]; Sim [1996]; Riches [2000]; Esler [2003; 2006]; Duling [2003, 2005]; Buell [2002, 2005]; Buell and Hodge [2004]).
3. English lacks a noun corresponding to the adjective 'ethnic', and 'ethnic group' proves stylistically cumbersome. It has become fashionable in the literature to use the French term *ethnie,* a practice I will draw upon at various places in the pages that follow.

10. *Jesus as an Ethnic Entrepreneur*

which a particular group finds itself. Indeed, one could fairly assert that it is the creative utilization of an *ethnie's* shared past to address present challenges and future hopes which energizes the whole process of ethnic identity formation. The past shared by Second-Temple Judeans centered, of course, around the defining Old Testament narratives that recorded their common history as God's chosen people. As we saw in an earlier chapter, post-Maccabean Jews generally recast the story of Israel's history in ways that decidedly reinforced their social boundaries, as they awaited God's intervention on their behalf. Jesus, too, took part in this creative historiographical project, as he reinterpreted Israel's past in terms of his own life and ministry. For Jesus, however, God's intervention had already begun, the kingdom had arrived, and Yahweh was writing a decisive new chapter in the story of his relationship with his people. This meant that Jesus and those who resisted his program for Israel's renewal had very different ideas about just how their shared past was to be utilized to address present needs. These competing perspectives, in turn, generated correspondingly divergent ways of constructing the ethnic identity of the people of God in the context of Gentile hegemony.

1. *'Ethnic Group' and 'Ethnicity': Some Definitions*

Weber's classic definition will serve well as a point of departure for our consideration of ethnicity. He defined ethnic groups as

> those human groups that entertain a subjective belief in their common descent because of similarities of physical type or of customs or both, or because of memories of colonization and migration; conversely, it does not matter whether or not an objective blood relationship exists.[4]

More recently, Yinger has defined an *ethnie* as

> a segment of a larger society whose members are thought, by themselves or others, to have a common origin and to share important segments of a common culture and who, in addition, participate in shared activities in which the common origin and culture are significant ingredients.[5]

Somewhat similarly, Smith identifies an ethnic group as a cultural collectivity that 'emphasizes the role of myths of descent and historical memories, and that is recognized by one or more cultural differences like religion, customs, language, or institutions'.[6] Finally, Schermerhorn views an ethnic group as

---

4. Weber (1968: 389).
5. Yinger (1994: 3).
6. A. Smith (1991: 20).

a collectivity within a larger society having real or putative common ancestry, memories of a shared historical past, and a cultural focus on one or more symbolic elements defined as the epitome of their peoplehood.[7]

Central to ethnic identity, according to these definitions, are (a) a common past or history of some sort and (b) certain cultural practices that distinguish an ethnic group in its current social context. As we saw in our survey of Jewish literature earlier in the book, Second-Temple Judeans exhibited both of these key characteristics. To adopt Schermerhorn's terminology, above, Jews enjoyed a 'common ancestry' in Abrahamic descent, 'memories of a shared historical past' articulated in the grand narratives of the Hebrew Scriptures (as well as more recent Maccabean historiography), and 'a cultural focus on one or more symbolic elements' expressed in various purity practices associated with distinctions between sacred and profane times, territory, and foods.

A final aspect of ethnicity may prove most important. Jenkins refers to ethnic differentiation as 'the social construction of "us" and "them", marked in cultural terms', and the literature increasingly insists that ethnic identity is, to a great degree, a constructed, not an objective, reality.[8] Ethnicity is therefore not a static concept that can be understood 'by merely listing the empirical cultural traits of groups...or describing their empirical or "true" history'.[9] An *ethnie's* cultural traits, and the degree to which ethnic identity is important to group members, often change over time, and the shared past of a group, in particular, is always open to renegotiation. Ethnographers have discovered, in fact, that it is ultimately quite irrelevant whether or not an ethnic group's shared history 'really happened'. What is important,

---

7. Schermerhorn (1970: 12). Hutchinson and Smith have recently modified Schermerhorn's definition to include 'a link with a homeland' (1996: 7). The application in the present connection should be quite transparent.

8. Jenkins (1997: 46). As Olyan recently observed, 'Both self-definition and its counterpart, the constitution of the "Other" are unending, interconnected 'projects' that all groups pursue continuously' (2004: 1 n. 1). Ethnicity is, of course, a key aspect of this social definitional project. Duling provides a brief and lucid summary of the various schools of thought that characterize contemporary ethnicity theory, including the constructionist approach advocated above (2005: 126-27).

With Duling (2005: 131) I reject Denzey's assertion that it is 'dangerously anachronistic' to utilize modern conceptions of ethnicity to describe ancient social phenemonena (Denzey 2002: 495). To be sure, the Greek term ἔθνος had a broader semantic range than the expression 'ethnic group', as used in contemporary scholarship (Duling 2005: 129-30). And models devised from the study of contemporary societies must not be forcibly imposed on the social realia of Mediterranean antiquity. Where the data happen to fit the model, however—and this is particularly the case in the application of ethnic identity theory to Judaism and early Christianity—the model admirably serves its purpose as a heuristic device that helps to shed new light upon ancient texts and artifacts.

9. Eller (1999: 11).

rather, is that the members of the group enjoy a collective consciousness of their common origins, that is, that their shared history functions in the present 'to maintain group cohesiveness, sustain and enhance identity, and to establish social networks and communicative patterns'.[10] In summary, ethnicity, to borrow from Eller, is 'a complex reworking, remembering, sometimes reinvention, and always employment of culture in the light and service of present and even future considerations'.[11]

We encountered just such an employment of culture in an earlier chapter, with the competing stories of Samaritan origins told by Samaritans and Judeans, respectively. These opposing narratives cannot both be historically accurate, of course, and it is likely that neither relates the actual events of Samaritan history. Rather, each story has been creatively constructed for the purpose of legitimizing (in the case of the Samaritan version) or delegitimizing (in the case of the Jewish version) Samaritan claims to belong to the historical people of Yahweh. Eller's 'employment of culture in the light and service of present and even future considerations' can also be observed in the treatment of sacred times, sacred food, and sacred space by post-Maccabean Judeans. Both Jesus and his contemporaries reworked these vital cultural indicia of Judean ethnicity to address contemporary challenges in first-century Roman Palestine, and, in each case, there resulted some modification of the ethnic contours of the people of God. The respective goals and strategies of Jesus and those who opposed him were so distinct, however, that conflict—leading to an ultimate 'parting of the ways' and the birth of what might fairly be identified as a new ethnic group among Jesus' later followers—was inevitable.

2. *Aspects of a Shared Past: A Threefold Typology*

All *ethnies*, and practically all scholarly treatments of ethnicity, make some reference to the past. Eller identifies three aspects of an ethnic group's shared past which I find particularly useful for considering the strategies of Jesus in group identity formation.[12]

10. Patterson (1975: 305).
11. Eller (1999: 5). The quotation calls for some qualification. Jenkins, an avowed social constructionist, nevertheless observes,

> To say that ethnic identity is transactional and changeable, is really to say that it *may* be; it doesn't mean that it *always* is, or *has* to be... The recognition that ethnicity is neither static nor monolithic should not be taken to mean that it is definitively and perpetually in a state of flux. There are questions to be asked about how and why ethnicity is more or less flexible in different places and times (1997: 51, author's italics).

12. Eller includes a fourth sub-heading, *Past as Resource*, and I have considerably reworked and adapted much of what he has presented in the other three sections, as well (1999: 28-41). I have also reversed the order of Eller's list, in favor of a more chronological approach.

Past as Myth—Eller uses the term 'myth' in the anthropological sense of 'remote and unprovable history' and 'charter for the group's existence and culture in the present'.[13] Gurr and Harff find in myths of ethnicity various kinds of narratives, including stories 'of origin; of migration and liberation; of descent; of an heroic age; of communal decline, conquest, and exile; and of rebirth, with a summons to action'.[14] It should be abundantly clear that the Torah account of Abraham and his descendants—including, preeminently, the Exodus narratives of liberation from Egypt and the constitution of the Israelites as the people of Yahweh at Sinai—constituted Israel's myth of origins, *par excellence*. Although I am more optimistic than most about the historical reliability of the Old Testament accounts, it must be emphasized again that the veracity of the narratives is not at issue in the present connection.[15] What we are after here is the utilization of Israel's story of origins to establish or reinforce boundaries and thereby reconstruct Jewish ethnicity during the post-Maccabean era. As Eriksen relates,

> While many historians try to find out what *really* happened. . .most anthropologists would rather concentrate on showing the ways in which historical accounts are used as tools in the *contemporary* creation of identities and in politics. Anthropologists would stress that history is not a product of the past but a response to requirements of the present.[16]

The way in which a group will use its myth of origins to construct an ethnic identity will vary depending upon the setting in which the group finds itself.[17] As my earlier survey of Jewish literature demonstrated, Judeans often reworked the biblical narratives so as to emphasize social exclusivism,

---

13. Eller (1999: 40).
14. Gurr and Harff (1994: 12-13).
15. For a positive evaluation of the basic historical worth of the account of the Israelites' exodus from Egypt, see now Hoffmeier (1996).
16. Eriksen (1993: 72). Aguilar observes, 'History is indeed a post-factual commentary and a guided interpretation of social events, guided more by memories and intuitions than by systematic reconstructions of true facts gathered and understood as "authentic data" ' (2000: 64).
17. As Fishman properly observes, 'Current needs and problems are always a factor in ethnicity. The past always needs to be recaptured, used, interpreted, and exploited to solve current problems' (1980: 90). This is true of all aspects of ethnic identity. Students of ancient Greek ethnicity are familiar with the fivefold definition of Greekness given by Herodotus (*Hist.* 8.144.2). Konstan maintains that Herodotus's catalogue of ethnic markers was specifically crafted to emphasize Hellenic unity and thereby subvert the possibility of Athenian dominance in the wake of the Persian Wars (2001: 30). Later, during the Roman imperial period, Greekness was defined and negotiated primarily in relation to Romanness. On the Roman side, discourse about Greekness served as a way of articulating the boundaries of Roman identity. On all this see Buell (2005: 40-41), who appropriately adds, 'Similarly, ideas about what constitutes a *Ioudaios* shift over time and need to be evaluated in context' (41).

an issue vital to the preservation of their identity in a Gentile-dominated world. Texts representing the literary genre of the rewritten Torah reinterpreted various aspects of Israel's myth of origins so as to underscore the importance of Jewish identity markers. In the case of *Jubilees*, for example, we discover that the angels were circumcised at creation and Abraham observed the Feast of Booths generations before the giving of the Law at Sinai. All of this colorfully exhibits what Eller has described as 'a complex and empirically (i.e. case-by-case) specific amalgamation of *remembering, forgetting, interpreting*, and *inventing*', which typifies the way in which ethnic groups adapt their stories of origins to meet contemporary social needs.[18] So fundamental, in fact, was the exodus narrative to Judean ethnic identity that non-Jews, too, joined in the creative enterprise, although with decidedly different intentions. As we saw in an earlier chapter, certain pagan elites radically rewrote the Jewish myth of origins in an attempt to delegitimize Jewish claims to an honorable past. By the early second century CE, the dominant story told by Tacitus and his peers thus portrayed the first Israelites as diseased persons whom Pharaoh had expelled from Egypt.

We should interpret Jewish convictions about divine election as a particular aspect of Israel's myth of origins. The two, however, are not identical. Myths of common ancestry and remote origins (as discussed above) are ubiquitous among ethnic groups in traditional societies. Collective memories of divine election, in contrast, are not. Although Israel was not unique, even in antiquity, in holding to a belief in divine election, such a conception is not a particularly common one among aggregates—ancient or modern—that can otherwise be identified as ethnic groups. Social scientists thus view a 'myth of ethnic election' as a marked intensification of a group's myth of remote origins, one which is 'even more important [than the latter] for ethnic survival'.[19]

Assuming that this understanding is accurate, we will expect representatives of an *ethnie* who have such a conception to draw eagerly upon the idea of election especially during those periods in the group's history when members perceive their social identity to be somehow threatened or compromised. This, we might recall, is precisely what we found (Chapter 3) in the marked emphasis on Israel's unique status as Yahweh's chosen people in Pseudo-Philo's *Biblical Antiquities*. Again and again in Pseudo-Philo we encountered references to Israel's election which have no parallels in the Masoretic Text. Just as post-Maccabean Judeans reworked Israel's broader myth of origins in the service of current needs and challenges, so also

---

18. Eller (1999: 41, author's italics).

19. Smith (1992: 441). Smith traces the effectiveness of 'myths of ethnic election' in the survival of a number of ethnic groups throughout the history of the Middle East and Europe (1992).

persons like the author of Pseudo-Philo underscored their people's 'myth of ethnic election' in ways that went far beyond the traditions handed down to them from previous generations.

Past as History—Eller includes under this heading three phases: 'ancient (formative) past, colonial past, and recent political past'.[20] I am interested in the latter two in the present connection, given the political domination and colonization of the East by Alexander and his successors, beginning in the late fourth century BCE. Particularly relevant here are the memories of military defeat and corresponding longings for group redemption and revenge which commonly characterize the collective consciousness of an ethnic group. Such sentiments tenaciously persist in the minds of group members, sometimes for centuries. Speaking of the past as history, Eller notes,

> Groups will, in fact, go to great lengths to 'discover' and systematize a past in which they were either prior to, superior to, or dominant over rival groups or in which they were damaged or shamed by those groups; both are equally calls to action.[21]

In their experiences with the Syrian Greeks, post-Maccabean Jews had readily at hand a treasure house of historical resources to draw upon in order to 'systematize a past' (to adopt Eller's terminology) to speak to present exigencies. Judeans had been severely 'damaged' and 'shamed' by the edict of Antiochus IV and the ensuing profanation of the temple in 167 BCE. Soon, however, they showed themselves 'superior to' and became 'dominant over' their colonial oppressors, regaining their sacred temple and ultimately winning national independence in their struggles with the Syrian dynasty.

The decades that followed this defining period in Judean history generated a number of literary works that narrated the events of the Maccabean era in ways that sharply emphasized ethnic boundary markers of circumcision, Sabbath observance, and the food laws (1, 2 Maccabees and *4 Maccabees*). By the time the Romans took control of Judea in 63 BCE, the Jews had revived and extensively recrafted their biblical Deuteronomistic ideology of sin, repentance, and divine restoration, in the light of more recent Maccabean history. Syrian oppression thus found its explanation in the adoption by Judeans of foreign cultural values and practices:

> 16 For this reason heavy disaster overtook them, and those whose ways of living they admired and wished to imitate completely became their enemies and punished them. 17 It is no light thing to show irreverence to the divine laws—a fact that later events will make clear (2 Macc. 4.16-17).

Maccabean ideology correspondingly attributed Hasmonean military successes to divine intervention in response to the obedience of faithful martyrs

---

20. Eller (1999: 30).
21. Eller (1999: 31).

who refused to abide by the Syrian proscription of circumcision and the levitical dietary laws. As the author of 2 Maccabees pointedly explained, '[T]he Jews were invulnerable, because they followed the laws ordained by him' (8.36). The Maccabean historiographical enterprise thus functioned preeminently as an exercise in the construction of ethnic identity, and its message was one that would powerfully resonate among Jews during the Roman period, when God's people once again found themselves living under the heavy hand of an imperial oppressor.[22]

Past as Tradition or Cultural Past—Here we have to do with present cultural practices that are perceived by an *ethnie* to represent the way in which things have always been. Eller summarizes:

> Thus, the language the group has 'always' spoken, the religion it has always followed or that it converted to at some ancient time, the customs, the clothes, the stories and music, the values and morals—these things are effective identifiers and legitimizers of the group.[23]

Torah observation immediately comes to mind as the primary way in which 'past as tradition' found expression among Second-Temple Jews. Concerns for the preservation of distinctions between sacred and profane times, space, and foods—expressed in practices like Sabbath-keeping, the celebration of annual festivals, and exclusive table fellowship—all fall within the purview of this aspect of the construction and preservation of ethnic identity. An ethnic group's traditions, moreover, like its myth of origins, generally change over time to address current social needs. Contrast, for example, the intense preoccupation with boundaries and purity characteristic of our period with the relatively relaxed approach to such issues that pervades the Hebrew Scriptures. Discontinuity between current cultural practices, on the one hand, and tradition remembered, on the other, becomes particularly acute in a literate society with a sacred text, and efforts on the part of Pharisees and others to trace their oral traditions back into Israel's earlier history betray an *ethnie's* need for assurance that 'what we really are' corresponds to 'what we were'.[24]

---

22. Thus, Aguilar remarks, of 1 Maccabees,

> The production of this sort of narrative is important for successive generations of Jews because it shows that a small nation can stand against a mighty power if and only if such a nation has a common bond of ethnicity and identity related to a common myth of origin (2000: 62).

Aquilar's post-structuralist treatment of 1 Maccabees helpfully emphasizes the role the text plays as 'a myth of ethnic continuity' (2000: 63).

23. Eller (1999: 29).

24. Eller (1999: 29). See the Mishnah (*m. Peah* 2.6; *m. Abot* 1.1-5; *m. Eduy.* 8.7; *m. Yad.* 4.3) for rabbinic efforts to trace oral law back to Moses. Instone-Brewer dates *m. Peah* 2.6 to pre-70 CE (2004: 134).

3. Considering the Aims of Jesus

Jesus' social agenda can profitably be viewed against the background of ethnic identity formation, as outlined above. In what follows I will maintain that in his relativization of natural family ties, and in his challenges to current purity practices that reinforced Jewish social exclusivism, Jesus radically reconstructed Israel's myth of origins (*Past as Myth*) and forcefully contested its current cultural values (*Past as Tradition or Cultural Past*), thereby implicitly undermining nationalistic interpretations of recent history which prevailed among the Pharisees and others during the post-Maccabean period (*Past as History*).

We need not revisit the gospel evidence for Jesus and purity, which filled the pages of several previous chapters. It is enough to note, in view of the above discussion, that Jesus' distinctly alternative approach to the defining symbols of sacred space, sacred times, and sacred food reflects a desire on his part to relativize a central aspect of Jewish ethnic identity in light of the arrival of the reign of Yahweh. As our consideration of ethnicity reveals, behaviors like Sabbath-keeping, and the scruples associated with exclusive table fellowship, were not simply isolated religious practices. They constituted the living expressions of Israel's cultural past, and, as such, were central to Judean identity during our period (*Past as Tradition or Cultural Past*). As he challenged and subverted these practices, therefore, Jesus functioned as somewhat of an 'ethnic entrepreneur', redrawing ethnic boundaries and reconstructing the ethnic identity of the people of God. In his particular approach to purity, moreover, Jesus decidedly rejected current nationalistic interpretations of recent Maccabean history, interpretations that had placed the observation of these Jewish distinctives at the heart of what it meant to be a faithful Jew in the context of pagan domination (*Past as History*).

Jesus also raised questions about the ethnic identity of God's people by the ways in which he adapted and significantly reworked Israel's myth of origins (*Past as Myth*). Recall Eller's definition of an ethnic myth of origins as 'remote and unprovable history' that serves as a 'charter for the group's existence and culture in the present'. Jewish feasts, such as Tabernacles and Passover, revived Israel's sacred history for Second-Temple Judeans on a yearly basis, and they did so in a profoundly dramatic way. Hundreds of thousands of the faithful gathered annually in Jerusalem to celebrate God's great acts in Israel's distant past, when Yahweh redeemed his people from Egyptian slavery and cared for them as they wandered in the wilderness before entering the promised land. Jesus boldly redefined these powerful yearly reminders of Israel's remote history in terms of his own life and ministry. The implications of these activities for Jesus' understanding of ethnicity and boundary preservation should by now be quite transparent.

Finally, Jesus' subordination of natural family ties to his kingdom designs also functioned as a pointed challenge to the way in which Israel's myth of origins was utilized by Jesus' opponents, especially where the issue of Abrahamic descent was concerned. To properly appreciate the implications of Jesus' teachings about family and lineage for the reconfiguration of social boundaries, it will be helpful briefly to consider the close connection between kinship and ethnicity in ancient Mediterranean society.

4. *Kinship and Ethnicity*

As mentioned above, ethnicity is generally associated with a real or putative shared ancestry of some sort. As a result, most ethnographers now include 'myth of common ancestry' as a key component in their taxonomies of the various characteristics exhibited by ethnic groups, and ethnicity is regularly likened to kinship in the anthropological literature.[25] Eller, for example, refers to ethnicity as 'a kind of kinship writ large'.[26] Fischer suggests that 'ethnicity may be the maximal case of societally organized intimacy and kinship experience'.[27] It should be pointed out that the objective reality of a consanguine family bond is not necessary required here. Data, in fact, show that most ethnic groups contain several genetic strains. Connor rightly emphasizes that

> it is not *what is* but *what people perceive as is* which influences attitudes and behavior. And a subconscious belief in the group's separate origin and evolution is an important ingredient of national psychology.[28]

This perceived connection between kinship and ethnicity will be particularly vibrant, moreover, where lineage family systems are the norm, as was

---

25. Hutchinson and Smith (1996: 7). Thus, when Herodotus describes the Ionians, Dorians, Herakleeidai, and Akhaians, he cites stories of the origins of these groups, which are based on genealogies traced from the eponymous ancestors Helen, Doros, Aiolos, Ion, and Akhaois (Duling 2005: 132; Hall 1997: 43). As Duling notes, the names 'Israelite' and Ἰουδαῖος suggest the eponymous ancestors Jacob/Israel and Judah, respectively (2005: 132).

26. Eller (1999: 60). Similarly, Fishman: 'Ethnicity has always been experienced as a kinship phenomenon, a continuity within the self and within those who share an intergenerational link to common ancestors' (1980: 84).

27. Fischer cited by Eller (1999: 9).

28. Connor (1994: 198). Yet, as Van den Berghe properly observes, perception will generally have some basis in reality:

> A myth, to be effective, has to be believed, and a myth of ethnicity will only be believed if members of an ethnic group are sufficiently alike in physical appearance and culture, and have lived together and intermarried for a sufficient period (at a minimum three or four generations) for the myth to have developed a substantial measure of biological truth (1995: 361).

the case with the patrilineal kinship groups of Mediterranean antiquity. To relativize family ties in such a setting, therefore, is to challenge bonds of ethnicity and thereby undermine ethnic identity at the broader societal level.[29]

A good bit of evidence can be found for just such a connection between kinship and ethnicity among post-Maccabean Judeans. Abrahamic descent was, of course, central to the Jews' myth of common ancestry, and Abraham and the patriarchs figure again and again in literature written during the period, often in close contextual proximity to themes of Jewish exclusivism.[30] Note, for example, the association of Abrahamic descent with the ethnic badge of sacred food in the following speech of the aged martyr Eleazar from *4 Maccabees*:

> 17 'Never may we, the children of Abraham, think so basely that out of cowardice we feign a role unbecoming to us! 18 For it would be irrational if having lived in accordance with truth up to old age and having maintained in

---

29. Readers schooled in anthropological theory will detect a transition at this point from the discursive, social constructionist approach to ethnicity which characterized arguments in the earlier portions of the chapter to the use of a primordial model in the discussion of the relationship between kinship and ethnicity which follows (the term 'primordial' was first used in the literature by Shils [1957]). The debate over constructivism versus primordialism has unfortunately been a heated and often misleading one, as any cursory review of the dialogue between the two schools of anthropological theory will attest (Eller and Coughlan [1993]; Grosby [1994]; Jenkins [1997: 44-50]; Eller [1999: 71-83]; Esler [2003: 44-48]). The primordial model, in particular, has fallen out of favor in many circles, and this is somewhat unfortunate, since distaste for primordialism is due, at least in part, to a misunderstanding of the approach as it was framed by some of its earliest proponents (Geertz [1963]). It is quite fair, I think, to describe ethnicity in primordial terms when ethnic ties are viewed from the emic perspective of cultural insiders—particularly when these insiders belong to a traditional society where lineage kinship structures are the norm (Hutchinson and Smith helpfully label this phenomenon 'participant's primordialism' [1996: 9]; see also Grosby [1994]). It is hardly controversial to assert, for example, that a first-century Palestinian Jew would have viewed his or her ethnic identity as 'a primordial phenomenon, a singular form of sociality or solidarity, based on emotional connection to long-standing, objective, and fixed social characteristics'—whatever an outside analyst might say about the ultimately socially constructed nature of such an outlook (Eller [1999: 78]). On this see Esler (2003: 46-47) and Scott (1990). Current studies increasingly distance themselves from the primordialism-versus-constructivism debate, preferring instead to analyze how 'discourses of race and ethnicity rely upon the notion of fixity or primordiality even while they are also always under negotiation and flux' (Buell [2005: 7] cites as examples Stoler [1997: 198-200], Malkin [2001: 6, 15-16], and Baumann [1999: 90]).

30. Preoccupation with ancestral lineage can be traced back to the early postexilic period. Schwartz, for example, sees the principle of descent displacing that of territoriality as the most important mark of Jewish self-identity, when Judeans returned from exile in Babylon with Ezra and Nehemiah (1992: 7-9).

accordance with law the reputation of such a life, we should now change our course 19 and ourselves become a pattern of impiety to the young by setting them an example in the eating of defiling food... 22 Therefore, O children of Abraham, die nobly for your religion!' (*4 Macc.* 6.17-19, 22)

Horowitz has observed that 'the language of ethnicity is the language of kinship'.[31] The use of kinship terminology in close association with important symbols of Jewish ethnic identity such as 'law' and 'covenant' in Maccabean literature affirms the truth of this assertion for Jesus' social world. The beginning of the Maccabean revolt finds the patriarch Mattathias exclaiming,

> 19 'Even if all the nations that live under the rule of the king obey him, and have chosen to obey his commandments, everyone of them abandoning the religion of their ancestors, 20 I and my sons and my brothers will continue to live by the covenant of our ancestors (διαθήκη πατέρων ἡμῶν)' (1 Macc. 2.19-20).

The key family term 'ancestors' appears often in 1 Maccabees, generally in close association with Jewish distinctives of law and covenant. Thus, Mattathias before he dies urges his sons, 'Now, my children, show zeal for the law, and give your lives for the covenant of our ancestors (διαθήκης πατέρων)' (2.50). Judas draws upon the same theme shortly thereafter, exhorting his band of faithful warriors,

> 9 'Remember how our ancestors were saved at the Red Sea, when Pharaoh with his forces pursued them. 10 And now, let us cry to Heaven, to see whether he will favor us and remember his covenant with our ancestors and crush this army before us today' (4.9-10).

The term 'ancestors' surfaces yet again, this time in connection with the vital ethnic badge of sacred space, when Simon, justifying his conquests to an agent of the Syrian king, asserts,

> 33 'We have neither taken foreign land nor seized foreign property, but only the inheritance of our ancestors, which at one time had been unjustly taken by our enemies. 34 Now that we have the opportunity, we are firmly holding the inheritance of our ancestors' (15.33-34).

In 2 Maccabees, as well, kinship terminology and the theme of Jewish identity occur in close proximity. As a result of Antiochus's edict, the reader is told, 'People could neither keep the sabbath, nor observe the festivals of their ancestors (πατρῴους ἑορτάς), nor so much as confess themselves to be Jews' (6.6). The phrase 'laws of our ancestors' occurs twice in the work (2 Macc. 7.2, 37; τοὺς πατρίους νόμους), and the author pointedly refers to Antiochus's edict, which proscribed such vital ethnic badges as Sabbath

---

31. Horowitz (1985: 57).

observance and Jewish dietary practices, as 'the overthrow of [the Jews'] ancestral way of life' (8.17).

In his study of ethnic identity formation Eller includes as a central ingredient under the rubric *Past as Tradition* 'the language the group has "always" spoken', and some scholars, in fact, isolate language as a distinct feature of ethnicity.[32] Evidence abounds associating language with social identity in the ancient world, and this is not surprising, given the role played by language in the construction and reinforcement of ethnic boundaries.[33] 2 Maccabees specifically identifies the Hebrew language as a bond that connects the story's Judean protagonists to their ethnic heritage, and it does so, once again, by recourse to the familiar term 'ancestor' (see above). Five times in 2 Maccabees we encounter the expression 'ancestral language' (ἡ πάτριος φωνή [7.8, 21, 27; 12.37; 15.29]).[34] Particularly revealing is the way in which the author uses the expression in 2 Maccabees 7, where the 'language of [their] ancestors' is generally reserved for interaction between the Jewish protagonists, while the Jews address the king in Greek. The mother, for example, encourages the lads 'in the language of their ancestors' (2 Macc. 7.21).

With a single exception (2 Macc. 8.17), the words 'ancestors/ancestral' in the texts cited above all translate a term from the Greek word-group πατρ*. Van Henten maintains that adjectives derived from πατρ* are used in 2 Maccabees 'in connection with Jewish culture and religion as opposed to Greek customs'.[35] This is an important observation, particularly in view of the semantic field of the πατρ* word-group. The use of this root to refer both to one's distant ancestors and to the father of one's immediate family speaks forcefully to the close connection in the Jewish mindset between kinship and ethnicity. Due to the lineage orientation of Jewish kinship, Second-Temple Jews will have sensed a close familial connection with the patriarchs, their ethnic progenitors, through a multi-generational patriline.[36] The broad semantic field of the πατρ* word-group reflects this connection.

---

32. Eller (1999: 29). Duling, for example, lists 'common language' as one of nine distinct components of his model of ethnicity (2005: 128, 133). The power of language, in this regard, is self-evident to those of us who witnessed the resurrection of spoken Hebrew after Israel was established as a state in 1948. See, too, Bartlett's fascinating treatment of the relationship between language and ethnicity in medieval European history (Bartlett [1994: 198-204]).

33. Herodotus, for example, refers to 'the kinship of all Greeks in blood and speech' (*Hist.* 8.144.2).

34. With van Henten (1999: 66-68) we may assume that the Hebrew language is here in view, although the 'ancestral language' is not specifically identified in the text.

35. Van Henten (1999: 58).

36. Wright is therefore quite correct to assert that Israel 'thought of itself as a blood family' (Borg [2000: 43]).

In such a socio-linguistic context the boundary line between the conceptual categories of family and ethnicity tends to blur considerably.

The association of kinship and ethnicity encourages us, in turn, to interpret Jesus' counter-cultural approach to family relations against the background of Jewish ethnic identity. By subordinating natural family ties under the overarching rubric of loyalty to his surrogate family of followers, Jesus sought to address more than the inevitable conflict of interests that would result in the lives of disciples with competing family loyalties. Given the close connection between kinship and ethnicity among Jesus' Jewish contemporaries, we may assume that Jesus' challenges to natural family loyalty functioned simultaneously as pointed challenges to Judean ethnicity. This was particularly the case where Jesus relativized the role of father in the patrilineal kinship groups to which his followers belonged, and it becomes patently transparent in those gospel traditions that question the soteriological efficacy of Abrahamic descent.

5. Jesus and Patriarchy

Elliott appropriately cautions against anachronism in the employment of social scientific models in the study of ancient texts, rightly labeling as an 'idealistic fallacy' the popular theory that Jesus was an egalitarian.[37] While Elliott is more directly concerned here with matters of status and social stratification than with the issue of patriarchy, those who are interested in Jesus' attitude towards gender roles would do well to keep Elliott's timely admonition in view. We must take care not to project modern views of gender back onto the world of Mediterranean antiquity. It nevertheless remains the case that Jesus challenged patriarchy and relativized the role of father in the patrilineal family in some rather striking and memorable ways during his earthly ministry.[38] In my view, however, he did not do so intentionally to ameliorate the way in which patriarchy functioned in the natural family systems of his day. For example, I do not think that Jesus subverted patriarchal authority chiefly to elevate the role of women in the Jewish family. Although we can reasonably draw some secondary implications about Jesus' convictions concerning relations in the natural family from the anti-patriarchal traditions in the Gospels, the connection between kinship and ethnicity outlined above suggests that Jesus' primary intentions here related more directly (and more broadly) to his desire to redefine the ethnic boundaries of God's people in terms of his surrogate family of followers. Jesus' challenge to Jewish patriarchy, then, represented, at a most

---

37. Elliott (2002: 87).
38. Horsley elaborates upon what he describes as the synoptic tradition's 'sharp criticism of the traditional patriarchal forms' (1989: 123).

profound level, a challenge to the prevailing assumption that Jewish ethnicity was coterminous with membership in the people of Yahweh.

Passages cited in the previous chapter to illustrate Jesus' attitude toward family ties in general can profitably be reconsidered in the present connection. The exhortation to the potential disciple in Mt. 8.20-21 reveals much about Jesus' view of the inviolable paternal bond that characterized family life in the Mediterranean world: 'Another of his disciples said to him, "Lord, first let me go and bury my father". But Jesus said to him, "Follow me, and let the dead bury their own dead"'. The promise to Peter, who claims to have left all to follow Jesus, is also informative along these lines:

> 29 Jesus said, 'Truly I tell you, there is no one who has left house or brothers or sisters or mother or father or children or fields, for my sake and for the sake of the good news, 30 who will not receive a hundredfold now in this age—houses, brothers and sisters, mothers and children, and fields with persecutions—and in the age to come eternal life' (Mk 10.29-30).

As has been noted by commentators for some time, the term 'father', which appears in the list of family relations that have been left behind to join the Jesus movement (v. 29), is noticeably missing from the catalogue of relations gained in Jesus' fictive family of followers (v. 30). The emphasis throughout the gospel traditions upon God as Father of both Jesus and his followers most likely accounts for the absence of a human father figure in the surrogate kinship group described in Mk 10.30, above. Matthew 23.9 is to be similarly explained: 'And call no one your father on earth, for you have one Father—the one in heaven'.[39] Given the relationship between kinship and ethnicity in post-Maccabean Judaism, Jesus' elevation of 'father' to the divine realm in his new family not only subverts the role and authority of fathers in the natural families of his followers. Jesus' strategy also intentionally contests current assumptions about the broader contours of Jewish ethnicity.[40]

---

39. Catchpole, too, interprets the saying in Mt. 23.9 in connection with the absence of 'father' in Mk 10.30. He argues for the authenticity of the Matthean text, and he assumes that Mk 10.28-30 goes back to Jesus, as well (Catchpole [2006: 95-96])

Theissen also sees the exclusiveness of God as father reflected in Mk 3.35, where 'father' is lacking in Jesus' list of surrogate family relations: 'Whoever does the will of God is my brother and sister and mother'. Catchpole concurs (2006: 96). Here, however, the absence of the term is probably to be understood biographically, as due to the (apparently) early death of Joseph, an explanation that Theissen himself acknowledges in part (1998: 218).

40. At this point a comparison with Qumran proves illuminating. Qumran, like the Gospels, uses surrogate family language to delineate the social boundaries of the community: 'sons of light/darkness' (1QS 3-4; cf. 1QH 9.34-36: 'Until I am old Thou wilt care for me; for my father knew me not and my mother abandoned me to Thee. For Thou art a father to all [the sons] of Thy truth'.). But whereas Jesus directly

A similar theme surfaces in the dispute over Abrahamic descent related in John 8.[41] The fatherhood of God and the fatherhood of Abraham both figure in the debate, and Jesus places his opponents in a distinctly unfavorable position with respect to their paternity on both accounts.[42] We pick up the dialogue in vv. 31-33, where the Abrahamic descent of Jesus' interlocutors enters into the discussion:

> 31 Then Jesus said to the Jews who had believed in him, 'If you continue in my word, you are truly my disciples; 32 and you will know the truth, and the truth will make you free'. 33 They answered him, 'We are descendants of Abraham and have never been slaves to anyone. What do you mean by saying, "You will be made free"?' (Jn 8.31-33).

Jesus' initial response affirms the Abrahamic patriline of his questioners, while at the same time drawing attention to the inappropriateness of their behavior in light of such a claim:

> 34 Jesus answered them, 'Very truly, I tell you, everyone who commits sin is a slave to sin. 35 The slave does not have a permanent place in the household; the son has a place there forever. 36 So if the Son makes you free, you will be free indeed. 37 I know that you are descendants of Abraham; yet you look for an opportunity to kill me, because there is no place in you for my word. 38 I declare what I have seen in the Father's presence; as for you, you should do what you have heard from the Father' (8.34-38).

As the verbal conflict escalates, Jesus presses the incongruity of claiming Abraham as one's father while at the same time trying to kill Jesus, a man sent from God, thus suggesting that his dialogue partners may not be the genuine offspring of Abraham after all:

challenges natural family solidarity and the Abrahamic bloodline, Qumran is much more conservative along these lines, insisting, for example, that the community's priests have a proper lineage pedigree as the 'sons of Zadok' (1QS 5). The Dead Sea community thus becomes a subset or 'faithful remnant' (CD 1) of the true Israel, and the fictive family language at Qumran serves to reinforce these intra-Jewish boundaries. The Jesus traditions, in contrast, employ surrogate kinship language alongside anti-family sayings that directly subvert the Abrahamic patriline. What results is a fictive family model with potentially porous boundaries where Jewish ethnicity is concerned.

41. Although the author of the Gospel has certainly crafted the text in view of his own theological concerns, we need not be skeptical concerning the general historicity of the narrative, since the story coheres thematically with Jesus' critiques of patriarchy in the passages cited above, and it parallels John the Baptizer's relativization of the soteriological efficacy of the Abrahamic bloodline found in the double tradition (Mt. 3.9; Lk. 3.8).

42. Moloney correctly notes that the debate in John 8 'at all times swivels around the question of origins' (2002: 166), a question, I might add, that is central to ethnicity and ethnic identity formation.

39 They answered him, 'Abraham is our father'. Jesus said to them, 'If you were Abraham's children, you would be doing what Abraham did, 40 but now you are trying to kill me, a man who has told you the truth that I heard from God. This is not what Abraham did. 41 You are indeed doing what your father does' (8.39-41a).

Jesus' opponents may be 'descendants (σπέρμα) of Abraham' (vv. 33, 37) but they are not 'Abraham's children (τέκνα)' (v. 39).[43] The debate finally crescendoes in a series of forceful assertions by Jesus about the paternity of his opponents, assertions that would have been utterly scandalous in the cultural setting in which the dialogue occurred:

They said to him, 'We are not illegitimate children; we have one father, God himself'. 42 Jesus said to them, 'If God were your Father, you would love me, for I came from God and now I am here. I did not come on my own, but he sent me. 43 Why do you not understand what I say? It is because you cannot accept my word. 44 You are from your father the devil, and you choose to do your father's desires. He was a murderer from the beginning and does not stand in the truth, because there is no truth in him. When he lies, he speaks according to his own nature, for he is a liar and the father of lies' (8.41b-44).

Here, again, Jesus renegotiates the boundaries of ethnic identity, this time directly challenging the soteriological confidence his contemporaries placed in their status as children of Abraham. By refusing to acknowledge the legitimacy of his opponents' claim to Abrahamic ancestry, and assigning their spiritual paternity to the devil instead of God, Jesus has effectively

---

43. The wrangling over Abrahamic descent must be heard against the background of a number of socio-cultural scripts and assumptions, one unique to Judeans, others common to the broader Mediterranean world. On the Jewish side, Catchpole suggests that appealing to one's status as the offspring of Abraham 'bases the confidence of the present generation on security achieved by the righteousness of the patriarchs in the past' (2006: 34). Participation in the patriline thus guarantees participation in the patriarchs' deeds of righteousness. Catchpole cites as evidence for such an outlook Josephus's expansion of a speech of Nehemiah:

Fellow Jews, you know that God cherishes the memory of our fathers Abraham, Isaac, and Jacob, and because of their righteousness does not give up his providential care for us (Josephus, *Ant.* 11.169).

Jesus responds with a familiar *topos,* one of a more universal nature: like father, like child. The deeds of Jesus' adversaries betray in his view a patent lack of genuine solidarity with father Abraham. The *imitatio* theme, moreover, represents a subset of a broader cultural script that utterly permeated the world of Roman antiquity, namely, the notion that a male's primary source of honor—in a society in which honor counted for everything—was his patriline. To publicly challenge the legitimacy of a claim to Abrahamic ancestry therefore constitutes one of the greatest interpersonal offenses imaginable among Jewish males in the ancient Mediterranean world.

positioned his dialogue partners decidedly beyond the boundaries of his ethnically reconstituted people of God.[44]

6. Conclusion

The following chart summarizes the findings of the previous Chapters under the rubric of ethnic identity formation:[45]

Aspects of Ethnicity	Raw Materials	Post-Maccabean Judaism	Jesus of Nazareth
Myth of Remote Origins	Torah's Narrative of Israelite Origins	Reinterpreted Biblical Narratives to Support a Stridently Nationalistic Agenda	Reinterpreted Biblical Narratives in Terms of his Own Life and Ministry
Putative Shared Ancestry	Abrahamic Descent and Patrilineal Kinship Structure	Emphasized Abrahamic Descent and the Preservation of the Purity of the Bloodline	Relativized the Abrahamic Bloodline and Reconstituted God's People as a Surrogate Family
Shared Recent History	Syrian Oppression and Judean Independence	Explained Recent History by Means of a Deuteronomistic Theology That Focused upon Faithfulness to Badges of Ethnic Solidarity	Rejected the Idea that Yahweh's Intervention on Israel's Behalf Depended on Carefully Maintaining Badges of Jewish Ethnicity
Distinguishing Cultural Practices	Food, Festivals, Sabbath-Keeping, Circumcision	Increasingly Defined Such Practices as Non-Negotiable Badges of Jewish Identity	Consistently Challenged Current Practices Related to Food, Festivals, and Sabbath
A Link with a Homeland	Canaan as the Promised Land; Jerusalem Temple as Yahweh's Dwelling Place	Intensified Focus upon Sacred Space and Territorialism in Response to Threats to the Temple	Intentionally Relativized Distinctions between Sacred and Profane Space

---

44. Perhaps even more scandalous, given the connotations of the phrase in antiquity, is Jesus' castigation of scribes and Pharisees as a 'brood of vipers', as related in Matthew's Gospel (12.34; 23.33). That the insult would have been interpreted as a challenge to the efficacy of Abrahamic descent is supported by the juxtaposition of the two ideas in John's proclamation in Mt. 3.7-9. On the widespread ancient belief that vipers killed their mothers during the birth process, see Keener (2005).

45. The aspects of ethnicity in the left-hand column have been taken (with some alteration and adaptation) from Hutchinson and Smith (1996: 6-7). The authors refer to them as 'features' that *ethnies* 'habitually exhibit' (6).

The column to the left lists five significant cultural characteristics that typically contribute to an ethnic group's sense of identity and social solidarity. The next column outlines the raw materials that Jesus and his contemporaries had at their disposal in each of these categories, as they sought to reconstruct Jewish ethnicity to address the perceived needs of the people of God in the context of Roman hegemony. Except for the events of recent Maccabean history all of these raw materials were found in the Hebrew Scriptures. The third and fourth columns contrast the social agenda of post-Maccabean Judaism with that of Jesus of Nazareth and thereby underscore in summary form Jesus' radically alternative vision for redefining the ethnic contours of a renewed Israel in light of the inbreaking of the kingdom of God.

a. *'Why This New Race?'*
Sometime after the destruction of the temple in 70 CE, an anonymous Rabbi quoted Yahweh as follows: '"I am God for all those who come into the world, nevertheless I have conferred My name particularly on My people Israel"'.[46] By the time this statement was committed to writing (c. third century CE), the tension between these two biblical realities had preoccupied Judeans in the East for centuries. In the case of the Jesus movement, it was the former idea that finally won the day. Sometime between the middle of the first and the second centuries, early Christianity, which had its origins as a Jewish renewal movement in Roman Palestine, became increasingly Gentile in composition, ultimately parting ways with Judaism and establishing its own social identity in the eastern empire.

Christianity, however, was not to become simply another alternative among the various religious options in the Greco-Roman world. As several leaders of the early Christian movement properly insisted, and as outsiders apparently observed, as well, the Christian project was much more all encompassing—Christians in the empire constituted something akin to a 'third race'.[47] While such a description calls for a good deal of qualification,

---

46. *Mek. Mishpatim* 20, cited by Sanders (1977: 87).
47. Tertullian relates, 'We are indeed said to be the 'third race' of men', though he resists the notion (*Ad nat.* 1.8). The author of the *Epistle to Diognetus* begins the letter by asking, 'Why this new race?' (*Ep. Diog.* 1.1). Clement of Alexandria talks about Greeks and Jews now being gathered into 'one race' (*Strom.* 6.6). See, also, Aristides, *Apology*, which identifies 'three kinds of humans in this world: worshippers of so-called gods, Jews, and Christians' (*Apol.* 2.2).

Complicating the analysis of early Christian self-definition is the fact that Christians saw themselves as ethnically inclusive, yet continued to utilize symbols and concepts related to ethnicity to define boundaries between themselves and other groups in the empire. Thus Paul can categorically assert that there is 'no longer Jew or Greek' (Gal. 3.28), while simultaneously appropriating a key component of ethnicity—putative

one can hardly deny the intentional reconstruction of ethnic identity reflected in passages like the following from Paul's letter to the Galatians:[48]

> 26 for in Christ Jesus you are all children of God through faith. 27 As many of you as were baptized into Christ have clothed yourselves with Christ. 28 There is no longer Jew or Greek, there is no longer slave or free, there is no longer male and female; for all of you are one in Christ Jesus. 29 And if you belong to Christ, then you are Abraham's offspring, heirs according to the promise (Gal. 3.26-29).

As I have now argued in detail, it appears that the social and ideological trajectory for Paul's vision for a multi-ethnic people of God was established some decades earlier, when Jesus began to reengineer the ethnic values and practices of his Jewish contemporaries during his earthly ministry in Roman Palestine.

It should be abundantly clear from the above discussion that the manner in which post-Maccabean Judeans utilized the powerful symbols of food, territory, and calendar to differentiate themselves from other people-groups

---

ancestry—to define the contours of the new group he is describing: 'you are Abraham's offspring' (v. 29). On the conscious use by Christian leaders of ethnic discourse to make universalizing claims about Christianity, see the insightful work of Buell, who seeks to demonstrate that 'saying that Christianity is open to all was not mutually exclusive with defining Christians as members of an ethnic or racial group' (Buell [2005: 138]; see also Buell [2002]). As Buell convincingly argues, early Christians used ethnic reasoning both (a) to define Christianness as a distinct category in contrast to other peoples, and (b) to present Christianness as 'inclusive, since it is a category formed out of individuals from a range of different races' (Buell 2005: 3). I would emphasize, however, in a way that Buell has not, that the degree to which the early Christians engaged in the latter aspect of this self-definitional project marked them out as rather exceptional among the various people-groups of the empire.

48. Buell and Hodge (2004) discuss Paul's use of ethnic reasoning in this verse. For the implications of texts like Gal. 3.26-29 for social relations between Jews and Gentiles in the newly-constituted people of God, Horrell's essay is to be consulted (2000). Horrell effectively challenges Tomson's thesis that *'the observance of distinct sets of commandments by Jewish and gentile Christians was the basic principle of Paul's missionary work'* (Tomson [1996: 268, author's italics]; see also Tomson [1990]). Such a perspective erects an artificial firewall between Paul's symbolic universe (his theology) and his ethical convictions. Insights from the sociology of knowledge encourage us to anticipate a strong connection between Paul's soteriology and his vision for relations among his converts in the *ecclesia,* and a careful reading of the pertinent texts (Gal. 2.14-21; 1 Cor. 7.18-20; and Rom. 14.1–15.13) serves precisely to confirm such an expectation. As Horrell rightly concludes,

> Paul's emphatic and repeated declaration that in Christ there is no longer Jew and Gentile reflects not just a soteriological conviction, but a profound statement about the identity and unity of the new community which God has created, a statement which shapes and structures social interaction in the congregations in real and sometimes controversial ways (Horrell [2000: 343]).

in the empire constitutes a classic example of the construction and preservation of ethnic identity in the context of foreign domination and colonization. The social agenda of Jesus of Nazareth may be similarly understood. Jesus intentionally and systematically went after vital markers of Jewish identity in what can only be described as a competing attempt to reconstitute the ethnicity of the people of Yahweh, in order to provide direction for the future in the face of present needs and challenges.

And not only is Jesus' deconstruction of Jewish nationalism to be viewed in terms of ethnic identity formation. As demonstrated above, we should interpret the more positive aspects of Jesus' social program along these lines, as well. The connection between kinship and ethnicity in Jesus' social world encourages us to interpret Jesus' surrogate family construct and his corresponding subversion of Jewish patriarchy as intentional challenges to an ethnic understanding of the people of God that had prevailed since Sinai. By substituting a surrogate family model of social organization for the traditional notion of God's people as the lineal descendants of Abraham, and forcefully challenging the values of post-Maccabean Jewish nationalism, Jesus thus laid the conceptual foundation for his movement to transcend the boundaries of ethnic Judaism in the decades to follow.

CONCLUSION

JEWS AND THE PEOPLE OF GOD

'The Jesus tradition shattered Jewish exclusivism.'
Graydon Snyder[1]

The concluding chapter offers a condensed overview of materials canvassed in the course of the presentation, followed by some closing methodological considerations. I will first summarize what we have learned about the social environment of post-Maccabean Judaism, and then provide an abbreviated synopsis of Jesus' alternative approach to matters of purity and social boundaries. The discussion continues with some further reflections about historical methodology, and it concludes with a comment or two about the significance of the historical Jesus for those of us who claim to be his followers today.

1. *Summary*

The watershed events that occurred during the reign of the Seleucid dynast Antiochus IV indelibly marked the worldview of Judeans in the East during the post-Maccabean era. The threat to Jewish identity which climaxed in Antiochus's proscription of socio-religious practices in 167 BCE continued for generations to fuel concerns among Judeans about social boundary preservation. Of particular interest for our purposes are the specific behaviors that Antiochus prohibited: circumcision, Sabbath-keeping, the observation of the dietary laws, and activities related to the traditional temple cult. References to such practices surface again and again in Jewish literature penned in the wake of the Maccabean revolt, where the goal, in every instance, is the preservation of social boundaries between Jews and Gentiles.

The early Christians, in contrast, began to distance themselves from these Jewish distinctives, as they sought to reconstruct the identity of the new covenant people of God in terms of surrogate family. We can locate the genesis of this boundary-breaking agenda in the ministry of Jesus of Nazareth, who repeatedly conflicted with Jewish leaders over the vital identity markers of Sabbath, temple, and exclusive table fellowship. The

1. Snyder (1999: 156).

events of 167–164 BCE thus significantly inform our understanding of the teachings and activities of Jesus in the context of first-century Judaism, and they clarify Jesus' seminal contribution to the gradual transition from *ethnos* to *oikos* that later characterized the movement he established.

Antiochus's program in 167 BCE was an intentional one. Jewish particularism had long been closely connected to Israelite monotheism. Israel was to worship Yahweh alone, as utterly unique among the ancient Near Eastern pantheon of gods, and the Hebrew Scriptures directed Israel to replicate Yahweh's otherness, in this regard, by remaining distinct from surrounding peoples through a series of socially defining practices related to sacred times, sacred territory, and sacred food. By the late Greek period, the primary badges of Jewish identity recognized by both Jews and Gentiles included abstinence from pork, the observation of the Sabbath and the festal calendar, and the rite of circumcision. It was no accident, then, that Antiochus outlawed these very practices in his attempt to constitute his kingdom as 'one people' (1 Macc. 1.41). And we are not surprised to discover that these same badges of social identity increasingly captured the attention of Judeans in the East, as they sought to negotiate their place in the world in the decades of Jewish independence, and later Roman occupation, which followed the Syrian conflict.

a. *Post-Maccabean Jewish Historiography*
Literature produced in the wake of the Hellenization crisis attests to a growing concern to safeguard the boundary between Jew and Gentile by careful attention to Jewish cultural distinctives. We can profitably view the strategies of the authors of these documents as characteristic expressions of the process of ethnic identity formation and preservation. Ethnic groups typically construct and reinforce their identity and social boundaries by reinterpreting for current generations both the remote and the recent historical experiences of the group. Second-Temple Jews had much to work with on both counts. Judeans possessed in the Hebrew Scriptures a dramatic and powerful chronicle of ancient origins which marked them out as the chosen people of God. And the more recent pogrom of Antiochus IV, along with the ensuing exploits of the Hasmonean warriors and their party, provided Jews with additional raw materials to utilize in the service of the markedly particularistic historiography that came to characterize much of the literature of the period.

A number of writers sought to recraft Israel's story of origins to speak more forcefully to contemporary concerns. The authors of *Jubilees*, Pseudo-Philo's *Biblical Antiquities*, Judith, and the Additions to Esther each rewrote and elaborated upon narratives from the Hebrew Scriptures in such a way as to reinforce Judean particularism, by emphasizing the need to maintain the familiar badges of Jewish identity.

Events of recent history proved even more serviceable for the construction and preservation of Jewish ethnicity. The glorious exploits of the people of Yahweh during the early Hasmonean era, already cast in decidedly nationalistic terms in 1 Maccabees, received a profoundly ideological framework in 2 Maccabees and *4 Maccabees*, where faithfulness to the food laws was elevated to the apex of religious fidelity through the adaptation and reframing of Israel's traditional Deuteronomistic theology of sin, judgment, repentance, and deliverance. The authors of 2 Maccabees and *4 Maccabees* thus trace the suffering experienced at the hands of the Seleucids to a failure on Israel's part to remain loyal to the vital badges of socio-religious identity outlined above. In the words of one Maccabean historian, 'It is no light thing to show irreverence to the divine laws' (2 Macc. 4.17). Jewish leaders like Jason and his Hellenizing companions, who compromised with Greek culture and thereby blurred the social boundary that distinguished Jew from Gentile, brought upon their people divine chastisement in the form of the edict and activities of Antiochus IV.

Jason's apostasy contrasts directly in these documents with the faithfulness of Eleazar and the mother and her seven sons, whose martyrdoms are graphically narrated in 2 Maccabees and *4 Maccabees*. The unswerving devotion of these pious Jews to the Torah's dietary mandates explains, in turn, the change of Jewish fortunes and the ensuing victories of Judas and his brothers: '[W]hat was forsaken in the wrath of the Almighty was restored again in all its glory when the great Lord became reconciled' (2 Macc. 5.20). Yahweh's favor now returned to his people, and suddenly 'the Jews were invulnerable, because they followed the laws ordained by him' (2 Macc. 8.36).

These engaging works of Jewish literature thus tell us much about the outlook of Judeans in the East during the post-Maccabean era. Such documents reflected and reinforced the conviction among Jesus' contemporaries that obedience to commandments in the Torah regarding circumcision, Sabbath, and diet constituted the epitome of faithfulness to Yahweh. Indeed, according to the worldview that came to characterize much of post-Maccabean Judaism, the national integrity of the people of God depended for its very survival upon the preservation of Israel's badges of covenant loyalty.

b. *The Widespread Influence of Nationalistic Ideology*
Several lines of evidence attest to the widespread influence of the socio-religious agenda championed in the literature mentioned above. First of all, we have reason to believe that a number of these works enjoyed widespread distribution. Josephus used 1 Maccabees as an important source for his *Antiquities of the Jews* some two centuries after the document had been written, and 2 Maccabees, on its part, served as a useful resource for the authors of *3* and *4 Maccabees* in the service of their own exclusivist historiographical agendas. The Hasmonean protagonists of these narratives

seem, in fact, to have become national heroes among the populace, for many Judean families named their sons after Judas, Jonathan, and Simon in the decades following the Maccabean revolt. The book of *Jubilees,* as well, proved highly influential. The popularity of the narrative at Qumran is widely known, and Josephus's knowledge of the work now suggests an appreciation for the markedly particularistic orientation of *Jubilees* on the part of Jews whose theological and social horizons ranged far beyond the narrow confines of Essene sectarianism.

The popularity of literature produced in the wake of the Maccabean revolt is not our only evidence for the persistent influence of Jewish nationalistic ideology and praxis. The genesis of purity groups like the Essenes and Pharisees, and archaeological data from Palestine, also attest to the growing concern with boundaries and social identity that characterized Jewish values and behaviors during the post-Maccabean period. Both the Pharisees and the Essenes practiced exclusive table fellowship. Their efforts, in this regard, resulted in a repositioning—now between sectarian and non-sectarian Jews—of the social boundary that had traditionally separated Judeans from Gentiles. And the expansionist approaches to purity that characterized the period were not confined to the interests and behaviors of Jewish sectarians. Material remains uncovered in both Judea and Galilee forcefully attest to widespread purity practices on the part of a broad cross-section of the population. Immersion pools (*miqwaoth*) and stone vessels, both of which were utilized in the service of ritual purity, have been unearthed throughout Roman Palestine, in elite and non-elite Jewish settings alike.

And then there were the annual feasts, and a regrettable succession of abuses on the part of Roman leaders, each of which further fueled the fires of Jewish exclusivism and ethnic solidarity. The yearly festivals, already associated in the Hebrew Scriptures with deliverance from Egyptian slavery and the corresponding establishment of Israel as Yahweh's covenant people, took on an increasingly nationalistic flavor during our period. Outbreaks of violence between Jewish pilgrims and imperial forces in Jerusalem vividly testify to the cognitive dissonance that obtained in the Jewish mind between images of freedom and national sovereignty associated with festivals like Passover, on the one hand, and the stark reality of foreign occupation, on the other. And the manner in which the Romans exercised their authority did little to ameliorate the defensive social posture of their subject peoples. Roman abuses, beginning with Pompey's brazenly offensive foray into the temple in 63 BCE, and crescendoing in the Caligula debacle a century later, only confirmed fears among Judeans that Gentile occupation had the potential to seriously compromise the social integrity of the particular people of Yahweh.

Such were the values and social contours of the world in which Jesus of Nazareth lived and ministered. It was a religious and cultural environment that compelled any self-proclaimed leader of a Jewish renewal movement to weigh in with clarity and conviction on matters related to national identity and ethnic boundary preservation. If we are to trust the message of the canonical Gospels, Jesus did not disappoint in this regard. Jesus is distinctly remembered for stirring up controversy on these very issues. His disturbing teachings and actions related to Sabbath, temple, and table fellowship scandalized numbers of his contemporaries in first-century Galilee.

c. *Jesus and Jewish Boundaries*
We began our survey of the Gospels with an examination of Jesus' approach to sacred times. Sabbath controversy is a theme deeply embedded in the gospel tradition, and with good reason, if the first such story narrated in Mark's Gospel is at all indicative of Jesus' general attitude toward the seventh day. By paralleling his disciples' act of gleaning grain on the Sabbath with David's lawless consumption of the shewbread in 1 Samuel 21, Jesus raised serious questions about the function of the Sabbath in the context of the arrival of the dominion of God (Mk 2.23-28). Intentional Sabbath healings furthered Jesus' disconcerting agenda, an agenda that inevitably elicited opposition from those concerned to preserve this essential badge of Jewish ethnicity (Mk 3.1-6).

Equally striking was Jesus' reinterpretation of major Jewish festivals in terms of his own life and ministry. According to John's Gospel Jesus boldly claimed to represent the eschatological fulfillment of promises associated with the feast of Tabernacles (John 7–8). And by replacing Passover with the commemorative meal that came to be known as the Lord's Supper, Jesus completely disassociated a most important feast on Israel's annual calendar from traditional themes of deliverance from slavery and national sovereignty. In each case, by challenging Israel's sacred times Jesus destabilized the conception of God's people as an ethno-national entity, a conception that had prevailed since Sinai.

The way in which Jesus relativized sacred space also troubled numbers of his contemporaries. The Jerusalem temple served as the central locus of the 'ten degrees of holiness' that characterized Jewish territorial convictions during the post-Maccabean era, and it was the temple that received much of Jesus' critique, in this regard. Echoes of Jesus' prediction of the destruction of the edifice found their way into all four Gospels, as well as the book of Acts. Not unrelated to these predictions was the action in the temple courts during the final week of Jesus' life, an event that proves particularly informative for ascertaining Jesus' perspective on Jewish sacred space. The Old Testament excerpts he cited to explain his treatment of the moneychangers and merchants suggest that Jesus confronted perceived abuses in temple polity which discouraged, rather than encouraged, Gentile worship in the temple courts. In Jesus' view, the time had arrived for Isaiah's prophecy concerning the salvation of the nations to be fulfilled, and the marginalization of Gentiles in Yahweh's dwelling place could no longer be tolerated.

Jesus' interaction with the Samaritan woman at the well of Jacob further underscores his indifference towards current conceptions of Jewish territoriality, and here the connection between Jesus' treatment of sacred space and his desire to renegotiate ethnic boundaries becomes quite transparent. The narrator pointedly informs us that 'Jews do not share things in common with Samaritans' (Jn 4.9). Yet Jesus not only crossed an intractable social boundary to request a drink of water from the Samaritan woman's utensil, but proceeded to assert that 'the hour is coming when you will worship the Father neither on this mountain nor in Jerusalem'—a direct affront to the ethno-territorial convictions of Judeans and Samaritans alike (v. 21).

Equally disturbing to his opponents was Jesus' practice of inclusive table fellowship. By the first century CE, purity of food, which had for generations divided Jews and Gentiles at table, now separated sectarian from non-sectarian Jews among groups like the Pharisees and the Essenes. Jesus shared a table with Jews of every social and ritual stripe, thereby repositioning the boundary of the people of Yahweh, once again, where the Torah had essentially placed it, namely, between Judeans and Gentiles. In his teaching, moreover, Jesus seems to have gone even farther. Parables of reversal portrayed Gentiles at the eschatological table of Yahweh, and Jesus' assertion that 'it is not what goes into the mouth that defiles a person' (Mt. 15.11) set a trajectory that would in some circles result in the conviction that Jesus had effectively 'declared all foods clean' (Mk 7.19).

The cultural values and social codes that characterized life in post-Maccabean Jewish Palestine thus prove indispensable to a proper understanding of Jesus' attitude towards purity and nationalism. His consistently subversive approach to traditional distinctions between sacred and profane times, space, and food must not be interpreted merely as a critique of corrupt or legalistic religion. Given the sociological function of these practices, the challenges to Sabbath, temple, and exclusive table fellowship can only be understood as an intentional attempt on the part of Jesus to destabilize the socio-ethnic boundaries of the people of Yahweh in view of the inbreaking of the kingdom of God in his own life and ministry. Jesus' establishment of his followers as a surrogate family is to be understood as the constructive side of the same social project.

d. *Jesus' New Family*

For Jesus, the alternative to a stridently nationalistic Israel was a surrogate family model of social organization, which no longer defined the eschatological people of Yahweh in ethnic terms. Now it is the person who 'does the will of God' who belongs to Jesus' group, regardless of his or her familial connection to the patriline of Abraham (Mk 3.35). The fictive family construct came with its own set of relational expectations for its members. Here Jesus and his followers drew upon behaviors that ideally typified relations among siblings in the lineage groups of the Mediterranean world. Central to such behaviors were the sharing of material resources and high degrees of relational loyalty and affective solidarity.

As we saw in Chapter 9, moreover, the establishment of Jesus' followers as a surrogate family helps to interpret and prioritize much of what Jesus says about family in the Gospels. We may acknowledge at the outset that Jesus generally encouraged the fulfillment of natural family obligations. Such commitments, however, were of secondary importance to Jesus' overarching social agenda. For where natural family ties conflicted with commitment to the fictive family of Yahweh, Jesus expected loyalty to the latter to take priority over loyalty to one's patriline. This, in turn, explains the presence in the Gospels of passages in which Jesus is less than affirming of natural family relations. The surrogate family texts and the anti-family traditions in the Gospels are thus to be read together.

e. *Jesus as an Ethnic Entrepreneur*
Current thinking about the construction of social identity sheds much light upon the agendas and activities of both Jesus and those who resisted his program for Israel's renewal. Jewish nationalism during the post-Maccabean period transparently constitutes an exercise in the construction and preservation of ethnic identity. The genre of the rewritten Bible, interpretations of more recent events by Maccabean historians, and cultural practices related to purity and boundary preservation all served to establish and reinforce the social contours of the Jewish people during the Roman occupation of Palestine.

Ethnic identity theory also significantly illuminates the ministry of Jesus, since Jesus intentionally destabilized or reinterpreted each of these markers of social identity. By claiming to represent in his person the fulfillment of the high points on Israel's festal calendar, and by relativizing vital badges of Jewish national identity, Jesus essentially rewrote Israel's remote history in light of his own life and ministry and forcefully registered his disapproval of those popular interpretations of more recent history that had encouraged Judeans to adopt a defensive posture over against the Gentiles and even, in some cases, over against their fellow-Jews. Insights from social anthropology thus encourage us to interpret the activities of both Jesus and his contemporaries, in this regard, as attempts to reconstruct Jewish ethnicity to address current socio-cultural needs.

Jesus' critique of patriarchy and the establishment of his followers as a surrogate family are to be similarly understood. We earlier considered in some detail the connection that obtains between kinship and ethnicity. The link often characterizes the insider perspective of members of an *ethnie*, particularly in traditional societies, where lineage kinship structure generally obtains, and where a sense of common ancestry (real or imagined) functions as a vital social bond. The connection between kinship and ethnicity surfaces repeatedly in post-Maccabean Jewish literature, becoming most apparent when the authors of these works utilize family language to describe their cultural traditions. This conceptual link between one's immediate patriline and the broader ethnic group, in turn, informs our understanding of the manner in which Jesus subverted the role of the father in the natural family systems of his day. It also helpfully elucidates Jesus' pointed rejection of the confidence that his contemporaries placed in the soteriological efficacy of Abrahamic descent. And, perhaps most significantly, the connection between kinship and ethnicity explains the corresponding establishment of Jesus' followers as a surrogate family. By undermining Jewish patriarchy and organizing his disciples as a fictive family, Jesus laid a foundation for the later expansion of early Christianity beyond the boundaries of ethnic Judaism.

Ethnic identity theory thus demonstrates that Jesus' counter-cultural approach to Israel's symbols of national identity, on the one hand, and the organization of his followers in terms of surrogate family, on the other, constitute two aspects of a singular overarching social project—a project that sought to renegotiate the ethnic contours of the people of Yahweh in view of the arrival of the kingdom of God.

2. Opening the Canopy of Historical Methodology

I expect that the Jesus who has surfaced during the course of my presentation will strike some as being a bit too Christian. For as Dunn has recently observed,

> when Jesus is seen as some sort of bridge figure between Judaism and Christianity, any attempt to pull him more firmly to one side provokes protest from those who suspect his relation to the other side has been compromised.[2]

Those who insist on finding in Jesus a typical Jew whose life was characterized by commonly held convictions about purity and nationalism will undoubtedly construe my analysis as an attempt to pull Jesus too far down the Christian side of the historical watershed. The opposite approach, however, comes with its own set of problems. Interpreters who prefer wholly to confine Jesus to the Jewish side of the historical divide must struggle, on their part, to explain the origins of the movement that Jesus established, a movement that becomes rather anomalous if Jesus lived and died in ways that some minimalist interpreters suggest he did. Scholars of both persuasions clearly have their historical challenges to face.

2. Dunn (2002: 449).

As mentioned in the introduction, and as evidenced throughout the book, I have cast my lot with those who take a robust view of the historical integrity of the Gospels and who, as a result, are left with a Jesus who stands out in some rather striking ways from his contemporaries in first-century Jewish Palestine. The payoff here, of course, is the explanatory power that such a Jesus provides for the genesis of early Christianity. Such a position has much to commend it, as illustrated, I trust, by the analysis of the preceding chapters. It is also a position that accords well with my social location as an evangelical scholar, and, as such, it lends itself quite nicely to the application of a bit of non-traditional, open-canopy historical methodology.

I am under the distinct impression that few of my colleagues who have devoted their lives to the study of Christian origins are professing atheists. Many of us, indeed, identify ourselves as Christians. We see the God of Israel (however we might define 'God') as somehow present in the teachings and activities of Jesus of Nazareth. And we engage in our daily routines and responsibilities as if we live under an open canopy. When we turn to the task of historical analysis, however, we generally do so as practicing atheists. God is simply not allowed to break through the closed canopy of naturalistic methodology in order to be counted as a causative agent in the unfolding of historical events.[3] Theissen and Merz distinguish, in this regard, between 'religious imagination', which is 'concerned with access to God' and 'historical imagination', which is 'concerned with access to a past reality'.[4] It is the latter that typically characterizes the work of the professional historian of early Christianity.[5] Accordingly, in the preceding pages I have attempted to elucidate Jesus' activities relating to post-Maccabean Jewish nationalism through the use of traditional, closed-canopy historical methodology, generally resisting the temptation to default to divine intervention as some sort of *deus ex machina* to conveniently solve otherwise intractable historical problems.

Although much can be gained from the traditional approach to historical analysis outlined above, our postmodern *Zeitgeist* properly encourages us to question the viability of the artificial firewall that modernist thinking has erected between the material and the immaterial, between the natural and the numinous, between (to adopt Theissen's terminology) 'historical imagination' and 'religious imagination'. DeSilva is quite on target, in this

---

3. Meyer insightfully remarks, in this regard, about 'the many reductionistic philosophies which, whether or not they have won the historians' conscious agreement, have exercised a decisive remote control over historical-Jesus work' (1979: 16).

4. Theissen and Merz (1998: 13).

5. As C.S. Evans has suggested, there are some distinct benefits related to a closed canopy historiography, even for Christian scholars who reject naturalism as a metaphysical worldview (1999: 199-201).

regard, to interpret the modernist program as 'but a methodological institutionalization of a post-Enlightenment worldview'.[6] It is in this spirit that I propose to open the canopy of historical methodology, so to speak, and consider for a moment how the appropriation of a bit of 'religious imagination' might inform our understanding of the activities of Jesus.[7]

a. *An Open Canopy and an Anomalous Jesus*
The explanatory power of an open canopy manifests itself in several ways. First of all, at the risk of oversimplification, it appears that, in the end, each of us must choose to some degree between an anomalous Jesus movement and an anomalous Jesus. To operate under the rubric of methodological naturalism and reduce Jesus to a Jewish Cynic sage or a social reformer is to render anomalous the character of the movement that took root in Jerusalem immediately after his crucifixion. To give credence, instead, to the claims of the canonical Gospels is to embrace a Jesus who is decidedly unique among his contemporaries. In either case, we deal with anomaly. And in either case, scholars doing history under the closed canopy of methodological naturalism should feel discomfort, for, as Sanders has rightly observed, historians have 'grave difficulty with the category "unique"'.[8]

If, however, as many of us assume, God was, indeed, present in some extraordinary way in the person of Jesus of Nazareth, then I suggest that anomaly finds reasonable explanation. One of Israel's great prophets quoted Yahweh as follows:

> 'For my thoughts are not your thoughts,
>   nor are your ways my ways', says the LORD.
> 'For as the heavens are higher than the earth,
>   so are my ways higher than your ways
>   and my thoughts than your thoughts' (Isa. 55.8-9).

The prophet's point is a familiar one to those versed in the extended story of Yahweh's relationship with his people, as narrated in the Hebrew Scriptures. The God of Israel is ever Other when he appears in salvation history to challenge and confront the various societal domination structures and selfish personal behaviors that characterize human life on this planet. An encounter between Yahweh and his people will inevitably be marked by a healthy degree of socio-cultural anomaly. It will not be otherwise with Yahweh's anointed agent, Jesus of Nazareth, in the context of first-century Roman Palestine.

---

6. DeSilva (2004: 128).
7. For a helpful treatment of the relationship between historical analysis and the Christian faith see Minear (2002).
8. Sanders (1985: 320).

b. *An Open Canopy and Jesus' Mighty Deeds*

Secondly, removing the shackles of methodological naturalism from the study of Jesus renders the miracles fair game for historical inquiry. The common assertion that Jesus' miracles are not historically accessible obtains only if the interpreter's metaphysic is a naturalistic one, or if he or she has chosen to work within the confines of a closed-canopy historical methodology. Once we begin to allow that God was somehow present in the life and ministry of Jesus, the miracles in the Gospels become no less accessible to historical analysis than Jesus' teachings or other apparently mundane activities.[9]

Jesus' miraculous deeds, moreover, are not unrelated to the aspects of his ministry addressed in the preceding chapters and, particularly, to the anomalous nature of those activities, as discussed above. For apart from the crowd appeal of the miracles, it is reasonable to wonder why a Galilean peasant with such marginal views on social boundaries and Jewish ethnicity would have been taken seriously by Jewish leaders who were responsible

---

9. The issue inevitably reduces itself to one of worldview, as aptly noted by Blomberg (1999: 27). It has become quite commonplace among Christian scholars to bracket one's own worldview in order to adopt a naturalistic methodology for the purpose of historical analysis. In spite of his pointed comments explicitly eschewing a naturalistic metaphysic (1992: 93; 1996: 187), methodologically Wright's analysis of Jesus generally proceeds along these very lines (as demonstrated by C.S. Evans [1999: 188-95]; see also Twelftree [2004: 202]).

Meier's extensive treatment of the miracle traditions is similarly conceived (1994: 509-1038). At one point in his discussion Meier offers a revealing observation:

> The curious upshot of our investigation is that, viewed globally, the tradition of Jesus' miracles is more firmly supported by the criteria of historicity than are a number of other well-known and often readily accepted traditions about his life and ministry... Put dramatically but without too much exaggeration: if the miracle tradition from Jesus' public ministry were to be rejected in toto as unhistorical, so should every other Gospel tradition about him (Meier [1994: 630]).

Meier's methodology, however, does not allow him to treat the miracles as he does the 'other well-known and often readily accepted traditions', that is, to affirm the historical occurrences of the miracles. Rather, Meier is willing as a historian only to affirm that Jesus was *believed* by his contemporaries to have performed miracles. The reason: 'a positive judgment that a miracle has taken place is always a philosophical or theological judgment. Of its nature it goes beyond any judgment that a historian operating precisely as a historian can make' (1994: 514).

For Meier, however, 'a historian operating precisely as a historian' is a historian who plies his or her trade under the rubric of methodological naturalism. Such a perspective has, of course, already invoked *a priori* judgments of a philosophical or theological nature, even if, for the professing Christian scholar, those judgments only affect one's historical methodology. Meier recognizes this and has consciously chosen to work within the confines of such a program. I have chosen otherwise in the discussion that follows (see the helpful discussion and bibliography in Twelftree [1999: 17-53, 437-38]).

for preserving Israel's traditions in the context of Gentile occupation. An iconoclast, or a bit of a pest? Perhaps. A serious threat to the socio-religious status quo? Apart from the miracles and the crowds they attracted, we have reason to wonder whether Jesus would have attracted the opposition that he did. To appreciate why this is so, we must pause for a moment to acquaint ourselves with another 'Jesus', who prophesied against Israel's most sacred space during the years leading up to the destruction of the temple by the Romans in 70 CE, and who was simply dismissed as a fool by those in power.

c. *Jesus ben Ananias and Jesus of Nazareth*
In his narrative of the war with Rome, Josephus digresses to relate a series of 'manifest portents' that accurately 'foretold the coming desolation' of Jerusalem at the hands of the Romans (Josephus, *War* 6.288). Josephus highlights as the most notable of these portents the activities of a 'rude peasant' named Jesus ben Ananias, who stood in the temple at the feast of Tabernacles in the autumn of 62 CE and began to prophesy as follows:

> 'A voice from the east, a voice from the west, a voice from the four winds; a voice against Jerusalem and the sanctuary, a voice against the bridegroom and the bride, a voice against all the people' (Josephus, *War* 6.301).

For our purposes it is important to appreciate how those in power reacted to this Jesus and his anti-temple rhetoric.

Josephus informs us that the Jewish leaders 'arrested the fellow and severely chastised him'. Jesus would not be dissuaded from his prophetic activity, however, so the Jews finally brought him to Albinus, the Roman governor, who scourged him 'to the bone'. When Albinus questioned Jesus, the prophet 'answered him never a word, but unceasingly reiterated his dirge over the city, until Albinus pronounced him a maniac and let him go'. According to Josephus, Jesus continued to wander throughout the streets and alleys of the capital, prolonging his dirge day and night for seven years and five months, until he was finally killed not by his fellow Judeans but, rather, by a stone hurled from a Roman catapult during the siege of the capital (Josephus, *War* 6.300-09). The Romans thus dismissed Jesus ben Ananias as a madman, and his fellow-Judeans proceeded to tolerate the prophet's anti-temple rhetoric until he died, more than seven years later. We may profitably compare this response with the reaction of Jewish and Roman leaders to Jesus of Nazareth, some four decades earlier.

Evans enumerates a number of fascinating parallels between Jesus of Nazareth's action in the temple and the prophetic activity of Jesus ben Ananias.[10]

---

10. Evans (1993: 106). To these parallel historical experiences listed by Evans we can add the broader typological category of oracular prophet, a category shared by both

The parallels come to an abrupt halt, however, in the markedly contrasting treatments the two men finally received at the hands of the Romans. Jesus of Nazareth was crucified by Pilate. Jesus ben Ananias was scourged and dismissed as a fool by Albinus. And it was not only the Romans who dealt differently with the two Jesuses. Jewish authorities reacted in distinct ways, as well. Significant hostility toward Jesus of Nazareth surfaced in Jewish circles early in his ministry in Galilee, and it continued relatively unabated until he was delivered over to the Romans in 30 CE.[11] Pharisees and others apparently perceived in the activities of Jesus an ongoing threat of some kind.

Things were otherwise for the Jesus of Josephus's narrative. After he was dismissed as a madman by the Romans, Jesus ben Ananias continued prophesying against Israel's sacred space for some seven years, unmolested by scribal authorities and other Jews in positions of power in the capital—all this during a period of Judean history that was much more volatile than the late 20s, when Jesus of Nazareth ministered in Galilee.[12] These divergent responses call out for some explanation.

Evans attributes the more severe treatment of Jesus of Nazareth to the messianic ideas he entertained and to the large group of followers he had amassed.[13] It is the latter that proves most illuminating. The multitudes that followed Jesus surely became a cause of concern to Pilate, the Roman governor charged with maintaining stability in the volatile setting of first-century Judea. And Jesus' popularity apparently troubled Jewish authorities, as well. The crowds therefore offer the best explanation for the different reactions of both Jews and Romans to Jesus of Nazareth and Jesus ben Ananias, respectively. Jesus of Nazareth attracted crowds of followers. Jesus ben Ananias did not. For this reason, the latter could be dismissed as

---

Jesus of Nazareth and Jesus ben Ananias. Wright, for example, finds the category of prophet an important one for understanding the historical Jesus, and he identifies Jesus more specifically as an oracular and leadership prophet (1996: 162-68). The former type of prophetic ministry (oracular) accords well with the activities of Jesus ben Ananias, as described by Josephus. Wright lists a number of statements of Jesus in the Gospels that fall into the category of oracles of judgment (1996: 183-84). For the categorical schema see Webb (1991) and Horsley and Hanson (1985: 160-89).

11. According to Mark, after Jesus' first recorded Sabbath healing, 'the Pharisees went out and immediately conspired with the Herodians against him, how to destroy him' (Mark 3.6). There are exceptions, of course, such as the invitation Jesus received to dine in the home of Simon the Pharisee (Luke 7).

12. Evans is not quite accurate, therefore, when he asserts that 'both [Jesuses] encountered deadly opposition from the ruling priests' (2001: 486). Potentially deadly, perhaps. But the Roman dismissal of Jesus ben Ananias apparently led to a cessation of formal opposition to the prophet on the part of Jewish authorities, as well. Otherwise we are hard-pressed to explain Jesus ben Ananias's ensuing seven-year public ministry.

13. Evans (1993: 110).

an iconoclastic fool and allowed to continue his prophetic activity unimpeded. Jesus of Nazareth could not.

But this raises a further question. Why did Jesus of Nazareth attract the following that he did, given his unpopular attitude towards purity and nationalism? Both Jesus of Nazareth and Jesus ben Ananias directly challenged symbols of Judean identity that were viewed as sacred and inviolable by the majority of their contemporaries. We should hardly expect such a program to attract much popular attention in the socio-religious context of first-century Palestine, an expectation confirmed, in the case of Jesus ben Ananias, by his solitary prophetic ministry. Jesus ben Ananias seems to have attracted no following at all.

It is interesting to note, in this regard, that messianic and prophetic figures who did generate a following during our period all seem to have adopted a more traditional, nationalistic posture over against Roman occupation. They reinterpreted Israel's myth of origins in ways that reinforced, rather than subverted, Jewish identity and ethnicity. Josephus relates:

> Deceivers and imposters, under the pretence of divine inspiration fostering revolutionary changes, they persuaded the multitude to act like madmen, and led them out into the wilderness under the belief that God would there give them signs of freedom (Josephus, *War* 2.259).

The nationalistic orientation of these movements is quite transparent in Josephus's references to 'revolutionary changes', 'the wilderness', and 'signs of freedom'. The latter two expressions, in particular, hearken back to Israel's defining experience of deliverance from Egyptian slavery, here interpreted anew in ways that only served to fuel the fires of desire for liberation from Roman hegemony. At various points in his narrative Josephus describes in some detail the exploits of various charismatic messianic or prophetic figures, each of whom (a) promised deliverance from pagan oppression, (b) drew a large popular following, and (c) met their end at the hands of the Romans.[14]

Given the persistence of Maccabean ideology during our period, and the popularity of charismatic figures who championed a nationalistic agenda, we are not surprised to discover that Jesus ben Ananias, who called down doom upon the most important tangible symbol of Jewish socio-religious identity, engaged in his seven-year prophetic ministry as a solitary individual. His message was not a particularly popular one. This, however, renders the contrast with Jesus of Nazareth all the more striking. For in spite of the similarly subversive nature of his anti-nationalistic agenda, Jesus of Nazareth attracted a large following.

---

14. Horsley (1985) remains the most helpful treatment of these popular resistance movements.

The Gospels tell us why. And here is where doing history under an open canopy that admits Jesus' miracles as evidence into the historical court of inquiry proves quite illuminating. For the gospel narratives consistently ascribe Jesus' crowd appeal to his mighty works of exorcism and healing. Repeatedly in the first three chapters of Mark, for example, the narrator portrays the gathering of the multitudes as a characteristic response to Jesus' miraculous healings (1.28, 33, 45; 2.2, 12; 3.7-8). It is the miracles that attract the crowds. And it is the crowds, in turn, that demand a response on the part of Pharisees and others in positions of leadership to Jesus of Nazareth's decidedly subversive social agenda.

To summarize, apart from the miracles, an anomalous Galilean peasant who publicly challenged his people's deeply treasured badges of ethnic identity and solidarity through some sort of prophetic activity would probably have been dismissed (like Jesus ben Ananias) as relatively inconsequential by Pharisees and others in positions of power or influence in post-Maccabean Jewish Palestine. But then there were the miracles and the crowds that they drew. And here is where an open canopy methodology which renders Jesus' mighty deeds accessible to historical inquiry appears to possess significant explanatory power. For those in authority could not easily ignore a Jewish peasant who attracted multitudes of people, as he authenticated his destabilizing challenges to Jewish ethnicity and social boundaries with miracles like those recorded in the Gospels.[15] Once his opponents failed in their attempts to marginalize Jesus by attributing his mighty works to Satan, they had no other option but to engage in more extreme measures, in order to put a halt to the potential influence of Jesus' counter-cultural social agenda. For those of us willing to exercise a bit of Theissen and Merz's 'religious imagination', then, and embrace an open canopy historiography, the severe resistance Jesus encountered at the hands of Pharisees and others finds adequate explanation in the considerable crowd appeal of Jesus' miraculous authentication of his radically deconstructive approach to Jewish nationalism and ethnic boundaries.[16]

---

15. Meier similarly relates Jesus' miracles to his teaching and to the opposition he encountered: '[Jesus'] miracle-working activity not only supported but also dramatized and actuated his eschatological message, and it may have contributed to some degree to the alarm felt by the authorities who finally brought about his death' (1994: 970). The idea that Jesus authenticated his teaching through the exorcisms and healing miracles is a common one in the literature. Loader, for example, finds Jesus' authority over the powers, as portrayed in Mk 1.21-28, inseparable from his authority as a teacher: 'The exorcistic power confirms the legitimacy of the claim to teaching authority' (2002: 16). Kazen specifically connects Jesus' miracles to his indifference to purity: 'Jesus' attitude to impurity was thus corroborated by his authority as a "man of deed" ' (2002: 297).

16. Readers uncomfortable with an open canopy approach may feel that the emphasis upon Jesus' miracles compromises the arguments laid out in the earlier chapters of the

3. *A Brief Epilogue: Jesus Then and Now*

The Jesus uncovered in the course of my study differs not only from his Second-Temple Jewish contemporaries. He also stands out as rather distinct from many of us who claim to be his followers today. With his exorcisms, his apocalyptic worldview, and his radical ethic, Jesus, as Theissen observes, belongs 'on the margin of our culture'.[17] And this is only to be expected. For serious reflection about any figure from antiquity must traverse not only two millennia of time. A significant socio-cultural gap must be bridged, as well. We should, therefore, be immediately suspicious of any portrayal of Jesus which conveniently aligns itself with a contemporary ideological agenda. We should not expect the Jesus of first-century Palestine, for example, to satisfy the academic left's desire for 'a counter-culture Jesus who serves as an iconic precedent for all anti-establishment restiveness'.[18] Nor will the Jesus of history be easily co-opted by the conservative right in support of radical individualism, unbridled consumerism, or the uninformed and forceable imposition of these values upon peoples ill-equipped and unwilling to align themselves with decidedly Western ways of life.

This is not to fold the cards of historical inquiry and assume, with much postmodern historiography, that our contemporary cultural prisons allow us no access to the world of a first-century Palestinian Jew. On the contrary, as evidenced throughout my discussion, I am rather optimistic about our ability at least partially to access the world of Jesus and the early Christians. And I am equally confident that the historical Jesus has relevance for those of us who identify ourselves as Christians today. Nevertheless, as Hartley has so poignantly noted, 'The past is a foreign country: they do things differently there'.[19] Those of us who count ourselves as followers of Jesus of Nazareth in the twenty-first century must figure out how they did things there before we can figure out how to do things here. In the present case, our attempt to figure out how they did things there has led us to a Jesus who (a) deconstructed an ethnic understanding of the people of God that had prevailed since Sinai and (b) established in its place a surrogate family

---

book. It should be noted, however, that the above discussion does not depend upon the historicity of the miracles, as such, but only upon the conviction on the part of Jesus' contemporaries that Jesus performed such mighty deeds (see on Meier, n. 9, above). One could, therefore, conceivably remain within the confines of a traditional historical methodology, bracket the issue of Jesus' miracles as historical events, and still make the case outlined above. I have chosen, instead, to adopt an overtly open canopy approach at this point in the discussion.

17. Theissen and Winter (2002: 255).

18. I was unable to improve upon James Dunn's description of what he labels the 'neo-liberal' Jesus (Dunn [2003: 64]).

19. Hartley (1953), cited by Dunn (2003: 28 n. 11).

model that would one day include persons of every ethnic background. The implications of such a program are considerable.

Theissen has recently utilized the distinction between nature and culture to underscore the timeless relevance of Jesus of Nazareth for human beings of all eras and backgrounds. Nature, in Theissen's thinking, relates to the process of selection, where the principle of the 'survival of the fittest' reigns supreme. 'Culture' in contrast, 'begins where the weak, who would have no (or only minimal) chance for survival, receive the opportunity for a new (or better) life by intentional human conduct'. Culture's drive to reduce the pressure of selection is traditionally facilitated through 'the technological manipulation of the environment, social institutions that foster equality, and ethically motivated convictions'.[20]

For Theissen, the Bible stands squarely on the side of culture, in this regard, representing, as it does, 'a sharp protest against the principle of selection'.[21] This protest manifests itself in various forms throughout the Hebrew Scriptures but finds its clearest and most significant expression in the dominion of God as proclaimed by Jesus of Nazareth, where the weak are not only protected but given priority in Yahweh's social economy. This, in turn, renders Jesus, a figure far removed from the modern world in time and culture, eminently accessible to us today:

> If one sees in the figure of Jesus—precisely in the one who seems bizarre and forcign to us—an antiselection protest, then this figure turns out to belong not on the margin of our culture but at its center, at least for those who know that they must be committed to the program of reducing the pressure of selection for those of our fellow human beings who are weaker or who, as the 'less well-adjusted', don't fit in.[22]

All of this finds particular application in the present connection, since the principle of selection, and the corresponding axiom of 'the survival of the fittest', are inextricably linked to biology, kinship, and ethnic solidarity. This means that Jesus' comprehensive rejection of ethnic boundary preservation in favor of an alternative surrogate family model of social organization directly subverts the natural, selective propensities of human beings. Again, in the words of Theissen:

> Jesus' ethic may be too radical for us, but it only makes a break with previous biological evolution. It places a question against family solidarity founded on biology—love for those genetically related—and calls instead for love for enemies, love for those not genetically (or culturally) related—the very opposite of conduct governed by biology.[23]

---

20. Theissen and Winter (2002: 254).
21. Theissen and Winter (2002: 254).
22. Theissen and Winter (2002: 255).
23. Theissen and Winter (2002: 255).

I find Jesus even more radical than Theissen implies. For not only did he destabilize and call into question genetically (and, by extension, ethnically) based social solidarity. Jesus intentionally adopted his culture's most powerful symbol of familial solidarity—brotherhood—as the central metaphor for his own anti-selective approach to human relations: 'you are all brothers' (Mt. 23.8). As mentioned in an earlier chapter, a direct correlation obtains between altruistic behavior among relatives, on the one hand, and the number of genes shared by these persons, on the other. Siblings share more of the genetic code than any persons of the same generation (50%), and they typically exhibit a closer relational bond, where altruistic behavior is concerned, than any other family relation. For Jesus to hijack the commanding symbol of brotherhood and use it to define relations among a surrogate family of followers who shared no biological connection was to 'protest against the principle of natural selection' in a most profound and fundamental way.[24]

Specific points of contemporary contextualization are manifold. I will mention but two. First, Jesus' expansive social agenda appears to leave little room for the subjective, individualistic emphasis upon Jesus as 'personal savior', which continues to characterize much popular evangelical theology in the West today. It is hardly accidental that such an outlook all too easily facilitates the competitive (and therefore selective) propensities of persons in capitalistic societies, who tend to accumulate status and wealth for themselves as individuals while ignoring the needs of other persons—not to mention other Christians—in less fortunate circumstances. Jesus' vision for a renewed people of God was just that—a vision for a *people* who would experience life together as family under the reign of Yahweh. Jesus' surrogate family model thus poses no small challenge to Western Christians, many of whom have been socialized to embrace a solitary, individualistic version of the Christian faith that bears little resemblance to the community-orientated approach of Jesus and his early followers. So much for the positive aspect of Jesus' social project.

Jesus' deconstruction of Jewish nationalism also contains a message for contemporary Christians. The Jesus of the canonical Gospels speaks forcefully to those among us who would seek, in any form, to champion an ethnic or nationalistic approach to religion today. We are all too aware of the horrors perpetrated by ethnic groups and nation states that have sought to legitimize their violent and self-promoting tendencies by grounding them in appeals to religious dogma. Here, the survival of the fittest and natural selection manifest themselves in a most transparent and regrettable way. And here, I submit, lies the most pointed message of the Jesus who has surfaced in my study for those of us who claim to be his followers today.

---

24. Theissen and Winter (2002: 254).

Persons who wish to return to an era behind the cross, so to speak, and revive a nationalistic model of socio-religious identity by aligning Christianity with the platform of a nation state or a political party of any persuasion, will find no encouragement in a Jesus who subverted and destabilized religious nationalism at every turn during his ministry in Palestine more than two millennia ago.[25] Those who seek to pattern their lives after Jesus of Nazareth will vigorously resist both the ethnicization and the nationalization of the people of God. For as Jesus' great apostle so clearly understood, 'There is no longer Jew or Greek, there is no longer slave or free, there is no longer male and female; for all of you are one in Christ Jesus' (Gal. 3.28).

---

25. Nor, I might add, does Jesus' vision align itself with the viewpoint of certain modern church theorists who have unwittingly promoted the ethnic and cultural balkanization of the church through the appropriation of unbiblical ideas such as the homogeneous church growth principle.

BIBLIOGRAPHY

Aasgaard, R.
    2004   *My Beloved Brothers and Sisters: Christian Siblingship in Paul. Early Christianity in Context* (JSNTSup, 265; London/New York: T. & T. Clark).

Abel, F.-M.
    1946   'La fête de la Hanoucca', *RB* 53.4: 540-46.
    1949   *Les livres des Maccabées* (Paris: J. Gabalda).

Adler, W.
    1998   'Review: A Commentary on Pseudo-Philo's Liber antiquitatum biblicarum. With Latin text and English translation', *CBQ* 60.1: 160-61.

Ådna, J.
    1993   *Jesu Kritik am Tempel. Eine Untersuchung zum Verlauf und Sinn der sogenannten Tempelreinigung Jesu, Markus 11, 15-17 und Parallelen* (Oslo: Norwegian Lutheran School of Theology).
    1999   'Jesus' Symbolic Action in the Temple (Mark 11:15-17). The Replacement of the Sacrificial Cult by his Atoning Death', in B. Ego, A. Lange and P. Pilhofer (eds.), *Gemeinde ohne Tempel. Zur Substituierung und Transformation des jerusalemer Tempels und seines Kults im Alten Testament, antiken Judentum und frühen Christentum* (Tübingen: J.C.B. Mohr), pp. 461-73.
    2000   *Jesus Stellung zum Tempel. Die Tempelaktion und das Tempelwort als Ausdruck seiner messianischen Sendung* (WUNT, 2.119; Tübingen: J.C.B. Mohr).

Aguilar, M.I.
    2000   'Rethinking the Judean Past: Questions of History and a Social Archaeology of Memory in the First Book of the Maccabees', *BTB* 30.2: 58-67.

Albright, W.F., and C.S. Mann
    1971   *Matthew* (AB, 26; Garden City, NY: Doubleday).

Alexander, P.S.
    1997   'Jerusalem as the Omphalos of the World: On the History of a Geographical Concept', *Judaism* 46: 147-58.

Allison, D.C.
    1989   'Who Will Come from East and West? Observations on Matt 8:11-12–Luke 13:28-29', *Irish Biblical Studies* 11: 158-70.
    1999   *The Sermon on the Mount: Inspiring the Moral Imagination* (New York: Crossroad).

Alon, G.
    1977   *Jews, Judaism, and the Classical World* (Jerusalem: Magnes Press).

Alter, R.
    1981   *The Art of Biblical Narrative* (New York: Basic Books).

Anderson, H.
  1976   *The Gospel of Mark* (NCB; London: Oliphants).
  1985   '3 Maccabees (First Century B.C.): A New Translation and Introduction', in *OTP* (ed. J.H. Charlesworth; New York: Doubleday), pp. 509-29.
  1985b   '4 Maccabees (First Century A.D.): A New Translation and Introduction', in *OTP* (ed. J.H. Charlesworth; New York: Doubleday), pp. 531-64.

Anderson, R.T.
  1992   'Samaritans', in *ABD* (ed. D.N. Freedman; New York: Doubleday), V, pp. 940-47.

Arlandson, J.
  1997   *Women, Class, and Society in Early Christianity: Models from Luke–Acts* (Peabody, MA: Hendrickson).

Aune, D.E.
  1987   *The New Testament in its Literary Environment* (Philadelphia: Westminster Press).
  1988   *Greco-Roman Literature and the New Testament: Selected Forms and Genres* (SBLSBS, 21; Atlanta: Scholars Press).

Aymer, M.P.
  2006   Review of *Conflict and Identity in Romans: The Social Setting of Paul's Letter* (by Philip F. Esler [Minneapolis: Fortress Press, 2003]). *Review of Biblical Literature* (ed. J.G.van der Watt; Atlanta: SBL), pp. 483-88.

Bacchiocchi, S.
  1977   *From Sabbath to Sunday: A Historical Investigation of the Rise of Sunday Observance in Early Christianity* (Rome: Pontifical Gregorian University Press).

Bach, K., and L.J. Harnish
  1979   *Linguistic Communication and Speech Acts* (Cambridge, MA: MIT Press).

Bailey, J.L.
  1993   'Sermon on the Mount: Model for Community', *Concordia Theological Monthly* 20: 85-94.

Bailey, K.E.
  1980   *Through Peasant Eyes* (Grand Rapids: Eerdmans).

Banks, R.
  1975   *Jesus and the Law in the Synoptic Tradition* (SNTSMS, 28; Cambridge: Cambridge University Press).

Bar-Kochva, B.
  1989   *Judas Maccabaeus: The Jewish Struggle against the Seleucids* (Cambridge: Cambridge University Press).

Barrett, C.K.
  1978   *The Gospel according to St John* (Philadelphia: Westminster Press).

Bartchy, S.S.
  1992   'Table Fellowship', in *DJG* (ed. J.B. Green and S. McKnight; Downers Grove, IL: InterVarsity Press), pp. 796-800.

Bartlett, R.
  1994   *The Making of Europe* (Harmondsworth: Penguin Books).

Barton, S.C.
  1994   *Discipleship and Family Ties in Mark and Matthew* (SNTSMS, 80; Cambridge: Cambridge University Press).

Baslez, M.-F.
  2004   'Polémologie et histoire dans le Livre de Judith', *RB* 111.3: 362-76.

Bauckham, R.
- 1988 'Jesus' Demonstration in the Temple', in B. Lindars (ed.), *Law and Religion: Essays on the Place of the Law in Israel and Early Christianity* (Cambridge: James Clarke), pp. 72-89.
- 1998a *The Gospels for All Christians: Rethinking the Gospel Audiences* (Grand Rapids: Eerdmans).
- 1998b 'Introduction', in R. Bauckham (ed.), *The Gospels for All Christians: Rethinking the Gospel Audiences* (Grand Rapids: Eerdmans), pp. 1-48.
- 1999 *God Crucified: Monotheism and Christology in the New Testament* (Grand Rapids: Eerdmans).
- 2006 *Jesus and the Eyewitnesses: The Gospels as Eyewitness Testimony* (Grand Rapids: Eerdmans).

Baumann, G.
- 1999 *The Multicultural Riddle: Rethinking National, Ethnic, and Religious Identities* (New York: Routledge).

Baumgarten, J.
- 1992 'A New Qumran Substitute for the Divine Name and Mishnah Sukkah 4.5', *JQR* 83.1-2: 1-5.

Beasley-Murray, G.R.
- 1999 *John* (Word Biblical Commentary, 36; Waco, TX: Word Books).

Becker, A.H., and A.Y. Reed
- 2003 *The Ways That Never Parted: Jews and Christians in Late Antiquity and the Early Middle Ages* (Tübingen: Mohr Siebeck).

Becker, J.
- 1998 *Jesus of Nazareth* (Berlin: W. de Gruyter).

Beckwith, R.T.
- 1996 *Calendar and Chronology, Jewish and Christian: Biblical, Intertestamental and Patristic Studies* (Leiden: E.J. Brill).
- 1997 'The Temple Scroll and its Calendars. Their Character and Purpose', *RevQ* 69: 3-19.

Begg, C.T.
- 1996 'Samuel's Anointing of David in Josephus and Pseudo-Philo', *Rivista di storia e letteratura religiosa* 32.3: 491-529.
- 1997a 'The Massacre of the Priests of Nob in Josephus and Pseudo-Philo', *Estudios bíblicos* 55.2: 171-98.
- 1997b 'The Ceremonies at Gilgal/Ebal according to Pseudo-Philo: LAB 21,7-10', *EphTheolLov* 73.1: 72-83.
- 2000 'The Retellings of the Story of Judges 19 by Pseudo-Philo and Josephus: A Comparison', *Estudios bíblicos* 58.1: 33-49.

Berger, K.
- 1972 *Die Gesetzesauslegung Jesu. Ihr historischer Hintergrund im Judentum und im Alten Testament. I. Markus und Parellelen* (WMANT, 40; Neukirchen–Vluyn: Neukirchener Verlag).

Bergler, S.
- 1998 'Jesus, Bar Kochba und das messianische Laubhüttenfest', *JSJ* 29.2: 143-91.

Betz, H.D.
- 1995 *The Sermon on the Mount* (Hermeneia; Minneapolis: Fortress Press).
- 1997 'Jesus and the Purity of the Temple (Mark 11:15-18): A Comparative Religion Approach', *JBL* 116.3: 455-72.

Bickerman, E.J.
  1933 'Ein jüdischer Festbrief vom Jahre 124 v. Chr. (II Macc. 1.1-9)', *ZNW* 32: 233-54.
  1937/1979 *The God of the Maccabees* (Leiden: E.J. Brill).
  1944 'The Colophon of the Greek Book of Esther', *JBL* 63.3: 339-62.
  1945 'The Date of Fourth Maccabees', in S. Goldman and B. Cohen (eds.), *Louis Ginzberg Jubilee Volume* (New York: The American Academy for Jewish Research), pp. 105-12.
  1976 *Studies in Jewish and Christian History* (Arbeiten zur Geschichte des antiken Judentums und des Urchristentums, 9; Leiden: E.J. Brill).

Bird, M.F.
  2005 'When the Dust Finally Settles: Coming to a Post-New New Perspective', *Criswell Theological Review* 2.2: 57-69.

Blomberg, C.L.
  1987 *The Historical Reliability of the Gospels* (Downers Grove, IL: InterVarsity Press).
  1990 *Interpreting the Parables* (Downers Grove, IL: InterVarsity Press).
  1992 *Matthew* (New American Commentary; Nashville: Broadman).
  1999 'The Wright Stuff', in C.C. Newman (ed.), *Jesus and the Restoration of Israel: A Critical Assessment of N.T. Wright's* Jesus and the Victory of God (Downers Grove, IL: InterVarsity Press), pp. 18-39.
  2001 *The Historical Reliability of John's Gospel: Issues and Commentary* (Downers Grove, IL: InterVarsity Press).
  2004 'The Most Often Abused Verses in the Sermon on the Mount', *Southwestern Journal of Theology* 46.3: 1-17.
  2005 *Contagious Holiness: Jesus' Meals with Sinners* (New Studies in Biblical Theology, 19; Downers Grove, IL: InterVarsity Press).

Bock, D.L.
  1994 *Luke* (Baker Exegetical Commentary on the New Testament, 1; Grand Rapids: Baker Book House).
  1996 *Luke* (Baker Exegetical Commentary on the New Testament, 2; Grand Rapids: Baker Book House).

Bockmuehl, M.
  2001 '1QS and Salvation at Qumran', in D.A. Carson, P.T. O'Brien and M.A. Seifrid (eds.), *Justification and Variegated Nomism. I. The Complexities of Second Temple Judaism* (Grand Rapids: Baker Academic), pp. 381-414.

Bohak, G.
  1999 'Theopolis: A Single-Temple Policy and its Singular Ramifications', *JJS* 50.1: 3-16.

Bonneau, N.R.
  1973 'The Woman at the Well: John 4 and Genesis 24', *The Bible Today* 67: 1252-59.

Booth, R.P.
  1986 *Jesus and the Laws of Purity: Tradition History and Legal History in Mark 7* (JSNTSup, 13; Sheffield: JSOT Press).

Borg, M.J., and N.T. Wright.
  2000 *The Meaning of Jesus* (San Francisco: HarperSanFrancisco).

Boring, M.E., K. Berger and C. Colpe
    1995   *Hellenistic Commentary to the New Testament* (Nashville: Abingdon Press).

Botha, J.E.
    1991   *Jesus and the Samaritan Woman: A Speech Act Reading of John 4:1-42* (NovTSup, 65; Leiden: E.J. Brill).

Bovon, F.
    1991   *L'évangile selon Saint Luc 1–9* (Geneva: Labor et Fides).

Boyarin, D.
    2004   *Border Lines: The Partition of Judaeo-Christianity* (Philadelphia: University of Pennsylvania Press).

Brass, P.R.
    1991   *Ethnicity and Nationalism* (London: Sage Publications).

Braun, W.
    1995   *Feasting and Social Rhetoric in Luke 14* (SNTSMS, 85; Cambridge: Cambridge University Press).

Brett, M.G.
    1996   *Ethnicity and the Bible* (Biblical Interpretation Series, 19; Leiden: E.J. Brill).

Bringmann, K.
    1983   *Hellenistische Reform und Religionsverfolgung in Judäa* (Abhandlungen der Akademie der Wissenschaften in Göttingen, Philologisch-Historische Klasse 3.132; Göttingen: Vandenhoeck & Ruprecht).

Brown, R.
    1979   *The Community of the Beloved Disciple* (New York: Paulist Press).

Brown, R.E.
    1966   *The Gospel according to John*, I (New York: Doubleday).

Buchanan, G.W.
    1991   'Symbolic Money-Changers in the Temple?', *NTS* 37.2: 280-90.

Buell, D.K.
    2002   'Race and Universalism in Early Christianity', *Journal of Early Christian Studies* 10.4: 429-68.
    2005   *Why This New Race: Ethnic Reasoning in Early Christianity* (New York: Columbia University Press).

Buell, D.K., and C.J. Hodge
    2004   'The Politics of Interpretation: The Rhetoric of Race and Ethnicity in Paul', *JBL* 123.2: 235-52.

Bultmann, R.
    1926   'The New Approach to the Synoptic Problem', *JR* 6.4: 337-62.
    1963   *The History of the Synoptic Tradition* (Oxford: Blackwell).

Burke, T.J.
    2003   *Family Matters: A Socio-Historical Study of Kinship Metaphors in 1 Thessalonians* (JSNTSup, 247; London: T. & T. Clark).

Burkett, D.R.
    1999   *The Son of Man Debate* (SNSTMS, 107; Cambridge: Cambridge University Press).

Burridge, R.A.
    1992   *What Are the Gospels? A Comparison with Graeco-Roman Biography* (SNTSMS, 70; Cambridge: Cambridge University Press).

>   1998   'Gospel Genre and Audiences', in R. Bauckham (ed.), *The Gospels for All Christians: Rethinking the Gospel Audiences* (Grand Rapids: Eerdmans), pp. 113-45.

Cahill, L.S.
>   1987   'The Ethical Implications of the Sermon on the Mount', *Interpretation* 41.2: 144-56.

Carmichael, C.M.
>   1980   'Marriage and the Samaritan Woman', *NTS* 26: 332-46.

Carson, D.A.
>   1982   *From Sabbath to Lord's Day: A Biblical, Historical and Theological Investigation* (Grand Rapids: Zondervan).
>   1991   *The Gospel according to John* (Grand Rapids: Eerdmans).

Carson, D.A., and P.T. O'Brien (eds.)
>   2001   *Justification and Variegated Nomism: The Complexities of Second Temple Judaism* (WUNT, 2.140; Tübingen: J.C.B. Mohr).

Carter, Warren
>   1994   *What are they Saying about Matthew's Sermon on the Mount?* (New York: Paulist Press).

Casey, M.
>   1991   *From Jewish Prophet to Gentile God: The Origins and Development of New Testament Christology* (Louisville, KY: Westminster/John Knox Press).
>   1997   'Culture and Historicity: The Cleansing of the Temple', *CBQ* 59.2: 306-32.
>   1998   *Aramaic Sources of Mark's Gospel* (SNTSMS, 102; Cambridge: Cambridge University Press).

Catchpole, D.R.
>   1977   'Tradition History', in I.H. Marshall (ed.), *New Testament Interpretation: Essays on Principles and Methods* (Exeter: Paternoster Press), pp. 165-80.
>   2006   *Jesus People: The Historical Jesus and the Beginnings of Community* (Grand Rapids: Baker).

Champlin, E.
>   2003   *Nero* (Cambridge, MA: Harvard University Press).

Charlesworth, J.H.
>   1988   *Jesus within Judaism: New Light from Exciting Archaeological Discoveries* (New York: Doubleday).
>   1992   'The Dead Sea Scrolls and the Historical Jesus', in J.H. Charlesworth (ed.), *Jesus and the Dead Sea Scrolls* (New York: Doubleday), pp. 1-74.

Chilton, B.D.
>   1994   *A Feast of Meanings: Eucharistic Theologies from Jesus through Johannine Circles* (Leiden: E.J. Brill).
>   1996   *Pure Kingdom: Jesus' Vision of God* (Studies in the Historical Jesus; Grand Rapids: Eerdmans).
>   2000   *Rabbi Jesus: An Intimate Biography* (New York: Doubleday).
>   2003   'Jesus, Levitical Purity, and the Development of Primitive Christianity', in R. Rendtorff and R.A. Kugler (ed.), *The Book of Leviticus* (Leiden: E.J. Brill), pp. 358-82.

Coggins, R.J.
    1975   *Samaritans and Jews: The Origins of Samaritanism Reconsidered* (Atlanta: John Knox Press).

Cohen, S.J.D.
    1979   *Josephus in Galilee and Rome: His Vita and Development as a Historian* (Leiden: E.J. Brill).
    1999   *The Beginnings of Jewishness. Boundaries, Varieties, Uncertainties* (Berkeley: University of California Press).

Collins, J.J.
    1992   'Essenes', in *ABD* (ed. D.N. Freedman; New York: Doubleday), II, pp. 619-26.
    2000   *Between Athens and Jerusalem: Jewish Identity in the Hellenistic Diaspora* (Grand Rapids: Eerdmans).

Coloe, M.
    1999   'Like Father, like Son: The Role of Abraham in Tabernacles: John 8:31-59', *Pacifica* 12: 1-11.

Connor, W.
    1994   *Ethno-Nationalism: The Quest for Understanding* (Princeton, NJ: Princeton University Press).

Corley, K.
    1993   *Private Women, Public Meals: Social Conflict in the Synoptic Tradition* (Peabody, MA: Hendrickson).
    1997   'Wisdom's Rescue: A New Reading of the Tabernacles Discourse (John 7:1–8:59)', *JBL* 116.1: 95-116.

Cowley, A.E.
    1913   'The Book of Judith', in R.H. Charles (ed.), *The Apocrypha and Pseudepigrapha of the Old Testament in English* (Oxford: Oxford University Press), pp. 242-67.

Cranfield, C.E.B.
    1959   *The Gospel according to Saint Mark* (Cambridge Greek Testament Commentary; Cambridge: Cambridge University Press).
    1991   '"The Works of the Law" in the Epistle to the Romans', *JSNT* 43: 89-101.

Craven, T.
    1983   *Artistry and Faith in the Book of Judith* (SBLDS, 70; Chico, CA: Scholars Press).
    2003   'The Book of Judith in the Context of Twentieth-Century Studies of the Apocryphal/Deuterocanonical Books', *Currents in Biblical Research* 1.2: 187-229.

Cresswell, T.
    1996   *In Place, out of Place: Geography, Ideology, and Transgression* (Minneapolis: University of Minnesota Press).

Cross, F.M., and D.W. Perry
    1997   'A Preliminary Edition of a Fragment of 4QSam^b [4Q52]', *BASOR* 306: 63-74.

Crossan, J.D.
    1973   'Mark and the Relatives of Jesus', *NovT* 15.2: 81-113.
    1983   *In Fragments: The Aphorisms of Jesus* (San Francisco: Harper & Row).
    1991   *The Historical Jesus. The Life of a Mediterranean Jewish Peasant* (San Francisco: Harper).

Crossan, J.D., and J.L. Reed
    2001   *Excavating Jesus: Beneath the Stones, behind the Text* (San Francisco: Harper).

Crossley, J.G.
    2003   'Halakah and Mark 7:4: "…and beds"', *JSNT* 25.4: 433-47.
    2004   *The Date of Mark's Gospel: Insights from the Law in Earliest Christianity* (JSNTSup, 266; London: T. & T. Clark).

Crown, A.D.
    1984   *A Bibliography of the Samaritans* (ATLA Bibliography Series, 10; Metuchen: American Theological Library Assocation and Scarecrow Press).
    1989   *The Samaritans* (Tübingen: J.C.B. Mohr).

Cullmann, O.
    1961   'Out of Season Remarks on the "Historical Jesus" of the Bultmann School', *Union Seminary Quarterly Review* 16.2: 131-48.

Culpepper, R.A.
    1983   *Anatomy of the Fourth Gospel: A Study in Literary Design* (Foundations and Facets; Philadelphia: Fortress Press).

Cummins, S.A.
    2001   *Paul and the Crucified Christ in Antioch* (SNTSMS, 114; Cambridge: Cambridge University Press).

Dahl, N.A.
    1976   'The Early Church and Jesus', in N.A. Dahl (ed.), *Jesus in the Memory of the Early Church* (Minneapolis: Fortress Press), pp. 167-75.

Daise, M.A.
    2005   '"The Days of Sukkot of the Month of Kislev": The Festival of Dedication and the Delay of Feasts in 1QS 1:13-15', in G. Boccaccini (ed.), *Enoch and Qumran Origins: New Light on a Forgotten Connection* (Grand Rapids: Eerdmans), pp. 119-28.

Daube, D.
    1950   'Jesus and the Samaritan Woman: The Meaning of *sygchraomai*', *JBL* 69.2: 137-47.
    1972/73   'Responsibilities of Master and Disciples in the Gospels', *NTS* 19: 1-15.

Davies, P.R.
    1983   'Calendrical Change and Qumran Origins: An Assessment of VanderKam's Theory', *CBQ* 45.1: 80-89.
    2001   'Didactic Stories', in D.A. Carson, P.T. O'Brien and M.A. Seifrid (eds.), *Justification and Variegated Nomism*. I. *The Complexities of Second Temple Judaism* (Grand Rapids: Baker Academic), pp. 99-133.

Davies, W.D.
    1974   *The Gospel and the Land: Early Christianity and Jewish Territorial Doctrine* (Berekley and Los Angeles: University of California Press).

Davies, W.D., and D.C. Allison, Jr
    1991   *The Gospel according to Saint Matthew*, II (ICC; Edinburgh: T. & T. Clark).

Deines, R.
    1993   *Jüdische Steingefässe und pharisäische Frömmigkeit: Ein archäologisch-historischer Beitrag zum Verständnis von Joh 2,6 und der jüdischen Reinheitshalacha zur Zeit Jesu* (WUNT, 2.52; Tübingen: Mohr Siebeck).

1997   *Die Pharisäer: Ihr Verständnis im Spiegel der christlichen und jüdischen Forschung seit Wellhausen und Graetz* (WUNT, 101; Tübingen: Mohr Siebeck).
2001   'The Pharisees between "Judaisms" and "Common Judaism"', in D.A. Carson, P.T. O'Brien and M.A. Seifrid (eds.), *Justification and Variegated Nomism*. I. *The Complexities of Second Temple Judaism* (Grand Rapids: Baker Academic), pp. 443-504.

Denzey, N.
2002   'The Limits of Ethnic Categories', in A.J. Blasi, J. Duhaime and P.-A. Turcotte (eds.), *Handbook of Early Christianity: Social Science Approaches* (Walnut Creek, CA: Altamira Press), pp. 489-507.

Derouchie, J.S.
2004   'Circumcision in the Hebrew Bible and Targums: Theology, Rhetoric, and the Handling of Metaphor', *BBR* 14.2: 175-203.

Derrett, J.D.M.
1977   'Judaica in St Mark', in J.D.M. Derrett (ed.), *Studies in the New Testament*. I. *Glimpses of the Legal and Social Presuppositions of the Authors* (Leiden: E.J. Brill), pp. 85-100.

DesCamp, M.T.
1997   'Why Are These Women Here? An Examination of the Sociological Setting of Pseudo-Philo through Comparative Reading', *JSP* 16: 53-80.

deSilva, D.A.
2002   *Introduction to the Apocrypha* (Grand Rapids: Baker Book House).
2004   'Embodying the Word: Social-Scientific Interpretation of the New Testament', in S. McKnight and G.R. Osborne (eds.), *The Face of New Testament Studies* (Grand Rapids: Baker Academic), pp. 118-29.
2006   'Judith the Heroine? Lies, Seduction, and Murder in Cultural Perspective', *BTB* 36.2: 55-61.

Dexinger, F.
1981   'Limits of Tolerance in Judaism: The Samaritan Example', in E.P. Sanders (ed.), *Jewish and Christian Self-Definition* (Philadelphia: Fortress Press), pp. 88-114.

Dimante, D.
1995   'The Qumran Manuscripts: Contents and Significance', in D. Dimant and L.H. Schiffman (eds.), *Time to Prepare the Way in the Wilderness: Papers on the Qumran Scrolls by Fellows of the Institute for Advanced Studies of the Hebrew University, Jerusalem, 1989–1990* (Leiden: E.J. Brill), pp. 23-58.

Doering, L.
1999   *Schabbat: Sabbathalacha und -praxis im antiken Judentum und Urchristentum* (TSAJ, 78; Tübingen: Mohr Siebeck).

Donaldson, T.L.
1989   'Zealot and Convert: The Origin of Paul's Christ–Torah Antithesis', *CBQ* 51.4: 655-82.

Doran, R.
1981   *Temple Propoganda: The Purpose and Character of 2 Maccabees* (CBQMS, 12; Washington: Catholic Biblical Association of America).
1999   'Independence or Co-Existence: The Responses of 1 and 2 Maccabees to Seleucid Hegemony', *SBLSP* 38: 94-103.

Douglas, M.
    1966   *Purity and Danger: An Analysis of Concepts of Pollution and Taboo* (London: Routledge & Kegan Paul).
    1975   'Deciphering a Meal', in M. Douglas (ed.), *Implicit Meanings: Essays in Anthropology* (London and Boston: Routledge & Kegan Paul).

Downing, G.F.
    1992   *Cynics and Christian Origins* (Edinburgh: T. & T. Clark).

Draper, J.A., and G.O. West
    1989   'Anglicans and Scripture in South Africa', in F. England and T.J.M. Paterson (eds.), *Bounty in Bondage* (Johannesburg: Raven).

Duling, D.C.
    2003   '"Whatever Gain I Had…": Ethnicity and Paul's Self-Identification in Phil. 3:5-6', in D.B. Gowler, G. Bloomquist and D.F. Watson (eds.), *Fabrics of Discourse. Essays in Honor of Vernon K. Robbins* (Harrisburg, PA: Trinity Press International), pp. 222-41.
    2005   'Ethnicity, Ethnocentrism, and the Matthean *Ethnos*', *BTB* 35.4: 125-43.

Dunn, J.D.G.
    1983   'The Incident at Antioch (Gal. 2:11-18)', *JSNT* 18: 3-75.
    1983b   'The New Perspective on Paul', *BJRL* 65.2: 95-102.
    1988a   *Romans 1–8* (Word Biblical Commentary, 38a; Waco, TX: Word Books).
    1988b   *Romans 9–16* (Word Biblical Commentary, 38b; Waco, TX: Word Books).
    1988c   'Pharisees, Sinners and Jesus', in P. Borgen and J. Neusner (eds.), *The Social World of Formative Christianity and Judaism* (Philadelphia: Fortress Press), pp. 264-89.
    1990   *Jesus, Paul, and the Law: Studies in Mark and Galatians* (Louisville, KY: Westminster/John Knox Press).
    1991   *The Partings of the Ways between Christianity and Judaism and their Significance for the Character of Christianity* (Philadelphia: Trinity Press International).
    1992a   'Jesus, Table Fellowship, and Qumran', in J.H. Charlesworth (ed.), *Jesus and the Dead Sea Scrolls* (New York: Doubleday), pp. 254-72.
    1992b   'Yet Once More—"The Works of the Law": A Response', *JSNT* 46: 99-117.
    2000   '"Are You the Messiah?" Is the Crux of Mark 14:61-62 Resolvable?', in D.G. Horrell and C.M. Tuckett (eds.), *Christology and Community: New Testament Essays in Honour of David R. Catchpole* (Leiden: E.J. Brill), pp. 1-22.
    2002   'Jesus and Purity: An Ongoing Debate', *NTS* 48.4: 449-67.
    2003   *Jesus Remembered* (Grand Rapids: Eerdmans).
    2005   *The New Perspective on Paul: Collected Essays* (WUNT, 185; Tübingen: Mohr Siebeck).
    2005b   *A New Perspective on Jesus: What the Quest for the Historical Jesus Missed* (Grand Rapids: Baker).

Duran, N.
    2005   'Having Men for Dinner: Deadly Banquets and Biblical Women', *BTB* 35.4: 117-24.

Edwards, J.R.
    2002   *The Gospel according to Mark* (Grand Rapids: Eerdmans).

Eisenbaum, P.
    2005   'Paul, Polemics, and the Problem of Essentialism', *BibInt* 13.3: 224-38.
Eller, J., and R. Coughlan
    1993   'The Poverty of Primordialism: The Demystification of Ethnic Attachments', *Racial Studies* 16.2: 183-202.
Eller, J.D.
    1999   *From Culture to Ethnicity to Conflict: An Anthropological Perspective on International Ethnic Conflict* (Ann Arbor, MI: University of Michigan Press).
Elliott, J.H.
    1993   *What Is Social-Scientific Criticism? Guides to Biblical Scholarship* (Minneapolis: Fortress Press).
    2002   'Jesus Was Not an Egalitarian. A Critique of an Anachronistic and Idealist Theory', *BTB* 32.2: 75-91.
Elliott, M.A.
    2000   *The Survivors of Israel* (Grand Rapids: Eerdmans).
Elliott, N.
    2005   'An American "Myth of Innnocence" and Contemporary Pauline Studies', *BibInt* 13.3: 239-49.
Endres, J.C.
    1987   *Biblical Interpretation in the Book of Jubilees* (CBQMS, 18; Washington, DC: Catholic Biblical Association of America).
Engle, A.
    1977   'An Amphorisk of the Second Temple Period', *PEQ* 109: 117-22.
Enloe, C.
    1980   'Religion and Ethnicity', in P. Sugar (ed.), *Ethnic Diversity and Conflict in Eastern Europe* (Santa Barbara: ABC-Clio), pp. 347-71.
Ensor, P.W.
    1996   *Jesus and his 'Works': The Johannine Sayings in Historical Perspective* (WUNT, 2.85; Tübingen: Mohr Siebeck).
Eppstein, V.
    1964   'The Historicity of the Cleansing of the Temple', *ZNW* 55: 42-58.
Eriksen, T.H.
    1993   *Ethnicity and Nationalism: Anthropological Perspectives* (London: Pluto Press).
Eshel, H.
    2005   '4Q390, the 490-Year Prophecy, and the Calendrical History of the Second Temple Period', in G. Boccaccini (ed.), *Enoch and Qumran Origins: New Light on a Forgotten Connection* (Grand Rapids: Eerdmans), pp. 102-10.
Esler, P.F.
    1987   *Community and Gospel in Luke–Acts* (SNTSMS, 57; Cambridge: Cambridge University Press).
    2003   *Conflict and Identity in Romans: The Social Setting of Paul's Letter* (Minneapolis: Fortress Press).
    2006   'Paul's Contestation of Israel's (Ethnic) Memory of Abraham in Galatians 3', *BTB* 36.1: 23-34.
Eslinger, L.
    1993   'The Wooing of the Woman at the Well: Jesus, the Reader, and Reader-

Response Criticism', in M.W.G. Stibbe (ed.), *The Gospel of John as Literature* (Leiden: E.J. Brill), pp. 165-82.

Evans, C.A.
  1989a 'Jesus' Action in the Temple and Evidence of Corruption in the First Century Temple', *SBLSP* 28: 522-39.
  1989b 'Jesus' Action in the Temple: Cleansing or Portent of Destruction?', *CBQ* 51.2: 237-70.
  1992 'Opposition to the Temple: Jesus and the Dead Sea Scrolls', in J.H. Charlesworth (ed.), *Jesus and the Dead Sea Scrolls* (New York: Doubleday), pp. 235-53.
  1993 'Jesus and the "Cave of Robbers": Toward a Jewish Context for the Temple Action', *BBR* 3: 93-110.
  1995 'Jesus and Predictions of the Destruction of the Herodian Temple', in C.A. Evans (ed.), *Jesus and his Contemporaries: Comparative Studies* (Leiden: E.J. Brill), pp. 367-80.
  2001 *Mark 8:27–16:20* (Word Biblical Commentary, 34b; Nashville: Thomas Nelson).
  2001b 'Scripture-Based Stories in the Pseudepigrapha', in D.A. Carson, P.T. O'Brien and M.A. Seifrid (eds.), *Justification and Variegated Nomism.* I. *The Complexities of Second Temple Judaism* (Grand Rapids: Baker Academic), pp. 57-72.

Evans, C.S.
  1999 'Methodological Naturalism in Historical Biblical Scholarship', in C.C. Newman (ed.), *Jesus and the Restoration of Israel: A Critical Assessment of N.T. Wright's Jesus and the Victory of God* (Downers Grove, IL: InterVarsity Press), pp. 180-205.

Falk, D.
  2001 'Prayers and Psalms', in D.A. Carson, P.T. O'Brien and M.A. Seifrid (ed.), *Justification and Variegated Nomism.* I. *The Complexities of Second Temple Judaism* (Grand Rapids: Baker Academic), pp. 7-56.

Feeley-Harnik, G.
  1981 *The Lord's Table: Eucharist and Passover in Early Christianity* (Philadelphia: University of Pennsylvania Press).

Feldman, L.H.
  1993 *Jew and Gentile in the Ancient World: Attitudes and Interactions from Alexander to Justinian* (Princeton, NJ: Princeton University Press).
  2001 'The Destruction of Sodom and Gomorrah according to Philo, Pseudo-Philo, and Josephus', *Henoch* 23.2-3: 185-19.
  2002a 'The Portrayal of Phinehas by Philo, Pseudo-Philo, and Josephus', *JQR* 92.3-4: 315-45.
  2002b 'The Plague of the First-born Egyptians in Rabbinic Tradition, Philo, Pseudo-Philo, and Josephus', *RB* 109.3: 403-21.
  2003a 'The Command, according to Philo, Pseudo-Philo, and Josephus, to Annihilate the Seven Nations of Canaan', *Andrews University Seminary Studies* 41.1: 13-29.
  2003b 'Questions about the Great Flood, as Viewed by Philo, Pseudo-Philo, Josephus, and the Rabbis', *ZAW* 115.3: 401-22.

Fewell, D.N., and G.A. Phillips
  1997 'Drawn to Excess, or Reading Beyond Betrothal', *Semeia* 77: 23-58.

Fischer, M.
    1986   'Ethnicity and the Post-Modern Arts of Memory', in J. Clifford and G. Marcus (eds.), *Writing Culture: The Poetics and Politics of Ethnography* (Berkeley: University of California Press), pp. 194-233.

Fischer, T.
    1990   'Hasmoneans and Seleucids: Aspects of War and Policy in the Second and First Centuries B.C.E.', in A. Kasher (ed.), *Greece and Rome in Eretz Israel: Collected Essays* (Jerusalem: Palestinian Exploration Society), pp. 3-19.

Fischer, T., and H. Anderson
    1992   'Maccabees, Books of', in *ABD* (ed. D.N. Freedman; New York: Doubleday), IV, pp. 439-54.

Fishman, J.
    1980   'Social Theory and Ethnography', in P. Sugar (ed.), *Ethnic Diversity and Conflict in Eastern Europe* (Santa Barbara: ABC-Clio), pp. 84-97.

Fisk, B.N.
    2001   *Do You Not Remember? Scripture, Story and Exegesis in the Rewritten Bible of Pseudo-Philo* (JSPSup, 37; Sheffield: Sheffield Academic Press).

Fitzmyer, J.A.
    1981   *The Gospel according to Luke* (AB, 28; New York: Doubleday).

France, R.T.
    2002   *The Gospel of Mark* (The New International Greek Text Commentary; Grand Rapids: Eerdmans).

Francis, M.
    1988   'The Samaritan Woman', *Asia Journal of Theology* 2: 117-48.

Freyne, S.
    2004   *Jesus, a Jewish Galilean: A New Reading of the Jesus Story* (London: T. & T. Clark).

Fredriksen, P.
    1999   *Jesus of Nazareth, King of the Jews: A Jewish Life and the Emergence of Christianity* (New York: Knopf).

Fuglseth, K.S.
    2005   *Johannine Sectarianism in Perspective: A Sociological, Historical, and Comparative Analysis of Temple and Social Relationships in the Gospel of John, Philo, and Qumran* (NovTSup, 119; Leiden: E.J. Brill).

Funk, R.W.
    1996   *Honest to Jesus: Jesus for a New Millennium* (San Francisco: Harper).

Funk, R.W., and R.W. Hoover
    1993   *The Five Gospels: The Search for the Authentic Words of Jesus* (New York: Macmillan).
    1998   *The Acts of Jesus* (San Francisco: HarperCollins).

Gafni, I.M.
    1989   'Josephus and 1 Maccabees', in L.H. Feldman and G. Hata (eds.), *Josephus, the Bible, and History* (Detroit: Wayne State University Press), pp. 116-31.

Gager, J.G.
    1974   'The Gospels and Jesus: Some Doubts about Method', *JR* 54: 244-72.
    1983   *The Origins of Anti-Semitism: Attitudes toward Judaism in Pagan and Christian Antiquity* (New York: Oxford University Press).

Gardner, A.E.
    1984   'The Relationships of the Additions to the Book of Esther to the Maccabean Crisis', *JSJ* 15: 1-8.

Garlington, D.B.
    2005   'The New Perspective on Paul: An Appraisal Two Decades Later', *Criswell Theological Review* 2.2: 17-38.

Gaston, L.
    1970   *No Stone on Another* (NovTSup, 23; Leiden: E.J. Brill).
    2005   'The Impact of the New Perspectives on Judaism and Improved Jewish–Christian Relations on the Study of Paul', *BibInt* 13.3: 250-54.

Gathercole, S.J.
    2002   *Where is Boasting? Early Jewish Soteriology and Paul's Response in Romans 1–5* (Grand Rapids: Eerdmans).

Geertz, C.
    1963   'The Integrative Revolution: Primordial Sentiments and Civil Politics in the New States', in C. Geertz (ed.), *Old Societies and New States* (New York: Free Press), pp. 105-57.
    1973   *Thick Description: Toward an Interpretive Theory of Culture* (New York: Basic Books).

Gehring, R.H.
    2004   *House Church and Mission* (Peabody, MA: Hendrikson).

Gerhardsson, B.
    1991   'Illuminating the Kingdom: Narrative Meshalim in the Synoptic Gospels', in H. Wansbrough (ed.), *Jesus and the Oral Gospel Tradition* (Sheffield: Sheffield Academic Press).

Giblin, C.H.
    1999   'What Was Everything He Told Her She Did?', *NTS* 45.1: 148-52.

Gnilka, J.
    1963.   'Matthäusgemeinde und Qumran', *BZ* 7: 63-43.
    1978.   *Das Evangelium nach Markus* (EKKNT, 1; Neukirchen–Vluyn: Neukirchener Verlag).
    1997.   *Jesus of Nazareth* (Peabody, MA: Hendrickson).

Goldenberg, R.
    1979   'The Jewish Sabbath in the Roman World up to the Time of Constantine the Great', in *ANRW* 19.1 (ed. H. Temporini and W. Haase; Berlin: W. de Gruyter), pp. 414-47.

Goldstein, J.
    1976   *1 Maccabees* (AB, 41; Garden City, NY: Doubleday).
    1983b   'The Date of the Book of Jubilees', in *Proceedings of the American Academy for Jewish Research* (Philadelphia: American Academy for Jewish Research), pp. 63-86.

Goldstein, J.A.
    1983a   *II Maccabees* (AB, 41a; Garden City, NY: Doubleday).

Grabbe, L.
    1992a   *Judaism from Cyrus to Hadrian*, I (Minneapolis: Fortress Press).
    1992b   *Judaism from Cyrus to Hadrian*, II (Minneapolis: Fortress Press).

Green, J.B.
    1997   *The Gospel of Luke* (New International Commentary on the New Testament; Grand Rapids: Eerdmans).

Grigsby, B.H.
 1986 '"If Any Man Thirsts...": Observations on the Rabbinic Background of John 7,37-39', *Bib* 67.1: 100-108.

Grosby, S.
 1994 'The Verdict of History: The Inexpungeable Tie of Primordality—A Response to Eller and Coughlan', *Ethnic and Racial Studies* 17.2: 164-71.

Gruen, E.S.
 1998 *Heritage and Hellenism: The Reinvention of Jewish Tradition* (Hellenistic Culture and Society, 30; Berkeley: University of California Press).
 2004 *Diaspora: Jews amidst Greeks and Romans* (Cambridge: Harvard University Press).
 2005 'Greeks and Jews: Mutual Misperceptions in Josephus' *Contra Apionem*', in C. Bakhos (ed.), *Ancient Judaism in its Hellenistic Context* (Leiden: E.J. Brill), pp. 31-51.

Guelich, R.A.
 1982 *The Sermon on the Mount: A Foundation for Understanding* (Dallas: Word Books).
 1989 *Mark 1–8:26* (Word Biblical Commentary, 34a; Dallas: Word Books).

Gundry, R.H.
 1985 'Grace, Works, and Staying Saved in Paul', *Bib* 66.1: 1-38.
 1993 *Mark: A Commentary on his Apology for the Cross* (Grand Rapids: Eerdmans).

Gundry-Volf, J.
 1995 'Spirit, Mercy, and the Other', *Theology Today* 51.4: 508-23.

Gurr, T.R., and B. Harff
 1994 *Ethnic Conflict in World Politics* (Boulder, CO: Westview Press).

Haas, P.
 1990 'The Maccabean Struggle to Define Judaism', in J. Neusner, P. Borgen, E.S. Frerichs and R. Horsley (eds.), *Religion, Literature, and Society in Ancient Israel, Formative Christianity and Judaism* (Atlanta: Scholars Press), pp. 49-65.

Haenchen, E.
 1984 *A Commentary on the Gospel of John: Chapters 1–6* (Hermeneia; Philadelphia: Fortress Press).

Hagner, D.A.
 1993. 'Paul and Judaism: The Jewish Matrix of Early Christianity: Issues in the Current Debate', *BBR* 3: 111-30.
 1995 *Matthew 14–28* (Word Biblical Commentary, 33b; Dallas: Word Books).

Hakola, R.
 2005 *Identity Matters: John, the Jews and Jewishness* (NovTSup, 118; Leiden: E.J. Brill).

Hall, E.T.
 1976 *Beyond Culture* (Garden City, NY: Doubleday).
 1983 *The Dance of Life: The Other Dimensions of Time* (Garden City, NY: Doubleday).

Hall, J.M.
 1997 *Ethnic Identity in Greek Antiquity* (Cambridge: Cambridge University Press).

Halpern-Amaru, B.
   1999   *The Empowerment of Women in the Book of Jubilees* (Leiden: E.J. Brill).
   2001   'Flavius Josephus and the Book of Jubilees: A Question of Source', *HUCA* 72: 15-44.
Hammerton-Kelly, R.
   1979   *God the Father: Theology and Patriarchy in the Teaching of Jesus* (Philadelphia: Fortress Press).
Hanson, K.C., and D.E. Oakman
   1998   *Palestine in the Time of Jesus: Social Structures and Social Conflicts* (Minneapolis: Fortress Press).
Hanson, P.D.
   1975   *The Dawn of Apocalyptic: The Historical and Sociological Roots of Jewish Apocalyptic Eschatology* (Philadelphia: Fortress Press).
Harland, P.A.
   2005   'Familial Dimensions of Group Identity: 'Brothers' (ἀδελφοί) in Associations of the Greek East', *JBL* 124.3: 491-513.
Harrington, D.J.
   1988   'A Decade of Research on Pseudo-Philo's Biblical Antiquities', *JSP* 2: 3-12.
Hartley, L.P.
   1953   *The Go-Between* (London: Hamish Hamilton).
Harvey, A.E.
   1982   *Jesus and the Constraints of History* (London: Gerald Duckworth).
Hayward, C.T.R.
   1996   *The Jewish Temple: A Non-Biblical Sourcebook* (London: Routledge).
Hayward, R.
   1987   *The Targum of Jeremiah* (The Aramaic Bible, 12; Wilmington, DE: Michael Glazier).
   1997   'Review of Jacobson, A Commentary on Pseudo-Philo's Liber antiquitatum biblicarum (1996)', *JJS* 38.2: 363-66.
Hellerman, J.H.
   2000a 'Challenging the Authority of Jesus: Mark 11:27-33 and Mediterranean Notions of Honor and Shame', *JETS* 34.2: 213-28.
   2000b 'Wealth and Sacrifice in Early Christianity: Revisiting Mark's Presentation of Jesus' Encounter with the Rich Young Ruler', *Trinity Journal* 21.2: 143-64.
   2001   *The Ancient Church as Family* (Minneapolis: Fortress Press).
   2005   *Reconstructing Honor: Carmen Christi as Cursus Pudorum* (SNTSMS, 132; Cambridge: Cambridge University Press).
Helyer, L.
   2002   *Exploring Jewish Literature of the Second Temple Period* (Downers Grove, IL: InterVarsity Press).
Hempel, C.
   2000   'The Place of the Book of Jubilees at Qumran and Beyond', in T.H. Lim (ed.), *The Dead Sea Scrolls in their Historical Context* (Edinburgh: T. & T. Clark), pp. 187-96.
Hengel, M.
   1974   *Judaism and Hellenism: Studies in their Encounter in Palestine during the Early Hellenistic Period*, I (Philadelphia: Fortress Press).

    1981   *The Charismatic Leader and his Followers* (New York: Crossroad).
    1983   *Between Jesus and Paul* (London: SCM Press).
Hengel, M., and R. Deines
    1995   'E.P. Sanders' "Common Judaism", Jesus and the Pharisees', *JTS* 46.1: 1-70.
Henten, J.W. van
    1995   'Judith as an Alternative Leader: A Rereading of Judith 7-13', in A. Brenner (ed.), *A Feminist Companion to Esther, Judith and Susanna* (Sheffield: Sheffield Academic Press), pp. 224-52.
    1997   *The Maccabean Martyrs as Saviours of the Jewish People: A Study of 2 & 4 Maccabees* (Supplements to the Journal for the Study of Judaism, 57; Leiden: E.J. Brill).
    1999   'The Ancestral Language of the Jews in 2 Maccabees', in W. Horbury (ed.), *Hebrew Study from Ezra to Ben-Yehuda* (Edinburgh: T & T Clark), pp. 53-68.
Hill, C.C.
    1992   *Hellenists and Hebrews: Reappraising Division within the Earliest Church* (Minneapolis: Fortress Press).
Himmelfarb, M.
    2005   'Jubilees and Sectarianism', in G. Boccaccini (ed.), *Enoch and Qumran Origins: New Light on a Forgotten Connection* (Grand Rapids: Eerdmans), pp. 129-31.
Hjelm, I.
    2000   *The Samaritans and Early Judaism* (JSOTSup, 303; Sheffield: Sheffield Academic Press).
Hoffmeier, J.K.
    1996   *Israel in Egypt: The Evidence for the Authenticity of the Exodus Tradition* (Oxford: Oxford University Press).
Holst, R.
    1976   'The Anointing of Jesus: Another Application of the Form-Critical Method', *JBL* 95.3: 435-46.
Holtzmann, H.
    1911   *Lehrbuch der neutestamentlichen Theologie*, I (Tübingen: J.C.B. Mohr).
Hooker, M.D.
    1991   *The Gospel according to Mark* (London: A. & C. Black).
    2000   'Creative Conflict: The Torah and Christology', in D.G. Horrell and C.M. Tuckett (eds.), *Christology and Community: New Testament Essays in Honour of David R. Catchpole* (Leiden: E.J. Brill), pp. 117-36.
Horowitz, D.
    1985   *Ethnic Groups in Conflict* (Berkeley: University of California Press).
Horrell, D.G.
    1999   'Social-Scientific Approaches to New Testament Interpretation. Retrospect and Prospect', in D.G. Horrell (ed.), *Social-Scientific Approaches to New Testament Interpretation* (Edinburgh: T. & T. Clark), pp. 1-27.
    2000   '"No Longer Jew or Greek" Paul's Corporate Christology and the Construction of Christian Community', in D.G. Horrell and C.M. Tuckett (ed.), *Christology and Community: New Testament Essays in Honour of David R. Catchpole* (Leiden: E.J. Brill), pp. 321-44.

Horsley, R.A.
    1989   *Sociology and the Jesus Movement* (New York: Crossroad).
    1998   'Submerged Biblical Histories and Imperial Biblical Studies', in *The Postcolonial Bible* (ed. R.S. Sugirtharajah; Sheffield: Sheffield Academic Press), pp. 152-73.

Horsley, R.A., and J.S. Hanson
    1985   *Bandits, Prophets, and Messiahs: Popular Movements at the Time of Jesus* (San Francisco: Harper & Row).

Houlden, J.L.
    1983   'A Response to James Dunn', *JSNT* 18: 58-67.

Houston, W.
    1993   *Purity and Monotheism: Clean and Unclean Animals in Biblical Literature* (JSOTSup, 140; Sheffield: Sheffield Academic Press).

Hübner, H.
    1973   *Das Gesetz in der synoptischen Tradition* (Witten: Luther).

Hurtado, L.
    2003   *Lord Jesus Christ: Devotion to Jesus in Earliest Christianity* (Grand Rapids: Eerdmans).

Hutchinson, J., and A.D. Smith
    1996   *Ethnicity* (Oxford: Oxford University Press).

Ilan, T.
    2002   *Lexicon of Jewish Names in Late Antiquity* (Tübingen: Mohr Siebeck).

Instone-Brewer, D.
    2004   *Traditions of the Rabbis from the Era of the New Testament: Prayer and Agriculture*, I (Grand Rapids: Eerdmans).

Jackson, R.H., and R. Henrie
    1983   'Perception of Sacred Space', *Journal of Cultural Geography* 3: 94-107.

Jacobson, A.D.
    1995   'Divided Families and Christian Origins', in R.A. Piper (ed.), *The Gospel behind the Gospels: Current Studies on 'Q'* (Leiden: E.J. Brill), pp. 361-80.

Jacobson, H.
    1996   *A Commentary on Pseudo-Philo's Liber antiquitatum biblicarum. With Latin text and English translation* (Leiden: E.J. Brill).

Jenkins, R.
    1997   *Rethinking Ethnicity* (London: Sage Publications).

Jeremias, J.
    1963   *The Parables of Jesus* (New York: Charles Scribner's Sons).
    1966   *The Eucharistic Words of Jesus* (London: SCM Press).
    1971   *The Proclamation of Jesus* (New Testament Theology, 1; London: SCM Press).
    1982/1958   *Jesus' Promise to the Nations* (Philadelphia: Fortress Press).

Jones, L.P.
    1997   *The Symbol of Water in the Gospel of John* (JSNTSup, 145; Sheffield: Sheffield Academic Press).

Judge, E.A.
    1994   'Judaism and the Rise of Christianity: A Roman Perspective', *Tyndale Bulletin* 45.2: 355-68.

Kahl, W.
 1998 'Ist es erlaubt, am Sabbat Leben zu retten oder zu töten? (Marc. 3:4)', *NovT* 40.4: 313-35.

Karris, R.J.
 1985 *Luke: Artist and Theologian* (New York: Paulist Press).

Kasfir, N.
 1979 'Explaining Ethnic Political Participation', *World Politics* 31.3: 365-88.

Kawashima, R.S.
 2003 'The Jubilee Year and the Return of Cosmic Purity', *CBQ* 65.3: 370-89.

Kazen, T.
 2002 *Jesus and Purity Halakhah: Was Jesus Indifferent to Purity?* (ConBNT, 38; Stockholm: Almqvist & Wiksell).

Keck, L.E.
 2000 *Who is Jesus? History in the Perfect Tense* (Columbia: University of South Carolina).

Kee, H.C.
 1970 *Jesus in History: An Approach to the Study of the Gospels* (New York: Harcourt).
 1977 *Community of the New Age: Studies in Mark's Gospel* (London: SCM Press).
 1989 'The Import of Archaeological Investigations of Galilee for Scholarly Reassessment of the Gospels'. Paper delivered to the Society of Biblical Literature: Anaheim CA.

Keener, C.S.
 1999 *A Commentary on the Gospel of Matthew* (Grand Rapids: Eerdmans).
 2003 *The Gospel of John: A Commentary* (Peabody, MA: Hendrickson).
 2005 '"Brood of Vipers" (Matthew 3.7; 12.34; 23.33)', *JSNT* 28.1: 3-11.

Keesing, R.M.
 1975 *Kin Groups and Social Structure* (New York: Holt, Rinehart & Winston).

Kelley, S.
 2002 *Racializing Jesus: Race, Ideology, and the Formation of Modern Biblical Scholarship* (New York: Routledge).

Kennell, N.M.
 2005 'New Light on 2 Maccabees 4:7-15', *JJS* 56.1: 10-24.

Kiilunen, J.
 1985 *Die Vollmacht in Widerstreit: Untersuchungen zum Werdegang von Mk 2,1–3,6* (Annales Academiae Scientiarum Fennicae/Dissertationes Humanarum Litterarum, 40; Helsinki: Suomalainen Tiedeakatemia).

Kim, S.
 2001 *Paul and the New Perspective: Second Thoughts on the Origin of Paul's Gospel* (Grand Rapids: Eerdmans).

Kingsbury, J.D.
 1988 'On Following Jesus', *NTS* 34.1: 45-59.
 1989 *Conflict in Mark: Jesus, Authorities, Disciples* (Minneapolis: Fortress Press).

Kissinger, Warren S.
 1975 *The Sermon on the Mount: A History of Interpretation and Bibliography* (Metuchen: Scarecrow Press).

Klawans, J.
 2000 *Impurity and Sin in Ancient Judaism* (Oxford: Oxford University Press).

2002 'Interpreting the Last Supper: Sacrifice, Spiritualization, and Anti-Sacrifice', *NTS* 48.1: 1-17.

Klemm, H.G.
1969–70 'Das Wort von der Selbstbestattung der Toten', *NTS* 16: 60-75.

Kloppenborg, J.S., and J.W. Marshall (eds.)
2005 *Apocalypticism, Anti-Semitism and the Historical Jesus: Subtexts in Criticism* (JSNTSup, 275; London: T. & T. Clark).

Klosinski, L.E.
1988 *The Meals in Mark* (Claremont, CA: Claremont Graduate School).

Knibb, M.A.
1989 *Jubilees and the Origins of the Qumran Community: An Inaugural Lecture* (London: King's College).

Koester, C.R.
1995 *Symbolism in the Fourth Gospel* (Minneapolis: Fortress Press).

Konstan, D.
2001 'To Hellenikon Ethnos: Ethnicity and the Construction of Ancient Greek Identity', in I. Malkin (ed.), *Ancient Perceptions of Greek Ethnicity* (Cambridge, MA: Harvard University Press), pp. 29-50.

Kraft, R.A., and G.W.E. Nickelsburg
1986 *Early Judaism and its Modern Interpreters* (Atlanta, GA: Scholars Press).

Kruse, H.
1954 '"Dialektische Negation" als semitisches Idiom', *VT* 4: 385-400.

Kuhn, H.-W.
1971 *Ältere Sammlungen im Markusevangelium* (SUNT, 8; Göttingen: Vandenhoeck & Ruprecht).

Kugel, J.
1996 'The Holiness of Israel and the Land in Second Temple Times', in M.V. Fox and A. Hurowitz (eds.), *Texts, Temples, and Traditions: A Tribute to Menahem Haran* (Winona Lake, IN: Eisenbrauns), pp. 21-32.

Kunin, S.D.
1998 *God's Place in the World. Sacred Space and Sacred Place in Judaism* (New York: Cassell).

Kvanvig, H.S.
2005 'Jubilees: Read as Narrative', in G. Boccaccini (ed.), *Enoch and Qumran Origins: New Light on a Forgotten Connection* (Grand Rapids: Eerdmans), pp. 75-83.

Lane, W.L.
1974 *The Gospel according to Mark* (Grand Rapids: Eerdmans).

Lieu, J.
1994 '"The Parting of the Ways": Theological Construct or Historical Reality?', *JSNT* 56: 101-19.

Lightfoot, R.H.
1950 *The Gospel Message of Mark* (Oxford: Oxford University Press).

Lindars, B.
1982 *The Gospel of John* (NCB; Grand Rapids: Eerdmans).

Loader, W.R.G.
2002 *Jesus' Attitude to the Law: A Study of the Gospels* (Grand Rapids: Eerdmans).

Loffreda, S.
1993 *Recovering Capharnaum* (Jerusalem: Franciscan Printing Press).

Longenecker, R.N.
    1991   *Eschatology and Covenant: A Comparison of 4 Ezra and Romans 1–11* (Sheffield: Sheffield Academic Press).

Lührmann, D.
    1987   *Das Markusevangelium* (HNT, 3; Tübingen: J.C.B. Mohr).

Luz, U.
    1991   'Das Primatwort Matthäus 16.17-19 aus wirkungsgeschichtlicher Sicht', *NTS* 37.3: 415-33.

Maccini, R.G.
    1994   'A Reassessment of the Woman at the Well in John 4 in Light of the Samaritan Context', *JSNT* 53: 35-46.

Maccoby, H.
    1999   *Ritual and Morality: The Ritual Purity System and its Place in Judaism* (Cambridge: Cambridge University Press).

Mack, B.L.
    1988   *A Myth of Innocence* (Philadelphia: Fortress Press).

Magen, Y.
    1990   'Mount Gerizim—A Temple City [Hebrew]', *Qadmoniot* 23.3-4: 70-96.
    1993   'Mount Gerizim', in E. Stern (ed.), *New Encyclopedia of Archaeological Excavations in the Holy Land* (New York: Simon & Schuster), pp. 484-92.
    2000   'Mount Gerizim—A Temple City [Hebrew]', *Qadmoniot* 33.2: 74-118.

Magness, J.
    2002   *The Archaeology of Qumran and the Dead Sea Scrolls: Studies in the Dead Sea Scrolls and Related Literature* (Grand Rapids: Eerdmans).

Malina, B.J.
    1986   *Christian Origins and Cultural Anthropology: Practical Models for Biblical Interpretation* (Atlanta: John Knox Press).
    1991   'Reading Theory Perspective: Reading Luke–Acts', in J. Neyrey (ed.), *The Social World of Luke–Acts* (Peabody, MA: Hendrickson), pp. 3-23.
    1988   'A Conflict Approach to Mark 7', *Forum* 4.3: 3-30.
    2001   *The Social Gospel of Jesus: The Kingdom of God in Mediterranean Perspective* (Minneapolis: Fortress Press).

Malina, B.J., and R.L. Rohrbaugh
    1992   *Social Science Commentary on the Synoptic Gospels* (Minneapolis: Fortress Press).

Malkin, I.
    2001   *Ancient Perceptions of Greek Ethnicity* (Cambridge, MA: Harvard University Press).

Manson, T.W.
    1949   *The Sayings of Jesus* (London: SCM Press).

Marcus, J.
    1992   'The Jewish War and the Sitz im Leben of Mark', *JBL* 111.3: 441-62.

Marshall, I.H.
    1978   *The Gospel of Luke* (The New International Greek Testament Commentary; Grand Rapids: Eerdmans).
    1992   'Church', in *DJG* (ed. J. Green and S. McKnight; Downers Grove, IL: InterVarsity Press).

Martin, R.A.
  1975 'Syntax Criticism of the LXX Additions to the Book of Esther', *JBL* 94.1: 65-72.
Marxsen, W.
  1969 *The Beginnings of Christology: A Study in its Problems* (Facet Books Biblical Series, 22; Philadelphia: Fortress Press).
Mayer-Haas, A.J.
  2003 *«Geschenk aus Gottes Schatzkammer» (bSchab 10b): Jesus und der Sabbat im Spiegel der neutestamentlichen Schriften* (Neutestamentliche Abhandlungen, NF, 43; Münster: Aschendorff).
McCane, B.
  1990 'Let the Dead Bury their Own Dead', *HTR* 83.1: 31-43.
McKnight, S.
  2004 'Jesus of Nazareth', in S. McKnight and G.R. Osborne (eds.), *The Face of New Testament Studies* (Grand Rapids: Baker Academic), pp. 149-76.
McLaren, J.S.
  1991 *Power and Politics in Palestine* (JSNTSup, 63; Sheffield: Sheffield Academic Press).
McVann, M.
  1993 'Family-Centeredness', in J.J. Pilch and B.J. Malina (eds.), *Biblical Social Values and their Meaning* (Peabody, MA: Hendrickson), pp. 70-73.
Meier, J.P.
  1991 *A Marginal Jew* (ABRL, 1; New York: Doubleday).
  1994 *A Marginal Jew* (ABRL, 2; New York: Doubleday).
  2001 *A Marginal Jew* (ABRL, 3; New York: Doubleday).
Méndez-Moratalla, F.
  2004 *The Paradigm of Conversion in Luke* (JSNTSup, 252; London: T. & T. Clark).
Metzdorf, C.
  2003 *Die Tempelaktion Jesu. Patristische und historisch-kritische Exegese im Vergleich* (WUNT, 2.168; Tübingen: Mohr Siebeck).
Metzger, B.M.
  1977 *Oxford Annotated Apocrypha: RSV* (New York: Oxford University Press).
Meyer, B.F.
  1979 *The Aims of Jesus* (London: SCM Press).
Meyers, C.L., and E.M. Meyers
  1993 *Zechariah 9–14* (AB, 25C; New York: Doubleday).
Meyers, E.M., and J.F. Strange
  1981 *Archaeology, the Rabbis, and Early Christianity* (Nashville: Abingdon Press).
Millar, F.
  1978 'The Background to the Maccabean Revolution: Reflections on Martin Hengel's *Judaism and Hellenism*', *JJS* 29: 1-21.
  2006 'Transformations of Judaism under Graeco-Roman Rule: Responses to Seth Schwartz's *Imperialism and Jewish Society*', *JJS* 57.1: 139-58.
Miller, G.T.
  1995 'Isaiah 25:6-9', *Int* 49.2: 175-78.
Miller, R.J.
  1991 'The (A)historicity of Jesus' Temple Demonstration: A Test Case in

Milns, R.D.
        Methodology', in D.J. Lull (ed.), *SBL 1991 Seminar Papers* (Atlanta: Scholars Press), pp. 235-52.
    1992   'Alexander the Great', in *ABD* (ed. D.N. Freedman; New York: Doubleday), I, pp. 146-50.

Minear, P.
    2002   *The Bible and the Historian: Breaking the Silence about God in Biblical Studies* (Nashville: Abingdon Press).

Moloney, F.J.
    2002   'Narrative and Discourse at the Feast of Tabernacles: John 7:1–8:59', in J. Painter, R.A. Culpepper and F.F. Segovia (eds.), *Word, Theology, and Community in John* (St Louis: Chalice Press), pp. 155-69.

Montefiore, C.G.
    1914   *Judaism and St Paul* (London: Max Goschen).

Moo, D.J.
    1984   'Jesus and the Authority of the Mosaic Law', *JSNT* 20: 3-49.

Moore, C.A.
    1973   'On the Origins of the LXX Additions to Esther', *JBL* 92.3: 382-93.
    1977   *Daniel, Esther, and Jeremiah: The Additions* (AB, 44; Garden City, NY: Doubleday).
    1985   *Judith* (AB, 40; Garden City, NY: Doubleday).

Mørkholm, O.
    1966   *Antiochus IV of Syria* (Classica et Medievalia Dissertationes, 8; Copenhagen: Gyldendalske Boghandel).

Morris, L.
    1992   *The Gospel according to Matthew* (Grand Rapids: Eerdmans).

Murphy, F.J.
    1993   *Pseudo-Philo: Rewriting the Bible* (London: Oxford University Press).

Murphy-O'Connor, J.
    2000   'Jesus and the Money Changers (Mark 11:15-17; John 2:13-17)', *RB* 107.1: 42-55.

Mussner, F.
    1979   *Traktat über die Juden* (Munich: Kösel).

Najman, H.
    1999   'Interpretation as Primordial Writing: Jubilees and its Authority Conferring Strategies', *JSJ* 30.4: 379-410.

Nanos, M.
    2005   'How Inter-Christian Approaches to Paul's Rhetoric Can Perpetuate Negative Valuations of Jewishness—Although Proposing to Avoid that Outcome', *BibInt* 13.3: 250-53.

Nash, M.
    1989   *The Cauldron of Ethnicity in the Modern World* (Chicago: University of Chicago Press).

Neusner, J.
    1971   *The Rabbinic Traditions about the Pharisees* (Leiden: E.J. Brill).
    1973a   *The Idea of Purity in Ancient Judaism* (Leiden: E.J. Brill).
    1973b   *From Politics to Piety: The Emergence of Rabbinic Judaism* (Englewood Cliffs, NJ: Prentice–Hall).
    1977–86   *The Tosefta* (New York: Ktav).

1981	*Judaism, the Evidence of the Mishna* (Chicago: University of Chicago Press).
1986	*Reading and Believing: Ancient Judaism and Contemporary Gullibility* (Atlanta: Scholars Press).
1989	'Money-Changers in the Temple: The Mishnah's Explanation', *NTS* 35.2: 287-90.
1991	'Mr Maccoby's Red Cow, Mr Sanders's Pharisees—and Mine', *JSJ* 23.1: 81-98.
1992	'Mr Sanders's Pharisees and Mine', *BBR* 2: 143-69.

Neyrey, J.H.

1979	'Jacob Traditions and the Interpretation of John 4:10-26', *CBQ* 41.3: 419-37.
1991	'Ceremonies in Luke–Acts: The Case of Meals and Table Fellowship', in J.H. Neyrey (ed.), *The Social World of Luke–Acts* (Peabody, MA: Hendrikson), pp. 361-87.
1994	'What's Wrong with This Picture? John 4, Cultural Stereotypes of Women, and Public and Private Space', *BTB* 24.2: 77-91.
2002a	'Spaces and Places, Whence and Whither, Homes and Rooms: "Territoriality" in the Fourth Gospel', *BTB* 32.2: 60-74.
2002b	'Spaced Out: "Territoriality" in the Fourth Gospel', *HTS Teologiese Studies/Theological Studies* 58.2: 632-63.

Nickelsburg, G.W.E.

1981	*Jewish Literature between the Bible and the Mishnah* (Philadelphia: Fortress Press).

Nikiprowetzky, V.

2000	'Le sabbat et les armies dans l'histoire ancienne d'Israël', *Revue des études juives* 159.1-2: 1-17.

Nodet, E.

1986	'La dédicace, les Maccabées et le messie', *RB* 93.3: 321-75.

Nolland, J.

1989	*Luke 1–9:20* (Word Biblical Commentary, 35a; Dallas: Word Books).
1993	*Luke 9:21–18:34* (Word Biblical Commentary, 35b; Dallas: Word Books).

Nongbri, B.

2005	'The Motivations of the Maccabees and Judean Rhetoric of Ancestral Tradition', in C. Bakhos (ed.), *Ancient Judaism in its Hellenistic Context* (Leiden: E.J. Brill), pp. 85-111.

Okure, K.

1988	*The Johannine Approach to Mission: A Contextual Study of John 4:1-42* (WUNT, 2.31; Tübingen: J.C.B. Mohr).

Olyan, S.M.

2004	'Purity Ideology in Ezra–Nehemiah as a Tool to Reconstitute Community', *JSJ* 35.1: 1-16.

Orton, D.E.

1989	*The Understanding Scribe* (Sheffield: JSOT Press).

Overman, J.A.

1996	*Church and Community in Crisis: The Gospel according to Matthew* (The New Testament in Context; Valley Forge, PA: Trinity Press International).

Paesler, K.
　1999　　　*Das Tempelwort Jesu: Die Traditionen von Tempelzerstörung und Tempelerneurung im Neuen Testament* (FRLANT, 184; Göttingen: Vandenhoeck & Ruprecht).

Patterson, O.
　1975　　　'Context and Choice in Ethnic Allegiance: A Theoretical Framework and Caribbean Case Study', in N. Glazer and D.P. Moynihan (eds.), *Ethnicity: Theory and Experience* (Cambridge: Harvard University Press), pp. 305-49.

Pesch, R.
　1980　　　*Das Markusevangelium* (HTKNT, 2; Freiburg: Herder).

Plummer, A.
　1896/1975　*A Critical and Exegetical Commentary on the Gospel according to Luke* (ICC; Edinburgh: T. & T. Clark).

Poon, W.C.K.
　2003　　　'Superabundant Table Fellowship in the Kingdom: The Feeding of the Five Thousand and the Meal Motif in Luke', *ET* 114.7: 224-30.

Poirier, J.C.
　1996　　　'Why Did the Pharisees Wash their Hands?', *JJS* 47.2: 217-33.
　2003　　　'Purity beyond the Temple in the Second Temple Era', *JBL* 122.2: 247-65.

Price, S.R.F.
　1996　　　'The Place of Religion: Rome in the Early Empire', in A. Bowman, E. Champlin and A. Lintott (eds.), *The Augustan Empire, 43 B.C.–A.D. 69* (CAH, 10; Cambridge: Cambridge University Press), pp. 812-47.

Purvis, J.D.
　1992　　　'Samaria (City)', in *ABD* (ed. D.N. Freedman; New York: Doubleday), V, pp. 914-21.

Räisänen, H.
　1982　　　'Jesus and the Food Laws: Reflections on Mark 7:15', *JSNT* 16: 79-100.
　1986　　　*The Torah and Christ* (Suomen eksegeettisen seuran julkaisuja, 45; Helsinki: Finnish Exegetical Society).

Rankin, O.S.
　1930　　　*The Origins of the Festival of Hanukkah* (Edinburgh: T. & T. Clark).

Reed, J.L.
　1992　　　*The Population of Capernaum* (Occasional Papers of the Institute of Antiquity and Christianity, 24; Claremont, CA: Institute for Antiquity and Christianity).
　2000　　　*Archeology and the Galilean Jesus* (Harrisburg, PA: Trinity Press International).

Regev, E.
　2000　　　'Pure Individualism: The Idea of Non-Priestly Purity in Ancient Judaism', *JSJ* 31.2: 176-202.
　2005　　　'The Ritual Baths near the Temple Mount and Extra-Purification before Entering the Temple Courts', *IEJ* 55.2: 194-204.

Reich, R.
　1981　　　'Archaeological Evidence of the Jewish Population at Hasmonean Gezer', *IEJ* 31: 48-52.

Reid, B.E.
- 1995 '"Do You See This Woman?" Luke 7:36-50 as a Paradigm for Feminist Hermeneutics', *BR* 40: 37-49.

Reinmuth, E.
- 1997 'Beobachtungen zur Rezeption der Genesis bei Pseudo-Philo (LAB 1–8) und Lukas (Apg 7.2-17)', *NTS* 43.4: 552-69.

Resseguie, J.L.
- 1991 'Automatization and Defamiliarization in Luke 7.36-50', *Literature and Theology* 5: 137-50.

Rhodes, D., J. Dewey, and D. Michie
- 1999 *Mark as Story: An Introduction to the Narrative of a Gospel* (Minneapolis: Fortress Press).

Richardson, P.
- 1992 'Why Turn the Tables? Jesus' Protest in the Temple Precincts', *SBLSP* 31: 507-23.
- 2000 'First-Century Houses and Q's Setting', in D.G. Horrell and C.M. Tuckett (eds.), *Christology and Community: New Testament Essays in Honour of David R. Catchpole* (Leiden: E.J. Brill), pp. 63-83.
- 2004 *Building Jewish in the Roman East* (Baylor TX: Baylor University Press).

Riches, J.K.
- 1982 *Jesus and the Transformation of Judaism* (New York: Seabury).
- 2000 *Conflicting Mythologies. Identity Formation in the Gospels of Mark and Matthew* (Edinburgh: T. & T. Clark).

Riesner, R.
- 1985 'Essener und Urkirche in Jerusalem', *Bibel und Kirche* 40.2: 64-76.

Rietz, H.W.M.
- 2005 'Synchronizing Worship: Jubilees as a Tradition for the Qumran Community', in G. Boccaccini (ed.), *Enoch and Qumran Origins: New Light on a Forgotten Connection* (Grand Rapids: Eerdmans), pp. 111-18.

Rohrbaugh, R.L.
- 2007 *The New Testament in Cross-Cultural Perspective* (Matrix: The Bible in Mediterranean Context; Eugene, OR: Cascade Books).

Rordorf, W.
- 1962 *Der Sonntag: Geschichte des Ruhe- und Gottesdiensttags im ältesten Christentum* (Abhandlungen zur Theologie des Alten und Neuen Testaments, 43; Zürich: Zwingli).

Roth, C.
- 1960 'The Cleansing of the Temple and Zechariah xiv 21', *NovT* 4.3: 174-81.

Routledge, R.
- 2002 'Passover and the Last Supper', *Tyndale Bulletin* 53.2: 203-21.

Rubenstein, J.L.
- 1995 *The History of Sukkot in the Second Temple and Rabbinic Periods* (Brown Judaic Studies, 302; Atlanta: Scholars Press).

Rudolph, D.J.
- 2002 'Jesus and the Food Laws: A Reassessment of Mark 7:19b', *EQ* 74.4: 291-311.

Ruiten, J.T.A.G.M. van
- 1999 'Eden and the Temple. The Rewriting of Genesis 2:4–3:24 in the Book

of Jubilees', in G. Luttikhuizen (ed.), *Paradise Interpreted* (Leiden: E.J. Brill), pp. 63-94.
2000 *Primaeval History Interpreted: The Rewriting of Genesis I–II in the Book of Jubilees* (Leiden: E.J. Brill).
2004 'A Literary Dependency of *Jubilees* on *1 Enoch?* A Reassessment of a Thesis of J.C. VanderKam', *Henoch* 26.2: 205-209.

Ruzer, S.
2004 '"Love your Enemy" Precept in the Sermon on the Mount in the Context of Early Jewish Exegesis: A New Perspective', *RB* 111.2: 193-208.

Sack, R.D.
1986 *Human Territoriality. Its Theory and History* (Cambridge: Cambridge University Press).

Saldarini, A.J.
1984 *Jesus and Passover* (New York: Paulist Press).
1994 *Matthew's Christian-Jewish Community* (Chicago: Chicago University Press).

Samuel, G.
1990 *Mind, Body and Culture: Anthropology and the Biological Interface* (Cambridge: Cambridge University Press).

Sanders, E.P.
1977 *Paul and Palestinian Judaism* (Philadelphia: Fortress Press).
1983 *Paul, the Law, and the Jewish People* (Philadelphia: Fortress Press).
1985 *Jesus and Judaism* (Philadelphia: Fortress Press).
1990 *Jewish Law from Jesus to the Mishnah: Five Studies* (London: SCM Press).
1992 *Judaism: Practice and Belief 63 BCE–66 CE* (Philadelphia: Trinity Press International).
2000 'The Dead Sea Sect and Other Jews', in T.H. Lim (ed.), *The Dead Sea Scrolls in their Historical Context* (Edinburgh: T. & T. Clark), pp. 7-43.

Sariola, H.
1990 *Markus und das Gesetz* (Annales Academiae Scientiarum Fennicae. Dissertationes humanarum litterarum, 56; Helsinki: Suomalainen Tiedeakatemia).

Schaefer, K.R.
1993a 'The Ending of the Book of Zechariah: A Commentary', *RB* 100.2: 165-238.
1993b 'Zechariah 14 and the Composition of the Book of Zechariah', *RB* 100.3: 368-98.

Schäfer, P.
1997 *Judeophobia: Attitudes toward Jews in the Ancient World* (Cambridge: Harvard University Press).

Schermerhorn, R.A.
1970 *Comparative Ethnic Relations* (New York: Random House).

Schiffman, L.H.
1975 *The Halakhah at Qumran* (Leiden: E.J. Brill).
1994 *Reclaiming the Dead Sea Scrolls* (Philadelphia: Jewish Publication Society).

Schillebeeckx, E.
1979 *Jesus: An Experiment in Christology* (New York: Crossroad).

Schlosser, J.
 1990 'La parole de Jésus sur la fin du Temple', *NTS* 36.3: 398-414.
Schmithals, W.
 1979 *Das Evangelium nach Markus* (Ökumenischer Taschenbuchkommentar zum Neuen Testament, 2; Würzburg: Echter).
Schnackenburg, R.
 1987 *The Gospel according to St John*, II (New York: Crossroad).
 1995 *All Things Are Possible to Believers: Reflections on the Lord's Prayer and the Sermon on the Mount* (Louisville, KY: Westminister/John Knox Press).
Schreiner, T.R.
 1993 *The Law and its Fulfillment: A Pauline Theology of the Law* (Grand Rapids: Baker Book House).
Schubert, K.
 1957 'The Sermon on the Mount and the Qumran Texts', in K. Stendahl (ed.), *The Scrolls and the New Testament* (New York: Harper & Brothers), pp. 118-28.
Schürer, E.
 1973/1885 *The History of the Jewish People in the Age of Jesus Christ*, I (Edinburgh: T. & T. Clark).
Schwartz, D.R.
 1979 *Priesthood, Temple, Sacrifice: Opposition and Spiritualization in the Late Second Temple Period* (Jerusalem: Hebrew University).
 1992 *Studies in the Jewish Background of Christianity* (WUNT, 60; Tübingen: J.C.B. Mohr).
Schwartz, S.
 1991 'Israel and the Nations Roundabout: 1 Maccabees and the Hasmonean Expansion', *JJS* 42.1: 16-38.
 1993 'A Note on the Social Type and Political Ideology of the Hasmonean Family', *JBL* 112.2: 305-09.
 2004 *Imperialism and Jewish Society: 200 B.C.E. to 640 C.E.* (Princeton, NJ: Princeton University Press).
Schweitzer, A.
 1906/2001 *The Quest of the Historical Jesus* (Minneapolis: Fortress Press).
Schweizer, E.
 1970 *The Good News according to Mark* (Richmond, VA: John Knox Press).
Scott, G.M., Jr
 1990 'A Resynthesis of the Primordial and Circumstantialist Approaches to Ethnic Group Solidarity: Towards an Explanatory Model', *Ethnic and Racial Studies* 13: 147-71.
Seeley, D.
 1993 'Jesus' Temple Act', *CBQ* 55.2: 263-83.
 2000 'Jesus' Temple Act Revisited: A Response to P.M. Casey', *CBQ* 62.1: 55-63.
Seland, T.
 1995 *Establishment Violence in Philo and Luke: A Study in Non-Conformity to the Torah and Jewish Vigilante Reactions* (Leiden: E.J. Brill).
Shead, A.G.
 2002 'An Old Testament Theology of the Sabbath Year and Jubilee', *Reformed Theological Review* 61.1: 19-33.

Shils, E.
    1957   'Primordial, Personal, Sacred and Civic Ties', *British Journal of Sociology* 7: 113-45.
Sievers, J.
    1990   *The Hasmoneans and their Supporters: From Mattathias to the Death of John Hyrcanus* (University of South Florida Studies in the History of Judaism, 6; Atlanta: Scholars Press).
Sim, D.C.
    1996   'Christianity and Ethnicity in the Gospel of Matthew', in M.G. Brett (ed.), *Ethnicity and the Bible* (Leiden: E.J. Brill), pp. 171-95.
Simon, M.
    1986   *Verus Israel: A Study of the Relations between Christians and Jews in the Roman Empire (AD 135–425)* (Oxford: Oxford University Press).
Smallwood, E.M.
    1970   *Philonis Alexandrini Legatio ad Gaium: Text and Commentary* (Leiden: E.J. Brill).
Smith, A.D.
    1991   *National Identity* (Reno: University of Nevada Press).
    1992   'Chosen Peoples: Why Ethnic Groups Survive', *Ethnic and Racial Studies* 15.3: 440-49.
Smith, B.D.
    1991   'The Chronology of the Last Supper', *WTJ* 53.1: 29-45.
Smith, C.W.F.
    1962–63 'Tabernacles in the Fourth Gospel and Mark', *NTS* 9: 130-46.
Smith, D.E.
    1987   'Table Fellowship as a Literary Motif in the Gospel of Luke', *JBL* 106.4: 613-38.
    2003   *From Symposium to Eucharist: The Banquet in the Early Christian World* (Minneapolis: Fortress Press).
Smith, D.M.
    1999   *John* (Abingdon New Testament Commentaries; Nashville: Abingdon Press).
Smith, J.E.
    2005   'The New Perspective on Paul: A Select and Annotated Bibliography', *Criswell Theological Review* 2.2: 91-111.
Smith, M.
    1973   *The Secret Gospel: The Discovery and Interpretation of the Secret Gospel according to Mark* (New York: Harper & Row).
Snyder, G.F.
    1999   *Inculturation of the Jesus Tradition: The Impact of Jesus on Jewish and Roman Cultures* (Harrisburg, PA: Trinity Press International).
Söding, T.
    2000   '"Was kann aus Nazareth schon Gutes kommen?" (Joh 1.46): Die Bedeutung des Judeseins Jesu im Johannesevangelium', *NTS* 46.1: 21-41.
Staley, J.L.
    1988   *The Print's First Kiss: A Rhetorical Investigation of the Implied Reader in the Fourth Gospel* (Atlanta: Scholars Press).
Stanton, G.N.
    1975   'Form Criticism Revisited', in M.D. Hooker and C. Hickling (eds.), *What about the New Testament?* (London: SCM Press), pp. 13-27.

Stein, R.H.
  1992 'The Last Supper', in *DJG* (ed. J.B. Green, S. McKnight and I.H. Marshall; Downers Grove, IL: InterVarsity Press), pp. 444-50.
Stern, M.
  1974 *Greek and Latin Authors on Jews and Judaism*, 1 (Jerusalem: The Israel Academy of Sciences and Humanities).
Stern, S.
  2001 *Calendar and Community: A History of the Jewish Calendar, 2nd Century BCE to 10th Century CE* (New York: Oxford University Press).
Stettler, H.
  2004 'Sanctification in the Jesus Tradition', *Bib* 85.2: 153-78.
Stoler, A.L.
  1997 'Racial Histories and their Regimes of Truth', *Political Power and Social Theory* 11: 183-206.
Stuhlmacher, P.
  2000 'Matt 28:16-20 and the Course of Mission in the Apostolic and Postapostolic Age', in J. Ådna (ed.), *The Mission of the Early Church to Jews and Gentiles* (Tübingen: J.C.B. Mohr), pp. 17-43.
Sturcke, H.
  2005 *Encountering the Rest of God: How Jesus Came to Personify the Sabbath* (TVA Dissertationen, Zürich: Theologischer Verlag).
Svartvik, J.
  2000 *Mark and Mission: Mk 7:1-23 in its Narrative and Historical Contexts* (ConBNT, 32; Stockholm: Almqvist & Wiksell).
Swanson, T.D.
  1994 'To Prepare a Place: Johannine Christianity and the Collapse of Ethnic Territory', *JAAR* 62.2: 241-63.
Talbert, C.H.
  1977 *What Is a Gospel? The Genre of the Canonical Gospels* (Philadelphia: Fortress).
  1993 'Worship in the Fourth Gospel and its Milieu', in R.B. Sloan and M.C. Parsons (eds.), *Perspectives on John: Method and Interpretation in the Fourth Gospel* (Lewiston, NY: Edwin Mellen Press), pp. 337-56.
Taylor, N.H.
  1996 'Palestinian Christianity and the Caligula Crisis. Part I. Social and Historical Reconstruction', *JSNT* 61: 101-24.
Taylor, R.B.
  1988 *Human Territorial Functioning: An Empirical Evolutionary Perspective on Individual and Small Group Territorial Cognitions, Behaviors and Consequences* (Cambridge: Cambridge University Press).
Taylor, V.
  1966/1981 *The Gospel according to Mark* (Grand Rapids: Baker Book House).
Tcherikover, V.
  1961 *Hellenistic Civilization and the Jews* (Philadelphia: Jewish Publication Society of America).
Theissen, G.
  1991 *The Gospels in Context: Social and Political History in the Synoptic Tradition* (Minneapolis: Fortress Press).
  1992a 'The Wandering Radicals: Light Shed by the Sociology of Literature

on the Early Transmission of the Jesus Sayings', in G. Theissen (ed.), *Social Reality and the Early Christians* (Minneapolis: Fortress Press), pp. 33-59.

1992b '"We Have Left Everything..." (Mark 10:28): Discipleship and Social Uprooting in the Jewish-Palestinian Society of the First Century', in G. Theissen (ed.), *Social Reality and the Early Christians* (Minneapolis: Fortress Press), pp. 60-93.

1996 'Historical Skepticism and the Criteria of Jesus Research, or My Attempt to Leap across Lessing's Yawning Gulf', *SJT* 49: 147-76.

1999 *The Religion of the Earliest Churches: Creating a Symbolic World* (Minneapolis: Fortress Press).

Theissen, G., and A. Merz
1998 *The Historical Jesus: A Comprehensive Guide* (Minneapolis: Fortress Press).

Theissen, G., and D. Winter
1997 *Die Kriterienfrage in der Jesusforschung: Vom Differenzkriterium zum Plausibilitätskriterium* (Novum Testamentum et orbis antiquus, 34; Freiburg, Switzerland: Universitätsverlag).

2002 *The Quest for the Plausible Jesus* (Louisville, KY: Westminster/John Knox Press).

Thompson, M.B.
2002 *The New Perspective on Paul* (Cambridge: Grove Books Limited).

Thurén, L.
2000 *Derhetoricizing Paul: A Dynamic Perspective on Pauline Theology* (WUNT, 124; Tübingen: Mohr Siebeck).

Thyen, H.
1980 '"Das Heil kommt von den Juden"', in D. Lührmann and G. Strecker (eds.), *Kirche. Festschrift für Günther Bornkamm zum 75. Geburtstag* (Tübingen: Mohr Siebeck), pp. 163-84.

Tilly, M.
2002 *Jerusalem—Nabel der Welt: Überlieferung und Funktionen von Heiligtumstraditionen im antiken Judentum* (Stuttgart: W. Kohlhammer).

Tomson, P.J.
1988 'Zavim 5:12—Reflections on Dating Mishnaic Halakhah', in A. Kuyt and N.A. van Uchelen (eds.), *History and Form: Dutch Studies in the Mishnah: Papers Read at the Workshop 'Mishnah'* (Amsterdam: University of Amsterdam Press), pp. 53-69.

1990 *Paul and the Jewish Law* (Minneapolis: Fortress Press).

1996 'Paul's Jewish Background in View of his Law Teaching in 1 Corinthians 7', in J.D.G. Dunn (ed.), *Paul and the Mosaic Law* (Tübingen: J.C.B. Mohr), pp. 251-70.

Torrey, C.C.
1941 *Documents of the Primitive Church* (London and New York: Harper & Brothers).

Townsend, R.B.
1913 'The Fourth Book of Maccabees', in R.H. Charles (ed.), *The Apocrypha and Pseudepigraph of the Old Testament* (Oxford: Clarendon Press).

Trocmé, E.
1975 *The Formation of the Gospel according to Mark* (London: SPCK).

Turner, M.M.B.
  1982 'The Sabbath, Sunday, and the Law in Luke/Acts', in D.A. Carson (ed.), *From Sabbath to the Lord's Day: A Biblical Historical and Theological Investigation* (Grand Rapids: Zondervan), pp. 99-157.

Twelftreee, G.H.
  1999 *Jesus the Miracle Worker* (Downers Grove, IL: InterVarsity Press).
  2004 'The History of Miracles in the History of Jesus', in S. McKnight and G.R. Osborne (eds.), *The Face of New Testament Studies* (Grand Rapids: Baker Academic), pp. 191-208.

Ulfgard, H.
  1998 *The Story of Sukkot: The Setting, Shaping, and Sequel of the Biblical Feast of Tabernacles* (BGBE, 34; Tübingen: Mohr Siebeck).

Van Belle, G.
  2001 '"Salvation is from the Jews": The Parenthesis in John 4:22b', in R. Bieringer, D. Pollefeyt and F. Vandecasteele-Vanneuville (eds.), *Anti-Judaism and the Fourth Gospel: Papers of the Leuven Colloquium, 2000* (Assen: Royal van Gorcum), pp. 370-400.

Van den Berghe, P.
  1995 'Does Race Matter?', *Nations and Nationalism* 1.3: 357-68.

VanderKam, J.C.
  1979 'The Origin, Character, and Early History of the 364-Day Calendar: A Reassessment of Jaubert's Hypotheses', *CBQ* 41.3: 390-411.
  1981 '2 Maccabees 6.7a and Calendrical Change in Jerusalem', *JSJ* 12: 52-74.
  1987 'Hanukkah: Its Timing and Significance according to 1 and 2 Maccabees', *JSP* 1: 23-40.
  1992a 'Jubilees, Book of', in *ABD* (ed. D.N. Freedman; New York: Doubleday), III, pp. 1030-32.
  1992b 'The Jubilees Fragments from Qumran Cave 4', in J.T. Barrera and L.V. Montaner (eds.), *The Madrid Qumran Congress* (Leiden: E.J. Brill), pp. 635-48.
  1994 'Putting Them in their Place: Geography as an Evaluative Tool', in J.C. Reeves and J. Kampen (eds.), *Pursuing the Text: Studies in Honor of Ben Zion Wacholder on the Occasion of his Seventieth Birthday* (Sheffield: Sheffield Academic Press), pp. 46-69.
  1994/2000 'Genesis 1 in Jubilees 2', in J.J. Collins (ed.), *From Revelation to Canon: Studies in the Hebrew Bible and Second Temple Literature* (Supplements to the Journal for the Study of Judaism; Leiden: E.J. Brill), pp. 500-21.

Vermes, G.
  1993 *The Religion of Jesus the Jew* (London: SCM Press).
  1995 *The Dead Sea Scrolls in English* (London: Penguin Books).

Vouga, F.
  1988 *Jesus et la loi selon la tradition synoptique* (Geneva: Labor et Fides).

Watson, F.
  1997 *Text and Truth: Redefining Biblical Theology* (Grand Rapids: Eerdmans).
  1998 'Toward a Literal Reading of the Gospels', in R. Bauckham (ed.), *The Gospels for All Christians: Rethinking the Gospel Audiences* (Grand Rapids: Eerdmans), pp. 195-217.

Webb, R.L.
    1991   *John the Baptizer and Prophet: A Socio-Historical Study* (JSNTSup, 62; Sheffield: JSOT Press).

Weber, M.M.
    1968   *Economy and Society*, I (New York: Bedminster).

Wedderburn, A.J.
    2006   'Jesus' Action in the Temple: A Key or a Puzzle?', *ZNW* 97.1: 1-22.

Weiss, H.
    1994   'The Sabbath among the Samaritans', *JSJ* 25.2: 252-73.
    1996   'Sabbatismos in the Epistle to the Hebrews', *CBQ* 58.4: 674-89.
    1998   'The Sabbath in the Writings of Josephus', *JSJ* 29.4: 363-90.

Wenham, D.
    1998   'A Historical View of John's Gospel', *Themelios* 23.2: 5-21.

West, G.O.
    1993   'The Interface between Trained Readers and Ordinary Readers in Liberation Hermeneutics. A Case Study: Mark 10:17-22', *Neotestamentica* 27.1: 165-80.

Westerholm, S.
    1978   *Jesus and Scribal Authority* (ConBNT, 10; Lund: C.W.K. Gleerup).
    1992   'Clean and Unclean', in *DJG* (ed. J.B. Green and S. McKnight; Downers Grove, IL: InterVarsity Press), pp. 125-32.
    2003   *Perspectives Old and New on Paul: The 'Lutheran' Paul and his Critics* (Grand Rapids: Eerdmans).

Williams, M.H.
    1995   'Palestinian Jewish Personal Names in Acts', in R. Bauckham (ed.), *The Book of Acts in its Palestinian Setting* (Grand Rapids: Eerdmans), pp. 79-113.
    2005   'Jewish Festal Names in Antiquity—A Neglected Area of Onomastic Research', *JSJ* 36.1: 21-40.

Wilson, S.G.
    1973   *The Gentiles and the Gentile Mission in Luke–Acts* (SNTSMS, 23; Cambridge: Cambridge University Press).
    1983   *Luke and the Law* (Cambridge: Cambridge University Press).

Wintermute, O.S.
    1985   'Jubilees', in *OTP* (ed. J.H. Charlesworth; Garden City, NY: Doubleday), pp. 35-142.

Wise, M.O.
    1992   'Feasts', in *DJG* (ed. J.B. Green and S. McKnight; Downers Grove, IL: InterVarsity Press), pp. 234-41.

Witherington, B.I.
    1984   *Women in the Ministry of Jesus* (SNTSMS, 51; Cambridge: Cambridge University Press).
    1990   *The Christology of Jesus* (Minneapolis: Fortress Press).
    1994   *Jesus the Sage: The Pilgrimage of Wisdom* (Minneapolis: Fortress Press).
    2001   *The Gospel of Mark: A Socio-Rhetorical Commentary* (Grand Rapids: Eerdmans).
    2005   *The Problem with Evangelical Theology* (Waco, TX: Baylor University Press).

Wright, N.T.
- 1992 *The New Testament and the People of God* (Minneapolis: Fortress Press).
- 1996 *Jesus and the Victory of God* (Minneapolis: Fortress Press).
- 1997 *What Saint Paul Really Said: Was Paul of Tarsus the Real Founder of Christianity?* (Grand Rapids: Eerdmans).
- 1998 'Jesus and the Identity of God', *Ex auditu* 14: 42-56.

Wyckoff, E.J.
- 2005 'Jesus in Samaria (John 4:4-42): A Model for Cross-Cultural Ministry', *BTB* 35.3: 89-98.

Yadin. Y.
- 1985 *The Temple Scroll* (New York: Random House).

Yinger, K.L.
- 1999 *Paul, Judaism, and Judgment according to Deeds* (SNTSMS, 105; Cambridge: Cambridge University Press).

Yinger, M.
- 1994 *Ethnicity: Source of Strength? Source of Conflict?* (Albany: SUNY Press).

York, J.O.
- 1991 *The Last Shall Be First: The Rhetoric of Reversal in Luke* (JSNTSup, 46; Sheffield: JSOT Press).

Zuntz, G.
- 1984 'Wann wurde das Evangelium Marci geschrieben?', in H. Cancik (ed.), *Markus-Philologie* (Tübingen: Mohr Siebeck), pp. 47-71.

INDEXES

INDEX OF ANCIENT SOURCES

OLD TESTAMENT

Genesis		34.15-16	25	*Leviticus*	
1	68	41.45	204	7.20-27	83
1.14	70	43.32	205	11.13-14	60
1.14-19	70			11.44-45	21
2	66	*Exodus*		12.2-5	66
2.1-3	128	2	198	12.4	66
2.2-3	128	2.15	198	18.5	116
2.3	128	11–13	159	19.9-10	127
2.8-14	67	11.7	160, 163	19.18	282
3	68	12.1-13	159	19.30	37
3.21	68	12.14-20	159	20.22-26	21
3.23-24	67	12.15-16	128	20.24	24
10	67	12.43-49	160	20.26	21
11	74	12.48	26	21.17-24	225
12	73	13.6	128	23.1-2	146
12.1-3	20	16	128, 129	23.33-36	146
12.6-7	194	16.22-30	123	23.36	147
15	20, 67	16.23, 26	128	23.40	152
15.18-21	23	16.28	128	23.42-43	146
17	64	17	150	26.1-45	83
17.3-8	20	17.1-7	149		
17.10-14	25	19.5-6	210	*Numbers*	
17.25	64	20.4-6	245	15.32-36	123
21.4	64	20.8-11	128	20.8-13	149
22.16-18	20	20.11	128	23.9	10
24	198	20.13	282	25.1-13	32
25.8	275	24.18	61	25.10-14	246
27.46–28.2	72	30.16	182	25.14	247
28–29	198	31.12-17	23	29	147
28.6	198	31.14	23, 132	29.12-38	147
28.10-18	190	34.21	123, 127, 129		
28.16-18	190			*Deuteronomy*	
29.10	198	35.2	141	4.1	116
33.19	190	35.2-3	123	4.24	245
33.20	190			5.9	245
34	25, 72				

Index of References

5.14-15	22	*2 Kings*		*Isaiah*	
6.15	245	17	191	1.1-17	238
10.16	232	19	24	12.2	150
11.29-30	194			12.3	149
12.5	194	*2 Chronicles*		20.1-6	179
14.2	21	8.13	147	25.6	213
14.3-21	21			25.6-9	222
16.5-6	26	*Ezra*		40.1-11	259
16.14	152	3.1-6	153	43.5-6	222
16.16	147	4.1-3	191	49.8-21	259
17.6	278	4.4-5	191	49.12	222
19.15	278			51.1-16	259
21.18-21	273	*Nehemiah*		52.1-12	259
23	127	4.7-8	191	55.8-9	318
23.3-6	282	8.17	147	56	183, 185, 187
23.24	126	9.13-14	68		
23.25	126	10.31	123	56.3, 6	184
25.17-19	282	13.3	23	56.6-7	181
26.12-13	127	13.4-8	23	56.7	181, 183, 185, 187, 221
27.12	194	13.15-22	23, 123		
31.10-13	150	13.17-18	83	56.7b-c	183
34.1-4	74	13.23-27	23	56.7c	181
				58.1-14	238
Joshua		*Esther*		65.1-7	83
5.4-7	26	1.1	84	65.4	83
9.6	226	2.9	87		
22	74, 75	2.20 (LXX)	87	*Jeremiah*	
22.28b-29	74	3.8	86	3.18	222
22.30-34	75	3.13	84	4.4	232
		4.17	85	7	180, 186
Judges		5.1-2	85	7.4	24
17	77	9.24-28	87	7.5-11	186
18.31	180	9.26-31	151	7.6	187
19	77	10.3	84	7.6, 9	186
				7.11	179, 180, 186, 187
1 Samuel		*Psalms*			
21	131, 132, 313	2.6	24	7.12-14	180
		3.4	24	7.21-23	238
21.1	132	15.1	24	7.34	180
21.1-9	131	24.3	24	9.25-26	232
26.19	24	36.7-9	213	17.19-27	83
26.20	24	43.3	24	17.21-22	123
		78.60	180	19.1-9, 11-15	179
2 Samuel		106.34-39	82	27.1-15	179
5–7	24	106.40-43	82		
		106.41-42	83	*Ezekiel*	
1 Kings		107.3	222	4.13	83
6–8	24	137.5-6	24	7.22	52
18	246	139.21	282	12.1-16	179

Ezekiel (cont.)		14.3-4	147	12.2-4	80		
22.4	83	14.5-15	147	12.6-9	240		
28.13	66	14.7	148, 150	12.9	81		
31.9	66	14.8	148, 149,	12.10-13.10	81		
44.9	232		150	12.19	240		
45.1-4	25	14.8-11	259	13.10	81		
47.1-12	150	14.9	148	14.1-15.7	81		
47.2	149	14.16	148	14.10	79		
		14.16-21	148				
Daniel		14.17	148, 150	*1 Maccabees*			
1.3-16	240	14.17-18	149	1.11	45, 69		
7	133	14.21b	185	1.15	39		
7.13	134			1.21-23	40		
7.13-14	133	*Malachi*		1.29, 37, 39	40		
9.27	248	3.1-3	258	1.41	310		
10.3	240			1.41-42	1, 86		
11.31	248	*Additions to Esther*		1.41-50	29		
12.11	248	10.4–11.1	85	1.43	30		
		10.4–16.24	84	1.44-48	1		
Hosea		10.7-13	87	1.45-46, 54	40		
3.4-5	258	11.2–12.6	84	1.45-48	34		
6.4-6	238	11.6-9	85	1.48	40		
6.6	126, 201	11.10	85	1.48b-49	43		
9.3	83	11.10-12	84	1.54	29, 247		
14.4-8	259	13.1-7	84	1.60-61	40		
		13.3-5	86	1.60-62	34		
Joel		13.4	86	1.62-63	240		
2.18-32	259	13.8–14.19	85	1.62-64	44		
2.21-27, 32b	259	13.15-16	86	1.63	44		
2.28-32a	259	14.5, 15-17	87	2.7-13	40		
		14.17	87, 240	2.19-20	299		
Amos		15.1-16	85	2.19-22	32		
5.21-24	201	16.1-24	85	2.23	247		
5.21-27	238			2.24-26	32		
8.4-8	83	*Baruch*		2.25	249		
		4.36-37	222	2.26-27	246		
Micah		5.5	222	2.27-28	33		
2.12-13	259			2.28	248		
		Judith		2.34	43		
Zephaniah		4.12	79	2.40-41	43		
3.9-20	259	5.20-21	79	2.41	136		
		8.6	79	2.46	40		
Zechariah		9.4	246	2.50	299		
2.12	25	9.8, 13	79	2.54	246		
8.3-8	259	10	80	2.58	246		
13.1-2, 8-9	258	11.9-10	80	2.68	53		
14	147, 149,	11.11-14	80	3.43	40		
	155, 185	11.12	83	3.43-45	40		
14.1-2	147	12.2	240	3.45	40, 41		

Index of References

3.49-51	41	3	51	7.8, 21, 27	300
4.9-10	299	3.1	39, 51	7.21	300
4.36	41	3.1-40	50	8.5–15.36	50
4.37-59	41	3.1–15.36	46, 48	8.16-17	47
4.58	41	3.12	46	8.17	300
4.59	43	3.18	47, 51	8.26-27	48
7.37-38	41	3.24	38	8.36	53, 144, 295, 303
7.46	41	3.25	38		
9.54-56	41	3.29	38	9.4-5	52
10.25	43	3.38	47	10.6	152, 248
10.34	43	3.38-39	38	10.7	152
11.63-74	42	3.39	175	10.6-8	152
13.3	42	4.1–5.10	50	11.24-25	47, 50
13.3b-6	44	4.7-15	32	11.25	47
13.6	44	4.9-10	32	11.31	50
13.42	42	4.10	30	12.37	300
14.4-15	42	4.11-15	30, 52	12.38	48
14.4, 6	42	4.12-14	68	14.33	52
14.7	42	4.13	52	15.1-5	49
14.15	42	4.13-17	50	15.17-18	48
14.27	42	4.16-17	52, 294	15.29	300
14.27-45	42	4.17	37, 39, 311	15.32	52
14.29, 31-32, 36	42	5.11–6.17	50	15.37-39	48
14.31	42	5.15-16, 21	38		
15.33-34	299	5.17-18	51	Sirach	
		5.20	7, 53, 311	3.6-8, 12-15	275
2 Maccabees		5.21	51	25.1	281
1.1–2.18	48	5.25-26	48	45.23-24	246
1.7	25	5.27	49	48.1-3	246
1.9	151, 154	6.1	47	50.25-26	193
1.10	151	6.2	47		
1.18	151	6.6	48, 299	Tobit	
1.27-29	46	6.10	34, 46	1.10-13	240
2.19	46	6.11	48	4.3-4	275
2.19-32	46, 48	6.18–7.42	34, 49	6.14-15	275
2.21	38, 175	6.18-8.4	50		
		7.2, 37	49, 299	Wisdom	
				12.3	25

New Testament

Matthew		5.3-12	222, 280	5.22	278
3.7-9	305	5.5	280	5.22-24	279
3.9	221, 288, 303	5.8	232	5.43	283, 284
		5.9	280	5.43a	282
3.12	259	5.16, 45, 48	281	5.43b	282
3.17	277	5.21	282	5.43-48	281, 283, 284
4.13	271	5.21-24	280, 282		
5–7	284	5.21-42	282	5.45	283

Matthew (cont.)		15.3-6	271	1.14-15	137, 274
5.45, 47-48	282	15.10-20	229	1.15	7, 137
5.47	278	15.11	96, 97,	1.16-20	274
6.1	4, 6, 8, 9,		232, 233,	1.21	135, 271
	14, 15, 18,		235, 240,	1.21-28	323
	26, 32, 281		256, 314	1.28, 33, 45	323
7.3-5	278, 279,	15.11b	232	1.29-31	271
	280, 282	15.11, 17-18	232, 233	1.40	140
7.9-11	280, 281	15.12-20	255	1.40-45	241
7.11, 21	281	15.17-18	232	1.44	237, 240
8.5-12	257	15.18	232, 235	2	134
8.10	221	15.18-20	233	2.1	135, 271
8.10-12	224	15.20	96, 230,	2.1–3.6	122, 140
8.11-12	98, 222,		232, 233,	2.1-10	140
	234		256	2.2, 12	323
8.12	222	15.24	221	2.10	133, 134
8.20	271	15.39	227	2.10-11	133
8.20-21	302	16.17-19	278	2.13-17	98
8.21	277	17.11	137	2.15-17	140, 214
8.21-22	274, 275	18	278	2.16	121, 212
8.22	286	18.15	278, 279	2.18-22	140
9.1	271	18.15-17	278	2.19	232
9.9-13	214	18.15-18,		2.23	126, 127
10.5	189, 221	21-22	278	2.23-28	125, 126,
10.21	268	18.15-20	268		135, 139,
10.32-33	277	18.17	278, 279		140, 234,
10.34-38	272	18.21	278, 279		313
10.38	273	18.21-35	269	2.23-3.6	98, 121,
11.2-3	259	18.35	278, 279		124, 139,
11.18-19	214	19.3-9	271		241
11.19	98	21.12-13	177	2.24	129, 130,
11.20-22	221, 224,	23.8	270, 278,		132, 141
	227		326	2.25-26	131.132
11.23	271	23.9	277, 302	2.26	130, 132
11.25-27	277	23.23	233, 237,	2.27	132, 133,
12.1-14	124		238, 240,		134, 139
12.6	167		241	2.28	132, 133,
12.7	126	23.25	232		134
12.32	133	23.33	305	3.1	135
12.34	305	25.40	278	3.1-6	121, 122,
12.41	221, 224,	26.6-13	215		134, 135,
	227	26.17-19	164		313, 138,
12.46-50	276	26.60-61	98, 173		139, 140
12.49-50	278	27.40	98, 173	3.2	141
13.54-56	276	28.10	278	3.3	135
15	227, 233,	28.19-20	256	3.4	139
	256			3.4-5	137
15.1-2	232	*Mark*		3.6	121, 122,
15.1-20	228	1.1-3	137		140, 141,
					143, 321

3.7	135	10.13-16	271	6.1-11	124
3.7-8	323	10.17-21	105	6.20-23	222
3.20	271	10.17-22	103, 104	6.41-42	280
3.31-35	2, 4, 276, 286	10.17, 19, 21, 28-30	105	6.42	280
3.34	280	10.18	104	7	321
3.35	265, 286, 302, 314	10.21	104, 105	7.9	221
		10.26	232	7.29-30	220
4.10-11	255	10.28	271	7.33-34	214
5.19	240	10.28-29	280	7.36	215
5.25-34	241	10.28-30	268, 276, 302	7.36-50	98, 213, 215, 217, 219
6.1-3	276	10.28-31	2	7.37	215, 217
6.1-6	276	10.29	302	7.38	215, 218
6.30-44	98, 226	10.29-30	286, 302	7.39	215, 217, 218
6.43	226	10.30	302		
7	227, 228, 233, 256	10.42-45	207	7.40-43	218
7.1-5	228, 232	11.15	184	7.44	218
7.1-23	228	11.15-16	180, 188	7.44, 45, 46	219
7.3-4	210, 212	11.15-18	177, 179, 188	7.44-46	218
7.9-13	271			7.47	217
7.14-16	228	11.15-33	121	7.47-48	217
7.14-23	229	11.16	185, 186	7.47-50	220
7.15	96, 228, 232, 233, 234, 238, 241, 257, 263	11.17	179, 180, 184, 186, 187, 188, 221	7.50	221
				8.19-21	276
				8.21	280
				9.10-17	226
		11.17a	181, 187	9.52-55	189
7.17	257	11.17b	179	9.58	271
7.17-23	228, 255	12.41-44	241	9.59-60	274
7.18	59, 232	13	248, 251	9.61-62	274
7.19	228, 232, 233, 255, 256, 314	13.1	176	10.7-8	233
		13.1-2	172	10.13-14	221, 224, 227
		13.2	98, 176		
7.19c	228, 235	13.14	248, 251, 252	10.15	271
7.24-30	241			10.29-37	190
7.27	221	14.3-9	215	10.38-42	98, 271
8	227	14.12-17	164	11.11-13	280
8.1-10	98, 226, 234	14.12-26	277	11.18-20	142
		14.22, 24	165	11.32	221, 224, 227
8.3	226	14.57-58	98, 173		
8.5	227	15.29-30	98, 173	11.37-38	219
8.8	226	15.43	277	11.37-54	98
8.10	227			11.39	232
9.12	137	*Luke*		11.42	237
9.33-37	207	3.3	220	12.10	133
9.39	232	3.8	221, 303	12.53	271
10	104	4.25-27	222	13.10-17	98, 124, 141
10.2-9	271	5.29-32	214	13.12	135

Luke (cont.)		3.1	199	7.1	145
13.14	138, 142	4	189, 190,	7.1-10	156
13.15	142		196, 197,	7.1–10.21	145
13.16	142		199, 201	7.2	145
13.22-29	223	4.1-6	190	7.11-12	156
13.22	223	4.4	197	7.14	156
13.25, 26	223	4.4-5	190	7.15	156
13.28	223	4.4-9	197	7.16-18	156
13.28-29	222, 257	4.4-42	189	7.19-24	156
13.29	223	4.5	190, 197	7.21	156
14	224	4.6	197, 198,	7.21-24	125, 143
14.1	224		199	7.25-36	157
14.1-6	98, 124, 142	4.7	200	7.28-29	156
		4.7-8	191	7.37-38	158
14.1-24	98, 224	4.7-18	199	7.37-39	145, 154, 157
14.2-6	224	4.7, 9	197		
14.4	135	4.9	191, 196, 197, 199, 201, 314	7.37b-38	158
14.7-11	207, 224			7.38	158
14.12-14	224			7.49	212
14.15	219, 224	4.10	197	7.53–8.11	156
14.15-24	257	4.10-11, 13-14	158	8	303
14.16-17	225			8.12	145, 154, 157, 158
14.16-21	224	4.11	196		
14.16-24	225, 234	4.11-14	197	8.16-19	156
14.21	224, 225	4.12	190, 197	8.31-33	303
14.22-24	225	4.15	199	8.33, 37	304
14.23	225	4.16	199	8.33-58	154
14.25-27	273	4.17-19	199	8.34-38	303
14.26	273, 285, 286, 287	4.20	199, 201	8.39	304
		4.20-21	190	8.39-41a	304
14.27	273	4.21	200, 210, 314	8.41b-44	304
15.1-2	214			9.1-16	125, 143
17.11-19	190	4.21-24	200, 201	9.16	123
18.9	117	4.21, 23	201	10.22	145, 244
18.9-14	207	4.22	200, 201	11	271
19.9	221	4.23	201	12.1-8	215
19.1-10	98	4.39-41	189	21.3	271
19.45-46	177	5	157		
21.1-4	241	5.1	145	Acts	
22.7-13	164	5.1-9	156	1.6	137, 259
22.19	165	5.1-17	98	2	235, 253
22.19-20	262	5.1-18	125, 143	2.17-21	259
22.24-27	207	5.1–10.42	145	2.43-47	268
		5.6	135	2.46	253
John		5.11, 15, 16, 19, 20, 29	157	2.46-47	165
2.13	145			2.47	253
2.14-17	177	5.17	157	3.25	237
2.18-22	173	6.1	145	4.1-22	253
2.19	98	6.4	145	5.17-39	253
		7-8	156, 313	5.42	253

Index of References

6.11	237	5.9-10	254	2.7-10	263
6.12	237	12.10	269	2.11-14	255
6.13	264	14.1–15.13	307	2.14-21	307
6.13-14	98, 173, 237	14.5	124, 166	3	111
		14.14	256, 263	3.26	3, 265
7	252	14.20	263	3.26-29	307
7.48-50	237			3.28	202, 306, 327
7.48-60	264	*1 Corinthians*			
10	237	3.16	202	3.28-29	76
10.1–11.18	255	6.5-6	279	3.29	307
10.13	97	6.7-8	269	4.10	124
10.14	230, 236, 254	7	262		
		7.10	262	*Ephesians*	
10.28	237	7.10-11	262	2.14-15	202
10–11	236	7.12	262		
11.8	230	7.18-20	307	*Philippians*	
12	253	7.19	60	1.7-8	269
12.1-4	264	9.5	271	3.6	247
15	228, 236, 237, 256	9.14	262	4.1	269
		11	262		
15.1	256	11.2, 23	261	*Colossians*	
15.4	256	11.23-25	262	2.16-17	124
15.1-29	255	11.23-26	163	2.17	166
18.11	271	11.25	165		
20.6	151	15.1, 3	261	*1 Thessalonians*	
20.7	165	15.1-5	263	3.6-8	269
20.31	271	15.1-8	101		
21.17-26	253	15.3	254	*Titus*	
		16.2	165	1.15	263
Romans					
2.6-10	116	*Galatians*		*Hebrews*	
3	110	1.9	261	4.9	138
3.20	111	1.14	247		
3.21-26	254	1.18	261	*1 John*	
3.27	111	2	236	3.10-17	268
4	111	2.7	263	3.17	268

Pseudepigrapha

1 Enoch		1.33-35	54	5.25-30	55
55.4	142	3.20	57	6.17-19, 22	55, 299
62.13-14	213	4.9	56	6.27-29	57
90.6-21	60	4.10	56	7.6	55
		4.11-12	56	8.2	55
3 Maccabees		4.12	57	8.2, 12, 29	56
1.3	34	4.19-21	57	8.7-8	56
		4.25	56	9.23-24	57
4 Maccabees		4.26-5.3	54	11.16, 25	56
1.1	54	5.6-7	54	13.2	56
1.34	54	5.23	55	17.8-10	58

17.20-22	58	16.20-21, 25,		*Psalms of Solomon*	
18.1-5	58	27, 29, 31	152	2.1-2, 26-29	132
18.4	144	16.20-31	156	2.26-27	132
18.12	246	16.21	156	8.16-18	132
		16.25b	155	17.12	132
Jubilees		1625b-26	155		
1.9	65	22.16	35, 61, 62,	Pseudo-Philo's	
1.9b	65		71	*Biblical Antiquities*	
1.9b-10, 14	65	23.29	142	1-8	75
2	70	25.1-10	72	6-7	73
2.9	70	25.4	72, 198	7.4	74
2.17-18	69	27.8-9	72	9.3	76
2.19-20	69	30	72	9.5	78.198
2.29-30	129	30.7-17	72	9.13-15	77
2.30-32	70, 123	30.8-18	246	12-24	73
3.9	66	30.11-14	73	13.7	150
3.12	66	32	154	18.13	78
3.13-14	66	32.22	190	19.10	25, 74
3.31	68	35.22	267	22.1-2	75
4.24-25	66	36.4-11	268	22.7	75
4.26	66	50.1-13	70	22.9	75
6	71	50.6-13	123	23.12	75
6.32-35	71			25.13	77
6.35	75	*Joseph and Aseneth*		30.2	76
6.36-37	71	6.1	204	31.5	76
8–10	67	7.1	204, 240	35.1-3	76
8.19	172	8.5	240	39.7	76
9.14-15	67	10.13	205	44.6-7	77
10.29-34	67	12.5	205	45.3	77
15	63	20.1, 8	206		
15.25-27	64, 77	21.13-14	205	*Testament of Judah*	
15.28-32	64			25.3	142
15.33-34	65	*Letter of Aristeas*			
15.34	65	142	204	*Testament of Moses*	
16.14a	64	228	275	10.1	142
16.14b	64				
16.17-19	155	*Life of Adam and Eve*		*Testament of Simeon*	
16.20-21	154	60.1	138	6.6	142

OTHER ANCIENT REFERENCES

DEAD SEA SCROLLS		1QS		6.2-5	62
1QH		1.10	282, 284	11	115
9.34-36	302	1.14	152	11.9-14	115
15.18-20	115	3-4	302		
		5	303	1QpHab	
1QH[a]		5-6	278	11.13	232
1	115	5.5	232	12.7-9	96

Index of References

1Q28a [1QSa]	
1.1	212
2.3-10	225

4Q52	
frg. 7, line 7	131

4Q514	62

4QMMT	148

4QShirShabb	70

CD	
1	303
4.3	96
5.6-7	96
6.18-19	96
7.6-7	283
9	278
10.14-11.18	124
10.22-23	129
11.13-14	124
12.19	283

RABBINIC WORKS
Mishnah

m. Abot.	
1.1-5	295

m. Ber.	
5.2	70
5.5	157
8.1	208
8.2-8	208
8.5	70
9.5	186

m. Dem.	
2.3a	209

m. Eduy.	
8.7	295

m. Hag.	
1.1	169

m. Kel.	
1.6-9	169

1.7-9	25
10.1	231

m. Ker.	
1.7	186

m. Mak.	
1.8-9	141

m. Ohal.	
18.7	169

m. Peah	
2.6	295
4.5	127

m. Sanh.	
5.1	141
7.8	141

m. Shab.	
7.2	124, 127
15.1-2	124

m. Sheb.	
9.9	216

m. Sheq.	
1.3	182
1.5	182

m. Sot.	
9.15	157

m. Suk.	
4.1, 8	152
4.5-5.1	149
5.1	149
5.2-4	150
5.3	150
5.4	157
5.6	152

m. Yad.	
4.3	295

m. Yoma	
8.6	136, 138

Talmud

b. Ber.	
28b	212

b. Meg.	
31a	149

b. Shab.	
118b	144

b. Suk.	
51b	167

b. Sot.	
12a	77

b. Zeb.	
113a	74

b. B. Bat.	
4a	167

y. Shab.	
7.2	129

Tosefta

t. Ber.	
5.29	220

t. Shab.	
9.17	129

t. Sheq.	
1.6	182

t. Suk.	
3.3-9	149
3.11-12	149
3.18	149

Other

Exod. Rab.	
1.24	77

Cant. Rab.	
1.15	74

Mekhilta	
109b	132

Mekhilta Mishpatim
20   306

SAMARITAN TRADITIONS
Memar Marqah
II.10   190

Samaritan Pentateuch
Deut.
12.5   194
27.3-4   194

CHRISTIAN LITERATURE
Aristides
Apology
2.2   306

Augustine
De civitate Dei
6.11   16

Clement of Alexandria
Stromateis
6.6   306

Didache
4   271

Epistle to Diognetus
1.1   306

Eusebius
Historia ecclesiastica
2.1.4   263
3.39.3-4   263

3.39.15   255
5.20.4-7   263

Praeparatio evangelica
4.11   201
4.12-13   201

Gospel of Thomas
53   255
55   273
89   232
101   273

Tertullian
Ad nationes
1.8   306

GRECO-ROMAN

Ammonius
Diff.
243   18

Apollonius of Tyana
Epistulae
26   201

Dio Cassius
37.17.1   20
37.17.3   15, 19

Diodorus Siculus
1.28.2-3   17
1.55.5   17
34-35.1.1-2 14
40.3   28
40.3.4   14
40.3.8   21

Epictetus
Dissertationes
1.11.12-13   14
1.22.4   14

Frontinus
Strategemata
2.1.17   16

Herodotus
Histories
2.104.3   17
8.144.2   292, 299

Hippocrates
Fragments
33   15

Horace
Satirae
1.9.70   17, 19

Justin
Historiae philippicae
2.14-15   15

Josephus
Vita
49   278
74-75   215
197   210

Antiquitates judaicae
3.244-45   152
4.219   278
7.356   104
7.374   104
7.384   104
8.100   150, 153

8.280   104
8.300   104
8.394   104
9.236   104
9.277-91   191
9.290   193
11.19-30,
84-119   191
11.169   304
12.10   189
12.136   19
12.237-13.229 39
12.253   248
12.272-77   136
13.74-79   189
13.242-43   147
13.252   43
13.255-57   193
13.298, 401 129
13.318   59
13.319   18
14.71-72   132
14.116   19
14.237   43
15.267-91   253
15.267-425   184
15.380   184
15.391-402   176
15.417   171

15.421	185	7.1-4	175	Philo	
15.425	184	7.4	176	*Quis rerum divinarum*	
17.149-54	253	7.264	34	*heres sit*	
17.213	162			168	104
18.14	129	*Contra Apionem*		171-73	104
18.29	163	1.3	161		
18.29-30	195	1.40	161	*In Flaccum*	
18.55-59	253	1.209-11	15	41	250
18.85-86	189	1.229	161		
18.88-89	189	1.239	14	*Legatio ad Gaium*	
18.261-64	251	2.20-21	16	117	251, 252
18.261-308	249	2.103	184	196	251, 252
18.265	251, 252	2.106	186	200-202	250
18.271	251, 252	2.137	15, 19	200-207	250
18.277	251	2.205-06	275	207-333	249
20.100-103	34			226	251
20.102	254	Livy		347	249
20.106-07	162	5.52.2-3	167	361	15
20.106-12	162				
20.109	163	Martial		*Quod omnis probus*	
20.118	195	*Epigrammaton libri*		*liber sit*	
		4.4	17	75	201
Bellum judaicum		7.30	18		
1.145-47	43	8.82	18	*De migratione Abrahami*	
1.157-60	43	11.94	19	89-93	34
2.10	162				
2.97	31	Meleager		*De sacrificiis*	
2.124-27	272	*Anthologia graeca*		54-57	110
2.166	129	5.160	17		
2.184-203	249			*De specialibus legibus*	
2.224-26	162	Ovid		2.41	123
2.226-27	162	*Ars amatoria*		2.41-222	123
2.232-46	195	1.76	17	2.63	104
2.259	322	1.416	17		
2.280	163			*Vita Mosis*	
2.409	174	*Remedia amoris*		2.22	129
2.517	43	219-20	17		
3.307-15	189			Plato	
3.516-19	136	Perseus		*Alcibiades*	
5.184-247	176	*Satirae*		2.149E	201
5.194	171	2.69-75	201		
5.222-23	170	5.180-84	19	Plutarch	
5.459	174, 175			*Alexander*	
6.250-66	175, 176	Petronius		1.5	31
6.285-87	175	*Satyricon*			
6.288	320	68.8	18	*Cicero*	
6.300-09	320	102.14	18	7.4	13
6.301	180, 320				
7.1	175	*Fragments*		*De fraterno amore*	
		37	14, 18	491B	267, 281

De superstitione		Strabo		Tibullus	
8	16	*Geographia*		1.18	17
		16.2.37	14, 19, 69		
Moralia				Xenophon	
1.615D	219	Suetonius		*Memorabilia*	
		Divus Iulius		1.3.1-3	201
Quaestiones conviviales		48	207		
4.5.1-3	14				
		Domitianus			
Polybius		12.2	18		
26.1	251				
		Tacitus			
Seneca		*Historiae*			
Epistulae		5.2-5	12		
41	201	5.3	12, 161		
95.47	16	5.4	12		
108.22	15	5.5	11, 12, 13		

INDEX OF AUTHORS

Aasgaard, R. 266
Abel, F.-M. 45, 152
Adler, W. 73
Ådna, J. 178, 241, 253
Aguilar, M.I. 29, 292, 295
Albright, W.F. 278
Alexander, P.S. 67
Allison, D.C. 133, 223, 273, 279
Alon, G. 211
Alter, R. 198
Anderson, H. 48, 49, 50, 58, 59, 163
Anderson, R.T. 191, 193
Arlandson, J. 219
Aune, D.E. 93
Aymer, M.P. 10

Bacchiocchi, S. 124
Bach, K. 106
Bailey, J.L. 285
Bailey, K.E. 220
Banks, R. 125, 130, 228
Bar-Kochva, B. 39
Barnett, P. 144, 251
Barrett, C.K. 158, 200
Bartchy, S.S. 207, 211, 214, 226
Bartlett, R. 300
Barton, S.C. 274, 276, 277, 278, 286
Baslez, M.-F. 78
Bauckham, R. 5, 92, 93, 94, 179, 244, 260, 261, 262, 263
Baumann, G. 298
Baumgarten, J. 149
Beasley-Murray, G.R. 145, 150, 158, 194
Becker, A.H. 120
Becker, J. 213, 229, 273
Beckwith, R.T. 71, 124
Begg, C.T. 73
Berger, K. 228, 275
Bergler, S. 148, 155, 187
Betz, H.D. 178, 179, 180, 184, 185, 279
Bickerman, E.J. 30, 37, 58, 69, 84, 154

Bird, M.F. 113
Blomberg, C.L. 87, 98, 190, 213, 214, 215, 218, 226, 227, 277, 285, 319
Bock, D.L. 215, 217, 218, 220
Bockmuehl, M. 115
Bohak, G. 168
Bonneau, N.R. 198
Booth, R.P. 228, 232, 237
Borg, M.J. 300
Boring, M.E. 275
Botha, J.E. 106, 198, 199
Bovon, F. 217
Boyarin, D. 120
Brass, P.R. 2
Braun, W. 225
Brett, M.G. 288
Bringmann, K. 30, 33
Brown, R.E. 92, 158, 189
Buchanan, G.W. 178, 183
Buell, D.K. 120, 288, 292, 298, 307
Bultmann, R. 92, 121, 201
Burke, T.J. 266
Burkett, D.R. 133, 134
Burridge, R.A. 93

Cahill, L.S. 285
Carmichael, C.M. 198
Carson, D.A. 110, 124, 158, 194
Carter, W. 279
Casey, P.M. 5, 122, 126, 129, 131, 136, 137, 163, 164, 179, 183, 184, 185
Catchpole, D.R. 5, 127, 129, 135, 163, 179, 214, 216, 232, 236, 275, 302, 304
Champlin, E. 167
Charlesworth, J.H. 135, 282
Chilton, B.D. 163, 213, 228
Coggins, R.J. 196, 200
Cohen, S.J.D. 20, 39
Collins, J.J. 84, 85, 160, 282
Coloe, M. 154
Colpe, C. 275

Connor, W. 177, 297
Corley, K. 217
Cory, C. 158
Coughlan, R. 298
Cowley, A.E. 78
Cranfield, C.E.B. 104, 105, 110, 135
Craven, T. 78, 79
Cresswell, T. 168
Cross, F.M. 131
Crossan, J.D. 90, 132, 134, 163, 216, 232, 270, 276
Crossley, J.G. 126, 129, 130, 179, 186, 248, 251
Crown, A.D. 191
Cullmann, O. 99
Culpepper, R.A. 158
Cummins, S.A. 2, 53

Dahl, N.A. 99
Daise, M.A. 71, 151, 152
Daube, D. 131, 196
Davies, P.R. 71
Davies, W.D. 133, 184, 223, 273
Deines, R. 20, 210, 211, 231, 243
Denzey, N. 290
Derouchie, J.S. 25
Derrett, J.D.M. 131
DesCamp, M.T. 77
deSilva, D.A. 8, 54, 58, 78, 79, 81, 84, 85, 88, 243, 244, 318
Dewey, J. 135
Dexinger, F. 193
Dimante, D. 62
Doering, L. 17, 43
Donaldson, T.L. 245
Doran, R. 45, 50, 53
Douglas, M. 208
Downing, G.F. 5
Draper, J.A. 103
Duling, D.C. 20, 288, 290, 297, 300
Dunn, J.D.G. 94, 108, 109, 110, 111, 115, 120, 140, 143, 171, 208, 210, 212, 213, 214, 216, 219, 222, 225, 228, 230, 231, 233, 234, 240, 245, 246, 247, 253, 255, 270, 273, 286, 287, 316, 324
Duran, N. 79, 80

Edwards, J.R. 171, 176, 226
Eisenbaum, P. 119

Eller, J.D. 288, 290, 291, 293, 294, 295, 297, 298, 300
Elliott, J.H. 8, 301
Elliott, M.A. 212
Elliott, N. 118, 119
Endres, J.C. 64
Engle, A. 149
Enloe, C. 77
Ensor, P.W. 157
Eppstein, V. 184
Eriksen, T.H. 292
Eshel, H. 71
Esler, P.F. 10, 92, 195, 208, 288, 298
Eslinger, L. 198
Evans, C.A. 171, 177, 179, 180, 184, 185, 187, 206, 320, 321
Evans, C.S. 100, 317, 319

Falk, D. 115
Feeley-Harnik, G. 206
Feldman, L.H. 11, 73
Fewell, D.N. 196
Fischer, M. 297
Fischer, T. 37, 48, 49, 50
Fishman, J. 292, 297
Fisk, B.N. 73
Fitzmyer, J.A. 220
France, R.T. 135, 139, 140, 226
Francis, M. 199
Fredriksen, P. 163, 230, 236, 239
Freyne, S. 42, 94, 202, 223, 241
Fuglseth, K.S. 8, 169, 170, 201, 253
Funk, R.W. 163, 270

Gafni, I.M. 39, 243
Gager, J.G. 11, 99
Gardner, A.E. 85
Garlington, D.B. 116
Gaston, L. 119
Gathercole, S.J. 116
Geertz, C. 105, 298
Gehring, R.H. 135
Gerhardsson, B. 261
Giblin, C.H. 199
Gnilka, J. 99, 121, 135, 229, 270, 279
Goldenberg, R. 17
Goldstein, J.A. 45, 63, 69, 151, 153
Grabbe, L. 1, 30, 45
Green, J.B. 218, 220

Index of Authors

Grigsby, B.H. 149, 158
Grosby, S. 298
Gruen, E.S. 59, 161
Guelich, R.A. 122, 137, 140, 143, 227, 279
Gundry, R.H. 116, 125, 130, 133, 134, 135, 140, 141, 186, 215, 228, 232, 233, 240, 276, 284
Gundry-Volf, J. 200
Gurr, T.R. 292

Haas, P. 51
Haenchen, E. 201
Hagner, D.A. 107, 108, 110, 112, 116, 117, 118
Hakola, R. 189, 200, 201
Hall, E.T. 106
Hall, J.M. 297
Halpern-Amaru, B. 63, 72
Hammerton-Kelly, R. 270, 273
Hanson, J.S. 321, 322
Hanson, K.C. 171
Hanson, P.D. 147
Harff, B. 292
Harland, P.A. 266
Harnish, L.J. 106
Harrington, D.J. 73
Hartley, L.P. 324
Harvey, A.E. 99, 230
Hayward, C.T.R. 19
Hayward, R. 73, 187
Hellerman, J.H. 2, 104, 137, 207, 266, 267, 270, 277
Helyer, L. 54, 78, 84
Hempel, C. 62
Hengel, M. 30, 34, 69, 210, 237, 275
Henrie, R. 168
Henten, J.W. van 45, 49, 50, 51, 58, 78, 79, 300
Hill, C.C. 237
Himmelfarb, M. 62
Hjelm, I. 191
Hoffmeier, J.K. 292
Hodge, C.J. 288, 307
Holst, R. 215
Holtzmann, H. 96
Hooker, M.D. 130, 163, 233
Hoover, R.W. 163
Horowitz, D 299

Horrell, D.G. 8, 307
Horsley, R.A. 118, 301, 321, 322
Houlden, J.L. 229
Houston, W. 170
Hübner, H. 228
Hurtado, L. 5, 92, 228, 237
Hutchinson, J. 195, 200, 290, 297, 298, 305

Ilan, T. 244
Instone-Brewer, D. 70, 127, 149, 186, 208, 209, 212, 215, 220, 295

Jackson, R.H. 168
Jacobson, A.D. 273
Jacobson, H. 73
Jenkins, R. 288, 290, 298
Jeremias, J. 99, 164, 184, 216, 225
Jones, L.P. 158, 198, 200
Judge, E.A. 120

Kahl, W. 137, 142
Karris, R.J. 213
Kasfir, N. 288
Kawashima, R.S. 25, 27
Kazen, T. 101, 211, 217, 218, 228, 230, 231, 233, 239, 323
Keck, L.E. 209
Kee, H.C. 92, 99, 136, 270
Keener, C.S. 149, 158, 176, 189, 190, 197, 200, 201, 223, 226, 305
Keesing, R.M. 285
Kelley, S. 119
Kennell, N.M. 32
Kiilunen, J. 127, 131
Kim, S. 111
Kingsbury, J.D. 140
Kissinger, W.S. 279
Klawans, J. 62, 163, 210, 217, 232, 233, 253
Klemm, H.G. 275
Kloppenborg, J.S. 119
Klosinski, L.E. 206
Knibb, M.A. 62
Koester, C.R. 158
Konstan, D. 292
Kraft, R.A. 212
Kruse, H. 238
Kugel, J. 168

Kuhn, H.-W. 121
Kunin, S.D. 168
Kvanvig, H.S. 72

Lane, W.L. 226
Lieu, J. 120
Lightfoot, R.H. 184
Lindars, B. 158, 189, 190, 196, 198, 200
Loader, W.R.G. 121, 126, 127, 130, 228, 230, 232, 233, 238, 239, 240, 241, 323
Loffreda, S. 136
Longenecker, R.N. 111
Lührmann, D. 121
Luz, U. 278

Maccini, R.G. 196
Maccoby, H. 211
Mack, B.L. 163, 178
Magen, Y. 193, 194
Magness, J. 172
Malina, B.J. 106, 202, 216, 228, 276
Malkin, I. 298
Mann, C.S. 278
Manson, T.W. 273
Marcus, J. 179, 233, 241
Marshall, I.H. 215, 217, 220, 223, 224, 225, 273
Marshall, J.W. 119
Martin, R.A. 85
Marxsen, W. 99
Mayer-Haas, A.J. 124
McCane, B. 275
McKnight, S. 90, 100, 119
McLaren, J.S. 174, 195, 249
McVann, M. 276
Meier, J.P. 121, 189, 191, 196, 200, 216, 245, 319, 323, 324
Méndez-Moratalla, F. 217, 218, 220
Merz, A. 90, 122, 125, 135, 136, 143, 163, 164, 189, 210, 229, 232, 233, 234, 253, 257, 302, 317
Metzdorf, C. 178
Metzger, B.M. 50
Meyer, B.F. 232, 238, 317
Meyers, C.L. 147
Meyers, E.M. 136, 147
Michie, D. 135
Millar, F. 33, 102

Miller, G.T. 213
Miller, R.J. 178
Milns, R.D. 31
Minear, P. 318
Moloney, F.J. 145, 146, 148, 150, 154, 158, 303
Montefiore, C.G. 113
Moo, D.J. 126
Moore, C.A. 78, 81, 85, 87
Mørkholm, O. 1
Morris, L. 223
Murphy, F.J. 73
Murphy-O'Connor, J. 96, 182
Mussner, F. 200

Najman, H. 62
Nanos, M. 119
Nash, M. 207
Neusner, J. 148, 182, 183, 209, 211, 231
Neyrey, J.J. 190, 197, 198, 201, 202, 219, 235
Nickelsburg, G.W.E. 50, 78, 106, 212
Nikiprowetzky, V. 137
Nodet, E. 152
Nolland, J. 217, 220, 223, 273
Nongbri, B. 1, 33

Oakman, D.E. 26, 171
O'Brien, P.T. 110
Okure, K. 198
Olyan, S.M. 23
Orton, D.E. 92
Overman, J.A. 226, 278, 279, 280, 285

Paesler, K. 179, 185
Patterson, O. 291
Perry, D.W. 131
Pesch, R. 105, 229
Phillips, G.A. 196
Plummer, A. 215, 218
Poirier, J.C. 211
Poon, W.C.K. 226
Price, S.R.F. 167
Purvis, J.D. 191, 193

Räisänen, H. 233, 238
Rankin, O.S. 152
Reed, A.Y. 120
Reed, J.L. 136, 216, 231, 232

Index of Authors

Regev, E. 170, 211
Reich, R. 231
Reid, B.E. 217
Reinmuth, E. 75
Resseguie, J.L. 220
Rhodes, D. 135
Richardson, P. 182, 231
Riches, J.K. 21, 120, 167, 172, 202, 277, 284, 286, 288
Riesner, R. 283
Rietz, H.W.M. 70
Rohrbaugh, R.L. 103, 106, 276
Rordorf, W. 124, 125
Roth, C. 185
Routledge, R. 164
Rubenstein, J.L. 146, 148, 149, 150, 151, 153, 154
Rudolph, D.J. 228, 233, 256
Ruiten, J.T.A.G.M. van 64, 66
Ruzer, S. 284

Sack, R.D. 168
Saldarini, A.J. 26, 277
Samuel, G. 105
Sanders, E.P. 43, 62, 99, 104, 107, 108, 109, 113, 121, 126, 129, 143, 163, 171, 178, 179, 182, 184, 185, 209, 210, 213, 216, 219, 222, 223, 228, 230, 231, 236, 264, 306, 318
Sariola, H. 105, 121
Schaefer, K.R. 147, 148, 158
Schäfer, P. 11
Schermerhorn, R.A. 290
Schiffmann, L.H. 129, 282
Schillebeeckx, E. 99
Schlosser, J. 172
Schmithals, W. 104
Schnackenburg, R. 158, 279
Schreiner, T.R. 110
Schubert, K. 282
Schürer, E. 31
Schwartz, D.R. 24, 175, 177, 180, 181, 183, 298
Schwartz, S. 33, 44, 45, 102
Schweitzer, A. 90
Schweizer, E. 121, 135
Scott, G.M. 298
Seeley, D. 178, 185
Seland, T. 245

Shead, A.G. 137
Shils, E. 298
Sievers, J. 33
Sim, D.C. 288
Simon, M. 256
Smallwood, E.M. 249
Smith, A.D. 75, 195, 200, 289, 290, 292, 297, 298, 305
Smith, B. 164
Smith, C.W.F. 156
Smith, D.E. 214
Smith, D.M. 199, 201
Smith, J.E. 108
Smith, M. 90
Snyder, G.F. 124, 166, 201, 206, 309
Söding, T. 200
Staley, J.L. 198
Stanton, G.N. 139
Stein, R.H. 164
Stern, M. 15, 16, 17, 18
Stern, S. 71
Stettler, H. 222, 240, 263
Stoler, A.L. 298
Strange, J.F. 136
Stuhlmacher, P. 222
Sturcke, H. 70, 124, 128, 130, 142, 144
Svartvik, J. 228, 232
Swanson, T.D. 201

Talbert, C.H. 93, 201
Taylor, N.H. 252
Taylor, R.B. 168
Taylor, V. 134, 140, 163, 229
Tcherikover, V. 30
Theissen, G. 69, 90, 94, 95, 96, 97, 99, 100, 101, 122, 125, 135, 136, 143, 163, 164, 179, 189, 210, 229, 232, 233, 234, 242, 248, 249, 251, 252, 253, 257, 270, 302, 317, 324, 325, 326
Thompson, M.B. 108
Thurén, L. 111
Thyen, H. 200
Tilly, M. 67
Tomson, P.J. 228, 307
Torrey, C.C. 251
Townsend, R.B. 249
Trocmé, E. 276
Turner, M.M.B. 142
Twelftree, G.H. 226, 227, 319

Ulfgard, H. 153

Van Belle, G. 200
Van den Berghe, P. 297
VanderKam, J.C. 33, 62, 63, 67, 68, 69, 70, 71, 151, 152, 153, 245
Vermes, G. 230, 282
Vouga, F. 228

Watson, F. 93
Webb, R.L. 321
Weber, M.M. 289
Wedderburn, A.J. 178, 182, 184, 188, 257
Weiss, H. 16, 83, 138, 193
Wenham, D. 156
West, G.O. 103, 104
Westerholm, S. 108, 114, 131, 217, 228, 263
Williams, M.H. 244

Wilson, S.G. 208, 223
Winter, D. 94, 95, 96, 97, 99, 100, 101, 242, 324, 325, 326
Wintermute, O.S. 63, 67, 68, 72
Wise, M.O. 22
Witherington, B.I. 109, 110, 112, 132, 133, 215, 227, 253
Wright, N.T. 2, 5, 90, 91, 100, 109, 111, 131, 139, 163, 179, 232, 255, 275, 300, 321
Wyckoff, E.J. 189

Yadin, Y. 282
Yinger, M. 116, 289

York, J.O. 217, 220, 225

Zuntz, G. 251

Index of Subjects

Caligula 247-54
circumcision 17-19, 25-26, 39-40, 46, 63-65, 76-77
cultural scripts 102-107

dietary laws 13-15, 21, 43-44, 49-50, 55-56, 71, 80-81, 204-35

election 21, 75-76
eschatology 257-60
ethnicity 195-96, 288-91
ethnicity and kinship 297-301
ethnicity, Jesus and 296-308, 315-16
ethnic identity formation 291-95, 305-06

family values, Mediterranean 266-70
family, Jesus and 270-87

gentiles 44-45, 86-87, 221-33
Greco-Roman perspective 11-20,

historiography 3, 37-39, 50-53, 56-59, 118-19, 310-11, 316-23
Hanukkah 48, 151-53
Hellenization 27-32

intermarriage 72, 77-78

legalism 113-20

Maccabean revolt 2, 32-33
Maccabean ideology (see also *historiography*) 81-84, 87, 151-53, 243-45, 311-13

methodology 4-6, 91-102, 316-23

New Perspective 2, 107-112
nationalism 112-20

Passover 22, 158-65
patriarchy, Jesus and 301-05
Paul 107-13, 260-63
Pharisees 209-13
Purim 87
purity, Jesus and 239-40

rewritten Bible 61, 78

Sabbath 15-17, 22-23, 43, 48-49, 68-71, 79, 123-44
Samaritans 188-202
sectarianism 61-63, 213-21
space, sacred (see also *temple, territoriality*) 23-25, 65-68, 73-75, 167-203
surrogate kinship 268-70, 275-85

Tabernacles, Feast of 145-58
table fellowship see *dietary laws*
temple 40-43, 46-48, 79, 169-77
temple, Jesus' action in 177-88
territoriality 167-68
tradition history 91-102

zeal 245-47

www.ingramcontent.com/pod-product-compliance
Lightning Source LLC
Chambersburg PA
CBHW052048230426
43671CB00011B/1826